EXCELLENCE
IN BUSINESS COMMUNICATION

EXCELLENCE

IN BUSINESS COMMUNICATION

EXCELLENCE
IN BUSINESS COMMUNICATION
THIRD EDITION

J *ohn V. Thill*

Chief Executive Officer
Communication Specialists of America

C *ourtland L. Bovée*

Professor of Business Communication
C. Allen Paul Distinguished Chair
Grossmont College

McGRAW-HILL, INC.

New York   St. Louis   San Francisco   Auckland   Bogotá
Caracas   Lisbon   London   Madrid   Mexico City   Milan   Montreal,
New Delhi   San Juan   Singapore   Sydney   Tokyo   Toronto

This book was set in Minion by York Graphic Services, Inc.
The editors were Karen Westover and Linda Richmond;
the designer was Karen K. Quigley;
the production supervisor was Elizabeth J. Strange.
R. R. Donnelley & Sons Company was printer and binder.

Cover photos: Comstock; center photo, Bob Pizaro/Comstock

NOTE TO STUDENTS

A study guide for this textbook can be obtained from college bookstores under the title *Study Guide, Excellence in Business Communication,* Third Edition, by John V. Thill and Courtland L. Bovée.

You can use the *Study Guide* throughout the course for reviewing the content of this textbook, for developing communication skills, and for increasing your knowledge of business communication. It is also an ideal aid when preparing for tests.

If the *Study Guide* is not in stock, ask the bookstore manager to order a copy from the publisher.

EXCELLENCE IN BUSINESS COMMUNICATION

This book is printed on acid-free paper.

2 3 4 5 6 7 8 9 0 DOC DOC 9 0 9 8 7 6

ISBN 0-07-006907-7

Library of Congress Cataloging-in-Publication Data

Thill, John V.
    Excellence in business communication / John V. Thill, Courtland L.
Bovée.—3rd ed.
       p.   cm.
    Includes bibliographical references and index.
    ISBN 0-07-006907-7
    1. Business communication—United States—Case studies.
I. Bovée, Courtland L.   II. Title.
IN PROCESS
658.4′5—dc20

CONTENTS IN BRIEF

Checklists xvii
Preface xix

Part I   FOUNDATIONS OF BUSINESS COMMUNICATION 1
Chapter 1: Communicating Successfully in an Organization 2
Chapter 2: Understanding Business Communication 21
Chapter 3: Communicating Interculturally 39
Chapter 4: Communicating Through Technology 59

Part II   THE WRITING PROCESS 75
Chapter 5: Planning Business Messages 76
Chapter 6: Composing Business Messages 94
Chapter 7: Revising Business Messages 116

Part III   LETTERS, MEMOS, AND OTHER BRIEF MESSAGES 145
Chapter 8: Writing Direct Requests 146
Chapter 9: Writing Routine, Good-News, and Goodwill Messages 170
Chapter 10: Writing Bad-News Messages 202
Chapter 11: Writing Persuasive Messages 232

Part IV   REPORTS AND PROPOSALS 263
Chapter 12: Writing Short Reports 264
Chapter 13: Planning Long Reports 294
Chapter 14: Writing Long Reports 319

Part V   EMPLOYMENT MESSAGES 369
Chapter 15: Writing Résumés and Application Letters 370
Chapter 16: Interviewing for Employment and Following Up 400

Part VI   ORAL COMMUNICATION 425
Chapter 17: Listening, Interviewing, and Conducting Meetings 426
Chapter 18: Giving Speeches and Oral Presentations 444

Appendix A: Format and Layout of Business Documents 465
Appendix B: Documentation of Report Sources 484
Appendix C: Fundamentals of Grammar and Usage 495
Appendix D: Correction Symbols 513

References R-1
Acknowledgments A-1
Indexes I-1

CONTENTS

Checklists xvii
Preface xix

Part I   FOUNDATIONS OF BUSINESS COMMUNICATION 1

Chapter 1   COMMUNICATING SUCCESSFULLY IN AN ORGANIZATION 2

On the Job: FACING A COMMUNICATION DILEMMA AT SATURN 2

Communication, Business, and You 3
Internal Communication 3
  Formal Communication Channels 4
  Informal Communication Channels 6
External Communication 7
  Formal Contacts with Outsiders 7
  Informal Contacts with Outsiders 10
Characteristics of Effective Communication 11
  An Open Communication Climate 11
  A Commitment to Ethical Communication 11
  An Understanding of Intercultural Communication 13
  A Proficiency in Communication Technology 14
  An Audience-Centered Approach to Communication 15
  An Efficient Flow of Communication Messages 15
Applying What You've Learned 17

On the Job: SOLVING A COMMUNICATION DILEMMA AT SATURN 17

Questions for Discussion 19
Exercises 19
BEHIND THE SCENES AT AMTRAK 8

Chapter 2   UNDERSTANDING BUSINESS COMMUNICATION 21

On the Job: FACING A COMMUNICATION DILEMMA AT BEN & JERRY'S
HOMEMADE 21

The Basic Forms of Communication 22
  Nonverbal Communication 22
  Verbal Communication 24
The Process of Communication 25
  Formulating a Message 26
  Overcoming Communication Barriers 27
How to Improve Communication 33
  Create the Message Carefully 34
  Minimize Noise 34
  Facilitate Feedback 35

On the Job: SOLVING A COMMUNICATION DILEMMA AT BEN & JERRY'S HOMEMADE 35

Questions for Discussion 37
Document for Analysis 37
Exercises 38
BEHIND THE SCENES AT FEDERAL EXPRESS 32

Chapter 3   COMMUNICATING INTERCULTURALLY 39

On the Job: FACING A COMMUNICATION DILEMMA AT APPLE COMPUTER 39

The Basics of Intercultural Business Communication 39
  Understanding Culture 40
  Recognizing Cultural Differences 41
  Dealing with Language Barriers 44
  Dealing with Ethnocentric Reactions 47
Tips for Communicating with People from Other Cultures 47
  Learning About a Culture 48
  Developing Intercultural Communication Skills 50
  Negotiating Across Cultures 52
  Handling Written Communication 53
  Handling Oral Communication 54

On the Job: SOLVING A COMMUNICATION DILEMMA AT APPLE COMPUTER 56

Questions for Discussion 58
Exercises 58
BEHIND THE SCENES AT PARKER PEN 50

Chapter 4   COMMUNICATING THROUGH TECHNOLOGY 59

On the Job: FACING A COMMUNICATION DILEMMA AT METROPOLITAN LIFE INSURANCE 59

Technology and the New World of Business Communication 60
Technology in Written Communication 61
  Creating Printed Documents 61
  Creating Electronic Documents 68
Technology in Oral Communication 69
  Individual Communication 69
  Group Communication 70
How Technology Is Changing Communication 70

On the Job: SOLVING A COMMUNICATION DILEMMA AT METROPOLITAN LIFE INSURANCE 72

Questions for Discussion 73
Exercises 74
BEHIND THE SCENES AT MIKE'S VIDEO 64

Part II	**THE WRITING PROCESS** 75	
Chapter 5	**PLANNING BUSINESS MESSAGES** 76	
On the Job:	FACING A COMMUNICATION DILEMMA AT MATTEL 76	

Understanding the Composition Process 77
Defining Your Purpose 78
  Common Purposes of Business Messages 78
  How to Test Your Purpose 79
Analyzing Your Audience 79
  Develop Your Audience's Profile 80
  Satisfy Your Audience's Information Needs 80
  Satisfy Your Audience's Motivational Needs 81
  Satisfy Your Audience's Practical Needs 83
Establishing the Main Idea 84
  Use Prewriting Techniques 84
  Limit the Scope 85
Selecting the Appropriate Channel and Medium 86
  Oral Communication 86
  Written Communication 86
  Electronic Communication 89

On the Job: SOLVING A COMMUNICATION DILEMMA AT MATTEL 91

Questions for Discussion 92
Exercises 93
BEHIND THE SCENES AT ALLSTATE INSURANCE 82

Chapter 6 **COMPOSING BUSINESS MESSAGES** 94
On the Job: FACING A COMMUNICATION DILEMMA AT DRAKE BEAM MORIN 94

Organizing Your Message 95
  What Good Organization Means 95
  Why Good Organization Is Important 97
  How Good Organization Is Achieved 97
Formulating Your Message 103
  Your First Draft 103
  Your Style and Tone 104

On the Job: SOLVING A COMMUNICATION DILEMMA AT DRAKE BEAM MORIN 111

Questions for Discussion 113
Documents for Analysis 114
Exercises 114
BEHIND THE SCENES AT GENERAL ELECTRIC 104

Chapter 7 **REVISING BUSINESS MESSAGES** 116
On the Job: FACING A COMMUNICATION DILEMMA AT McDONALD'S 116

Editing Your Message 117
  Evaluate Your Content and Organization 118
  Review Your Style and Readability 118
  Assess Your Word Choice 118

Rewriting Your Message 125
  Create Effective Sentences 125
  Develop Coherent Paragraphs 134
Producing Your Message 136
Proofing Your Message 137

On the Job: SOLVING A COMMUNICATION DILEMMA
            AT McDONALD'S 138

Questions for Discussion 141
Documents for Analysis 141
Exercises 142
BEHIND THE SCENES AT LA JOLLA PLAYHOUSE 132

Part III   LETTERS, MEMOS, AND OTHER BRIEF MESSAGES 145

Chapter 8   WRITING DIRECT REQUESTS 146

On the Job: FACING A COMMUNICATION DILEMMA AT
            BARNES & NOBLE 146

Intercultural Requests 147
Organizing Direct Requests 147
  Direct Statement of the Request or Main Idea 148
  Justification, Explanation, and Details 148
  Courteous Close with Request for Specific Action 149
Placing Orders 149
Requesting Routine Information and Action 151
  Requests to Company Insiders 152
  Requests to Other Businesses 153
  Requests to Customers and Other Outsiders 154
Requesting Claims and Adjustments 158
Making Routine Credit Requests 160
Inquiring About People 162

On the Job: SOLVING A COMMUNICATION DILEMMA AT
            BARNES & NOBLE 162

Questions for Discussion 164
Documents for Analysis 165
Cases 165
BEHIND THE SCENES AT THE PHOENIX SYMPHONY 156

Chapter 9   WRITING ROUTINE, GOOD-NEWS, AND
            GOODWILL MESSAGES 170

On the Job: FACING A COMMUNICATION DILEMMA AT
            CAMPBELL SOUP COMPANY 170

Organizing Positive Messages 171
  Clear Statement of the Main Idea 171
  Necessary Details 171
  Courteous Close 172
Writing Positive Replies 172
  Acknowledging Orders 172
  Replying to Requests for Information and Action 173
Responding Favorably to Claims and Adjustment Requests 178

Handling Routing Credit Requests 180
   Approving Credit 180
   Providing Credit References 182
Conveying Positive Information About People 183
   Recommendation Letters 183
   Good News About Employment 184
Writing Directives and Instructions 185
Conveying Good News About Products and Operations 186
Writing Goodwill Messages 188
   Congratulations 189
   Messages of Appreciation 189
   Condolences 191

On the Job: SOLVING A COMMUNICATION DILEMMA AT
CAMPBELL SOUP COMPANY 193

Questions for Discussion 195
Documents for Analysis 195
Cases 196
BEHIND THE SCENES AT CITIBANK 174

Chapter 10   **WRITING BAD-NEWS MESSAGES 202**

On the Job: FACING A COMMUNICATION DILEMMA AT CREATIVE
ASSOCIATES 202

Organizing Bad-News Messages 203
   Indirect Plan 203
   Direct Plan 208
Conveying Bad News About Orders 209
Communicating Negative Answers and Information 212
   Providing Bad News About Products 212
   Denying Cooperation with Routine Requests 213
   Declining Requests for Favors 215
Refusing Adjustment of Claims and Complaints 216
Refusing to Extend Credit 218
Conveying Unfavorable News About People 219
   Refusing to Write Recommendation Letters 219
   Rejecting Job Applications 221
   Giving Negative Performance Reviews 221
   Terminating Employment 221

On the Job: SOLVING A COMMUNICATION DILEMMA AT CREATIVE
ASSOCIATES 223

Questions for Discussion 225
Documents for Analysis 225
Cases 226
BEHIND THE SCENES AT AMERICA WEST 208

Chapter 11   **WRITING PERSUASIVE MESSAGES 232**

On the Job: FACING A COMMUNICATION DILEMMA AT UNITED
NEGRO COLLEGE FUND 232

Motivating with Persuasive Messages 233
   Needs and Appeals 233
   Emotion and Logic 233

Credibility 234
Semantics 234
Organizing Persuasive Messages 235
Writing Persuasive Requests for Action 236
Writing Sales Letters 238
Planning Sales Letters 239
Composing Sales Letters 240
Packaging Sales Letters 246
Writing Collection Messages 247
The Collection Context 247
The Collection Series 250

On the Job: SOLVING A COMMUNICATION DILEMMA AT UNITED
NEGRO COLLEGE FUND 254

Questions for Discussion 256
Documents for Analysis 256
Cases 257
BEHIND THE SCENES WITH JOHN KEIL 242

Part IV   REPORTS AND PROPOSALS 263

Chapter 12   WRITING SHORT REPORTS 264

On the Job: FACING A COMMUNICATION DILEMMA AT FEDERAL
EXPRESS 264

What Makes a Good Report 265
Accuracy 265
Good Judgment 267
Responsive Format, Style, and Organization 267
Planning Short Reports 269
Deciding on Format and Length 269
Establishing a Basic Structure 270
Organizing Short Reports 272
Organizing Informational Memos and Reports 272
Organizing Analytical Reports 275
Making Reports and Proposals Readable 280
Choosing the Proper Degree of Formality 281
Developing Structural Clues 283

On the Job: SOLVING A COMMUNICATION DILEMMA AT FEDERAL
EXPRESS 287

Questions for Discussion 291
Exercises 291
Cases 292
BEHIND THE SCENES AT THE SAN DIEGO ZOO 268

Chapter 13   PLANNING LONG REPORTS 294

On the Job: FACING A COMMUNICATION DILEMMA AT
HARLEY-DAVIDSON 294

Five Steps in Planning Reports 295
Defining the Problem 295
Asking the Right Questions 296
Developing the Statement of Purpose 296

Outlining Issues for Investigation 297
  Developing a Logical Structure 298
  Following the Rules of Division 300
  Preparing a Preliminary Outline 300
Preparing the Work Plan 302
Conducting the Research 302
  Reviewing Secondary Sources 304
  Collecting Primary Data 304
Analyzing and Interpreting Data 308
  Calculating Statistics 308
  Drawing Conclusions 309
  Developing Recommendations 310
Preparing the Final Outline 311

On the Job: SOLVING A COMMUNICATION DILEMMA AT
HARLEY-DAVIDSON 313

Questions for Discussion 316
Exercises 317
BEHIND THE SCENES AT GANNETT COMPANY 312

Chapter 14 WRITING LONG REPORTS 319

On the Job: FACING A COMMUNICATION DILEMMA AT PENN STATE 319

Report Production 319
Components of a Formal Report 320
  Prefatory Parts 321
  Text of the Report 325
  Visual Aids 329
  Supplementary Parts 337
Components of a Formal Proposal 357
  Prefatory Parts 357
  Text of the Proposal 358

On the Job: SOLVING A COMMUNICATION DILEMMA AT
PENN STATE 362

Questions for Discussion 364
Exercises 364
Cases 365
BEHIND THE SCENES AT THE ROCKY MOUNTAIN
INSTITUTE 322

REPORT WRITER'S NOTEBOOK: CREATING COLORFUL
VISUAL AIDS WITH COMPUTERS 336

REPORT WRITER'S NOTEBOOK: ANALYZING A FORMAL
REPORT: AN IN-DEPTH CRITIQUE 338

Part V EMPLOYMENT MESSAGES 369

Chapter 15 WRITING RÉSUMÉS AND APPLICATION LETTERS 370

On the Job: FACING A COMMUNICATION DILEMMA AT PINKERTON 370

Thinking About Your Career 371
  What Do You Have to Offer? 371
  What Do You Want to Do? 371
  Where Do You Find Employment Information? 372

Writing a Résumé 373
Controlling the Format and Style 373
Tailoring the Contents 374
Choosing the Best Organizational Plan 379
Writing the Perfect Résumé 383
Writing an Application Letter 384
Writing the Opening Paragraph 385
Summarizing Your Key Selling Points 387
Writing the Closing Paragraph 389
Writing the Perfect Application Letter 389
Writing Other Types of Employment Messages 390
Writing Job-Inquiry Letters 390
Filling Out Application Forms 391
Writing Application Follow-Ups 392

On the Job: SOLVING A COMMUNICATION DILEMMA AT
PINKERTON 394

Questions for Discussion 397
Documents for Analysis 397
Cases 398
BEHIND THE SCENES AT MOBIL CORPORATION 376

Chapter 16 **INTERVIEWING FOR EMPLOYMENT
AND FOLLOWING UP 400**

On the Job: FACING A COMMUNICATION DILEMMA AT
HERMAN MILLER, INC. 400

Interviewing with Potential Employers 401
The Interview Process 401
What Employers Look For 402
What Applicants Need to Find Out 403
How to Prepare for a Job Interview 403
How to Be Interviewed 408
Following Up After the Interview 413
Thank-You Message 414
Inquiry 415
Request for a Time Extension 416
Letter of Acceptance 417
Letter Declining a Job Offer 417
Letter of Resignation 418

On the Job: SOLVING A COMMUNICATION DILEMMA AT
HERMAN MILLER, INC. 419

Questions for Discussion 422
Documents for Analysis 422
Cases 422
BEHIND THE SCENES AT IBM 410

Part VI ORAL COMMUNICATION 425

Chapter 17 **LISTENING, INTERVIEWING, AND CONDUCTING
MEETINGS 426**

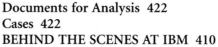

On the Job: FACING A COMMUNICATION DILEMMA AT ROCKPORT 426

Communicating Orally 427
  Speaking 427
  Listening 428
Conducting Interviews on the Job 430
  Categorizing Interviews 430
  Planning Interviews 432
Participating in Small Groups and Meetings 434
  Understanding Group Dynamics 435
  Arranging the Meeting 437
  Contributing to a Productive Meeting 438

On the Job: SOLVING A COMMUNICATION DILEMMA AT ROCKPORT 440

Questions for Discussion 442
Exercises 442
BEHIND THE SCENES AT 3M 436

Chapter 18   **GIVING SPEECHES AND ORAL PRESENTATIONS 444**

On the Job: FACING A COMMUNICATION DILEMMA AT
THE KEYS GROUP 444

Preparing to Speak 445
  Defining Your Purpose 445
  Analyzing Your Audience 445
  Planning Your Speech or Presentation 446
Developing Formal Speeches and Presentations 449
  The Introduction 450
  The Body 451
  The Close 452
  The Question-and-Answer Period 453
  The Visual Aids 454
Mastering the Art of Delivery 456
  Preparing for Successful Speaking 458
  Delivering the Speech 458
  Handling Questions 459

On the Job: SOLVING A COMMUNICATION DILEMMA AT
THE KEYS GROUP 461

Questions for Discussion 463
Exercises 463
BEHIND THE SCENES WITH CHARLES OSGOOD 456

Appendix A   **FORMAT AND LAYOUT OF BUSINESS DOCUMENTS 465**

First Impressions 465
  Paper 465
  Customization 466
  Appearance 466
Letters 466
  Standard Letter Parts 467
  Additional Letter Parts 470
  Letter Formats 473
Envelopes 475
  Addressing the Envelope 476
  Folding to Fit 478

International Mail 478
Memos 478
Time-Saving Messages 480
Reports 481
  Margins 481
  Headings 482
  Spacing and Indentions 482
  Page Numbers 482
Meeting Documents 482

Appendix B DOCUMENTATION OF REPORT SOURCES 484

Secondary Sources 484
  A Library's Resources 484
  Computerized Databanks 486
  Note Cards 486
Copyright and Fair Use 486
Source Notes 487
  Mechanics 488
  Form 488
Bibliographies 491
  Mechanics 491
  Examples 492
Reference Citations 493
  Author-Date System 493
  Key-Number System 493
  MLA Simplified Style 493
Further Information on Documentation 494

Appendix C FUNDAMENTALS OF GRAMMAR AND USAGE 495

1.0 Grammar 495
  1.1 Nouns 496
  1.2 Pronouns 497
  1.3 Verbs 498
  1.4 Adjectives 500
  1.5 Adverbs 501
  1.6 Other Parts of Speech 501
  1.7 Sentences 501
2.0 Punctuation 505
  2.1 Periods 505
  2.2 Question Marks 505
  2.3 Exclamation Points 505
  2.4 Semicolons 505
  2.5 Colons 505
  2.6 Commas 505
  2.7 Dashes 506
  2.8 Hyphens 507
  2.9 Apostrophes 507
  2.10 Quotation Marks 507
  2.11 Parentheses 507
  2.12 Ellipses 508
  2.13 Underscores and Italics 508
3.0 Mechanics 508

3.1   *Capitals 508*
3.2   *Abbreviations 508*
3.3   *Numbers 509*
3.4   *Word Division 509*
4.0 Vocabulary 509
4.1   *Frequently Confused Words 509*
4.2   *Frequently Misused Words 511*
4.3   *Frequently Misspelled Words 511*
4.4   *Transitional Words and Phrases 512*

Appendix D   **CORRECTION SYMBOLS 513**

Content and Style 513
Grammar, Usage, and Mechanics 515
Proofreading Marks 516

References R-1
Acknowledgments A-1
Organization/Product/Name Index I-1
Subject Index I-5

CHECKLISTS

- Checklist for Doing Business Abroad 48
- Checklist for Communicating with a Culturally Diverse Workforce 52
- Checklist for Dictation 62
- Checklist for Planning Business Messages 90
- Checklist for Composing Business Messages 111
- Checklist for Revising Business Messages 138
- Checklist for Orders 151
- Checklist for Routine Requests 158
- Checklist for Claims and Requests for Adjustment 160
- Checklist for Positive Replies 178
- Checklist for Favorable Responses to Claims and Adjustment Requests 181
- Checklist for Credit Approvals 182
- Checklist for Goodwill Messages 192
- Checklist for Bad News About Orders 212
- Checklist for Refusals to Make Adjustments 217
- Checklist for Credit Refusals 220
- Checklist for Unfavorable News About People 222
- Checklist for Persuasive Requests for Action 238
- Checklist for Sales Letters 248
- Checklist for Collection Messages 252
- Checklist for Short Informal Reports 286
- Checklist for Formal Reports and Proposals 360
- Checklist for Résumés 384
- Checklist for Application Letters 392
- Checklist for Interviews 412
- Checklist for Follow-Up Messages 419
- Checklist for Interviews on the Job 434
- Checklist for Meetings 439
- Checklist for Speeches and Oral Presentations 460

PREFACE

Excellence in Business Communication, Third Edition, provides an exciting and dynamic new way of bringing the real world into the classroom. This is the first textbook that offers business communication experience through real-world simulations featuring actual companies. These simulations provide a unique opportunity for students to apply concepts to real events and to sharpen their business communication problem-solving skills.

Students are introduced to a cross section of real people—men and women who work for some of America's most fascinating companies and who, on a typical day, encounter a variety of communication problems. In each chapter, students are asked to help these businesspeople find solutions to their communication problems. Moreover, students find it easy to relate to the highly visible companies featured, including such well-respected giants as McDonald's, Mattel, Federal Express, Barnes & Noble, and Ben & Jerry's, to name just a few.

Excellence in Business Communication is the next step in the evolution of business communication textbooks. Of course, this text covers all the basic principles and presents them in a traditional sequence. But its real-life simulations, engaging writing style, and eye-opening graphics all bring the subject to life, capturing the essence of business communication as no other text has done before. We believe this book will instill in students both respect for the field of business communication and confidence that the subject can be understood and mastered.

The textbook itself is the centerpiece of a comprehensive teaching and learning package that targets a single goal: to demonstrate how business communication works in the real world, thus helping students understand the concepts behind effective communication while developing and refining their own abilities.

F EATURES LINK CONCEPTS TO THE REAL WORLD

Excellence in Business Communication, Third Edition, paints a vivid picture of the world of business communication. It offers an overview of the wide range of communication skills that are used by businesspeople to present ideas clearly and persuasively. It also gives specific examples of the communication techniques that have led to sound decision making and effective teamwork. In addition, its insights into the way organizations operate help clarify student career interests by identifying the skills needed for a lifetime of career success.

On-the-Job Simulations

The opportunity to learn by doing is what sets this textbook apart from others. Students not only learn from other people's successes and failures but also make "on the job" decisions about communication problems. To understand our commitment to this concept, glance at the table of contents. You'll also see that this textbook was written with the cooperation of many well-known businesses, including Saturn, Campbell Soup, Apple Computer, Harley-Davidson, and Metropolitan Life.

Each chapter opens with an exclusive concept, On the Job: Facing a Communication Dilemma. This slice-of-life vignette summarizes a communication problem being faced by an actual company. The solution to the dilemma is found in the concepts presented in the chapter, and the dilemma reappears from time to time throughout the chapter to dramatize the connection between the principles discussed and life on the job.

But we don't stop there. Each chapter ends with another exclusive feature, On the Job: Solving a Communication Dilemma. These simulations are factually based on real companies, and they expand on the chapter-opening dilemma. Students are asked to solve the dilemma by applying the principles discussed in the text, by making decisions about the communication process, and by selecting the best alternatives from the choices offered. Not only do these simulations give students the opportunity to practice real-world decision making, they also tie the textual information to real-life examples, providing a concrete basis for analyzing the chapter principles. This chapter-spanning feature provides a dimension of reality unmatched by other textbooks in the field.

Behind the Scenes Special Features

Boxed and carefully placed within each chapter, Behind the Scenes sidebars extend the chapter material by focusing on real people, real products, and real companies. We personally interviewed accomplished business communicators at actual companies to provide insights into the business world that cannot be found in other textbooks. Eighteen Behind the Scenes special features bring even more of the world of business into the classroom. Examples include

- Behind the Scenes at the Phoenix Symphony: Orchestrating Direct Requests
- Behind the Scenes at the San Diego Zoo: Even Tapirs Leave a Paper Trail
- Behind the Scenes at 3M: The Keys to Masterful Meetings

The discussion questions at the end of each of these special features give students numerous opportunities to analyze business communication principles and practices.

Gallery of Business Communication Professionals

Another unique feature of this text is the inclusion of full-color photographs with incisive captions that focus on 72 highly successful communication professionals from business, industry, government, and the media. Among the individuals featured are Paul Fireman (Reebok), William Gates (Microsoft), Michael Eisner (Disney), Dan Rather (CBS News), and Sandra Day O'Connor (U.S. Supreme Court).

Strategically placed in the margins throughout each chapter, these captions with accompanying photographs expand the amount of insight to be gained from this book. Each caption relates specifically to the text and gives a communication expert's view about a particular aspect of business communication, adding a new dimension to student learning.

Example after Example of Letters, Memos, and Reports

Throughout *Excellence in Business Communication,* Third Edition, you'll find numerous up-to-date sample documents, many collected in our consulting work. These superb business examples provide students with benchmarks for achievement.

The chapters on letters and memos contain outstanding examples from numerous types of organizations and from people working in a variety of functional areas. Many of these documents are fully formatted, and some are presented on the letterheads of such well-known companies as TWA, J. C. Penney, Black & Decker, General Mills, and Mattel Toys. Accompanying sentence-by-sentence analyses help students see precisely how to apply the principles discussed in the text. Poor and improved examples illustrate common errors and effective techniques for correcting them.

The report-writing chapters give numerous examples, too. And the last chapter of the report unit illustrates the step-by-step development of a long report, which appears in its entirety to show how all the parts fit together.

Real-World Issues

The boundaries of business communication are always expanding. So in addition to covering all the traditional subjects, *Excellence in Business Communication,* Third Edition, provides material to help students manage a myriad of current issues in business communication:

- *The process approach.* Because both the communication product and the process to achieve it are so important in today's business world, we have strengthened the process approach while maintaining the strong product orientation.
- *Ethics.* Every message, whether verbal or nonverbal, communicates something about our values and ethics. Thus students must be given the means to anticipate and analyze the ethical dilemmas they will face on the job. Moreover, adhering to high ethical standards takes on a new importance in this age of wavering business behavior. Ethical questions addressed in this book include how much to emphasize the positive in business messages (Chapter 6), how to handle negative information in recommendations (Chapter 9), where to draw the line between persuasion and manipulation in sales letters (Chapter 11), and how to construct visual aids without misleading the audience (Chapter 16). Taking an ethical position in the face of pressures and temptations requires more than courage—it requires strong communication skills.
- *Crisis communication.* Whether it's the bombing of the World Trade Center or the deaths from contaminated hamburger served at Jack in the Box fast-food outlets, recent catastrophes emphasize the value of planning for crisis communication (Chapter 1).
- *Communication barriers.* The shift toward a service economy means that more and more careers will depend on interpersonal skills. Instead of working on an assembly line, people will be interacting with other people, making it vital for people to overcome communication barriers (Chapter 2).
- *Cultural diversity.* The changing nature of the domestic workforce requires strong communication skills to relate to older workers, women, members of various socioeconomic groups, immigrants, and others. Moreover, with such international agreements as Europe 1992, the North American Free Trade Agreement (NAFTA), and the new General Agreement on Tariffs and Trade (GATT), the continuing globalization of business necessitates strong skills to communicate effectively with people from other cultures (Chapter 3).

- *Business technology.* Advances in communication technology are altering the way people communicate in organizations. Students will be using more computerized interaction and less hard copy. To survive in the business world of today and tomorrow, students will need to master new machines and become comfortable with new communication channels such as the Internet, the global electronic network (Chapter 4).
- *Law.* The increasing tendency of people to sue makes it important to understand the legal implications of written and oral communication, such as the pitfalls of writing recommendation letters (Chapter 9).
- *Employment search.* More and more people are making radical midcareer job changes, whether by choice or because their companies are downsizing and flattening hierarchies. These people need to master new communication skills as well as any information pertaining to their new jobs (Chapter 12).

A THOROUGH REVISION

When preparing the Third Edition of *Excellence in Business Communication*, we dedicated ourselves to a thorough revision. We have not only shifted the placement of two critical chapters but also entirely restructured and rewritten the technology chapter. With an eye to emphasizing and integrating important topics, we have critically evaluated virtually every sentence in the text, making literally hundreds of refinements. Members of the academic and business communities have carefully reviewed the third edition, and we have tested it in the classroom. Instructors, businesspeople, and students have all praised its competent coverage of subject matter, its up-to-date examples, its flexible organization, and its authentic portrayal of business. Here is an overview of the major content changes in the Third Edition:

- *Chapter 1: Communicating Successfully in an Organization.* Now appearing before the chapter on theory, draws students into the course, showing the importance of business communication, management, and organizational networks; now introduces six vital themes that recur throughout the book: open communication climate, ethics, intercultural messages, technological tools, audience-centered thinking, and efficient message flow.
- *Chapter 2: Understanding Business Communication.* Integrates a more comprehensive discussion of communication barriers, offering tips on how to overcome them; now includes gender and intercultural differences in the section on types of nonverbal behaviors; simplifies and clarifies the discussion of the communication process.
- *Chapter 3: Communicating Interculturally.* Now an introductory chapter rather than an ending chapter; maintains its emphasis on introducing the idea of culture and how intercultural differences can block successful communication; increases the emphasis on cultural diversity in the U.S. workforce; decreases emphasis on intercultural writing and speaking so that this material can be covered throughout the text in relevant chapters; relates intercultural problems as an extension of the barriers to communication that are presented in Chapter 2.
- *Chapter 4: Communicating Through Business Technology.* Now appears as an introductory chapter rather than as an ending chapter; emphasizes how technology affects communication; offers guidance about when it is appropriate to use various tools; introduces ways that technological tools can help students produce messages; updates current developments in terms of practical, on-the-job usefulness.

- *Chapter 5: Planning Business Messages.* Emphasizes the composition process explained throughout Chapters 5, 6, and 7; clarifies this process by presenting it as comprising various tasks, regardless of order; strengthens the presentation of the tasks involved in planning (defining your purpose, analyzing your audience, establishing your main idea, and selecting the appropriate channel and medium); includes a discussion of electronic channels in addition to discussions of oral and written channels.

- *Chapter 6: Composing Business Messages.* Strengthens chapter organization and flow; simplifies presentation of the tasks involved in composing business messages (organizing and formulating).

- *Chapter 7: Revising Business Messages.* Clarifies organization to emphasize revision tasks (editing, rewriting, producing, and proofing your message); now incorporates producing messages, including design elements to consider and the types of design decisions that must be made; places proofing messages in the proper context (discussing mechanics and format along with electronic grammar and spell checkers).

- *Chapter 8: Writing Direct Requests.* Now incorporates the issues of intercultural customs and expectations into a well-balanced discussion of direct requests; updates samples and real-life examples.

- *Chapter 9: Writing Routine, Good-News, and Goodwill Messages.* Updates and strengthens discussion of routine, good-news, and goodwill messages, cautioning students to consider the intercultural differences in their audiences; integrates other vital topics such as ethics, technology, and the audience-centered approach.

- *Chapter 10: Writing Bad-News Messages.* Integrates a more intercultural view of bad-news messages while maintaining an emphasis on ethics and centering attention on the audience.

- *Chapter 11: Writing Persuasive Messages.* Sharpens learning objectives; tightens chapter organization (especially with regard to sales letters) to more clearly reflect the composition process.

- *Chapter 12: Writing Short Reports.* Adds a table of the six most common uses of reports; includes a new interim progress report; incorporates more real-world business examples; simplifies language regarding research and logical reasoning.

- *Chapter 13: Planning Long Reports.* Now defines *hypothesis;* simplifies language regarding factoring; strengthens discussion of basing recommendations on analysis and conclusions rather than assumptions; clarifies the tasks in the planning and research process.

- *Chapter 14: Writing Long Reports.* Strengthens material on report production, discussing collaborative efforts, technological equipment, scheduling, and gathering reviews; now defines and discusses ethics of plagiarism.

- *Chapter 15: Writing Résumés and Application Letters.* Clarifies exactly what employers want a résumé to indicate about a candidate; adds material on intercultural differences that affect how students present themselves in résumés and application letters; strengthens the discussion of résumé inflation and the ethics of accuracy; adds material on getting a job electronically.

- *Chapter 16: Interviewing for Employment and Following Up.* Incorporates a discussion of illegal interview questions and how to handle them; amplifies the discussion of specific interviewing techniques, including warning against sounding overrehearsed by memorizing answers to common interview questions; more clearly defines the type of interviews students can expect during each step in the employment process.

- *Chapter 17: Listening, Interviewing, and Conducting Meetings.* Incorporates communication by telephone into the discussion of oral communication; integrates chapter discussion by reducing number of bulleted lists; expands guidelines to improve listening.

- *Chapter 18: Giving Speeches and Oral Presentations.* Adds material on using translators and interpreters when giving presentations abroad; expands discussion of presentation software and multimedia in oral presentations.
- *Appendix A: Format and Layout of Business Documents.* Amplifies the importance of format and layout, while retaining the convenience of presenting all formatting material in one well-organized component chapter.
- *Appendix B: Documentation of Report Sources.* Focuses on the clearest ways for documenting sources; strengthens the material on bibliographies.
- *Appendix C: Fundamentals of Grammar and Usage.* Now an appendix rather than a component chapter; strengthens the description and discussion of grammatical rules and usage problems.
- *Appendix D: Correction Symbols.* Clarifies the use of correction symbols and abbreviations so that students can easily understand teacher evaluations and can readily use proofreading marks when evaluating their own work.

*T*OOLS THAT HELP DEVELOP SKILLS AND ENHANCE COMPREHENSION

Having an accurate picture of how businesspeople communicate is important, but students need more if they are to develop usable skills. That's why, in *Excellence in Business Communication,* Third Edition, we've included a number of helpful learning tools.

Lively, Conversational Writing Style

Read a few pages of this textbook; then read a few pages of another textbook. We think you'll immediately notice the difference. The lucid writing style in *Excellence in Business Communication* makes the material pleasing to read and easy to comprehend. It stimulates interest and promotes learning. The writing style also exemplifies the principles presented in this book. In addition, we have carefully monitored the reading level of *Excellence in Business Communication* to make sure it's neither too simple nor too difficult.

Checklists

To help students organize their thinking when they begin a communication project, make decisions as they write, and check their own work, we've included numerous checklists throughout the book. Appearing as close as possible to the related discussion, the checklists are reminders, not "recipes." They provide useful guidelines for writing, without limiting creativity. Students will find them handy when they're on the job and need to refresh their memory about effective communication techniques.

Documents for Analysis

In this textbook we have provided a selection of documents that students can critique and revise—22 documents in 9 chapters. Documents include letters and memos, a letter of application, and a résumé. This hands-on experience in analyzing and improving sample documents will help students revise their own.

Exercises and Cases

A wealth of exercises and cases, many of them memo-writing tasks, provide assignments like those that students will most often face at work. The exercises and cases deal with all types and sizes of organizations, domestic and international. And we have written them for a variety of majors: management, marketing, accounting, finance, information systems, office administration, and many others. With such variety to choose from, students will have ample opportunity to test their problem-solving skills. In *Excellence in Business Communication,* Third Edition, most cases feature real companies. Examples include

- Corporate Service: Letter requesting feedback from Office Depot's newest customers
- Thank you, Japan: Letter from Xerox acknowledging an order
- No, No, No: Policy memo to "60 Minutes" producers
- Risky Business: Memo explaining credit refusal by Digital Equipment
- Safety First: Memo pressing for a new security system at Hertz

These cases are yet another tool for demonstrating the role of communication in the real business world.

Learning Objectives

Each chapter begins with a concise list of goals that students are expected to achieve by reading the chapter and completing the simulations, exercises, and cases. These objectives are meant to guide the learning process, motivate students to master the material, and aid them in measuring their success.

Margin Notes

Short summary statements that highlight key points and reinforce learning appear in the margins of *Excellence in Business Communication,* Third Edition. They are no substitute for reading the chapters but are useful for quickly getting the gist of a section, rapidly reviewing a chapter, and locating areas of greatest concern.

End-of-Chapter Discussion Questions

Questions for Discussion are designed to get students thinking about the concepts introduced in each chapter. The questions may also prompt students to stretch their learning beyond the chapter content. Not only will students find them useful in studying for examinations, but the instructor may also draw on them to promote classroom discussion of issues that have no easy answers.

Appendixes

Excellence in Business Communication, Third Edition, contains four appendixes: Appendix A, Format and Layout of Business Documents, discusses formatting for all types of documents in one convenient place. Appendix B, Documentation of Report Sources, presents information on conducting secondary research and gives basic guidelines for handling reference citations, bibliographies, and source notes. Appendix C, Fundamentals of Grammar and Usage, is a primer in brief, presenting the basic tools of language. Appendix D, Correction Symbols, provides convenient symbols for students to use when revising documents.

Color Art and Strong Visual Program

To enliven the book and heighten student interest, *Excellence in Business Communication* is the first text in this market to be printed in full color throughout. We believe you'll agree that the book has been attractively printed and that the dramatic use of color gives it exceptional visual appeal. Also, in each chapter, students learn from a rich selection of carefully crafted illustrations—graphs, charts, tables, and photographs—that demonstrate important concepts.

Book Design

The state-of-the-art design is based on extensive research and invites students to delve into the content. It also makes reading easier, reinforces learning, and increases comprehension. For example, the special features do not interfere with the flow of text material, a vital factor in maintaining attention and concentration. The design of this book, like much communication, has the simple objective of gaining interest and making a point.

A TEACHING/LEARNING PACKAGE THAT MEETS REAL NEEDS

The instructional package for this textbook is specially designed to simplify the task of teaching and learning. The instructor may choose to use the following supplements.

Instructor's Resource Manual

This comprehensive paperback book is an instructor's toolkit. Among the many things it provides are a section about collaborative writing, suggested solutions to exercises, suggested solutions and fully formatted letters for *every* case in the letter-writing chapters, and a grammar pretest and posttest. The *Instructor's Resource Manual* also has an answer key to selected exercises in the *Study Guide*.

Video Exercises

Now you can add an exciting new dimension to your course with seven professionally produced videos, one for each part of the text. Developed by the authors specifically for this book, these business communication video exercises are easy to use and are closely integrated with the content of the text to help students successfully apply important concepts and principles.

For the instructor, *Video Exercise Teaching Notes* includes teaching objectives, a list of the concepts covered in the video, discussion questions, and suggested answers to the discussion questions and video exercises.

Test Bank

This manual is organized by text chapters and includes a mix of multiple-choice, true-false, and fill-in questions for each chapter, approximately 1,500 objective items in all, carefully written and reviewed to provide a fair, structured program of evaluation.

You can also get the complete test bank on computer disk, or you can get even more flexibility with McGraw-Hill's phone-in customized test service.

Testing Services

Two major programs are available:

1. *Computerized Test Bank.* A powerful microcomputer program allows the instructor to create customized tests using the questions from the test bank, self-prepared items, or a combination. This versatile program incorporates a broad range of test-making capabilities, including question editing and scrambling to create alternative versions of a test. This program is available for both MacIntosh and IBM computers.
2. *Customized Test Service.* Through its Customized Test Service, McGraw-Hill will supply adopters of *Excellence in Business Communication,* Third Edition, with custommade tests of items selected from the test bank. The test questions can be renumbered in any order. Instructors will receive an original test, ready for reproduction, and a separate answer key. Tests can be ordered by mail or by phone, using a toll-free number.

Acetate Transparency Program

A set of 100 large-type transparency acetates, available to adopters on request, helps bring concepts alive in the classroom and provides a starting point for discussing communication techniques. All transparencies are keyed to the *Instructor's Resource Manual,* and many contrast poor and improved solutions to cases featured in the textbook.

Report Card: Classroom Management Software

This software makes compiling students' grades accurate and easy and is available for both IBM PC/PC-XT and Apple II.

Business Communication Update Newsletter

Issued four times a year and filled with stimulating ideas, this newsletter is written exclusively for instructors of business communication. The newsletter provides interesting materials that can be used in class, and it offers practical ideas about teaching methodology.

Study Guide

This paperback book contains a wealth of material reinforcing the information presented in the textbook. Students who are interested in maximizing their learning will appreciate its fill-in-the-blank chapter outlines, self-scoring quizzes on chapter contents, skill-building exercises, supplementary readings, and vocabulary and spelling exercises. In addition, to help students brush up on their English skills, the study guide includes an extensive review of grammar, punctuation, and mechanics interspersed with reinforcement exercises.

Computer Software for Students

The instructor may also choose to use our *Gregg Reference Manual Software.* Also available is *Activities in Business Communication.* Three modules—dealing with job-search strategies, vocabulary development, and writing style—contain innovative learning activities. All the modules are interactive learning tools, so students are continually reinforced by word and sound. Also available is the McGraw-Hill College Version of WordPerfect for the IBM PC and compatibles. It assists composition on a word processor and permits inserting, deleting, or moving text; correcting; automatic formatting; and storing material. For additional information on software, videos, and other ancillary materials, please contact your McGraw-Hill sales representative.

P ERSONAL ACKNOWLEDGMENTS

Excellence in Business Communication is the result of the concerted efforts of a number of people. A heartfelt thanks to our many friends, acquaintances, and business associates who agreed to be interviewed so that we could bring the real world into the classroom.

Our thanks to Terry Anderson, whose outstanding communication skills and organizational ability assured this project's clarity and completeness.

We are grateful to Randy Stevens for her proofreading skills; to Jackie Estrada for her expert assistance and sound advice; to Lianne Stevens Downey for her tenacity and inventiveness; and to Marie Painter for her diligence and specialized skills in word processing.

We also feel it is important to acknowledge and thank the Association for Business Communication, an organization whose meetings and publications provide a valuable forum for the exchange of ideas and for professional growth.

Thanks to the many individuals whose valuable suggestions and constructive comments contributed to the success of this book. The authors are deeply grateful for the efforts of Anita S. Bednar, Central State University; Donna Cox, Monroe Community College; Sauny Dills, California Polytechnic State University—San Luis Obispo; Charlene A. Gierkey, Northwestern Michigan College; Sue Granger, Jacksonville State University; Bradley S. Hayden, Western Michigan University; Michael Hignite, Southwest Missouri State; Cynthia Hofacker, University of Wisconsin—Eau Claire; Louise C. Holcomb, Gainesville College; Larry Honl, University of Wisconsin—Eau Claire; Kenneth Hunsaker, Utah State University; Robert O. Joy, Central Michigan University; Paul Killorin, Portland Community College; Al Lucero, East Tennessee State University; Rachel Mather, Adelphi University; Betty Mealor, Abraham Baldwin College; Mary Miller, Ashland University; Richard Profozich, Prince George's Community College; Brian Railsback, Western Carolina University; John Rehfuss, California State University—Sacramento; Joan C. Roderick, Southwest Texas State University; Jean Anna Sellers, Fort Hays State University; Carla L. Sloan, Liberty University; Michael Thompson, Brigham Young University; Betsy Vardaman, Baylor University; Billy Walters, Troy State University; George Walters, Emporia State University; F. Stanford Wayne, Southwest Missouri State; Robert Wheatley, Troy State University; Rosemary B. Wilson, Washtenaw Community College; and Beverly C. Wise, SUNY—Morrisville.

We appreciate the insightful comments and helpful suggestions of the individuals who reviewed the manuscript for this edition. They include John Beard, Wayne State University; Belinda Wood Droll, Millikin University; Helen Gratta, Des Moines Area Community College; Lorita S. Langdon, Columbus State Community College; and Rita Sloan Tilton, University of Nevada, Las Vegas.

We also want to extend our warmest appreciation to the very devoted professionals at McGraw-Hill. They include Robert Christie, Gary Burke, Karen Westover, Dan Loch, and the outstanding McGraw-Hill sales representatives. Finally, we thank editor Linda Richmond for her dedication and expertise, and we are grateful to copyeditor Lynn Anderson, designer Karen Quigley, and production supervisor Elizabeth Strange for their superb work.

John V. Thill
Courtland L. Bovée

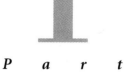

al Communication · External Communication · Characteristics of Effective Communication

FOUNDATIONS

rms of Communication · The Process of Communication · How to Improve Communication

OF BUSINESS

ltural Business Communication · Tips for Communicating with People from Other Cultures

COMMUNICATION

Other Cultures · Technology in Oral Communication · How Technology Is Changing Communication

Chapter 1
Communicating Successfully in an Organization

Chapter 2
Understanding Business Communication

Chapter 3
Communicating Interculturally

Chapter 4
Communicating Through Technology

After studying this chapter, you will be able to

Discuss how communication affects your business future

Explain how organizations use internal communication

List the distinctions between formal and informal communication channels

Describe the two departments responsible for external communication

Analyze how companies communicate successfully in a crisis

Discuss the six factors that contribute to effective business communication

COMMUNICATING SUCCESSFULLY IN AN ORGANIZATION

*O*n the Job

FACING A COMMUNICATION DILEMMA AT SATURN

Tuning Up Communication with Employees, Dealers, and Customers

Starting a new car company is anything but easy. Just ask Richard (Skip) LeFauve. As president of Saturn, LeFauve leads the team of innovators in Spring Hill, Tennessee, who have the daunting task of luring U.S. car buyers back from foreign manufacturers. LeFauve believes that maintaining a constant and open flow of information inside and outside the plant is essential if Saturn is to achieve its goal.

Saturn's parent, General Motors, once dominated the U.S. market but lost ground as smaller, more fuel-efficient imports became popular. Worse, many buyers considered cars from Honda and other foreign automakers to be better built and more reliable than U.S. cars. Losses mounted during the 1980s as GM struggled to redesign cars and factories and to cut costs through massive layoffs and plant closings.

Then GM started Saturn and an entirely new way of approaching the automotive business. The state-of-the-art factory stresses quality rather than quantity, and instead of working within the traditional boss-worker structure, managers and employees work together in teams, making decisions by consensus. These teams decide everything about Saturn's operation, including who does what job, how to engineer parts, how to advertise the car, and what the company's long-range strategy will be. Even Saturn's contract with the United Auto Workers union was a departure from the norm.

Long before the first Saturn rolled off the assembly line, LeFauve had to start thinking about communication. How could he help employees share their ideas? What could he do to foster a good relationship with the union? How could he communicate Saturn's unique qualities to car buyers?[1]

COMMUNICATION, BUSINESS, AND YOU

Organizations like Saturn bend over backward to see that communication both inside and outside the company is open, honest, and clear. Your ability to communicate increases productivity, both yours and your organization's. It shapes the impressions you make on your colleagues, employees, supervisors, investors, and customers. It allows you to perceive the needs of these stakeholders (your first step toward satisfying them), and it helps you respond to those needs. Whether you run your own business, work for an employer, invest in a company, buy or sell products, design computer chips, run for public office, or raise money for charities, your communication skills determine your success.[2]

Saturn

Regardless of the field you're in or the career you choose, your chances of being hired by an organization are better if you possess strong communication skills. Out of 120 job descriptions appearing in one issue of the *National Business Employment Weekly* (published by *The Wall Street Journal*), almost every listing included this requirement: "The persons we seek must have strong oral and written communication skills."[3]

Employers want people who can communicate.

That's because every member of an organization is a link in the information chain. The flow of information along that chain is a steady stream of messages, whether from inside the organization (staff meetings, progress reports, project proposals, research results, employee surveys, persuasive interviews) or from outside the organization (loan applications, purchasing agreements, help-wanted ads, distribution contracts, product advertisements, sales calls). Your ability to receive, evaluate, use, and pass on information affects your company's effectiveness, as well as your own.

Within the company, you and your co-workers use the information you obtain from one another and from outsiders to guide your activities. The work of the organization is divided into tasks and assigned to various organizational units, each reporting to a manager who directs and coordinates the effort. This delegation of responsibility depends on the constant flow of information up, down, and across the organization. So by feeding information to your boss and peers, you help them do their jobs—and vice versa.

Ask yourself what information your co-workers and supervisors need from you, and then figure out how you can supply it.

If you are a manager, your day consists of a never-ending series of meetings, casual conversations, speaking engagements, and phone calls, interspersed with occasional time for reading or writing. From these sources you cull important points and then pass them on to the right people. In turn, you rely on your employees to provide you with useful data and to interpret, transmit, and act on the messages you send them.

Managers make and carry out decisions by collecting facts, analyzing them, and transmitting directions to lower-level employees.

If you are a relatively junior employee, you are likely to find yourself on the perimeter of the communication network. Oddly enough, this puts you in an important position in the information chain. Although your span of influence may be limited, you are in a position to observe firsthand things that your supervisors and co-workers cannot see: a customer's immediate reaction to a product display, a supplier's momentary hesitation before agreeing to a delivery date, a funny whirring noise in a piece of equipment, or a slowdown in the flow of customers. These are the little gems of information that managers and co-workers need to do their jobs. If you don't pass that information along, nobody will—because nobody else knows. Such an exchange of information within an organization is called **internal communication.**

Employees serve as the eyes and ears of an organization, providing direct impressions from the front line.

You are a contact point in both the external and internal communication networks.

INTERNAL COMMUNICATION

Communication among the members of an organization is essential for a business to be effective, so each organization approaches internal communication differently. In

Each organization has its own approach to transmitting information throughout the organization.

a small business with only five or six employees, much information can be exchanged casually and directly. In a large organization like Saturn, transmitting the right information to the right people at the right time is a real challenge.

Formal Communication Channels

The formal flow of information follows the official chain of command.

The **formal communication network** is the official structure of an organization, which is typically shown as an organization chart like the one in Figure 1.1. Such charts summarize the lines of authority, each box representing a link in the chain of command and each line representing a formal channel for the transmission of official messages. Information may travel down, up, and across an organization's formal hierarchy.

When managers depend too heavily on formal channels for communicating, they risk encountering **distortion,** or misunderstanding. Every link in the communication chain opens up a chance for error. So by the time a message makes its way all the way up or down the chain, it may bear little resemblance to the original idea. As a consequence, people at lower levels may have only a vague idea of what top management expects of them, and executives may get an imperfect picture of what's happening lower down the chain.

The communication climate suffers when management distorts or ignores information from below or when management limits the flow of information to employees.

One way to reduce such distortion is to reduce the number of levels in the organizational structure. The fewer the links in the communication chain, the less likely it is that misunderstandings will occur.[4] Generally speaking, bigger corporations have more levels. However, as Figure 1.2 illustrates, size doesn't necessarily force a company to have a hierarchy with many levels. By increasing the number of people who report to each supervisor, the company can reduce the number of levels in the organization and simplify the communication chain. In other words, a flat structure (having fewer levels) and a wide span of control (having more people reporting to each supervisor) are less likely to introduce distortion than are a tall structure and a narrow span of control. The best way to fight distortion is to make sure communication flows freely down, up, and across the organization chart.

Figure 1.1
Formal Communication Network

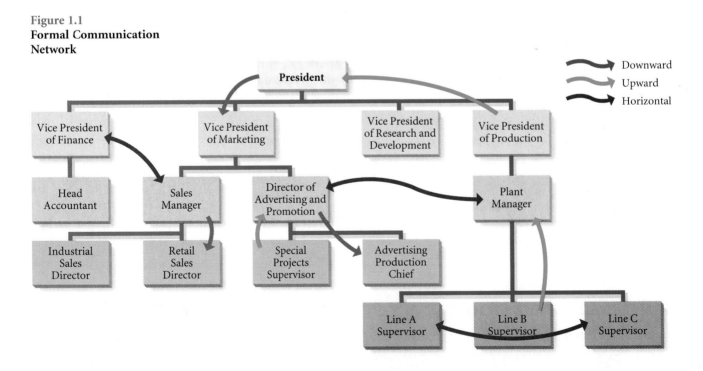

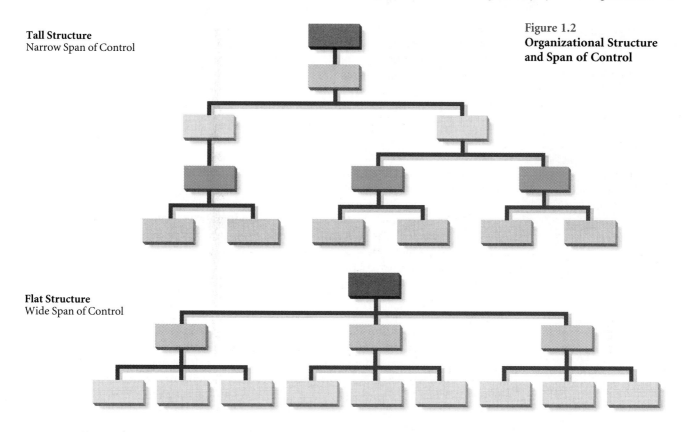

Tall Structure
Narrow Span of Control

Figure 1.2
**Organizational Structure
and Span of Control**

Flat Structure
Wide Span of Control

Downward Information Flow

In most organizations, decisions are made at the top and then flow down to the people who will carry them out.[5] Downward messages might take the form of a casual conversation or a formal interview between a supervisor and an individual employee, or they might be communicated orally in a meeting, in a workshop, or on videotape. Messages might also be written in a memo, training manual, newsletter, bulletin board announcement, or policy directive. From top to bottom, each person in the organization must be careful to understand the message, apply it, and pass it along.

Most of what filters downward is geared toward helping employees do their jobs. Typical messages include briefings on the organization's mission and strategies, instructions on how to perform various jobs, explanations of policies and procedures, feedback on employee performance, and motivational pep talks. In hard times, downward communication is especially important, letting employees know how the organization is doing, what problems it faces, and what's expected to happen in the future. "One of the most important communication obligations I have is the release of information to employees in advance of its public release," says Avon CEO Hicks Waldron. It keeps them "in tune with what's going on in the business."[6]

> Managers direct and control the activities of lower-level employees by sending messages down through formal channels.

Upward Information Flow

Upward communication is just as vital as downward communication. To solve problems and make intelligent decisions, managers must learn what's going on in the organization. Since they can't be everywhere at once, executives depend on lower-level employees to furnish them with accurate, timely reports on problems, emerging trends, opportunities for improvement, grievances, and performance.

> Messages directed upward provide managers with the information they need to make intelligent decisions.

Robert M. Beavers is senior vice president/zone manager at McDonald's Corporation. Having worked his way up from the bottom, he is now responsible for six regional offices: Phoenix, Denver, San Francisco, Sacramento, Los Angeles, and San Diego. He credits his success to good communication. No matter what the industry, says Beavers, it's communicating with people that makes the difference.

Official channels also permit messages to flow from department to department.

Informal communication travels along the organization's unofficial lines of activity and power.

The grapevine is an important source of information in most organizations.

The danger, of course, is that employees will report only the good news. People are often afraid to admit their own mistakes or to report data that suggest their boss was wrong. Companies try to guard against the "rose-colored glasses" syndrome by creating reporting systems that require employees to furnish vital information on a routine basis. Many of these reports have a "red flag" feature that calls attention to deviations from planned results.

Other formal methods for channeling information upward include group meetings, interviews with employees who are leaving the company, and formal procedures for resolving grievances. At the Walt Disney Company, two favorite methods are employee surveys (which give people a chance to comment anonymously on a wide range of issues) and focus groups (which allow employees to share their insights on specific subjects).

In recent years, many companies have also set up suggestion systems that encourage employees to submit ideas for improving the business. At Herman Miller, a Michigan manufacturer of office furniture, people who submit suggestions are publicly honored at departmental meetings, and those with the most outstanding ideas are invited to a special annual dinner with the CEO. The savings or profits created by the suggestions are set aside and spent for something that benefits all the employees.[7]

Horizontal Information Flow

In the formal communication network, horizontal communication flows from one department to another, either laterally or diagonally. It helps employees coordinate tasks, and it's especially useful for solving complex and difficult problems.[8] For example, in Figure 1.1, the sales manager might write a memo to the vice president of finance, outlining sales forecasts for the coming period; or the plant manager might phone the director of advertising and promotion to discuss changes in the production schedule.

Companies that encourage horizontal communication report dramatic increases in productivity, largely because cooperation between employees from various departments breaks down the bureaucratic barriers that inhibit innovation and camouflage problems. Ever since Federal Express started emphasizing horizontal teamwork, service problems have declined. By working across department lines, one team of clerks single-handedly solved a billing problem costing the company $2.1 million a year.[9]

In many companies, advanced technology provides the physical foundation for communication between departments. For example, Sun Microsystems uses a worldwide computer network to link its 13,000 employees in the United States, England, Scotland, Brazil, Japan, Germany, the Netherlands, France, and Hong Kong. Whether implemented through technology or teamwork, horizontal communication is crucial. Without it, co-workers aren't able to share information, and the results are missed deadlines, duplicated efforts, increased costs (due to rework), decreased product quality, and deteriorating employee relationships.[10]

Informal Communication Channels

Formal organization charts illustrate how information is supposed to flow. In actual practice, however, lines and boxes on a piece of paper cannot prevent people from talking with one another. Every organization has an **informal communication network**—a grapevine—that supplements official channels. As people go about their work, they have casual conversations with their friends in the office. They joke around and discuss their apartments, their families, restaurants, movies, sports, and other people in the company.

Although many of these conversations deal with personal matters, business is often discussed as well. In fact, about 80 percent of the information that travels along

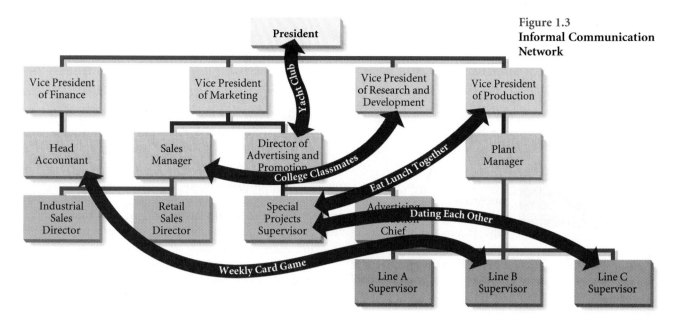

Figure 1.3
Informal Communication Network

the grapevine pertains to business, and 75 to 95 percent of it is accurate.[11] Figure 1.3 illustrates a typical informal communication network, which is often the company's real power structure.

Some top executives are wary of the informal communication network, possibly because it threatens their power to control the flow of information. However, attempts to quash the grapevine generally have the opposite effect. Informal communication increases when official channels are closed or when the organization faces periods of change, excitement, or anxiety. Instead of trying to eliminate the grapevine, sophisticated companies minimize its importance by making certain that the official word gets out.

One service, called In Touch, helps executives keep up with grapevine news by providing an 800 number that employees can call anonymously with any problems or worries.[12] Better yet, successful managers tap into the grapevine themselves to avoid being isolated from what's really happening. Hewlett-Packard trains its managers in **Management by Walking Around (MBWA),** encouraging them to be interested in employees' personal lives as well as their work lives. Saturn's Richard LeFauve encourages informal communication by having all employees eat in the same cafeterias (rather than providing separate facilities for top management).

E XTERNAL COMMUNICATION

Just as the internal communication network carries information up, down, and across the organization, the **external communication network** carries information in and out. Companies constantly exchange messages with customers, vendors, distributors, competitors, investors, journalists, and government and community representatives. Some of this communication is carefully orchestrated, and much occurs informally.

Formal Contacts with Outsiders

Even though a lot of the communication that occurs with outsiders is casual and relatively unplanned, most organizations attempt to control the information they convey to customers, investors, and the general public. Two departments are particularly

Jack Welch started out in an engineering job in General Electric's plastics business. Now chairman and CEO, Welch believes GE must increase competitiveness and productivity. Thus he has declared war on what he sees as GE's excessive bureaucracy, and he encourages management to bypass formal communication channels and communicate directly with employees.

BEHIND THE SCENES AT AMTRAK
Keeping an Image on Track

You saw the familiar silver Amtrak trains with their red, white, and blue stripes in *Midnight Run, Rain Man,* and *Witness,* but you didn't see them in *Throw Momma from the Train* or in *Planes, Trains and Automobiles.* That's because Amtrak wants its trains and stations portrayed favorably to the public. As senior director of public affairs, Sue Martin manages Amtrak's communications with external audiences. She works with news and travel media, consumer groups such as the National Association of Railroad Passengers, travel industry organizations, Amtrak riders, the general public, and the motion picture industry.

Martin's work with the motion picture industry is a small but highly visible demonstration of how an organization communicates externally. Amtrak is the only national passenger railroad in the United States, and its trains and stations are much sought after for movie scenes. "Typically," says Martin, "producers come to Amtrak with a movie idea involving a train setting. They ask a lot of questions, and we discuss what we would be able to do for them."

Scripts are reviewed carefully. Some are refused because of the way a train employee is portrayed or the way a murder is staged. But Amtrak works with producers to make scripts acceptable. For instance, *Witness*'s opening scene was originally set on a bus, but it was agreed to replace the bus ride with a train trip through beautiful Pennsylvania Dutch country—to keep the murder scene at Amtrak's 30th Street Station in Philadelphia. If a script portrays Amtrak positively, a meeting is set up with the producer to decide what is possible to do and to negotiate contracts covering Amtrak's costs and insurance. When completed, the movie serves Amtrak in two ways: Showing a train or an interesting station to millions of moviegoers gives the railroad visibility, and

---

External communication links the organization with the outside world of customers, suppliers, competitors, and investors.

important in managing the flow of external messages: the marketing department and the public relations department. Of course, not all companies have separate departments or even distinct positions for these roles, but every organization communicates with outsiders and depends on one or more employees to perform marketing and public relations tasks.

The Role of Marketing and Public Relations

The marketing and public relations departments are responsible for managing much of the organization's formal communication with outsiders.

Marketing and public relations are closely related and are often confused, but the two departments differ. As a consumer, you are often on the receiving end of marketing messages: face-to-face or telephone conversations with salespeople, direct-mail solicitations, TV and radio commercials, newspaper and magazine ads, product brochures, and mail-order catalogs. Although these messages are highly visible, they are only a small part of marketing communication. In addition to advertising and selling products, the typical marketing department also handles product development, physical distribution, market research, and customer service, all of which involve both sending and receiving information. Basically, marketing has three responsibilities: (1) to find out who customers are and what they want, (2) to develop products that satisfy those needs, and (3) to get the products into the customers' hands.

Marketing focuses on selling goods and services, whereas public relations is more concerned with developing the organization's overall reputation.

The public relations (PR) department (also called the corporate communication department) manages the organization's reputation, addressing audiences such as employees, customers, investors, government agencies, and the general public. Whereas marketing messages are usually openly sponsored and paid for by the company, public relations messages are carried by the media when they are considered newsworthy. In fact, professional PR people view their role as disseminating news about the business to the organization's various audiences. The communication tools used by PR departments include news releases, lobbying programs, special events, booklets and

fees from the movie company generate revenues— $80,000 in a recent year.

In her work serving all Amtrak departments, Martin and her nine-member staff rely heavily on recognized, formal channels of communication. "We are the communicators for the company. We help others plan, decide on strategy, and carry out public relations, whether it's crisis management, publicity, or marketing communications. We recently created a crisis-response workshop for field managers." Her staff helps Amtrak employees deal with the public, even exercising control over how and when employees speak with the media. Martin's department writes and edits press releases, columns for the on-train magazine (*Express*), and direct mailings to consumer groups. Informal communication also has a role, "but in public affairs work," says Martin, "informal channels are hard to manage."

Even though you may not be directly responsible for public relations like Sue Martin, you may be called on to speak to outsiders on behalf of your company. Your concern will be to create and distribute messages that, in Martin's words, "help the public see that the corporation's interests are actually the public's interests."

Apply Your Knowledge

1. Review the following list of events that Sue Martin's department might have to deal with: (a) the five-year anniversary of the most serious fatal accident involving an Amtrak train, (b) a well-known travel writer is planning to see America by train for a series of articles, and (c) a railroad historical society wants to launch an annual excursion over Amtrak's most historic routes. Which would be the most complex (requiring you to work with others inside and outside Amtrak)? Which would consume the most of your time? Which would benefit Amtrak's image the most? Explain.

2. A train en route from Chicago to Seattle has been trapped by an avalanche in a remote, mountainous region of Montana. Passengers include a U.S. senator, a famous football commentator known for his fear of flying, and a pregnant woman on her way to a lifesaving medical procedure (which can be performed only in Spokane, Washington). As you plan for press coverage of the incident, consider the factors you would face. Which factors can you control? Which are out of your control? How can you offset those factors you can't control?

brochures about the organization, letters, annual reports, audiovisual materials, speeches and position papers, tours, and internal publications for employees.

Crisis Communication

One of the most visible functions of the PR department is to help management plan for and respond to crises. A good PR professional constantly scans the business environment looking for potential problems and then alerts management to the implications and suggests the best course of action. Disneyland, for example, has anticipated the possibility of an earthquake and is prepared to provide food, water, and medical care for 10,000 people for five days. The park also has specially trained employees who would coordinate rescue efforts using walkie-talkies, cellular phones, and a public-address system. In an emergency, visitors would be assembled in "safe havens" away from major structures.[13]

Disasters of earthquake proportions fall into the category of public relations nightmares created by sudden, violent accidents. Plane crashes, oil spills, chemical leaks, and product defects all belong to this group. The other type of crisis is the sort that builds slowly and occurs because of a company's conscious, but ill-founded, decisions. One example is R. J. Reynolds's attempt to introduce a cigarette aimed at African Americans (who have historically suffered higher rates of smoking-related illness than other groups). RJR badly miscalculated the public's probable reaction to the new product. Antismoking activists accused the company of sleazy and cynical business practices, and the U.S. Department of Human Services blasted the firm for promoting a "culture of cancer." The barrage of bad press prompted RJR to cancel the introduction of Uptown cigarettes.[14]

According to public relations professionals, when disaster strikes, a defensive posture is generally counterproductive. The best course is to be proactive, admit your mis-

Table 1.1	DO'S AND DON'TS OF CRISIS COMMUNICATION

Do's	Don'ts
Do prepare for trouble. Identify potential problems in advance, appoint and train a predesignated response team, and prepare and test a crisis management plan. **Do** set up a news center for company representatives and the media (equipped with phones, typewriters, and other electronic tools for preparing news releases). **Do** issue at least two news updates a day and have trained personnel on call to respond to questions around the clock. **Do** provide complete information packets to the media as soon as possible. **Do** prevent conflicting statements and provide continuity. Appoint a single person (trained in advance) to speak for the company. **Do** tell receptionists to direct all calls to the information center. **Do** tell the whole story—openly, completely, and honestly. If you are at fault, apologize. **Do** demonstrate the company's concern by your statements and your actions.	**Don't** blame anyone for anything. **Don't** speculate in public about unknown facts. **Don't** decline to answer questions. **Don't** release information that will violate anyone's right to privacy. **Don't** use the crisis to pitch products or services. **Don't** play favorites with media representatives.

Most experts recommend handling a crisis with candor and honesty.

takes, and apologize (see Table 1.1). That's what AT&T did when its long-distance service was out of commission for nine hours in January 1990, hanging up 80 million callers. That's also what Johnson & Johnson did in its now classic handling of the Tylenol poisoning scare in 1982.

Don't ignore the impact of a crisis on employees.

When disaster hits, most companies respond, to some degree, through their public relations department, but they often ignore the audience that is likely to be hit hardest—employees. When the New York *Daily News* faced a violent 21-week union strike, morale sank. "Everyone was on edge, and even minor work-related problems were blown out of proportion," said Dawna Fields, manager of public affairs. To minimize the impact of any crisis on employees, be sure to communicate honestly, openly, and often; actively encourage employees to share their concerns; and use caution when sharing personal opinions.[15]

Informal Contacts with Outsiders

Every employee informally accumulates facts and impressions that contribute to the organization's collective understanding of the outside world.

As a member of an organization, you are automatically an informal conduit for communicating with the outside world. In the course of your daily activities, you unconsciously absorb bits and pieces of information that add to the collective knowledge pool of your company. During a trip to the shopping mall, you notice how a competitor's products are selling; as you read the paper, you pick up economic and business news that relates to your work; when you have a problem at the office, you ask your family or friends for advice.

What's more, every time you speak for or about your company, you send a message. In fact, if you have a public-contact job, you don't even have to say anything. All you have to do is smile. Many outsiders form their impressions of your organization on the basis of the subtle, unconscious clues you transmit through your tone of voice, facial expression, and general appearance.

Top managers rely heavily on informal contacts with outsiders to exchange information that might be useful to their companies. Although much of the networking involves interaction with fellow executives, plenty of high-level managers recognize the value of keeping in touch with "the real world." For example, when Stanley Gault was chairman of Rubbermaid, he cornered travelers in airports to ask for ideas on new products. Xerox executives spend one day each month handling customer complaints, and senior executives at Hyatt Hotels serve as bellhops. As Wal-Mart founder Sam Walton used to say when someone asked why he visited Kmart stores: "It's all part of the educational process. I'm just learning."[16]

Washington Post *Company chairman Katharine Graham is a helpful, supportive manager who encourages communication. Such clues as her simple, tasteful office, with its soft lighting, neutral colors, and casual seating, help establish that role.*

CHARACTERISTICS OF EFFECTIVE COMMUNICATION

If effective communication determines business success, then the outstanding companies are those that have built the best internal and external communication networks. Just what does that mean? What characteristics produce effective communication? Six factors are involved:

- Fostering an open communication climate
- Committing to ethical communication
- Understanding the difficulties involved in intercultural communication
- Becoming proficient in communication technology
- Using an audience-centered approach to communication
- Creating and processing messages efficiently

An Open Communication Climate

An organization's communication climate is a reflection of its **corporate culture**—the mixture of values, traditions, and habits that give a place its atmosphere or personality. Some companies tend to choke off the upward flow of communication, believing that debate is time consuming and unproductive. Other companies, like Saturn, foster candor and honesty. Their employees feel free to confess their mistakes, to disagree with the boss, and to express their opinions.

The organization's communication climate affects the quantity and quality of the information that passes through the pipeline.

Many factors influence an organization's communication climate, including the nature of the industry, the company's physical setup, the history of the company, and passing events. However, one of the most important factors is the style of the top-management group.[17] Of all the many ways to categorize management styles, one of the most widely used is Douglas McGregor's Theory X and Theory Y.[18] Theory X managers consider workers to be lazy and irresponsible, motivated to work only by fear of losing their jobs. So these managers adopt a directive style. Theory Y managers, on the other hand, assume that people like to work and to take responsibility when they believe in what they are doing. So these managers adopt a more supportive management style. Yet another management approach, called Theory Z, was developed by William Ouchi.[19] Like athletic coaches, Theory Z managers encourage employees to work together as a team. Although the company still looks after employees, it also gives them the opportunity to take responsibility and to participate in decision making.

The management style of the top executives influences the organization's communication climate.

The trend today is toward any style that encourages an open communication climate. Only in such a climate do managers spend more time listening than issuing orders, and only there do workers not only offer suggestions but also help set goals and collaborate on solving problems.[20]

Today more and more companies are recognizing the value of an open communication climate.

A Commitment to Ethical Communication

The second factor contributing to effective communication is the organization's commitment to **ethics,** the principles of conduct that govern a person or a group. Former Supreme Court Justice Potter Stewart defined ethics as "knowing the difference between what you have a right to do and what is the right thing to do."[21]

Ethics are the principles of conduct that govern a person or group.

Ethics play a crucial role in communication. Language itself is made up of words that carry values. So merely by saying things a certain way, you influence how others perceive your message, and you shape expectations and behaviors.[22] Likewise, when an organization expresses itself internally, it influences the values of its employees; when it communicates externally, it shapes the way outsiders perceive it. **Ethical communication** includes all relevant information, is true in every sense, and is not deceptive in any way.

Ethics affect every aspect of business communication. When sending an ethical message, you are accurate and sincere. You avoid language that manipulates, discriminates, or exaggerates. You do not hide negative information behind an optimistic attitude, you don't state opinions as facts, and you portray graphic data fairly. You are honest with employers, co-workers, and clients, never seeking personal gain by making others look better or worse than they are. You don't allow personal preferences to influence your perception or the perception of others, and you act in good faith. On the surface, such ethical practices appear fairly easy to recognize. But deciding what is ethical can be quite complex.

Ethical Dilemmas and Lapses

> Conflicting priorities and the vast gray areas between right and wrong pose ethical problems for an organization's communicators.

An **ethical dilemma** involves choosing among alternatives that aren't clear cut (perhaps two conflicting alternatives are both ethical and valid, or perhaps your alternatives lie somewhere in the vast gray area between right and wrong). Suppose you're president of a company that's losing money. You have a duty to your shareholders to try to cut your losses and to your employees to be fair and honest. After looking at various options, you conclude that you'll have to lay off 500 people immediately. You suspect you may have to lay off another 100 people later on, but right now you need those 100 workers to finish a project. What do you tell them? If you confess that their jobs are shaky, many of them may quit just when you need them most. However, if you tell them that the future is rosy, you'll be stretching the truth.

Unlike a dilemma, an **ethical lapse** is making a clearly unethical or illegal choice. Suppose you have decided to change jobs and have discreetly landed an interview with your boss's largest competitor. You get along great with the interviewer, who is impressed enough with you to offer you a position on the spot. Not only is the new position a step up from your present job, but the pay is double what you're getting now. You accept the job and agree to start next month. Then, as you're shaking hands with the interviewer, she asks that when you begin your new job, you bring along profiles of your present company's ten largest customers. Do you comply with her request? How do you decide between what's ethical and what is not?

Legal Considerations

> Laws provide ethical guidelines for certain types of messages.

One place to look for guidance is the law. If saying or writing something is clearly illegal, you have no dilemma: You obey the law. For example, human resource management is closely regulated by laws. If you are interviewing a job applicant, the law says that you cannot ask questions relating to the candidate's race or religion. However, regardless of whether a specific situation is covered by law, be aware of the legal implications of anything you say or write on the job. For better or for worse, that innocent memo you wrote for the files could end up as evidence in court. So before you commit words to paper, ask yourself whether you would want to defend your remarks before a judge and jury.

Moral Considerations

> Moral considerations result from your own judgment and principles.

Although legal considerations will resolve some ethical questions, you'll often have to rely on your own judgment and principles. You might apply the Golden Rule: Do unto others as you would have them do unto you. You might examine your motives: If your intent is honest, the message is ethical, even though it may be factually incorrect; if your intent is to mislead or manipulate the audience, the message is unethical, regardless of whether it is true. You might look at the consequences of your decision and opt for the solution that provides the greatest good to the greatest number of people. You might also ask yourself a set of questions:[23]

- Is this decision legal? (Does it violate civil law or company policy?)
- Is it balanced? (Does it do the most good and the least harm? Is it fair to all concerned in the short term as well as the long term? Does it promote positive win-win relationships?)
- Is it a decision you can live with? (Does it make you feel good about yourself? Does it make you proud? Would you feel good about your decision if a newspaper published it? If your family knew about it?)
- Is it feasible? (Can it work in the real world? Have you considered your position in the company, your company's competition, its financial and political strength, the likely costs or risks of your decision, and the time available?)

Organizational Considerations

Ethical communication promotes long-term business success and profit. However, improving profits isn't reason enough to be ethical; as soon as the cost of being ethical outweighed the benefits, ethical choices would no longer be possible. As the CEO of Quaker Oats points out: "Making a profit is to a business what eating is to a human being. It is absolutely necessary; if you don't eat, you die. But very few of us would consider eating to be the purpose of human life."[24] However, if an organization can't point to increased profits to motivate employees to be ethical, what can it do?

First and foremost, the personal influence of chief executives and managers plays an important role. They can begin encouraging ethical behavior and decision making by being more receptive communicators, which requires mastering many of the skills presented in this text. They can also send the right message to employees by rewarding ethical behavior. Managers can lay out an explicit ethical policy, and in fact, more and more companies are using written codes to help employees determine what is acceptable. In addition, managers can use ethics audits to monitor ethical progress and to point up any weaknesses that need to be addressed.[25]

> Organizations can foster ethical behavior by
> - Helping top managers become more sensitive communicators
> - Rewarding ethical actions
> - Using ethics audits

Beyond leading to success in business, being ethical is simply the right thing to do. Moreover, it's contagious. Others will follow your example when they observe you being ethical and see the success you experience both in your interpersonal relationships and in your career.[26]

An Understanding of Intercultural Communication

The third factor contributing to a positive communication climate is understanding intercultural communication. Not only are more and more businesses crossing national boundaries to compete on a global scale, but the makeup of the global and domestic workforce is changing rapidly. In fact, the U.S. Department of Labor projects that by the turn of the century, 85 percent of the people entering the workforce will be women, minorities, and immigrants.[27] So whether you work abroad or at home, you will be encountering more and more cultural diversity in the workplace. To compete successfully in today's multicultural environment, you will face communication barriers not only of language but of culture as well.

> Intercultural communication plays an important role both abroad and at home.

Numerous countries use English for business and commerce. But even if English is your native language, you'll want to avoid common mistakes that can lead to misunderstanding and miscommunication:[28]

- Avoid using combinations of words that could easily be replaced by one word: Say *delay* instead of *put off*, and say *maintain* instead of *keep up*.
- Avoid using slang that is easily misinterpreted: Say *contact* instead of *keep in touch with*.
- Avoid using acronyms without first spelling out the meaning: Explain that *ASAP* means "as soon as possible."
- Avoid being satisfied with poor listening skills: Try to obtain frequent feedback.
- Avoid using pretentious terminology and jargon: Try to use simple, clear language.
- Avoid using terms that may mean something different in another culture: Do your best to find out whether identical words mean different things in different cultures (e.g., in England, *napkin* means "diaper," not "table linen").

Of course, even if you learn a foreign language to improve your relationship with business associates or employees, be aware that *speaking* a language is not the same as *communicating* in it.[29]

Culture determines how we perceive and thus how we communicate.

Culture controls our daily lives in many unsuspected ways. It determines what we notice in our environment and how we notice it. Culture also determines custom and social convention. For example, in Hong Kong, Korea, and Taiwan, the triangle is considered a negative shape, although it's considered positive or neutral in the United States. In Kenya the number 7 is considered bad luck, but in some Slavic cultures it's good luck. Although red is a positive color in Denmark, it's linked with witchcraft and death in many African countries. And in Bulgaria a nod means "no" and shaking the head side-to-side means "yes."

Intercultural communication is discussed in detail in Chapter 3.

Understanding cultural differences in perception, greetings, and gestures is critical to businesspeople, as you'll see in Chapter 3. You'll see how the need for intercultural understanding has grown and how specific cultural differences affect communication. Chapter 3 also gives you important tips for communicating with people from other cultures.

A Proficiency in Communication Technology

The fourth factor contributing to effective organizational communication is the ability to use and adapt to technology. The increasing speed of communication and the growing amount of information to be communicated are only two results of the ever-changing technology you will encounter on the job. To succeed, businesspeople today make sure they can understand, use, and adapt to the technological tools of communication.

As we move into the next century, technology is determining who we communicate with, how often we communicate, and what sort of devices we use to communicate. More and more employees are finding computer screens at their desks and using portable computers at home or on the road. Moreover, both employees and organizations are becoming increasingly accessible through fax, car phone, cellular phone, electronic mail, voice mail, and satellite communication. Of course, business success depends on words rather than on the technological tools used to manipulate those words. However, today's businesses operate at such a fast pace, communicate across such great distances, and demand such professional-looking documents that you are left with no option but to master the technological tools and processes necessary to compete.[30]

Debbie Fields, founder of Mrs. Fields Cookies, uses a chain-wide interactive computer and electronic mail system to instruct store managers, to plan work schedules, and even to screen job applicants. The computer system makes it easy to maintain the two-way communication between store managers and headquarters that is so necessary.

Chapter 4 tells you about the impact of technology on communication, about when it's appropriate to use various tools, and about the specific tools that can help you research, compose, revise, and produce messages. Although many of you may have grown up using computers and feel comfortable with the ever-changing face of technological developments, many of you may feel apprehensive about computers or anything technical. Chapter 4 is an overview of the types of technological tools you'll encounter on the job. If you wish to learn more about communication technology, or if you would like more specific information, consult the reference notes at the end of the book for this section and for Chapter 4, and consult your instructor and your school librarian.

Technology's effects on communication are discussed in detail in Chapter 4.

An Audience-Centered Approach to Communication

The fifth factor contributing to effective organizational communication is an **audience-centered approach,** keeping your audience in mind at all times during the process of communication. Your ability to empathize with, be sensitive to, and generally consider your audience's feelings is the best way to be effective in your communication. Because you care about your audience, you take every step possible to get your message across in a way that is meaningful to your audience. You might actually create lively individual portraits of readers and listeners to predict how they will react. You might simply try to put yourself in your audience's position. You might try adhering strictly to guidelines about courtesy, or you might be able to gather research about the needs and wants of your audience. Whatever your tactic, the point is to write and speak from your audience's point of view.

Using an audience-centered approach means keeping your audience in mind at all times when communicating.

The audience-centered approach is more than an approach to business communication; it's actually the modern approach to business in general (behind such concepts as total quality management and total customer satisfaction). The advantages of using this approach include making your communication successful by making it mean something to your audience, by enhancing your own credibility (because your audience perceives your sincerity), and by staving off uncountable ethical questions (because when you concentrate on the benefits to your audience, your concern for others reduces the chance of an ethical lapse).

Centering your attention on your audience supports the other five factors that contribute to effective communication. Because you want to know what your audience's needs are and what they think of your message, you will work for an open communication climate inside and outside your organization. Because you sincerely wish to satisfy the needs of your audience, you will approach communication situations with good intentions and high ethical standards. Because you need to understand your audience, you will do whatever it takes to understand intercultural differences and barriers. Because you make a practice of anticipating your audience's expectations, you will choose the appropriate technological tools for your message and make the best use of them. Finally, because you value your audience's time, you will prepare and communicate oral and written messages as efficiently as possible.

Your audience-centered approach will support the other five factors of effective communication: open climate, ethical commitment, intercultural understanding, technological expertise, and efficient message flow.

An Efficient Flow of Communication Messages

The sixth factor contributing to effective organizational communication is an efficient flow of communication messages. Think for a minute about the logistics of moving all those messages, both within the organization and to and from the outside world. A few statistics may help you see the problem in perspective:

Although organizations need to document their activities, they also need to manage the flow of messages as efficiently as possible.

- For every white-collar employee on the payroll, the typical organization maintains 18,000 pages of paper, enough to fill a four-drawer filing cabinet. The size of the file increases by 4,000 pages a year.[31]
- Some 30 billion documents a year are created in the United States, costing more than $100 billion. Many of these documents are filed away, but 75 to 85 percent of the time we don't look at the information again.

Routine communication is essential to business, but it represents a major expense.

- U.S. companies waste $2.6 billion each year on unnecessary photocopies. Roughly one-third of the copies made are tossed into the trash.
- One financial services company, Fidelity Investments, sends out 53 million pieces of mail every year and receives 15 million pieces from its customers. Its annual postal bill is $12 million, not including the amount it spends on direct-marketing efforts.

Those are just the routine written messages. How many meetings are a waste of time? How much effort is wasted handling messages during a crisis? The volume of messages is greater in large organizations than in small ones, but all companies can hold down the costs and maximize the benefits of their communication activities by reducing the number of messages, speeding up the preparation of messages, and training employees in communication skills.

Reduce the Number of Messages

One useful way to reduce the number of messages is to think twice before sending one. The world is adrift in a sea of information. Only about 13 percent of the mail that executives receive is of immediate value, and not surprisingly, they tend to give it short shrift. They also tend to ignore many of the internal messages they receive. One study found that five CEOs received 40 routine reports in five weeks and responded to only 2 of them.[32]

Organizations save time and money by sending only necessary messages.

It takes time and resources to produce letters, memos, and even electronic messages, so organizations have to be concerned with how many messages they create. The average cost of dictating, transcribing, and mailing a business letter is between $12.28 and $18.54.[33] If a message must be put into writing, a letter or memo is a good investment. If a message is important but doesn't require a written format, consider making a quick phone call, sending an electronic message, or having a face-to-face chat. If the message merely adds to the information overload, it's better left unsent.

Speed Up the Preparation of Messages

By streamlining the preparation of messages, companies make sure that information is transmitted in a timely manner.

Because the value of so much information depends on its timeliness, people in business try to transmit messages as quickly as possible. Aside from the tools of technology, one thing that helps speed up the process is making sure that written messages are prepared correctly the first time around. Of course, eliminating errors entirely is an unrealistic goal, but if you're given an unclear writing assignment, ask for more guidance. If you're handing out assignments, be sure to explain what you want.

Another way to speed up message preparation is through standardization. Most organizations use form letters for handling repetitive correspondence, and most employ a standard format for routine memos and reports. Although following a "formula" may inhibit your creativity, it reduces your writing time. It also saves the reader's time because the familiar format enables people to absorb the information more quickly.

Train the Writers and Speakers

In-house training benefits even experienced communicators.

Recognizing the importance of efficient communication, many companies train employees in communication skills. The American Society for Training and Development surveyed major employers and found that 41 percent provide writing-skills programs for their employees.[34] Many others offer seminars and workshops on handling common oral communication situations such as dealing with customers, managing subordinates, and getting along with co-workers.

Even though you may ultimately receive training on the job, you can start mastering business communication skills right now, in this course. Perhaps the best place to begin is with an honest assessment of where you stand. In the next few days, watch how you handle the communication situations that arise. Try to figure out what you're doing right and what you're doing wrong. Then in the months ahead, try to focus on building your competence in areas where you need the most work. One of the great advantages of taking a course in business communication is that you get to practice in an environment that provides honest and constructive criticism. A course of this kind also gives you an understanding of acceptable techniques, so you can avoid making costly mistakes on the job.

This book is designed to provide the kind of communication practice that will prepare you for whatever comes along later in your career. The next chapter introduces some concepts of communication in general so that you will be better able to analyze and predict the outcome of various situations. Chapters 3 and 4 discuss intercultural and technological communication. Chapters 5, 6, and 7 explain how to plan and organize business messages and how to perfect their style and tone. The following chapters deal with specific forms of communication: letters and memos, résumés and application letters, reports, interviews and meetings, and speeches and presentations. As you progress through this book, you will also meet many business communicators like Richard LeFauve of Saturn. Their experiences will give you an insight into what it takes to communicate effectively on the job.

> Focus on building skills in the areas where you've been weak.

> Practice using all communication skills so that you can learn from your mistakes.

A PPLYING WHAT YOU'VE LEARNED

Taking what you learn in a business communication course and applying it to the real world can sometimes be a challenge. One good way to prepare is to practice your new skills on a real communication situation. Each chapter in this book gives you that opportunity.

In this chapter, you've met Saturn's Richard LeFauve, and throughout the book, you'll meet a cross section of real people—men and women who work for some of America's most fascinating organizations. On a typical day, these people encounter a variety of communication problems. At the beginning of this chapter, you read about the challenge faced by Saturn as it tried to approach the automotive business in an entirely new way. You'll read about an organization's situation at the beginning of each chapter in a slice-of-life vignette titled "On the Job: Facing a Communication Dilemma." After reading the vignette, think about the organization's communication problems as you read through the chapter and become familiar with the various concepts presented there.

At the end of each chapter is an innovative simulation called "On the Job: Solving a Communication Dilemma." Each simulation is designed to hone your communication skills. You'll play the role of a person at the organization introduced in the vignette and you'll face a situation you'd encounter on the job in that organization. Each simulation starts by explaining how the organization actually solved its communication dilemma. Then you are presented with several communication scenarios, each with several possible courses of action. It's up to you to recommend one course of action from the available choices.

If you don't like any of the alternatives, you may devise your own solution (if your instructor agrees). In fact, some of the questions have more than one acceptable answer, and some have no truly satisfactory answers. That's how it happens for people on the job, too. You will consider the concepts you learn in each chapter, apply your own judgment, and then pick the answer that you think is best. Think about each possible answer carefully, and think about why each one is either a wise or an unwise choice. Your instructor may assign the simulations as homework, as teamwork, as material for in-class discussion, or in a host of other ways. These scenarios let you explore various communication ideas and apply the concepts and techniques fromthe chapter.

Now you're ready for the first simulation. As you tackle each question, think about the material you covered in this chapter, and consider your own experience as a communicator. You'll probably be surprised to discover how much you already know about business communication.

O n the Job

SOLVING A COMMUNICATION DILEMMA AT SATURN

In addition to the ordinary challenges of launching a new business, Richard LeFauve and the Saturn team used communication to overcome traditional notions of management-labor relations, foreign competition, and consumer skepticism. The stakes were high: Saturn's parent, General Motors, was spending more than $5 billion to prove that a U.S. manufacturer could successfully build—and sell—a quality car. So both internal and external communication were crucial.

From the start, top management set Saturn apart from other U.S. car companies by tearing down the communication barriers between managers and workers. For example, instead of providing separate dining halls for executives and workers, Saturn managers expect all employees to eat in the same cafeterias, which encourages managers and employees to exchange ideas through informal communication channels. Saturn also improved internal communication by organizing its 5,000 production employees into small work teams of up to 15 people. Aided by an adviser from management and an adviser from the union, each team was given responsibility for managing its own budget, ordering repairs, hiring new employees, and taking other actions to keep quality and productivity high. This team organization opened up the communication climate and sped the flow of information among top management, team advisers, and production workers.

Another milestone in internal communication is the labor contract signed by GM management and the United Auto Workers union. Other GM operations are covered by a 597-page UAW contract that is renegotiated every three years. But the Saturn agreement is just 28 pages long; both efficient and flexible, it is a living document that will never expire (although it can be altered if both parties agree). As a result, labor relations and communication at Saturn are collaborative, not combative. Other sites have experienced angry confrontations between labor and management over plant closings and other cost-cutting steps. But Spring Hill has avoided such problems because its contract has allowed both sides to be flexible when dealing with issues as they arose.

LeFauve and his team used external communication to communicate the Saturn "difference" to car buyers. Saturn team members built a reasonably priced, reliable car to satisfy customers—but they didn't stop there. They used an audience-centered approach to completely overhaul the showroom experience, setting fixed prices (so that buyers don't have to haggle) and throwing out the hard-sell approach. Saturn trained dealer personnel in communication skills so that they could understand what customers wanted and could fulfill those needs.

Saturn also used external communication in a unique advertising campaign. Unlike most ads used by competitors, early Saturn ads didn't show cars winding over mountain roads, and they didn't talk about performance details. Instead, the ads featured the real people who were building and driving Saturns and talked about the satisfaction those people derived from their cars. This audience-centered approach distinguished Saturn from the pack and helped build a strong emotional bond between the public, the product, and the company behind the product.

For the first two years, sales were so strong that the Spring Hill factory couldn't keep up with demand. Then sales slowed, in part because of a limited product line (Saturn offered no trucks or large cars) and in part because rivals were introducing attractive cars to compete directly with Saturn models. General Motors had to delay building a second Saturn plant and had to postpone an overhaul of the Saturn design. Given these challenges, Richard LeFauve and his Saturn team are keeping communication lines open to smooth the bumpy ride ahead.

Your Mission: You are head of plant communications for Saturn's Spring Hill operation. In this position, you're responsible for both internal and external communication. Use your knowledge of communication to choose the best response for each of the following situations. Be prepared to explain why your choice is best:

1. Over the past few months, you've learned of several occasions on which employees in other GM divisions had ideas that could have helped Saturn, but no one in Spring Hill heard about them. At the same time, you know that many ideas used at Saturn could help other divisions. Which is the best way to make sure that GM personnel can exchange ideas in a timely fashion?

   a. Install computerized communication systems throughout the organization so that every time someone has an idea, he or she can instantly transmit it to everyone else electronically.

   b. Establish both formal and informal horizontal communication links. For example, engine designers across the company should have their own formal communication network so that they can regularly share and discuss new ideas.

   c. Establish a corporate "idea-sharing" policy, in which anyone with a useful new idea is required to report it to his or her supervisor. The idea then moves up the corporate ladder, and the people at the top make sure it reaches everyone in the company.

   d. Install bulletin boards around the Saturn plant so that people with new ideas can post their thoughts and people who need help can post requests for assistance.

2. Although the information that Saturn employees receive from the grapevine is usually accurate, a blatantly false rumor concerning the company's future has been circulating for several days. What's the first step you should take to handle this?

   a. Identify the opinion leaders throughout the plant—union leaders and production employees who are known to be good sources of inside information—and invite them to a private session with management. Explain why the rumor is false, giving them complete data on the issue. Ask them to share the information with their colleagues.

   b. Publish a memorandum to all employees, insisting that the rumor is false and stating the facts.

   c. Instruct all managers to tell their teams that the rumor is false.

   d. Call a companywide meeting at which Richard LeFauve can explain the facts and publicly state that the rumor is false.

3. Assume that Saturn's shipping and receiving team is falling behind schedule. The management adviser says that many team members are just going through the motions and not putting their hearts into their jobs. As one way of improving performance, she wants to send a memo to everyone in the department. Which of the following approaches would you recommend that she use?
   a. Tell employees that the group's performance is not as good as it could be, and solicit their ideas on how things might be improved.
   b. Threaten to fire the next employee you see giving less than 100 percent, even though you know company policy prevents you from actually doing so.
   c. Ask employees to monitor one another and to report to the department manager any instances of laziness or carelessness.
   d. Tell all employees that the department better shape up or heads are going to roll.
4. When visiting the painting facility, you see the following four signs; which one communicates its point most clearly?
   a. "If dangerous fumes are present, all employees must wear respirators."
   b. "All employees must wear respirators while painting."
   c. "All persons must wear respirators in this area at all times."

d. "WARNING: Dangerous fumes present while painting operations are under way."
5. Crisis communication is among your responsibilities, and at ten o'clock on a Sunday night, you receive a phone call from the plant manager. A minor explosion in the production department spilled about a thousand barrels of toxic metal-cleaning solution into a creek that runs by the facility. You know the media will soon find out. Which of the following is the best response?
   a. To keep the media from exaggerating the spill, tell them that a "small amount" of chemicals was spilled and that you're not even sure whether the chemicals are dangerous.
   b. Give the media full access to Saturn managers, and provide them with a written description of the incident and of the company's efforts to clean up the spill. Tell them as much as you know about the dangers of such spills.
   c. Distribute a written statement to the media that says, "Until further notice, Saturn managers will be unavailable for public comment regarding the alleged chemical spill."
   d. Distribute a written statement to the media that emphasizes the division's past record of safety and environmental consciousness. Talk about Saturn's recycling program, efforts to encourage employees to carpool, and so on; avoid any discussion of the chemical spill.[35]

Questions for Discussion

1. Why do you think good communication in an organization improves employees' attitudes and performance?
2. Whenever you report negative information to your boss, she never passes it along to her colleagues or supervisors. You believe the information is important, but who do you talk to? Your boss? Your boss's supervisor? A co-worker who also reports to your boss? A co-worker who reports to a different boss? Explain.
3. Pick three jobs that you might like to have after you graduate. What communication skills do you think would be most important to you in these positions?

4. Because of your excellent communication skills, your boss always asks you to write his reports for him. When you overhear the CEO complimenting him on his logical organization and clear writing style, he responds as if he'd written all those reports himself. You're angry, but he's your boss. What can you do?
5. To save time and money, your company is considering limiting all memos to one page or less. Is that a good idea?
6. As long as you make sure that everyone involved receives some benefit and no one gets hurt, is it okay to make a decision that's just a little unethical?

Exercises

1. Name three ways you might encourage your employees to give you feedback on daily operations. Briefly explain your answer.
2. Your boss often uses you as a sounding board for her ideas. Now she seems to want you to act as an unofficial messenger, passing her ideas along to the staff and informing her of their responses. Are you comfortable with this arrangement? Write a short paragraph explaining your feelings.

3. In less than a page, explain why you think each of the following is or is not ethical:
   a. De-emphasizing negative test results in a report on your product idea
   b. Taking a computer home to finish a work-related assignment
   c. Telling an associate and close friend that she'd better pay more attention to her work responsibilities before management fires her

d. Recommending the purchase of excess equipment to use up your allocated funds before the end of the fiscal year so that your budget won't be cut next year

4. Your boss wants to send a message welcoming employees recently transferred to your department from your Hong Kong branch. They all speak English, but your boss asks you to review his message for clarity. What would you suggest your boss change in the following paragraph?

> I wanted to welcome you ASAP to our little family here in the States. It's high time we shook hands in person and not just across the sea. I'm pleased as punch about getting to know you all, and I for one will do my level best to sell you on America.

5. What would be the most efficient way (phone call, interview, memo, or newsletter) of handling the following communication situations? Briefly explain your answers.
   a. Informing everyone in the company of your department's new procedure for purchasing equipment
   b. Leaving final instructions for your secretary to follow while you're out of town
   c. Disciplining an employee for chronic tardiness
   d. Announcing the installation of ramps for employees using wheelchairs

6. What are your strengths and weaknesses as a writer and as a speaker? Consider your personality, training, and preferences. Present your analysis in a way that will help your instructor plan this course to meet your needs.

UNDERSTANDING BUSINESS COMMUNICATION

After studying this chapter, you will be able to

List the general categories of nonverbal communication

Explain the four channels of verbal communication

Identify the steps in the communication process

Describe what can go wrong when you're formulating messages

Discuss communication barriers and how to overcome them

Summarize what you can do to improve communication

On the Job

FACING A COMMUNICATION DILEMMA AT BEN & JERRY'S HOMEMADE

Serving Up Ice Cream and a Strong Social Message

Every company communicates with customers, employees, and various other groups. For Ben & Jerry's Homemade, of Waterbury, Vermont, communication has a special importance. The company makes more than premium ice cream; it makes an unusual effort to operate as a force for social change. Co-founders Ben Cohen and Jerry Greenfield intended to start an ice cream parlor and then sell it once the business got going, but something always forced them to keep at it—a new competitor, the need to replace or fix equipment. Almost in spite of itself, Ben & Jerry's has grown beyond its founders' expectations. But Cohen and Greenfield don't want to run a conventional business. They want their company not only to contribute to society but also to help save the rain forests, encourage conservation, help family farmers, and support other important causes.

This mission presents Ben & Jerry's with some unusual communication challenges. Perhaps the most important is keeping the founders' vision alive as the company grows. Back when the operation involved only Cohen, Greenfield, and a handful of employees, communicating the company's social goals was a fairly easy task. But with more employees, more suppliers, customers spread across the nation, and even shareholders (once the company went public and sold stock to investors), communication has become a big challenge indeed. Just one example: Cohen and Greenfield worry that some of the managers they've hired have lost touch with the original message and are more interested in generating profits than in fostering social change.

How can Cohen and Greenfield use communication to keep their vision alive in the minds of customers, employees, and investors? What is the process of communication, and how can the managers at Ben & Jerry's use it to keep the company true to the founders' vision? How can misunderstandings arise in business communication, and how can Ben & Jerry's avoid them?[1]

*T*HE BASIC FORMS OF COMMUNICATION

Ben & Jerry's Homemade

As Cohen and Greenfield are well aware, effective communicators have many tools at their disposal. They know how to put together the words that will convey their meaning. They reinforce their words with gestures and actions. They look you in the eye, listen to what you have to say, and think about your feelings and needs. At the same time, they study your reactions, picking up the nuances of your response by watching your face and body, listening to your tone of voice, and evaluating your words. They absorb information just as efficiently as they transmit it, relying on both nonverbal and verbal cues.

Nonverbal Communication

Nonverbal communication is the process of communicating without words.

The most basic form of communication is **nonverbal communication,** all the cues, gestures, vocal qualities, spatial relationships, and attitudes toward time that allow us to communicate without words. Anthropologists theorize that long before human beings used words to talk things over, our ancestors communicated with one another by using their bodies. They gritted their teeth to show anger; they smiled and touched one another to indicate affection. Although we have come a long way since those primitive times, we still use nonverbal cues to express superiority, dependence, dislike, respect, love, and other feelings.[2]

Nonverbal communication differs from verbal communication in fundamental ways. For one thing, it's less structured, which makes it more difficult to study. You can't pick up a book on nonverbal language and master the vocabulary of gestures, expressions, and inflections that are common in our culture. We don't really know how people learn nonverbal behavior. No one teaches a baby to cry or smile, yet such forms of self-expression are almost universal. Other types of nonverbal communication, such as the meaning of colors and certain gestures, vary from culture to culture.

Nonverbal communication has few rules and often occurs unconsciously.

Nonverbal communication also differs from verbal communication in terms of intent and spontaneity. We generally plan our words. When we say, "Please get back to me on that order by Friday," we have a conscious purpose. We think about the message, if only for a moment. However, when we communicate nonverbally, we sometimes do so unconsciously. We don't mean to raise an eyebrow or blush. Those actions come naturally. Without our consent, our emotions are written all over our faces.

The Importance of Nonverbal Communication
Although nonverbal communication is often unplanned, it has more impact than does verbal communication alone. Nonverbal cues are especially important when conveying feelings, accounting for 93 percent of the emotional meaning that is exchanged in any interaction.[3] Of course, the total impact of any message is probably most affected by the blending of nonverbal and verbal communication.[4]

Nonverbal communication is more reliable than verbal communication.

One advantage of nonverbal communication is its reliability. Most people can deceive us much more easily with words than they can with their bodies. Words are relatively easy to control; body language, facial expressions, and vocal characteristics are not. By paying attention to these nonverbal cues, we can detect deception or affirm a speaker's honesty. Not surprisingly, we have more faith in nonverbal cues than we do in verbal messages. If a person says one thing but transmits a conflicting message non-verbally, we almost invariably believe the nonverbal signal.[5] So if you can read other people's nonverbal messages correctly, you can interpret their underlying attitudes and intentions and respond appropriately.

Nonverbal communication is important for another reason: It can be efficient for both the sender and the receiver. You can transmit a nonverbal message without even thinking about it, and your audience can register the meaning unconsciously. At the same time, when you have a conscious purpose, you can often achieve it more economically with a gesture than with words. A wave of the hand, a pat on the back, a wink—all are streamlined expressions of thought.

Nonverbal communication is important because it's so efficient.

The Types of Nonverbal Communication

Nonverbal communication falls into general categories: facial expressions and eye behavior, gestures and postures, vocal characteristics, personal appearance, touching behavior, and use of time and space. But remember, the meaning of nonverbal communication lies with the observer, who both reads specific signals and interprets them in the context of a particular situation and a particular culture.

- *Facial expressions and eye behavior.* Your face is the primary site for expressing your emotions; it reveals both the type and the intensity of your feelings.[6] Your eyes are especially effective for indicating attention and interest, influencing others, regulating interaction, and establishing dominance.

The face and eyes command particular attention as a source of nonverbal messages.

- *Gestures and postures.* By moving your body, you can express both specific and general messages, some voluntary and some involuntary. A wave of the hand, for example, has a specific and intentional meaning, such as "hello" or "good-bye." Other gestures are unintentional and express a more general message. Slouching or leaning forward is an unconscious signal that reveals whether you feel nervous or confident, assertive or passive.

- *Vocal characteristics.* Like body language, your voice carries both intentional and unintentional messages. Your voice can create various impressions. Consider the sentence "What have you been up to?" If you repeat that question four or five times, changing your tone of voice and stressing various words, you can convey quite different messages. However, the tone and volume of your voice, your accent and speaking pace, and all the little *um*'s and *ah*'s that creep into your speech say a lot about you, your emotions, and your relationship with the audience.

Body language and tone of voice reveal a lot about a person's emotions and attitudes.

- *Personal appearance.* Your appearance helps establish your social identity. People respond to us on the basis of our physical attractiveness. Although an individual's body type and facial features impose limitations, most of us are able to control our attractiveness to some degree. Our grooming, our clothing, our accessories, our "style"—all modify our appearance.

Physical appearance and personal style contribute to our identity.

- *Touching behavior.* Touch is an important vehicle for conveying warmth, comfort, and reassurance. Even the most casual contact can create positive feelings. The accepted norms of touching vary, depending on the gender, age, relative status, and cultural background of the persons involved. In business situations, touching suggests dominance, so a higher-status person is more likely to touch a lower-status person than the other way around. Touching has become controversial, however, because it can sometimes be interpreted as sexual harassment.

Your use of touch, your attitude toward time, and your use of space (all of which are affected by culture) help establish your social relationships.

- *Use of time and space.* Like touch, time and space can be used to assert authority. In many cultures, people demonstrate their importance by making other people wait; they show respect by being on time. People can also assert their status by occupying the best space. In U.S. companies, the chief executive usually has the corner office and the prettiest view. Apart from serving as a symbol of status, space can determine how comfortable people feel talking with one another. When people stand too close or too far away, we feel ill at ease.

Nonverbal communication can be different for men and women.

Attitudes toward punctuality, comfort zones, and all other nonverbal communication vary from culture to culture. In addition, gender has an impact on nonverbal communication. For example, women are generally better than men at decoding nonverbal cues. In social settings and business meetings, women have less personal space and are touched more often than men (both observations indicating less power for women). Moreover, even though sitting at the head of a conference table symbolizes power for a man, if a woman is at the head and at least one man is sitting elsewhere, observers assume that the man is in charge.[7]

Improve nonverbal skills by paying more attention to cues, both yours and those of others.

To improve nonverbal skills in the United States, pay more attention to nonverbal cues (especially facial expressions), engage in more eye contact, and probe for more information when verbal and nonverbal cues conflict. Most employees are frustrated and distrustful when their supervisors give them conflicting signals. So try to be as honest as possible when communicating your emotions.[8]

Verbal Communication

Verbal communication is the process of communicating with words.

Although you can express many things nonverbally, there are limits to what you can communicate without the help of language. If you want to discuss past events, ideas, or abstractions, you need symbols that stand for your thoughts. **Verbal communication** consists of words arranged in meaningful patterns. In the English language, the pool of words is growing; there are currently about 750,000, although most people in the United States recognize only about 20,000 of them.[9] To create a thought with these words, we arrange them according to the rules of grammar, putting the various parts of speech in the proper sequence. We then transmit the message in spoken or written form, anticipating that someone will hear or read what we have to say.

Language is composed of words and grammar.

Speaking and Writing

As Figure 2.1 illustrates, businesspeople tend to prefer oral communication channels to written ones. It's generally quicker and more convenient to talk to somebody than

Figure 2.1
Business Time Spent on Communication Channels

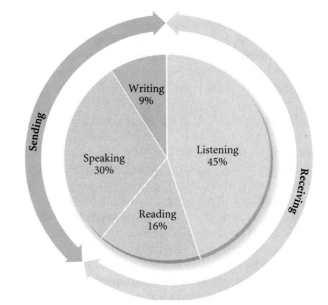

to write a memo or letter. Furthermore, when you're speaking or listening, you can pick up added meaning from nonverbal cues and benefit from immediate feedback. For maximum impact, use both written and spoken channels. Citicorp used multiple channels when explaining its new employee-benefits plan. Employees received a printout of their benefits, a computer disk, an extensive workbook, brochures, special face-to-face training meetings, a take-home video, and access to a hot line. With so many choices available, employees were able to use the media they felt most comfortable with.[10]

Businesspeople rely more heavily on oral than on written communication channels for sharing information on a day-to-day basis, but they often put important messages in writing.

Listening and Reading

Take another look at Figure 2.1. Apart from underscoring the importance of oral communication, it illustrates another interesting fact: People spend more time *receiving* information than transmitting it. Listening and reading are every bit as important as speaking and writing.

Effective business communication depends on skill in receiving messages as well as skill in sending them.

Unfortunately, most of us aren't very good listeners. Immediately after hearing a ten-minute speech, we typically remember only half of what was said. A few days later, we've forgotten three-quarters of the message.[11] To some extent, our listening problems stem from our education, or lack of it. We spend years learning to express our ideas, but few of us ever take a course in listening. Nevertheless, developing better listening abilities is crucial if we want to foster the understanding and cooperation so necessary for an increasingly diverse workforce.[12]

At the same time, our reading skills often leave a good deal to be desired. Studies indicate that approximately 20 percent of the adults in the United States are functionally illiterate; 14 percent cannot fill out a check properly; 38 percent have trouble reading the help-wanted ads in the newspaper; and 26 percent can't figure out the deductions listed on their paychecks.[13] Even those who read adequately often have trouble extracting the important points from a document, so they can't make the most of the information contained in it.

Although listening and reading differ, both require a similar approach. The first step is to register the information, which means that you must tune out distractions and focus your attention. You must then interpret and evaluate the information, respond in some fashion, and file away the data for future reference. The most important part of this process is interpretation and evaluation. While absorbing the material, you must decide what is important and what isn't. One approach is to look for the main ideas and the most important supporting details, rather than trying to remember everything you read or hear. If you can discern the structure of the material, you can also understand the relationships among the ideas.

To absorb information, you must concentrate, evaluate, and retain what you read or hear.

If you're listening as opposed to reading, you have the advantage of being able to ask questions and interact with the speaker. Instead of just gathering information, you can cooperate in solving problems. This interactive process requires additional listening skills, which Chapter 17 discusses.

T HE PROCESS OF COMMUNICATION

Whether you are speaking or writing, listening or reading, communication is more than a single act. Instead, it is a chain of events that can be broken into five phases, as Figure 2.2 illustrates:[14]

The communication process consists of five phases linking sender and receiver.

- The sender has an idea.
- The idea becomes a message.
- The message is transmitted.
- The receiver gets the message.
- The receiver reacts and sends feedback to the sender.

1. *The sender has an idea.* You conceive an idea and want to share it.
2. *The idea becomes a message.* When you put your idea into a message that your receiver will understand, you are **encoding,** deciding on the message's form (word,

Figure 2.2
The Communication
Process

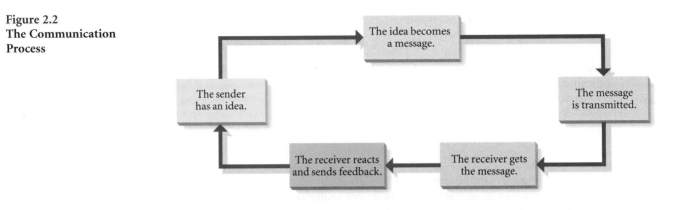

facial expression, gesture), length, organization, tone, and style—all of which depend on your idea, your audience, and your personal style or mood.

3. *The message is transmitted.* To physically transmit your message to your receiver, you select a **communication channel** (verbal, nonverbal, spoken, or written) and **medium** (telephone, computer, letter, memo, report, face-to-face exchange, etc.). The channel and medium you choose depend on your message, the location of your audience, your need for speed, and the formality of the situation.

4. *The receiver gets the message.* For communication to occur, your receiver must first get the message. If you send a letter, your receiver has to read it before understanding it. If you're giving a speech, the people in your audience have to be able to hear you, and they have to be paying attention. Your receiver must cooperate by **decoding** your message, absorbing and understanding it. Then the decoded message has to be stored in the receiver's mind. If all goes well, the message is interpreted correctly; that is, the receiver assigns the same basic meaning to the words as the sender intended and responds in the desired way.

5. *The receiver reacts and sends feedback to the sender.* **Feedback** is your receiver's response, the final link in the communication chain. After getting the message, your receiver responds in some way and signals that response to you. Feedback is the key element in the communication process because it enables you to evaluate the effectiveness of your message. If your audience doesn't understand what you mean, you can tell by the response and refine your message.

Feedback is your audience's response. It permits you to evaluate your message's effectiveness.

The process is repeated until both parties have finished expressing themselves, but communication is effective only when each step is successful.

Formulating a Message

Communication is a dynamic process. Your idea can't be communicated if you ignore, fail, or skip any step in that process. Unfortunately, the process can be interrupted before it really begins—while you're trying to put your idea into words. Several things can go wrong when you're formulating a message, including indecision about the content of your message, lack of familiarity with the situation or the receiver, and difficulty in expressing ideas.

Estée Lauder credits the success of her skin-care products company, in part, to her communication policy. She keeps herself open to input and feedback from everyone she deals with: customers, retailers, employees, suppliers, and managers.

Indecision About Content
Deciding what to say is the first hurdle in the communication process. Many people make the mistake of trying to convey everything they know about a subject.

Unfortunately, when a message contains too much information, it's difficult to absorb. If you want to get your point across, decide what to include and what to leave out, how much detail to provide, and what order to follow. If you try to explain something without first giving the receiver adequate background, you'll create confusion. Likewise, if you recommend actions without first explaining why they are justified, your message may provoke an emotional response that inhibits understanding.

Include only the information that is useful to your audience, and organize it in a way that encourages its acceptance.

Lack of Familiarity with the Situation or the Receiver

Creating an effective message is difficult if you don't know how it will be used. Unless you know why the report is needed, you are forced to create a very general document, one that covers a little bit of everything. In the process, you're likely to leave out some important information and to include some irrelevant material.

Ask why you are preparing the message and for whom you are preparing it.

Lack of familiarity with your audience is an equally serious handicap. You need to know something about the biases, education, age, status, and style of your receiver in order to create an effective message. If you're writing for a specialist in your field, for example, you can use technical terms that might be unfamiliar to a layperson. If you're addressing a lower-level employee, you might approach a subject differently than if you were talking to your boss.

Difficulty Expressing Ideas

Lack of experience in writing or speaking can also prevent a person from developing effective messages. Some people are unable to develop an effective message because they lack expertise in using language. Such problems can be overcome, but only with some effort. The important thing is to recognize the problem and take action. Taking courses in communication at a college is a good first step. Many companies offer their own in-house training programs in communication; others have tuition reimbursement programs to help cover the cost of outside courses. Self-help books are another good, inexpensive alternative. You might even join a professional organization or other group (such as Toastmasters or the League of Women Voters) to practice your communication skills in an informal setting.

An inability to put thoughts into words can be overcome through study and practice.

Overcoming Communication Barriers

The fact is that innumerable barriers to communication can block any phase of the communication process. **Noise** is any interference in the communication process that distorts or obscures the sender's meaning, and such communication barriers can exist between people and within organizations.[15] Effective communicators do all they can to reduce such barriers. By thinking about some of these barriers, you increase your chances of overcoming them.

Communication barriers exist between people and within organizations.

Communication Barriers Between People

When you send a message, you intend to communicate meaning, but the message itself doesn't contain meaning. The meaning exists in your mind and in the mind of your receiver. To understand each other, you and your receiver must share similar meanings for words, gestures, tone of voice, and other symbols.

Differences in Perception   The world constantly bombards us with information: sights, sounds, scents, and so on. Our minds organize this stream of sensation into a mental map that represents our **perception** of reality. In no case is the map in a person's mind the same as the world itself, and no two maps are exactly alike. As you view the world, your mind absorbs your experiences in a unique and personal way. For

Perception is our individual interpretation of the world around us.

As anchor of NBC's "Evening News," Tom Brokaw addresses a nationwide audience daily. He must be careful to use words that mean the same thing to everyone, regardless of background or region of the country. Straightforward and simple is best, says Brokaw. Your chances of being misunderstood decrease if you are as accurate and as specific as you can be.

Filtering is screening out or abbreviating information before passing the message on to someone else.

Your denotative (literal) and connotative (subjective) definitions of words may differ dramatically from those of other people.

example, if you go out for pizza with a friend, each of you will notice different things. As you enter the restaurant, one of you may notice the coolness of the air-conditioning; the other may notice the aroma of pizza. Because your perceptions are unique, the ideas you want to express differ from other people's. As senders, we choose the details that seem important and focus our attention on the most relevant and general. As receivers, we try to fit new details into our existing pattern. If a detail doesn't quite fit, we are inclined to distort the information rather than rearrange the pattern.

Overcoming perceptual barriers can be difficult. Try to predict how your message will be received, anticipate your receiver's reactions, and shape the message accordingly—constantly adjusting to correct any misunderstanding. Try not to apply the same solution to every problem, but look for solutions to fit specific problems. Frame your messages in terms that have meaning for your audience, and try to find something useful in every message you receive.[16]

Incorrect Filtering   **Filtering** is screening out or abbreviating information before a message is passed on to someone else. In business, the filters between you and your receiver are many: secretaries, assistants, receptionists, and answering machines, to name a few. Just getting through by telephone can take a week if you're calling someone who's protected by layers of gatekeepers. Worse yet, your message may be digested, distilled, and probably distorted before it's passed on to your intended receiver. Those same gatekeepers may also translate, embellish, and augment your receiver's ideas and responses before passing them on to you. To overcome filtering barriers, try to establish more than one communication channel (so that information can be verified through multiple sources), eliminate as many intermediaries as possible, and decrease distortion by condensing message information to the bare essentials.

Language Problems   When you choose the words for your message, they impose their own barriers on it. For example, the language of a lawyer differs from that of an accountant or a doctor, and the difference in their vocabularies affects their ability to recognize and express ideas.

Barriers also exist because words can be interpreted in more than one way. Language uses words as symbols to represent reality: Nothing in the word *cookie* automatically ties it to the physical thing that is a cookie. We might just as well call a cookie a zebra. Language is an arbitrary code that depends on shared definitions, but there's a limit to how completely any of us can share the same meaning for a given word.

Even on the literal (denotative) level, words are imprecise. People in the United States generally agree on what a cookie is. However, your idea of a cookie is a composite of all the cookies you have ever tasted or seen: oatmeal cookies, chocolate chip cookies, sugar cookies, and vanilla wafers. Someone from another culture may have a different range of cookie experiences: meringue, florentine, and spritz. You both agree on the general concept of cookie, but the precise image in your minds differs.

On the subjective (connotative) level, the differences are even greater. Your interpretation of the word *cookie* depends partly on how you feel about cookies. You may have very pleasant feelings about them: You may remember baking them with your mother or coming home from school on winter afternoons to cookies and milk. Or you may be on a diet, in which case cookies will be an unpleasant reminder that you think you're too fat and must say no to all your favorite foods.

To overcome language barriers, use the most specific and accurate words possible. Always try to use words your audience will understand. Increase the accuracy of your messages by using language that describes rather than evaluates and by presenting observable facts, events, and circumstances.

Poor Listening   Perhaps the most common barrier to reception is simply a lack of attention on the receiver's part. We all let our minds wander now and then, regardless of how hard we try to concentrate. People are especially likely to drift off when they are forced to listen to information that is difficult to understand or that has little direct bearing on their own lives. If they are tired or concerned about other matters, they are even more likely to lose interest. As already mentioned, too few of us listen well.

To overcome listening barriers, verify your interpretation of what's been said (by paraphrasing what you've understood). Empathize with speakers (by trying to view the situation through their eyes), and resist jumping to conclusions. Clarify meaning by asking nonthreatening questions, and listen without interrupting.

Listening ability decreases when information is difficult to understand and when it has little meaning for your audience.

Differing Emotional States   Every message contains both a content meaning, which deals with the subject of the message, and a relationship meaning, which suggests the nature of the interaction between sender and receiver. Communication can break down when the receiver reacts negatively to either of these meanings. You may have to deal with people when they are upset—or when you are. You may also have conflicting emotions about the subject of your message or the audience for it.

To overcome emotional barriers, be aware of the feelings that arise in you and in others as you communicate, and attempt to control them. For example, choose neutral words to avoid arousing strong feelings unduly. Avoid attitudes, blame, and other subjective concepts. Most important, be alert to the greater potential for misunderstanding that accompanies emotional messages.

Your audience may react either to the content of a message or to the relationship between sender and receiver that it implies.

In business communication, try to maintain your objectivity.

Differing Backgrounds   Differences in background can be one of the hardest communication barriers to overcome. When your receiver's life experience differs substantially from yours, communication becomes more difficult. Age, education, gender, social status, economic position, cultural background, temperament, health, beauty, popularity, religion, political belief, even a passing mood can all separate one person from another and make understanding difficult. Communicating with someone from another country is probably the most extreme example of how background may impede communication, and culture clashes frequently arise in the workplace (see Chapter 3). But you don't have to seek out a person from an exotic locale to run into cultural gaps. You can misunderstand even your best friends and closest relatives, as you no doubt know from personal experience.

To overcome the barriers associated with differing backgrounds, avoid projecting your own background or culture onto others. Clarify your own and understand others' backgrounds, spheres of knowledge, personalities, and perceptions. Moreover, don't assume that certain behaviors mean the same thing to everyone.

Try to understand the other person's point of view, and respect the inevitable differences in background and culture.

As corporate vice president of human resources at Avon Products, Marcia Worthing long ago recognized the impact of differing cultural backgrounds. Her solution was to institute cultural-sensitivity courses to help employees deal with the growing changes both in the customer base and in the workforce.

Communication Barriers Within Organizations

Although all communication is subject to misunderstandings, business communication is particularly difficult. The material is often complex and controversial. Moreover, both the sender and the receiver may face distractions that divert their attention. Further, the opportunities for feedback are often limited, making it difficult to correct misunderstandings.

Information Overload   Too much information is as bad as too little because it reduces the audience's ability to concentrate effectively on the most important messages. People facing information overload sometimes try to cope by ignoring some of the messages, by delaying responses to messages they deem unimportant, by answering

Roger Plummer is president of Ameritech Information Systems, which sells communications systems to business clients in five states. Plummer believes communication must bridge the gap between corporate philosophy and the individual. He says every employee must represent the company's view in all business communications—even though this is sometimes difficult to do.

Business messages rarely have the benefit of the audience's full and undivided attention.

only parts of some messages, by responding inaccurately to certain messages, by taking less time with each message, or by reacting only superficially to all messages.

To overcome information overload, realize that some information is not necessary, and make necessary information easily available. Give information meaning, rather than just passing it on, and set priorities for dealing with the information flow.

Message Complexity   When formulating business messages, you communicate both as an individual and as a representative of an organization. Thus you must adjust your own ideas and style so that they are acceptable to your employer. On occasion, you may even be asked to write or say something that you disagree with personally.

Business messages may also deal with subject matter that can be technical or difficult to express. Imagine trying to write interesting insurance policies, instructions on how to operate a scraped-surface heat exchanger, or guidelines for checking credit references. These topics are dry, and making them interesting is a real challenge.

To overcome the barriers of complex messages, keep them clear and easy to understand. Use strong organization, guide readers by telling them what to expect, use concrete and specific language, and stick to the point. Be sure to ask for feedback so that you can clarify and improve your message.

Message Competition   Communicators are often faced with messages that compete for attention. If you're talking on the phone while scanning a report, both messages are apt to get short shrift. Even your own messages may have to compete with a variety of interruptions: The phone rings every five minutes, people intrude, meetings are called, and crises arise. In short, your messages rarely have the benefit of the receiver's undivided attention.

To overcome competition barriers, avoid making demands on a receiver who doesn't have the time to pay careful attention to your message. Make written messages visually appealing and easy to understand, and try to deliver them when your receiver has time to read them. Oral messages are most effective when you can speak directly to your receiver (rather than to intermediaries or answering machines). Also, be sure to set aside enough time for important messages that you receive.

Status barriers can be overcome by a willingness to give and receive bad news.

Differing Status   Employees of low status may be overly cautious when sending messages to managers and may talk only about subjects they think the manager is interested in. Similarly, higher-status people may distort messages by refusing to discuss anything that would tend to undermine their authority in the organization. Moreover, belonging to a particular department or being responsible for a particular task can narrow your point of view so that it differs from the attitudes, values, and expectations of people who belong to other departments or who are responsible for other tasks.

To overcome status barriers, keep managers and colleagues well informed. Encourage lower-status employees to keep you informed (by being fair-minded and respecting their opinions). When you have information that you're afraid your boss might not like, be brave and convey it anyway.

For communication to be successful, organizations must create an atmosphere of fairness and trust.

Lack of Trust   Building trust is a difficult problem. Other organization members don't know whether you'll respond in a supportive or responsible way, so trusting can be risky. Without trust, however, free and open communication is effectively blocked, threatening the organization's stability. Just being clear in your communication is not enough.

To overcome trust barriers, be visible and accessible. Don't insulate yourself behind assistants or secretaries. Share key information with colleagues and employees, communicate honestly, and include employees in decision making.

Inadequate Communication Structures   Organizational communication is affected by formal restrictions on who may communicate with whom and who is authorized to make decisions. Designing too few formal channels blocks effective communication. Strongly centralized organizations reduce communication capacity and decrease the tendency to communicate horizontally. Organizations with many levels of hierarchy tend to provide too many vertical communication links, so messages become distorted as they move through the organization's levels. To overcome structural barriers, offer opportunities for communicating upward, downward, and horizontally (using such techniques as employee surveys, open-door policies, newsletters, memos, and task groups). Try to reduce hierarchical levels, increase coordination between departments, and encourage two-way communication.

Structural barriers block upward, downward, and horizontal communication.

Incorrect Choice of Medium   If you choose an inappropriate communication medium, your message can be distorted so that the intended meaning is blocked. You can select the most appropriate medium by matching your choice with the nature of the message and of the group or the individual who will receive it. **Media richness** is the value of a medium in a given communication situation. It's determined by a medium's ability (1) to convey a message using more than one informational cue (visual, verbal, vocal), (2) to facilitate feedback, and (3) to establish personal focus (see Figure 2.3).

Your choice of a communication channel and medium depends on the

- Message
- Audience
- Need for speed
- Situation

Face-to-face communication is the richest medium because it is personal, it provides immediate feedback, it transmits information from both verbal and nonverbal cues, and it conveys the emotion behind the message. Telephones and other interactive electronic media aren't as rich; although they allow immediate feedback, they don't provide visual nonverbal cues such as facial expressions, eye contact, and body movements. Written media can be personalized through addressed memos, letters, and reports, but they lack the immediate feedback and the visual and vocal nonverbal cues that contribute to the meaning of the message. The leanest media are generally impersonal written messages such as bulletins, fliers, and standard reports. Not only do they lack the ability to transmit nonverbal cues and give feedback, they also eliminate any personal focus.

To overcome media barriers, choose the richest media for nonroutine, complex messages. Use rich media to extend and to humanize your presence throughout the organization, to communicate caring and personal interest to employees, and to gain employee commitment to organizational goals. Use leaner media to communicate simple, routine messages. You can send information such as statistics, facts, figures, and conclusions through a note, memo, or written report.[17]

**Figure 2.3
A Continuum of Media Richness**
To ensure effective communication, be sure to use richer media for messages that are complex, ambiguous, and nonroutine.

Closed Communication Climate   As discussed in Chapter 1, communication climate is influenced by management style, and a directive, authoritarian style blocks the free and open exchange of information that characterizes good communication. To overcome climate barriers, spend more time listening than issuing orders. Make sure you respond constructively to employees, and encourage employees and colleagues to offer suggestions, help set goals, participate in solving problems, and help make decisions.

Unethical Communication   An organization cannot create illegal or unethical messages and still be credible or successful in the long run. Relationships within and out-

*B*EHIND THE SCENES AT FEDERAL EXPRESS
When It Absolutely, Positively Has to Be Perfect

As senior manager of Federal Express's LBE (Latrobe, Pennsylvania) Station, Jon Sutton helps bring to life an automated system that picks up and delivers nearly 2 million priority packages every day. Air express delivery is big business, and Federal Express's share of the revenues exceeds $7 billion annually. The company has become the runaway leader by combining state-of-the-art technology with clear and effective interpersonal communication.

When you dial a Federal Express call center toll-free to start your package on its way, someone answers you within three rings, despite a daily volume of 250,000 calls. The customer service representative places your pickup order in the COSMOS computer system and sends it on-line to the dispatch center at a station near you. From there, the order is sent to the courier over DADS, a mobile unit linked with each Federal Express van, and your package is scheduled for pickup. When the courier arrives, he or she runs an on-line scanner over your package's number, letting COSMOS know where it is. Then every step of delivery is tracked as the package travels through the system: to the sending station, the airplane, the airport sorting hub, the receiving station, the delivering courier, and finally the recipient.

People make this high-tech system work. Sutton uses a variety of communication skills to help his 52-member team meet both management's and customers' demanding expectations: 100 percent perfection. As Sutton points out, "The company's philosophy, People-Service-Profits, is the key. If you take good care of your people, they will provide good service, which in turn will provide Federal Express with a profit."

To take good care of his people, Sutton relies heavily on meetings: face-to-face meetings with individuals, weekly 15-minute work-group meetings to get the word out on things that affect the couriers or customer service agents, and informal monthly meetings with the work groups to bring out issues on a more human scale. "That's the time to tell it like it is," says Sutton. "You don't like

---

Ethical messages are crucial to any organization's credibility and success.

side the organization depend on trust and fairness. To overcome ethics barriers, make sure your messages include all the information that ought to be there. Make sure that information is adequate and relevant to the situation. Also make sure your message is completely truthful, not deceptive in any way.

Communication can be blocked by inefficiency.

Inefficient Communication Producing worthless messages wastes time and resources, and it contributes to the information overload already mentioned. Reduce the number of messages by thinking twice before sending one. Then speed up the process, first, by preparing messages correctly the first time around and, second, by standardizing format and material when appropriate. Be clear about the writing assignments you accept as well as the ones you assign.

Your audience is more likely to receive your message accurately if nothing physical interrupts or distorts the message.

Physical Distractions Communication barriers are often physical: bad connections, poor acoustics, illegible copy. Although noise of this sort seems trivial, it can completely block an otherwise effective message. Your receiver might also be distracted by an uncomfortable chair, poor lighting, or some other irritating condition. In some cases, the barrier may be related to the receiver's health. Hearing or visual impairment or even a headache can interfere with reception of a message. These annoyances don't generally block communication entirely, but they may reduce concentration.

To overcome physical barriers, exercise as much control as possible over the physical transmission link: If you're preparing a written document, make sure its appearance doesn't detract from your message. If you're delivering an oral presentation, choose a setting that permits the audience to see and hear you without straining. When you are the audience, learn to concentrate on the message rather than the distractions.

the way I part my hair? You want to know why something is done the way it is? You can suggest a change in a van's route to improve our efficiency? Speak up!" Sutton understands that people are often reluctant to bring up problems, so he prompts discussions by starting with something like "I overheard someone say . . ."

Nonverbal techniques play an equally important role. "Watching is very important to me," says Sutton. A person's facial expression or behavior lets Sutton know how things are going. And he shows his own feelings: "Just a subtle look, a glance, or a hint of action can often get my point across without having to say anything."

About written communication, Sutton says he usually writes only memos and then only when "procedures change or when I want to praise someone or something, update people, remind them of something, or clarify a point." He doesn't want any misunderstandings when it affects his team's work.

To succeed as a manager, Sutton advises, you first have to know how to listen: "Always, always listen. And I mean listen to everything, both verbally and nonverbally." Beyond that, he recommends that you should be willing to talk about anything: "You have to be able to discuss matters openly to get to the bottom of a problem and get it resolved." Such an approach will help you

run a high-pressure operation flawlessly. At Federal Express, this approach is expected to work 100 percent of the time.

Apply Your Knowledge

1. How should Jon Sutton handle these problems: (a) There are areas in certain courier routes where communications via the DADS computer unit are cut off. (b) A new courier picks up the package at one office in a building on his route, but he unknowingly misses pickups at two other offices in the same building. (c) A seasoned courier leaves a small package in the back of his van when he returns to the station, clocks out, and goes home. Which communication techniques are most appropriate to use in each situation?

2. In the past three months as Jon Sutton's assistant, you've been disappointed in the pace and outcome of your monthly open-forum meetings. No one speaks up, and no suggestions are made; people just eye one another nervously, seeming anxious to get it over with and get back to work. What would you do to encourage greater participation? What specific communication techniques would you use? Include at least two strategies each of oral, written, and nonverbal communication.

H OW TO IMPROVE COMMUNICATION

As you learn how to overcome more and more communication barriers, you become more and more successful as a business communicator. Think about the people you know. Which of them would you call successful communicators? What do these people have in common? Chances are, the individuals on your list share five traits:

- *Perception.* They are able to predict how you will receive their message. They anticipate your reaction and shape the message accordingly. They read your response correctly and constantly adjust to correct any misunderstanding.
- *Precision.* They create a "meeting of the minds." When they finish expressing themselves, you share the same mental picture.
- *Credibility.* They are believable. You have faith in the substance of their message. You trust their information and their intentions.
- *Control.* They shape your response. Depending on their purpose, they can make you laugh or cry, calm down, change your mind, or take action.
- *Congeniality.* They maintain friendly, pleasant relations with you. Regardless of whether you agree with them, good communicators command your respect and goodwill. You are willing to work with them again, despite your differences.

Effective communication requires perception, precision, credibility, control, and congeniality.

Effective communicators overcome the main barriers to communication by creating their messages carefully, minimizing noise in the transmission process, and facilitating feedback.

Create the Message Carefully

You want to create a bridge of words that leads audience members from their current position to your point. The best way to create messages carefully is to focus on your audience so that you can help them understand and accept your message:

In general terms, your purpose is to bring your audience closer to your views.

- *Learn about your audience.* Learn about the members of your audience—their current position, what they know now, and what they need to know. Even without hard facts, you can project yourself into your audience's position by using your common sense and imagination.

Give your audience a framework for understanding the ideas you communicate.

- *Tell your audience what to expect.* Guide your audience through your message. Tell them at the outset what they can expect to gain. Tell them the purpose and the main points of your message. Even if you don't want to reveal controversial ideas at the beginning of a message, you can still give a preview of the topics you plan to cover. By telling them how to categorize the information in your message, you eliminate the discrepancy between your mental filing system and theirs, making it easier for people to follow your message without getting lost.

To make your message memorable
- Use words that evoke a physical, sensory impression
- Use telling statistics

- *Reach your audience with concrete, specific language.* Help your audience understand and remember the message by balancing your general concepts with specific illustrations. At the beginning, state the overall idea; then develop that idea by using vivid, concrete examples to help the audience visualize the concept.

The key to brevity is to limit the number of ideas, not to shortchange their development.

- *Keep your audience focused.* Eliminate any information that doesn't directly contribute to your purpose. Audiences need only a few pertinent facts, enough information to answer their questions or facilitate their decisions. With few exceptions, one page is better than two, especially in a business environment where so many messages compete for attention. Of course, you have to be careful to develop each main idea adequately. You're better off covering three points thoroughly rather than eight points superficially. If an idea is worth including, it's worth explaining.

Tie the message to your audience's frame of reference.

- *Show your audience how new information relates to existing ideas.* Indicate how new ideas are related to the files that already exist in the minds of audience members. The meaning of the new concept is clarified by its relationship to the old, and such connections help make the new ideas more acceptable.

By highlighting and summarizing key points, you help your audience understand and remember the message.

- *Remind your audience of your key points.* Call attention to the most important points in your message with your words, your format, and your body language. When you come to an important idea, say so. Underscore key points by using headlines, bold type, indented lists, charts, graphs, maps, diagrams, and illustrations. Before you conclude your message, take a moment or two to review the essential points. Restate the purpose, and show how the main ideas relate to it. This simple step helps your audience remember the message.

Minimize Noise

Even the most carefully constructed message will fail to achieve results if it does not reach your audience. As far as possible, try to eliminate potential sources of interference. Then make sure your choice of communication channel and medium doesn't interfere with your message. Choose the method that will be most likely to attract your audience's attention and enable them to concentrate on the message. If a written document seems the best choice, try to make it physically appealing and easy to comprehend. Use an attractive, convenient format, and pay attention to such details as the choice of paper and the quality of type. If possible, deliver the document when you know the reader will have time to study it.

The careful choice of channel and medium helps focus your audience's attention on your message.

If the message calls for an oral delivery channel, try to eliminate physical barriers. The location should be comfortable and quiet, with adequate lighting, good acoustics, and few visual distractions. In addition, think about how your own appearance will affect the audience. An outfit that screams for attention creates as much noise as a squeaky air-conditioning system. Another way to reduce interference, particularly in oral communication, is to deliver your message directly to the intended audience. The more people who filter your message, the greater the potential for message distortion.

Facilitate Feedback

In addition to minimizing noise, giving your audience a chance to provide feedback is crucial. Unfortunately, one thing that makes business communication difficult is the complexity of the feedback loop. If you're talking face-to-face with another person, feedback is immediate and clear. However, if you're writing a letter, memo, or report that will be read by several people, feedback will be delayed and mixed. Some of the readers will be enthusiastic or respond promptly; others will be critical or reluctant to respond, and revising your message to take into account their feedback will be difficult.

When you formulate a message, think about the amount of feedback you want to encourage. Although feedback is generally useful, it reduces your control over the communication situation. You need to know whether your message is being understood and accepted, but you may not want to respond to comments until you have completed your argument. If you are communicating with a group, you may not have the time to react to every impression or question.

So think about how you want to obtain feedback, and choose a form of communication that suits your needs. Some channels and media allow more feedback than others do. If you want to adjust your message quickly, talk to the receiver face-to-face or by phone. If feedback is less important to you, use a written document or give a prepared speech.

Feedback is not always easy to get, even when you encourage it. In some cases, you may have to draw out the other person by asking questions. If you want to know specific things, ask specific questions, but also encourage your audience to express general reactions; you can often learn something very interesting that way.

Regardless of whether the response to your message is written or oral, encourage people to be open and to tell you what they really think and feel. Of course, you have to listen to their comments, and you must do so objectively. You can't say "Please tell me what you think" and then get angry at the first critical comment. So try not to react defensively. Your goal is to find out whether the people in your audience have understood and accepted your message. If you find that they haven't, don't lose your temper. After all, the fault is at least partially yours. Instead of saying the same thing all over again, only louder this time, try to find the source of the misunderstanding. Then revise your message. Sooner or later, if you keep trying, you'll succeed. You may not win the audience to your point of view, but at least you'll make your meaning clear, and you'll part with a feeling of mutual respect.

> Make feedback more useful by
> - Planning how and when to accept it
> - Being receptive to your audience's responses
> - Encouraging frankness
> - Using it to improve communication

On the Job

SOLVING A COMMUNICATION DILEMMA AT BEN & JERRY'S HOMEMADE

Communication—with customers, the public, investors, and government officials—plays a key role in Ben & Jerry's success. Whether it's a company meeting, a tour of the facilities, or involvement in various social and environmental causes, the company works energetically to communicate its messages.

To begin with, the communicators at Ben & Jerry's never miss an opportunity to get their messages across to customers and the general public. The labels on most food products discuss ingredients and taste, but Ben & Jerry's labels go a step beyond, showing information about world peace, the environment, and other causes. Some products are even designed to convey messages. For example, a percentage of sales from Peace Pops goes to promoting world peace, and Rainforest Crunch is made with nuts from the South American rain forest (which supports the native people directly and gives them a financial incentive to nurture the forest instead of cutting it down). Both labels and products act as transmission channels for Ben & Jerry's messages.

Publicly owned companies are required to publish annual reports for their shareholders, and these reports are usually slick and glossy, heaping praise on the company's managers and employees. An annual report from Ben & Jerry's, on the other hand, is likely to be illustrated with whimsical drawings of cows, ice cream cones, and endangered species. The content can include such features as a "social assessment," in which an outside observer evaluates the company's success in meeting its social goals. Investors, employees, government officials, and other readers can have no doubt about the company's orientation after reading these reports.

In addition to communicating with customers and shareholders, communicating with employees is crucial to the success of any business. At Ben & Jerry's, internal communication ranges from meetings in which all employees are encouraged to speak their minds about company policies and practices to the following formal mission statement (which is also published in the annual report):

■ *Product Mission.* To make, distribute, and sell the finest quality all-natural ice cream and related products in a wide variety of innovative flavors made from Vermont dairy products.
■ *Economic Mission.* To operate the company on a sound financial basis of profitable growth, increasing value for our shareholders and creating career opportunities and financial rewards for our employees.
■ *Social Mission.* To operate the company in a way that actively recognizes the central role that business plays in the structure of society by initiating innovative ways to improve the quality of life in a broad community: local, national, and international.

This mission statement clearly communicates what the company's leaders consider important. It also gives every employee and franchisee—the people and organizations who own individual Ben & Jerry's stores—a framework in which to make decisions and take action. By communicating what the company is about and what it wants to accomplish, Cohen and Greenfield can keep their unusual business effort alive and well.

Your Mission: You've recently been hired to assist Dave Stigman, Ben & Jerry's director of communications. This role covers internal communication with employees and franchisees as well as external communication with customers, suppliers, the news media, and the general public. You have three responsibilities: (1) developing guidelines and practices to help the company communicate more effectively, (2) helping

individual employees and managers with specific communication problems, and (3) acting as the company's official voice by talking to reporters, welcoming tour groups, and so on.

In the following hypothetical situations, select the best choice from the available options. Keep in mind that in some of the situations, two or three options might be attractive, so you'll have to pick the best one carefully. In other situations, none of the options may look particularly strong, but you still need to pick the best one from the choices offered. Use good judgment and common sense to help identify the best answer in each situation, and be prepared to explain why your choice is best.

1. A reporter from *The New York Times* is writing an article on fat and cholesterol in the American diet. She wants to know how Ben & Jerry's can claim to be so socially responsible when the company sells products that aren't exactly healthy. The article is running in tomorrow's editions, so the reporter doesn't have time to let you think about it and call back with an answer. Which is the best response?
   a. You know that anything you say might provoke a negative reaction, so you simply say, "I'm sorry, we don't comment on health-related issues."
   b. You know that you have to establish some credibility, and pretending that a steady diet of ice cream is acceptable is not the way to do that, so you say, "We don't encourage anyone to eat excessive amounts of ice cream. We do believe, however, that modest amounts of ice cream can be compatible with a generally healthy lifestyle that includes a balanced diet and regular exercise."
   c. You want to take control of the conversation, so you tell her that "until we conduct our own research, we're not willing to accept without question the negative image that the medical profession has created for ice cream."
   d. You know that you can't control what your customers eat, so you say, "We can't be held responsible for our customers' health. After all, we make only ice cream, and people could have unhealthy eating habits that extend beyond dessert."

2. The manager of one of the production plants realizes that his communication skills are important for several reasons: He holds primary responsibility for successful communication inside the plant, he needs to communicate with the managers who report to him, and his style sets an example for other managers. He asks you to sit in on face-to-face meetings for several days to observe any nonverbal messages that he may be sending. You witness the following four habits; which do you think is the most negative?
   a. He rarely comes out from behind his massive desk when meeting with people in his office; at one point he gave an employee a congratulatory handshake, and the employee had to lean way over his desk just to reach him.
   b. When an employee hands him a report and then sits down to discuss it, he alternates between making eye contact and making notes on the report.
   c. He is consistently pleasant, even if the person he is meeting is delivering bad news.

d. He interrupts meetings to answer the phone, rather than letting an assistant get the phone; then he apologizes to visitors for the interruption.

3. Say that a weak economy has forced the company to lay off 5 percent of its employees. Knowing that this is an emotionally charged issue, the company president asks you to recommend the best way to break the news to those who will lose their jobs.

   a. Soften the blow by writing an article for the company newsletter, describing the plans to lay off 5 percent of the workforce.

   b. It is the responsibility of individual managers to tell the employees who report to them. However, the president should send a brief personal letter to all affected employees, noting their accomplishments and wishing them luck in finding new jobs.

   c. The president owes it to the employees to meet with them individually and break the news.

   d. On bulletin boards around the company, post a list of employees to be laid off.

4. At a recent companywide meeting, employees were told that shareholders have been pressuring company management to pay them a higher dividend, and the board of directors has agreed. (Dividends are a portion of the company's profits set aside for shareholders; higher dividends mean less money is available for other purposes.) Then, when the employees returned to work, they found the latest issue of the company newsletter, in which an article by Jerry Greenfield asked employees to voluntarily shorten their lunch periods to increase ice cream production so that more money can be given to charities. Which of the following scenarios best describes the effect of the two messages?

   a. The two messages are compatible; shareh[olders get] more money from the existing profit mar[gin; char]ities will get more from the employees' w[orking] hours. You don't foresee any problems.

   b. Employees will actually work less because they'll resent the shareholders' request for higher dividends.

   c. Employees will begin to question the wisdom of the company's charitable contributions.

   d. Confusion is the most likely result because the two messages conflict. Some employees are likely to think that their sacrifice of working longer for the same pay is going to benefit the shareholders, not the charities.

5. The human resources manager is writing a letter to all employees explaining that health insurance is getting more expensive and that employees will have to pay 10 percent more for coverage. The company and the employees share the cost of coverage, and the company decides how much of the cost its employees have to pay. The manager asks you to read four possible openings for the letter. Which would you recommend that she use?

   a. "If you follow the news, you are certainly aware of the skyrocketing costs of health insurance; those increases are now going to affect all of us here at Ben & Jerry's."

   b. "You're probably aware of the increasing costs of health insurance. Although we have been doing everything possible to keep your insurance payments from rising, we've unfortunately reached a point where the company can no longer absorb all the increases by itself."

   c. "Your health insurance premiums have increased by 10 percent, effective immediately."

   d. "We're pleased to announce that the company has found a way to improve its profitability by decreasing the amount it spends on health insurance."[18]

Questions for Discussion

1. How can nonverbal communication help you run a meeting? How can it help you show approval, express reservations, and regulate the flow of conversation?

2. How can you as a receiver help a sender successfully communicate a message?

3. Which communication channels are more susceptible to noise, written or spoken? Why?

4. "A good business writer can make any piece of writing interesting." Do you agree? Explain.

5. Do you believe it's easier to communicate with members of your own sex? Why or why not?

6. Under what circumstances might you want to limit the feedback you receive from an audience of readers or listeners?

Document for Analysis

Read the following memo; then (1) analyze the strengths or weaknesses of each sentence and (2) revise the memo so that it follows this chapter's guidelines.

It has come to my attention that many of you are lying on your time cards. If you come in late, you should not put 8:00 on your card. If you take a long unch, you should not put 1:00 on your time card. I will not stand for this type of cheating. I simply have no choice but to institute a time-clock system. Beginning next Monday, all employees will have to punch in and punch out whenever they come and go from the work area.

The time clock will be right by the entrance to each work area, so you have no excuse for not punching in.

Anyone who is late for work or late coming back from lunch more than three times will have to answer to me. I don't care whether you had to take a nap or if you girls had to shop. This is a place of business, and we do not want to be taken advantage of by slackers who are cheaters to boot.

It is too bad that a few bad apples always have to spoil things for everyone.

Exercises

1. Write a short description of your classroom's communication potential. What furniture is in the room? How is the room arranged? Are students seated in rows? In a circle? Where is the instructor's space? At the front of the room? In the middle? What are the acoustics like? Are there any windows in the room? Do they offer pleasing views? Could they be distracting? Are there any chalkboards or other visual aids that might affect communication? Is the temperature comfortable? Are heaters or air conditioners noisy? Explain how these and other factors influence the communication that goes on in your classroom. Conclude your description with a statement about the kind of communication your classroom encourages (an inflexible atmosphere for one-way lectures? an open forum of give and take? an intimate setting for private conversations between members of small groups?).

2. Describe the kinds of vocal signals and body movements you will use to highlight the key points of a speech you're presenting next week.

3. Without intruding, observe and analyze three face-to-face interactions (perhaps between a customer and a cashier at a supermarket checkout, between students in your college cafeteria, between your roommates or family members, etc.). Describe how the nonverbal behaviors you observe give the participants clues about what's being said.

4. Think of a communication experience you have had recently. In a paragraph or two, identify the sender, message, transmission channel and medium, receiver, and feedback. Also identify any barriers that affected the communication.

5. Briefly describe a miscommunication you've had with a co-worker, fellow college student, friend, or family member. Can you identify what barrier(s) prevented your successful communication? Please explain.

6. Some business communicators supply too much information, which makes it difficult for the recipient to sort out the most important points. Here is the first draft of a memo written by a busy office manager to her immediate supervisor. Rephrase it so that it gets to the point more quickly and fits easily onto a half-sheet memo form.

I can't ever remember being so frustrated in my life! Here is what happened. I ordered six regional U.S. maps last week at $17 each against our office equipment budget, but Mr. Olson in purchasing said that I had to place the order against the office supplies budget because the maps cost less than $25 each. The problem is, of course, that we are going to be overspent this year in the office supplies budget, but we still have equipment money because we got such a good price on the terminals I ordered last month. Anyway, Olson and I went round and round about this. He wouldn't budge, and I couldn't budge, but I do see a possible way out of the dilemma. Do you think that I could put the order through again, this time for a single set of U.S. maps costing $102? You'll probably be hearing from Mr. Olson, so I wanted to alert you to the problem and get your advice. We do need the maps!

COMMUNICATING INTERCULTURALLY

After studying this chapter, you will be able to

Define culture *and* intercultural communication

Discuss nine ways people can differ culturally

Summarize how to learn about a particular culture

Discuss some general skills to help communicate in any culture

Identify some of the common sources of misunderstanding that occur in written and oral intercultural communication

Explain the importance of speaking and listening more effectively when communicating face-to-face with people from other cultures

On the Job

FACING A COMMUNICATION DILEMMA AT APPLE COMPUTER
A Yen for Computer Profits

After Apple Computer's optimistic start, the sun seemed to be setting on the company's future in Japan. Based in Cupertino, California, Apple began selling personal computers in Japan in 1979. With virtually no competitors, top managers were confident of success. After all, they had a hot product, and they saw Japan as the first step in the quest for global sales and profits.

Ten years later, Apple had gained only a tiny share of the Japanese market. Despite this dismal performance, the company wasn't about to leave Japan. "If you call yourself a global company, it's a misnomer if you're not strong in Japan," says Ian Diery, president of Apple Pacific.

Apple was in trouble because it didn't understand Japanese customers' needs or the country's business climate. The computer maker faced more than language barriers. It had to learn about its Japanese customers, make and sell products to fit the needs of those customers, and learn about how to do business in Japan. All this required effective intercultural communication.

If you were in charge of Apple in Japan, how would you learn about the values and needs of Japanese customers? What messages would you send to persuade Japanese customers to try Apple products? How would you overcome the language barrier and the problems caused by a bad image?[1]

*T*HE BASICS OF INTERCULTURAL BUSINESS COMMUNICATION

Apple is by no means alone in its multinational focus. More and more companies around the world are hopping national borders to conduct business. Thanks to ad-

Apple Computer

The globalization of business is accelerating as more companies cross national borders to find customers, materials, and money.

Cultural diversity is the degree to which the population is made up of people from varied national, ethnic, racial, and religious backgrounds.

vances in telecommunication and transportation, companies can quickly and easily span the globe in search of new customers, new sources of materials, and new sources of money. Even firms that once thought they were too tiny to expand into a neighboring city have discovered that they can tap the sales potential of overseas markets with the help of fax machines and overnight delivery services. With this rise of international business, companies are finding that good communication skills are essential for meeting customers, making sales, and working more effectively with colleagues in other countries.

Of course, communicating across national borders is only one way your communication skills will be challenged. Communicating across language and cultural barriers at home will also challenge your skills. First, if you work in the local branch of a foreign firm or if your company does business with local branches of foreign firms, you may find that differences in language and culture interfere with your message exchange. Second, no matter where you work, you'll face language and cultural barriers as you communicate with members of an increasingly diverse domestic workforce. Few countries have an entirely homogeneous population. A country's workforce reflects its **cultural diversity,** the degree to which the population is made up of people from various national, ethnic, racial, and religious backgrounds. People also differ in terms of their gender, age, physical abilities, family status, and educational background, which contribute to the diversity of the workforce. Without leaving your own country, you're likely to come into contact with people from a variety of backgrounds who work in your company, industry, and community.

As discussed in Chapter 2, differences in background can be a difficult communication barrier to overcome. When you plan to communicate with people of another culture—whether in another country or in your own country—it's important to be aware of cultural differences. Consider the communication challenge that Mazda's managers faced when the Japanese auto manufacturer opened a plant in the United States. Mazda officials passed out company baseball caps and told their U.S. employees that they could wear the caps at work, along with their mandatory company uniform (blue pants and khaki shirts). The employees assumed that the caps were a *voluntary* accessory, and many decided not to wear them. This upset the Japanese managers, who regarded failure to wear the caps as a sign of disrespect. Managers acknowledged that the caps were voluntary but believed that employees who really cared about the company would *want* to wear the caps. However, the U.S. employees had a different view: They resented being told what they should want to do, and they began cynically referring to all Mazda's directives as "mandatory-voluntary."[2] Even though communicating with people from other cultures can be challenging, your ability to foster successful communication among people of differing cultures will bolster your success in business and in your career. To overcome cultural barriers to communication, first learn what *culture* actually means.

Understanding Culture

Culture is a shared system of symbols, beliefs, attitudes, values, expectations, and norms for behavior.

Subcultures are distinct groups that exist within a major culture.

You belong to several cultures. The most obvious is the culture you share with all the people who live in your own country. You also belong to other cultural groups, including an ethnic group, a religious group, and perhaps a profession that has its own special language and customs. **Culture** is a shared system of symbols, beliefs, attitudes, values, expectations, and norms for behavior. All members of a culture have similar assumptions about how people should think, behave, and communicate, and they tend to act on those assumptions in much the same way. Distinct groups that exist within a major culture are more properly referred to as **subcultures.** Groups that might be considered subcultures in the United States are Mexican Americans, Mormons, wrestling fans, Russian immigrants, and Harvard graduates.

By bridging cultural differences, you can successfully achieve **intercultural communication,** the process of sending and receiving messages between people of different cultures. You will be most effective when you learn to identify the differences between sender and receiver and to accommodate those differences without expecting either culture to give up its own identity.[3] Most of us need special training in identifying cultural differences before we can feel comfortable communicating with someone from another culture.

Recognizing Cultural Differences

Cultural differences can affect your ability to send and receive messages. When you write to or speak with someone in another culture, you encode your message using the assumptions of your own culture. However, the receiver decodes it according to the assumptions of the other culture, so your meaning may be misunderstood. The greater the difference between the sender's culture and the receiver's culture, the greater the chance for misunderstanding.[4]

Consider the U.S. computer sales representative who called on a client in China. Hoping to make a good impression, the salesperson brought an expensive grandfather clock as a gift. Unfortunately, the differences between the sender's culture and the receiver's culture interfered with the communication process. Instead of being pleased, the Chinese client was deeply offended, because in China receiving a clock as a gift is considered bad luck.[5]

Such problems arise when we assume, wrongly, that other people's attitudes and lives are like ours. As a graduate of one training program said: "I used to think it was enough to treat people the way I wanted to be treated. But [after taking the course] . . . I realized you have to treat people the way *they* want to be treated."[6] Acknowledging and exploring these differences is an important step toward understanding how culture affects the communication process.

Social Values

Although the United States is home to millions of people having different religions and values, the major influence is the Puritan work ethic. The predominant U.S. view is that money solves many problems, that material comfort (earned by individual effort) is a sign of superiority, and that people who work hard are better than those who don't. By and large, people in the United States assume that people from other cultures also dislike poverty and value hard work. In fact, many societies condemn materialism, and some prize a more carefree lifestyle.

As a culture, people in the United States are goal-oriented. They want to get their work done efficiently, and they assume that everyone else does too. They think they're improving things if they can figure out a way for two people using modern methods to do the same work as four people using the "old way." In countries such as India and Pakistan, where unemployment is high, creating jobs is more important than working efficiently. Executives in these countries would rather employ four workers than two, and their values influence their actions as well as the way they encode and decode messages.

Roles and Status

Culture dictates the roles people play, including who communicates with whom, what they communicate, and in what way. For example, in many countries women still don't

During Nelson Mandela's decades of struggling for human rights and democracy, he has been the victim of, and the victor over, cultural differences. Now president of South Africa, Mandela is working to reassure the members of all cultures that he and his government value all minorities for their contributions.

Intercultural communication is the process of sending and receiving messages between people of different cultures.

A society's culture affects its members' view of the world and thus their responses to people and events.

People from the United States emphasize hard work, material success, and efficiency more than many other people do.

People from other cultures demonstrate their status differently than do people in the United States.

play a prominent role in business, so female executives who visit these countries may find that they're not taken seriously as businesspeople. Culture can define roles by the way people refer to one another. In the United States people show respect for superiors and top managers by addressing them as "Mr. Roberts" or "Mrs. Gutierrez." However, in China it's customary to show respect for organizational rank by addressing businesspeople according to their official titles, such as "President" or "Manager."[7]

Concepts of status also differ. Most U.S. executives send status signals that reflect materialistic values. The big boss has a large corner office, deep carpets, an expensive desk, and handsome accessories. In other cultures status is communicated in other ways. The highest-ranking executives in France sit in the middle of an open area, surrounded by lower-level employees. In the Middle East fine possessions are reserved for the home, and business is conducted in cramped and modest quarters. An executive from another culture who assumes that such office arrangements indicate a lack of status would be making a big mistake.

Decision-Making Customs

Many cultural groups take longer than U.S. and Canadian businesspeople to reach decisions, and many rely more heavily on group consensus.

In the United States and Canada, businesspeople try to reach decisions as quickly and efficiently as possible. The top people are concerned with reaching an agreement on the main points, and they leave the details to be worked out later by others. In Greece this approach would backfire. A Greek executive assumes that anyone who ignores the details is being evasive and untrustworthy. Spending time on each little point is considered a mark of good faith. Similarly, Latin Americans prefer to make their deals slowly, after much discussion.

Cultures also differ in terms of who makes the decisions. In the United States many organizations are dominated by a single figure who says yes or no to the major deals. It is the same in Pakistan, where you can get a decision quickly if you reach the highest-ranking executive.[8] In other cultures, decision making is shared. In Japan a negotiating team arrives at consensus through an elaborate, time-consuming process. Agreement must be complete—there is no majority rule. And like businesses everywhere, Japanese firms expect their managers to follow the same decision-making process regardless of whether they're in Tokyo or in Toledo, Ohio.

Concepts of Time

Although businesspeople in the United States, Germany, and some other nations see time as a way of organizing the business day efficiently, other cultures see time as more flexible.

Differing perceptions of time are another factor that can lead to misunderstandings. German and U.S. executives see time as a way to plan the business day efficiently, focusing on only one task during each scheduled period. Because time is so limited, German and U.S. executives try to get to the point quickly when communicating.

However, executives from Latin America and Asia see time as more flexible. In these cultures, building a foundation for the business relationship is more important than meeting a deadline for completing a task. Seen in this light, it's not surprising that people in such cultures do not observe strict schedules. Instead, they take whatever time is needed to get to know one another and explore the background issues.[9]

If a salesperson from Chicago called on a client in Mexico City and was kept waiting 30 minutes in the outer office, that salesperson would feel angry and insulted, assuming the client attaches a low priority to the visit. In fact, the Mexican client doesn't mean to imply anything at all by this delay. In Mexico, a wait of 30 minutes is a matter of course; the workday isn't expected to follow a rigid, preset schedule.[10]

Concepts of Personal Space

People from various cultures have different "comfort zones."

Like time, space means different things in different cultures. The classic story of a conversation between a U.S. executive and a Latin American executive is that the interaction may begin at one end of a hallway and end up at the other, with neither party aware of having moved. During the conversation the Latin American executive instinctively moves closer to the U.S. executive, who unconsciously steps back, resulting in an intercultural dance across the floor.

People in Canada and the United States usually stand about five feet apart during a business conversation. This distance is uncomfortably close for people from Germany or Japan. But to Arabs or Latin Americans, this distance is uncomfortably far. Because of these differing concepts of personal space, a Canadian manager may react negatively (without knowing exactly why) when a Latin American colleague moves closer during their conversation. And the Latin American colleague may react negatively (again, without knowing why) when the Canadian manager backs away.

Cultural Context

One of the ways we assign meaning to a message is according to its **cultural context,** the pattern of physical cues and implicit understanding that convey meaning between two members of the same culture. However, people convey contextual meaning differently from culture to culture. In a **high-context culture** such as South Korea or Taiwan, people rely less on verbal communication and more on the context of non-verbal actions and environmental setting to convey meaning. The rules of everyday life are rarely explicit in high-context cultures. As they grow up, people learn how to recognize situational cues (such as gestures and tone of voice) and how to respond as expected.[11]

In a **low-context culture** such as the United States or Germany, people rely more on verbal communication and less on circumstances and implied meaning to communicate. Expectations are usually spelled out in a low-context culture through explicit statements, such as "Please wait until I'm finished" or "You're welcome to browse." In this way, a businessperson in a low-context culture not only explains his or her own actions but also cues the other person about what to do or what to expect next.[12]

Imagine the confusion and frustration of someone from a low-context culture (such as Apple) trying to sell products to a client from a high-context culture (such as Japan). Using a typically Western approach to advertising, Apple ran hard-sell messages in a country that prefers soft-sell image building. The result was slow sales and a small market share for Apple in Japan.

Body Language

Gestures help members of a culture clarify confusing messages, but differences in body language are a major source of misunderstanding during intercultural communication. Furthermore, don't make the mistake of assuming that someone from another country who speaks your language has mastered the body language of your culture. Instead, learn some of the basic differences in the way people supplement their words with body movement. Take the signal for *no*. People in the United States and Canada shake their heads back and forth; people in Bulgaria nod up and down; people in Japan move their right hands; people in Sicily raise their chins. Or take eye contact. Businesspeople in the United States assume that a person who won't meet their gaze is evasive and dishonest. In many parts of Latin America and Asia, however, keeping your eyes lowered is a sign of respect. Among many Native American groups, it's a sign of disrespect for children to maintain eye contact with adults.[13] So when some teachers scold Native American students by saying, "Look at me when I'm talking to you," they only create confusion.

Sometimes people from different cultures misread an intentional signal sent by body language; sometimes they overlook the signal entirely or assume that a meaningless gesture is significant. An Arab man indicates a romantic interest in a woman by run-

Although U.S. businesspeople rely more on words to convey meaning, people in other cultures rely more on situational cues and implicit understanding.

Stacy L. Coleman is a vice president at the Chase Manhattan Private Bank where she helps teams learn to focus on the customer. Listening to clients is key, says Coleman. Understanding them in a cultural context is essential to satisfying their needs for products or services.

Variations in the meaning of body language can cause problems because people are unaware of the messages they are transmitting.

ning a hand backward across his hair; most Westerners would not understand the significance of this gesture.[14] On the other hand, an Egyptian might mistakenly assume that a Westerner who exposes the sole of his or her shoe is offering a grave insult.

Social Behavior and Manners

The rules of polite behavior vary from country to country.

What is polite in one culture may be considered rude in another. In Arab countries it's impolite to take gifts to a man's wife but acceptable to take gifts to his children. In Germany giving a woman a red rose is considered a romantic invitation, inappropriate if you are trying to establish a business relationship with her. In India you might be invited to visit someone's home "anytime." If you're not familiar with the culture, you may be reluctant to make an unexpected visit, and you might therefore wait for a definite invitation. But your failure to take the invitation literally is an insult, a sign that you do not care to develop the friendship.

In any culture, rules of etiquette may be formal or informal. Formal rules are the specifically taught "rights" and "wrongs" of how to behave in common social situations, such as table manners at meals. When formal rules are violated, members of a culture can explain why they feel upset. In contrast, informal social rules are more difficult to identify and are usually learned by watching how people behave and then imitating that behavior. Informal rules govern how males and females are supposed to behave, when it is appropriate to use a person's first name, and so on. When informal rules are violated, members of a culture are likely to feel uncomfortable, although they may not be able to say exactly why.[15]

Legal and Ethical Behavior

People often encounter differing standards of legal and ethical behavior in the course of doing business in other countries.

From culture to culture, what is considered legal and ethical behavior varies widely. In some countries companies are expected to pay government officials extra fees for approving government contracts. These payments aren't illegal or unethical, merely routine. However, the same payments are seen as bribes in the United States, Sweden, and many other countries, where they are both illegal and unethical. In fact, U.S.-based companies are generally not allowed to bribe officials anywhere in the world. (The U.S. Foreign Corrupt Practices Act, which governs company payments to foreign officials, allows a few exceptions, such as small payments that speed but don't actually influence government actions.)[16]

When you conduct business around the world, you may also find that other legal systems differ from what you're accustomed to. In the United Kingdom and the United States, someone is innocent until proven guilty, a principle that is rooted in English common law. In Mexico and Turkey, someone is presumed guilty until proven innocent, a principle that is rooted in the Napoleonic code.[17] These distinctions can be particularly important if your firm must communicate about a legal dispute in another country.

Dealing with Language Barriers

Although three out of four companies polled in a recent survey said that cultural differences frequently complicate their international business relationships, only one in three complained of significant language problems. Nevertheless, U.S. businesspeople may underestimate linguistic barriers because the burden of adjustment generally rests with "the other side." Most multinational business is conducted in English, which is the official language in more than 40 countries and the most commonly studied second language in countries considered to be major trading partners of the United States.[18]

English is the most prevalent language in international business, but it's a mistake to assume that everyone understands it.

Still, language differences can trip you up even if you're a U.S. executive doing business in an English-speaking country. A U.S. paper products manufacturer learned this the hard way while trying to crack the English market for paper napkins by using its usual advertising slogan: "There is no finer paper napkin for the dinner table." Unfortunately for the U.S. company, *napkin* is the British term for *diaper*.[19]

Misunderstandings involving vocabulary, pronunciation, or usage are also likely when U.S. businesspeople deal with people who use English as a second language (and some 650 million people fall into this category). Some of these millions are extremely fluent; others have only an elementary command of English. Although you may miss a few subtleties when dealing with those less fluent in your own language, you'll still be able to communicate. However, don't assume that the other person understands everything you say. Your message can be mangled by slang, idioms, and local accents. One group of English-speaking Japanese employees who transferred to Toyota's U.S. office had to enroll in a special course to learn that "Jeat yet?" means "Did you eat yet?" and that "Cannahepya?" means "Can I help you?"

> Watch for clues to be sure that your message is getting through to people who don't speak your language.

When you deal with people who don't speak your language at all, you have three options: You can learn their language, use an intermediary or a translator, or teach them your language. Becoming fluent in a new language requires a major commitment. At the U.S. State Department, foreign service officers take six months of language training and then continue their studies at their foreign posts. Even the Berlitz method, famous for the speed of its results, requires a month of intensive effort. Language courses can be quite expensive, as well. So unless you're planning to spend several years abroad or to make frequent trips over an extended period, learning another language may take more time and more money than you can afford.

> If you have a long-term business relationship with people of another culture, it is helpful to learn their language.

A more practical approach is to use an intermediary or a translator. An experienced translator can analyze a message, understand its meaning in the cultural context, consider how to convey the meaning in another language, and then use verbal and nonverbal signals to encode or decode the message for someone from another culture. If your company has an overseas subsidiary, you may want to seek help from local employees who are bilingual. You can also hire bilingual professionals such as advertising consultants and lawyers.

The option of teaching other people to speak your language doesn't appear to be very practical at first glance. However, many multinational companies do offer language training programs for employees. Tenneco is a U.S.-based company that instituted an English-language training program—in this case, for its Spanish-speaking employees in a New Jersey plant. The training concentrated on practical English for use on the job, and thanks to the classes, both accidents and grievances declined and productivity improved.[20] In general, the magnitude of the language barrier depends on whether you are writing or speaking. Written communication is generally easier to handle.

Barriers to Written Communication

Because so many international business letters are written in English, U.S. firms don't always worry about translating their correspondence. One survey of 100 companies engaged in international business revealed that between 95 and 99 percent of their business letters to other countries are written in English. Moreover, 59 percent of the companies reported that the letters they receive from people in other countries are usually written in English, although they also receive letters written in Spanish and French.[21]

Regardless of where they're located, some multinational companies ask all their employees to use English when writing to employees in other lands. For example, Nissan employees use English for internal memos to colleagues in other countries, even though the corporation is based in Japan. Similarly, English is the official business language of Philips, the global electronics giant based in the Netherlands.[22]

Most routine business correspondence is written in English, but marketing messages are generally translated into the language of the country where the product is to be sold.

However, many other forms of written communication have to be translated. Advertisements are almost always translated into the language of the culture in which the products are being sold. Warranties, repair and maintenance manuals, and product labels require translation, as well. In addition, many multinational companies translate policy and procedure manuals for use in overseas offices. Reports from foreign branches to the home office may be written in one language and then translated into another. One multinational company, E. I. Du Pont de Nemours & Company, translates roughly 70,000 pages of documents per year.[23]

When documents are translated literally, communication can break down. For example, the advertising slogan "Come alive with Pepsi" was once mistranslated for German audiences as "Come out of the grave" and for Thai audiences as "Bring your ancestors back from the dead."[24] Part of the message is almost inevitably lost during any translation process. So it's critical to consider the meaning of the message and the way it will appear to the receiver when translating from one language into another.

Barriers to Oral Communication

Differences in pronunciation, vocal inflections, and vocabulary can pose problems when you're speaking to people from other cultures.

Oral communication usually presents more problems than written communication. If you've ever studied another language, you know it's easier to write in that language than to conduct a conversation. Even if the other person speaks your language, you may have a hard time understanding the pronunciation if the person isn't proficient. For example, many nonnative English speakers can't distinguish between the English sounds *v* and *w,* so they say "wery" for "very." At the same time, many people from the United States cannot pronounce the French *r* or the German *ch.*

In addition people use their voices in different ways, which can lead listeners to misunderstand their intentions. Russian speakers, for instance, speak in flat, level tones in their native tongue. When they speak English, they maintain this pattern, and non-Russian listeners may assume that the speakers are bored or rude. Middle Easterners tend to speak more loudly than Westerners and may therefore mistakenly be considered more emotional. On the other hand, the Japanese are soft-spoken, a characteristic that implies politeness or humility to Western listeners.

Also confusing are idiomatic expressions (which must be understood as a whole rather than as a sum of the meanings of their elements). If a U.S. executive tells an Egyptian executive that a certain product "doesn't cut the mustard," chances are communication will fail. The words don't make sense because the definition of each word does not add up to the meaning of the expression (that a certain product "isn't satisfactory"). Even when the words do make sense, their meanings may differ according to the situation. For example, suppose you are dining with a German woman who speaks English quite well. You inquire, "More bread?" She says, "Thank you," so you pass the bread. She looks confused; then she takes the breadbasket and sets it down without taking any. In German, *thank you* (*danke*) can also be used as a polite refusal. If the woman had wanted more bread, she would have used the word *please* (*bitte* in German).

When speaking in English to people who speak English as a second language, you may find these guidelines helpful:

- *Try to eliminate noise.* Pronounce words clearly, stop at distinct punctuation points, and make one point at a time.
- *Look for feedback.* Be alert to signs of confusion in your listener. Realize that nods and smiles don't necessarily mean understanding.
- *Rephrase your sentence when necessary.* If someone doesn't seem to understand you, choose simpler words; don't just repeat the sentence in a louder voice.
- *Don't talk down to the other person.* Try not to overenunciate, and don't "blame" the

listener for not understanding. Use phrases such as "Am I going too fast?" rather than "Is this too difficult for you?"

- *Use objective, accurate language.* Avoid throwing around adjectives such as *fabulous,* which people from other cultures might consider unreal and overly dramatic.
- *Let other people finish what they have to say.* If you interrupt, you may miss something important. You'll also show a lack of respect.

Dealing with Ethnocentric Reactions

Although language and cultural differences are significant barriers to communication, these problems can be overcome by maintaining an open mind. Unfortunately, many of us lapse into **ethnocentricism,** the tendency to judge all other groups according to our own group's standards, behaviors, and customs. When we make such comparisons, we too often decide that our group is superior.[25]

By reacting ethnocentrically, you ignore the distinctions between your own culture and another person's culture. You assume that others will act the same way you do, that they will operate from the same assumptions, and that they will use language and symbols the same way you do. If they do not, you may mistakenly believe that they are in error, that their way is invalid, or that it's inferior to your own. An ethnocentric reaction makes you lose sight of the possibility that your words and actions will be misunderstood. It also makes you more likely to misinterpret or belittle the behavior of others.

Ethnocentric people are often prone to **stereotyping,** attempting to predict individuals' behavior or character on the basis of their membership in a particular group or class. When someone first starts to investigate the culture of another group, he or she may stereotype characteristics as a way of understanding the common tendencies of that group's members, but the next step is to move beyond the stereotypes to relationships with real people. Unfortunately, when ethnocentric people stereotype an entire group of people, they do so on the basis of limited, general, or inaccurate evidence, and they frequently develop biased attitudes toward the group.[26] They fail to communicate with individuals as they really are. Instead of talking with Abdul Karhum, unique human being, ethnocentric people think only about talking to an Arab. Although they've never met an Arab, they may already believe that all Arabs are, say, hagglers. Abdul Karhum's personal qualities become insignificant in the face of such preconceptions. Everything he says and does will be forced to fit the preconceived image, even if it's wrong.

Often both parties in an intercultural exchange are guilty of ethnocentrism, stereotyping, and prejudice. Little wonder, then, that misunderstandings arise. Fortunately, a healthy dose of open-mindedness can prevent a lot of problems.

T IPS FOR COMMUNICATING WITH PEOPLE FROM OTHER CULTURES

You may never completely overcome linguistic and cultural barriers or ethnocentric tendencies, but you can communicate more effectively with people from other cultures if you work at it. Once you've acknowledged that cultural differences exist, the next step is to learn as much as possible about the cultures in which you plan to do business. You can also develop general skills for dealing with cultural diversity in your own and in other countries. If you'll be negotiating across cultures, it's important to learn how to conduct yourself and what to expect. Finally, you'll want to consider how to handle both written and oral communication with people from other cultures.

After serving as chairman of the Joint Chiefs of Staff and winning popular acclaim during the Persian Gulf War, General Colin Powell is changing roles—retiring from 35 years in the U.S. Army to lecture and write his memoirs. Born in Harlem and raised in the South Bronx, Powell has always made a special effort to serve as a role model for young African Americans. Now lecturing and writing his memoirs, he advises students that racism is the other person's problem and to reach down inside themselves: Rely on yourself, says Powell, just like I did.

Ethnocentrism is the tendency to judge all other groups according to your own group's standards, behaviors, and customs and to see other groups as inferior by comparison.

Stereotyping is the attempt to categorize individuals by trying to predict their behavior or character on the basis of their membership in a particular group.

Learning About a Culture

Learning as much as possible about another culture will enhance your ability to communicate with its members.

When you're preparing to do business with people from a particular culture, you'll find that you can communicate more effectively if you study that culture in advance. Apple has learned that before advertising a new product in another culture, company researchers must thoroughly investigate that culture to see what its people want and need. That way, Apple marketers can shape the advertising message to the language and customs of the particular culture.

If you're planning to live in another country or to do business there repeatedly, you might want to learn the language. The same holds true if you'll be working closely with a subculture that has its own language, such as Vietnamese Americans. Even if you're doing business in your own language, you show respect by making the effort to learn the subculture's language. In addition, you'll learn something about the culture and the customs of its people. If you don't have the time or the opportunity to learn a new language, at least learn a few words.

Read books and articles about the culture and talk to people who have done business with that culture's members. Concentrate on learning something about the culture's history, religion, politics, values, and customs. Find out about a country's sub-

CHECKLIST FOR DOING BUSINESS ABROAD

A. Social Customs

1. How do people react to strangers? Are they friendly? Hostile?
2. How do people greet each other?
3. What are the appropriate manners when you enter and leave a room? Bowing? Nodding? Shaking hands?
4. How are names used for introduction?
5. What are the attitudes toward touching people?
6. How do you express appreciation for an invitation to lunch or dinner?
7. Does custom dictate how, when, or where people are expected to sit in social or business situations?
8. Are any phrases, facial expressions, or hand gestures considered rude?
9. How close do people stand when talking?
10. How do you attract the attention of a waiter in a restaurant? Do you tip the waiter?
11. When is it rude to refuse an invitation? How do you refuse politely?
12. What are the acceptable eye contact patterns?
13. What gestures indicate agreement? Disagreement? Respect?
14. What topics may be discussed in a social setting? In a business setting? What topics are unacceptable?

B. Concepts of Time

1. How is time expressed?
2. What are the generally accepted working hours?
3. How do people view business appointments? View time in social situations?

C. Clothing and Food

1. What occasions require special clothing? What colors are associated with mourning? Love? Joy?
2. Is some clothing taboo for one sex? What is appropriate business attire for men and women?
3. What are the attitudes toward human body odors?
4. When do people eat? How do they use their hands/utensils?
5. What places, food, and drink are appropriate for business entertainment? Where is the seat of honor?

D. Political Patterns

1. How stable is the political situation? How does this affect business inside and outside the country?
2. How is political power manifested? Military power? Economic strength?
3. What are the traditional institutions of government?
4. What channels are used for expressing political opinions? Official government positions? Unofficial government positions?
5. What information media are important? Who controls them?

cultures, especially its business subculture, and any special rules or protocol. Seasoned business travelers can give you tips on intercultural communication. For example,

- In Spain let a handshake last five to seven strokes; pulling away too soon may be interpreted as rejection. In France, however, the preferred handshake is a single stroke.
- Don't give a gift of liquor in Arab countries.
- In Pakistan don't be surprised when businesspeople excuse themselves in the middle of a meeting to conduct prayers. Muslims pray five times a day.
- Allow plenty of time to get to know the people you're dealing with in Africa; they're suspicious of people in a hurry.
- You'll insult your hosts if you turn down food, drink, or hospitality of any kind in Arab countries. But don't accept too quickly, either. A polite refusal (such as "I don't want to put you to any trouble") is expected before you finally accept.
- Stress your company's longevity when dealing with German, Dutch, and Swiss firms.

These are just a few examples of the variations in customs that make intercultural business so interesting. This chapter's Checklist for Doing Business Abroad can help you start your investigation of another culture.

6. In social or business situations, is it appropriate to talk politics?

E. Workforce Diversity
 1. Is the society homogeneous?
 2. What minority groups are represented?
 3. What languages are spoken?
 4. How diverse is the workforce?
 5. What are the current immigration patterns? How is workforce composition affected?

F. Religion and Folk Beliefs
 1. To which religious groups do people belong? Is one predominant?
 2. How do religious beliefs influence daily activities?
 3. Which places are sacred? Which objects? Events?
 4. Is there a tolerance for minority religions?
 5. How do religious holidays affect business and government activities?
 6. Does religion affect attitudes toward smoking? Drinking? Gambling?
 7. Does religion require or prohibit eating specific foods? At specific times?
 8. Which objects or actions portend good luck? Bad luck?

G. Economic and Business Institutions
 1. What are the primary resources and products?
 2. What vocational and technological training is offered?

3. What are the attitudes toward education?
 a. Do most businesspersons have a college degree?
 b. Are women educated as well as men?
4. Are businesses generally of one type?
 a. Are they large public corporations?
 b. Are they owned or controlled by the government?
 c. Are they family businesses?
5. Is it appropriate to do business by telephone?
6. Do managers make business decisions unilaterally, or do they involve employees?
7. Do any customs involve exchanging business cards?
8. How are status and seniority shown in an organization? In a business meeting?
9. Are businesspeople expected to socialize before conducting business?

H. Ethics, Values, and Laws
 1. Is money or a gift expected for arranging a business transaction? What are the legal, ethical, and business consequences of giving? Of not giving?
 2. What ethics and laws affect business transactions?
 3. Which is more important, competitiveness or cooperation?
 4. What are the attitudes toward work? Toward money?
 5. Is politeness more important than factual honesty?
 6. How is a *friend* defined? What are a friend's duties?
 7. What virtues are admired?

*B*EHIND THE SCENES AT PARKER PEN
Do as the Natives Do, But Should You Eat the Roast Gorilla Hand?

If offered a roast gorilla hand, you should eat it—so says Roger E. Axtel, vice president of The Parker Pen Company. In his 18 years of living and traveling in the 154 countries where Parker sells pens, Axtel learned that communicating with foreign nationals demands more than merely learning their language. The gorilla hand (served rising from mashed yams) was prepared for a meal in honor of a U.S. family-planning expert who was visiting a newly emerged African nation. The guest of honor was expected to eat it, so he did. Learning the behavior expected of you as you conduct business internationally can be daunting if not intimidating. Axtel recommends the following basic rules to help you get off to a good start.

1. *What's in a name?* The first transaction between even ordinary citizens—and the first chance to make an impression for better or worse—is an exchange of names. In the United States, there is little to get wrong. Not so elsewhere. In the Eastern Hemisphere, where name frequently denotes social rank or family status, a mistake can be an outright insult, and so can using someone's given name without permission. One overseas deputy director for an international telecommunications corporation always asks, "What would you like me to call you?" He advises that it's "better to ask several times than to get it wrong." Even then, "I err on the side of formality." Another frequent traveler insists his company provide him with a list of key people he will meet—country by country, surnames underlined—to be memorized on the flight over.

2. *Eat, drink, and be wary.* Away from home, eating is a language all its own. No words can match it for saying "glad to meet you . . . glad to be doing business with you . . . glad to have you here." Mealtime is no time for a thanks-but-no-thanks response. Accepting what is on your plate is tantamount to accepting host, country, and company. So no matter how tough things may be to swallow, swallow. Often what's offered constitutes your host country's proudest culi-

Developing Intercultural Communication Skills

Learning all you can about a particular culture is a good way to figure out how to send and receive intercultural messages more effectively. However, don't expect ever to understand another culture completely. No matter how much you study German culture, for example, you'll never be a German or share the experience of having grown up in Germany. Also, don't fall into the overgeneralization trap; don't look at people as stereotypical "Italians" or "African Americans" and then never move beyond that view. The trick is to learn useful general information and, at the same time, be aware of and open to variations and individual differences.

Learning general intercultural communication skills will help you adapt in any culture, which is important if you interact with people from a variety of cultures or subcultures.

This is especially important if you interact with people from a variety of cultures or subcultures. You may not have the time or interest to learn a lot about every culture, but you can communicate more effectively if you develop general skills that will help you adapt to any culture:[27]

- *Take responsibility for communication.* Don't assume it's the other person's job to communicate with you.
- *Withhold judgment.* Learn to listen to the whole story and accept differences in others without judging them.
- *Show respect.* Learn how respect is communicated—through gestures, eye contact, and so on—in various cultures.

nary achievements. Squeamishness comes not so much from the thing itself as from your unfamiliarity with it. After all, an oyster has remarkably the same look and consistency as a sheep's eye (a delicacy in Saudi Arabia). Most business travelers say there's no alternative to taking at least a few bites. It helps to slice unfamiliar food very thin so that you minimize the texture and the reminder of where it came from. Another useful dodge is not knowing what you're eating. What's for dinner? Don't ask.

3. *Clothes can make you or break you.* Wherever you are, try not to look out of place. Wear something you look natural in, that you know how to wear, and that fits in with your surroundings. For example, a woman dressed in a tailored suit, even with high heels and flowery blouse, looks startlingly masculine in a country full of diaphanous saris. More appropriate attire might be a silky, loose-fitting dress in a bright color. With few exceptions, the general rule everywhere, whether for business, eating out, or even visiting people at home, is that you should be very conservative.

4. *English spoken here—you hope.* Many people outside the United States speak English. Even where people from the United States aren't understood, their language often is. Of course, some languages are incom-prehensible when pronounced by outsiders, but no matter how you twist most native tongues, some meaning gets through—or at least you get an A for effort. Memorizing a toast or greeting nearly always serves to break the ice, if not the communication barrier.

Apply Your Knowledge

1. Select a non-English-speaking nation that trades with the United States. With the help of either a foreign-language instructor or a bilingual dictionary, type or print the accepted translation for the following business terms: (1) contract, (2) sale, (3) delivery date, (4) dupli-cate copies, and (5) negligence. Separately, show three friends the list of translated terms only. Ask each to pro-nounce the terms. In your notebook, spell phonetically the pronunciations you hear. When finished, compare the pronunciations. How different are they? Which terms produced the greatest variety?

2. Should colleges and universities that offer a business major require a separate degree or certification program for international business? What courses from the cur-riculum at your school would you require for such a degree/certificate? What new courses can you suggest?

- *Empathize.* Imagine the other person's feelings and point of view. Consider what he or she is trying to communicate and why.
- *Tolerate ambiguity.* Learn to control your frustration when placed in an unfamiliar or confusing situation.
- *Look beyond the superficial.* Don't be distracted by such things as dress, appearance, or environmental discomforts.
- *Be patient and persistent.* If you want to communicate with someone from another culture, don't give up easily.
- *Recognize your own cultural biases.* Learn to identify when your assumptions are different from the other person's.
- *Be flexible.* Be prepared to change your habits and attitudes when communicating with someone from another culture.
- *Emphasize common ground.* Look for similarities to work from.
- *Send clear messages.* Make both your verbal and nonverbal signals clear and consistent.
- *Increase your cultural sensitivity.* Learn about variations in customs and practices so that you'll be more aware of potential areas for miscommunication.
- *Deal with the individual.* Communicate with each person as an individual, not as a stereotypical representative of another group.
- *Learn when to be direct.* Investigate each culture so that you know when to send your message in a straightforward manner and when to be indirect.

Ford Motor Company chair-man Alex Trotman says his experience leading a multina-tional corporation has taught him that intercultural com-munication helps all parties by bringing forward the best ideas, regardless of their ori-gin. Whether you're learning about a specific culture or de-veloping general skills, advises Trotman, remember to keep an open mind.

CHECKLIST FOR COMMUNICATING WITH A CULTURALLY DIVERSE WORKFORCE

A. Accepting Cultural Differences
1. Adjust communication to employees' educational level.
2. Encourage employees to openly discuss their culture's customs so that differences won't seem strange.
3. Create a forum for all employees to become familiar with the cultures represented in the company.
4. Provide training to help employees recognize and overcome ethnocentric reactions and stereotyping.
5. Provide books, articles, and videotapes on various cultures.
6. Help stamp out negative or stereotyped labels by noticing how people identify their own groups.

B. Handling Oral and Written Communications
1. Define and explain key terms that people will need to know on the job.
2. Repeat and recap information frequently to emphasize important points.
3. Use familiar words wherever possible.
4. Don't cover too much information at one time.
5. Be specific and explicit, using descriptive words, exact measurements, and examples wherever possible.
6. Give reasons for following a certain procedure, and explain what happens if the procedure is not followed.
7. Use written summaries and visual aids (when appropriate) to clarify your points.
   - a. Give employees written information they can take to review later.
   - b. Use pictures that show actions (especially when explaining safety procedures).
   - c. Use international symbols (such as ∅), which are understood cross-culturally.
   - d. Augment written material with videos to make the material come alive.

8. If possible, demonstrate the wrong way and then the right way when explaining a tool or a task.
9. Reduce barriers caused by language differences.
   - a. Offer managers training in the language of the employees they supervise.
   - b. Train employees in the language used by most people in the company (and by most customers).
   - c. Ask bilingual employees to translate when needed, rotating the assignment to avoid resentment.
   - d. Recruit bilingual employees and managers, or provide trained translators to offer more flexibility with linguistic differences.
   - e. Print health and safety instructions in two or more languages so that all employees understand.

C. Assessing How Well You've Been Understood
1. Be alert to facial expressions and other nonverbal signs that indicate confusion or embarrassment.
2. Encourage employees to ask questions in private and in writing.
3. Observe how employees use the information you've provided to do their jobs, and review any points that may have been misunderstood.
4. Research the nonverbal reactions of other cultures so that you're prepared to spot the more subtle signs of misunderstanding.

D. Offering Feedback to Improve Communication
1. Focus on the positive by explaining what *should* be done rather than on the negative by discussing what *shouldn't* be done.
2. Offer feedback in terms of behaviors and conditions, not judgments about the person.
3. Be supportive when giving feedback, and reassure people that their skills and contributions are important.

These skills will help you communicate with anybody, regardless of culture. For more ideas on how to improve communication in the workplace, see this chapter's Checklist for Communicating with a Culturally Diverse Workforce.

Negotiating Across Cultures

Whether you're trying to make a sale, buy a business, or rent an office, negotiating with people from other cultures can test your communication skills. First, you may find that your approach to negotiation differs from the approach of the people you're negotiating with. For example, negotiators from the United States tend to take a relatively impersonal view of negotiations. They see their goals in economic terms and usually presume trust of the other party, at least at the outset. In contrast, Chinese and Japanese negotiators prefer a more sociable negotiating atmosphere. They try to forge personal ties as the basis for building trust throughout the negotiating process. In their view, any immediate economic gains are less important than establishing and maintaining a long-term relationship. Unlike U.S., Chinese, and Japanese negotiators, French negotiators are likely to be somewhat less personal. They may favor an atmosphere of formal hospitality and start by distrusting the other party.[28]

Second, cultures differ in their tolerance for open disagreement. Although U.S. negotiators typically enjoy confrontational, debate-oriented negotiation, Japanese negotiators shun such tactics. To avoid the unpleasant feelings that might result from open conflict, Japanese companies use a go-between or a third person to assist in the negotiation. Chinese negotiators also try to prevent public conflict. They make concessions slowly and stay away from proposal-counterproposal methods. If you try to get a Chinese negotiating team to back down from a position it has taken, you will cause its members to lose face—and you will very likely lose the deal.

In addition, negotiators from other cultures may use different problem-solving techniques, protocol, schedules, and decision-making methods. If you learn about your counterparts' culture before you start to negotiate, you'll be better equipped to understand their viewpoints. Moreover, showing flexibility, courtesy, patience, and a friendly attitude will go a long way toward finding a solution that works for both sides.

People from other cultures often have different approaches to negotiation and may vary in their tolerance for open disagreement.

Handling Written Communication

Unless you are personally fluent in the language of your intended audience, you will ordinarily write in your own language and, if needed, have your letters or other written materials translated by a professional translator. Be especially concerned with clarity:

- Use short, precise words that say exactly what you mean.
- Rely on specific terms and concrete examples to explain your points.
- Stay away from slang, idioms, jargon, and buzzwords. Abbreviations, acronyms (such as CAD/CAM), and unfamiliar product names may also lead to confusion.
- Construct sentences that are shorter and simpler than those you might use when writing to someone fluent in your own language.
- Use short paragraphs. Each paragraph should stick to one topic and be no more than eight to ten lines long.
- Help readers follow your train of thought by using transitional phrases. Precede related points with expressions like *in addition* and *first, second, third.*

Your word choice should also reflect the relationship between you and your audience. Many non-U.S. cultures use a more elaborate style, so your audience will expect more formal language in your letter. Consider a letter written by a supplier in Germany to a nearby retailer (see Figure 3.1). This letter might sound stilted to a U.S. reader, but it is typical of business letters in many other countries. In Germany, business letters usually open with a reference to the business relationship and close with a compliment to the recipient. Of course, be careful not to carry formality to extremes, or you'll sound unnatural.

International business letters generally have a formal tone and a relatively elaborate style.

Letter writers in other countries also use various techniques to organize their thoughts. If you are aware of some of these practices, you'll be able to concentrate on the message without passing judgment on the writers. Letters from Japanese businesspeople, for example, are slow to come to the point. They typically begin with a re-

Figure 3.1
German Business Letter, with Translation
The addressee's title, *Geschäftsführer*, literally means "business leader." A common English translation would be "managing director." Also note that in German letters, the sender's title is not included under the typed name on the closing block.

Furtwangen Handcrafts
Kussenhofstrasse 150
Furtwangen, Germany

Herrn
Karl Wieland
Geschäftsführer
Schwarzwald-Geschenke
Friedrichstraße 98

70174 Stuttgart
GERMANY

15. Mai 1996

Sehr geehrter Herr Wieland,

da die Touristensaison bald beginnt, möchten wir die Gelegenheit ergreifen, Ihnen unsere neue Reihe handgeschnitzter Kuckucksuhren vorzustellen. Im letzten Jahr waren Sie so freundlich, zwei Dutzend unserer Uhren zu kaufen. In Anerkennung unserer guten Geschäftsbeziehungen bieten wir Ihnen nunmehr die Möglichkeit, die neuen Modelle auszuwählen, bevor wir diese Reihe anderen Geschäften zum Kauf anbieten.

Wie Sie wissen, verwenden unsere Kunsthandwerker nur das beste Holz. Nach altbewährten Mustern, die von Generation zu Generation weitergereicht werden, schnitzen sie sorgfältig jedes Detail von Hand. Unsere Uhrwerke sind von hervorragender Qualität, und wir testen jede Uhr, bevor sie bemalt und versandt wird. Auf alle Furtwangener Kunsthandwerk-Uhren geben wir eine Garantie von 5 Jahren.

Beiliegend erhalten Sie eine Ausgabe unserer neuesten Broschüre und ein Bestellformular. Um unserer Wertschätzung Ausdruck zu verleihen, übernehmen wir die Versandkosten, wenn Sie vor dem 15. Juni bestellen.

Wir wünschen Ihnen weiterhin viel Erfolg in Ihrer neuen Stuttgarter Niederlassung. Wir sind davon überzeugt, daß Sie mit Ihrer größeren Ausstellungsfläche und erweitertem Angebot Ihre Stammkunden zufriedenstellen werden und viele neue Besucher gewinnen werden.

Mit freundlichen Grüßen

Frederick Semper

Frederick Semper

mark about the season or weather. This is followed by an inquiry about your health or congratulations on your success. A note of thanks for your patronage might come next. After these preliminaries, the main idea is introduced.

Handling Oral Communication

Face-to-face communication lets you establish a personal relationship with people from other cultures and gives you the benefit of immediate feedback.

Some transactions simply cannot be handled without face-to-face contact. In many countries, business relationships are based on personal relationships, and until you establish a rapport, nothing happens. In addition, personal contact gives you the benefit of immediate feedback so that you can clarify your own message as well as the other person's. As a consequence, executives in charge of international operations often have a hectic travel schedule. When Apple's CEO was the head of the international division, he spent nearly 70 percent of his time meeting with managers and high-level contacts in other countries.

```
Mister
Karl Wieland
Business Leader
Black Forest Gifts
Friedrichstrasse 98

70174 Stuttgart
GERMANY


                                              May 15, 1996

Very honorable Mister Wieland,

As the tourist season will begin soon, we would like to
seize the opportunity to introduce our new line of hand-
carved cuckoo clocks to you.  Last year you were so friendly
as to buy two dozen of our clocks.  In recognition of our
good business relationship, we now offer you the opportunity
to select the new models before we offer this line to other
businesses for purchase.

As you know, our artisans only use the best wood.  According
to time-honored patterns which are passed on from generation
to generation, they carefully carve every detail by hand.
Our clockworks are of superior quality, and we test every
clock before it is painted and shipped.  We give you a
guarantee of five years on all Furtwangen Handcrafts clocks.

Enclosed you receive a copy of our newest brochure and an
order form.  To express our appreciation, we take over the
shipping costs if you order before June 15.

We continue to wish you a lot of success in your new
Stuttgart location.  We are convinced that you will satisfy
your regular clientele with your larger exhibition area and
expanded stock and will gain many new visitors.


With friendly greetings



Frederick Semper
Sales Leader
```

When using oral communication, be alert to the possibilities for misunderstanding. Recognize that you may inadvertently be sending conflicting signals or misreading the other person's cues. To help overcome language and cultural barriers, follow these suggestions:

- Try to be aware of unintentional meanings that may be read into your message. Clarify your true intent with repetition and examples.
- Listen carefully and patiently. If you do not understand a comment, ask the person to repeat it.
- Recognize that gestures and expressions mean different things in different cultures. If the other person's body language seems at odds with the message, take time to clarify the meaning.
- Adapt your conversation style to the other person's. If the other person appears to be direct and straightforward, follow suit. If not, adjust your style to match.

- At the end of a conversation, be sure that you and the other person agree on what has been said and decided. Clarify what will happen next.
- If appropriate, follow up by writing a letter or memo summarizing the conversation and thanking the person for meeting with you.

In short, take advantage of the other person's presence to make sure that your message is getting across and that you understand his or her message too.

On the Job

SOLVING A COMMUNICATION DILEMMA AT APPLE COMPUTER

To officials at Apple Computer, Japan looked like a communicator's dream: 99.7 percent literacy and a compact geographical area that supports 4 national newspapers, 250 local papers, 20,000 magazines, and 5 national broadcasting networks. Thanks to this comprehensive media network, advertisers in Japan can efficiently blanket the entire country with a single message—a sharp contrast to the situation in most countries, where few national media exist and many separate messages must be sent in a variety of media to cover an entire region or country. But despite the winning combination of effective media, literate customers, and few competitors, Apple failed to capture any significant market share during its first ten years in Japan.

For one thing, Apple didn't understand Japanese customers' needs and expectations. In this market, top quality and superior service are important requirements. Unfortunately, Apple's early models were of poor quality. Worse, the original models were geared to English-language users. On top of these errors, the company put a high price on its products, which made lower-priced products seem like bargains.

In addition, Apple didn't adapt its communications to the Japanese market. The company simply translated its U.S. advertising into Japanese. However, Apple's hard-sell advertising messages were at odds with the low-key image ads that Japanese customers were accustomed to seeing. "In the United States, most companies stick to product advertising: 'Buy my product, it's a great solution and it's cheap,'" says Ian Diery, president of Apple Pacific. "In Japan, companies focus on name-awareness advertising. You rarely advertise price. You build an image as a very reliable company."

After nearly ten years of slow sales, Apple changed its approach. The company improved quality and introduced computers with Japanese-language capabilities. Apple also concentrated on communicating its commitment to meeting customer needs and its increased sensitivity to the local business climate. Now Apple's CEO makes a point of traveling to Japan four or five times a year. These visits are a tangible demonstration of the market's importance. In addition, the company has taken steps to have its stock listed on the Tokyo Stock Exchange, which is like a "stamp of approval in Japan

for business," says Diery. The computer maker is establishing a high profile by sponsoring Japanese events such as Janet Jackson concerts and the Japanese Ladies Professional Golf Association tournament (linking its name with one of the country's most popular sports). Finally, to help build a trendy image for itself, Apple worked with Tokyo retailers to launch an "Apple Collection" of shirts, jackets, mugs, and other items.

By 1992 Apple had increased its share of Japan's $7 billion computer market to 6 percent. Of course the company is actively pursuing even tougher goals. To meet them, Ian Diery and his team will be carefully crafting international communications in the Japanese market.

Your Mission: You've been named special assistant to Ian Diery. He wants to continue building sales in Japan, and he has asked you to study the market. You want to stay in touch with the needs of your customers, and you want to consider the interests of the distributors who handle your products. Although your knowledge of Japan and the Japanese language may be limited, use your skill in intercultural communication to determine the best response to each of the following situations. Be prepared to explain why your choice is best:

1. Apple Japan has started a training program in which newly hired Japanese managers spend a month at corporate headquarters in California to learn about the parent company. You are working with a trainee who learned English in high school and college, but you aren't sure whether he understands everything you say. Each time you discuss something with him, the trainee smiles shyly and nods. How can you be sure your message is getting through?

   a. Speak slowly and distinctly, and ask whether the trainee understands specific phrases or instructions. Also, pause frequently and repeat or write down anything he doesn't understand.

   b. You need feedback, so ask the trainee to repeat word for word what you've said. That way, you'll know that he understands.

   c. To be sure the trainee receives your message, write everything down. He can refer to the written explanation later to check his comprehension.

d. You will be better able to convey your message if you talk loudly and use larger hand gestures to clarify your meaning and to keep the listener's interest.

2. To improve sales of Macintosh computers in Japan, managers from your new Japanese advertising agency have traveled to California to meet with the Macintosh product managers. One of the agency managers transferred to Japan from the United States, so he's fluent in English, but the others are not. Which of the following approaches is the most effective way to explain the product's background so that the Japanese agency can develop new advertising?

a. Use videotape to overcome the language barrier. Prepare a tape showing the product when it was first launched in Japan, and include clips from every commercial previously used. Use narration or subtitles in both Japanese and English.

b. Use videotape as suggested in (a), but also include a report, in Japanese and in English, showing the product's sales history, customer information, and a profile of the Japanese personal computer market.

c. Videotape can't adequately convey the tradition and quality of the Macintosh. Write a detailed report (translated into Japanese) that describes the product's global history.

d. To avoid possible misunderstanding, stick to oral rather than written communication. Make a speech in English that covers sales history and customer information, and show slides of Macintosh commercials used in the past. At the end of the speech, offer to answer any questions that the ad agency people have.

3. To learn more about the Japanese market, you plan to travel to Tokyo, Osaka, and Yokohama. You'd like to see how Apple products are sold in the corporate market, and you'd also like to gain a better understanding of the distribution system. What is the best way to arrange to visit your distributors?

a. Before you go, write a brief but formal letter in English to the head of each distributor. Introduce yourself as Ian Diery's assistant, and request permission to meet with several salespeople who sell to the corporate market. Stress your interest in learning more about their needs as distributors, and ask when it would be convenient for you to visit.

b. Your boss knows many of the distributors in Japan, so you should carry a letter of introduction from him (translated into Japanese), which you can show to each distributor. This personal introduction will open doors for you, and it will explain your visit and your objective once you get to Japan.

c. Instead of taking the time to write and then waiting for an answer, it would be quicker to telephone the heads of each distributor. Through an interpreter, you can stress that you are interested in their views of the market for Apple products and in learning how the Japanese distribution system operates. Let them know that you

are eager to see them as soon as possible, and press for a definite date on which you can visit their offices.

d. To get the background you need, start by making unannounced visits to several customers. Look at how these customers use their Macintoshes. Then visit your distributors' executive offices to meet with top managers.

4. Since you will be speaking English during your visit to Japan, which of the following is the best way to overcome communication barriers?

a. Repeat each sentence two or three times, until you're sure that people catch your meaning.

b. Learn how to say "Do you understand me?" in Japanese so that you can find out whether your meaning has been received.

c. Write down your words so that people can read as well as listen to what you are trying to say.

d. Use simpler words if people don't seem to understand you.

5. Diery has received a letter from the head of Mitsukoshi, a large Japanese department store chain. The retailer plans to hold a computer expo and wants Apple Pacific to display some Macintosh computers that are under development but not yet for sale. Diery says he won't show prototypes because they don't always work as they should, and if people have problems, they may get the impression that all Macintosh products are of poor quality. Diery asks you to write to Mitsukoshi and offer to demonstrate only the current Macintosh products. Which of the following introductory paragraphs is best?

a. We are in receipt of your correspondence of July 7, in which you raised the possibility of having Apple demonstrate Macintosh products in the upcoming Mitsukoshi computer expo. We at Apple concur wholeheartedly with your plan to show off the latest computer technology. Much to our regret, however, we are unable to comply with your request to display prototypes.

b. Thanks for dropping us a note about the computer expo you plan to hold. You're right, people would probably like playing with new computer technology. You can count on us to give you a hand. But please understand that our lips are sealed about Macintosh products under development.

c. Thank you for your interest in displaying Apple products at your computer expo. We agree that the people who attend will enjoy seeing the latest in computer technology, and we will gladly help you by demonstrating our current Macintosh computers.

d. Thanks for thinking of us. We sure would like to help you, but our hands are tied. You know what they say about counting your chickens before they hatch. We can't show off any Mac before its time. That just wouldn't be good business sense.[29]

Questions for Discussion

1. Your office in Turkey needs the supplies that have been sitting in Turkish customs for a month. Should you bribe a customs official to speed up delivery? Explain.
2. Your offices in Canada and Venezuela have differing concepts of time. How can you minimize potential problems?
3. In intercultural communication, why is written communication less of a problem than oral communication?
4. Your company has relocated to a U.S. city where a Vietnamese subculture is strongly established. How can you improve communication between your managers and the Vietnamese Americans you are now hiring?
5. What are some of your own stereotypes and prejudices? For example, what are your beliefs about Germans? Japanese? Saudi Arabians? Cubans? Ethiopians? Mexicans? Tahitians?
6. What are some of the issues to consider when deciding whether to accept a job overseas?

Exercises

1. Investigate the foreign-language department at your school. In less than a page, describe the languages offered and the cultural aspects covered.
2. In teams, develop a brief handbook to help students from other countries know what to expect when they arrive to study at your school.
3. How do both intentional and unintentional forms of nonverbal communication convey meaning? Working with another student, give an example of each from your own culture. In a short paragraph for each, explain how the communication might be misunderstood (or overlooked) by someone from another culture.
4. Locate someone, preferably a businessperson, who has spent some time in another country, and interview him or her about the experience. What preparation did the person have before going to the country? In what ways was the preparation adequate? Inadequate? In hindsight, how might he or she have prepared differently? Ask for anecdotes about particular communication problems or mistakes. Briefly summarize your findings.
5. Team up with two other students and list ten examples of slang (in your own language) that would probably be misinterpreted or misunderstood during a business conversation with someone from another culture. Next to each example, suggest other words you might use to convey the same message. Do the alternatives mean *exactly* the same thing as the original slang or idiom? Summarize your findings in a brief report to the class.
6. Suppose you transferred to a college in another country. How would you learn appropriate classroom behavior? Make a list of what you would need to know.

COMMUNICATING THROUGH TECHNOLOGY

C h a p t e r

After studying this chapter, you will be able to

Describe the technological tools now available for creating printed documents

Discuss the internal and external databases used in business research

Analyze the benefits and limitations of spell checkers and grammar checkers

Explain the role of electronic mail in today's business organizations

Describe the technologies available for group communication

Assess the ways technology is changing business communication

On the Job
FACING A COMMUNICATION DILEMMA
AT METROPOLITAN LIFE INSURANCE
Taming the Paper Tiger

Picture the insurance business for a minute. What do you see? William D. Livesey sees paper, piles and piles of paper: policies, responses to claims, statements of benefits, descriptive booklets. As Metropolitan Life Insurance Company's vice president of group insurance, national accounts, Livesey is ultimately responsible for producing hundreds of thousands of words per year. He supervises about 75 employees who provide administrative services to support Metropolitan Life's group insurance accounts. His department handles group life, health, and disability coverage for major corporations like General Electric, AT&T, Rockwell International, and Mobil Oil.

Every time one of these major customers revamps its insurance benefits, Metropolitan Life faces many tasks, including revising the descriptive booklets used by each corporate customer to explain its benefits package to its employees. That may not sound like much, but try producing or revising 125 booklets a month. Throw in all the other documents the insurance business ordinarily generates, and it all adds up to a pretty big job.

If you were William Livesey, how would you manage this problem of paper? What machines might help you manage this paperwork? What innovations have been made in office technology that could reduce the sea of paper faced by businesses like Metropolitan Life?[1]

TECHNOLOGY AND THE NEW WORLD OF BUSINESS COMMUNICATION

Metropolitan Life Insurance Company

As Metropolitan Life and other companies try to compete in the global economy, they are always looking for better ways to communicate. In addition to the machines needed by Metropolitan Life to manage paperwork, technology now provides businesses with faster, more efficient equipment for every aspect of communication. You'll probably use most or all of the technologies discussed in this chapter, as well as some innovations that we can only dream about right now. The better you understand the technological issues involved, the more effective you'll be as a communicator.

If a typewriter and a postage stamp were your only communication tools, you wouldn't have to spend much time thinking about how to create documents or send messages. When you have word processors, laser printers, fax machines, satellite video links, computer mail, voice recognition systems, and dozens of other options, the choices you make as a communicator are more complicated. In today's business office, you not only have to think about what you're going to say and how you're going to say it, you also have to decide which technological tools you'll use to do so. No hard rules dictate which tool to use in each case (partly because the technology keeps changing), but here are some general guidelines:

Technology gives business communicators more options, but it also requires more decisions and more skills.

General guidelines for choosing communication technology include considering
■ Audience expectations
■ Time and cost
■ Message type
■ Presentation needs

■ *Audience expectations.* What would you think if your college tried to deliver your diploma by fax? It would probably seem a little strange. You expect the college to use a certain set of technologies (such as mail delivery or a phone-in system). Business audiences have similar expectations for various kinds of messages. Knowing what people expect is part of getting to know your audience.

■ *Time and cost.* Time is often the biggest factor in your technology choice. You'd probably choose the phone to send an urgent message, for instance. Many of the technologies discussed in this chapter were designed specifically to help people communicate faster, but cost can be an issue as well, both how much you have to spend and how much is appropriate for the situation. Spending $500 to create a presentation for customers might be appropriate; however, spending that much to tell your colleagues when you'll be on vacation would be wasteful.

■ *Nature of the message.* What you need to say in a document also affects your choice of technologies. For instance, business messages often require some sort of visual support (diagrams, photographs, or tables). A telephone call wouldn't be a good choice in such cases, but a printed report would be. If you need to convey emotion and excitement, delivering your message in person might be best. However, if you can't visit every member of your audience, sending your message on videotape might be a good substitute.

■ *Presentation needs.* Sometimes the way you need to present your document will dictate which tools you use. If you're sending a report to an important client, you might want to stretch your budget to use typeset printing, color graphics, and professional binding. However, for short internal messages you probably wouldn't want to spend the time or the money to present things so nicely.

As you'll see throughout this chapter, some tools can create more than one type of message or document. Likewise, you may have two or three technological options when it comes to one particular message or document. The trick is to pick the tool that does the best overall job in each situation.

*T*ECHNOLOGY IN WRITTEN COMMUNICATION

When preparing written documents, you can take advantage of technological developments at every step. You're probably familiar with some of these, but others are becoming more popular. In a well-equipped office, you'll have a variety of tools to help you create both printed and electronic documents.

Creating Printed Documents

Whether you're writing a one-paragraph memo or a 500-page report, technology can help you create a more effective document with less time and effort. Some of these tools apply only to printed documents; others can help you with electronic documents as well. **Word processors** are the predominant tools for creating printed documents. In the most basic sense, you can think of a word processor as a computerized typewriter, but today's word-processing software can do far more than you could ever attempt on a typewriter. For a text entry that involves two or more people developing a single document, you can use *group authoring tools.* These are multiuser word processors that help people work together without getting in one another's way. The systems keep track of revisions, let people attach electronic notes to one another's sections, enforce a common format for all sections, and take care of other issues that come up in any collaborative writing project. These special word processors are often embodied in a class of software called *groupware,* which can include a variety of computing and communication tools to help people work together.[2]

In the same way that word processors were created to emulate mechanical typewriters, **desktop publishing (DTP)** software was created to computerize the process of assembling finished pages. If you wanted a first-class report with photos and drawings, the old way of doing things involved cutting out strips of printed text and pasting them onto a blank page along with the photos and drawings. DTP software does the same thing, only it all happens on your computer screen. Word processing and DTP are the core technologies for creating printed documents, and like Metropolitan Life, you can take advantage of a growing selection of specialized tools as well. The following sections present a brief overview of document creation to give you a better idea of how the various pieces of hardware and software can help you with planning, composing, revising, producing, distributing, and storing first-class documents.

Planning Documents

Some of the writing you'll do on the job requires very little planning. For a memo to your staff regarding the company picnic or a letter to customers thanking them for placing orders, you can often collect a few facts and get right down to writing. In other cases, however, you won't be able to start writing until you've done extensive research. This research often covers both the audience you'll be writing to and the subject matter you'll be writing about. Technology can help with these research tasks and with outlining your thoughts once you've done your research.

Researching Audience and Content   Sometimes the information you need for a document can be found inside your company, in its sales records, existing research reports, and other *internal sources.* Other times the information you need will be found outside the company by searching through books, magazines, and other *external sources.* Technology can help in both cases.

Founder of TBS Superstation and CNN, Ted Turner is a pioneer in the cable TV industry. The challenge of technology, says Turner, is managing it to create our world—instead of merely being dragged along by it.

The most common software for creating printed documents is word processing.

The software most appropriate for assembling finished pages with graphics elements is desktop publishing (DTP).

Research is often one of the most important steps in business communication, and technology provides several helpful tools, including

- Databases
- Statistical analysis software
- Text retrieval software
- CD-ROM information sources

Much of your company's internal information may be stored in one or more **databases**—collections of facts ranging from financial figures to the text of reports. For information on sales trends, you might use a computer to search through your company's sales records. You can use *statistical analysis* software to sort through numerical data and *text retrieval* software to sort through reports and other textual material.

The list of external sources of business information is long and getting longer all the time. If you need some recent forecasts on household income, you can tap into Econbase, a database of economic forecasts and projects. If you need to see whether Congress passed any tax laws in the last week that might affect your company, you can try accessing Tax Notes Today, which explains all recent government actions regarding federal and state taxes.[3] These and thousands of other databases, on topics ranging from accounting to zoology, are available to anyone with a properly equipped computer—usually for a fee.

A recent addition to the communicator's research toolbox is **CD-ROM,** a type of compact disk that can be read by special computer equipment. An individual CD-ROM can contain either a single volume of information or collections of documents ranging from back files of newspapers to sets of books on a particular subject. For example, the Microsoft Bookshelf collection contains seven volumes helpful for writers and speakers, including a dictionary, a thesaurus, and an atlas.[4] Other CD-ROM offerings include back issues of *The Wall Street Journal,* the names and addresses of business executives, and government trade statistics.[5]

Outlining   Once you've collected the necessary information for your report, the next step is to outline how you want to present your ideas. You've probably outlined reports, possibly using note cards to arrange and sort the various sections. Computer-based outliners perform the same function, only without the need to fill out all those cards. You type in the titles of your sections; then you can quickly move sections around, experimenting with order and organization. Computer outliners further boost your productivity by saving you from retyping the section titles once you've finished outlining.

CHECKLIST FOR DICTATION

A. Preparation for Dictation
1. Review the operating instructions for the dictation equipment, and see that it is working properly.
2. Gather all notes, files, and reference materials that you may need to use during the dictation session.
3. Plan the message.
   - a. Determine your purpose.
   - b. Think about the audience's needs and interests.
   - c. Organize your thoughts into logical groups, and decide on the sequence of points.

B. Dictation Procedures
1. Start with messages that have the greatest priority.
2. Speak clearly and distinctly, in a natural tone of voice.
3. Avoid eating, gum chewing, smoking, and other audible distractions while you are dictating.

4. Provide full instructions for the transcriber.
   - a. Identify yourself and your department, indicating where you can be reached if the transcriber has any questions.
   - b. Identify the form of the message—letter, memo, report, slide presentation, or whatever—and specify whether you want a draft or a final copy.
   - c. Request any special stationery you want used, and specify any special format instructions, such as margin widths, single or double spacing, and block format or indented paragraphs.
   - d. Indicate how many copies are required, who should receive them, and how copies should be filed.
   - e. Identify enclosures, and if necessary, tell the transcriber where they can be found.

Composing Documents

When you're ready to start writing, the computer once again demonstrates how it can enhance the communication process. Composing a document on your computer involves keyboarding, of course, but that's just the beginning. Technology now offers a number of ways to get text into your document, and you're no longer limited to text, either. Software makes it relatively easy to add a wide variety of graphic elements to your document, and even audio notes if you have the right equipment.

Entering Text   Composing means sitting at the keyboard and typing. Word processors help make this as painless as possible, giving you the ability to erase and move text easily. The fact that you're on a computer, however, opens up possibilities for text entry that typewriter-bound communicators can only dream about.

To start with, if you don't know how to keyboard or don't like to, your worries may be over sooner than you think. *Pen-based computers* let you write with an electronic stylus on a special pad that converts your handwriting to text the computer can recognize. Pen-based systems aren't completely accurate yet, but some of the world's largest computer firms are working to perfect them and free users from their keyboards.[6] With some computers, you don't have to write or type at all. *Voice recognition systems* convert your voice to text, freeing you from keyboard or pen input. Some experts predict that computers of the future won't even have keyboards, relying instead on voice input.[7] Such breakthroughs are particularly important for people with physical impairments, giving them the means of becoming more active communicators.

Of course, not everyone uses a computer or even a typewriter to create documents. Some executives still give their secretaries handwritten rough drafts. Many *dictate* messages and documents, either to an assistant or into a *dictation system.* These systems are like elaborate tape recorders that allow secretaries to play back the recordings while typing the information into a computer file. (You can see that the computerized voice recognition systems just discussed are a natural development of dictation systems.) For many executives, dictation remains an important skill.[8] This chapter's Checklist for Dictation offers some handy pointers to review (as a reminder, not a recipe).

Technology provides a number of options for entering text into a document:

- Keyboarding (typing)
- Pen-based computers
- Voice recognition systems
- Dictation systems
- Scanning

---

  f. Describe special mailing and transmission requirements.
  g. Specify the turnaround time for each message.
  h. Spell out clearly the name and address of each person who is to receive the message.
5. Use the pause or stop button on the dictation machine if you need to think through a statement or locate additional material.
6. Clarify ambiguous grammar, spelling, and punctuation.
  a. Clearly enunciate plurals, past-tense endings, and sounds that might be confused (such as *b* and *p*).
  b. Spell out personal and company names, homophones (words that sound alike but are spelled differently), and trade or technical terms.
  c. Specify punctuation where a question may arise: periods, commas, colons and semicolons, question marks, exclamation points, hyphens, dashes, parentheses, and quotation marks.

  d. Specify capitalization: "all caps" for an entire word, "initial cap" for the first letter of a word.
  e. Identify the use of underlining, indention, and columns.
  f. Dictate long or unusual numbers digit by digit.
  g. Indicate paragraph endings by saying "paragraph."
7. Make corrections as soon as you notice that you have made a mistake or that revision is needed.
8. Conclude the dictation by saying "end of dictation" and thanking the transcriber.

C. Dictation Follow-Up
1. Proofread the typed document carefully; then double-check to be certain that any required changes were made.
2. Sign or initial the final version.
3. Ask the transcriber for feedback on how to improve your dictation technique.

Some of the text that business communicators use in their documents is "prewritten," already appearing in other documents. When Metropolitan Life offers similar coverage to various companies, it can use standard, prewritten material in the employee-benefits booklets. Any standard block of text used in various documents without changing it is called a *boilerplate.* With a good word processor, you don't have to retype the boilerplate each time you write a press release. You simply store the paragraph the first time you write it and then pop it into a document whenever you need it. Not only does this save time, it also reduces mistakes, since you're not retyping the paragraph every time you use it. A related concept also applies to manipulating existing text. If you're a national sales manager compiling a report that includes summaries from your four regional managers, you can use your word processor's *file merge* capability to combine the four documents into one, saving yourself the trouble of retyping each one.

> A boilerplate is any standard block of text used in various documents without changing it.

Using a boilerplate or file merge assumes that the text you want to include is in electronic format, saved on a computer disk. But sometimes you have only a printed version of a document. In such cases you can use a *scanner,* a device that essentially takes a picture of a printed document and converts it to an electronic format that your computer can handle. Scanners produce just a visual image of the document, though, and the process requires an additional step if you want to use the words from the document as normal input to your word processor. A technology called *optical character recognition (OCR)* lets your computer "read" the scanned image, picking out the letters and words that make up the text.

Adding Graphics and Sound   Computers can do some amazing things with text entry, but that's only part of the story. With the right equipment, you can add full-color pictures and even sound recordings to your documents. The software for creating busi-

---

*B*EHIND THE SCENES AT MIKE'S VIDEO
Video Club Thrives on Office Technology

Mike's Video in State College, Pennsylvania, serves the students of Penn State University and the surrounding community. Since opening in 1984, the company has grown from one club to four clubs and has opened a TV and appliance store. In the process, owners Mike Negra, Alan Abruzzo, and Wanda White have learned to communicate using a wide and constantly changing array of technological products.

Mike's Video has been successful because it communicates effectively with its club members, employees, and suppliers. Technology has had an impact on every aspect of the company's communication, from auto-dial telephones to electronic mail, from word processing on a Macintosh Plus with laser printer to faxing newsletter articles to their publisher in Arkansas. Something that has to go out fast is handwritten and faxed, not typed and mailed.

Wanda White manages operations: "The PC does our letters, puts together our club newsletter, and does our signs, business cards, stationery, forms, anything that needs printing." Alan Abruzzo purchases videos (14,000 copies of 3,800 titles at last count), TVs, VCRs, and stereos. The telephone and fax machine are his tools: "I order all the movies from seven distributors through telemarketers. Appliance manufacturers send their specials overnight on the fax machine, and I can call in an order the next day. If we're planning a large purchase, I solicit bids by telephone, then get responses and send out the contract and order by fax." As president, Mike Negra travels for the company and oversees appliances. He uses a cellular phone to help him keep on top of things: "With our Centrex system, I can call one store and be switched to any phone in our company."

Most important, technology gives Mike's Video the ability to satisfy its customers. "Our club members are

ness visuals falls into two basic groups: *presentation software* and *graphics software*. Presentation software helps you create overhead transparencies and other visuals for meetings, discussed later in the chapter.

Graphics software ranges from products that can create simple diagrams and flow-charts to comprehensive tools designed for artists and graphic designers. You can create your pictures from scratch, use *clip art* (collections of simple images), or scan in drawings or photos. Much of the graphic design and artwork that you see in business publications was created with software packages such as CorelDRAW and Macromedia's Freehand.

Inserting your visuals into a document used to be a chore, but increasing standardization of computer file formats has made the task somewhat easier. Say you want to distribute some ideas you have for a new corporate logo, and you want to include your sketches in a memo. You've already created several logos in CorelDRAW, but your memo was created in Microsoft Word. No problem—you simply save the CorelDRAW file in a special transfer format, then switch to your memo in Microsoft Word and activate the Insert Picture command. The logos pop into your memo, and you can shrink or enlarge them as needed to fit.

Adding sound bites to your documents is an exciting new way to get your message across. Several systems now allow you to record a brief message or other sound and attach it to particular places in a document. Of course, to actually hear the sound, the person receiving the memo has to load the memo into a computer that also has sound capability.

Graphics software can add a visual element to your message.

Revising Documents

When it's time to revise and polish your message, your word processor can help in a variety of ways, starting with the basics of adding, deleting, and moving text. *Cut and*

---

amazed at how efficient we are," says White. "Our computer system and telephones allow us to be on top of the service details in a timely and expedient way." Negra adds: "When you call a club to buy a TV, you are switched to the appliance store without having to redial. When you call your club to rent a certain movie, our computer can tell us which store has it. Then if you return it to another of our clubs while you're out running around, your club knows instantly that you've returned it, so there are no delays when you show up to rent a new movie."

All of this does have drawbacks. Abruzzo believes it's less personal than face-to-face communication: "I've done business with some people almost daily for five years, and I've never met them." For Negra, the struggle is keeping the problems of a small business on the minds of large manufacturers: "To a distributor in Pittsburgh, our success was important. We had a rep visiting us, and if we bought $100,000 in TVs from her, that made us important to her. But now we deal directly with the manufacturer in St. Louis. To him, our $100,000 doesn't look so big, so we don't get the attention we need." For White, who handles personnel, there

is the danger of missed communication: "When I put a message out on our system, the club reps logging on get their messages all right, but there's no body language, tone, or inflection to measure. It's just black words on a white screen."

"But don't forget," says Negra, "technology is merely a tool. We can train people to operate it. When we hire students for part-time work or a salesperson for our store, we look for people with good communication skills. To make the technology work for us, our people have to understand the communication process. All you need to know about the technology is how to use it."

Apply Your Knowledge

1. Suggest as many ways as you can for the people at Mike's Video to personalize their use of the technology described.

2. How would these problems affect operations at Mike's Video: (1) An employee tampers with the movie inventory database. (2) A fire destroys one club. (3) Power fails throughout State College. (4) A customer insists, "The computer's wrong; I did return the five movies."

paste is a term used in both word processing and desktop publishing to indicate cutting a block of text out of one section of a document and pasting it in somewhere else. The *search-and-replace function* helps you track down words or phrases and change them if you need to. This can be a great time-saver in long documents if you need to change a word or phrase that appears in a number of places.

Spell checkers, computerized thesauruses, and grammar checkers can all help with the revision process, but they can't take the place of good writing and editing skills.

Beyond the basic revision tools, three advanced functions can help bring out the best in your documents. A *spell checker* compares your document with an electronic dictionary stored on your disk drive, highlights words it doesn't recognize, and suggests correct spelling(s). Spell checkers are a wonderful way to weed major typos out of your documents, but it's best not to use them as replacements for good spelling skills. If you use *their* when you mean to use *there,* your spell checker will fly right past the error, since *their* is in fact spelled correctly. If you're in a hurry and accidently omit the *p* at the end of *top,* your spell checker will read *to* as correct. Or if you mistakenly type the semicolon instead of the *p,* your spell checker will read *to;* as a correctly spelled word.

A computer *thesaurus* gives you alternative words, just as your printed thesaurus does. Not only can a computer thesaurus give you answers faster and more easily than a printed thesaurus, it may also be able to do things your printed thesaurus could never do. The electronic version of the American Heritage dictionary provides a thesaurus and a special WordHunter function that gives you the term when all you know is part of the definition. If you're racking your brain to remember the word that means a certain quantity of paper, you simply type *quantity AND paper* and then WordHunter searches for every definition in the dictionary that includes those two terms. In a few seconds the word *ream* pops into view, and you say, "Aha! That's the word I was looking for."

The third major revision tool is the *grammar checker,* which tries to do for your grammar what a spell checker does for your spelling. The catch here is that checking your spelling is much easier than checking your grammar. A spell checker simply compares each word in your document with a list of correctly spelled words. A grammar checker has to determine whether you're using words correctly and constructing sentences according to the complex rules of composition. Since the computer doesn't have a clue about what you're trying to say, determining whether you've said it correctly is monstrously difficult. Moreover, even if you've used all the rules correctly, a grammar checker still can't tell whether your document communicates clearly. However, grammar checkers can perform some helpful review tasks and point out things you should consider changing, such as passive voice, long sentences, and words that tend to be misused or overused.[9]

Susan Mersereau is vice president and general manager of Weyerhaeuser Information Systems. As such, Mersereau heads the group responsible for the company's worldwide telecommunications program, linking voice and data communications, electronic mail, fax, and videoconferencing facilities. To manage change, says Mersereau, you must control vast amounts of information, which is something technology can help you do.

Producing Finished Documents

Consider the memo shown in Figure 4.1. Many simple hardware and software packages are capable of producing documents like this one, combining text and graphics so that the appearance is both professional and inviting. It's important that you balance the graphics and text. The bar chart in this memo is centered to give a formal impression, and the color used in the graphic is balanced by the letterhead logo. The manner in which you package your ideas has a lot to do with how successful your communication will be. A document that looks tired and out of date will give that impression to your readers—even if your ideas are innovative. Today's computer software makes it easy for anyone to produce great-looking documents in a hurry. Both word processors and desktop publishing software can help you in three ways:

■ *Adding a first-class finish.* From selecting attractive typefaces to adding color graphics, you can use your computer tools to turn a plain piece of text into a dazzling and

CalPlus

9408 SEPULVEDA WAY, LOS ANGELES, CALIFORNIA 97402 (805) 555-4103

MEMO

TO: Alden Maxwell, V.P., Marketing

FROM: Louise Ellison, Manager, Promotions

DATE: April 14, 1996

SUBJECT: Using sports as a selling tool for promoting our new calcium-plus soft drink

After doing a little research, I'm more convinced than ever that sponsoring a sporting event would be an excellent way to build awareness of our new calcium-plus soft drink.

The experiences of other companies show that

For example, Volvo has found that it can reach as many people by spending $3 million on tennis tournaments as it can by spending $25 million on media advertising.

If we decide to go forward with a sponsorship, our first priority should be to identify a sport that is popular with our target customers. As the chart below indicates, auto racing is currently the number-one sport among corporate sponsors, possibly because it appeals to both men and women:

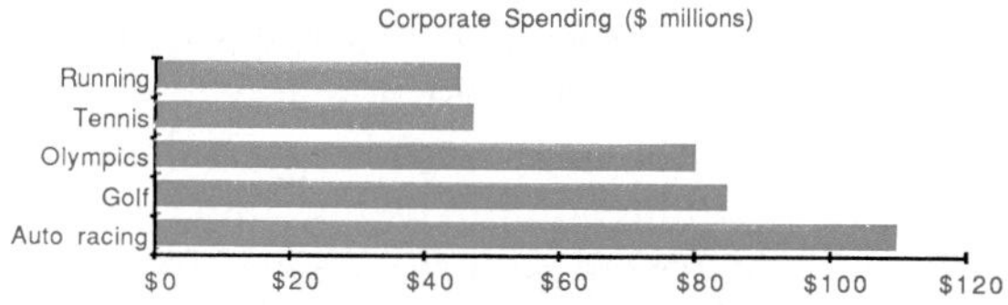

Although the "mainstream" sports currently receive the lion's share of coroporate dollars, we might achieve more impact with a lesser-known event. Timberline Company has really scored with its sponsorship of the Idatarod dog-sled race across Alaska, a contest that appeals to customers for rugged footwear.

Over the next few days, I plan to do some more research to identify sporting events that would give us the most exposure among the health-conscious women who represent our primary market. I hope to pinpoint three or four possibilities and prepare some preliminary cost estimates for discussion at the Tuesday staff meeting.

Figure 4.1
The Importance of Appearance
An attractive, contemporary appearance can help you get your message across more effectively.

persuasive document. Used improperly, however, these same tools can turn your text into garish, high-tech rubbish. Knowing how to use the tools of technology is a key issue for today's business communicators.

- *Managing document style.* With so many design and formatting choices at your fingertips, it's important to maintain consistency throughout your document. *Style sheets* are collections of formatting rules available in high-end word processors and DTP packages that can save a lot of formatting effort. Every time you need to add a section to your report, for instance, your style sheet can ensure that every section is formatted consistently (with the same typeface, margins, word spacing, etc.). You can also use style sheets to make sure that all the documents created by everyone in a department or even an entire company have a consistent look.
- *Generating supporting elements.* If you've ever written a report with footnotes or endnotes, an index, and a table of contents, you know how much work these supporting elements can be. Fortunately, computers can help here as well. A good word

Computer software can help you add a first-class look to your most important business documents.

processor can keep track of your footnotes, renumbering them all every time you add or delete references. For indexes and tables of contents, you simply flag the terms you want to include, and the software assembles the lists for you.

High-end word processors can now handle most aspects of final document production, but many communicators prefer to finish off their documents with desktop publishing instead. In addition to giving you more control over spacing, graphics, color, and other elements, DTP makes many layout and design tasks easier. Moving a column of text, for instance, can be quite difficult with most word processors. But by using DTP, you can grab it, move it wherever you want, and resize it along the way if you like.

Printing and Distributing Documents

With a finished document, you're ready to print and distribute copies to your audience. *Printers* come in a variety of shapes, sizes, and capabilities, from low-cost portables that fit into your briefcase to high-resolution color units that can print photographs with startling accuracy. Like Metropolitan Life, many businesses today are equipped with laser printers, which produce a printed image by drawing with a low-power laser beam. For results that look the very best, pages can be printed using a *typesetter* or an *imagesetter,* both of which are similar in concept to laser printers but which produce sharper images.

Laser printers are a popular way of producing documents in business today.

Technology does some of its most amazing feats when it's time to distribute your documents. For multiple copies of your document, you can print as many as you like on your office printer or print a single copy or reproduce it with a *photocopier.* For high-volume or complex reproduction (involving colors or photographs, for instance), you'll want to take your document to a *print shop,* a company that has the special equipment needed for such jobs.

When you need to send the same document (sales letter, invoice, or other customer communication) to a large number of people, *mail merge* automatically combines a standard version of the document with a list of names and addresses. It will produce one copy for each person on your mailing list, saving you the trouble of inserting the name and address each time. The names and addresses can come from your own customer database or from mailing lists you can rent from firms that specialize in collecting names and addresses.

Fax machines are now an integral part of the business communication process, providing fast transmission of printed documents all over the world.

Fax machines have had a major impact on the distribution of printed documents. Using regular telephone lines, you can transmit (fax) an exact reproduction (facsimile) of a document from one machine to another. Fax machines are indispensable for international business, particularly since they overcome the delay problems of regular mail and the time-zone problems of trying to contact someone by telephone.[10]

Creating Electronic Documents

A growing number of business documents are never put onto paper; they're written on a computer and sent along telephone lines or other connections to be read on other computers. **Electronic mail,** called **E-mail,** refers to documents created, transmitted, and read entirely on computers (see Figure 4.2). E-mail **networks** vary greatly in size. Small private-office setups, sometimes called *local area networks (LANs),* connect people in a single company. National and international networks such as MCI Mail and CompuServe can be accessed by the general public,[11] and businesses are rushing to use the global network known as Internet.[12]

Electronic mail (E-mail) helps businesses communicate faster and more informally, bypassing some of the barriers that restrict printed documents and face-to-face communication.

For the people who use it, E-mail has changed the style of business communication in three dramatic ways. First, it has opened new channels of communication in-

Subject: Thanks for your help

Address:	TO: Dave Johnson, 70003,2424	1 recipient
From:	Debra Young, 70004,336	4/20/93 8:39 AM
Receipt	Importance: Normal	Sensitivity: Normal

Dave,

Thanks so much for your help in capturing those screen shots for the slide presentation. All went well, and I couldn't have done it without you.

Hope your trip to Arizona is successful. Take care.

Debra

[In-Basket] [File It] [Reply] [Forward] [Delete] [Cancel]

Figure 4.2
Electronic Mail
This screen from an E-mail session shows how the system helps you communicate with anyone connected to the system—anywhere in the world—whether you're sending, receiving, or filing messages.

side the organization. With most E-mail systems, anybody can send messages to just about anybody else. Lower-level employees who may otherwise have no contact with upper management can send E-mail messages to top managers as easily as to their own colleagues.

Second, E-mail is usually an informal communication medium. Experienced users don't worry much about formatting or document design. The idea is to get your point across as quickly as possible, and the typical system doesn't give you many tools for formatting, anyway. In fact, people who spend any amount of time making their messages look nice are viewed as novices.[13]

Third, E-mail has a curious way of encouraging people to drop the inhibitions that normally govern their messages. People sometimes write things in E-mail that they wouldn't dream of saying in person or typing in a document.[14] This new openness can be beneficial, helping companies communicate better and circulating useful opinions from a wider variety of people. However, as you can imagine, such openness can also create tension and interpersonal conflict.

*T*ECHNOLOGY IN ORAL COMMUNICATION

Written documents are only part of the business communication picture. Oral communication is just as important, whether it's face-to-face or on the phone, whether it's with one other person or with a group. Here's a quick look at the technologies used to improve communication among individuals and groups.

Individual Communication

If you threw out fax machines, E-mail, and computers, most businesses could survive. Just don't touch the phone—that's a company's real lifeline. Phones link businesses with their customers, suppliers, news media, investors, and all the other parties that affect their success. Phones keep employees in touch with one another and give them quick access to the people and the information they need to do their jobs.

As it has in every other aspect of communication, technology has transformed the way businesspeople use their phones. Business phone systems have become less and less like the phone you use at home; many act like computers with phones attached.

John L. Sims is vice president of strategic resources for Digital Equipment Corporation, which leads the world in computer network technology. At Digital, employees stay on-line with the company's own VAX stations, a family of computerized workstations. Machines can't do it alone, says Sims. It takes good people to use them.

Technologies for one-on-one oral communication include the basic telephone and advanced options such as voice mail.

Call management systems give companies better control over both the calls that come in and the calls that go out. For inbound calls, a *PBX (private branch exchange)* system can screen and route calls. Some are run by a human operator; others are partly or completely computerized. To reach employees who are out of the office, a company can equip them with *pagers,* small radio receivers that signal employees to call the office. For outbound calls, computers can track who called whom, automatically dial numbers from a list of potential customers, and perform other time- and money-saving tasks.

The combination of phones and computers has also created an entirely new method of communication. *Voice mail* is similar to E-mail in concept, except that it doesn't require each user to have a computer (only a Touch-Tone phone), and it lets you send, store, and retrieve spoken, rather than written, messages. Much more than a glorified answering machine, voice mail sends verbal messages to any number of "mailboxes" on the system. Messages can be several minutes long, and you can review your recordings before releasing them. When people need to get their messages, they enter a confidential code; then they can listen to, delete, and forward messages to other people on the system. Voice mail solves time-zone difficulties when communicating across the country or internationally. It can also reduce a substantial amount of interoffice paperwork.[15]

Voice mail can make employees more productive, but it's not universally loved. The biggest complaint comes from customers who try to call a company and reach a computerized voice mail system instead of a person. In a recent survey, 95 percent of the people questioned said they prefer reaching a person on their first call to a business.[16] Businesses that use voice mail need to balance the productivity gains with the potential effects on customer satisfaction.

Group Communication

Technologies for group presentations include teleconferencing, videoconferencing, presentation tools, and group decision-making systems.

Technology can also lend a hand when people need to communicate in groups. Group communication used to take place in person, in the same room, but technology has given people a new degree of freedom. Through *teleconferencing* (which encompasses audioconferencing and videoconferencing via phone lines and satellite), it's now possible to conduct meetings with people who are scattered across the country or around the globe.[17]

In more traditional gatherings, when all participants can meet in one location, technology provides an array of presentation tools to make meetings more productive and interesting. *Overhead transparencies* are clear sheets of plastic with printed images that can be projected onto a screen for viewing by large numbers of people. You might use *35-mm slides* (just like the slides you can produce with a camera), or you could make use of a *computer-driven presentation* in which the computer's display is transferred to a large-screen television. Presentation software can help you create these visual materials. But beyond visuals, technology can even help groups make decisions and formulate plans. You can connect everyone through computers using *group decision support systems,* which range from simple vote-counting systems to advanced tools that help people consider a decision from various points of view.[18]

HOW TECHNOLOGY IS CHANGING COMMUNICATION

As Metropolitan's William Livesey can attest, communication technology is changing the way we do business. Some of the effects are unquestionably positive; others are not. On the positive side, technology can increase the flow of information, improve teamwork, change organizational structures, and decrease communication costs. On the other hand, there are technology's negative effects: It can produce information overload, burden people with more and more unwanted messages, isolate some people from employment opportunities, and blur the line between work life and home life. Consider the following effects:

- *Increasing and changing the flow of information.* Businesspeople can now get more information on more subjects faster than ever before. Although much of this information is useful, technology makes it easy to bury yourself and your company in information you really don't need. By pressing just a few keys or buttons, you can send E-mail, voice mail, and faxes to hundreds or even thousands of people—whether they actually need the information or not. Of course, technology can also help you sort through all that information to find just the bits you need. In addition, technology is changing the nature of information flow. Although corporate structure used to define the flow, E-mail in particular frees communication from the confines of the organizational chart. In the electronic office, anyone can send messages to anyone else with equal access, a big change from the old days, when messages just moved up and down the chain of command.[19]
- *Making it easier for people to communicate.* Technology makes it easier and faster to reach more people than ever before, both inside and outside the company. E-mail facilitates internal communication, voice mail overcomes time zones and even working hours, and faxes are being accepted as purchase orders by mail-order houses and as money transfers by banks.[20]
- *Changing the organizational structure.* Communication technology has loosened the strings that bind the traditional company together. In many firms, it is no longer necessary for co-workers or even entire departments to be in a single location. **Telecommuting** lets people work (linked through computers, phones, and faxes) where it is most convenient for them—whether at home, in a suburban satellite office (where people can work close to home but away from the company's main office), or on the road (while traveling to sell products or service customer accounts). Telecommuting can cover a lot more territory than the area around town. Chris Leinberger is one of the three top executives at Lesser & Weitzman, the largest U.S. real estate consulting business. The firm's clients are located in major urban centers around the country, but Leinberger lives and works on a ranch outside Sante Fe, New Mexico, where faxes and E-mail keep him in touch with company offices across the country.[21]
- *Improving profits.* Communication technology can boost profits directly because it costs less for people to produce and distribute messages and documents. It can improve profits indirectly by making a company more competitive, say, by searching databases to uncover a new market opportunity.
- *Isolating people with no access to technology.* Businesses and individuals who don't have E-mail, faxes, or other technological tools tend to be left out of the communication flow. This presents a challenge to young people who lack experience with communication technology but who are applying for jobs that require some knowledge of it.
- *Increasing the pressure to perform.* E-mail, faxes, and other technologies that speed up and extend the reach of business communication can increase the pressure on those people who use them. From home computers to car phones to portable fax machines, technology can make it easy to feel that you're always "plugged in" and that you're expected to respond instantly to every message that comes in, whether you're at home, on a business trip, or on vacation.

The development and evolution of technology is changing business communication, and its effects are both positive and negative.

Katherine M. Hudson is vice president and director of corporate information systems at Eastman Kodak Company. Hudson and her worldwide team lead the corporate information systems division, which is responsible for Kodak's global computing and telecommunications. Such networks allow us to exchange ideas more readily, says Hudson, but people still have to dream up the ideas to communicate.

Remember several key points about technology: First, even though it helps you communicate with more people more efficiently, it doesn't solve *all* your problems. For one thing, it adds to the complexity of your job—learning to use the voice-mail system, the computer-messaging network, the desktop publishing system, and any other tools at your disposal. Second, it doesn't come cheap; companies spend millions of dollars on all the communication equipment employees use. Third, whether in the form of handwritten notes, electronic newsletters, or global videoconferences, communication efforts are only as good as the people involved. Technology cannot do the thinking, planning, or communicating. Human beings must do that. Only those who learn to balance the complexity and expense of technology with good communication skills will succeed in business and in the future.

On the Job

SOLVING A COMMUNICATION DILEMMA AT METROPOLITAN LIFE INSURANCE

To manage the mountains of paper needed to support its business, Metropolitan Life has moved aggressively into new technology. This philosophy extends into every part of the business. For William Livesey, the primary objective in producing employee-benefits booklets for corporate accounts is satisfying the customer. He wants to provide clear, attractive booklets in the smallest amount of time so that Metropolitan's corporate customers always have up-to-date explanations of their insurance coverage for their employees. Livesey assigns 20 people to handle the workload of roughly 125 booklets a month.

Until recently, the job of producing the booklets involved a division of labor between Metropolitan's internal employees and outside typesetting and printing services. This arrangement, however, introduced inevitable delays. As Livesey points out, "the Ping-Pong effect" was inherently inefficient: paper bounced back and forth between Metropolitan and its contractors in the course of typesetting, proofreading, making revisions, and printing the booklets.

When Metropolitan decided to reorganize its national accounts activities and move to new quarters, Livesey seized the opportunity to overhaul the procedures for producing the booklets. He invested in an electronic publishing system, including personal computers and laser printers, which now enables Metropolitan to create professionally styled documents internally.

With the new system, Metropolitan has cut three to four weeks off the time required to produce new and revised booklets. Livesey notes, "We have regained control of the process, eliminated the time delays caused by the middlemen, and greatly improved the responsiveness to customers." Not only that, Metropolitan is saving money. Livesey estimates that the system will more than pay for itself in 18 months.

Although creating and revising descriptive booklets is the main application for the system, it is also used to produce Metropolitan's financial reports, charts, and forms. Livesey says, "Those have been an unexpected bonus of having this system at our disposal."

Your Mission: You supervise the 20-person department that produces employee-benefits booklets. Your responsibilities involve everything from writing the text to laying out pages and reproducing the booklets. Choose the best solutions for the following situations, and be prepared to explain why your choice is best:

1. One of Metropolitan's major customers has revised its group insurance benefits. The customer has asked you to provide details on how you intend to handle the revision of its benefits booklet, which is bound in a loose-leaf three-ring binder. You estimate that roughly half the pages in the existing booklet will be affected by the changes. What will you tell the customer?
   a. Ask the customer to return all existing employee-benefits booklets, and then take out the old pages and insert the new ones.
   b. Enter the changes to the existing text on Metropolitan's electronic publishing system, and then print as many completely new booklets as the customer requires.
   c. Revise the pages in question, and then send copies of those pages to the customer for insertion into the benefits booklets.
   d. Describe the changes in a cross-referenced addendum that supplements the existing booklet, and then print and ship enough copies of the addendum so that all the customer's employees can have their own copy.
2. Livesey has asked you to shop for some new software that can be used with the electronic publishing system to make transparencies for oral presentations. What is the first step to take?

a. Buy an assortment of magazines that cover the subject of computer software, and read articles on the various programs available.

b. Contact the company that manufactures the hardware Metropolitan is currently using, ask for a listing of compatible software programs for making transparencies, and write to all the software companies for sales literature.

c. Talk to the people at Metropolitan who use transparencies in their oral presentations, and determine what they are looking for in graphics capabilities, clip art, color, and various types and sizes of print.

d. Attend a trade show that features electronic publishing hardware and software so that you can see the alternatives firsthand.

3. Livesey has asked you to look into supplementing the descriptive booklets with videotapes that explain each customer's group insurance benefits. What is the first step you should take in conducting your investigation?

a. Develop a rough outline for such a videotape; then call up a cross section of the customers and ask them what they think of the idea.

b. Find out whether Metropolitan's competitors provide videotape explanations of group insurance benefits.

c. Develop a rough outline for such a videotape, and then ask some outside producers to give you an idea of how much it would cost to produce and update tapes for each of your major customers.

d. Attend a videotape equipment show to determine what equipment Metropolitan would need to purchase to produce its own training films.

4. The sales and marketing department has persuaded Metropolitan to install a toll-free hot line that allows group insurance customers to call with questions during business hours. Livesey has asked you to recommend the best way to keep the hot-line operators informed on the details of each customer's insurance benefits coverage. What would you propose?

a. Give each hot-line operator a copy of the benefits booklet for each customer.

b. Provide each hot-line operator with a computer terminal that has access to the texts of all the insurance booklets created on the electronic publishing system. Program the computers so that the operators can quickly access the appropriate information for each group insurance customer. (Set up a read-only safeguard so that the operators cannot inadvertently alter the text.)

c. Prepare a fact sheet that provides answers to the most frequently asked questions. Instruct the hot-line operators to direct questions not covered by the fact sheet to the sales representative who handles that customer's account.

d. Have a fax machine at the telephone service center to allow the hot-line operators to provide the inquiring customers with copies of the appropriate pages from the benefits booklet when questions arise.

5. One of your most experienced booklet writers has notified you that her spouse has been relocated to another city by his employer. Rather than quit, the employee has proposed setting up a home office in the city where she and her spouse will be living so that she can "commute" to Metropolitan Life via long-distance phone lines. What pieces of equipment would you need to provide to enable the employee to continue to make a productive contribution to your department?

a. A typewriter and a generous supply of envelopes and postage stamps.

b. A computer and draft-quality printer linked by telephone to Metropolitan Life's electronic publishing system, together with the software required to produce the booklets.

c. A duplicate of the entire electronic publishing system, including a computer terminal, laser printer, color plotter, photocopy machine, and fax machine, along with the related software.

d. A complete teleconferencing setup to allow the employee to attend meetings at Metropolitan's headquarters, together with all the input and output devices required to tie into the electronic publishing system.[22]

Questions for Discussion

1. Is it important for everyone in a company to know how to use the latest technological tools for document preparation? Why or why not?

2. Would you choose word-processing or desktop publishing software as a tool for writing memos to your staff? Why?

3. Considering how fast and easy it is, should E-mail replace meetings and other face-to-face communication? Why or why not?

4. Why are companies interested in group technologies such as teleconferencing and groupware?

5. How could a global corporation such as Coca-Cola take advantage of technology to keep its people around the world in touch with one another?

6. What are the implications for companies that can't afford communication technology and for employment candidates who have no experience with such technology?

Exercises

1. You are responsible for recommending word-processing software to the headquarters staff at Federal Express. Using computer magazines such as *Windows* and *PCNovice,* read reviews of leading word-processing products. According to your research, select the one product you think is best, and write a brief recommendation.

2. List the technological skills you already have and could discuss in a job interview. Can you type? Have you used electronic typewriters, computer keyboards, E-mail, computer networks? Have you used photocopiers, calculators, answering machines, voice-mail systems? What experience do you have with video cameras, video players, videoconferencing equipment? Which brands, models, or systems are you familiar with? Which software do you have experience using?

3. Interview several local businesspeople or college administrators to find out
   a. What communication technology they use
   b. What tasks they use the technology for
   c. The advantages of using the technology
   d. The disadvantages of using the technology
   Write a one-page summary of your findings.

4. Visit a computer store and see a *multimedia* computer in action. These PCs are equipped to handle videotape, high-quality sound, and other nontraditional elements—in addition to perfoming word processing and the more typical computer functions. After seeing what these machines can do, make a list of the ways multimedia computers could enhance business communication.

5. Your boss refuses to adopt computers for communication purposes—choosing to rely on dictation, typewriters, and simple face-to-face contact. What arguments might you use to persuade your boss to give communication technology a try? Be prepared to discuss your arguments in class.

6. Using whatever type of dictation equipment is available to you (perhaps a simple tape recorder), dictate one of the sample letters in Component Chapter A (following the steps in this chapter's Checklist for Dictation). Let the tape sit for at least two days; then try to transcribe the letter from your dictation.

on Process · Defining Your Purpose · Analyzing Your Audience · Establishing the Main Idea

THE WRITING

nd Medium · Organizing Your Message · Formulating Your Message · Editing Your Message

PROCESS

Producing Your Message · Proofing Your Message · Understanding the Composition Process

Chapter 5
Planning Business Messages

Chapter 6
Composing Business Messages

Chapter 7
Revising Business Messages

PLANNING BUSINESS MESSAGES

After studying this chapter, you will be able to

Describe the basic tasks in the composition process

Test the purpose of your business messages

Develop an audience profile

Analyze the needs of your audience

Establish the main idea of your messages

Select an appropriate channel and medium for transmitting a particular message to a particular audience

On the Job

FACING A COMMUNICATION DILEMMA AT MATTEL

The "Bimbo" with a Brain

Dressed in a zebra-striped bathing suit, she made her grand entrance in 1959, a curvaceous blonde with a mane of platinum hair. Though decades have passed, she's still one of America's hottest items. You know her. Her name is Barbie, and she's some doll.

Since Barbie's debut, the Mattel toy company has sold over 500 million of the petite 11-inch-tall dolls. In fact, 90 percent of all U.S. girls between the ages of 4 and 10 own at least one Barbie. Many also own her boyfriend, Ken, and a group of her girl-friends, not to mention her $200 dream house, her red Ferrari, her vacation hideaway, her horse, her cats, and her incredible, ever-expanding wardrobe. Barbie's appeal is practically universal. She appears in 67 countries around the world, modified in facial characteristics and clothing to suit local tastes: Asian Barbie, Greek Barbie, Icelandic Barbie, Peruvian Barbie . . .

Still, not everybody loves her. Feminists complain that Barbie is a materialistic bubblehead concerned only with possessions, popularity, and appearances. Susan Reverby, director of the women's studies program at Wellesley College, sums it up by saying that Barbie is a "bimbo." Reverby won't allow her own little girl to play with Barbie. "I don't want my daughter to think that being a woman means she has to look like Barbie and date someone like Ken," Reverby says.

The people at Mattel are sensitive to the criticism. Jill Barad, president and chief operating officer, has set out to redeem Barbie's reputation by giving her a career. Hailed as one of the most powerful women in corporate America, Barad herself is a role model for many women. She has tried to add a new dimension to Barbie's appeal by giving her not just one job, but many. After plunging into the work force in 1983 as an employee of McDonald's, Barbie has gone on to bigger and better things. She's been an astronaut, a surgeon, a veterinarian, an Olympic athlete, and the leader of a rock band—and she has the clothes to prove it.

Barad faces the communication challenge of sending a message that will satisfy both Barbie's critics and her faithful fans. The critics want Barbie to be a strong, serious woman with a social conscience—the type of person who volunteers at a settlement house for homeless people after putting in a ten-hour day on Wall Street. The fans want Barbie to be what she has always been—a popular, pretty girl who wears glamorous clothes and has fun all the time.

How can Jill Barad plan messages that will appease one group without upsetting the other? What consideration should she give her purpose? Her audience? What are the best communication channel and medium for her messages?[1]

Mattel

*U*NDERSTANDING THE COMPOSITION PROCESS

Jill Barad's dilemma is not unique. In your own career, you'll face a variety of communication assignments. Some of your tasks will be routine, needing little more than jotting a few sentences down on paper or into an E-mail message; others will be more complex, requiring reflection, research, and careful document preparation. Regardless of the job you hold, the amount of time you actually spend composing messages, or the complexity of your task, effective communication is the key.[2]

For your business messages to be effective, they must be well planned, well organized, and well constructed. But how can you achieve all that if you can't even think of what to say or how to say it? Many people feel overcome by the thought of composing a message. You can gain control over your messages by separating the various composition activities into a process. Your final message and the process you use to achieve it are irrevocably linked, so successful communicators like Jill Barad concentrate on both.[3]

The process presented here will be most valuable to you if you view it not as a recipe but as a way of understanding the various tasks involved.[4] The composition process varies with the situation, the communicator, and the organization. So the various stages do not necessarily occur in 1-2-3 order. Communicators often jump back and forth from one stage to another.

The **composition process** may be viewed as ten separate stages that fall into three simple categories—planning, composing, and revising (see Figure 5.1):

- *Planning.* During the planning phase, you think about the fundamentals of your message: your reason for communicating, your audience, the main idea of your message, and the channel and medium that will best convey your thoughts. The stages of planning include defining your purpose, analyzing your audience, establishing your main idea, and selecting the appropriate channel and medium.
- *Composing.* Having collected all the information you'll need, you decide on the organization of ideas and the tone you'll adopt. Then you formulate the message, committing your thoughts to words, creating sentences and paragraphs, and selecting illustrations and details to support your main idea. The stages of composing include organizing your message and formulating your message.
- *Revising.* Having formulated your thoughts, you step back to see whether you have expressed them adequately. You review the content and organization of your message, its overall style and readability, and your word choice. You revise and rewrite until your message comes across as clearly and effectively as possible. Then once you have produced the message (as an oral, written, or electronic message), you proof it for details such as grammar, punctuation, and format. The stages of revision include editing your message, rewriting your message, producing your message, and proofing your message.

The composition process helps you gain control over your messages.

Figure 5.1
Tasks in the Composition Process

Planning	Define purpose
	Analyze audience
	Establish main idea
	Select channel and medium
Composing	Organize message
	Formulate message
Revising	Edit message
	Rewrite message
	Produce message
	Proof message

Technology affects the composition process.

Technology has an impact on the composition process. For example, word processing increases productivity and effectiveness by streamlining the process. Because word processing is immediate, you can perform "fingertip thinking"—you can key in all your thoughts without worrying about how they're related or organized. Instead of writing an outline in pen, you can plan on the computer and reorganize your plans with greater ease. Whether you write your first draft quickly without concern for phrasing or grammar or write slowly while deliberately revising as you go, you can do it more easily on a computer without writing it out by hand first. Word processing also makes it much easier for you to revise your rough drafts and incorporate other people's comments.[5]

Collaboration affects the composition process.

In many organizations, the process of preparing a message is a team effort, with more than one writer working on a document.[6] Such **collaborative writing** reduces the distance between you and your receiver by allowing you to bounce ideas off other people. Moreover, your collaborative messages reflect multiple perspectives by synthesizing the knowledge, values, attitudes, and assumptions of team members.[7] You might sit down with your boss to plan a memo and then work independently during the writing phase. After completing a rough draft, you might ask your boss to review the message and suggest revisions, which you would then incorporate. If your message is particularly long and important, the process might involve more people: an editor, a team of writers, typists, graphic artists. For efforts of this type, the review and revision stages might be repeated several times to respond to input from various departments. Of course, deadline pressures must also be considered; if the message was due yesterday, you would compress the process.

Scheduling affects the composition process.

In fact, allotting your time properly is an important consideration. Any realistic schedule would give you the time you need for thoroughly planning, composing, and revising your message, but business messages are often composed under pressure and on a schedule that is anything but realistic. Especially when time is short, carefully schedule yourself, and stick to your schedule. Of the time you're given, try using roughly half for planning, gathering material, and immersing yourself in the subject matter. Try using less than a quarter of your time for composing, and use more than a quarter of the time for revising (so that you don't shortchange important final steps such as polishing and proofing).[8]

Chapter 6 discusses composing business messages, and Chapter 7 covers revising business messages. The rest of this chapter focuses on planning business messages, the first category of the composition process. The result of planning can be as simple as a handwritten checklist of topics to cover in a phone conversation, or it can be a detailed strategy that spells out scheduling and collaborative responsibilities, objectives, audience needs, and media choices.

DEFINING YOUR PURPOSE

When planning a business message, think about your purpose. Of course you want to maintain the goodwill of the audience and create a favorable impression for your organization. You also have a particular goal you want to achieve. That purpose may be straightforward and obvious (like placing an order), or it may be more difficult to define (like Barad's purpose of satisfying both critics and fans of Barbie).

Common Purposes of Business Messages

Business messages commonly have a **general purpose:** to inform, to persuade, or to collaborate with your audience. These purposes determine both the amount of audi-

Pulitzer Prize–winning columnist William Safire writes political columns for The New York Times. *When planning how to organize your thoughts in writing, says Safire, use a combination of your experience, intuition, and common sense.*

ence participation you need and the amount of control you have over your message. If your message is intended strictly to inform, you require little interaction with your audience; you control the message. If your message is persuasive, you require a moderate amount of audience participation, so you retain a moderate amount of message control. Finally, if you seek collaboration from your audience, you require maximum audience participation, so your control of the message is reduced.

Beyond having a general purpose, your messages also have a **specific purpose.** Ask yourself, "What should my audience do or think after reviewing this message?" Then state your purpose as precisely as possible, identifying the members of the audience who should respond. Here are some examples:

Your general purpose may be to inform, persuade, or collaborate.

To determine the specific purpose, think of how the audience's ideas or behavior should be affected by the message.

General Purpose	*Specific Purpose*
To inform	To present last month's sales figures to the vice president of marketing
To persuade	To convince the marketing director of the need to hire more sales representatives
To collaborate	To help the personnel department develop a training program for new members of the sales staff

How to Test Your Purpose

Once you've established your purpose, pause for a moment to consider whether it's worth pursuing at this time. There's no point in creating a message that is unlikely to accomplish its purpose. So before you decide to pursue the message, ask yourself these questions:

- *Is the purpose realistic?* Most people resist change. So if your purpose involves a radical shift in action or attitude, you'll do better to go slowly. Instead of suggesting your whole program at once, consider proposing the first step. View your message as the beginning of a learning process.
- *Is this the right time?* An idea that is unacceptable when profits are down may easily win approval when business improves. If an organization is undergoing changes of some sort, you may want to defer your message until things stabilize and people can concentrate on your ideas.
- *Is the right person delivering the message?* Some people have more leverage in an organization than others do. Even though you may have done all the work yourself, your boss may have a better chance of accomplishing results because of her or his higher status. Also bear in mind that some people are simply better writers or speakers than others. If the stakes are high and you lack experience or confidence, you might want to play a supporting role rather than take the lead.
- *Is the purpose acceptable to the organization?* As the representative of your company, you are obligated to work toward the organization's goals. Your messages should reflect the organization's priorities.

Defer a message, or do not send it at all,

- *If the purpose is not realistic*
- *If the timing is not right*
- *If you are not the right person to deliver the message*
- *If the purpose is not acceptable to the organization*

As vice president of consumer market development for General Motors, Shirley Young is responsible for recommending ways to improve customer satisfaction as well as ways to enhance marketing effectiveness. Given such broad involvement, Young's business messages include all three common purposes: informing, persuading, collaborating.

*A*NALYZING YOUR AUDIENCE

Once you are satisfied that you have a legitimate purpose in communicating, take a good look at your intended audience. Who are the members, what are their attitudes, and what do they need to know? The answers to these questions will indicate something about the material you'll cover and the way you'll cover it.

Develop Your Audience's Profile

If you're communicating with someone you know well, perhaps your boss or a co-worker, audience analysis is relatively easy. You can predict their reactions pretty well without a lot of research. On the other hand, if your audience is made up of strangers, you'll have to do some investigating to learn about them and use common sense to anticipate their reactions.

Ask yourself some key questions about your audience:

- Who are they?
- What is their probable reaction to your message?
- How much do they already know about the subject?
- What is their relationship to you?

- *Determine audience size and composition.* Audience size affects the amount of audience participation in oral presentations and the degree of formality in written documents. Audience size also affects the diversity of backgrounds and interests you'll encounter, so you need to look for the common denominators that tie the members of an audience together. At the same time, you want to respond to the particular concerns of individuals. Because a marketing manager and a production or finance manager need different information, be sure to include a variety of evidence that touches on everyone's area of interest.

- *Identify the primary audience.* When several people will be receiving your message, try to identify those who are most important to your purpose. If you can reach these decision makers or opinion molders, the other members of the audience will fall into place. Although higher-status people usually make the decisions, occasionally a person in a relatively low position may have influence in one or two particular areas.

- *Estimate the audience's probable reaction.* Your approach to organizing your message depends on the probable reaction of your audience in general and of key decision makers within that audience. If you expect a favorable response with very little criticism or debate, you can be straightforward about stating your conclusions and recommendations. You can also use a bit less evidence to support your points. On the other hand, when you face a skeptical audience, you may have to introduce your conclusions and recommendations more gradually and provide more proof.

- *Gauge the audience's level of understanding.* If you and your audience share the same general background, you can assume audience members will understand your material without any difficulty. If not, you'll have to decide how much you need to educate them. The trick is to provide the information they need without being stodgy or obvious.

- *Define your relationship with the audience.* If you're unknown to your audience, you'll have to earn their confidence before you can win them to your point of view. If you're communicating with a familiar group, your credibility has already been established, so you can get down to business immediately. You can build credibility or overcome people's preconceptions of you by providing ample evidence for any material outside your usual area of expertise. Your status relative to your audience also affects the style and tone of your presentation, depending on whether you're addressing your boss, your peers, employees of lower status, customers, or suppliers.

In the race against Nike for market share, Reebok International's founder and chairman, Paul Fireman, plans his advertising messages for specific audiences rather than trying to appeal to the entire shoe market at one time—he uses sniper shots, not shotgun blasts.

Satisfy Your Audience's Information Needs

The key to effective communication is determining your reader's needs and then responding to them. You do that by telling people what they need to know in terms that are meaningful to them. A good message answers all the audience's questions. For example, if you're ordering office supplies, your supplier needs to know the number and type of items you want, when and where to deliver them, and the price you're prepared to pay. If you leave out any of the necessary information, your order will not be filled correctly.

- *Find out what the audience wants to know.* In many cases the audience's information needs are readily apparent. When Jill Barad answers letters requesting information about Barbie, all she normally has to do is respond to the consumers' questions. However, some people aren't particularly good at telling you what they want. Your boss might tell you, "Find out everything you can about the Polaroid Corporation, and write a memo on it." That's a pretty big assignment. Ten days later, you submit your 25-page report, and instead of heaping you with praise, your boss says: "I don't need all this. All I want is their five-year financial record." So when you get a vague request, pin it down. One good approach is to restate the request in more specific terms. Another approach is to get a fix on the assignment's priority. You might ask, "Should I drop everything else and devote myself to this for the next week?"
- *Anticipate unstated questions.* Try to think of information needs that your audience may not even be aware of. Suppose your company has just hired a new employee from out of town, and you've been assigned to coordinate this person's relocation. At a minimum, you would write a welcoming letter describing your company's procedures for relocating employees. With a little extra thought, however, you might decide to include some information about the city: perhaps a guide to residential areas, a map or two, brochures about cultural activities, or information on schools and transportation facilities.
- *Provide all the required information.* Once you've defined your audience's needs, be certain to satisfy those needs completely. One good way to test the thoroughness of your message is to use the journalistic approach: Check to see whether your messages answer *who, what, where, when, why,* and *how.* Whenever you request any action, take particular care to explain exactly what you are expecting. Until readers get a clear picture of what they're supposed to do, they can't possibly do it. If you want them to send you a check for $5, tell them; if you want them to turn in their time cards on Friday by 3:00 P.M., say so.
- *Be sure the information is accurate.* There's no point in answering all your audience's questions if the answers are wrong. In business, you have a special duty to check things before making a written commitment, especially if you're writing to someone who is outside the company. Your organization is legally bound by any promises you make, so make sure your company is able to follow through. Of course, honest mistakes are possible. You may sincerely believe that you have answered someone's questions correctly and then later realize that your information was wrong. If that happens, the most ethical thing for you to do is contact the person immediately and correct the error. Most people will respect you for your honesty.
- *Emphasize ideas of greatest interest to the audience.* When deciding how to respond to your audience's information needs, remember that some points will be of greater interest and importance than others. The head of engineering and someone from the shipping department will be interested in different things. If you don't know the audience, or if you're communicating with a group of people, you'll have to use your common sense to identify points of particular interest. Such factors as age, job, location, income, or education can give you a clue. Remember that your main goal as a business communicator is to tell your audience what they need to know.

Alfred F. Boschulte is vice president of carrier services for NYNEX Service Company, managing business relationships with more than 200 interexchange telecommunications carriers in New York and New England. Boschulte maintains that customer information needs must be anticipated; just meeting them is not enough.

Five questions to ask yourself that will help you satisfy the audience's information needs:

- What does the audience want to know?
- What does the audience need to know?
- Have I provided all desired and necessary information?
- Is the information accurate?
- Have I emphasized the information of greatest interest to the audience?

Satisfy Your Audience's Motivational Needs

Some types of messages, particularly persuasive messages and bad news, are intended to motivate audience members to change their beliefs or behavior. The problem is that

Rely mainly on reason to win your audience to your point of view, but don't overlook their underlying emotions.

people resist ideas that conflict with their existing beliefs and practices. They may selectively screen out threatening ideas or distort your message to fit their preconceived map of reality.

To overcome resistance, arrange your message so that the information will be as acceptable as possible. One approach is to use rational arguments, presented in an objective tone. If you're arguing that a loan applicant should reduce his existing debts before he borrows more, you might use cause-and-effect reasoning to prove your point: "Adding this amount to your current debt might endanger your credit standing." Another approach is to support your position with information or statistics: "A study of debt as a percentage of income suggests that this loan would put you over the safe limit." Presenting both sides of an argument is yet another rational approach that is often quite effective. You could point out how both the bank and the individual might benefit if the loan were approved but then conclude your argument by stating the risks. Two-sided approaches like this increase your credibility and defuse your audience's counterarguments.[9]

Although appealing to reason is often the best approach, you might try convincing your audience by appealing to emotion. When attempting to sell a product, you might suggest that the item would enhance your customer's status or confer social acceptability. You can also build a convincing case by making the audience respect your honesty and fairness. Readers accept the product because they trust the spokesperson. Your credibility with an audience depends on their perception of your competence and integrity. People are more likely to believe you if they feel comfortable with you: if you have similar backgrounds, have friends in common, wear the same style of clothes, en-

If an audience trusts you, they are more likely to agree with you.

*B*EHIND THE SCENES AT ALLSTATE INSURANCE
Editing for Action: Fine Print that Insures Success

"My job is to help management create the future," says Patrick Williams. To carry out that heady challenge for his employer, Allstate Insurance Company, Williams edits one of the nation's top all-employee publications, *Allstate Now*. Part of the 85-member corporate relations department at the company's headquarters in Northbrook, Illinois, Williams plans his maga-paper (a magazine that's put out in an eight-page newspaper-size format) to play a key role in helping employees participate in the Allstate story.

For Allstate's management, communicating with employees is critical to the future of the company. All employees must know where the company is going, what it is trying to achieve, and whether they are going to help it get there. Throughout the corporate relations department, therefore, the attitude is proactive—not telling people what has happened but helping them make things happen. For Williams, that means careful planning.

The planning actually begins at the highest level of the company. The board of directors meets annually with corporate relations management to formulate a communication policy for the coming year. The directors address such issues as where Allstate is going, how communication can help the company get there, what issues the employees must understand to get the company there, and how management can help employees understand these issues. Working within the framework established at that meeting, Williams plans the articles that will appear in each monthly issue of *Allstate Now*.

Eight weeks before publication, Williams meets with his editorial board, which is made up of ten managers of Allstate's various departments, including law, planning, sales, underwriting, advertising, and human resources—the people who plan the future of the company and give it direction. Listening closely to learn what they think is ahead, Williams decides what Allstate employees will need to hear about. "On the other hand," he quickly points out, "it is equally important to listen to employees, my readers in the company, to learn their information needs. My job as editor is to bring these two groups together."

joy the same sports, and aspire to the same goals. To establish rapport, you need to emphasize these common denominators.

Satisfy Your Audience's Practical Needs

Many business messages are directed toward people who are themselves in business— your customers, suppliers, co-workers. So regardless of where these people work or precisely what they do, they'll probably receive your communication under distracting circumstances:

- First-level supervisors are involved in at least 200 separate activities or incidents in an 8-hour day.
- Most activities are very brief. One study of supervisors shows that one activity is carried out every 48 seconds.
- A study of chief executives reports that periods of desk work average 10 to 15 minutes each.
- Responding to mail takes less than 5 percent of a manager's time, and most executives react to only about 30 percent of the mail they receive.[10]

In other words, many in your audience will review your message under difficult circumstances with many interruptions, and they are likely to give it a low priority. So make your message as convenient as possible for them. Try to be brief. Generally speaking, a 5-minute talk is easier to follow than a 30-minute presentation; a two-paragraph

Remember that your audience
- *May have little time*
- *May be distracted*
- *May give your message a low priority*

Presenting the required information in a convenient format will help your audience understand and accept your message.

Every issue must include four articles, each demonstrating one of Allstate's "Four Commitments"—to customers, to community and society, to employees, and to being the best. Williams then has to consider whether the content is appropriate to the publication or whether it could be better communicated by others in a memo or at a meeting. He also asks himself whether the article is what his readers want: "Is the subject technical or financial? Is the article full of data to be digested? Is it new, important, complex, or controversial?" Finally, with all these factors in mind, Williams selects articles and plans their organization and approach by asking himself, "How will this story, its picture and headline, help the company and employees?" He does not ask whether the story is amusing or entertaining but "Will it help the company and employees?"

The next step is to create and design the articles. Photographs are decided on first because they have to be set up and shot. Meanwhile, Williams and his staff interview the appropriate people. The format of each article is determined by its purpose. For example, the purpose of one article, which had to convey both good news and bad news, was to inform, reestablish trust, and allay fears. To accomplish that, Williams believed that readers needed to hear "the sound of another person's voice." In this case, the voice was to be that of a top manager. He invited several Allstate employees to join the interview session, and they posed questions for the top manager to answer. This lively question-and-answer session provided the basis of the article.

The result of all that careful planning? Eight weeks after an editorial board discussion, nearly 50,000 employees arrived on a Friday morning to find the latest issue of *Allstate Now* on their desks. When they finished reading it, they had been unobtrusively assured, through words and pictures, of their important place in creating Allstate's future.

Apply Your Knowledge

1. As editor of *Allstate Now*, how would you plan to communicate the following changes at Allstate as being in the best interests of the employees: (a) dropping the slogan "The Good Hands People," (b) moving corporate headquarters from Illinois to Texas, (c) acquiring the home and auto insurance divisions of a major competitor?

2. Imagine you're planning articles for *Allstate Now*. List the advantages and disadvantages of the following changes: (a) expanding the publication from 8 to 16 pages per issue, (b) publishing every two weeks instead of monthly, (c) receiving permission to use color photographs and a second color in the design.

letter is more manageable than one that's two pages long, and a two-page memo is more likely to be read than a ten-page report.

If your written message has to be long, make it easy for readers to follow so that they can pick it up and put it down several times without losing the thread of what you're saying. Begin with a summary of key points, use plenty of headings, and put important points in list format so that they'll stand out. Put less important information in separate enclosures or appendixes, and use charts and graphs to dramatize important ideas.

If you're delivering a long message orally, be sure to give listeners an overview of the message's structure, and then express your thoughts clearly and logically. You might also use flip charts, slides, or handouts to help listeners understand and remember key points. You're the guide, leading your audience through your message by telling them where they've been and where they're going.

> Devices that make your messages easier to comprehend include summaries and overviews, headings, lists, enclosures, appendixes, handouts, charts, and graphs.

E STABLISHING THE MAIN IDEA

Regardless of an issue's complexity, one central point sums up everything. This is your theme, your main idea. Everything else in the message either supports this point or demonstrates its implications.

A topic and a main idea are different. The **topic** is the broad subject of the message. The **main idea** makes a statement about the topic—one of many possible statements—that provides a rationale, explains your purpose in terms that the audience can accept. Barad might give a presentation on the topic of Barbie's image with the aim of persuading critics that Barbie has become an acceptable role model for young girls. Her main idea might be that Barbie's careers and culturally diverse friends have made the doll a better person.

The main idea has to strike a response in the intended audience. It has to motivate people to do what you want by linking your purpose with their own. When you're preparing a brief letter, memo, or meeting, the main idea may be pretty obvious, especially if you're dealing with simple facts that have little or no emotional content for the audience. In such cases the main idea may be nothing more than "Here is what you wanted." If you're responding to a request for information about the price and availability of your company's products, your main idea would be something like "We have these items at competitive prices."

> The main idea is the "hook" that sums up why a particular audience should do or think as you suggest.

Finding the "angle" or "hook" is more complicated when you're trying to convince someone (see Chapter 11) or when you have disappointing information to convey (see Chapter 10). In these situations, look for a main idea that will establish a good relationship between you and your audience. Focus on some point of agreement or common interest. In longer documents and presentations, in which a mass of material needs to be unified, the problem of establishing a main idea becomes still more challenging. You need to identify a generalization that encompasses all the individual points you want to make. For tougher assignments like these, you may need to take special measures to come up with a main idea.

Use Prewriting Techniques

Identifying the main idea often requires creativity and experimentation. The best approach is to **brainstorm,** letting your mind wander over the possibilities and testing various alternatives against your purpose, your audience, and the facts at your disposal. How do you generate those possibilities? Successful communicators use various prewriting approaches:

- *Storyteller's tour.* Turn on your tape recorder and pretend that you've just run into an old friend on the street. She says, "So, what are you working on these days?" Give her an overview of your message, focusing on your reasons for communicating, your major points, your rationale, and the implications for your intended audience. Listen critically to the tape; then repeat the exercise until you are able to give a smooth, two-minute summary that conveys the gist of your message. The summary should reveal your main idea.

- *Random list.* On a clean sheet of paper or a computer screen, list everything that pops into your head pertaining to your message. When you've exhausted the possibilities, study the list for relationships. Sort the items into groups, as you would sort a deck of cards into suits. Look for common denominators; the connection might be geographic, sequential, spatial, chronological, or topical. Part of the list might break down into problems, causes, and solutions; another part, into pros and cons. Regardless of what categories finally emerge, the sorting process will help you sift through your thoughts and decide what's important and what isn't.

- *FCR worksheet.* If your subject involves the solution to a problem, you might try using an FCR worksheet to help you visualize the relationships among your findings (F), your conclusions (C), and your recommendations (R). For example, you might find that you're losing sales to a competitor who offers lower prices than you do (F). From this, you might conclude that your loss of sales is due to your pricing policy (C). This conclusion would lead you to recommend a price cut (R). To make an FCR worksheet, divide a sheet of paper or a computer screen into three columns. List the major findings in the first column; then extrapolate conclusions and write them in the second column. These conclusions form the basis for the recommendations, which are listed in the third column. An analysis of the three columns should help you focus on the main idea.

- *Journalistic approach.* For informational messages, the journalistic approach may provide a good point of departure. The answers to six questions—*who, what, where, when, why,* and *how*—should clarify the main idea.

- *Question-and-answer chain.* Perhaps the best approach is to look at the subject from your audience's perspective. Ask yourself: "What is the audience's main question? What do they need to know?" Examine your answers to those questions. What additional questions emerge? Follow the chain of questions and answers until you have replied to every conceivable question that might occur to a reasonable audience. By thinking about your material from their point of view, you are more likely to pinpoint the main idea.

Some techniques for establishing the main idea:

- Storyteller's tour
- Random list
- FCR worksheet
- Journalistic approach
- Question-and-answer chain

Limit the Scope

There's a limit to how much you can communicate in a given number of words. What can be accomplished depends on the nature of the subject, the audience members' familiarity with the topic, their receptivity to your conclusions, and your existing credibility. In general, presenting routine information to a knowledgeable audience that already knows and respects you takes fewer words. Building consensus about a complex and controversial subject takes longer, especially if the audience is composed of skeptical or hostile strangers.

The main idea should be geared to the length of the message.

Although you may have to adjust your message to fit the time or space available, don't change the number of major points. Regardless of how long the message will be, stick with three or four major points—five at the very most. According to communication researchers, that's all your audience will remember.[11] So if you're delivering a long message, say, a 60-minute presentation or a 20-page report, the major points can be developed in considerable detail. You can spend about ten minutes or ten paragraphs (or more than three pages of double-spaced, typewritten text) on each of your key points and still have room for the introduction and conclusion. If your message is brief, four minutes or one page, you'll have only a minute or a paragraph each for the introduction, conclusion, and major points.

S ELECTING THE APPROPRIATE CHANNEL AND MEDIUM

The communication media available to businesspeople have mushroomed in the past two decades: audiotapes, videotapes, fax machines, electronic mail, voice mail, teleconferences—to name a few. You can now select not only from the traditional oral and written channels but also from the newer electronic channel, which includes some features of the other two. Your selection of channel and medium can make the difference between effective and ineffective communication.[12] So when choosing a channel (whether oral, written, or electronic) and a medium (whether face-to-face conversation, telephone conversation, E-mail, voice mail, videotape, written report, etc.), do your best to match your selections to your message and your intentions.[13]

Various types of messages require various communication channels.

Various cultures tend to favor one channel over another. For example, the United States, Canada, and Germany emphasize written media, whereas Japan emphasizes oral media—perhaps because its high-context culture carries so much of the message in nonverbal cues and "between the lines" interpretation.[14] Within the United States, the basic choice of oral, written, or electronic channels depends on the purpose, the audience, and the characteristics of the three communication channels (see Table 5.1).

Oral Communication

In general, use oral communication if your purpose is to collaborate with the audience.

The chief advantage of oral communication is the opportunity it provides for immediate feedback. This is the channel to use when you want the audience to ask questions and make comments or when you're trying to reach a group decision. Face-to-face communication is useful when you're presenting controversial information, because you can read the audience's body language and adjust your message accordingly. Face-to-face communication is the richest medium, but it's also one of the most restrictive; you and your audience must be in the same place at the same time. Even so, its richness makes it the standard for measuring the effectiveness of all other media.[15]

Your choice between a face-to-face conversation and a telephone or conference call would depend on the location of the audience, the importance of the message, and how much you need the sort of nonverbal feedback that only body language can reveal. In fact, oral communication can take many forms, including conversations, telephone calls, interviews, small group meetings, seminars, workshops, training programs, formal speeches, and major presentations. Chapters 17 and 18 explore these media in more detail.

Written Communication

Written communication increases the sender's control but eliminates the possibility of immediate feedback.

Written messages also take many forms. At one extreme are the scribbled notes people use to jog their own memories; at the other are elaborate, formal reports that rival magazines in graphic quality. Regardless of the form, written messages have one big advantage: They let you plan and control the message. A written format is appropriate when the information is complex, when a permanent record is needed for fu-

Table 5.1 **WHEN TO TALK IT OVER, WRITE IT OUT, OR APPLY TECHNOLOGY**		
Oral Messages Are Best If	**Written Messages Are Best If**	**Electronic Messages Are Best If**
You want immediate feedback from the audience	You need no immediate feedback	You need no immediate feedback, but you do need speed
Your message is simple and easy to accept	Your message is detailed and complex and requires careful planning	Your message is emotional, you may or may not need immediate feedback, but you're physically separated (videotape, teleconference)
You need no permanent record	You need a permanent, verifiable record	You need no permanent record, but you want to overcome time-zone barriers (voice mail, fax)
You can assemble the audience conveniently and economically	You need to reach an audience that is large and geographically dispersed	You need to reach an audience that is large and geographically dispersed, and you want to reach them personally (teleconference, videotape)
You want to encourage interaction to solve a problem or reach a decision	You want to minimize the chances of distortion that occur when a message is passed orally from person to person	You want to minimize oral distortion, but you're in a hurry and in a distant location (E-mail)

ture reference, when the audience is large and geographically dispersed, and when immediate interaction with the audience is either unimportant or undesirable.

For extensive coverage of letters and memos, see Chapters 8 through 11. Reports are thoroughly discussed in Chapters 14 through 18. In addition, Appendix B presents a detailed discussion of the accepted formats for business documents. Although many types of written communication are specialized, the most common are letters, memos, and reports.

Letters and Memos

With a few exceptions, most letters and memos are relatively brief documents, generally one or two pages long. Memos are the "workhorses" of business communication, used for the routine, day-to-day exchange of information within an organization. Letters go to outsiders, and they perform an important public relations function in addition to conveying a particular message. Memos are usually brief, lacking a salutation and emphasizing the needs of readers who have time only to skim messages. They can also be sent to any number of receivers, whereas a letter is sent to only one. Because of their open construction and method of delivery, memos are less private than letters. You can use memos to designate responsibility, communicate the same material to many people, communicate policy and procedure, confirm oral agreements or decisions, and place specific information on record.

Figure 5.2
A Typical Letter

Irma Cameron uses letterhead enhanced with her name to give a personal touch.

The formal salutation indicates Cameron's respect for a customer she doesn't know.

The body of the letter is brief but still includes a number of friendly remarks designed to maintain goodwill.

The signature also demonstrates a personal touch.

General Mills, Inc.
General Offices

Post Office Box 1113
Minneapolis, Minnesota 55440

IRMA K. CAMERON
Manager, Consumer Relations

May 6, 1996

Mr. Ron Philip
280 Lake Drive
Kalispell, MT 59901

Dear Mr. Philip:

Your letter was a day brightener for the Cheerio brand group and for us in the Consumer Relations Department. We were all delighted to learn how much you enjoy Cheerios.

You are right! Cheerios was first introduced in the same year you were born, 1941. Perhaps that explains your affection for those little Cheerioats, as the product was initially called.

Congratulations to you and your wife as you await the arrival of your baby. I am sending something separately to help welcome the newest member of your "Cheerios family."

Best wishes,

Irma K. Cameron

Irma K. Cameron
Manager, Consumer Relations

ss

Enclosure

General Offices and Betty Crocker Kitchens at Number One General Mills Boulevard

---

Letters and memos are organized according to their purpose; the relationship between writer and reader dictates their style and tone.

Letters (see Figure 5.2) and memos (see Figure 5.3) can be classified by function into four categories: direct requests; routine, good-news, and goodwill messages; bad-news messages; and persuasive messages. Their function determines their organization, but their style and tone are governed by your relationship with your audience.

Reports and Proposals

Reports are generally longer and more formal than letters and memos, and they have more components.

These factual, objective documents may be distributed either to insiders or to outsiders, depending on their purpose and subject. They come in many formats, including preprinted forms, letters, memos, and manuscripts. In length, they range from a few pages to several hundred. Generally, reports and proposals are longer than letters and memos, with a larger number of distinct elements. Reports and proposals also tend to be more formal than letters and memos. As in all forms of business communication, the organization, style, and tone of reports and proposals depend on the message's purpose, the relationship between writer and reader, and the traditions of the organization. Thus the basic composition process is much the same for all.

Figure 5.3
A Typical Memo

Every memo is headed with four pieces of information—to, from, subject, and date—even when a plain sheet of paper is used.

The writer, Irma Cameron, states her business right away.

Direct phrasing may be used more frequently in memos than in letters, especially when a boss is telling an employee what to do.

Common courtesy never hurts.

Electronic Communication

Although oral messages can be in person and face-to-face, they can also be transmitted electronically using voice mail, teleconferencing, audiotape, videotape, closed-circuit television, and so on. Similarly, although written messages can be handwritten, typed, or printed, they can also be transmitted electronically using faxes, E-mail, computer conferencing, and so on. Electronic media are useful when you need speed, when you're physically separated from your audience, when you need to overcome time-zone barriers, and when you need to reach a dispersed audience personally. Chapter 4 introduces the technological features of electronic media; following are a few pointers on when to select electronic media over traditional oral or written media:[16]

In general, use electronic communication for speed, to overcome time-zone barriers, and to reach a widely dispersed audience personally.

- *Voice mail* is usually used to replace short memos and phone calls that need no response. It is most effective for short, unambiguous messages.
- *Teleconferencing* is good for informational meetings, but it's ineffective for negotiation. It's an efficient alternative to a face-to-face meeting, but it can't totally simulate one. For example, teleconferencing discourages the "secondary" conversations that usually occur during a meeting of more than four or five people—which could either prevent participants from sharing valuable information or encourage them to focus on the topic.
- *Videotape* is often effective for reaching a large number of people with a motivational message. By communicating nonverbal cues, it can strengthen your image of sincerity and trustworthiness; however, it offers no opportunity for immediate feedback.
- *Fax* messages are usually used to overcome time-zone barriers when a hard copy is required. A fax has all the characteristics of a written message, except that it may lack the privacy of a letter, and depending on the quality of your audience's ma-

chine (thermal versus plain-paper, for example), your message may appear less crisp, perhaps even less professional, than other written messages.

- *E-mail* offers advantages of speed, lower cost, and increased access to other employees. This medium is best at communicating brief, noncomplex information that's time-sensitive, but its effectiveness depends on the skills of the people using it.
- *Computer conferencing* offers the advantage of democracy; that is, more attention is focused on an idea than on who communicates it. However, too much emphasis on the message (to the neglect of the person communicating it) can threaten corporate culture, which needs a more dynamic medium of communication.

Message planning encompasses valuable tasks that help you gain more control over the composition process. Use this chapter's Checklist for Planning Business Messages not as a recipe but as a reminder of what tasks and choices to address as you develop your business messages.

CHECKLIST FOR PLANNING BUSINESS MESSAGES

A. Purpose
1. Determine whether the purpose of your message is to inform, persuade, or collaborate.
2. Identify the specific behavior you hope to induce in the audience.
3. Make sure that your purpose is worthwhile and realistic.

B. Audience
1. Identify the primary audience.
2. Determine the size and composition of the group.
3. Analyze the audience's probable reaction to your message.
4. Determine the audience's level of understanding.
5. Evaluate your relationship with the audience.
6. Analyze the audience's informational, motivational, and practical needs.

C. Main Idea
1. Stimulate your creativity with brainstorming techniques.
2. Identify a "hook" that will motivate the audience to respond to your message in the way you intend.
3. Evaluate whether the main idea is realistic given the length limitations imposed on the message.
4. Collect any necessary information.

D. Channel and Medium
1. If your purpose is to collaborate, give an informal, relatively unstructured oral presentation to a small group.
2. If you are celebrating an important public occasion, give a prepared speech to a large audience.
3. If you need a permanent record, if the message is complex, or if immediate feedback is unimportant, prepare a written message.
   - a. Send a letter if your message is relatively simple and the audience is outside the company.
   - b. Send a memo if your message is relatively simple and the audience is inside the company.
   - c. Write a report if your message is objective and complex.
4. If you need to communicate quickly, overcome time-zone differences, or personally reach a widely dispersed audience, choose electronic communication.
   - a. Use voice mail if your message is short and clear.
   - b. Use teleconferencing for informational meetings.
   - c. Use videotape for sending motivational messages to a large number of people.
   - d. Use fax machines to overcome time-zone barriers.
   - e. Use E-mail for speed, lower cost, and increased access to other employees.
   - f. Use computer conferencing to focus attention on ideas instead of status.

On the Job

SOLVING A COMMUNICATION DILEMMA AT MATTEL

Convincing the world that Barbie is more than just a bimbo is not an easy task, but Jill Barad is doing her best with careful planning and a thorough understanding of her audience. Part of Barad's problem is that Mattel's purposes are mixed. On the one hand, the company wants Barbie to be a worthy role model for little girls. On the other hand, Mattel wants to sell dolls and accessories—and that means that Barbie must retain her traditional appeal. After all, 500 million people have voted with their pocketbooks for the Barbie doll whose number-one priority is what to wear. More than $1 billion in yearly doll sales is at stake. Barad knows that completely changing Barbie's image could jeopardize the doll's mystique and hurt sales.

To a great extent, that mystique depends on Barbie's lack of a strong identity. Mattel intentionally says very little about Barbie's character because it wants little girls themselves to decide what Barbie is like. Her bland personality and her wide assortment of clothes and accessories allow for endless possibilities. Barbie can be whatever a child wants her to be.

Still, an image of Barbie emerges from a variety of messages—advertising, public relations events, and *Barbie* magazine, a glossy publication sent to 650,000 members of Barbie's fan club. The magazine describes Barbie's clothes and activities. In a recent issue, for example, Ken took Barbie out to dinner at a "sumptuous restaurant." For the occasion, Barbie chose her "ravishing new pink ruffled evening dress." Perhaps the strongest statement about Barbie's personality was a two-hour cartoon special featuring her experiences with her all-girl rock band. But even there, Barbie's character remained a mystery. All she did on the show was sing and play music.

Although in many ways Mattel has reinforced the popular image of Barbie, the company has raised her consciousness. In the mid-1970s, the company surveyed mothers and asked their opinion of Barbie. Many responded that she lacked ambition and should get a job. According to Jill Barad, the public was delighted when Mattel reacted by launching Barbie's career. Now Barbie is a better person, says Barad, who comments that Barbie "does have talent and skills, and goes to work and makes money, and that's how she affords her car!" She has also embraced cultural diversity. Barbie's pals are African American, Asian, and Hispanic, and there are African American and Hispanic versions of Barbie herself.

Mattel is also winning points for Barbie by emphasizing the doll's therapeutic value. Children's Hospital in Los Angeles uses Barbie to help youngsters who are going through an amputation. The hospital staff removes Barbie's arm or leg, fits her with an artificial limb, and gives her to the child as a gift. Ellen Zaman, director of patient family services, notes, "It helps the children understand what will happen to them."

As a symbol of popular culture, Barbie has also gained a measure of respectability. Scholars write learned articles analyzing her significance. The Toy Manufacturers of America have acknowledged her unique place in the history of toys. The Smithsonian sponsored a special Barbie exhibit. For her 30th birthday, a crowd of toy manufacturers, collectors, and fans assembled at Lincoln Center to pay tribute to America's number-one doll. Needless to say, Barbie wowed them in her rose gown, her pink feather boa, and her lavish earrings.

Your Mission: You have recently joined Mattel's marketing department. One of your responsibilities is to respond to letters about Barbie. Your goal is to emphasize Barbie's positive qualities, to reinforce her popularity with youngsters, and to handle her critics as diplomatically as possible. Choose the best alternatives for handling the following correspondence, and be prepared to explain why your choice is best:

1. You have received a letter from Alice Brown, a reporter for *Ms.* magazine, who is writing an article tentatively entitled "Barbie: Reflection or Molder of Contemporary Values?" Brown has asked you for information about the marketing campaign that Mattel has employed to mold Barbie's image over the years. When responding to Brown's request, what should your purpose be?

   a. The general purpose is to inform. The specific purpose is to provide Brown with a brief summary of the evolution of Mattel's marketing campaign for Barbie over the past 30 years.

   b. The general purpose is to persuade. The specific purpose is to convince Brown that Barbie is a worthy role model for young girls and that the marketing campaign portrays Barbie as a socially aware, successful career woman.

   c. The general purpose is to collaborate. The specific purpose is to work with Brown to develop an article that examines the evolution of Mattel's marketing campaign for Barbie.

   d. The general purpose is to respond. The specific purpose is to convey details requested by a journalist.

2. Assume that your purpose is to convince Brown of Barbie's worthiness as a role model who is a socially aware, successful career woman. Does this purpose meet the tests suggested in the chapter?

   a. Yes. The purpose is realistic. The timing is right. You are the right person to send the message. And the purpose is acceptable to the organization.

   b. Not completely. Realistically, Brown may not accept Barbie as an admirable role model for young girls. Even though Barbie now has a career and some friends from other cultural backgrounds, her basic image has not changed a great deal.

c. The purpose is fine, but you are not the right person to send the message. Mattel's president should respond.

d. The timing is right for this message. Stress Barbie's involvement in social causes and in career activities. Show how unimportant fashion is to Barbie's new lifestyle.

3. When planning your reply, what assumptions can you safely make about your audience?

a. The audience includes not only Alice Brown but also the readers of *Ms.* magazine. Given their feminist bias, the readers will probably be hostile to business in general and Barbie in particular. They probably know virtually nothing about the toy business. Furthermore, they probably mistrust you because you are a Mattel employee.

b. Alice Brown will probably be the only person who reads the letter directly; she represents the primary audience, whereas the readers of her article are the secondary audience. Brown will be happy to hear from Mattel and will read the information with an open mind. As a journalist, Brown is probably intelligent and objective. However, she may not know a great deal about Mattel or about marketing. Although she is a stranger to you, she trusts your credibility as a Mattel spokesperson.

c. Alice Brown is probably the sole and primary audience for the letter. The fact that she is writing an article about Barbie suggests that she enjoyed playing with the doll as a child and that she knows a great deal about Barbie already. In all likelihood, she will respond positively to your reply and will trust your credibility as a Mattel representative.

d. Alice Brown may be an industrial spy working for a rival toy company. She will show your reply to people who work for your competitor; they will analyze the information and use it to improve their own marketing program at your expense.

4. Assume that your purpose is to inform Alice Brown that the approach to marketing Barbie has evolved in response to societal changes. Which of the following main ideas best supports this purpose?

a. Mattel's marketing department reports to a successful black woman who has improved Barbie's image with liberated women and ethnic minorities.

b. Barbie has learned to dress for success in the world of work.

c. In response to changes in society's values, Mattel has revised its marketing program to allow Barbie to appear as a strong, successful career woman who may be black, white, or Latino, and as a popular person with friends from many cultures.

d. Mattel keeps Barbie's personality a mystery so that children can use their imaginations to create the Barbie of their dreams.

5. Which channel and medium of communication should you use in replying to Alice Brown?

a. Call her on the phone to ask for clarification of her needs; then follow up with a letter report (4 to 20 pages, written in letter format).

b. Call her on the phone, ask for clarification of her needs, and answer her while you have her on the line.

c. Write a letter asking for clarification of her needs, and follow up with a letter report.

d. Send a form letter used for replying to all inquiries about Barbie.[17]

Questions for Discussion

1. Some writers argue that planning messages wastes time because they inevitably change their plans as they go along. How would you respond to this argument?

2. Your supervisor has asked you to prepare a message that, in your opinion, serves no worthwhile purpose. What do you do?

3. As editor of your company's newsletter, how would you go about discovering the needs of your fellow employees?

4. List several main ideas you might use if you were trying to persuade top management to invest in word-processing equipment and software.

5. As personnel manager, decide which medium would be best to use for explaining employee benefits to new employees. Explain your decision.

6. As a member of the public relations department, recommend the best medium to use for informing the local community that your toxic-waste cleanup program has been successful. Explain your recommendation.

Exercises

1. Make a list of the communication tasks you'll need to accomplish in the next week or so (a job application, a letter of complaint, a speech to a class, an order for some merchandise, etc.). For each, determine a general and a specific purpose.

2. List five messages you have received lately, such as direct-mail promotions, letters, phone solicitations, and lectures. For each, answer the following questions: Was the message well timed? Did the sender choose an appropriate channel and medium for the message? Did the appropriate person deliver the message?

3. Barbara Marquardt is in charge of public relations for a cruise line that operates out of Miami. She is shocked to read a letter in a local newspaper from a disgruntled passenger, complaining about the service and entertainment on a recent cruise. Marquardt will have to respond to these publicized criticisms in some way. What audiences will she need to consider in her response? What channels and media should she choose? If the letter had been published in a travel publication widely read by travel agents and cruise travelers, how might her course of action differ?

4. For each communication task below, write brief answers to three questions: Who is my audience? What is my audience's general attitude toward my subject? What does my audience need to know?

   a. A final-notice collection letter from an appliance manufacturer to an appliance dealer, sent ten days before initiating legal collection procedures
   b. An unsolicited sales letter asking readers to purchase computer disks at near-wholesale prices
   c. An advertisement for peanut butter
   d. Fliers to be attached to doorknobs in the neighborhood, announcing reduced rates for chimney cleaning or repairs
   e. A cover letter sent along with your résumé to a potential employer

5. Choose an electronic device that you know how to operate well (videocassette recorder, home computer, telephone answering machine, etc.). Write two sets of instructions for operating the device: one set for a reader who has never used that type of machine and one set for someone who is generally familiar with that type of machine but has never operated the specific model.

6. You're looking for a job as a salesperson, so you'd better be able to sell yourself first. What special qualities do you have that would make you a desirable sales employee? Use the techniques described in the chapter to come up with a main idea you can use in your efforts to market yourself. In no more than a paragraph, draft a statement of your main idea that tells your audience (potential employers) what to do or think about you and why.

COMPOSING BUSINESS MESSAGES

After studying this chapter, you will be able to

Identify the characteristics of a well-organized message

Explain why organization is important to both the audience and the communicator

Break a main idea into subdivisions grouped under logical categories

Arrange ideas in direct or indirect order, depending on the audience's probable reaction

Compose a message using a style and tone that are appropriate to your subject, purpose, audience, and format

Use the "you" attitude to interest the audience in your message

On the Job

FACING A COMMUNICATION DILEMMA AT DRAKE BEAM MORIN
Putting a Silver Lining on the Pink Slip

"Layoffs Hit Executive Suite in Wake of Merger"; "Thousands of Jobs in Jeopardy as Economy Continues to Decline"; "Pink Slips Flow at Local Company Following Loss of Major Contract." When headlines like these predict doom and gloom for the employees of one or more companies, most people feel at least a moment of vicarious apprehension about losing their jobs. However, at Drake Beam Morin, the country's largest outplacement firm, such bad news has a silver lining. When trouble strikes a company or an industry, outplacement executives see an opportunity to counsel those involved in the job termination process.

Outplacement services vary, but most of the leading firms like Drake Beam Morin provide help both for the managers involved in doing the firing and for the people who are losing their jobs. Managers are taught to handle the legal and emotional complexities of the dismissal process; terminated employees get help in coping with rejection and finding new jobs.

Corporations and dismissed employees clearly derive both psychological and practical benefits from such programs; however, the price is steep. Outplacement firms typically charge 15 percent of the fired executive's total annual compensation. In most cases, the employer picks up the tab. So if a company fires a manager who makes $100,000, providing the individual with outplacement service would cost $15,000. Since many terminations are cost-cutting moves involving a substantial number of employees, corporations naturally think twice before buying outplacement services. More often than not, the corporation is already obligated by law to provide other termination benefits, such as severance pay, accrued vacation time, and extended insurance coverage.

   If you worked for Drake Beam Morin, what sort of letter could you write to stimulate an executive's interest in your service? How important will organization be to your letter? Will an outline help? What style will work best? How will the tone of your letter affect potential clients?[1]

Organizing Your Message

Like Drake Beam Morin, all business communicators face the problem of compressing a complicated web of ideas into a linear message that proceeds point by point. People simply don't remember dissociated facts and figures, so successful communicators rely on organization to make their messages meaningful.[2] Before thinking about *how* to achieve good organization, however, think about *what* it means and *why* it's important.

Drake Beam Morin

What Good Organization Means

If you've ever received a disorganized message, you're familiar with the frustration of trying to sort through a muddle of ideas. Consider this letter from Jill Saunders, the office manager at Boswell & Sons, mapmakers:

Our president, Mr. Boswell, was in an accident last year, and he hasn't been able to work full-time. His absence has affected our business, so we don't have the budget we used to. His two sons are working hard, so we aren't bankrupt by any means, and soon Mr. Boswell will be coming back full-time.

Boswell & Sons has been doing business with Computertime since I was hired six years ago. Your building was smaller then, and it was located on the corner of Federal Avenue and 2nd N.W. Mr. Boswell bought our first laser printer there. I still remember the day. It was the biggest check I'd ever written. Of course, over the years, I've gotten used to larger purchases.

We have seven employees. Although all of them aren't directly involved in producing the maps we sell, they all need to have their computers working so that they can do their jobs. The 5-1/4-inch disk drive we bought for my assistant, Suzanne, has been a problem. We've taken it in for repairs three times in three months to the authorized service center, and Suzanne is very careful with the machine and hasn't abused it. She likes playing interactive adventure games on lunch breaks. It still doesn't work right, and she's tired of hauling it back and forth. We're all putting in longer hours to make up for Mr. Boswell's not being here, and none of us has a lot of spare time.

This is the first time we've returned anything to your store, and I hope you'll agree that we deserve a better deal.

   This letter displays the sort of disorganization that readers find frustrating. By taking a closer look at what's wrong, you can identify the four most common faults responsible for organization problems:

Most disorganized communication suffers from problems with content, grouping, or sequence.

- *Taking too long to get to the point.* Saunders wrote three paragraphs before introducing the topic: the faulty disk drive. Then she waited until the final paragraph to state her purpose: requesting an adjustment.

■ *Including irrelevant material.* Saunders introduced information that has no bearing on her purpose or her topic. Does it matter that the computer store used to be smaller or that it was in a different location? What difference does it make whether Saunders's boss is working only part-time or whether her assistant likes playing computer games during lunch?

■ *Getting ideas mixed up.* Saunders seems to be making six points: (1) her company has money to spend, (2) it's an old customer, (3) it pays by check, (4) it has purchased numerous items at the store, (5) the disk drive doesn't work, and (6) Saunders wants an adjustment. However, the ideas are in the wrong places. It would be more logical to begin with the fact that the machine doesn't work, and some of these ideas should be combined under the general idea that the company is a valuable cutomer.

■ *Leaving out necessary information.* The customer service representative may want to know the make, model, and price of the disk drive; the date on which it was purchased; the specific problems the machine has had; and whether the repairs were covered by the warranty. Saunders also failed to specify what she wants the store to do. Does she want a new disk drive of the same type? A different model? Or simply her money back?

> A message is well organized when all the pieces fit together in a coherent pattern.

Achieving good organization can be a challenge. Nevertheless, by working with these four common faults, you can establish what good organization means. Four guidelines can help you recognize a well-organized message:

■ The subject and purpose are clear.
■ All the information is related to the subject and purpose.
■ The ideas are grouped and presented in a logical way.
■ All necessary information is included.

Observing these four rules changes the previous letter so that the message can be easily and effectively communicated:

Boswell & Sons bought an Olympic Systems, Model PRS-2, 5-1/4-inch floppy disk drive from your store on November 15, during your pre-Christmas sale, when it was marked down to $199.95. We didn't use the unit until January, because it was purchased for my assistant, who unexpectedly took a six-week leave. You can imagine her frustration when she first tried using it and it didn't work.

We took the machine to the authorized service center and were assured that the problem was merely a loose connection. The service representative fixed the drive, but three weeks later it broke again--another loose connection. For the next month, the drive worked reasonably well, although the response time was occasionally slow. Two months ago, the drive stopped working again. Once more, the service representative blamed a loose connection and made the repair. Although the drive is working now, it isn't working very well. The response time is still subject to delay, and the motor seems to drag sometimes.

What is your policy on exchanging unsatisfactory merchandise? Although all the repairs have been relatively minor and have been covered by the one-year warranty, we are not satisfied with the drive. We would like to exchange it for a similar model from another manufacturer. If the new

As general manager of Ford's plastic products division, Ronald E. Goldsberry exemplifies the busy executive whose day is fragmented by such diverse activities as merger coordination, budget decisions, personnel problems, product decisions, and on and on. Goldsberry appreciates business messages that do not waste his time. He advises that you make sure the message is efficient, clear, and logical in organization.

drive costs more than the old one, we will pay the difference, even though we generally look for equipment with a heavy business discount.

Boswell & Sons has done business with your store for six years and until now has always been satisfied with your merchandise. We are counting on you to live up to your reputation for standing behind your products. Please let us hear from you soon.

Why Good Organization Is Important

You might be asking yourself whether it matters that the message is well organized, as long as the point is eventually made. Why not just let the ideas flow naturally and trust that the audience will grasp the meaning? By arranging your ideas logically and diplomatically, you help readers concentrate on your message. Readers are not obligated to pay attention to what they read, but with good organization, you can help them do so.

- *Helping your audience understand your message.* The less work required of your audience to figure out your message, the better they understand what you're trying to say. If you're interested in getting your message across, good organization is one of your handiest tools because it makes your message easier to understand and remember. A well-organized message satisfies the audience's need for information.
- *Helping your audience accept your message.* Good organization helps motivate your audience to accept your message. As the letter in Figure 6.1 shows, you can soften refusals, leave a better impression, and be more convincing by organizing messages diplomatically. You can also use good organization to enhance your credibility and add authority to your messages.
- *Saving your audience's time.* Well-organized messages are efficient. They contain only relevant ideas, so your audience doesn't waste time on superfluous information. Moreover, all the information in a well-organized message is in a logical place. The audience can follow the thought pattern without a struggle, and they can save even more time by looking for just the information they need instead of reading everything.
- *Simplifying your communication task.* Finally, being well organized helps you compose your message more quickly and efficiently. By thinking about what you're going to say and how you're going to say it before you begin to write, you can proceed more confidently. You can use your organizational plan to get some advance input from your boss to be sure you're on the right track *before* you spend hours working on a draft. If you're working on a large, complex project, you can use the plan to divide the writing job among co-workers to finish the assignment as quickly as possible.

The main reason for being well organized is to improve the chances that people will understand exactly what you mean.

Good organization also helps you get your ideas across without upsetting the audience.

Well-organized messages are efficient because they contain only relevant information.

Organizing what you're going to say before you start to write makes the job much easier.

How Good Organization Is Achieved

Understanding the *need* for good organization is half the battle. Knowing *how* to organize your messages well is the other half. At companies like Drake Beam Morin, employees achieve good organization by following the two-step process: First you define and group the ideas; then you establish their sequence with a carefully selected organizational pattern.

Define and Group Ideas

The brainstorming techniques described in Chapter 5 will help you generate your main idea, but they won't tell you how to develop it or how to group the supporting details

According to co-workers, Jane Pauley is a much better writer than most TV journalists—part of the reason for her success. Good organization is the key to good writing, says Pauley. Once you have defined the main idea, you decide how to break it down into logical pieces by considering your purpose and your subject matter.

Figure 6.1
Sample Letter Demonstrating the Importance of Good Organization

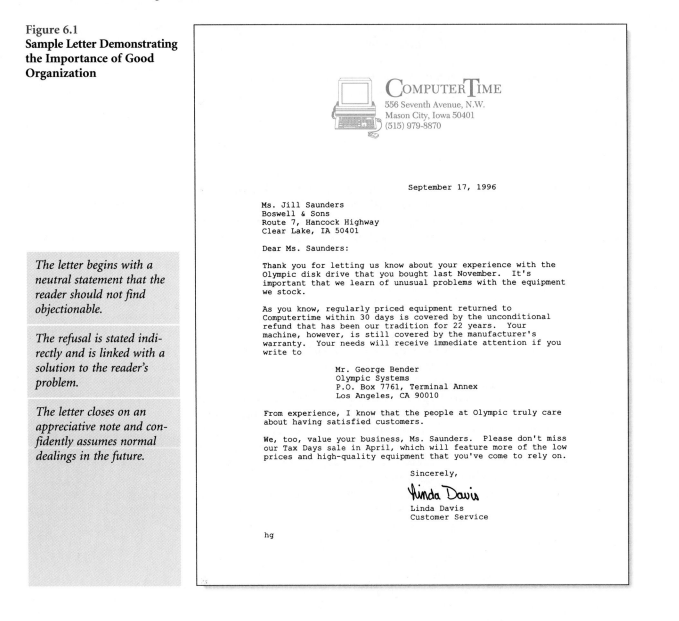

The letter begins with a neutral statement that the reader should not find objectionable.

The refusal is stated indirectly and is linked with a solution to the reader's problem.

The letter closes on an appreciative note and confidently assumes normal dealings in the future.

COMPUTERTIME
556 Seventh Avenue, N.W.
Mason City, Iowa 50401
(515) 979-8870

September 17, 1996

Ms. Jill Saunders
Boswell & Sons
Route 7, Hancock Highway
Clear Lake, IA 50401

Dear Ms. Saunders:

Thank you for letting us know about your experience with the Olympic disk drive that you bought last November. It's important that we learn of unusual problems with the equipment we stock.

As you know, regularly priced equipment returned to Computertime within 30 days is covered by the unconditional refund that has been our tradition for 22 years. Your machine, however, is still covered by the manufacturer's warranty. Your needs will receive immediate attention if you write to

Mr. George Bender
Olympic Systems
P.O. Box 7761, Terminal Annex
Los Angeles, CA 90010

From experience, I know that the people at Olympic truly care about having satisfied customers.

We, too, value your business, Ms. Saunders. Please don't miss our Tax Days sale in April, which will feature more of the low prices and high-quality equipment that you've come to rely on.

Sincerely,

Linda Davis

Linda Davis
Customer Service

hg

in the most logical and effective way. To decide on the final structure of your message, you need to visualize how all the points fit together. One way to do this is to construct an outline. Even if all you do is jot down three or four points on the back of an envelope, making a plan and sticking to it will help you cover the important details.

When you're preparing a long, complex message, an outline is indispensable because it helps you visualize the relationship among the various parts. Without an outline, you may be inclined to ramble. As you're describing one point, another point may occur to you—so you describe it. One detour leads to another, and before you know it, you've forgotten the original point. With an outline to guide you, however, you can communicate in a more systematic way, covering all the necessary ideas in an effective order and with proper emphasis. Following an outline also helps you express the transitions between points so that your message is coherent and the audience will understand the relationship among your ideas.

An outline or a schematic diagram will help you visualize the relationship among parts of a message.

You're no doubt familiar with the basic alphanumeric outline, which uses numbers and letters to identify each point and indents them to show which ideas are of equal status. (Chapter 13 tells more about the various formats that can be used in this type of outlining.) A more schematic approach illustrates the structure of your message in an "organization chart" like one that depicts a company's management structure (see Figure 6.2). The main idea is shown in the highest-level box, and like a top executive, it establishes the big picture. The lower-level ideas, like lower-level employees, provide the details. All the ideas are logically organized into divisions of thought, just as a company is organized into divisions and departments.[3]

Start with the Main Idea The main idea, placed at the top of an organization chart, helps you establish the goals and general strategy of the message. This main idea summarizes two things: (1) what you want your audience to do or think and (2) why they should do so. Everything in the message either supports this idea or explains its implications.

The main idea is the starting point for constructing an outline.

State the Major Points In an organization chart, the boxes directly below the top box represent the major supporting points, corresponding to the main headings in a conventional outline. These are the "vice presidential" ideas that clarify the message by expressing it in more concrete terms. To fill in these boxes, break the main idea into smaller units. Generally, try to identify three to five major points. If you come up with more than seven main divisions of thought, go back and look for opportunities to combine some of the ideas. The big question then is deciding what to put in each box.

The main idea should be supported by three to five major points, regardless of the message's length.

If your purpose is to inform and the material is factual, the groupings are generally suggested by the subject itself. They are usually based on something physical that you can visualize or measure: activities to be performed, functional units, spatial or chronological relationships, parts of a whole. When you're describing a process, the major support points are almost inevitably steps in the process. When you're describing a physical object, the vice presidential boxes correspond to the components of the object. When you're giving a historical account, each box represents an event in the chronological chain.

When your purpose is to persuade or collaborate, the major support points may be more difficult to identify. Instead of relying on a natural order imposed by the subject, develop a line of reasoning that proves your central message and motivates your audience to act. The boxes on the organization chart then correspond to the major elements in a logical argument. Basically, the supporting points are the main reasons why your audience should accept your message.

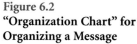

Figure 6.2
"Organization Chart" for Organizing a Message

Illustrate with Evidence   The third level on the organization chart shows the specific evidence you'll use to illustrate your major points. This evidence is the flesh and blood that helps your audience understand and remember the more abstract concepts. Say you're advocating that the company increase its advertising budget. To support this point, you could provide statistical evidence that your most successful competitors spend more on advertising than you do. You could also describe a specific case in which a particular competitor increased its ad budget and achieved an impressive sales gain. As a final bit of evidence, you could show that over the past five years, your firm's sales have gone up and down in unison with the amount spent on advertising.

If you're developing a long, complex message, you may need to carry the organization chart (or outline) down several levels. Remember that every level is a step along the chain from the abstract to the concrete, from the general to the specific. The lowest level contains the individual facts and figures that tie the generalizations to the observable, measurable world. The higher levels are the concepts that reveal why those facts are significant.

> Each major point should be supported with enough specific evidence to be convincing but not so much that it's boring.

The more evidence you provide, the more conclusive your case will be. If your subject is complex and unfamiliar or if your audience is skeptical, you'll need a lot of facts and figures to demonstrate your points. On the other hand, if your subject is routine and the audience is positively inclined, you can be more sparing with the evidence. You want to provide enough support to be convincing but not so much that your message becomes boring or inefficient.

Another way to keep the audience interested is to vary the type of detail. As you plan your message, try to incorporate the methods described in Table 6.1. Switch from facts and figures to narration; add a dash of description; throw in some examples or a reference to authority. Reinforce it all with visual aids. Think of your message as a stew, a mix of ingredients, seasoned with a blend of spices. Each separate flavor adds to the richness of the whole.

Establish Sequence with Organizational Patterns

Once you've defined and grouped your ideas, you're ready to decide on their sequence. You have two basic options:

- Direct approach *(deductive):* putting the main idea first, followed by the evidence
- Indirect approach *(inductive):* putting the evidence first and the main idea later

These two basic approaches may be applied either to short messages (memos and letters) or to long ones (reports, proposals, presentations). To choose between the two alternatives, you must first analyze your audience's likely reaction to your purpose and message. In general, the direct approach is fine when your audience will be receptive: eager, interested, pleased, or even neutral. If they'll be resistant to your message—displeased, uninterested, or unwilling—you'll have better results with the indirect approach.

> Use direct order if the audience's reaction is likely to be positive, indirect order if it is likely to be negative.

Bear in mind, however, that each message is unique. You can't solve all your communication problems with a simple formula. If you're sending bad news to outsiders, for example, an indirect approach is probably best. On the other hand, you might want to get directly to the point in a memo to an associate, even if your message is unpleasant. The direct approach might also be the best choice for long messages, regardless of the audience's attitude, because delaying the main point could cause confusion and frustration. Just remember that the first priority is to make the message clear.

> Short messages follow one of four organizational plans, depending on the audience's probable reaction.

Patterns for Short Messages   Once you've analyzed your audience's probable reaction and chosen a general approach, you can choose the most appropriate organizational

Table 6.1 SIX TYPES OF DETAILS		
Type of Detail	*Example*	*Comment*
Facts and figures	Sales are strong this month. We have received two new contracts worth $5 million and have a good chance of winning another with an annual value of $2.5 million.	Most common form of detail in business messages. Adds more credibility than any other form of development. May become boring if used in excess.
Example or illustration	We've spent four months trying to hire accounting graduates, and so far only one person has agreed to join our firm. One woman told me that she would love to work for us, but she can get $5,000 more a year elsewhere.	Adds life to a message, but one example does not prove a point. Idea must be supported by other evidence as well.
Description	Upscale burger restaurants appeal to people who still love the taste of a Big Mac but who want more than convenience and low prices. These restaurants feature attractive servers, wine and beer, half-pound burgers, and side dishes such as nachos or potato skins. "Atmosphere" is a key to success.	Useful when you need to explain how something looks or functions. Helps audience visualize subject by creating a sensory impression. Does not prove a point, but clarifies it and makes it memorable. Gives overview of object's function, operation, purpose, and major parts; relies on words that appeal to senses.
Narration	Under the former management, the company operated in a casual style. Executives came to work in blue jeans, meetings rarely started on time, and lunch rarely ended on time. When Mr. Wilson took over as CEO, however, the company got religion—financial religion. A Harvard M.B.A. who favors Brooks Brothers suits, Mr. Wilson has embarked on a complete overhaul of the operation. He has cut $12 million off expenses.	Good for attracting attention and explaining ideas, but lacks statistical validity.
Reference to authority	I talked with Jackie Lohman in the Cleveland plant about this idea, and she was very supportive. Jackie has been in charge of that plant for the past six years, and she believes we can speed up the line by 150 units per hour if we add another worker.	Bolsters a case and adds variety and credibility. Works only if "authority" is recognized and respected by audience, although he or she may be ordinary person.
Visual aid	Graphs, charts, tables	Essential when presenting specific information. Used more often in memos and reports.

pattern: direct request; routine, good-news, or goodwill message; bad-news message; persuasive message. Table 6.2 summarizes how each type of message is structured.

- *Direct requests.* The most straightforward business message is the direct request. This type of message uses the direct approach and lets you get to the point in the first paragraph; if you're talking with someone face-to-face or on the phone, you can get right down to business. Use this organizational pattern when your audience will be interested in complying or eager to respond. The direct approach is the most natural approach, perhaps the most useful and businesslike. This type of message is discussed in greater detail in Chapter 8.

  Direct requests get straight to the point because the audience usually wants to respond.

- *Routine, good-news, and goodwill messages.* Other messages use the direct approach

Table 6.2   **FOUR ORGANIZATIONAL PLANS FOR SHORT MESSAGES**

Audience Reaction	Organizational Pattern	Opening	Body	Close
Eager or interested	Direct request	Begin with the request or main idea.	Provide necessary details.	Close cordially and state the specific action desired.
Pleased or neutral	Routine, good-news, or goodwill message	Begin with the main idea or the good news.	Provide necessary details.	Close with a cordial comment, a reference to the good news, or a look toward the future.
Displeased	Bad-news message	Begin with a neutral statement that acts as a transition to the reasons for the bad news.	Give reasons to justify a negative answer; then state or imply the bad news, and make a positive suggestion.	Close cordially.
Uninterested or unwilling	Persuasive message	Begin with a statement or question that captures attention.	Arouse the audience's interest in the subject; then build the audience's desire to comply.	Request action.

The direct approach is effective for messages that will please the reader or cause no particular reaction.

when the audience will feel neutral about the message or will be pleased to hear from the writer. If you're providing routine information as part of your regular business, the audience will probably be neutral, neither pleased nor displeased. If you're announcing a price cut, granting an adjustment, accepting an invitation, or congratulating a colleague, the audience will be pleased to hear from you. Using the direct approach for routine, good-news, and goodwill messages has many advantages: You put your audience in a good frame of mind, you encourage readers to be receptive to whatever else you have to say, and you emphasize the pleasing aspect of your message by putting it right up front. This type of message is discussed in more detail in Chapter 9.

If you have bad news, try to put it somewhere in the middle, cushioned by other, more positive ideas.

■ *Bad-news messages.* This organizational pattern uses the indirect approach and is appropriate when the audience will be displeased about what you have to say. If you're turning down a job applicant, refusing credit, or denying a request for an adjustment, your audience will be disappointed. Astute businesspeople like those at Drake Beam Morin know that every person encountered may be a customer, a supplier, or a contributor or may influence someone who is a customer, a supplier, or a contributor. So they take a little extra care with their bad-news messages. They use the indirect approach, which is neither manipulative nor unethical. As long as you can be honest and reasonably brief, you're better off opening a bad-news message with a neutral point and putting the negative information after the explanation. This type of message is discussed further in Chapter 10.

Using the indirect approach gives you an opportunity to get your message across to a skeptical or hostile audience.

■ *Persuasive messages.* The indirect approach is also useful when you know your audience will resist your message (will be uninterested in your request or unwilling to comply without extra coaxing). Such resistance might be the likely reaction to a sales or collection letter, an unsolicited job application, or a request for a favor of some kind. Although you might argue that people are likely to feel manipulated by the indirect approach, the fact remains that you have to capture people's attention before you can persuade them to do something. If you don't, you really have no way to get the message across. You also have to get your audience to consider with an open mind what you have to say; to do this, you have to make an interesting point and provide supporting facts that encourage the audience to continue paying attention. Once you have them thinking, you can introduce your real purpose. This type of message is discussed at greater length in Chapter 11.

Patterns for Longer Messages   Most short messages can use one of the four basic organizational patterns. Longer messages (namely, reports and presentations) require a more complex pattern to handle the greater mass of information. These patterns can be broken into two general categories: informational and analytical.

> The organization of a longer message should reflect both the purpose of the message and the audience's probable reaction.

In general, the direct approach is used for informational reports and presentations, which provide nothing more than facts. Operating instructions, status reports, technical descriptions, and descriptions of company procedures all fall into this category. Long informational messages have an obvious main idea, often with a descriptive or "how-to" overtone. The development of subordinate ideas follows the natural breakdown of the material to be explained. Subtopics can be arranged in order of importance, sequentially, chronologically, spatially, geographically, or categorically.

> When your purpose is to inform, the major points are based on a natural order implied by the subject's characteristics.

Analytical reports and presentations are designed to lead the audience to a specific conclusion. When your purpose is to collaborate with your audience to solve a problem or to persuade them to take a definite action, your organizational pattern will highlight logical arguments or focus the audience's attention on what needs to be done. Your audience may respond in one of two ways to your material, and your choice of organizational plan should depend on the reaction you anticipate:

> When your purpose is to persuade or collaborate, the approach is analytical, with major points corresponding to logical arguments or to conclusions and recommendations.

- If you expect your audience to agree with you, use a structure that focuses attention on conclusions and recommendations.
- If you expect your audience to be skeptical about your conclusions and recommendations or hostile toward them, use a structure that focuses attention on the rationale that supports your point of view.

You'll learn more about organizing longer messages in Chapter 13. For now, the important thing is to master the basic steps in structuring a message.

F ORMULATING YOUR MESSAGE

Once you've completed the planning process, you're ready to begin composing the message. If your schedule permits, put your outline or organization chart aside for a day or two; then review it with a fresh eye, looking for opportunities to improve the flow of ideas. When you feel confident that your structure will achieve your purpose with the intended audience, you can begin to write.

Your First Draft

As you compose the first draft, don't worry about getting everything perfect. Just put down your ideas as quickly as you can. You'll have time to revise and refine the material later. You may discover as you go along that you can improve on your outline. Feel free to rearrange, delete, and add ideas, as long as you don't lose sight of your purpose.

> Composition is the process of drafting your message; polishing it is a later step.

*B*EHIND THE SCENES AT GENERAL ELECTRIC
The Making of an Annual Report

A company with publicly traded stock is required by the Securities and Exchange Commission (SEC) and by law to present an audited report of its financial status to its shareholders each year. This annual report enables the company's owners to make informed decisions before voting at the annual meeting. Annual reports are among the most common business messages created.

General Electric's stock is widely held, and each year the company spends more than $1.5 million to print and distribute 1.25 million annual reports. David Warshaw, manager of corporate communications at GE's headquarters in Fairfield, Connecticut, oversees the creation of these reports. It takes five months for one editor, two financial writers, and dozens of people elsewhere in the company to plan, compose, revise, and print the 70-page document. "The shareholder," says Warshaw, "is our primary audience, whether an individual investor with one share or a bank trust department with many thousands. But others read our report as well: job applicants, reporters, securities analysts, accounting teachers, and employees." Although legal requirements dictate the financial information to be included—which made up 48 of the 70 pages in a recent year—the format, text, and production quality are up to the individual company.

A small organization (or one in a single industry) can often select a theme for its annual report: quality, for example, or service. But the size and diversity of GE prohibits such an approach. Instead, Warshaw emphasizes the company's strategy as the main idea, both to guide the people working in various divisions as they write the copy and to give unity to the finished report: "Our strategic goals are (1) to be a global player and (2) to run businesses that are number one or number two in their global markets. The format calls on each of our 14 major businesses to comment on how they fit into that strategy. The financial results prove whether the strategy is working."

If you're writing the draft in longhand, leave space between lines so that you'll have plenty of room for making revisions. If you're using a typewriter, leave wide margins and double-space the text. Probably the best equipment for drafting the message is a word processor, which allows you to make changes easily. You might try dictating the message, particularly if you're practicing for an oral delivery or if you're trying to create a conversational tone.

Your Style and Tone

When composing the message, vary the style to create a tone that suits the occasion.

Style is the way you use words to achieve a certain **tone,** or overall impression. You can vary your style—your sentence structure and vocabulary—to sound forceful or passive, personal or impersonal, colorful or colorless. The right choice depends on the nature of your message and your relationship with the reader.

Your use of language is one of your credentials, a badge that identifies you as a member of a particular group. Try to make your style clear, concise, and grammatically correct, and try also to make it conform to the norms of your group. Every organization has its own stylistic conventions, and many occupational groups share a particular vocabulary.

Although style can be refined during the revision phase (see Chapter 7), you'll save time and a lot of rewriting if you compose your message in an appropriate style. Your tone is affected by planning-stage elements such as your purpose and your audience's probable reaction to your message. Other elements affecting the tone of your message include thinking about the relationship you want to establish with your audience, using the "you" attitude, emphasizing the positive, establishing credibility, being polite, and projecting your company's image.

A logical order is critical to the success of General Electric's annual report, especially given its length and complexity. "We want recipients to be able to understand the report, so to help them, we organize the sections from the general to the specific. We open with a letter from our chairman to all shareholders, which states our strategy and direction. Many recipients turn here first. It's probably the most-read section of the report, so it's written with all readers in mind."

A narrative section comes next. Taking a portfolio approach, each GE business (from appliances and financial services to the National Broadcasting Corporation) reports on its own activity. "That allows 14 large, independent, and diverse businesses to present themselves, their markets, their successes, and finally, their strategies and how these fit into the overall strategy as described in the chairman's opening letter."

Financial details make up the third and final section. "A lot is determined by what SEC regulations require. Using charts, tables, and even narrative, we provide various levels of information. Depending on the reader's level of interest and sophistication, all interested parties can find the detail they need."

Even illustration and design are considered part of the composition. "We decide what ideas we want illustrated by photographs, and the headlines and captions are chosen with the main idea in mind. That way, even if folks merely leaf through the report looking at pictures and reading captions, they'll get some idea about the status of the company."

Apply Your Knowledge

1. Two weeks before going to print with the annual report, you learn that the board of directors approved shortening your company's name from American Steel and Railroad Corporation to AMX. What impact would this have on the organization and composition of the report?

2. Two years ago, your company was doing well: You launched two new products, increased market share, and acquired an international distributor—all leading to record sales and earnings. However, last year was bad: Design problems caused you to recall one of your new products, a competitor introduced a product targeted at your leading brand, and three key executives resigned—which resulted in lower sales, less profit, and no dividend to stockholders. List the ways your annual report's organization and composition would differ for the two years.

Think About the Relationship You Want to Establish

The first step toward getting the right tone is to think about your relationship with the audience. Who are you, and who are they? Are you friends of long standing with common interests, or are you total strangers? Are you equal in status, experience, and education, or are you clearly unequal? Your answers to these questions will help you define your relationship with the audience so that you can give the right impression in your message.

If you're addressing an old friend, you can often take an informal tack. However, if you're in the lower echelon of a large organization, you generally adopt a respectful tone when communicating with the people above you. Moreover, some people who are proud of their status expect messages to show a deep appreciation of rank. Also, businesspeople in the United States are generally less formal than their counterparts in most other cultures.[4] So, to avoid embarrassment or misunderstanding when communicating across cultures, increase your level of formality.

Although various situations require various tones, most business communication sounds businesslike without being stuffy. The tone suggests that you and your audience are sensible, logical, unemotional people—objective, interested in the facts, rational, competent, and efficient. You are civilized people who share a mutual respect for each other.

To achieve this tone, avoid being too familiar. Don't mention things about anyone's personal life unless you know the individual very well. Such references are indiscreet and presumptuous. Avoid phrases that imply intimacy, such as "just between you and me," "as you and I are well aware," and "I'm sure we both agree." Also, be careful about sounding too folksy or chatty; the audience may interpret this tone as an attempt on your part to seem like an old friend when, in fact, you're not.

Humor is another type of intimacy that may backfire. It's fine to be witty in person with old friends. However, it's difficult to hit just the right note of humor in business messages, particularly if you don't know the readers very well. What seems humorous to you may be deadly serious to others.

To achieve a warm but business-like tone

- Don't be too familiar
- Use humor only with great care
- Don't flatter the other person
- Don't preach
- Don't brag
- Be yourself

Also avoid obvious flattery and abject fawning (or kowtowing). Although most of us respond well to honest praise and proper respect, we're suspicious of anyone who seems too impressed. When someone says, "Only a person of your outstanding intellect and refined tastes can fully appreciate this point," little warning lights flash in our minds. We suspect that we're about to be conned.

Avoid preaching to your audience, and don't offer help when it's neither asked for nor needed. Few things are more irritating than people who assume that they know it all and we know nothing. People who feel compelled to give lessons in business are particularly offensive. If, for some reason, you have to tell your audience something obvious, try to make the information unobtrusive. Place it in the middle of a paragraph, where it will sound like a casual comment as opposed to a major revelation. Alternatively, you might preface an obvious remark with "as you know" or some similar phrase.

Bragging is closely related to preaching and is equally offensive. When you praise your own accomplishments or those of your organization, you imply that you're better than your audience. References to the size, profitability, or eminence of your organization may be especially annoying (unless, of course, those in your audience work for the same organization). You're likely to evoke a negative reaction with comments like "We at McMann's, which is the oldest and most respected firm in the city, have a reputation for integrity that is beyond question."

Perhaps the most important thing you can do to establish a good relationship with your audience is to be yourself. People can spot falseness quickly, and they generally don't like it. If you don't try to be someone you're not, you'll sound sincere.

Use the "You" Attitude

The "you" attitude is best implemented by expressing your message in terms of the audience's interests and needs.

By using an audience-centered approach, you try to see your subject through your audience's eyes. You project this approach into your messages by adopting a **"you" attitude,** that is, by speaking and writing in terms of your audience's wishes, interests, hopes, and preferences. Talk about other people, and you're talking about what most interests them. Too many business messages have an "I" or "we" attitude, which sounds selfish and uninterested in the receiver: The message tells what the sender wants, and the recipient is expected to go along with it.

On the simplest level, you can adopt the "you" attitude by replacing terms that refer to yourself and your company with terms that refer to your audience. In other words, use *you* and *yours* instead of *I, me,* and *mine* or *we, us,* and *ours:*

Instead of This	*Use This*
To help us process this order, we must ask for another copy of the requisition.	So that your order can be filled promptly, please send another copy of the requisition.
We offer the typewriter ribbons in three colors: black, blue, and green.	Take your pick of typewriter ribbons in three colors: black, blue, and green.

Avoid using *you* and *yours*

- To excess
- When assigning blame
- If your organization prefers a more formal style

Using *you* and *yours* requires finesse.[5] If you overdo it, you're likely to create some rather awkward sentences. You also run the risk of sounding like a high-pressure carnival barker at the county fair. The "you" attitude is not intended to be manipulative or insincere. It is an extension of the audience-centered approach. In fact, the best way to implement the "you" attitude is to be sincere in thinking about your audience. It isn't just a matter of using one pronoun as opposed to another; it's a matter of genuine empathy. You can use *you* 25 times in a single page and still ignore your audience's true concerns. It's the thought that counts, not the pronoun. If you're talking to a retailer, try to think like a retailer; if you're dealing with a production supervisor, put yourself in his or her position; if you're writing to a dissatisfied customer, imagine how you would feel at the other end of the transaction. The important thing is your attitude toward the members of your audience and your appreciation of their position.

In fact, on some occasions, you'll do better to avoid using *you*. For instance, when someone makes a mistake and you want to point it out impersonally to minimize the possibility of ill will, you might say, "We have a problem," instead of "You caused a problem." Using *you* in a way that might sound dictatorial is also impolite:

> The word *you* does not always indicate a "you" attitude, and the "you" attitude can be displayed without using the word *you*.

Instead of This	*Use This*
You should never use that kind of paper in the copy machine.	That type of paper doesn't work very well in the copy machine.
You need to make sure the staff follows instructions.	The staff may need guidance in following instructions.

Keep in mind the attitudes and policies of your organization as well. Some companies have a tradition of avoiding references to *you* and *I* in their memos and formal reports. If you work for a company that expects a formal, impersonal style, confine your use of personal pronouns to informal letters and memos.

Emphasize the Positive

Another way of showing sensitivity to your audience is to emphasize the positive side of your message. Focus on the silver lining, not the cloud. Stress what is or will be instead of what isn't or won't be. Most information, even bad news, has at least some redeeming feature. If you can make your audience aware of that feature, you will make your message more acceptable.

> Explain what you have done, what you can do, and what you will do—not what you haven't done, can't do, or won't do.

Instead of This	*Use This*
It is impossible to repair this vacuum cleaner today.	Your vacuum cleaner will be ready by Tuesday.
We never exchange damaged goods.	We are happy to exchange merchandise that is returned to us in good condition.

In addition, when you're criticizing or correcting, don't hammer on the other person's mistakes. Avoid referring to failures, problems, or shortcomings. Focus instead on what the person can do to improve:

> When you are offering criticism or advice, focus on what the person can do to improve.

Instead of This	*Use This*
The problem with this department is a failure to control costs.	The performance of this department can be improved by tightening up cost controls.
You filled out the order form wrong. We can't send you the paint until you tell us what color you want.	So that your order can be processed properly, please check your color preferences on the enclosed card.

Show your audience how they will benefit from complying with your message.

If you're trying to persuade the audience to buy a product, pay a bill, or perform a service for you, emphasize what's in it for them. Don't focus on why *you* want them to do something. Instead of someone from Drake Beam Morin saying, "Please buy our service so that we can make our sales quota," the message would be more effective as "Our service can help you reduce the pain inherent in the process of termination." An individual who sees the possibility for personal benefit is more likely to respond positively to your appeal.

Avoid words with negative connotations; use meaningful euphemisms instead.

In general, try to state your message without using words that might hurt or offend your audience. Substitute mild terms (euphemisms) for those that have unpleasant connotations. Instead of advertising "cheap" merchandise, announce your bargain prices. Don't talk about "pimples and zits"; refer more delicately to complexion problems. You can be honest without being harsh. Gentle terms won't change the facts, but they will make those facts more acceptable:

Possibly Offensive	*Inoffensive*
toilet paper	bathroom tissue
used cars	resale cars
high-calorie food	high-energy food

On the other hand, don't carry euphemisms to extremes. If you're too subtle, people won't know what you're talking about. "Derecruiting" workers to the "mobility pool" instead of telling them they have six weeks to find another job isn't really very helpful. When using euphemisms, you walk a fine line between softening the blow and hiding the facts. It would not be ethical to speak to your community about relocating refuse when you're really talking about your plans for disposing of toxic waste. Such an attempt to hide the facts would very likely backfire, damaging your business image and reputation. In the final analysis, people respond better to an honest message delivered with integrity than they do to sugar-coated double-talk.

Establish Credibility

Because the success of your message may depend on the audience's perception of you, their belief in your competence and integrity is important. You want people to believe that you know what you're doing and your word is dependable. The first step in building credibility is to promise only what you can do and then to do what you promise.

Don't make false promises.

After that, just as your credibility is affected in person by your physical appearance, your professional manner, and your speaking style, so it is affected in writing by your document's physical appearance, its professionalism, and your writing style.

If you're communicating with someone you know well, your previous interactions influence your credibility. The other person knows from past experience whether you're trustworthy and capable. If the person is familiar with your company, the firm's reputation may be ample proof of your credibility.

But what if you are complete strangers? Even worse, what if the other person starts off with doubts about you? First and foremost, show an understanding of the other person's situation by calling attention to the things you have in common. If you're communicating with someone who shares your professional background, you might say, "As a fellow engineer [lawyer, doctor, teacher, or whatever], I'm sure you can appreciate this situation." Another approach is to use technical or professional terms that identify you as a peer.

To enhance your credibility,
- Show that you understand the other person's situation
- Establish your own credentials or ally yourself with a credible source
- Back up your claims with evidence, not exaggerations
- Use words that express confidence
- Believe in yourself and your message

You can also gain the audience's confidence by explaining your credentials, but be careful that you don't sound pompous. Generally, one or two aspects of your background are all you need to mention. Possibly your title or the name of your organization will be enough to impress the audience with your abilities. If not, perhaps you can mention the name of someone who carries some weight with your audience. You might begin a letter with "Professor Goldberg suggested that I contact you," or you could quote a recognized authority on a subject, even if you don't know the authority personally. The fact that your ideas are shared by a credible source adds prestige to your message.

Your credibility is also enhanced by the quality of the information you provide. If you support your points with evidence that can be confirmed through observation, research, experimentation, or measurement, your audience will recognize that you have the facts, and they will respect you. Exaggerated claims, on the other hand, are unethical and do more harm than good.

You risk losing credibility if you seem to be currying favor with insincere compliments. So support compliments with specific points:

When Body Shop founder Anita Roddick decided to use her business as a vehicle for social and environmental change, she focused worldwide attention on her credibility with customers. Indeed, as Roddick and her business have become symbols of social responsibility, they have drawn criticism and investigation. Any mistakes and errors will be magnified, says Roddick, but by emphasizing social issues in addition to profits, we are trying to change the focus of business.

Instead of This	*Use This*
My deepest heartfelt thanks for the excellent job you did. It's hard these days to find workers like you. You are just fantastic! I can't stress enough how happy you have made us with your outstanding performance.	Thanks for the fantastic job you did filling in for Gladys at the convention with just an hour's notice. Despite the difficult circumstances, you managed to attract several new orders with your demonstration of the new line of coffeemakers. Your dedication and sales ability are truly appreciated.

The other side of the credibility coin is too much modesty and not enough confidence. Try to avoid such words as *if, hope,* and *trust,* which express a lack of confidence on your part:

Instead of This	*Use This*
We hope this recommendation will be helpful.	We're glad to make this recommendation.
If you'd like to order, mail us the reply card.	To order, mail the reply card.

The ultimate key to being believable is to believe in yourself. If you are convinced that your message is sound, you can state your case with authority so that the audience has no doubts. When you have confidence in your own success, you automatically suggest that your audience will respond in the desired way. If you lack faith in yourself, however, you're likely to communicate an unsteady attitude that undermines your credibility.

Be Polite

The best tone for business messages is almost always a polite one. By being courteous to the people in your audience, you show consideration for their needs and feelings. You express yourself with kindness and tact.

Undoubtedly, you'll be frustrated and exasperated by other people many times in your career. When that happens, you'll be tempted to say what you think in blunt terms. To be sure, it's your job to convey the facts, precisely and accurately. Nevertheless, venting your emotions will rarely improve the situation and may jeopardize the goodwill of your audience. Instead, be gentle when expressing yourself:

Although you may be tempted now and then to be brutally frank, try to express the facts in a kind and thoughtful manner.

Instead of This	**Use This**
You really fouled things up with that last computer run.	Let me tell you what went wrong with that last computer run so that we can make sure things run smoothly next time.
You've been sitting on my order for two weeks now. When can I expect delivery?	As I mentioned in my letter of October 12, we are eager to receive our order as soon as possible. Please let us know when to expect delivery.

Use extra tact when writing to and when communicating with higher-ups and outsiders.

Of course, some situations require more diplomacy than others. If you know your audience well, you can get away with being informal. However, when corresponding with people who outrank you or with those outside your organization, you usually include an added measure of courtesy. In general, written communication requires more tact than oral communication. When you're speaking, your words are softened by your tone of voice and facial expression. You can adjust your approach depending on the feedback you get. Written communication, on the other hand, is stark and self-contained. If you hurt a person's feelings in writing, you can't soothe them right away. In fact, you may not even know that you have hurt the other person, because the lack of feedback prevents you from seeing his or her reaction.

Being courteous means taking the time to do a little extra for someone.

In addition to avoiding things that give offense, try to find things that might bring pleasure. Remember a co-worker's birthday, send a special note of thanks to a supplier who has done a good job, acknowledge someone's help, send a clipping to a customer who has expressed interest in a subject. People remember the extra little things that indicate you care about them as individuals. In this impersonal age, the human touch is particularly effective.

Another simple but effective courtesy is to be prompt in your correspondence. If possible, answer your mail within two or three days. If you need more time to prepare a reply, write a brief note or call to say that you're working on an answer. Most people are willing to wait if they know how long the wait will be. What annoys them is the suspense.

CEO William Gates wants Microsoft to maintain its image of competitiveness well into the future, when he predicts that his company's software "will be used in business, in the home, in the pocket, and in the car." But a company's image is also projected through its employees, so when you're speaking for your company, it's important to align your personal values with those of your organization.

Project the Company's Image

Even though establishing the right tone for your audience is your main goal, give some thought to projecting the right image for your company. When you communicate with outsiders on even the most routine matter, you serve as the spokesperson for your organization. The impression you make can enhance or damage the reputation of the entire company. Thus your own views and personality must be subordinated, at least to some extent, to the interests and style of the company.

You can save yourself a great deal of time and frustration if you master the company style early in your career. In a typical corporation, 85 percent of the letters, memos, and reports are written by someone other than the higher-level managers who sign them. Most of the time, managers reject first drafts of these documents for stylistic reasons. In fact, the average draft goes through five revisions before it is finally approved.[6]

You might wonder whether all this effort to fine-tune the style of a message is worthwhile. The fact is, people in business care very much about saying precisely the right thing in precisely the right way. Their willingness to go over the same document five times demonstrates just how important style really is. For a reminder of the tasks involved in composition, see this chapter's Checklist for Composing Business Messages.

CHECKLIST FOR COMPOSING BUSINESS MESSAGES

A. Organization
1. Recognize good organization.
   - a. Subject and purpose are clear.
   - b. Information is directly related to subject and purpose.
   - c. Ideas are grouped and presented logically.
   - d. All necessary information is included.
2. Achieve good organization through outlining.
   - a. Decide what to say.
     - i. Main idea
     - ii. Major points
     - iii. Evidence
   - b. Organize the message to respond to the audience's probable reaction.
     - i. Use the direct approach when your audience will be neutral, pleased, interested, or eager.
     - ii. Use the indirect approach when your audience will be displeased, uninterested, or unwilling.
3. Choose the appropriate organization plan.
   - a. Short messages
     - i. Direct request
     - ii. Routine, good-news, or goodwill message
     - iii. Bad-news message
     - iv. Persuasive message
   - b. Longer messages
     - i. Informational pattern
     - ii. Analytical pattern

B. Formulation
1. Compose your first draft.
   - a. Get ideas down as quickly as you can.
   - b. Rearrange, delete, and add ideas without losing sight of your purpose.
2. Vary the style to create a tone that suits the occasion.
   - a. Establish your relationship with your audience.
     - i. Use the appropriate level of formality.
     - ii. Avoid being overly familiar, using inappropriate humor, including obvious flattery, sounding preachy, bragging, and trying to be something you're not.
   - b. Extend your audience-centered approach by using the "you" attitude.
   - c. Emphasize the positive aspects of your message.
   - d. Establish your credibility to gain the audience's confidence.
   - e. Make your tone a polite one.
   - f. Use the style that your company prefers.

On the Job

SOLVING A COMMUNICATION DILEMMA AT DRAKE BEAM MORIN

Drake Beam Morin's success in selling outplacement services rests squarely on its sensitivity to its clients' attitudes and needs. Chairman William J. Morin points out that nobody likes to fire people: "Outplacement walks in the door and becomes a conscience-abating ingredient that helps management deal with a very unpleasant activity." Morin's clients want to make the termination process as easy as possible for both the dismissed employees and the company.

Drake Beam Morin satisfies that need. Like other leading outplacement firms, it has traditionally emphasized individual counseling for dismissed senior executives. The typical package includes psychological assessment, career counseling, résumé preparation, advice on interview techniques, and access to computerized job listings. Although the outplacement industry focuses on higher-level managers, many firms also offer one- to six-day group programs for middle managers and clerical workers.

In addition to counseling terminated workers, Morin and his staff teach managers how to dismiss people. Most managers responsible for doing the firing are extremely uncomfortable with the role of "bad guy." They need help handling the actual dismissal process and coping with their guilt. Through lectures and role-playing exercises, Drake Beam Morin teaches these managers techniques for dealing with dismissed workers' probable range of reactions. This training enables corporations to handle an extremely difficult situation with compassion, and it reduces the risk of lawsuits.

In addition, outplacement can save a company money by shortening the worker's job search and thus the corporation's severance payment obligations. With 35 offices across the country, Drake Beam Morin has a large network of "graduates" who, with the firm's help, have found responsible positions in major companies. When these executives need new employees, they often contact Drake Beam Morin. The job openings are entered into the firm's computerized job-lead databank, which lists some 4,000 positions paying salaries of $30,000 and up. These contacts, combined with Drake Beam Morin's other services, enable dismissed employees to find jobs more quickly than they could on their own. "We save about three months on the job search," says Morin.

A corporation also derives an important public relations benefit when it provides outplacement service for dismissed workers. Morin believes that by showing it cares about people, a company polishes its image and builds internal morale. Generally speaking, the survivors in a corporate layoff are apprehensive. Many of them identify more with their terminated co-workers than with the company. They worry that they might be the next to go if the company does not do well. Often, they are expected to assume additional duties or to take a pay cut until business improves. Under the circumstances, management needs all the help it can get to restore confidence.

Since its inception in 1967, Drake Beam Morin has communicated the benefits of its services to countless clients and, in the process, has earned its position as the leading firm in the outplacement business. During that same period, it has helped thousands of executives cope with one of business's most difficult situations—the loss of a job.

Your Mission: You are a counselor at Drake Beam Morin. Since one of your responsibilities is to find new business for the firm, you are always on the lookout for opportunities to sell your services. Needless to say, you are interested when an article in the morning paper announces that a local corporation plans to reorganize two of its divisions in a cost-cutting move. The final paragraph of the article suggests that several senior executives will lose their jobs:

> While management would not comment on layoffs and terminations growing out of the announced reorganization, the company is reportedly seeking ways to reduce costs in order to improve bottom-line performance. In two previous reorganizations, the company reduced levels of management, merged departments, and laid off workers for up to six months. "We seek to trim operations in order to better compete in the international marketplace," said incoming president Bob Waters.

Based on the article, you decide to contact the company's vice president of human resources about the possibility of providing outplacement services. You quickly draft a letter to the local company. Here is a copy of your draft. Read it and then select the best responses to the questions that follow. Be prepared to explain why your choice is best.

Have you ever been fired? If so, you know how painful the experience can be. Many people never recover. They are pulled into a downward spiral of failure that ends in despair and ruin for both themselves and their families. The people responsible for the termination decision also suffer an emotional burden. They are plagued by guilt, their loyalty to the company

erodes, and their productivity suffers. Ultimately, they too may lose their jobs.

This painful cycle can be avoided. Although no one can make termination a pleasant experience, a professional outplacement firm such as Drake Beam Morin can mitigate the problems inherent in the process. Using our proven workshop format, we will teach your managers how to terminate their colleagues with compassion and sensitivity. And we will help the dismissed employees regain their confidence and self-respect. With the aid of our trained staff of professional outplacement counselors, the terminated employees will soon find new positions. Many will look back on their dismissal as being the best thing that ever happened to them. Their bitterness and hostility will be defused, and they will be less inclined to bring legal action against you.

If you would like to learn more about how we can assist you as you face the difficult ordeal ahead, please contact me at 555-7765. I will be happy to meet with you in person and discuss our fees, which generally equal approximately 15 percent of the terminated employees' annual salaries.

1. Does the letter conform to the guidelines for good organization?
   a. No. The letter takes too long to get to the point. The opening question is too much of a gimmick—using an emotional, unprofessional tone and not providing any useful information. The description of the problem is unnecessary and melodramatic. The dire picture should be replaced by a more specific reference to the company and its need for help in handling the termination process. The letter's main fault is that it leaves out necessary information about the specific benefits of Drake Beam Morin's services. The brief reference to benefits should be expanded into several paragraphs, one that focuses on the benefits to terminated employees and one or two that present the benefits to the company. Another paragraph is needed to give background on Drake Beam Morin and to refer the reader to an enclosed brochure. The final paragraph should not mention fees; it should request an appointment and mention that a member of the firm will telephone to set a time.
   b. The letter is basically well organized, but some of the ideas are grouped and sequenced in an illogical manner. The opening paragraph should introduce Drake Beam Morin and describe its outplacement package. This should be followed by a reference to the newspaper article and a polite suggestion that the reader's company might need assistance. The third paragraph should provide information on financial arrangements, and the final paragraph should mention an enclosed brochure.
   c. The letter is very well organized. The purpose and subject are clear. All information is related to the subject

and purpose. The ideas are grouped and presented in a logical way. All necessary information is included.

    d. The letter leaves out necessary information such as the exact amount of time the company's employees can expect to search before finding new jobs.

2. You decide to rewrite the draft. Your first step is to develop an outline. What should you use as the main idea?

    a. Executives who are terminated after devoting their lives to a company often suffer from severe depression; to avoid causing unnecessary suffering, the company should provide outplacement counseling.

    b. If the company is looking for an outplacement counseling service, Drake Beam Morin is the best choice.

    c. The company should retain Drake Beam Morin because both the company and its terminated executives would benefit from the firm's outplacement service.

    d. By retaining Drake Beam Morin, the company can help avoid legal action on the part of terminated employees.

3. What basic points can be used to develop the main idea?

    a. Companies that fail to provide outplacement counseling often suffer serious consequences: They inflict lasting pain on decent, competent people; they make their remaining managers feel guilty; they face the prospect of lawsuits; and they weaken the morale of the remaining employees. Therefore, the company should hire Drake Beam Morin.

    b. Outplacement counseling involves a variety of services directed toward both the departing employees and the company that must terminate their employment. These services are expensive, but the cost is justified by the benefits. Drake Beam Morin is the finest outplacement firm in the country.

    c. Drake Beam Morin is the country's leading outplacement firm, with nearly 30 years of experience in outplacement counseling. The firm helps both the departing employees and the managers who must terminate their employment. Employees adjust more easily to termination, and they find new jobs more quickly. The organization's managers feel less distressed about having to hurt their associates, so they handle the termination process more smoothly (which minimizes the threat of lawsuits) and improve their image with the remaining employees.

    d. Compared with other outplacement firms, Drake Beam Morin has more experience, better resources, and a superior staff. Other outplacement firms are smaller and have fewer counselors available in the case of large-scale layoffs.

4. Which organizational plan should the letter follow?

    a. Indirect. Open with an attention-getting account of a company that botched the termination process and ended up losing several wrongful termination suits. Explain how Drake Beam Morin trains company managers to handle the terminations in a manner that minimizes the possibility of lawsuits. Discuss Drake Beam Morin's fee structure. Close with a request for an appointment.

    b. Indirect. Briefly mention the potential client's problem. Show generally how Drake Beam Morin can be of service. Explain how outplacement counseling benefits the terminated employee. Follow with a paragraph on the benefits the company will enjoy by providing this service. Give some background on Drake Beam Morin and refer the reader to an enclosed brochure for further information. Close with a request for an appointment.

    c. Indirect. Describe how the termination process creates emotional problems for both the dismissed employee and the manager responsible for the termination. Explain how outplacement counseling can reduce these problems. Describe Drake Beam Morin and mention the enclosed brochure. Close with a discussion of costs and contract terms.

    d. Direct. Ask for an appointment to discuss the company's problem. Describe Drake Beam Morin's services. Mention several successful assignments that are similar to the potential client's situation. Refer the reader to the enclosed brochure. Close by repeating your request for an appointment.

5. What is the best way to build the reader's confidence in you?

    a. Provide some background about your education, experience, and position in Drake Beam Morin.

    b. Mention a mutual acquaintance in the field of human resources.

    c. Describe Drake Beam Morin's services in objective, concrete terms and rely on the firm's reputation to establish your credibility.

    d. Use bold, assertive language that emphasizes your self-confidence.[7]

Questions for Discussion

1. When organizing the ideas for your business message, how can you be sure that what seems logical to you will also seem logical to your audience?

2. Do you think that cushioning bad news is manipulative of the audience?

3. Which organizational plan would you use to ask employees to work overtime to meet an important deadline, a direct request or a persuasive message? Why?

4. Which organizational plan would you use to let your boss know that you'll be out half a day next week to attend your

father's funeral, a routine message or a bad-news message? Why?

5. How can you mention the name of someone your audience respects without being considered a show-off name-dropper?

6. When composing business messages, how can you be yourself and project your company's image at the same time?

Documents for Analysis

DOCUMENT 6.A

The writer of the following outline is having trouble grouping ideas logically for an insurance information brochure. Revise the outline, paying attention to appropriate subordination of ideas. Rewrite where necessary to give phrases a more consistent sound.

ACCIDENT PROTECTION INSURANCE PLAN

   I. Coverage is only pennies a day
  II. Benefit is $100,000 for accidental death on common carrier
 III. Benefit is $100 a day for hospitalization as result of motor vehicle or common carrier accident
 IV. Benefit is $20,000 for accidental death in motor vehicle accident
  V. Individual coverage is only $17.85 per quarter; family coverage is just $26.85 per quarter
 VI. No physical exam or health questions
VII. Convenient payment--billed quarterly
VIII. Guaranteed acceptance for all applicants
 IX. No individual rate increases
  X. Free, no-obligation examination period
 XI. Cash paid in addition to any other insurance carried
XII. Covers accidental death when riding as fare-paying passenger on public transportation, including buses, trains, jets, ships, trolleys, subways, or any other common carrier
XIII. Covers accidental death in motor vehicle accidents occurring while driving or riding in or on automobile, truck, camper, motor home, or non-motorized bicycle

DOCUMENT 6.B

Read the following letter; then (1) analyze the strengths and weaknesses of each sentence and (2) revise the letter so that it follows this chapter's guidelines.

I am a new publisher with some really great books to sell. I saw your announcement in <u>Publishers Weekly</u> about the bookseller's show you're having this summer, and I think it's a great idea. Count me in, folks! I would like to get some space to show my books. I thought it would be a neat thing if I could do some airbrushing on T-shirts live to help promote my hot new title, <u>T-Shirt Art</u>. Before I got into publishing, I was an airbrush artist, and I could demonstrate my techniques. I've done hundreds of advertising illustrations and have been a sign painter all my life, so I'll also be promoting my other book, hot off the presses, <u>How to Make Money in the Sign Painting Business</u>.

I will be starting my PR campaign about May 1995 with ads in <u>PW</u> and some art trade papers, so my books should be well known by the time the show comes around in August. In case you would like to use my appearance there as part of your publicity, I have enclosed a biography and photo of myself.

P.S. Please let me know what it costs for booth space as soon as possible so that I can figure out whether I can afford to attend. Being a new publisher is mighty expensive!

Exercises

1. Indicate whether the direct or indirect approach would be best in each of the following situations; then briefly explain why.

  a. A letter asking when the next version of software will be available for your computer system

  b. A letter from a former employee requesting a letter of recommendation from a supervisor

  c. A letter turning down a request for credit

  d. An announcement that the executive lunchroom will be closed so that the space can be used to expand the employee cafeteria, which will now be used by everyone

  e. A request for a full refund on a cordless phone that has never worked properly

2. Suppose that end-of-term frustrations have produced this letter to Professor Anne Brewer from a student who feels he should have received a B in his accounting class:

> I think that I was unfairly awarded a C in your accounting class this term, and I am asking you to change the grade to a B. It was a difficult term. I don't get any money from home, and I have to work mornings at the Pancake House (as a cook), so I had to rush to make your class, and those two times that I missed class were because they wouldn't let me off work because of special events at the Pancake House (unlike some other students who just take off when they choose). On the midterm exam, I originally got a 75 percent, but you said in class that there were two different ways to answer the third question and that you would change the grades of students who used the "optimal cost" method and had been counted off 6 points for doing this. I don't think that you took this into account, because I got 80 percent on the final, which is clearly a B. Anyway, whatever you decide, I just want to tell you that I really enjoyed this class, and I thank you for making accounting so interesting.

Recast this letter into three or four clear sentences, showing how you would improve it.

3. Rewrite the following letter to Mrs. Bruce Crandall (1597 Church Street, Grants Pass, OR 97526) so that it conveys a helpful, personal, and interested tone:

> We have your letter of recent date to our Ms. Dobson. Owing to the fact that you neglected to include the size of the dress you ordered, please be advised that no shipment of your order was made, but the aforementioned shipment will occur at such time as we are in receipt of the aforementioned information.

4. Rewrite these sentences to reflect your audience's viewpoint:
   a. We request that you use the order form supplied in the back of our catalog.
   b. We insist that you always bring your credit card to the store.
   c. We want to get rid of all our manual typewriters to make room in our warehouse for the new electronic models, so we are offering a 25 percent discount on all sales this week.
   d. I am applying for the position of bookkeeper in your office. I feel that my grades prove that I am bright and capable, and I think I can do a good job for you.
   e. As requested, we are sending the refund for $25.

5. Revise these sentences to be positive rather than negative:
   a. Unfortunately, your order cannot be sent this week.
   b. To avoid the loss of your credit rating, please remit payment within ten days.
   c. We don't make refunds on returned merchandise that is soiled.
   d. Because we are temporarily out of Baby Cry dolls, we won't be able to ship your order for ten days.
   e. You failed to specify the color of the blouse that you ordered.

6. Provide euphemisms for the following words and phrases:
   a. stubborn
   b. wrong
   c. stupid
   d. strike (labor)
   e. incompetent

REVISING BUSINESS MESSAGES

After studying this chapter, you will be able to

Edit your messages for content and organization, style and readability, and word choice

Choose the most correct and most effective words to make your point

Rewrite sentences to clarify the relationships among ideas and to make your writing interesting

Rewrite paragraphs using the appropriate development technique

Choose the best design for written documents

Proof your messages for mechanics and format

On the Job

FACING A COMMUNICATION DILEMMA AT McDONALD'S

A Little More Polish on the Golden Arches, Please

If you hanker for a Big Mac, a Coke, and some fries, here's a job for you: being a quality-control representative for McDonald's. David Giarla has been one for ten years, and he still loves the smell of Egg McMuffins in the morning. On a typical day, he visits seven or eight McDonald's, samples the food, inspects the kitchen, surveys the storeroom, and chats with the manager and employees. If he likes what he eats and sees, everybody breathes a sigh of relief and goes back to flipping burgers and wiping tables. However, if the food, service, or facilities are not up to snuff, watch out. Giarla might file a negative report with headquarters. Moreover, if enough negative reports pile up, McDonald's might cancel the franchisee's license.

Giarla's aim, however, is not to get people into trouble. On the contrary, he wants store managers to succeed. He believes that by holding them to McDonald's high standards, he can help them build their businesses. When he spots a problem, he always points it out and gives the manager a chance to fix it before he files a negative report. His aim is to offer criticism in a diplomatic and constructive manner, and he usually succeeds.

Next time you're in a McDonald's, put yourself in Giarla's position. What would you tell the manager and employees to help them improve their operation? How would you phrase your suggestions? What words would you choose, and how would you arrange them in sentences and paragraphs?[1]

*E*DITING YOUR MESSAGE

Whether offering criticism or praise, David Giarla understands that once you have completed the first draft of your message, you owe it to both yourself and your audience to review and refine it. Plan to go over a document at least three times: once for content and organization, once for style and readability, and once for mechanics and format. The letter in Figure 7.1 has been thoroughly revised, using the proofreading marks shown in Appendix D.

The tendency is to separate revision from composition, but editing is an ongoing activity that occurs throughout the composition process. You edit and revise as you go along; then you edit and revise again after you've completed the first draft. Although the basic editing principles discussed here apply to both written and oral communication, the steps involved in revising a speech or an oral presentation are slightly different, as Chapter 18 explains.

McDonald's

Figure 7.1
Sample Revised Letter

November 12, 1996

Miss Louise Wilson
Corporate Travel Department
Brother's Electric Corporation
2300 Wacker Drive
Chicago, IL 60670

Dear Miss Wilson:

Thank you for your interest in
I enjoyed our recent conversation regarding the FG frequent-guest program
at the Commerce Hotel. We are
and am delighted to hear that the people at Brother's Electric
are thinking about joining. Incidentally, we are planning a
special Thanksgiving weekend rate, so keep that in mind in case
you happen to be in Chicago for the Holiday.

The enclosed brochure explains the details of the FG frequent-guest
program. As a corporate member, Brother's Electric will be entitled to a
20 percent discount on all rooms and services.
(the enclosed ID card,
Your FG ID card is enclosed. Use it whenever you make
reservations with us to obtain your corporate discount. We will
see to it that your executives are treated with special courtesy,
including free
and that they get to use the health club free.
Organizations enrolled in the frequent-guest program also qualify for discounts on
We also have excellent convention facilities and banquet
rooms. should you want to book a convention or meeting here. We
hope you and your company will take advantage of these facilities the
next time you book a convention.
outstanding world-class amenities. Please call me if you have
any questions. I will be happy to answer them.

Sincerely,

Mary Cortez
Account Representative

Content and organization: *Stick to the point, the main idea, in the first paragraph. In the middle, highlight the key advantage of the frequent-guest program and discuss details in subsequent paragraphs. Eliminate redundancies.*

Style and readability: *Reword to stress the "you" viewpoint. Clarify the relationships among ideas through placement and combination of phrases. Moderate the excessive enthusiasm, and eliminate words (such as amenities) that may be unfamiliar.*

Mechanics and format: *To prevent confusion, spell out the abbreviated phrase FG.*

Michael D. Eisner, chairman and CEO of the Walt Disney Company, appears to be the perfect heir of Walt Disney himself, possessing childlike enthusiasm, charisma, and creativity. His detail-oriented business sense is apparent too. For Eisner, careful review and revision of budgets, reports, and long-term strategic growth proposals are critical to running a company.

Evaluate Your Content and Organization

Ideally, let your draft "age" a day or two before you begin the editing process so that you can approach the material with a fresh eye. Then read through the document quickly to evaluate its overall effectiveness. At this point, you're mainly concerned with content, organization, and flow. Compare the draft with your original plan. Have you covered all points in the most logical order? Is there a good balance between the general and the specific? Do the most important ideas receive the most space, and are they placed in the most prominent positions? Have you provided enough support and double-checked the facts? Would the message be more convincing if it were arranged in another sequence? Do you need to add anything? On the other hand, what can you eliminate? In business, it's particularly important to weed out unnecessary material.

In the first phase of editing, spend a few extra moments on the beginning and ending of the message. These are the sections that have the greatest impact on the audience. Be sure that the opening of a letter or memo is relevant, interesting, and geared to the reader's probable reaction. In longer messages, check to see that the first few paragraphs establish the subject, purpose, and organization of the material. Review the conclusion to be sure it summarizes the main idea and leaves the audience with a positive impression.

Review Your Style and Readability

When editing a message's style and readability, ask yourself whether you've achieved the right tone for your audience. Look for opportunities to make the material more interesting through the use of lively words and phrases. At the same time, be particularly conscious of whether your message is clear and readable. Check your vocabulary and sentence structure to be sure you are relying mainly on familiar terms and simple, direct statements. You might even apply a readability formula to gauge the difficulty of your writing.

The most common readability formulas measure the length of words and sentences to give you a rough idea of how well educated your audience must be to understand your message. Figure 7.2 shows how one readability formula, the Fog Index, has been applied to a passage from a memo. (The "long words" in the passage have been underlined.) As the calculation shows, anyone who reads at a tenth-grade level should be able to read the passage with ease.

Of course, readability indexes can't be applied to languages other than English. Counting syllables makes no sense in other languages. For example, compare the English *forklift driver* with the German *Gabelstaplerfahrer*. Also, Chinese and Japanese characters don't lend themselves to syllable counting at all.[2]

Readability depends on word choice, sentence length, sentence structure, organization, and the message's physical appearance.

Although readability formulas can easily be applied, they ignore some important variables that contribute to reading ease, such as sentence structure, the organization of ideas, and the appearance of the message on the page.[3] To fully evaluate the readability of your message, ask yourself whether you have effectively emphasized the important information. Are your sentences easy to decipher? Do your paragraphs have clear topic sentences? Are the transitions between ideas obvious?

Assess Your Word Choice

The two key aspects of word choice are

- Correctness
- Effectiveness

As a business communicator, you have two things to pay attention to when choosing and revising your words: correctness and effectiveness.[4] Even though the "rules" of grammar are constantly changing to reflect changes in the way people speak, grammatical errors decrease your credibility with your audience. So if you have doubts about what is correct, don't be lazy. Look up the answer, and use the proper form of

SAMPLE PASSAGE

I called Global Corporation to ask when we will receive copies of their <u>insurance policies</u> and <u>engineering</u> reports. Cindy Turner of Global said that they are putting the <u>documents together</u> and will send them by Express Mail next week. She told me that they are late because most of the <u>information</u> is in the hands of Global's <u>attorneys</u> in Boston. I asked why it was in Boston; we had understood that the account is serviced by their <u>carrier's</u> Dallas branch. Turner explained that the account originally was sold to Global's Boston <u>division</u>, so all paperwork stays there. She promised to <u>telephone</u> us when the package is ready to ship.

FOG INDEX CALCULATION

1. Select a writing sample that is 100 to 125 words long. Count the number of words in each sentence. Treat independent clauses (stand-alone word groups containing a subject and predicate) as separate sentences (e.g., *In school we studied; we learned; we improved*—counts as three sentences). Count dates and other number combinations as single words. Then add all word counts for each sentence to get a total word count, and divide that by the number of sentences to get an average sentence length.

2. Count number of long words—that is, all words that have three or more syllables (underlined in the sample). Omit proper nouns, combinations of short words (such as *butterfly* and *anyway*), and verbs that gain a third syllable by adding *-es* or *-ed*, as in *trespasses* and *created*. Divide the number of long words by the total number of words in the sample to get a percentage of long words in the sample.

3. Add the numbers for average sentence length and percentage of long words. Multiply the sum by 0.4, and drop the number that follows the decimal point. The result is the number of years of schooling required to read the sample passage easily.

Average sentence length:

18 + 21 + 21 + 7 + 13 + 17 + 12 = 109 words ÷ 7 sentences = 16

Percentage of long words:

11 long words ÷ 109 words total = 10 percent

Fog Index:

16 + 10 = 26 × 0.4 = 10.4 = 10

Figure 7.2
The Fog Index

expression. Check the grammar and usage guide in this book (see Appendix A), or consult any number of special reference books available in libraries and bookstores. Most authorities agree on the basic conventions.

Just as important as using the correct words is choosing the best words for the job at hand. Word effectiveness is generally more difficult to achieve than correctness, particularly in written communication. Following are some of the techniques professional writers use to improve the effectiveness of their style.

If in doubt, check it out.

Plain English

Plain English is a way of writing and arranging language so that your audience can understand your meaning. If you've ever tried to make sense of an obtusely worded legal document or credit agreement, you can understand the movement toward requiring contracts and other such documents to be written in plain English. Because it's close to the way we speak, plain English is easily understood by anyone with an eighth- or ninth-grade education.[5]

Plain English is close to spoken English and can be more easily understood.

The growing focus on plain-English laws has already led to plain-English loan and credit card application forms, insurance policies, and real estate contracts. Even so, plain English does have some limitations. It lacks the precision necessary for scientific research, intense feeling, and personal insight. Moreover, it fails to embrace every culture and dialect equally.[6] Needless to say, it's intended for areas where English is the primary language; however, the lessons of plain English can also help you simplify messages intended for audiences who may speak English only as a second or even third language.

Functional Words and Content Words

Functional words (conjunctions, prepositions, articles, and pronouns) express relationships among content words (nouns, verbs, adjectives, and adverbs).

Words can be divided into two categories. Functional words express relationships and have only one unchanging meaning in any given context. They include conjunctions, prepositions, articles, and pronouns. Your main concern with functional words is to use them correctly. Content words are multidimensional and therefore subject to various interpretations. They include nouns, verbs, adjectives, and adverbs. These words carry the meaning of a sentence. Content words are the building blocks; functional words are the mortar. In the following sentence, all the content words are in italics:

> *Some objective observers* of the *cookie market give Nabisco* the *edge* in *quality,* but *Frito-Lay is lauded* for *superior distribution.*

Both functional words and content words are necessary, but your effectiveness as a communicator depends largely on your ability to choose the right content words for your message. So take a closer look at two important dimensions for classifying content words.

Denotation and Connotation   As you know from reading Chapter 2, content words have both a denotative and a connotative meaning. The **denotative meaning** is the literal, or dictionary, meaning. The **connotative meaning** includes all the associations and feelings evoked by the word.

Content words have both a denotative (dictionary) meaning and a connotative (associative) meaning.

Some words have more connotations than others. If you say that a person has failed to pass a test, you're making a strong statement; you suggest that she or he is inferior, incompetent, second rate. On the other hand, if you say that the person has achieved a score of 65 percent, you suggest something else. By replacing the word *failed,* you avoid a heavy load of negative connotations.

In business communication, generally use terms that are low in connotative meaning. Words that have relatively few possible interpretations are less likely to be misunderstood. Furthermore, because you are usually trying to deal with things in an objective, rational manner, avoid emotion-laden comments.

Abstraction and Concreteness   Content words also vary in their level of abstraction. An abstract word expresses a concept, quality, or characteristic instead of standing for a thing you can touch or see. Abstractions are usually broad, encompassing a category of ideas. They are often intellectual, academic, or philosophical. *Love, honor, progress, tradition,* and *beauty* are abstractions. Concrete terms are anchored in the tangible, material world. They stand for something particular: *chair, table, horse, rose, kick, kiss, red, green, two.* These words are direct and vivid, clear and exact.

The more abstract a word, the more it is removed from the tangible, objective world of things that can be perceived with the senses.

You might suppose that concrete words are better than abstract words because they are more precise. However, imagine trying to talk about business without referring to such concepts as *morale, productivity, profit, motivation,* or *guarantee.* Nevertheless, abstractions can be troublesome. They tend to be fuzzy and subject to many interpretations. They also tend to be boring. It isn't always easy to get excited about ideas, especially if they're not related to experience. The best way to minimize such problems is to blend abstract terms with concrete ones, the general with the specific. State the concept, and then pin it down with details expressed in more concrete terms. Save the abstractions for ideas that cannot be expressed any other way. For example, instead of referring to McDonald's principles of operation, Dave Giarla talks about specifics such as fast service, good food, and clean facilities.

In business communication, use concrete, specific terms whenever possible; use abstractions only when necessary.

Words That Communicate

Wordsmiths are journalists, public relations specialists, editors, letter and report writers—anyone who earns a living by crafting words. Unlike poets, novelists, or dramatists, wordsmiths do not try for dramatic effects. They are mainly concerned with being clear, concise, and accurate in their use of language. To reach this goal, they emphasize words that are strong, familiar, and short, and they avoid hiding them under unnecessary extra syllables. When you edit your message, do your best to think like a wordsmith.

Strong Words   Nouns and verbs are the most concrete words in any message, so use them as much as you can. Although adjectives and adverbs obviously have parts to play, use them sparingly. They often call for subjective judgments, and business communication strives to be objective. Verbs are especially powerful because they carry the action; they tell what's happening in the sentence. The more dynamic and specific the verb, the better. Instead of settling for *rise* or *fall*, look for something more meaningful and descriptive, like *soar* or *plummet*.

Dan Rather is managing editor and anchor of CBS Evening News. *Along with three others, he writes and heavily revises each evening's newscast right up to airtime. Rather is noted for his concern over each word he uses.*

Avoid Weak Phrases	*Use Strong Terms*
wealthy businessperson	tycoon
business prosperity	boom
hard times	slump

Familiar Words   You'll communicate best with words that are familiar to your readers. At the same time, bear in mind that words familiar to one reader might be unfamiliar to another:

Avoid Unfamiliar Words	*Use Familiar Words*
ascertain	find out, learn
consummate	close, bring about
peruse	read, study

Although familiar words are generally the best choice, beware of terms so common that they have become virtually meaningless. Readers tend to slide right by such clichés as these:

interface	time frame	strategic decisions
track record	frame of reference	dialogue
viable	prioritize	scenario

Familiar words are preferable to unfamiliar ones, but try to avoid overworked terms (clichés).

Also handle technical or professional terms with care. Used in moderation, they add precision and authority to a message. However, many people simply don't understand them, and even a technically sophisticated audience will be lulled to sleep by too many. Let your audience's vocabulary be your guide. If they share a particular jargon, you may enhance your credibility by speaking their language.

Short Words   Although certainly not true in every case, short words are generally more vivid and easier to read. Thus they often communicate better than long words:

Short words are generally more vivid than long ones and improve the readability of a document.

Avoid Long Words	*Use Short Words*
During the preceding year, the company accelerated productive operations.	Last year the company sped up operations.
The action was predicated on the assumption that the company was operating at a financial deficit.	The action was based on the belief that the company was losing money.

Turning verbs into nouns or adjectives weakens your writing style.

Camouflaged Verbs   In the words you use, watch for endings such as *-ion*, *-tion*, *-ing*, *-ment*, *-ant*, *-ent*, *-ence*, *-ance*, and *-ency*. Most of them change verbs into nouns and adjectives. In effect, the words that result are camouflaged verbs. Getting rid of these camouflaged verbs will strengthen your writing:

Avoid Camouflaged Verbs	*Use Verbs*
The manager undertook implementation of the rules.	The manager implemented the rules.
Verification of the shipments occurs weekly.	Shipments are verified weekly.

Bias-Free Language

Avoid biased language that might offend the audience.

Most of us like to think of ourselves as being sensitive, unbiased, ethical, and fair. Being fair and objective isn't enough, however; you must also *appear* to be fair.[7] **Bias-free language** avoids embarrassing, unethical blunders in language related to culture, gender, race, ethnic group, age, and disability.

Don't use slang, idioms, or restrictive viewpoints when communicating interculturally, and don't judge associates by their grammar or language structure.

Cultural Bias   Whether working with employees, other businesses, or customers at home or abroad, be careful to avoid cultural bias in your business messages. Avoid using slang ("The ball is now in your court"), acronyms ("FYI, the MIS is back on line"), or idioms ("You'll soon be moving up the organizational ladder").[8] Avoid using a restrictive viewpoint, for example, change *domestic sales* to *U.S.-based sales* in a letter to European readers. Also, if you're having your message translated into another language, the best way to avoid undetected cultural bias is to have it back-translated. Perhaps most important of all, avoid judging international associates and intercultural workers by their use of English. Employees and associates may misuse English grammar or structure, but that fact alone indicates nothing about their creativity or talent.

Replace words that inaccurately exclude women or men.

Gender Bias   For many years, the word *man* was used to denote humanity, describing a human being of either gender and any age. Today, however, *man* is associated more with an adult male human being. The fact that some of the most commonly used words contain the word *man* can create problems, and yet some simple solutions exist:

Unacceptable	*Preferable*
mankind	humanity, human beings, human race, people
if a man drove	if a person (or someone or a driver) drove
man-made	artificial, synthetic, manufactured, constructed, of human origin
manpower	human power, human energy, workers, workforce

Here are some simple ways to replace occupational terms that contain the word *man* with words that can represent people of either gender:

Unacceptable	*Preferable*
businessman	business executive, business manager, businessperson
salesman	sales representative, salesperson, sales-clerk
insurance man	insurance agent
foreman	supervisor

Avoid using female-gender words like *authoress* and *actress; author* and *actor* denote both women and men. Similarly, avoid special designations, such as *woman doctor* or *male nurse.* Use the same label for everyone in a particular group. Don't refer to a woman as *chairperson* and then call a man *chairman.*

The pronoun *he* has also traditionally been used to refer to both males and females. However, readers today interpret the pronoun as male, not as generic. Here are some simple ways to avoid this outdated usage:

Unacceptable	*Preferable*
The average worker . . . he	The average worker . . . he or she
The typical business executive spends four hours of his day in meetings.	Most business executives spend four hours a day in meetings.

Avoid identifying certain roles with a specific gender:

Unacceptable	*Preferable*
the consumer . . . she	consumers . . . they
the nurse/teacher . . . she	nurses/teachers . . . they
the judge . . . he	the judges . . . they

If you're discussing categories of people, such as bosses and office workers, avoid referring to the boss as *he* and the office worker as *she.* Instead, reword sentences so that you can use *they,* or reword them so that you don't have to use any pronoun. In today's business world, it's also appropriate sometimes to use *she* when referring to a boss and *he* when referring to an office worker. Another way to avoid bias is to make sure you don't always mention men first. Vary the traditional pattern with *women and men, gentlemen and ladies, she and he, her and his.* Finally, identify women by their own names, not by their role or marital status—unless it is appropriate to the context:

Unacceptable	*Preferable*
Phil Donahue and Marlo	Phil Donahue and Marlo Thomas
Phil Donahue and Ms. Thomas	Mr. Donahue and Ms. Thomas

The preferred title for women in business is Ms., unless the individual asks to be addressed as Miss or Mrs. or has some other title, such as Dr.

Racial and Ethnic Bias   The guidelines for avoiding racial and ethnic bias are much the same as those for avoiding gender bias. The central principle is to avoid language suggesting that members of a racial or ethnic group have the same stereotypical traits:

Eliminate references that reinforce racial or ethnic stereotypes.

Unacceptable	*Preferable*
disadvantaged black children	children from lower-income families
Jim Wong is an unusually tall Asian.	Jim Wong is tall.

The best solution is to avoid identifying people by race or ethnic origin unless such a label is relevant:

Unacceptable	*Preferable*
Mario M. Cuomo, Italian American governor of New York	Mario M. Cuomo, governor of New York

Age Bias   As with gender, race, and ethnic background, mention the age of a person only when it is relevant:

Avoid references to an individual's age or physical limitations.

Unacceptable	*Preferable*
Mary Kirazy, 58, has just joined our trust department.	Mary Kirazy has just joined our trust department.

When referring to older people, avoid such stereotyped adjectives as *spry, frail,* and *cute.*

Disability Bias   There is really no painless label for people with a physical, mental, sensory, or emotional impairment. However, if you must refer to such individuals in terms of their limitations, avoid using terms such as *handicapped, crippled,* or *retarded,* and be sure to put the person first and the disability second:[9]

Always refer to people first and their disabilities second.

Unacceptable	*Preferable*
Crippled workers face many barriers on the job.	Workers who have physical disabilities face many barriers on the job.

Most of all, avoid mentioning a disability unless it is pertinent. When it is pertinent, present the whole person, not just the disability, by showing the limitation in an unobtrusive manner:

Unacceptable	*Preferable*
An epileptic, Tracy has no trouble doing her job.	Tracy's epilepsy has no effect on her job performance.

The 1990 Americans with Disabilities Act guarantees equal opportunities for people who have or have had a condition that might handicap them. The goal of bias-free communication is to abandon stereotyped assumptions about what a person can do or will do and to focus on an individual's unique characteristics. So describe people without disabilities as *typical* rather than *normal.* People having disabilities are certainly *atypical* but not necessarily *abnormal.*[10]

REWRITING YOUR MESSAGE

As you edit your business message, you'll find yourself rewriting passages, sentences, and even whole sections to improve its effectiveness. First, remember that in your search for perfection, you're probably also facing a deadline, so try to stick to the schedule you set during the planning stage. Do your best to revise and rewrite thoroughly but also economically. Second, you'll probably want to keep copies of your revised versions. As you rewrite, you'll concentrate on how each word contributes to an effective sentence and how that sentence develops a coherent paragraph.

Create Effective Sentences

Words don't make much sense until they're combined into a sentence to express a complete thought. Thus, *Jill, receptionist, the, smiles,* and *at* can be organized into "Jill smiles at the receptionist." Now you can begin exploring the possibilities for improvement, looking at how well each word performs its particular function. Nouns and noun equivalents are the topics (or subjects) you're communicating about, and verbs and related words (or predicates) make statements about those subjects. In a more complicated sentence, adjectives and adverbs modify the subject and the statement, and various connectors hold the words together.

Vaughn Beals, CEO of Harley-Davidson, turned his company around by revising design, work flow, quality, and service. His close attention to detail improved his product's image, and so it is with communication. When you're striving for high-quality, error-free messages, you do a lot of revising.

The Three Types of Sentences

Sentences come in three basic varieties: First, a **simple sentence** has a single subject and a single predicate, although it may be expanded by nouns and pronouns serving as objects of the action and by modifying phrases. In the following examples, the subject is underlined once, and the predicate verb is underlined twice:

Profits have increased in the past year.

Second, a **compound sentence** expresses two or more independent but related thoughts of equal importance, joined by *and, but,* or *or.* In effect, a compound sentence is a merger of two or more simple sentences (independent clauses) that deal with the same basic idea:

Wage rates have declined by 5 percent, and employee turnover has been high.

The independent clauses in a compound sentence are always separated by a comma or by a semicolon (in which case the conjunction—*and, but, or*—is dropped).

Third, a **complex sentence** expresses one main thought (the independent clause) and one or more subordinate thoughts (dependent clauses) related to it, often separated by a comma. The subordinate thought, which comes first in the following sentence, could not stand alone:

Although you may question Gerald's conclusions, you must admit that his research is thorough.

When constructing a sentence, use the form that best fits the thought you want to express. The structure of the sentence should match the relationship of the ideas. If you have two ideas of equal importance, express them as two simple sentences or as one compound sentence. However, if one of the ideas is less important than the other, place it in a dependent clause to form a complex sentence. This compound sentence uses a conjunction to join two ideas that aren't truly equal:

Every sentence contains a subject (noun or noun equivalent) and a predicate (verb and related word).

To give your writing variety, use the three types of sentences:

- Simple
- Compound
- Complex

The chemical products division is the strongest in the company, and its management techniques should be adopted by the other divisions.

In the following complex sentence, the first thought has been made subordinate to the second. Notice how much more effective the second idea is when the cause-and-effect relationship has been established:

Because the chemical products division is the strongest in the company, its management techniques should be adopted by the other divisions.

In complex sentences, the placement of the dependent clause should be geared to the relationship between the ideas expressed. If you want to emphasize the idea, put the dependent clause at the end of the sentence (the most emphatic position) or at the beginning (the second most emphatic position). If you want to downplay the idea, bury the dependent clause within the sentence.

Most emphatic:	The handbags are manufactured in Mexico, *which has lower wage rates than the United States.*
Emphatic:	*Because wage rates are lower there,* the handbags are manufactured in Mexico.
Least emphatic:	Mexico, *which has lower wage rates,* was selected as the production site for the handbags.

To make your writing as effective as possible, balance all three sentence types. If you use too many simple sentences, you'll be unable to express the relationship among ideas. If you use too many long, compound sentences, your writing will sound monotonous. On the other hand, if you use an uninterrupted series of complex sentences, your message will be hard to follow.

Sentence Style

Of course, sentence style varies from culture to culture. German sentences are extremely complex, with a lot of modifiers and appositives; Japanese and Chinese languages don't even have sentences in the same sense that Western languages do.[11] Basically, whether a sentence in English is simple, compound, or complex, it should be grammatically correct, efficient, readable, interesting, and appropriate for your audience. In general, strive for straightforward simplicity.

Break long sentences into shorter ones to improve readability.

Keep Sentences Short   Long sentences are usually harder to understand than short sentences because they are packed with information that must all be absorbed at once. Most good business writing therefore has an average sentence length of 20 words or fewer. This figure is the average, not a ceiling. To be interesting, your writing should contain both longer and shorter sentences.

Long sentences are especially well suited for grouping or combining ideas, listing points, and summarizing or previewing information. Medium-length sentences (those with about 20 words) are useful for showing the relationships among ideas. Short sentences are tailor-made for emphasizing important information.

Active sentences are stronger than passive ones.

Rely on the Active Voice   Active sentences are generally preferable to passive sentences because they are easier to understand.[12] You're using **active voice** when the subject (the "actor") comes before the verb and the object of the sentence (the "acted upon") follows the verb: "John rented the office." You're using **passive voice** when the subject follows the verb and the object precedes it: "The office was rented by John."

As you can see, the passive verb combines the helping verb *to be* with a form of the verb that is usually similar to the past tense. Using passive verbs makes sentences longer and de-emphasizes the subject. Active verbs produce shorter, stronger sentences:

Avoid Passive Sentences	*Use Active Sentences*
Sales were increased by 32 percent last month.	Sales increased by 32 percent last month.
The new procedure is thought by the president to be superior.	The president thinks the new procedure is superior.

Of course, in some situations, using the passive voice makes sense. You may want to be diplomatic when pointing out a problem or error of some kind, so you might say, "The shipment was lost" rather than "You lost the shipment." The passive version seems less like an accusation because the emphasis is on the lost shipment rather than on the person responsible. Similarly, you may want to point out what's being done without taking or attributing either the credit or the blame, so you might say something like "The production line is being analyzed to determine the source of problems." You may want to avoid personal pronouns in order to create an objective tone, so in a formal report you might say, "Criteria have been established for evaluating capital expenditures."

Use passive sentences to soften bad news, to put yourself into the background, or to create an impersonal tone.

Eliminate Unnecessary Words and Phrases   Some words and combinations of words have more efficient, one-word equivalents. So you would avoid saying "This is to inform you that we have begun production" when "We have begun production" is enough.

Be on the lookout for
- *Inefficient phrases*
- *Redundancies*
- *Unneeded relative pronouns and articles*

Combinations to Avoid	*Efficient Equivalents*
for the sum of	for
in the event that	if
on the occasion of	on
prior to the start of	before

Other word combinations are redundant: Avoid saying "visible to the eye" because *visible* is enough—nothing is visible to the ear. Avoid saying "surrounded on all sides" because *surrounded* implies on all sides. Also take a close look at double modifiers. Do you really need to say "modern, up-to-date equipment," or would "modern equipment" do the job?

Relative pronouns such as *who, that,* and *which* frequently cause clutter, and sometimes even articles are excessive (mostly too many *the's*). However, well-placed relative pronouns and articles serve an important function by preventing confusion. For example, without *that,* the following sentence is ambiguous:

Confusing: The project manager told the engineers last week the specifications were changed.

Clear: The project manager told the engineers last week *that* the specifications were changed.

Clear: The project manager told the engineers *that* last week the specifications were changed.

Here are some other ways to prune your prose:

Poor	Improved
consensus of opinion	consensus
at this point in time	at this time, now
irregardless	(no such word; use *regardless*)
each and every	(either word, but not both)
due to the fact that	because
at an early date	soon (or a specific date)
at the present time	now
in view of the fact that	since, because
until such time as	when
we are of the opinion	we believe
with reference to	about
as a result of	because
for the month of December	for December

Avoid needless repetition.

In general, be on the lookout for the needless repetition of words or ideas. Try not to string together a series of sentences that all start with the same word or words, and avoid repeating the same word too often within a given sentence. Another way to save words is to use infinitives in place of some phrases. This technique not only shortens your sentences but makes them clearer as well:

Use infinitives to replace some phrases.

Poor	Improved
In order to be a successful writer, you must work hard.	To be a successful writer, you must work hard.
He went to the library for the purpose of studying.	He went to the library to study.
The employer increased salaries so that she could improve morale.	The employer increased salaries to improve morale.

Avoid Obsolete and Pompous Language   The language of business used to be much more formal than it is today, and a few out-of-date phrases remain from the old days. Perhaps the best way to eliminate them is to ask yourself: "Would I say this if I were talking face-to-face with someone?"

Astronomer Carl Sagan speaks at NASA news conferences (such as this one about Voyager's last pictures of our solar system), and he's known for his research on the possibilities of life in outer space. Sagan was creator and host of the public television series Cosmos, *and his book of the same name is the best-selling science volume of all time. More than a distinguished scientist, Sagan is highly skilled at translating scientific jargon into plain English, a valuable asset for any communicator.*

Obsolete	Up-to-Date
as per your letter	as in your letter (do not mix Latin and English)
hoping to hear from you soon, I remain	(omit)
yours of the 15th	your letter of June 15
awaiting your reply, we are	(omit)
in due course	today, tomorrow (or a specific time)
permit me to say that	(permission is not necessary; just say what you wish)
we are in receipt of	we have received

pursuant to	(omit)	Obsolete formal phrases can obscure meaning.
in closing, I'd like to say	(omit)	
attached herewith is	here is	
the undersigned	I; me	
kindly advise	please let us know	
under separate cover	in another envelope; by parcel post	
we wish to inform you	(just say it)	
attached please find	enclosed is	
it has come to my attention	I have just learned; Ms. Garza has just told me	
our Mr. Lydell	Mr. Lydell, our credit manager	
please be advised that	(omit)	

Being a good communicator, McDonald's Dave Giarla understands that pompous language sounds stiff, puffed up, and roundabout. People are likely to use pompous language when they are trying to impress somebody. In hopes of sounding imposing, they use big words, trite expressions, and overly complicated sentences.

The use of pompous language suggests that you are a pompous person.

Poor	*Improved*
Upon procurement of additional supplies, I will initiate fulfillment of your order.	I will fill your order when I receive more supplies.

Moderate Your Enthusiasm   An occasional adjective or adverb intensifies and emphasizes your meaning, but too many ruin your writing:

Business writing shouldn't be gushy.

Poor	*Improved*
We are extremely pleased to offer you a position on our staff of exceptionally skilled and highly educated employees. The work offers extraordinary challenges and a very large salary.	We are pleased to offer you a position on our staff of skilled and well-educated employees. The work offers challenges and an attractive salary.

Break Up Strung-Out Sentences   A strung-out sentence is a series of two or more sentences unwisely connected by *and*—in other words, a compound sentence taken too far. You can often improve your writing style by separating the string into individual sentences:

In many cases, the parts of a compound sentence should be separated into two sentences.

Poor	*Improved*
The magazine will be published January 1, and I'd better meet the deadline if I want my article included.	The magazine will be published January 1. I'd better meet the deadline if I want my article included.

Avoid Hedging Sentences   Sometimes you have to write *may* or *seems* to avoid stating a judgment as a fact. Nevertheless, when you have too many such hedges, you aren't really saying anything:

Don't be afraid to present your opinions without qualification.

Poor

I believe that Mr. Johnson's employment record seems to show that he may be capable of handling the position.

Improved

Mr. Johnson's employment record shows that he is capable of handling the position.

Avoid starting sentences with *it* and *there.*

Watch for Indefinite Pronoun Starters   If you start a sentence with an indefinite pronoun (an expletive) like *it* or *there,* odds are that the sentence could be shorter:

Poor

It would be appreciated if you would sign the lease today.

Improved

Please sign the lease today.

There are five employees in this division who were late to work today.

Five employees in this division were late to work today.

When you use the same grammatical pattern to express two or more ideas, you show that they are comparable thoughts.

Express Parallel Ideas in Parallel Form   When you have two or more similar (parallel) ideas to express, try to use a **parallel construction;** that is, use the same grammatical pattern. The repetition of the pattern tells readers that the ideas are comparable, and it adds a nice rhythm to your message. In the following examples, parallel construction makes the sentences more readable:

Poor

Ms. Simms had been drenched with rain, bombarded with telephone calls, and her boss shouted at her.

Improved

Ms. Simms had been drenched with rain, bombarded with telephone calls, and shouted at by her boss.

Parallelism can be achieved through a repetition of words, phrases, clauses, or entire sentences:

Parallel words:	The letter was approved by Clausen, Whittaker, Merlin, and Carlucci.
Parallel phrases:	We have beaten the competition in supermarkets, in department stores, and in specialty stores.
Parallel clauses:	I'd like to discuss the issue after Vicki gives her presentation but before Marvin shows his slides.
Parallel sentences:	In 1994 we exported 30 percent of our production. In 1995 we exported 50 percent.

Tell readers exactly where you want them to look.

Eliminate Awkward Pointers   To save words, business writers sometimes direct their readers' attention elsewhere with such expressions as *the above-mentioned, as mentioned above, the aforementioned, the former, the latter, respectively.* These words cause the reader to jump from one point in the message to another, a process that hinders effective communication. A better approach is to be specific in your references, even if you must add a few more words:

Poor

Typewriter ribbons for legal secretaries and beginning clerks are distributed by the Law Office and Stenographic Office, respectively.

Improved

Typewriter ribbons for legal secretaries are distributed by the Law Office; those for beginning clerks are distributed by the Stenographic Office.

Correct Dangling Modifiers   Sometimes a modifier is not just an adjective or adverb but an entire phrase defining a noun or verb. Be careful to construct your sentences so that this type of modifier refers to something in the main part of the sentence in a way that makes sense. Consider this sentence:

Walking to the office, a red sports car passed her.

The construction implies that the red sports car has the office and the legs to walk there. The modifier is said to be dangling because it has no real connection to the subject of the sentence—in this case, the sports car. This is what the writer is trying to say:

A red sports car passed her while she was walking to the office.

Flipping the clauses produces another correct sentence:

While she was walking to the office, a red sports car passed her.

Dangling modifiers make sentences confusing and sometimes ridiculous:

Poor	*Improved*
Working as fast as possible, the budget was soon ready.	Working as fast as possible, the committee soon had the budget ready.

The first example shows one frequent cause of dangling modifiers: passive construction in the independent clause. When the clause is made active instead of passive, the connection with the dangling modifier becomes more obvious.

Avoid Long Sequences of Nouns   When nouns are strung together as modifiers, the resulting sentence is hard to read. You can clarify the sentence by putting some of the nouns into a modifying phrase. Although you add a few more words, your audience won't have to work as hard to understand the sentence.

Poor	*Improved*
The window sash installation company will give us an estimate on Friday.	The company that installs window sashes will give us an estimate on Friday.

Keep Words Together That Work Together   To avoid confusing readers, keep the subject and predicate of a sentence as close together as possible. Otherwise, readers will have to read your sentence twice to figure out who did what.

Poor	*Improved*
A 10 percent decline in market share, which resulted from quality problems and an aggressive sales campaign by Armitage, the market leader in the Northeast, was the major problem in 1994.	The major problem in 1994 was a 10 percent loss of market share, which resulted from both quality problems and an aggressive sales campaign by Armitage, the market leader in the Northeast.

Side notes:

Make sure that an opening modifier phrase is really related to the subject of the sentence.

Passive construction is often the cause of dangling modifiers.

Stringing together a series of nouns may save a little space, but it causes confusion.

Subject and predicate should be placed as close together as possible, as should modifiers and the words they modify.

*B*EHIND THE SCENES AT THE LA JOLLA PLAYHOUSE
Greasepaint, Bright Lights, and Rewrites

On a typical midseason day at the La Jolla Playhouse, while the actors are rehearsing and the directors, composers, and designers are discussing endless set, score, and costume details, Constance Harvey is likely to be holed up in her office at a computer terminal, writing. No, she's not a playwright, but her job is almost as important to the internationally acclaimed regional theater. Harvey is the theater's publicist, and without the material she writes, the Playhouse could easily slip from public view. Harvey writes nearly every word the theater sends to reviewers, reporters, entertainment editors, television journalists, potential donors, and season subscribers. Her challenge is to attract local and national media attention to reach audiences, critics, and theater artists.

Every season is an eclectic mix of plays that might include anything from a period comedy performed by clown Bill Irwin to a musical by British rockers Ray Davies (*80 Days*) or Pete Townshend (*Tommy*)—and Harvey must capture the mood of each production. For example, the press release she wrote for Tennessee Williams's *The Glass Menagerie* demanded a quiet feeling, whereas her announcements about the performances of the wacky Flying Karamazov Brothers required a kind of verbal free fall. Harvey's messages must be full of information for calendar event editors—names, dates, times, locations, and so forth—and her copy must have appealing, pithy phrases that magazine editors can easily lift and use as two- or three-line descriptions of a play. When successful, her writing stirs interest and has a direct effect on ticket sales, donations, and future productions.

To accomplish all this, Harvey begins with an inflated first draft, which includes everything. Her ultimate objective is simplicity and completeness, but she's not afraid to be abstract and colorful—like her subject matter. The first draft goes to her assistant, who reads it for content. "I have two questions for that person," says Harvey. "Does it make sense, and what have I left out?" As she revises that first draft, Harvey keeps her assistant's comments in mind, but she also tries to anticipate the questions that might be asked by some of the theater critics who make up her primary audience. They are

---

The same rule applies to other parts of speech. Adjectives, adverbs, and prepositional phrases usually make the most sense when they're placed as close as possible to the words they modify:

Poor	*Improved*
We will deliver the pipe soon that you ordered last Tuesday.	We will soon deliver the pipe that you ordered last Tuesday.

Emphasize parts of a sentence by
- Giving them more space
- Putting them at the beginning or the end of the sentence
- Making them the subject of the sentence

Emphasize Key Thoughts   In every message, some ideas are more important than others. You can emphasize these key ideas through your choice of sentence style. One obvious technique is to give important points the greatest amount of space. When you want to call attention to a thought, use extra words to describe it. Consider this sentence.

The chairperson of the board called for a vote of the shareholders.

To emphasize the importance of the chairperson, you might give a fuller description of her:

The chairperson of the board, who has considerable experience in corporate takeover battles, called for a vote of the shareholders.

very important to the Playhouse, and over the years, Harvey has learned their needs and preferences. If her releases don't supply enough background about a play or an artist, or if her facts aren't straight, these critics call and let her know. Harvey also solicits input from the theater's associate artistic director, who gives her feedback on whether or not the press release falls in line with a production's artistic concept.

When she is finally satisfied with her second draft, she is ready to "proof it to death." She looks for errors in grammar and punctuation and reads the words aloud to test the rhythm. "To me, that's a dead giveaway," Harvey explains. "If the rhythm is off, then I don't know what I'm talking about, or I've missed the point. And if I've missed the point, then I'm not going to be able to convey it." She also makes sure she hasn't repeated a word too often. "There are only so many ways you can say *production,* and if I've said it already four or five times in the three preceding lines, it has to go." At the same time, she watches for passive voice. She has a bad habit of burying verbs in sentences, covering up more active and more interesting phrases.

"One of my rules of proofing is that three people have to see it, because I don't trust myself. I'm too familiar with the copy and the content." Nevertheless, embarrassing mistakes do slip by. Early in Harvey's career, no one noticed that the names of the producer and the artistic director were missing from a program's title page—until hours before the presses were scheduled to run. In the ensuing uproar, Harvey phoned the printer, who said it was too late for changes. She insisted, threatening to throw herself on the printing press if he didn't acquiesce. Eventually, he did add the missing names, albeit in the wrong places. Now Harvey keeps a special watch for mistakes in the standard boilerplate copy that everyone takes for granted.

Apply Your Knowledge

1. To demonstrate that writing can almost always be improved, select an article on any subject from a newspaper or magazine. (1) Make a list of the words you would exchange for more colorful, more precise, or less biased words. (2) List your revisions on a separate sheet. (3) Rewrite any sentences that could be enlivened by a more active voice. (4) Look for paragraphs that could be shortened or simplified without losing meaning.

2. One of the most frustrating problems business writers face is having their words and work misunderstood. List the steps you can take to avoid uttering "But that's not what I meant!"

You can increase the emphasis even more by adding a separate, short sentence to augment the first:

> The chairperson of the board called for a vote of the shareholders. She has considerable experience in corporate takeover battles.

Another way to emphasize an idea is to place it at either the beginning or the end of a sentence:

Less Emphatic	**More Emphatic**
We are cutting the *price* to stimulate demand.	To stimulate demand, we are cutting the *price*.

You can also call attention to a thought by making it the subject of the sentence. In the following example, the emphasis is on the person:

> *I* can write letters much more quickly using a computer.

In this version, the computer takes center stage:

> The *computer* enables me to write letters much more quickly.

Techniques like this one give you a great deal of control over the way your audience interprets what you have to say.

Develop Coherent Paragraphs

Paragraphs are functional units that revolve around a single thought.

A paragraph is a cluster of sentences all related to the same general topic. It is a unit of thought. A series of paragraphs makes up an entire composition. Each paragraph is an important part of the whole, a key link in the train of thought. As you edit a message, think about the paragraphs and their relationship to one another.

Elements of the Paragraph

Most paragraphs consist of a topic sentence, related sentences, and transitional elements.

Paragraphs vary widely in length and form. You can communicate effectively in one short paragraph or in pages of lengthy paragraphs, depending on your purpose, your audience, and your message. The typical paragraph contains three basic elements: a topic sentence, related sentences that develop the topic, and transitional words and phrases.

The topic sentence
- Reveals the subject of the paragraph
- Indicates how it will be developed

Topic Sentence   Every properly constructed paragraph is **unified;** it deals with a single topic. The sentence that introduces that topic is called the **topic sentence.** In informal and creative writing, the topic sentence may be implied rather than stated. In business writing, the topic sentence is generally explicit and often the first sentence in the paragraph. The topic sentence gives readers a summary of the general idea that will be covered in the rest of the paragraph. The following examples show how the topic sentence introduces the subject and suggests the way it will be developed:

> The medical products division has been troubled for many years by public relations problems. [In the rest of the paragraph, readers will learn the details of the problems.]

> To get a refund, you must supply us with some additional information. [The details will be described.]

Related Sentences   The sentences that explain the topic sentence round out the paragraph. These related sentences all have a bearing on the general subject and provide enough specific details to make the topic clear:

> The medical products division has been troubled for many years by public relations problems. Since 1991 the leading local newspaper has published 15 articles that portray the division in a negative light. We have been accused of everything from mistreating laboratory animals to polluting the local groundwater. Our facility has been described as a health hazard. Our scientists are referred to as "Frankensteins," and our profits are considered "obscene."

Paragraphs are developed through a series of related sentences that provide details about the topic sentence.

The developmental sentences are all more specific than the topic sentence. Each one provides another piece of evidence to demonstrate the general truth of the main thought. Also, each sentence is clearly related to the general idea being developed, which gives the paragraph its unity. A paragraph is well developed when it contains enough information to make the topic sentence convincing and interesting.

Transitional words and phrases show readers how paragraphs and the ideas within them are related.

Transitional Elements   In addition to being unified and well developed, effective paragraphs are **coherent,** that is, they are arranged in a logical order so that the audience can understand the train of thought. Coherence is achieved by using transitions that show how one thought is related to another. You can establish transitions in various ways:

- Use connecting words: *and, but, or, nevertheless, however, in addition,* and so on.
- Echo a word or phrase from a previous paragraph or sentence: "A system should be established for monitoring inventory levels. This system will provide . . ."
- Use a pronoun that refers to a noun used previously: "Ms. Arthur is the leading candidate for the president's position. She has excellent qualifications."
- Use words that are frequently paired: "The machine has a minimum output of . . . Its maximum output is . . ."

Some transitional devices:
- Connecting words (conjunctions)
- Repeated words or phrases
- Pronouns
- Words that are frequently paired

Five Ways to Develop a Paragraph

Paragraphs can be developed in many ways. Your choice of technique depends on your subject, your intended audience, and your purpose. Remember also that in actual practice, you'll often combine two or more methods of development in a single paragraph.

Before settling for the first approach that comes to mind, think about the alternatives. Think through various methods before committing yourself on paper or computer screen. If you fall into the easy habit of repeating the same old paragraph pattern time after time, your writing will be boring. Five of the more common techniques are illustration, comparison or contrast, cause and effect, classification, and problem and solution.

Five ways to develop paragraphs:
- Illustration
- Comparison or contrast
- Cause and effect
- Classification
- Problem and solution

Illustration   When you develop a paragraph by illustration, you give examples that demonstrate the general idea:

> Some of our most popular products are available through local distributors. For example, Everett & Lemmings carries our frozen soups and entrees. The J. B. Green Company carries our complete line of seasonings, as well as the frozen soups. Wilmont Foods, also a major distributor, now carries our new line of frozen desserts.

Comparison or Contrast   Similarities or differences among thoughts often provide a strong basis for paragraph development.

> In previous years, when the company was small, the recruiting function could be handled informally. The need for new employees was limited, and each manager could comfortably screen and hire her or his own staff. Today, however, Gambit Products must undertake a major recruiting effort. Our successful bid on the Owens contract means that we will be doubling our labor force over the next six months. To hire that many people without disrupting our ongoing activities, we will create a separate recruiting group within the personnel department.

Cause and Effect   When you develop a paragraph using the cause-and-effect technique, you focus on the reasons for something:

> The heavy-duty fabric of your Wanderer tent probably broke down for one of two reasons: (1) a sharp object punctured the fabric, and, without reinforcement, the hole was enlarged by the stress of erecting the tent daily for a week; or (2) the tent was folded and stored while still wet, which gradually rotted the fibers.

Classification   Paragraphs developed by classification show how a general idea is broken into specific categories:

> Successful candidates for our supervisor trainee program generally come from one of several groups. The largest group, by far, consists of recent graduates of accredited data-processing programs. The next-largest group comes from within our own company, as we try to promote promising clerical workers to positions of greater responsibility. Finally, we do occasionally accept candidates with outstanding supervisory experience in related industries.

Problem and Solution   Another way to develop a paragraph is to present a problem and then discuss the solution:

> Selling handmade toys by mail is a challenge because consumers are accustomed to buying heavily advertised toys from major chains. However, if we develop an appealing catalog, we can compete on the basis of product novelty and quality. In addition, we can provide craftsmanship at a competitive price: a rocking horse made of birchwood, with a hand-knit tail and mane; a music box with the child's name painted on the top; a real Indian tepee, made by a Native American artisan.

PRODUCING YOUR MESSAGE

Once you've planned, composed, edited, and rewritten your message, give some thought to its presentation. Oral presentations are discussed in Chapter 18, and visual aids are discussed in Chapter 14. In this section, you'll get an idea of the basic decisions necessary when designing written documents. Because people have trouble comprehending long, uninterrupted pages of text, you can use design elements such as white space, headings, and boldface type (just as this textbook does) to provide visual clues about the importance of various ideas and their relationships.[13]

Written documents require decisions about design elements.

- *White space.* The blank space free of text or artwork is known as **white space.** It provides contrast and gives readers a resting point. White space includes the open areas surrounding headings, in the margin, between columns, at the end of ragged lines, in paragraph indents (or between unindented paragraphs), and between lines of type. You'll decide how much white space to allow for each of these areas.

White space is free of text and artwork.

- *Margins and line justification.* Margins define the space around your text and between text columns. They're influenced by the way you place lines of type, which can be set (1) justified (flush on both the left and the right), (2) flush left with a ragged-right margin, (3) flush right with a ragged-left margin, or (4) centered. Justified type will "darken" your message's appearance and make it look more like a form letter, yet it's often used because it yields a higher word density. Flush-left–ragged-right type "lightens" your message's appearance, giving it an informal, contemporary feeling of openness. Centered type lends a formal tone to your message but makes your audience search for the beginning of each line, which slows reading. The same problem is true of flush-right–ragged-left type.

Flush-left–ragged-right type gives your message an open feeling.

- *Headings and captions.* Headings and subheadings are usually set larger than the type used for text and often in a separate typeface. They invite readers to become involved in your message, so avoid centering heads that contain more than two lines. Like centered text, they make your readers search for the beginning of each line. You can link headings as closely as possible with the text they introduce by providing more space above the heading than below it. Next to headings, captions are the most widely read part of a message, tying photographs and illustrations into the rest of your message. Although usually placed below the exhibits they describe, captions can be placed beside or above their exhibits.

Headings help your readers quickly identify the content and organization of your message.

- *Typefaces.* **Typeface** refers to the physical design of letters, numbers, and other characters, which makes your message look authoritative, friendly, expensive, classy, casual, and so on. **Serif typefaces** have small cross-lines (called serifs) at the ends of each letter stroke[14] (see Figure 7.3). Serif faces such as Times Roman are commonly used for text. Typefaces with rounded serifs can look friendly; those with squared serifs can look official. **Sans-serif typefaces** have no serifs. Faces such as Helvetica are ideal for display treatments that use larger type. Many great-looking documents

Serif typefaces are commonly used for text.

Serif Typeface	Sans-Serif Typeface
Times Roman is often used for text.	Helvetica is often used for headings.
TIMES ROMAN IS HARDER TO READ IN ALL CAPS.	HELVETICA IS A CLEANER FACE, EVEN IN ALL CAPS.

Figure 7.3
Common Typefaces
Although serif typefaces are considered easier to read than sans-serif are, both have a place in document design.

are based on a single sans-serif typeface for heads and subheads with a single serif typeface for text and captions. Using too many typefaces clutters the document.

- *Type styles.* Type style is any modification that lends contrast or emphasis to type. Using boldface type for subheads breaks up long expanses of text, but too much will darken your document's appearance. Use italic type for emphasis, to indicate a quote, or in captions. Be careful to avoid any style that slows your audience's reading. Underlining can interfere with your reader's ability to recognize the shapes of words, and using all capitals slows reading progress.[15] Shadowed or outlined type can seriously hinder legibility, so use these styles carefully.

> Sans-serif typefaces are commonly used for headings.

> Avoid using type styles that slow your readers down.

You decide on each design element according to its function. Effective design guides your readers through your message, so be sure to be consistent, balanced, restrained, and detail-oriented:

> For effective design, pay attention to
> - Consistency
> - Balance
> - Restraint
> - Detail

- *Consistency.* Be consistent in your design and use of certain elements within a message (and sometimes even from message to message). Throughout a message, be consistent in your use of margins, typeface, type size, and spacing (in paragraph indents, between columns, and around photographs). Also, be sure you're consistent in using all recurring elements, such as vertical lines, columns, and borders.
- *Balance.* To create a pleasing design, balance the space devoted to text, artwork, and white space.
- *Restraint.* Strive for simplicity in design. Don't clutter your message with too many design elements, too much highlighting, or too many decorative touches.
- *Detail.* Track all details that affect your design and thus your message. Headings and subheads that appear at the bottom of a column or a page (widows) can offend readers when the promised information doesn't appear until the next column or page. A layout that appears off balance can be distracting, and any typographical errors can sabotage an otherwise good-looking design.

Avoid last-minute compromises. Don't reduce type size or white space to squeeze in text. On the other hand, avoid increasing type size or white space to fill space. If you've planned your message so that your purpose, your audience, and your message are clear, you can design your document to be effective.[16]

PROOFING YOUR MESSAGE

When you proof your message, you ensure that it's letter perfect. Although grammar, spelling, punctuation, and typographical errors may seem trivial to some people, most readers will view your attention to detail as a sign of your professionalism. If a writer lets mechanical errors slip through, the reader automatically wonders whether the writer is unreliable in more important ways.

> Credibility is affected by your attention to the details of mechanics and format.

CHECKLIST FOR REVISING BUSINESS MESSAGES

A. Editing Your Message

1. Content and organization
   - a. Review your draft against the message plan.
   - b. Cover all necessary points in logical order.
   - c. Organize the message to respond to the audience's probable reaction.
   - d. Provide enough support to make the main idea convincing and interesting.
   - e. Eliminate unnecessary material; add useful material.
   - f. Be sure the beginning and ending are effective.

2. Style and readability
   - a. Be sure you've achieved the right tone.
   - b. Increase interest with lively words and phrases.
   - c. Make sure your message is readable.
     - i. Check vocabulary.
     - ii. Check sentence structure.
     - iii. Consider using a readability index.

3. Word choice
   - a. Use plain English.
   - b. Use concrete words that avoid negative connotations.
   - c. Rely on nouns, verbs, and specific adjectives and adverbs.
   - d. Select words that are strong, familiar, and short, while avoiding clichés and camouflaged verbs.
   - e. Use bias-free language.

B. Rewriting Your Message

1. Sentence style
   - a. Fit the sentence structure to the thought.
   - b. Tailor the sentence style to the audience.
   - c. Aim for an average sentence length of 20 words.
   - d. Write mainly in the active voice, but use the passive voice to achieve specific effects.
   - e. Eliminate unnecessary words and phrases.
   - f. Avoid obsolete and pompous language.
   - g. Moderate your enthusiasm.
   - h. Break up strung-out sentences.
   - i. Avoid hedging sentences.
   - j. Watch for indefinite pronoun starters.
   - k. Express parallel ideas in parallel form.
   - l. Eliminate awkward pointers.
   - m. Correct dangling modifiers.
   - n. Avoid long sequences of nouns.

Also, give some attention to the finer points of format. Have you followed accepted conventions and company guidelines for laying out the document on the page? Have you included all the traditional elements that belong in documents of the type you are creating? Have you been consistent in handling margins, page numbers, headings, exhibits, source notes, and other details? To resolve questions about format and layout, see Appendix B.

Electronic grammar and spell checkers can be helpful if you don't rely too heavily on them.

Finally, if you compose your business messages on a computer, many of the mechanical and grammatical problems discussed in this chapter can be checked electronically. Spell checkers and grammar checkers are discussed in Chapter 4. They're available either as part of word-processing programs or as stand-alone programs. Although both types of program can flag problem areas, they can't actually fix any of those errors for you. For a reminder of the tasks involved in revision, see this chapter's Checklist for Revising Business Messages.

On the Job

SOLVING A COMMUNICATION DILEMMA AT McDONALD'S

Over the past ten years, David Giarla has learned a great deal about the art of communication. By nature, he is a positive individual, and his communication style reflects that fact.

Although his job is to spot problems, you're more likely to hear him use words such as *outstanding, terrific,* and *delicious* rather than *bad, dreadful,* or *unacceptable.* Perhaps that's why

o. Keep subject and verb close together, and keep adverbs, adjectives, and prepositional phrases close to the words they modify.

p. Emphasize key points through sentence style.

2. Effective paragraphs

a. Be sure each paragraph contains a topic sentence, related sentences, and transitional elements.

b. Edit for unity, effective development, and coherence.

c. Choose a method of development that suits the subject: illustration, comparison or contrast, cause and effect, classification, problem and solution.

d. Vary the length and structure of sentences within paragraphs.

e. Mix paragraphs of different lengths, but aim for an average of 100 words.

C. Producing Your Message

1. Design elements

a. Use appropriate white space around headings, in margins, between columns, at line endings, in paragraph indents or between unindented paragraphs, and between lines of type.

b. Choose margins and line justification that won't darken your document.

c. Use headings to break up long passages and to guide your readers through your message.

d. Select typefaces that complement the tone of your message.

e. Use only as many type styles as you actually need, avoiding any style that slows reader progress.

2. Design decisions

a. Be consistent, balanced, restrained, and detail-oriented.

b. Avoid last-minute compromises.

D. Proofing Your Message

1. Mechanics and format

a. Review sentences to be sure they are grammatically correct.

b. Correct punctuation and capitalization errors.

c. Look for spelling and typographical errors.

d. Review the format to be sure it follows accepted conventions.

e. Apply the format consistently throughout the message.

2. Electronic grammar and spell checkers

a. Use electronic checkers to point up errors you might overlook.

b. Be aware of program limitations so that you don't rely too heavily on electronic checkers.

---

the managers and employees on his regular route always greet him with a smile.

Giarla calls on seven or eight McDonald's every day. If you work in one of his restaurants, you have a good chance of serving Giarla breakfast, lunch, a snack, or dinner on any given day. You know he's coming, but you don't know when—and that keeps you on your toes.

On a typical visit, Giarla pulls into the parking lot and checks for rubbish. The ideal McDonald's is blindingly clean from the street to the storeroom. He enters the restaurant. Are the lines moving quickly? They'd better be. Are the order takers smiling? You bet. A perky teenager behind the counter recognizes Giarla and asks, "Big Breakfast and a regular Diet Coke?" "Correctomundo," he replies.

He carries his tray to a table. Is it spotless? Yup. He inspects his food. Hmm. The biscuit looks a little small. He nibbles a hash brown, then heads for the kitchen. "Great hash browns," he says to the person at the deep fryer. "You should get a raise." He pauses a minute to inspect the dates stamped on the hamburger wrappers. Good. They're fresh. So are the cucumbers, cheese, and milk shake mix.

Business is picking up, so Giarla pitches in to help make Egg McMuffins. "These are going to be terrific," he announces. He finds that helping out builds rapport. He tries hard to cultivate goodwill between McDonald's headquarters and the restaurant managers and employees. He does not view himself as "the enemy spy." On the contrary, McDonald's is a team effort, and he is a coach—one of 300 field consultants who spend their days happily checking out the Golden Arches from coast to coast.

When Giarla spots the restaurant manager, he mentions the small-biscuit problem. He wonders whether someone could be overkneading the dough. He recommends that the biscuit maker review the McDonald's videotape that provides instructions for preparing biscuits and other items.

On to the next stop, where a helper crams too much food into a bag. More stops reveal more opportunities for improvement: a ceiling tile is stained and needs to be replaced; a cheeseburger bun is dented—probably because someone wrapped it too tightly; a storeroom is messy; a soft-serve cone is six inches high instead of the recommended three inches. Giarla calls attention to all these problems. You might expect the restaurant managers and employees to resent the criticism, but by and large they welcome his suggestions. Why? Because Giarla knows how to communicate.

Your Mission: You have recently joined McDonald's as a quality control representative. Like David Giarla, you cover seven or eight restaurants a day. Most of the managers are very cooperative, and most of the restaurants maintain very high standards, but there's one exception. Over the past few months, you have pointed out a variety of problems to a particular McDonald's manager. You have been friendly, polite, and constructive in your suggestions, yet nothing has been done to correct most of the problems. On your last visit, you warned the manager that you would have to file a negative report with headquarters if you didn't see some improvement immediately. You have decided to put your suggestions in writing and give the manager one week to take action. Here is the first draft of your letter. Using the questions that follow, analyze it according to the material in this chapter. Be prepared to explain your analysis.

Please correct the problems listed below. I will visit your facility within the next few days to monitor your progress. If nothing has been done toward rectifying these infractions of McDonald's principles of operation, you will be reported to headquarters for noncooperation and unsatisfactory levels of performance. As you know, I have mentioned these deviations from acceptable practice on previous visits. You have been given ample opportunity to comply with my suggestions. Your failure to comply suggests that you lack the necessary commitment to quality that has long been the hallmark of McDonald's restaurants.

On two occasions, I have ascertained that you are using expired ingredients in preparing hamburgers. On February 14, a package of buns with a freshness date of January 31 was used in your facility. Also, on March 2, you were using cheese that had expired by at least ten days. McDonald's is committed to freshness. All our ingredients are freshness dated. Expired ingredients should be disposed of, not used in the preparation of products for sale to the public. For example, you might contact local charities and offer the expired items to them free of charge, provided, of course, that the ingredients do not pose a health hazard (e.g., sour milk should be thrown out). The Community Resource Center in your area can be reached by calling 555-0909. Although I have warned you before about using old ingredients, the last time I visited your facility, I found expired ingredients in the storeroom.

Your bathrooms should be refurbished and cleaned more frequently. The paper towel dispenser in the men's room was out of towels the last time I was there, and the faucet on the sink dripped. This not only runs up your water bill but also creates a bad impression for the customer. Additionally, your windows need washing. On all my visits, I have noticed fingerprints on the front door. I have never, in fact, seen your door anything but dirty. This, too, creates a negative impression. Similarly, the windows are not

as clean as they might be. Also, please mop the floors more often. Nobody wants to eat in a dirty restaurant.

The most serious infraction pertains to the appearance of store personnel. Dirty uniforms are unforgivable. Also, employees, particularly those serving the public, must have clean fingernails and hands. Hair should be neatly combed, and uniforms should be carefully pressed. I realize that your restaurant is located in an economically depressed area, and I am aware that many of your employees are ethnic minorities from impoverished backgrounds and single-parent families. Perhaps you should hold a class in basic cleanliness for these people. It is likely that they have not been taught proper hygiene in their homes.

In addition, please instruct store personnel to empty the trash more frequently. The bins are constantly overflowing, making it difficult for customers to dispose of leftover food and rubbish. This is a problem both indoors and outdoors.

Also bear in mind that all patrons should be served within a few minutes of their arrival at your place of business. Waiting in line is annoying, particularly during the busy lunch hour, when people are on tight schedules. Open new lines when you must in order to accommodate the flow of traffic. In addition, instruct the order takers and order fillers to work more rapidly during busy times. Employees should not be standing around chatting with each other while customers wait in line.

As I mentioned above, I will visit your facility within a few days to check on your progress toward meeting McDonald's criteria of operation. If no visible progress has been made, I will have no alternative other than to report you to top management at headquarters. If you have any questions or require clarification on any of these items, please feel free to contact me. I can be reached by calling 555-3549.

1. How would you rate this draft in terms of its content and organization?
   a. Although the style of the letter needs work, the content and organization are basically okay.
   b. The draft is seriously flawed in both content and organization. Extensive editing is required.
   c. The content is fine, but the organization is poor.
   d. The organization is fine, but the content is poor.
2. What should be done to eliminate the biased tone of the fourth paragraph?
   a. Omit the last three sentences of the paragraph.
   b. Omit the last three sentences and add something like the following: "Please have your employees review the videotape that deals with McDonald's standards of personal appearance."

c. Revise the last three sentences along the following lines: "Given the composition of your labor force, you may need to stress the basics of personal hygiene."

3. Assume that you decide to retain the following passage: "McDonald's is committed to freshness. All our ingredients are freshness dated." How would you revise it? Explain your decision.

   a. Leave the passage as it is. The two simple sentences already do a good job of expressing the relationship of the ideas.
   b. "Because McDonald's is committed to quality, all our ingredients are freshness dated." A single complex sentence is the best vehicle for expressing the cause-and-effect relationship between McDonald's standards and its use of freshness dating on packages.
   c. "McDonald's is committed to quality, and all our ingredients are freshness dated." A compound sentence best reflects the relationship between the two ideas, which are of equal importance.
   d. "The freshness dates indicate McDonald's commitment to quality. Please observe them." A single simple sentence is the best vehicle for expressing the closely related ideas in the original version. The second sentence is added to make the implied point explicit.

4. Which of the following is the best alternative to this sentence: "If nothing has been done toward rectifying these infractions of McDonald's principles of operation, you will be reported to headquarters for noncooperation and unsatisfactory levels of performance."

   a. "If nothing has been done to correct these infractions, you will be reported to headquarters for noncompliance."
   b. "If you don't shape up immediately, headquarters will hear about it."
   c. "By correcting these problems promptly, you can avoid being reported to headquarters."
   d. "You can preserve your unblemished reputation by acting immediately to bring your facility into compliance with McDonald's principles of operation."

5. Take a look at the third paragraph of the letter. What is its chief flaw?

   a. There is no topic sentence.
   b. The topic sentence is too narrow for the ideas encompassed in the paragraph.
   c. The transition from the previous paragraph is poor.
   d. The paragraph deals with more than one subject.
   e. The topic sentence is not adequately developed with specific details in subsequent sentences.[17]

Questions for Discussion

1. You have so little time for your current project that you have to skip a few of the tasks in the composition process. You've already cut down everything you can in the planning and composing categories. Which tasks in the revision category would be best to cut: editing, rewriting, producing, or proofreading?

2. In what business situations might you want to use words of high connotative value?

3. How could cultural bias differ from racial and ethnic bias? What examples can you think of?

4. What specific techniques of style could you use to create a formal, objective tone? An informal, personal tone?

5. When you design your formal business letter, which elements are necessary to consider, and which are not?

6. Given the choice of only one, would you prefer to use a grammar checker or a spell checker? Why?

Documents for Analysis

Read the following documents; then (1) analyze the strengths and weaknesses of each sentence and (2) revise each document so that it follows this chapter's guidelines.

DOCUMENT 7.A

The move to our new offices will take place over this coming weekend. For everything to run smooth, everyone will have to clean out their own desk and pack up the contents in boxes that will be provided.

You will need to take everything off the walls too, and please pack it along with the boxes.

If you have alot of personal belongings, you should bring them home with you. Likewise with anything valuable. I do not mean to infer that items will be stolen, irregardless it is better to be safe than sorry.

On Monday, we will be unpacking, putting things away, and then get back to work. The least amount of disruption is anticipated by us, if everyone does their part. Hopefully, there will be no negative affects on production schedules, and current deadlines will be met.

DOCUMENT 7.B
Dear Ms. Giraud:

Enclosed herewith please find the manuscript for your book, Careers in Woolgathering. After perusing the first two chapters of your 1,500-page manuscript, I was forced to conclude that the subject matter, handicrafts and artwork using wool fibers, is not coincident with the publishing program of Framingham Press, which to this date has issued only works on business endeavors, avoiding all other topics completely.

Although our firm is unable to consider your impressive work at the present time, I have taken the liberty of recording some comments on some of the pages. I am of the opinion that any feedback that a writer can obtain from those well versed in the publishing realm can only serve to improve the writer's authorial skills.

In view of the fact that your residence is in the Boston area, might I suggest that you secure an appointment with someone of high editorial stature at the Cambridge Heritage Press, which I believe might have something of an interest in works of the nature you have produced.

Wishing you the best of luck in your literary endeavors, I remain

Arthur J. Cogswell

Editor

DOCUMENT 7.C
For delicious air-popped popcorn, please read the following instructions: The popper is designed to pop 1/2 cup of popcorn kernels at one time. Never add more than 1/2 cup. A half cup of corn will produce three to four quarts of popcorn. More batches may be made separately after completion of the first batch. Popcorn is popped by hot air. Oil or shortening is not needed for popping corn. Add only popcorn kernels to the popping chamber. Standard grades of popcorn are recommended for use. Premium or gourmet type popping corns may be used. Ingredients such as oil, shortening, butter, margarine, or salt should never be added to the popping chamber. The popper, with popping chute in position, may be preheated for two minutes before adding the corn. Turn the popper off before adding the corn. Use electricity safely and wisely. Observe safety precautions when using the popper. Do not touch the popper when it is hot. The popper should not be left unattended when it is plugged into an outlet. Do not use the popper if it or its cord has been damaged. Do not use the popper if it is not working properly. Before using the first time, wash the chute and butter/measuring cup in hot soapy water. Use a dishcloth or sponge. Wipe the outside of the popper base. Use a damp cloth. Dry the base. Do not immerse the popper base in water or other liquid. Replace the chute and butter/measuring cup. The popper is ready to use.

*E*xercises

1. Write a concrete phrase for each of these vague phrases:
   a. sometime this spring
   b. a substantial saving
   c. a large number attended
   d. increased efficiency
   e. expanded the work area
2. List words that are stronger than the following:
   a. ran after
   b. seasonal ups and downs
   c. bright
   d. suddenly rises
   e. moves forward
3. As you rewrite these sentences, replace the clichés with fresh, personal expressions:
   a. Being a jack-of-all-trades, Dave worked well in his new selling job.
   b. Moving Leslie into the accounting department, where she was literally a fish out of water, was like putting a square peg into a round hole, if you get my drift.
   c. I knew she was at death's door, but I thought the doctor would pull her through.
   d. Movies aren't really my cup of tea; as far as I am concerned, they can't hold a candle to a good book.
   e. It's a dog-eat-dog world out there in the rat race of the asphalt jungle.
4. Revise the following sentences using shorter, simpler words:
   a. The antiquated calculator is ineffectual for solving sophisticated problems.
   b. It is imperative that the pay increments be terminated before an inordinate deficit is accumulated.
   c. There was unanimity among the executives that Ms. Jackson's idiosyncrasies were cause for a mandatory meeting with the company's personnel director.
   d. The impending liquidation of the company's assets was cause for jubilation among the company's competitors.
   e. The expectations of the president for a stock dividend were accentuated by the preponderance of evidence that the company was in good financial condition.
5. Rewrite each of the following to eliminate bias:
   a. For an Indian, Maggie certainly is outgoing.

b. He needs a wheelchair, but he doesn't let his handicap affect his job performance.

c. She's too sensitive; when I criticized her performance, she asked me to explain.

d. A pilot must have the ability to stay calm under pressure, and then he must be trained to cope with any problem that arises.

e. "And what would you ladies like us to do about absenteeism?"

6. Rewrite each sentence so that it is active rather than passive:

a. The raw data are submitted to the data-processing division by the sales representative each Friday.

b. High profits are publicized by management.

c. The policies announced in the directive were implemented by the staff.

d. Our typewriters are serviced by the Santee Company.

e. The employees were represented by Janet Hogan.

7. Condense these sentences to as few words as possible:

a. We are of the conviction that writing is important.

b. In all probability, we're likely to have a price increase.

c. The price increase exceeded the amount of 5 cents.

d. We are engaged in the process of building this store.

e. Our goals include making a determination about that in the near future.

8. Write up-to-date versions of these phrases; write *none* if you believe there is no appropriate substitute:

a. as per your instructions

b. attached herewith

c. take the liberty of

d. this will acknowledge

e. according to our records

9. Remove all the unnecessary modifiers from these sentences:

a. Tremendously high pay increases were given to the extraordinarily skilled and extremely conscientious employees.

b. The union's proposals were highly inflationary, extremely demanding, and exceptionally bold.

10. Rewrite these sentences so that they no longer contain any hedging:

a. It would appear that someone apparently entered illegally.

b. It may be possible that sometime in the near future the situation is likely to improve.

c. Your report seems to suggest that we might be losing money.

d. I believe Nancy apparently has somewhat greater influence over employees in the typing pool.

e. It seems as if this letter of resignation means you might be leaving us.

11. Rewrite the sentences below to eliminate the indefinite starters:

a. There are several examples here to show that Elaine can't hold a position very long.

b. It would be greatly appreciated if every employee would make a generous contribution to Mildred Cook's retirement party.

c. It has been learned in Washington today from generally reliable sources that an important announcement will be made shortly by the White House.

d. There is a rule that states that we cannot work overtime without permission.

e. It would be great if you could work late for the next three Saturdays.

12. Present the ideas in these sentences in parallel form:

a. Mr. Hill is expected to lecture three days a week, to counsel two days a week, and must write for publication in his spare time.

b. The office workers were hired to receive callers, to operate the duplicating equipment, and a variety of duties were handled by them.

c. All the employees were given instruction in writing letters, using the photocopying machine, and how to keep all our accounts in alphabetical order.

d. She knows not only accounting, but she also reads Latin.

e. My Uncle Bill is young, ambitious, and he is rich.

13. Rewrite these sentences to clarify the dangling modifiers:

a. Running down the railroad tracks in a cloud of smoke, we watched the countryside glide by.

b. Lying on the shelf, Ruby saw the seashell.

c. Based on the information, I think we should buy the property.

d. Being cluttered and filthy, Sandy took the whole afternoon to clean up her desk.

e. After proofreading every word, the memo was ready to be signed.

14. Rewrite the following sentences to eliminate the long strings of nouns:

a. The focus of the meeting was a discussion of the bank interest rate deregulation issue.

b. Following the government task force report recommendations, we are revising our job applicant evaluation procedures.

c. The production department quality assurance program components include employee training, supplier cooperation, and computerized detection equipment.

d. The supermarket warehouse inventory reduction plan will be implemented next month.

e. The State University business school graduate placement program is one of the best in the country.

15. Rearrange the following sentences to bring the subjects closer to their verbs:

a. Trudy, when she first saw the bull pawing the ground, ran.

b. It was Terri who, according to Ted, who is probably the worst gossip in the office (Tom excepted), mailed the wrong order.

c. William Oberstreet, in his book *Investment Capital Reconsidered*, writes of the mistakes that bankers through the decades have made.

d. Judy Schimmel, after passing up several sensible investment opportunities, despite the warnings of her friends and family, invested her inheritance in a jojoba plantation.

e. The president of U-Stor-It, which was on the brink of bankruptcy after the warehouse fire, the worst tragedy in the history of the company, prepared an announcement for the press.

16. Write a paragraph on each of the following topics—one by illustration, one by comparison or contrast, one by discussion of cause and effect, one by classification, and one by discussion of problem and solution. Collect your various drafts and be prepared to explain the changes you made.

a. Types of cameras (or dogs or automobiles) available for sale

b. Advantages and disadvantages of eating at fast-food restaurants

c. Finding that first job

d. Good qualities of my car (or house, apartment, or neighborhood)

e. How to make a dessert recipe (or barbecue a steak or make coffee)

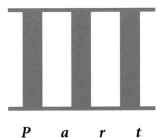

Organizing Direct Requests · Placing Orders · Requesting Routine Information and Action

LETTERS,

esting Claims and Adjustments · Making Routine Credit Requests · Inquiring about People

MEMOS, AND

ages · Writing Positive Replies · Responding Favorably to Claims and Adjustment Requests

OTHER BRIEF

quests · Conveying Positive Information About People · Writing Directives and Instructions

MESSAGES

ying Good News About Products and Operations · Writing Goodwill Intercultural Requests

Chapter 8
Writing Direct Requests

Chapter 9
Writing Routine, Good-News, and Goodwill Messages

Chapter 10
Writing Bad-News Messages

Chapter 11
Writing Persuasive Messages

After studying this chapter, you will be able to

Explain why you follow the customs of your audience when making requests across cultural boundaries

Clearly state the main idea of each direct request you write

Indicate your confidence that the request will be filled

Provide sufficient detail for the reader to be able to comply with your request

Clarify complicated requests with lists and tables

Close with a courteous request for specific action

WRITING DIRECT REQUESTS

n the Job

FACING A COMMUNICATION DILEMMA AT BARNES & NOBLE

May the Best Seller Win!

Lots of gloomy news has been written about the sad state of reading in the United States, but the book business has actually boomed in recent years. Consumers buy more than $13 billion worth of books each year—spending more on books than they do on going to the movies, buying or renting videotaped movies, and buying pre-recorded music. In fact, the U.S. book market has been expanding year by year, and at the forefront of this expansion is Leonard Riggio. As chairman and CEO of Barnes & Noble, Riggio is considered by many to be the most powerful person in publishing.

Riggio got his start as a clerk in a college bookstore and eventually opened six college bookstores of his own. His next move was becoming the principal owner of the Barnes & Noble Bookstore. After that he purchased the B. Dalton Bookseller, Bookstop, and Doubleday book chains. Today Barnes & Noble is the largest book retailer in the United States, with annual sales of more than $1.6 billion and an aggressive expansion plan. Despite its achievements, Riggio's chain is hardly alone in the book market.

Bookstores fall into three categories: (1) independent bookstores, which are individually owned outlets ranging from tiny specialty shops to warehouse-size giants; (2) regional chains, such as Kroch's in Chicago; and (3) big national chains such as Crown Books. Riggio competes to one degree or another with every category, but in terms of sheer size, the Kmart-owned bookstores, including the Borders and Waldenbooks chains, are his primary rivals.

As you read this chapter, put yourself in Leonard Riggio's shoes. To stay ahead of your competitors, you must send messages to customers and store managers, requesting both information and action. How can you obtain the information you need to make intelligent decisions? How would you phrase the requests you send to store managers so that they will respond with positive action in the race against Kmart's bookstores?[1]

INTERCULTURAL REQUESTS

Like so many U.S. executives, Leonard Riggio knows that making requests across cultural boundaries can be frustrating, depending on the degree of red tape, the language barrier, your familiarity with the cultural differences involved, and even the mail system in a particular region or country. Just deciding whether to make your request in writing can be tricky, depending on where you're doing business. On the one hand, paper-oriented countries such as France, Germany, and England use a steady stream of correspondence to lead up to meetings and negotiations.[2] On the other hand, some Arabic, Asian, and Latin American countries consider paperwork a poor second choice for conducting business.

Barnes & Noble

Whether written or oral, your request will be most effective if you follow the customs of your audience. Not all requests are organized directly. For example, an Arab letter would probably begin with a generalized blessing upon the reader and his or her family.[3] Other cultures begin with an explanation and work up to the request at the end of the message. So whenever you can, learn about the customs of your audience and follow them as far as possible.

ORGANIZING DIRECT REQUESTS

When you're addressing a U.S. or Canadian audience, when cultural differences are minimal, and when you can assume that your audience will be interested in what you have to say (or at least willing to cooperate with you), make a **direct request** by following the direct, or deductive, plan to organize your message. Present the request or the main idea first, follow up with necessary details, and close with a cordial statement of the action you want. This approach works well when your request requires no special tact or persuasion. For example, Barnes & Noble's store managers are certainly interested in helping Leonard Riggio increase book sales, just as distributors are interested in filling a Barnes & Noble order.

> For direct requests
> - State the request or main idea
> - Give necessary details
> - Close with a cordial request for specific action

People making direct requests may be tempted to begin with a personal introduction ("I am administrative assistant to the head of a large bookstore chain, and I'm interested in expanding our selection of reference books"). However, this type of beginning is usually a mistake. The essence of the message, the specific request, is buried and may get lost. A better way to organize a direct request is to state what you want in the first sentence or two and let the explanation follow this initial request.

Even though you expect a favorable response, the tone of your initial request is important. Instead of demanding immediate action ("Send me your catalog no. 33A"), soften your request with such words as *please* and *I would appreciate*. An impatient demand for rapid service isn't necessary because you can generally assume that your audience will comply with your request once the reason for it is understood.

> Assume that your reader will comply once he or she understands your purpose.

The middle part of a direct request usually explains the original request ("I would like to order a sample of several of your reference works to determine whether they would appeal to our customers"). Such amplifying details help your audience fulfill your request correctly.

When writing direct requests, says former NBC News correspondent and best-selling author Edwin Newman, get directly and clearly to the point by eliminating boastful, complicated vocabulary and words that impress or conceal.

In the last section, clearly state the action you're requesting. You may wish to tell the audience where to send the sought-after information or product, indicate any time limits, or list details of the request that were too complex or numerous to cover in the introductory section. Then close with a brief, cordial note reminding the audience of the importance of the request ("If the sample books sell well, you can expect to receive additional orders from Barnes & Noble on a monthly basis").

Now take a closer look at the three main sections of a direct request. Although this discussion focuses on letters and memos, remember that this organizational plan may be appropriate for brief oral messages as well.

Direct Statement of the Request or Main Idea

The general rule for the first part of a direct request is to write not only to be understood but also to avoid being misunderstood. If you request "1990 Census figures" from a government agency, the person who handles your request won't know whether you want a page or two of summary figures or a detailed report running to several thousand pages. So be as specific as possible in the sentence or two that begins your message.

Also, be aware of the difference between a polite request in question form (which requires no question mark) and a question that is part of a request:

Polite Request in Question Form	**Question That Is Part of a Request**
Would you please help us determine whether Kate Kingsley is a suitable applicant for a position as landscape designer.	Did Kate Kingsley demonstrate an ability to work smoothly with clients?

Use a period at the end of a request in question form that requires action; use a question mark at the end of a request that requires an answer in words.

Many direct requests include both types of statements, so be sure to distinguish between the polite request that is your overall reason for writing and the specific questions that belong in the middle section of your letter or memo.

Justification, Explanation, and Details

In the middle section
- Call attention to how the reader will benefit from granting your request
- Give details of your request

To make the explanation a smooth and logical outgrowth of your opening remarks, you might make the first sentence of your message's middle section you-oriented by stating a service-to-the-reader benefit. For instance, a Barnes & Noble manager might write, "By keeping Barnes & Noble informed about your products, you can expand your distribution channel. For example, if a unique readership exists for one of your new references, I can help you reach those customers."

Another possible approach for the middle section is to ask a series of questions, particularly if your inquiry concerns machinery or complex equipment. You might ask about technical specifications, exact dimensions, and the precise use of the product. The most important question is asked first. If cost is your main concern, you might begin with a question like "What is the price of your least expensive laser printer?" Then you may want to ask more specific but related questions about, say, the cost of toner cartridges and maintenance service.

Ask the most important question first; then ask related, more specific questions.

Use numbered lists when you're requesting several items or answers.

If you're requesting several items or answers, number the items and list them in logical order or in descending order of importance. Furthermore, so that your request can be handled quickly, ask only the questions that are central to your main request. Avoid asking for information that you can find on your own, even if your effort takes considerable time.

If you're asking many people to reply to the same questions, consider wording them so that they can be answered with a yes or no or with some other easily counted response. You may even want to provide respondents with a form or with boxes they can check to indicate their answers. If you need more than a simple yes or no answer, pose an open-ended question. For example, a question like "How fast can you repair computer monitors?" is more likely to elicit the information you want than "Can you repair computer monitors?" Keep in mind also that phrasing questions in a way that hints at the response you want is likely to get you less-than-accurate information. So try to phrase your questions objectively. Finally, deal with only one topic in each question. If the questions need amplification, keep each question in a separate paragraph.

When you prepare questions
- Ask only questions that relate to your main request
- Don't ask for information you can find yourself
- Make your questions open-ended and objective
- Deal with only one topic in each question

Other types of information that belong in this section include data about a product (model number, date and place of purchase, condition), your reason for being concerned about a particular matter, and other details about your request. Upon finishing this middle section, your audience should understand why the request is important and be persuaded to satisfy it.

Courteous Close with Request for Specific Action

Close your letter with two important elements: (1) a request for some specific response (complete with any time limits that apply) and (2) an expression of appreciation or goodwill. Help your reader respond easily by including your phone number, office hours, and other helpful information.

Close with
- A request for some specific response
- An expression of appreciation
- Information about how you can be reached

However, don't thank the reader "in advance" for cooperating. If the reader's reply warrants a word of thanks, send it after you've received the reply. If you're requesting information for a research project, you might offer to forward a copy of your report in gratitude for the reader's assistance. If you plan to reprint or publish materials that you ask for, indicate that you'll get any necessary permission. When asking for information about an individual, be sure to indicate that you'll keep all responses confidential.

P LACING ORDERS

Because they're usually processed without objection, and because they refer to a product that the reader knows about, orders are considered one of the simplest types of direct request. When placing an order, you don't need to excite your reader's interest; just state your needs clearly and directly.

To see what to include in a good order letter, examine any mail-order form supplied by a large firm: It offers complete and concise directions for providing all the information needed to fill an order. After the date, the order form probably starts with "Please send the following" or "Please ship." If you complete the rest of the form and mail it, these statements constitute a legal and binding offer to purchase the goods ordered. The supplier's shipment of those goods constitutes an acceptance of the offer and thus completes a legal contract.

Order letters are like good mail-order forms, although they also provide more room for explaining special needs.

Order blanks are arranged to document precisely the goods you want, describing them by catalog number, quantity, name or trade name, color, size, unit price, and total amount due. When drafting an order letter, follow the same format, presenting information about the items you want in column form, double-spacing between the items, and totaling the price at the end.

Order blanks provide space for delivery information, such as how and where to send the shipment. In your letter be sure to specify the delivery address, especially if it is not the address from which you send your letter. (Sometimes the billing and delivery addresses are different.) Also indicate how the merchandise is to be shipped: by truck, air freight, parcel post, air express, or delivery service. Unless you specify the mode of transportation, the seller chooses.

In any letter sent with money, mention the amount of payment, explain how the amount was calculated, and if necessary, explain to what account the amount should be charged. Again, the order form provides an excellent model. Most have spaces for showing unit prices, the total amount for each item, the cost of shipping and handling, the total amount of the payment, and the form of payment (check, money order, bank draft, or other means). Following is an example that follows the order-form format and adds important information:

Please ship by air express to the above address the following ten items, which are shown in your April sale catalog:

3-#256 Men's nylon raincoats (in gray); sizes 42 long (1), 40 regular (1), and 38 regular (1); @ $19.95	$ 59.85
2-#5823 Women's plastic rain-capes (in yellow); sizes medium (1) and small (1); @ $17.50	35.00
5-#353898 Unisex rain parkas (in red); sizes large (1), medium (3), and small (1); @ $23.95	119.75
Total sale	$214.60
Sales tax	15.02
Air express	45.73
Amount due	$275.35

The general request is stated first.

All necessary details are provided (in a format similar to an order form).

Information about such additional charges as tax and shipping was provided in the catalog, so to ensure quick processing of the order, the writer calculated the amount due.

I am enclosing a check for $275.35 to cover all charges. We need some of your famous rain gear for an upcoming field experiment to be conducted in the rain forest in the state of Washington. So please call us collect at once at (714) 833-9717 if you cannot deliver all ten items to us by May 9.

The closing paragraph sets a time limit and cordially requests a specific procedure if problems arise.

Not every item ordered through the mail is neatly displayed in a catalog or newspaper advertisement. If the goods are somewhat unusual, be thorough and clear when identifying them. For instance, the office manager of a company ordering specially cut lumber for a set of bookcases would need to be more descriptive:

When ordering a nonstandard item, include a complete description.

Please deliver the following pieces of cut lumber to the above address this Friday afternoon (August 12). We are having bookshelves built on Saturday to fit into two rather oddly shaped areas of our office.

CHECKLIST FOR ORDERS

A. Direct Statement of the Request
1. Use wording that indicates an order rather than a request: "Please send me" or "please ship" instead of "I want" or "I need," which are neither polite nor legally appropriate for a business order.
2. Open with a general description of your order that encompasses all the details.

B. Justification, Explanation, and Details
1. For complex orders, provide a general explanation of what the requested materials will be used for.
2. Provide all specifications: quantity, price (including discounts), size, catalog numbers, product description, shipping instructions (date and place), arrangements for payment (method, time, deposits), and cost totals.
3. Use a format that presents information clearly and makes it easy to total amounts.
4. Double-check the completeness of your order and the cost totals.

C. Courteous Close with Request for Specific Action
1. Include a clear summary of the desired action.
2. Suggest a future reader benefit, if possible.
3. Close on a cordial note.
4. Clearly state any time limits that apply to your order, and explain why they are important.

Be sure to cut the shelves to the following specifications, all from your finest-quality walnut, 3/4 inch thick and 6 inches wide:

    5 boards measuring 4 feet 3 inches
    6 boards measuring 4 feet 8 inches
    4 boards measuring 5 feet

So that I can have a check ready for your delivery person on Friday, please let me know by Thursday the total amount due. My phone number is 548-7907.

The added explanation of where and how the boards will be used helps the reader identify your needs accurately. In special cases, such as ordering machine parts, you may even make drawings of the parts you need and add an explanation of their particular use. (To remind yourself of the tasks involved in placing orders, see this chapter's Checklist for Orders.)

REQUESTING ROUTINE INFORMATION AND ACTION

When you need to know about something, elicit an opinion from someone, or suggest a simple action, you usually need only ask. In essence, simple requests say, "This is what I want to know [or what I want you to do], why I'm making the request, and why it may be in your interest to help me." Assuming that your reader is able and willing to do what you want, such a straightforward request gets the job done with a minimum of fuss.

Despite their simple organization, routine requests deserve a tactful touch. In many organizations, memos and letters like these are sent to hundreds or even thousands of employees, customers, clients, and shareholders. So the potential for creating a positive impression is second only to the risk of causing ill will through ambiguous wording or a discourteous tone. When writing a routine request, keep the purpose of your

When making a routine request, say

- *What you want to know*
- *Why you want to know*
- *Why it is in the reader's interest to help you*

Exactly what do you want the reader to understand or do as a result of reading your request for action?

message in mind. That is, ask yourself what you want recipients to understand or do as a result of reading the message. As you prepare the request, remember that even the briefest note can create confusion and hard feelings.

Requests to Company Insiders

A request in memo form

- Provides a permanent record
- Saves time and questions
- Tells precisely what is needed

Although requests to fellow employees are often oral and rather casual, some messages are better put into permanent, written form. A clear, thoughtfully written memo can save time and questions by helping readers understand precisely what is required.

A routine request follows the standard direct plan. Start with a clear statement of your reason for writing; then provide whatever explanation is needed to justify the request. Close with a specific account of what you expect, and include a deadline if appropriate. The memo in Figure 8.1 was sent to all employees of a relatively small manufacturing firm.

Figure 8.1
Memo Requesting Routine Action from Company Insiders

The basic request is stated at the beginning.

The next two paragraphs explain the problem that made the inquiry necessary.

The final paragraph requests action and, with a built-in questionnaire, makes a response easy.

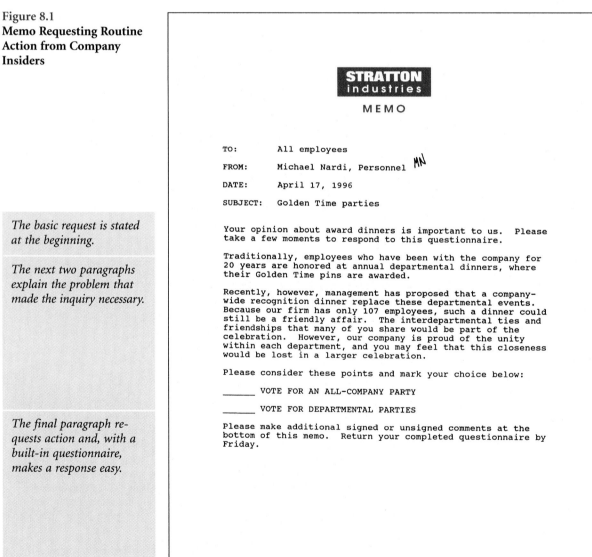

STRATTON industries

MEMO

TO: All employees

FROM: Michael Nardi, Personnel   MN

DATE: April 17, 1996

SUBJECT: Golden Time parties

Your opinion about award dinners is important to us. Please take a few moments to respond to this questionnaire.

Traditionally, employees who have been with the company for 20 years are honored at annual departmental dinners, where their Golden Time pins are awarded.

Recently, however, management has proposed that a company-wide recognition dinner replace these departmental events. Because our firm has only 107 employees, such a dinner could still be a friendly affair. The interdepartmental ties and friendships that many of you share would be part of the celebration. However, our company is proud of the unity within each department, and you may feel that this closeness would be lost in a larger celebration.

Please consider these points and mark your choice below:

_____ VOTE FOR AN ALL-COMPANY PARTY

_____ VOTE FOR DEPARTMENTAL PARTIES

Please make additional signed or unsigned comments at the bottom of this memo. Return your completed questionnaire by Friday.

In the following memo, the writer refers to a previous memo on the same topic and then makes a request for a response from employees:

How do you feel about adopting flextime in your department?

The memo begins with the central question.

Last week you received an explanation of flextime schedules as they could apply to our organization. Now we need your opinion of the proposal.

A little background information orients the reader.

1. Would you want to go on a flextime schedule? Please summarize your reasons.
2. The proposal listed four schedule patterns for employees to choose from. Which pattern now seems best for your department?
3. If your preferred schedule pattern is not available, what other pattern would suit you?
4. Should flextime be mandatory or optional?
5. If flextime is adopted, what problems might arise in your department?

The numbered questions focus responses so that they will be easier to tally.

Please write your answers directly on this sheet and return it to me by Friday. Complete responses will help us formulate the policy that will work best for our company.

Specific instructions for replying close the memo. The courteous tone helps ensure a prompt response.

As executive director of AT&T's new Switching Systems Technology Division of Bell Laboratories, Joseph S. Colson, Jr., is respected not only as a gifted engineer but also as a motivator of people. Known for his effective communication, Colson recommends that written requests spell out exactly the action requested.

This memo is matter-of-fact and assumes some shared background. Such a style is appropriate when you're communicating about a routine matter to someone in the same company.

Adjust the writing style in memos to accommodate shared reference points.

Requests to Other Businesses

Many letters to other businesses are requests for information about products, like a Barnes & Noble letter requesting a catalog from a reference book distributor. They are among the simplest of all letters to write because businesses welcome the opportunity to tell you about their goods and services. In fact, you can often simply fill out a coupon or response card and mail it to the correct address. In other cases you might write a brief note requesting further information about something you saw or heard in an advertisement. One or two sentences will most likely do the job. Companies commonly check on the effectiveness of their advertisements, so mention where you saw or heard about them.

When writing a letter in response to an advertisement
- *Say where you saw the ad*
- *Specify what you want*
- *Provide a clear and complete return address on the letter*

Of course, many inquiries are prompted by something other than an advertisement, and they demand a more detailed letter. If the letter will be welcome, or if the reader won't mind answering it, the direct approach is still appropriate. The following is such a letter:

If the reader is not expecting your letter, supply more detail.

As treasurer for the Washington Post Company, Leonade D. Jones manages the company's short-term investments, raises funds for potential acquisitions, manages the company's debt, and oversees $600 million in pension assets. Communication should clarify and expedite, not confuse or waste time, says Jones. So whenever you write to other businesses, state clearly what you want, and be specific about time limitations.

Would you please supply information and recommendations on the type of refrigerator we might install in the two-bedroom apartments we own and manage.

Ten refrigerators will be needed for our new apartment building, which is scheduled for completion within four months. Four other buildings are now under construction in the same complex and will need new appliances later.

Because we're considering your company as the supplier, please answer the following questions:

1. What size is appropriate for a two-bedroom apartment? 14 cubic feet? 16? 18?
2. Do you recommend putting self-defrosting refrigerators in rental units?
3. Do you provide service for the refrigerators you sell? If so, how quickly could you repair them in case of breakdown?
4. What models of apartment-size refrigerators do you carry, and what are their prices?
5. Which of your refrigerators has the best service record?

The refrigerators must be ordered within a month, so we would appreciate receiving your reply by March 26.

The overall request is stated at the beginning. Phrased politely in question form, it requires no question mark.

The explanation for the request keeps the reader's attention by hinting at the possibility of future business.

To avoid burdening the reader with an impossibly broad request, the writer asks a series of specific questions, itemized in a logical sequence.

To avoid receiving useless yes or no answers, the writer asks some open-ended questions.

The courteous close specifies a time limit.

This letter should bring a prompt and enthusiastic reply because the situation is clearly described, the possibility of current and future business is suggested, and the questions are specific and easy to answer. Also, the letter implies confidence in the opinion and assistance of the reader. Because the letter will be sent to a business and pertains to a possible sale, the writer did not enclose a stamped, preaddressed envelope.

If you're writing as an individual and are therefore not using letterhead stationery, be sure to write your address on the letter clearly and completely. Many inquiries are not answered because the address was illegibly handwritten or was written only on the return envelope, which was discarded by the recipient.

Requests to Customers and Other Outsiders

Requests to customers often spell out in detail

- What exactly is needed
- How filling the request will benefit them

Businesses often ask individuals outside the organization to provide information or to take some simple action: attend a meeting, return an information card, endorse a document, confirm an address, supplement information on an order. These messages are often short and simple, but some situations require a more detailed explanation. Readers might be unwilling to respond unless they understand how the request benefits them. So more complex letters, with several paragraphs of explanation, are sometimes necessary. When the same message must be sent to many people at the same time, it can be prepared as a form letter and perhaps individualized with a word processor. The following is an example of a well-planned, detailed form letter:

Under federal tax law, your pension payments are considered "wages" for income tax withholding purposes. To simplify your recordkeeping, you may choose to have us withhold taxes from your pension payments, or you may choose to receive the full payments and pay estimated taxes yourself.

The opening states the purpose of the letter in simple, reader-oriented terms. Providing details of the law convinces the reader that the request is warranted.

Here's how to decide which option is best for you:

First, estimate your total taxable income this year from all sources: the taxable portion of all pension payments you receive, dividends, interest, and salary from employment.

An explanation of procedures is another reader-oriented feature of the letter. To make a complex procedure easier to understand, the writer breaks the directions into two clearly defined steps.

Second, estimate your total tax liability for this year by using the income figure you just calculated and your present tax rates. Then subtract your payments of estimated taxes and other amounts withheld for you.

If your calculations show that you will have a tax liability, you may want us to withhold the taxable portion of your pension payments. Simply mark the appropriate box on the enclosed Tax Decision Form, fill in your Social Security number, sign and date the form, and mail it to us.

This paragraph begins to explain the particular action being requested. Again, clear directions are provided to help ensure a response.

If you do not want taxes withheld, mark the "no" box on the form, fill in your Social Security number, sign and date the form, and return it to us.

Providing boxes for the response helps readers comply with the request.

Please let us know your decision by November 1 so that we can begin withholding in January. If you need further information about the new requirements, call Larry Bender, our customer service representative, at (919) 744-2063. He is in the office Monday through Friday from 9:00 a.m. to 5:00 p.m.

The courteous close motivates action by specifying a person to talk to and a deadline for a reply.

BEHIND THE SCENES AT THE PHOENIX SYMPHONY
Orchestrating Direct Requests

Making direct requests is a way of life for Gail Warden, director of development for the Phoenix Symphony. Her job is to request donations, in-kind gifts, and grants to keep the symphony in business, competing with about 1,500 orchestras performing in the United States.

At the heart of Warden's efforts are direct-request letters. They are written to wealthy individuals known for their philanthropy, corporations that support community activities, and nonprofit foundations that contribute to the arts. Warden's letters vary in form because she has so many types of potential contributors, but the tone of her requests remains personalized as much as possible. "The accepted approach is to avoid writing personalized letters to top donors," says Warden, "but I do, and it's effective. They need to hear how much they're appreciated before I ask them for another gift."

A common type of letter Warden writes is to request a donation renewal from symphony sponsors. She opens with what she calls a "feel-good" paragraph:

Mr. Williams, you and your company have been generous donors to the Phoenix Symphony for several years. We have been grateful for that support. You know from your personal involvement with the arts how vital contributed income is to our organization's very existence, so when we say "thank you," it is heartfelt.

She then requests a new pledge: "I'm writing to invite your renewed support and to ask that you please continue for this season with a $1,000 contribution."

Another type of request letter is sent to donors originally solicited by one of the symphony's board mem-

---

Routine requests to customers can be used to reestablish communication.

Businesses sometimes need to reestablish a relationship with former customers. Frequently, customers who are unhappy about some purchase or about the way they were treated make no complaint: They simply stay away from the offending business. A letter of inquiry encouraging them to use idle credit accounts offers them an opportunity to register their displeasure and then move on to a good relationship. Additionally, a customer's response to an inquiry may provide the company with insights into ways to improve its products and customer service. Even if they have no complaint, customers still welcome the personal attention. Such an inquiry to the customer might begin this way:

When a good charge customer like you has not bought anything from us in six months, we wonder why. Is there some way we can serve you better?

When sending routine requests to individuals rather than other businesses, consider enclosing a stamped, preaddressed envelope.

Letters of inquiry sent to someone's home frequently include a stamped, preaddressed envelope to make a reply easier. Similar inquiry letters are sent from one business to another.

For example, the sales representatives of a housewares distributor might send a letter like this to their customers:

Because we haven't heard from you in a while, I thought it would be a good idea to touch base. In fact, I'd like to ask a favor.

The opening paragraph states the reason for the letter. The frank request arouses curiosity and encourages a frank response.

bers. The opening paragraph includes a reminder of the donor's response to the board member: "You were most generous with your response of a $1,000 contribution." Warden continues with a capsule description of the current successful symphony season, in effect explaining to the donors that their generosity helped make it all possible. Then she asks for a renewal.

A third type of request letter is what Warden calls a "cold renewal"—usually addressing patrons who haven't been solicited for two or three years because their gifts were for a longer term. Warden begins by reminding donors of their past generosity:

Last season your corporation completed a very generous three-year pledge to the Phoenix Symphony. We were pleased to recognize your company at the $1,000 Patrons level of giving throughout the three seasons. We hope that you and members of your company have had an opportunity to enjoy some of the wonderful concerts your generosity has helped make possible.

Warden then makes her direct request, only in this case she seeks a financial commitment for another two or three years instead of a specific sum. Because of this approach, she makes sure to include a reason: "We would like you to consider another multiyear pledge; your last pledge was extremely helpful to this organization in making short- and long-range plans." Warden then gives a clear example of the type of program the donor's funds support: "Please know that your corporation's contribution not only supports concerts in Symphony Hall but also enables us to have an extensive educational outreach program."

Apply Your Knowledge

1. Write direct requests for donations to your local art museum: (1) a renewal of a $3,000 donation from a regular corporate sponsor and (2) a renewal of a $5,000 gift from a wealthy patron whose husband recently died.

2. Write a "cold" request for a multiyear corporate donation to your local public broadcasting station.

Will you take a minute today to give us your honest opinion about our merchandise and service. Just jot your ideas, pro and con, at the bottom of this letter and rush it back in this afternoon's mail. Your response will help us help you.

This request for action is a device for uncovering trouble without actually suggesting that there might be trouble.

So that you'll have a good supply of order forms on hand, I'm enclosing some extra copies. Also the enclosed spring bulletin and update on our cooperative advertising program may help you plan your spring promotions.

This paragraph recognizes the possibility that nothing particular is wrong, that the customer just needs a little push.

Remember, Ms. Skovie, you can always count on us when you're in the market for high-style housewares. We have some new merchandise in today's most desirable colors that seems just right for your fashion-conscious customers. Do give us the opportunity to serve your needs soon. That's why we're here.

The actual request for action is left unstated until the end so that it will leave an impression.

To review material discussed here, see this chapter's Checklist for Routine Requests.

CHECKLIST FOR ROUTINE REQUESTS

A. Direct Statement of the Request
1. Phrase the opening to reflect the assumption that the reader will respond to your request favorably.
2. Phrase the opening so clearly and simply that the main idea cannot be misunderstood.
3. Write in a polite, undemanding, personal tone.
4. Preface complex requests with a sentence or two of explanation, possibly a statement of the problem that the response will solve.

B. Justification, Explanation, and Details
1. Justify the request, or explain its importance.
2. Explain to the reader the benefit of responding.
3. State desired actions in a positive and supportive, not negative or dictatorial, manner.
4. Itemize parts of a complex request in a numbered series.
5. List specific questions.
   - a. Don't ask questions that you could answer through your own efforts.
   - b. Arrange questions logically.
   - c. Number questions.
   - d. Word questions carefully to get the type of answers you need: numbers or yes's and no's if you need to tally many replies; more lengthy, detailed answers if you want to elicit more information.
   - e. Word questions to avoid clues about the answer you prefer so as not to bias the reader's answers.
   - f. Limit each question to one topic.

C. Courteous Close with Request for Specific Action
1. Courteously request a specific action, and make it as easy as possible to implement, possibly by enclosing a return envelope or explaining how you can be reached.
2. Indicate gratitude, possibly by promising to follow up in a way that will benefit the reader.
3. Clearly state any deadline or time frame, and briefly justify it if it is genuinely important.

REQUESTING CLAIMS AND ADJUSTMENTS

You are entitled to request an adjustment whenever you receive a product or experience service that doesn't live up to the supplier's standards.

Satisfied customers bring additional business to the firm, whereas angry or dissatisfied customers do not. In addition, angry customers complain to anyone who'll listen, creating poor public relations. So even though **claims** (or formal complaints) and **adjustments** (or claim settlements) may seem like unpleasant concepts, progressive organizations like Barnes & Noble want to know whether their customers and clients are dissatisfied with their services or merchandise. So if you have a complaint, it's in your best interest, and the company's, to bring your claim or request for an adjustment to the organization's attention. Communicate at once with someone in the company who can make the correction. A phone call or visit may solve the problem, but a written claim letter is better because it documents your dissatisfaction.

Tone is of primary importance; keep your claim businesslike and unemotional.

Your first reaction to a clumsy mistake or a defective product is likely to be anger or frustration, but the person reading your letter probably had nothing to do with the problem. A courteous, clear, concise explanation will impress the reader much more favorably than an abusive, angry letter. Asking for a fair and reasonable solution will increase your chances of receiving a satisfactory adjustment.

In your claim letter
- Explain the problem and give details
- Provide backup information
- Request specific action

In most cases, and especially in your first letter, assume that a fair adjustment will be made, and follow the plan for direct requests. Begin with a straightforward statement of the problem, and give a complete, specific explanation of the details. In the middle section of your claim letter, provide any information the adjuster will need to verify your complaint about faulty merchandise or unsatisfactory service. Politely request specific action in your closing, and suggest that the business relationship will continue if the problem is solved satisfactorily.

Companies usually accept the customer's explanation of what's wrong, so ethically speaking, it's important to be entirely honest when filing claims for adjustment or refund. Also, be prepared to back up your claim with invoices, sales receipts, canceled checks, dated correspondence, catalog descriptions, and any other relevant documents. Send copies and keep the originals for your files.

If the remedy is obvious, tell your reader exactly what will return the company to your good graces—for example, an exchange of merchandise for the right item or a refund if the item is out of stock. If you're uncertain about the precise nature of the trouble, you could ask the company to make an assessment. When you're dissatisfied with an expensive item, you might request that an unbiased third person either estimate the cost of repair or suggest another solution. Be sure to supply your telephone number and the best time to call (as well as your address) so that the company can discuss the situation with you if necessary.

The following two letters have been written to a gas and electric company. As you read them, compare the tones of the two versions. If you were the person receiving the complaint, which version would you respond to more favorably?

We have been at our present location only three months, and we don't understand why our December utility bill is $115.00 and our January bill is $117.50. Businesses on both sides of us, in offices just like ours, are paying only $43.50 and $45.67 for the same months. We all have similar computer and office equipment, so something must be wrong.

Small businesses are helpless against big utility companies. How can we prove that you read the meter wrong or that the November bill from before we even moved in here got added to our December bill? We want someone to check this meter right away. We can't afford to pay these big bills.

Here's the second version:

The utility meters may not be accurate in our office. Please send someone to check them.

We have been at our present location since December 1, almost three months. Our monthly bills are nearly triple those of neighboring businesses in this building, yet we all have similar offices, furnished with similar equipment. In December we paid $115.00, and our January bill was $117.50; the highest bills that neighboring businesses have paid were $43.50 and $45.67.

If your representative could check the operation of the meters, he or she could also see how much energy we are using. We understand that you regularly provide this helpful service to customers.

We would appreciate hearing from you this week. You can reach me by calling 878-2346 during business hours.

If you're like most people, you probably reacted more favorably to the second letter. A courteous approach is best for any routine request. If you must write a letter that gives vent to your anger, go ahead; but then tear that one up and write a letter that will actually help solve the problem. (This chapter's Checklist for Claims and Requests for Adjustment will remind you of the tasks involved in such messages.)

Generally, it's a good idea to suggest specific and fair compensation when asking for an adjustment. However, the following complaint is a case in which the customer does not request a specific adjustment but asks the reader to resolve the problem:

Lorraine C. Scarpa is a corporate communications consultant to a number of companies, including Dun & Bradstreet. Much of Scarpa's career has been spent identifying and serving the information needs of customers worldwide. For any claim or adjustment problem, advises Scarpa, be sure your request is straightforward and contains a complete explanation so that your audience can react effectively.

CHECKLIST FOR CLAIMS AND REQUESTS FOR ADJUSTMENT

A. Direct Statement of the Request
1. Write a claim letter as soon as possible after the problem has been identified.
2. State the need for reimbursement or correction of the problem.
3. Maintain a confident, factual, fair, unemotional tone.

B. Justification, Explanation, and Details
1. To gain the reader's understanding, praise some aspect of the product or the service.
2. Present facts honestly, clearly, and politely.
3. Eliminate threats, sarcasm, exaggeration, and hostility.
4. Specify the problem: Product failed to live up to advertised standards; product failed to live up to sales representative's claims; product fell short of company policy; product was defective; customer service was deficient.
5. Make no accusations against any person or company that you can't back up with facts.
6. Use a nonargumentative tone to show your confidence in the reader's fairness.
7. If necessary, refer to documentation (invoices, canceled checks, confirmation letters, and the like), but mail only photocopies.
8. Ask the reader to propose a fair adjustment, if appropriate.
9. If appropriate, present your idea of fair settlement, such as credit against the next order you place, full or partial refund of the purchase price of the product, replacement of the defective merchandise, performance of services as originally contracted, or repair of the defective merchandise.
10. Do not return the defective merchandise until you have been asked to do so.
11. Avoid uncertainty or vagueness that might permit the adjusters to prolong the issue by additional correspondence or to propose a less-than-fair settlement.

C. Courteous Close with Request for Specific Action
1. Summarize desired action briefly.
2. Simplify compliance with your request by including your name, address, phone number (including area code, if necessary), and hours of availability.
3. Note how complying with your request will benefit the reader.

A courteous approach gets the best results because it is non-threatening.

At our October 25 dinner meeting in your restaurant, your rum cake was a big success. You should know, however, that many who attended commented on three areas needing improvement:

1. Serving began half an hour late.
2. The roast beef was cold and tough.
3. The vegetables were cold and overcooked.

What can we do to guarantee that things go better at our next dinner meeting, which is scheduled for December 10?

In the past, we have been quite pleased with the quality of your food and service. Please call me at 372-9200, ext. 271, anytime this week to discuss this situation further.

MAKING ROUTINE CREDIT REQUESTS

The first step in requesting credit is to get an application form.

If your credit rating is sound, your application for business credit may be as direct as any other type of simple request. Whether the application is to a bank, a wholesaler or manufacturer, or a credit card company, the information needed is the same. You might phone the company for a credit application or write a letter as simple as this:

We would like to open a credit account with your company. Please send an application blank, and let us know what references you will need.

Before you get a credit account, you'll have to supply such information as the name of your company, the length of time you've been in business, the name of your bank, and the addresses of businesses where you have existing accounts. Businesses trying to establish credit are also expected to furnish a financial statement and possibly a balance sheet. In general, the lender wants proof that your income is stable and that you can repay the loan.

A request to buy on credit is sometimes included with a company's first-time order for goods. In such cases, the customer often sends copies of the latest financial statement along with the order letter. If a company's credit standing is good, it may ask with confidence for the order to be accepted on a credit basis. Because the main idea in this situation is to get permission to buy on credit, the letter should open with that request. Figure 8.2 is an example of the way an order may be combined with a

The second step is to supply the necessary information.

Order letters are often combined with a request for credit.

Figure 8.2
Letter Making a Routine Credit Request

ACTION HARDWARE

1411 S. Gillette Avenue
Tulsa, Oklahoma 74104
(918) 754-3121

August 5, 1996

OK Distributors, Inc.
2143 16th Street S.W.
Oklahoma City, OK 73108

Ladies and Gentlemen:

Please fill the following order on a credit basis. We would like to have a supply of your small appliances to include in our October promotion:

12 - #210 WR Electric Toasters @ $18.00		$ 216.00
12 - #486 XL Electric Table-Top Broilers @ $27.00		324.00
12 - #489 XL Electric Table-Top Broilers @ $32.00		384.00
6 - #862 XL Food Blenders @ $28.00		168.00
Total		$1,092.00

Since opening in January 1985, Action Hardware has enjoyed a steady improvement in business. We are capable of paying our bills promptly, as you'll see from the enclosed financial statements. You are welcome to phone us if you need more information for granting credit or if you need names of references.

Your WR and XL appliances are of the quality and price range sought by our customers. Because of the steady demand for them, we expect to place orders comparable to this one about every four months. This order could mark the beginning of a profitable relationship between our companies.

Sincerely,

Maggie Hastings
Maggie Hastings
Housewares Buyer

gh

Enclosures

The main idea is tied in with a statement implying a reader benefit.

The background details of the business are necessary if credit is to be granted.

The possibility of continuing orders is another reason for the reader to grant credit.

A request for credit

- Is supported by documentation
- Adopts a confident tone
- Hints at future business

request for credit. Notice that the request for credit is supported by documentation of financial stability. In addition, the writer has encouraged a favorable response by adopting a confident tone and mentioning the probability of future business.

I NQUIRING ABOUT PEOPLE

The need to inquire about people arises often in business. For example, some companies ask applicants to supply references before awarding credit, contracts, jobs, promotions, scholarships, and so on. If you're applying for a job and your potential employer asks for references, you may want to write a letter to a close personal or professional associate, asking for a letter of recommendation. Or, if you're an employer considering whether to hire an applicant, you may want to write directly to the person the applicant named as a reference. Whatever the situation, just remember that the approach to writing letters of inquiry about people is similar to the approach for requests already discussed; that is, such inquiries include a direct statement of the request (or main idea), a justification of the request (explanation of the situation with details), and a courteous close that includes a request for specific action.

O n the Job

SOLVING A COMMUNICATION DILEMMA AT BARNES & NOBLE

Leonard Riggio has reached the top of the U.S. bookselling market through a combination of building oversized bookstores, stocking books that interest each community, and employing effective communication to reach employees and customers. Of course, top managers in any business must clearly request the kinds of information they need from store managers. Riggio is using that information to help his company grow and evolve in the battle with competitors.

More and more of the book battles are being fought in "superstores," huge stores with up to 150,000 titles on the shelf (compared with 15,000 to 25,000 in the typical mall store). Barnes & Noble operates more than 268 superstores; the Crown chain, more than 60 superstores; and Kmart's Borders chain, more than 44 superstores. In addition to offering discount prices and a comprehensive selection of hardcover and paperback books, Barnes & Noble superstores regularly offer special events such as a children's story hour or a book signing by a local author.

Riggio is also working hard to increase sales in existing stores. A key technique, first introduced by Kmart's Waldenbooks chain and quickly imitated by Barnes & Noble's B. Dalton chain, is the frequent-purchase plan. Customers pay a modest membership fee and then get discounts on every purchase. Just like the frequent-flyer programs offered by airlines, the "BookSavers Club" at B. Dalton and the "Preferred Reader Program" at Waldenbooks are designed to attract and retain loyal customers.

As a lifelong lover of books, Riggio believes a bookstore should be a "marketplace of ideas." He wants to expose cus-

tomers to a wider variety of literary works. B. Dalton's "Discovery" program, for example, showcases books by both new and unknown writers. The program can boost a book's sales tenfold by bringing it to the attention of customers in B. Dalton stores.

Of course, rival bookstores are also working hard to communicate more effectively with customers. For instance, managers at Waldenbooks know what members of their Preferred Reader Program like, so they notify the fans of mystery novels when new mysteries are available, they alert computer users about new computer books, and so on. As the chains expand, the independents are fighting back by offering specialized books and individualized customer service. Competition is fierce, but Riggio's talent for communicating with customers and employees should keep his chain on top for a long time to come.

Your Mission: You have recently taken a job as Leonard Riggio's administrative assistant. He relies on you to draft letters to Barnes & Noble store managers and outside contacts. Using the principles outlined in this chapter for writing direct requests, handle each of the following letters to the best of your ability. Be prepared to explain your choices.

1. Riggio asks you to contact the store managers and find out whether the "Discovery" program is affecting sales. Which of the following is the best opening for this letter?

   a. I have recently joined Mr. Riggio's staff as his administrative assistant. He has asked me to write to you to obtain your input on the effectiveness of the "Discovery" program. Please reply to the following questions within five working days. [List of questions follows.]

b. Please tell us what you think of the "Discovery" program. Mr. Riggio is trying to evaluate its impact on our business. Within the next few days, can you take a few moments to jot down your thoughts on its effectiveness. Specifically, Mr. Riggio would like to know . . . [List of questions follows.]

c. By April 15, please submit written answers to the following questions on the "Discovery" program. [List of questions follows.]

d. Is the "Discovery" program working? You be the judge. We're polling all store managers for their reaction to the program. Is it thumbs up or thumbs down on "Discovery"?

2. Which of the following is the best choice for the middle section of the letter?

a. Specifically, has store business increased since the latest campaign began six weeks ago? If so, what is the percentage increase in sales over the previous six weeks? Over the comparable period last year? Have sales of the featured books increased during the past six weeks? Have customers mentioned the program? If so, have their comments been positive or negative? Has employee morale been affected by the program? How?

b. By replying to the following questions, you will help us decide whether to continue with the program as is, revise it, or drop it entirely:

    1. Has business increased in your store since the latest campaign began six weeks ago? If so, what is the percentage increase in sales over the previous six weeks? Over the comparable period last year?

    2. Have sales of the specific books you've promoted increased noticeably during the past six weeks? Please quantify.

    3. Have customers mentioned the program? If so, have their comments been positive or negative? Give some typical examples.

    4. Has employee morale been affected by the program? How?

c. By circling the response that most accurately reflects your store's experience, please answer the following questions regarding the "Discovery" program:

    1. Since the latest campaign began six weeks ago, sales have
        a. increased
        b. decreased
        c. remained about the same

    2. Sales of the specific books you've promoted have

        a. increased
        b. decreased
        c. remained about the same

    3. Customers (have/have not) mentioned the program. Their comments have been primarily (positive/negative).

    4. Employee morale (has/has not) been affected by the campaign.

d. Mr. Riggio needs to know the following: (1) How have overall store sales changed during the most recent campaign? (2) How have sales of the featured books changed during the "Discovery" campaign? (3) What do customers think of the campaign? Attach complimentary customer comments. (4) What do employees think of the campaign? Attach complimentary employee comments.

3. For a courteous close with a request for specific action, which of the following paragraphs is the best?

a. Thank you for your cooperation. Please submit your reply in writing by April 15.

b. Mr. Riggio is meeting with his senior staff on April 17 to discuss the program. He would like to have your reaction to the program in writing by April 15 so that he can present your views during that meeting. If you have any questions, please contact me at 697-2886.

c. You may contact me at 697-2886 if you have any questions or need additional information about this survey. Mr. Riggio requires your written response by April 15 so that he can discuss your views with his senior staff on April 17.

d. Thank you for your input. As the frontline troops in the battle for sales, you are in the best position to evaluate the results of the "Discovery" program. We here at corporate headquarters are doing our best to support you, but we need your feedback on our efforts. Please submit your written evaluation of the program by April 15 so that Mr. Riggio can use the results as ammunition in his meeting with senior staff on April 17.

4. Mr. Riggio has decided to order 795 large cutout cardboard displays of Mickey Mouse to promote a new line of children's books featuring the famous cartoon character. He has identified the item he needs in a catalog that features promotional materials licensed by the Walt Disney Company. Which of the following letters should you send to the vendor?

a. Please send 795 large cardboard cutouts of Mickey Mouse (item #90067-C in the April catalog) to the above address by parcel post. We need the shipment by April 25. I am enclosing a check for $4,397.50 to cover the order (795 @ $5.00), tax ($397.50), and shipping ($25).

b. This may seem like a "Mickey Mouse" request, but we need 795 cardboard cutouts of the famous rodent by April 25. Item #90067-C in your April catalog looks like it should do the trick. Please send the shipment to the above address. I am enclosing a check for $4,397.50.

Contact me immediately if Mickey is not available. We are counting on him to help us launch a new children's book at our stores on May 1.

c. We need some freestanding cardboard cutouts of Mickey Mouse to promote a new children's book that will go on sale in selected stores throughout the country on May 1. Item #90067-C, shown in the upper left corner of page 56 of your April catalog, appears to be well suited for our purpose. Please send 795 of these cutouts to me at our corporate headquarters, at the above address, by parcel post.

I am enclosing a check for $4,397 to cover all costs:

795 #90067-C @ $5.00 each	$3,975.00
Sales tax	397.50
Shipping and handling	25.00
Total sale	$4,397.50

Our May 1 book launch depends on our receiving the shipment by April 25, so please call me collect at 697-2886 if you cannot deliver all 795 cutouts by then.

d. Enclosed you will find $4,397.50 to cover 795 cardboard cutouts of Mickey Mouse, plus postage, tax, and shipping. This shipment should be sent to the above address by parcel post no later than April 25.

5. The Barnes & Noble warehouse has received its shipment of 795 Mickey Mouse cardboard cutouts. However, 50 of the displays are bent and cannot be used in promoting the new line of children's books. You have been asked to prepare a fax letter requesting an adjustment. Select the best version.

a. On March 25, we ordered 795 cardboard cutouts of Mickey Mouse (item #90067-C in your April catalog). When the shipment arrived last week, we discovered that 50 of the cutouts were bent. Whether the damage occurred during shipping or at your place of business, I do not know. However, I do know that we cannot use the cutouts in their present form. If you can replace them before April 25, please do so. We are withholding payment until the matter is straightened out.

b. Please call me immediately at 697-2886 to discuss a problem with the Mickey Mouse cutouts that we ordered from you. Fifty of them are bent and cannot be used in our nationwide book promotion scheduled for May 1.

Time is running short, I know, but we would really like you to replace the 50 damaged cutouts if you can do so in time for our promotion. If that is not possible, we will adjust our payment to reflect a sale of 745 cutouts as opposed to 795.

Thanks for your cooperation. The good cutouts are really cute, and we expect they will boost our book sales.

c. Of the 795 Mickey Mouse cardboard cutouts received last week, 50 are not in good condition. I inspected them myself, and several of us tried to fix the cutouts, but they don't look very good. Therefore, please replace these 50 before April 25.

d. Fifty of the Mickey Mouse cardboard cutouts that we ordered from your firm on March 25 arrived in poor condition. Can you replace them before April 25? If so, we would still like to use them in our May 1 book promotion.

I am enclosing a copy of the invoice for your convenience. As you can see, our original order was for 795 cutouts (catalog item #90067-C), priced at $5.00 each. Our bill for the total order is $4,397.50. We will send payment in full when we receive the 50 undamaged cutouts. If replacements are not available by April 25, we will send you a check for the 745 good cutouts, which we plan to use in any case. Including tax and handling costs, the adjusted total would be $4,139.50.

Would you like us to return the damaged items? Perhaps they can be salvaged for another purpose.

Please call me at 697-2886 any time this week to discuss the situation. We are eager to receive the replacement cutouts so that our bookstores can benefit from the Mickey Mouse display during our nationwide book promotion scheduled for May 1.[4]

Questions for Discussion

1. When organizing your requests, why is it important to know whether any cultural differences exist between you and your audience?

2. Why is it inappropriate to begin written requests to U.S. and Canadian businesses with a brief personal introduction?

3. What precautions should be taken when writing secondary questions in a direct request?
4. What is the most important element of an order letter: the legality of the offer, the clarity of the order, or the explanation of how items will be used?
5. Every time you send a direct-request memo to Ted Jackson, he delays or refuses to comply. You're beginning to get im-

patient. Should you send Jackson a memo to ask what's wrong? Complain to your supervisor about Jackson's attitude? Arrange a face-to-face meeting with Jackson? Bring up the problem at the next staff meeting? Explain.

6. You have a complaint against one of your suppliers, but you have no documentation. Should you request an adjustment anyway? Explain.

Documents for Analysis

Read the following letters; then (1) analyze the strengths or weaknesses of each sentence and (2) revise each letter so that it follows this chapter's guidelines.

DOCUMENT 8.A

Your ads in a recent local newspaper have caught my attention. I'd appreciate it greatly if you could send me accurate answers to these questions:

1. What information can you provide about the stainless steel ElectroPerk coffee pot? Does it work OK?
2. Can it be repaired when it breaks, and are repairs covered by a warranty or store policy? Or will I have to pay for repairs on faulty merchandise?
3. What is the price range on the machine?
4. Does it come with attachments? Do attachments cost extra? Is the machine hard to use?

Let me know the answers to these questions as soon as possible, please. I am evaluating equipment for my company and considering several other models.

DOCUMENT 8.B

I'm writing to inquire about your recent order for a custom wedding suit. You forgot to mention what

color you want and also failed to include your measurements. I'd like to clear up this confusion quickly so that we will be able to provide you with the suit before the wedding. When, exactly, is the happy day?

I know you must be busy getting ready for the wedding, but if you can spare the time, you might want to stop by in person to pick out your suit because we do offer an incredibly wide selection of fine wedding attire. At that time, you could also select an appropriate tie and shirt. I would also suggest that you choose clothing for your best man and ushers, assuming that you are having a large wedding. We can provide the best in both custom and rental formal attire for your entire wedding party, regardless of how large or small it is. Incidentally, you should also bring your fiancée along to coordinate the men's clothing with the bridesmaids' dresses. You know how picky women are about clothes.

If you can't come by in person, you should send me a letter stating your measurements and indicating your color and style preferences, or call me at 633-4296. After we receive this information, we will need at least two weeks to complete the suit. Thank you for your cooperation in this matter.

Cases

PLACING ORDERS

1. More mellow music: Memo about CD distribution at the Wherehouse This has been the busiest month you can remember since you started working for a Wherehouse Records outlet. Your boss asks you to contact the Wherehouse's West Coast distribution headquarters in Long Beach, California, to let them know you're out of certain titles and to pass on some special orders.

"Tell them we're selling New Age CDs like crazy, so they'd better increase our shipments," she explains as she gives you the list. "I think Music Design in Milwaukee distributes all

these titles—you might mention that in your memo. Ask them to send 1 each of the special orders, 5 each of the nature sounds, and 15 each of the other titles. Here." She reaches for a Music Design wholesale catalog and hands it to you. "Give them the item numbers and prices." You stop scribbling notes and glance at the list.

Your Task: Write a memo requesting a special supplement to your regular shipment from Wherehouse headquarters in Long Beach. Mention that Music Design's fall catalog carries all the compact discs on your list and that you have included their order numbers for easy reference. The special-order CDs are Gyuto Monks, *Tibetan Tantric Choir*, W50-172, $11.49 wholesale, $18.98 list; *Gregorian Chants of Hungary*, Vol. 3, Q1-103, $11.49 wholesale, $18.98 list; Gyume Monks, *Tantric Harmonics*, SR-103, $11.49 wholesale, $18.98 list; Lamas & Monks of the Four Great Orders, *Tibetan Ritual Music*, L6-102, $10.98 wholesale, $17.98 list. Order five CDs each of Atmosphere Collection/Brazilian Rainforest, *Jungle Journey/Evening Echoes*, RY-134, $6.59 wholesale, $10.98 list; Earth Sounds, *Cedar Creek*, P9-105, $9.69 wholesale, $15.98 list; Earth Sounds, *Ebb and Flow*, P9-103, $9.69 wholesale, $15.98 list; and Atmosphere Collection/A Week in Hawaii, *Midnight Rainshower*, RY-121, $6.59 wholesale, $10.98 list. The CDs you've run out of are Eric Tingstad, Nancy Rumbel, *In the Garden*, N1-259, $9.98 wholesale, $15.98 list; David Lanz, *Skyline Firedance* (double CD), N1-244, $10.79 wholesale, $17.98 list; David Arkenstone, *In the Wake of the Wind*, N1-256, $9.98 wholesale, $15.98 list; and *The Narada Wilderness Collection*, N1-233, $9.98 wholesale, $15.98 list.[5]

2. Fancy tea: Order letter from Guggenheim tea emporium
Following the popularity of coffeehouses in the United States is a new fascination with tea, and your boss, Miriam Novalle, is ready. Always a tea lover—and sensing the trend toward exotic, high-quality, loose-leaf, and even single estate (all plucked from one garden) teas—Novalle lost no time opening "T," a large tea emporium, café, and salon in the lower level of the Guggenheim Museum SoHo in New York City. Customers are delighted. Just as they learned to love (and pay a premium for) whole gourmet coffee beans in infinite variety, bottled mineral waters from all parts of the earth, and contemporary wines of distinction, people are beginning to discover what Novalle has always known: There's more to tea than a cup of hot water and a stale white bag.

Since coming to work for Novalle, you've learned that to make good tea, you first heat the teapot with boiling water, which you throw away because fresh boiling water must be poured over the leaves (not vice versa). The tea might be any one of the hundreds T carries—a delicate green tea from Japan or China or a black tea (the green leaves are withered and fermented) from Sri Lanka, India, or the Himalayan foothills. Herbal teas are always popular—chamomile in particular. But Novalle is most proud of the 30 special teas she orders from Mariage Frères, a top-of-the-line wholesaler in Paris.

In fact, this morning she asked you to send a new order to the French company. "We're running low on the Chinese Lapsang souchong, the Himalayan Assam, and the Castleton estate Darjeeling," says Novalle, glancing at her crowded emporium and calculating 200 cups per pound of loose tea. "I think we'd better order five pounds of each."

Your Task: Write the letter in English to Mariage Frères, 38 Rue de Rennes, 75014 Paris, France. Because foreign exchange rates fluctuate daily, ask to be billed for the exact cost of tea,

shipping, and handling as of the date your transaction is processed. Do what you can to strengthen the business relationship—Novalle is hoping for future discounts if her business keeps growing.[6]

3. Graphics plus: Letter ordering software from Computer Discount Warehouse C. J. Metschke began her business as a freelance technical writer, but she soon recognized that many of her clients needed desktop publishing services as well. She realized that by providing both, she could double, triple, or even quadruple her income. Thus was born The Monterey Press—your new employer. Business was so good that last summer, Metschke decided she could use some help. You started as an intern and now you're working for her as a part-time, salaried employee, honing your writing skills and learning new applications for desktop publishing software with every project that comes in.

Yesterday Metschke met with a prospective client who wants to publish a newsletter for cat lovers. They talked over all the details and came to an agreement. Unlike other newsletter clients, this self-publisher wants The Monterey Press to produce all the artwork for his newsletters.

"We're going to need some updated graphics software—a program that we can use to create original illustrations and one that works well with an optical scanner," explains Metschke as she shows you a mock-up of the newsletter. "I think the latest version of CorelDRAW offers both options. See if you can find it in our Computer Discount Warehouse catalog."

You dig the CDW catalog out of a file and find the software, CorelDRAW 4.0. The description says the program will do everything Metschke wants; it also provides more than 18,000 clip art images and a complete animation module. The software (catalog number CDW 29312) is priced at $359.13 for the 3.5-inch diskette format, plus $4.00 shipping and insurance.

Your Task: There's no order form in the catalog, so you need to write an order letter to CDW Computer Centers, Inc., 1020 E. Lake Cook Road, Buffalo Grove, IL 60089.[7]

REQUESTING ROUTINE INFORMATION AND ACTION

4. Maybe multimedia: Memo inquiring about computerized presentations at Rucker Fuller As a marketing vice president for Rucker Fuller office interiors in San Francisco, you've witnessed many new developments in business presentation technology. Your office furnishings and design firm was one of the first in the industry to build a special audiovisual room for showing professionally produced slide presentations to potential clients. However, that was back in the early 1980s. Now the latest developments in multimedia presentation software have caught your eye.

You've just read an article describing the features of new software packages designed to help ordinary business executives like you develop computerized presentations. According to the article, the new software not only allows you to include movies, slides, animation, audio, graphics, interactive sequences, and text, it also lets you program a time sequence for each element.

For instance, your computerized presentation might begin by playing a recorded sound track while the title slides into place on the screen. Then colorful circles spin around and land behind the title (simple animation you create yourself). An electronic narrator reads the title, while the Rucker Fuller logo appears in the lower right corner. The date of the presentation fades in, then out. At any point in the presentation, you can include an interactive option: The push of a button will bring up a selection of topics that you or your client can choose on the spot.

Your Task: You're no computer expert, and you need some advice. Write a memo asking Rucker Fuller's computer guru, Alison Blakesley, to research and recommend several timeline-based multimedia presentation software packages. You want to know how much these programs cost, which version has the best features, and whether they're as easy to use as the article indicates.[8]

5. Scientific frontier: Memo requesting a research update at Quantum Magnetics W. Barry Lindgren is a man of vision—as are all his colleagues at Quantum Magnetics in San Diego, California. Lindgren is president of a company that's exploring one of the scientific frontiers opened up by quantum physics. The company is using the latest developments in superconducting ceramics to develop ultrasensitive equipment that can detect extremely faint magnetic fluctuations at the molecular level.

Ultrasensitive magnetic sensors are already used in medicine as a diagnostic tool—known as magnetic resonance imaging (MRI)—to create images of internal organs that can reveal serious ailments. Soon doctors will be using devices that track magnetic fields produced by heart and brain activity. Quantum Magnetics has joined a dozen new firms racing to develop additional commercial uses for these sensors.

For example, the company has developed a prototype for a sensor that will detect hidden corrosion, metal fatigue, and microscopic stress fractures in aircraft frames—a device that could one day save lives. Working with IBM and under the sponsorship of the Federal Aviation Administration (FAA), Quantum Magnetics is also developing a scanner for use in airports to distinguish the minute magnetic signals of hidden explosives (and another to scan for illegal narcotics).

In fact, Lindgren received an inquiry from the FAA yesterday, asking for a report on the company's progress on a sensor that will determine whether a bottle packed in traveling luggage is holding a common alcoholic beverage or a high-energy liquid explosive. Lindgren will write the report, but first he needs an update from the research department. The FAA wants to know what's been done on the project for the last six months and what will be done during the next six.

The agency also wants an estimate of when a prototype sensor may be ready for testing.

Your Task: As Lindgren's administrative assistant, draft a memo to Andrew Hibbs, director of research, requesting the information Lindgren will need to respond to the FAA's query. Lindgren needs Hibbs's information by next Tuesday.[9]

6. Divine gifts: Letter to Translations gift shop customers According to magazines such as *Time* and *Newsweek,* angels are a subject of intense interest all over the world right now. Some say it began in 1990 with Sophy Burnham's *A Book of Angels,* in which she relates angel lore and dozens of highly dramatic tales of ordinary people who say they were helped by angelic presences. Others think angels are popular because they're nondenominational.

For you, the manager of Translations gift shop in Dallas, Texas, the love affair with angels has meant plenty of hours spent restocking shelves with angels: angel dolls, calendars, pins, watches, diaries, and thank-you notes. Business has been so good that the owners have decided to remodel the store to maximize display space and make more room for customers to browse (you're glad, because merchandise was getting damaged on busy days). Soon the store will be littered with plastic sheeting, stacked boards, paint buckets, and the lingering smell of sawdust. Since the owners can't afford the loss of income if they were to close during the remodeling (which could go on for a month), they need to encourage customers to come in and shop despite the mess.

Your Task: Co-owner Debbie Tompkins has asked you to help the situation by composing a form letter to the customers on Translations' mailing list, asking for their continued business and for their patience during the remodeling. As enticement, a 25 percent "Remodeling Special" discount coupon will accompany each letter, redeemable during the next four weeks only.[10]

7. Corporate service: Letter requesting feedback from Office Depot's newest customers When David Fuente took over as CEO of Office Depot, the Florida-based warehouse-style office supply chain consisted of only ten stores, valued at about $34 million. Now Office Depot has more than 400 stores, with about $2.6 billion in annual sales, and the company is still growing: Fuente wants to double the number of stores over the next five years.

What accounts for this phenomenal growth? Office Depot sells brand-name office supplies at 30 to 60 percent off the manufacturers' list prices, giving individuals and small businesses the same kind of price breaks large corporations have traditionally enjoyed. Morever, Office Depot's Business Services department offers on-the-spot faxing, photocopying, printing, and other services. Grateful small business owners are the foundation of Office Depot's fortunes.

Now Fuente wants to capture another market segment by selling the same goods to large corporations. As a marketing executive at corporate headquarters, you agree with him. Although most big companies have long-established relationships with regional suppliers whose prices are comparable, Fuente plans to win these large customers over by offering better service and consistently lower pricing. Your corporate sales executives are stressing Office Depot's efficient distribution network, strong buying power, and dependable delivery.

So far, Office Depot has won a few corporate accounts. To capitalize on this success, you have developed five open-ended questions about Office Depot's new corporate services. This brief survey will (1) identify problem areas and (2) gather positive feedback that your sales staff can use as testimonials. You designed the questionnaire so that it takes less than five minutes to complete, and as a way of saying thank you, Fuente is offering respondents an extra 10 percent discount (good for 90 days).

Your Task: Draft a form letter asking corporate purchasing agents to complete the questionnaire. Also, ask them to sign a line granting permission to use favorable comments as testimonials.[11]

8. Please tell me: Request for information about a product You're a consumer, and you've probably seen hundreds of products that you'd like to buy (if not, look at the advertisements in your favorite magazine for ideas). Choose a big-ticket item that is rather complicated, such as a stereo system or a vacation in the Caribbean.

Your Task: You surely have some questions about your chosen product's features, price, guarantees, local availability, and so on. Write to the company offering it, and ask four questions that are important to you. Be sure to include enough background information so that the reader can answer your questions satisfactorily.

If requested to do so by your instructor, mail a copy of your letter to the organization. After a few weeks, you and your classmates may wish to compare responses and answer this question: How well do companies respond to unsolicited inquiries?

REQUESTING CLAIMS AND ADJUSTMENTS

9. Spoiled in Argentina: Claim from California peach growers When President Carlos Menem of Argentina took office in 1989, he and his economy minister, Domingo Cavallo, decided that competition from foreign producers would stimulate Argentine business to provide better products at competitive prices. To the delight of Argentine shoppers, the import tariffs were lowered and goods began pouring in from all over the world: calculators and copy machines, scissors and automobiles, bicycles, toothpicks—and peaches.

When Menem's new policies took effect, California peach growers responded eagerly to the new market. Individual growers banded into the California Peach Growers Associ-

ation to ship their fruit to Edcadassa, the Argentine firm that oversees all imported goods while they await customs clearance at Ezeiza International Airport.

As supervisor of the Argentine project for the growers' association, you were extremely pleased with the success of the first few shipments; everything had gone smoothly. Then word came back from angry Argentine buyers that the fresh, firm California peaches they had expected arrived at their stores ready for the garbage bin. They refused to pay for the rotten fruit, and your growers lost $50,000.

You made inquiries and discovered that Edcadassa had been overwhelmed by the volume of imported goods flowing into Argentina (an average of 150 tons a day, compared with 60 tons two years before). Your peach shipment was lost in the confusion, and by the time it was cleared through customs, three weeks late, the peaches were already rotten. Since you'd shipped the fruit when it was at the perfect stage to make the journey, await the normal customs delay, and ripen gently in the supermarkets of Buenos Aires, you believe the responsibility for the shipment's destruction rests with Edcadassa.

Your Task: Write a letter to Edcadassa (Columbia 4300, 1425 Buenos Aires, Argentina) requesting full compensation for the ruined peaches.[12]

10. Missing makeup: Memo about an incomplete order at M.A.C. Greenwich Village When Canadian makeup artist Frank Toskan started M.A.C. (Make-Up Art Cosmetics) in his kitchen in 1985, he probably never dreamed how many of his lipsticks you'd be selling at his Greenwich Village store a decade later. Nonetheless, selling them you are, and you're also selling plenty of mascara, blush, professional makeup brushes, and even the T-shirts the company has become famous for: "Cruelty Free Beauty" (a plea against animal testing) and "Make Up, Make Out, Play Safe" (proceeds of which go to the Design Industries Foundation for AIDS).

When he began, Toskan was looking for professional-quality products to use himself. Now his customers love the company's social conscience (for every six used cases returned for recycling, they get a free lipstick) and its status among models and celebrities (Paula Abdul and Gloria Estefan certainly helped the bottom line). Mostly, however, they love the M.A.C. products, which come in 400 fashion colors. When some of those colors aren't in stock, they get angry.

Sure enough, your last shipment from M.A.C. headquarters in Canada was missing two of your best sellers: Russian Red and Chili Matte lipsticks. You specifically ordered three cases of each, but they were neither in the box nor listed on the packing list. You've been promising regulars all week ("Any day now"). You understand the reasons the company is having trouble keeping up with orders: It's been getting so much media coverage, its specialty stores are springing up across the United States, and more department stores are carrying the popular cosmetics. Nevertheless, you decide against excuses—your customers come first.

Your Task: As assistant manager, write a memo to M.A.C. Canada (233 Carleton St., Toronto, Ontario M58 2L2, Canada) explaining that your last order, dated March 2 and received April 17, was short the two items mentioned. Ask that they be shipped to the M.A.C. store in Greenwich Village immediately, via priority mail.[13]

MAKING ROUTINE CREDIT REQUESTS

11. To Russia with Toshiba: Letter from U S West requesting credit Your employer, U S West, recently signed on as the U.S. partner in a joint venture to rebuild Russia's decrepit phone system—a ten-year project that may cost as much as $40 billion. The agreement was a big coup for U S West, and your colleague Victor Pavlenko, head of the Russian investment unit, is still celebrating. But as a purchasing agent for the company, you've got an immediate problem to resolve.

A 12-member team of U S West executives is heading for Russia next week, and they're going to be seriously hampered without their desktop computers. They don't expect to find state-of-the-art equipment in Moscow, yet they've come to depend on computers for many routine tasks. So you've been asked to find the ideal portable equipment.

In addition to one PC configured for compatibility with the Russian power system, you've decided to purchase 12 Toshiba T3400CT portable notebook computers for team members. They weigh only four and a half pounds each but feature color monitors, 120-megabyte hard drives, and all the ports and features necessary to handle many of the functions of a full-size desktop computer. The notebook computers will provide essential, on-the-spot computerized assistance as team members travel to inspect various sites throughout Russia.

You've solicited price quotes from several corporate dealers (Toshiba doesn't sell direct), and a Denver company, Microage, has topped them all by offering free and immediate delivery.

Your Task: Write to Stanley Garlow at Microage (1400 S. Colorado Boulevard, Denver, CO 80222) ordering the 12 Toshiba T3400CTs on a credit basis. You were quoted a quantity discount price of $3,150 each. Mention U S West's stability, reputation, and recent business expansion, which should eliminate the need to include financial statements, but offer to provide more credit information if necessary.[14]

12. Canadian braids: Credit letter from Chassman & Bem Booksellers The American Booksellers Association Convention was one of the largest trade fairs you've attended since becoming a buyer for Chassman & Bem Booksellers. Although the Vermont retailer is considered a "small independent" store (compared to the big chains), owner Randy Chudnow's business has thrived because of his good service and large inventory. He financed your scouting trip particularly to round up new books by small publishers and individual authors.

So, forgoing the acres of high-tech displays in the main exhibit arena (some seven football fields' worth), you scoured the small-press exhibit hall for likely possibilities among the clutter of 3-D poster publishers, one-book authors, incense sellers, and alternative lifestyle hawkers. A corner booth caught your attention: Instead of the typical display of books on a table in front, a middle-aged woman was standing in the booth, patiently braiding the long hair of a weary conventiongoer who looked grateful to be sitting down. The braid swirled down the back of her head in an attractive S pattern you'd never seen before. The back wall of the booth sported dozens of photographs of various braided hairstyles.

The braid designer was Andrea Jeffery from Calgary, author of two self-published books on braiding. You've seen other books on hairstyling, but nothing with such detail. Ms. Jeffery pointed out that her books include precise directions on how the braiders should hold their hands to successfully duplicate her designs.

Back in Vermont, you decide to order some books from Andrea Jeffery. You want 50 copies each of *Braids and More* by Andrea Jeffery (ISBN 0-9693543-1-2) and *Braids and Styles for Long Hair* by Andrea Jeffery and Vickie Terner (ISBN 0-9693543-0-4). You'd like the transaction to be on a credit basis (90-day payment terms, no interest, payable in U.S. funds). The U.S. retail list price is $19.95 for each book, but your wholesale discount for ordering 50 or more copies is 50 percent (or $9.98 per book).

Your Task: Write the order letter, addressing it to Andrea Jeffery, P.O. Box 73054, #206, 2525 Woodview Dr. S.W., Calgary, Alberta, T2W 6E4, Canada.[15]

9

After studying this chapter, you will be able to

Decide when to write a routine, good-news, or goodwill message

Adjust the basic organizational pattern to fit the type of message you are writing

Add resale and sales promotion material when appropriate

Encourage your reader to take any desired action

Write credit approvals and recommendation letters

Use the correct form for such specialized messages as instructions, news releases, and goodwill letters

WRITING ROUTINE, GOOD-NEWS, AND GOODWILL MESSAGES

On the Job

FACING A COMMUNICATION DILEMMA AT CAMPBELL SOUP COMPANY

Food Giant Tries to Light a Fire Under Its Sales

For Zoe Coulson, staying on top of consumer demands and competitive pressures is a nonstop job. In her role as vice president of consumer affairs at Campbell Soup, Coulson plays a key role in making sure the company knows what consumers are thinking and what they want. Coulson must also keep customers happy by responding to questions and complaints, which requires strong writing skills and a good way with people. These tasks can be tough anywhere, but they're a special challenge in a company that's been struggling as much as Campbell Soup has been.

Campbell's products are found in virtually every U.S. kitchen, it has two-thirds of the U.S. soup market and major shares of other food markets both here and abroad, and it has a history of high-quality products stretching back nearly to the Civil War. It's hard to imagine how a company like this could find itself in such unpleasant straits. But in 1990 the New Jersey company was reeling from failed new products, ill-advised diversification, a controversial proposal to merge with Quaker Oats, and a bitter feud among the family members who control the company's stock. Even though sales had increased from just under $4 billion in 1985 to more than $6 billion in 1990, the company's net earnings on those sales had dropped from $198 million to a mere $4 million. Moreover, internal problems weren't all the company had to worry about. Consumer tastes were changing. Campbell's reliance on concentrated soups sold nationwide in uniform mixtures was less and less in line with regionalized tastes and a growing interest in convenience.

As the firm's in-house consumer advocate, Coulson is an important link between the public and the research kitchens. Her job is to find out what people are hungry for and then lobby the company to deliver—a role that constantly tests her communication skills. If you were Zoe Coulson, how would you communicate with the public to answer their inquiries and complaints? How would you plan and write positive business messages?[1]

ORGANIZING POSITIVE MESSAGES

Campbell Soup's Zoe Coulson understands that most business communication consists of messages that present neutral information, answer requests positively, and establish better relationships, so you'll probably get a lot of practice composing these **routine, good-news,** and **goodwill messages.** Understanding how positive messages are organized allows you to compose excellent examples quickly. Of course, intercultural positive messages are best when organized according to the audience's expectations, but when you're communicating with a U.S. or Canadian audience whose cultural differences are minimal, use the direct plan. Whether written or oral, positive messages begin with a clear statement of the main idea, clarify any necessary details, and end with a courteous close.

Campbell Soup Company

Clear Statement of the Main Idea

Almost all business communication has two basic purposes: (1) to convey information and (2) to produce in the audience a favorable (or at least accepting) attitude or response. When you begin a message with a statement of your purpose, you're preparing your audience for the explanation that follows. Make your opening clear and concise. The following introductory statements make the same point; however, one is cluttered with unnecessary information that buries the purpose, whereas the other is brief and to the point:

Organizational plan for routine, good-news, and goodwill messages:

- Main point
- Details
- Close

Instead of This	*Write This*
I am pleased to inform you that after deliberating the matter carefully, our personnel committee has recommended you for appointment as a staff accountant.	You've been selected to join our firm as a staff accountant, beginning March 20.

The best way to write a clear opening is to have a clear idea of what you want to say. Before you put one word on paper, ask yourself this: What is the single most important message I have for the audience?

Before you begin, have a clear idea of what you want to say.

Necessary Details

The middle part is typically the longest section of a routine, good-news, or goodwill message. Your reason for communicating can usually be expressed in a sentence or two, but you'll need more space or time to explain your point completely so that your audience will have no confusion or lingering doubt. The task of providing necessary details is easiest when you're responding to a series of questions. You can simply answer them in order, possibly in a numbered sequence.

Answer questions in the order they were asked.

In addition to being a television superstar and creator of the highly successful TV series "The Cosby Show," Bill Cosby is a popular Hollywood spokesperson (endorsing products for Kodak and Jell-O), a respected author, and a top performer in Las Vegas and throughout the country. Through it all, his passion is to change the images of African Americans in the media. Such positive messages, says Cosby, must be based on fact and performance if they are to create a lasting impact.

In addition to providing details in the middle section, maintain the supportive tone established at the beginning. This tone is easy to continue when your message is purely good news, as in this example:

As we discussed, your major responsibility as staff accountant in the internal accounting division will be to monitor our accounts receivable program. For this position, we're happy to offer you $2,750 monthly. You'll immediately be eligible for our health and pension plans and reduced membership fees at the Fitness and Racquet Club on Chestnut Avenue, near our office. Knowing how much you like to play squash, I'd also like to invite you to sign up right away for our Accountants' Squash Tournament, which begins next month.

When a routine message must convey mildly disappointing information, put the negative answer into as favorable a context as possible. Look at the following example:

Instead of This	*Write This*
No, we no longer carry the Sportsgirl line of sweaters.	The new Olympic line has replaced the Sportsgirl sweaters that you asked about. Olympic features a wider range of colors and sizes and more contemporary styling.

A bluntly negative explanation was replaced with a more complete description that emphasized how the audience could benefit from the change. Be careful, though: You can use negative information in this type of message only if you're reasonably sure the audience will respond positively to your message. (Otherwise, use the indirect approach, which is described more thoroughly in Chapter 10.)

Courteous Close

Make sure the audience understands what to do next and how that action will benefit them.

Your message is most likely to succeed if your audience is left with the feeling that you have their personal welfare in mind. In addition, if follow-up action is required, clearly state who will do what next. Highlighting a benefit to the audience, this closing statement clearly summarizes the desired procedure: "Mail us your order this week so that you can be wearing your Shetland coat by the first of October."

W *RITING POSITIVE REPLIES*

Many memos and business letters are written in response to an order, an inquiry, or a request. If the answer is yes or is straightforward information, the direct plan is appropriate.

Acknowledging Orders

Acknowledgment letters play a role in building goodwill.

An order acknowledgment is unnecessary if the products are being shipped or the services will be provided immediately. However, acknowledgments are appropriate for large orders, first orders, and orders that cannot be filled right away. You may use stock paragraphs, but to foster goodwill, personalize your message with your audience's name and specific product information.

The first paragraph states the good news: The order is being processed and the merchandise is on its way. The middle section demonstrates the professionalism of your firm with a clear, accurate summary of the transaction (when the delivery may be expected; the cost of the merchandise, shipping, and taxes; any problems that might have arisen; and perhaps your credit terms). Such messages end on a warm, personal note, with a look toward future dealings.

An order acknowledgment frequently does a bit of selling in the middle or closing section. Resale information bolsters the customer's confidence by pointing out the good points of a product or a company and by explaining how those good points will benefit the customer. Sales promotion—information about something you offer that the customer may not be aware of, may not have thought of buying, or hasn't yet purchased—takes advantage of the customer's obvious interest in your products. Sending along brochures or order blanks makes an additional purchase easier. Effective resale and sales promotion materials demonstrate the "you" attitude. Be sure to emphasize benefits to the customer rather than benefits to the company.

> Resale consists of information about the company or product that confirms the customer's good judgment in making the transaction.

> Sales promotion is information about goods or services that may supplement the customer's purchase.

The following letter was designed to leave the customer satisfied with the handling of the order and prepared to do more business with the writer's firm:

You'll receive your Span-a-Vision videocassette recorder in just over two weeks.	*The main message is stated clearly right at the start.*
Because you live in Massachusetts, you're exempt from the Illinois sales tax. So I'm enclosing a check for $26.15, the amount of the sales tax that you included in your payment.	*The middle section conveys specific details about the order.*
Mr. Harmon, you're going to enjoy your new VCR day after day. It's quite versatile, and to make it even more so, you might want to add a remote-control device. Wired and wireless models are pictured in the enclosed brochure. They let you fast-forward, rewind, and search--all without budging from your most comfortable chair!	*Resale and sales promotion build on the customer's goodwill toward the product and the company. The customer's name is mentioned, as in a personal conversation, to increase the feeling of friendliness.*
When your new VCR arrives, spend a few minutes with the user's manual. If you have any questions, call toll-free 1-800-441-6446 from 9:00 a.m. to 6:00 p.m. weekdays (Central Standard Time). One of our expert staff members will be happy to help you.	*In closing, the writer offers friendly, accessible help.*

Replying to Requests for Information and Action

Any request is important to the person making it, whether inside or outside the organization. That person's opinion of your company, your products, your department, and you yourself will be influenced by how promptly, graciously, and thoroughly the request is handled. Readers' perceptions are the reason Campbell's Zoe Coulson is so sensitive to the tone of her memos, letters, and other messages.

BEHIND THE SCENES AT CITIBANK
Solving Problems, Saving Business

Jane Wolchonok is the director of service quality for the northeast division of Citibank's Consumer Banking Group. She and her nine-member executive communications department handle the most serious and complicated service problems arising in the 230 regional branches in the New York metropolitan area. Here's what usually happens: A Citibank customer has a problem and is dissatisfied with the outcome or the lack of an outcome. The customer complains to a Citibank senior manager, and the complaint winds up in Wolchonok's department. Wolchonok not only oversees the resolution of such problems but also sets service quality priorities for the division. She also monitors the execution of various service programs.

"I wouldn't call our correspondence routine," Wolchonok quickly points out. "Anytime you deal with a person's money, tensions are heightened. Our responses to customer complaints must be prompt and correct, and they must address each customer's specific problem, which means our letters are anything but routine."

The events causing the problems aren't routine, either. And they're not usually the customer's fault. For example, "One of our customers made a $20,000 payment to reduce a credit line, but his account was credited with only $200. We investigated his complaint, found he was correct, and restored the missing $19,800—with interest. We not only wrote a letter telling the customer we corrected the problem, but we also sent along a small gift. Because of the size of the error, we wanted to emphasize the fact that we really regretted what had happened." On another occasion, the deposits of a customer were unaccounted for on three separate occasions over a six-month period. "First," says Wolchonok, "mislaying a deposit is a rare occurrence. Second, each lost deposit was in the same amount. It turned out that when the customer deposited his paycheck, he was writing his branch number in the space intended for his account number. Some processors caught it, but others didn't. When we didn't, the funds were misallocated."

When written on letterhead stationery, a reply legally commits the company to any promised action.

Admittedly, complying with a request isn't always easy. The information may not be immediately at hand, and decisions to take some action must often be made at a higher level. Furthermore, because a letter written on letterhead stationery is legally binding, plan your response carefully.

Fortunately, however, many requests are similar. For example, a human resources department gets a lot of inquiries about job openings. Companies usually develop form responses to handle repetitive queries like these. Although form responses are often criticized as being cold and impersonal, much time and thought may go into wording them, and computers permit personalization and the mixing of paragraphs. Thus a computerized form letter prepared with care may actually be more personal and sincere than a quickly dictated, hastily typed "personal" reply.

When a Potential Sale Is Involved

Prospective customers often request an annual report, a catalog, a brochure, a swatch of material, or some other type of sample or information to help them make a decision about a product encountered through advertising. A polite and helpful response may prompt them to buy. When the customer has not requested the information and is not looking forward to a response, you must use persuasive techniques like those described in Chapter 11. However, in a "solicited" sales letter, which the customer is anticipating, you may use the direct plan.

When answering requests involving a potential sale, you have three main goals:

Although some situations may be similar, Wolchonok doesn't use form letters. "Of course, we've developed some paragraphs we've come to rely on from time to time. But we customize every response to the spirit in which the customer has contacted us. We begin with a welcoming and orienting comment. In the case of the missing credit line payment, we might begin, 'Thank you for your letter to our chairman letting us know about our error with your line of credit.' That reminds our readers what we're writing about. In addition, I feel that taking responsibility for the error in the opening statement builds a bond between the customer and the bank. We go on to spell out the action we've taken, explaining why we've done things that way." Wolchonok also insists on a courteous close to point out that Citibank does not consider the customer's recent experience an acceptable level of service: "We made it clear to the fellow with the missing deposits, for example, that we held our own people accountable for catching his error."

Wolchonok's department creates approximately 6,000 letters a year, 90 percent of which deal with problem situations. "Of those," Wolchonok estimates, "ninety percent are favorably disposed of. That is, we resolve the situation to the customer's satisfaction. Our goal is nothing less than to restore the confidence of the cus-

tomer in the bank." So Wolchonok and her people make the unusual routine. "We know we've done our job right when a customer writes to thank us and to say that, based on his experience, he'd recommend Citibank to anyone." That's as good as goodwill gets in business today.

Apply Your Knowledge

1. Wolchonok has asked you to respond to an inquiry from a large depositor demanding to know why you closed a branch in her neighborhood. Outline the key points of your letter, and write the opening paragraph in the Citibank model.

2. The editor of a foreign-language newspaper (which serves a close-knit community where there are two busy branches) has written to Citibank's board members, pressing them to advertise in his publication. He states that he has a great deal of influence in the community, and he implies that he will use it against the bank if his request is not honored. How would you respond? Outline the key points of your letter, and write the opening paragraph.

---

1. To respond to the inquiry and answer all questions
2. To encourage the future sale
3. To leave your reader with a good impression of you and your firm

The following letter succeeds in meeting these three objectives:

Three main goals when a potential sale is involved:

- Responding to the immediate request
- Encouraging a sale
- Conveying a good impression of you and your firm

Here's the copy of "Brightening Your Bathroom" that you recently requested.

As beautiful as the full-color photographs are, you really need to inspect Brite-Tiles in person. Only then can you fully appreciate the sparkling colors, designer patterns, and overall quality. Baywood Hardware, 313 Front Street in Clear Lake, is the nearest outlet carrying Brite-Tiles. While you're there, ask the salesperson to explain how easy it is to install Brite-Tiles with our chemically compatible cements and grouts.

A clear, conversational statement of the main point is all that's required to start.

Key information—the address of the local store that carries the merchandise—is presented immediately, along with resale and sales promotion.

From antique Victorian to sleek contemporary, Brite-Tiles will help you achieve just the look you want. Spend a few moments now with the handy chart, "The Right Pattern for Your Decor," on page 5 of the enclosed booklet. Then you'll know which patterns to look for when you visit Baywood Hardware.

Mrs. Lyle, if you have any questions before or during installation, please phone our toll-free service hot line: 1-800-459-3678. You'll get easy-to-understand answers every time.

A reference to a specific page further emphasizes the benefits of the product. This suggestion also encourages the reader to take one more step toward an actual purchase.

The personal close confidently points toward the possible sale.

When No Potential Sale Is Involved

Two goals when no sale is involved:

- Responding to the request
- Leaving a favorable impression of your company or fostering a good working relationship

Some requests from outsiders and most requests from fellow employees are not opportunities to sell a product. In replies to those requests, you have two goals: (1) to answer all the questions honestly and completely and (2) to leave a favorable impression that prepares the way for future business or smooths working relationships. The following is a well-written response to a request from an outsider that does not involve an immediate sale:

Thanks for writing to ask us about the warranty on your Micro-9 computer. Here are the answers to your questions, in the order you asked them:

1. All needed repairs to your computer are covered by the warranty, with the exception of damage caused by abuse such as dents on the external frame, sheared wiring, or shorting from water penetration. If the cause of damage is in dispute, you may appeal your claim to our independent consumer panel. We will accept their decision.
2. When repair is needed, we'll be happy to pick up your computer and return it repaired for a total delivery charge of only $40. Whenever possible, pickups are made on a next-day basis--and always within two working days of your call.
3. Yes, you can buy a one-year computer service policy any time before the expiration of your 12-month warranty. You can renew this policy indefinitely.

A brief statement introduces the purpose of the letter.

Specific questions are answered clearly and fully, in the order asked and with consideration for the reader's needs.

Making sure you're 100 percent satisfied is always our goal, Ms. Worthington. Whenever you have more questions, just let me know. Also, be sure to let me know how you like your new Micro-9 computer.

A warm, personalized, appreciative close encourages goodwill.

A similar approach is appropriate for responding to requests from fellow employees, although a memo format is used. The memo in Figure 9.1 is a reply from the advertising director written to a housewares manager whose merchandise wasn't being featured correctly in regional newspaper ads. The tone of the memo, while still respectful, is a bit less formal than the tone in the previous letter. (See this chapter's Checklist for Positive Replies to review the primary tasks involved in this type of business message.)

When writing to a fellow employee, you can use a less formal tone.

Figure 9.1
Memo Replying to a Routine Request

WOOLWORTH CORPORATION

WOOLWORTH BUILDING
233 BROADWAY
NEW YORK, NEW YORK
10279-0003

Memorandum

TO: Avery Mendoza, Housewares Manager

FROM: Wilimina Simmons, Regional Advertising Director *WS*

DATE: August 24, 1996

SUBJECT: Sale ads for 12-ounce glass tumblers

At last we have traced the problem and corrected the newspaper ads you alerted us to in your memo:

1. Incorrect stock numbers have been corrected and cross-checked on all paperwork, both at the main warehouse and in advertising.

2. The ads that mistakenly featured 20-ounce glass tumblers have been revised to feature the 12-ounce glass tumblers you intended.

3. Ad layout people have been alerted to clear all future discrepancies with department managers.

Apparently, the housewares vendor transposed the item numbers for these glasses on the packing slips, and the error made its way all the way through inventory at our main warehouse and onto our stock-number sheets here in the advertising department. So every time you sent us your weekly features for 12-ounce glass tumblers (stock number HW779-898), our layout people traced the number on our stock sheets and mistakenly came up with 20-ounce tumblers.

I know you had to sell the more expensive 20-ounce tumblers for the 12-ounce sale price until we could get the ads corrected. I am sending a memo to your store manager, explaining the mix-up and taking full responsibility for it. If there is any way I can help you with ad features in the future, please contact me.

The good news is announced without any fanfare, and the specific actions are enumerated for easy reference.

The problem's cause and eventual solution are explained to demonstrate awareness and goodwill.

An appreciative, personal, cooperative close confirms the desire to foster good working relationships.

CHECKLIST FOR POSITIVE REPLIES

A. Initial Statement of the Good News or Main Idea

1. Respond promptly to the request.
2. Indicate in your first sentence that you are shipping the customer's order or fulfilling the reader's request.
3. Avoid such trite and obvious statements as "I am pleased to," "We have received," "This is in response to," or "Enclosed please find."
4. If you are acknowledging an order, summarize the transaction.
   a. Describe the merchandise in general terms.
   b. Express appreciation for the order and the payment, if it has arrived.
   c. Welcome a new customer aboard.
5. Convey an upbeat, courteous, you-oriented tone.

B. Middle, Informational Section

1. Imply or express interest in the request.
2. If possible, answer all questions and requests, preferably in the order posed.
   a. Adapt replies to the reader's needs.
   b. Indicate what you have done and will do.
   c. Include any necessary details or interpretations that the reader may need to understand your answers.
3. Provide all the important details about orders.
   a. Provide any necessary educational information about the product.
   b. Provide details of the shipment, including the approximate arrival time.
   c. Clear up any questions of charges (shipping costs, insurance, credit charges, or discounts for quick payment).
4. Use sales opportunities when appropriate.
   a. Enclose a brochure that provides routine information and specifications, if possible, pointing out its main value and the specific pages of potential interest to the reader.
   b. Call the customer's attention to related products with sales promotion material.
   c. Introduce price only after mentioning benefits, but make price and the method of payment clear.
   d. Send a credit application to new customers and cash customers, if desirable.
5. If you cannot comply with part of the request, perhaps because the information is unavailable or confidential, tell the reader why this is so, and offer other assistance.
6. Embed negative statements in positive contexts, or balance them with positive alternatives.

C. Warm, Courteous Close

1. Avoid clichés ("Please feel free to").
2. Direct a request to the reader ("Please let us know if this procedure does not have the effect you're seeking") or specify the action you want the reader to take, if appropriate.
   a. Make the reader's action easy.
   b. Refer to the reader benefit of fulfilling your request.
   c. Stimulate the reader to act promptly.
3. Use resale material when acknowledging orders to remind the reader of benefits to be derived from this order.
4. Offer additional service, but avoid suggestions of your answer's being inadequate, such as "I trust that," "I hope," and other doubtful statements.
5. Express goodwill or take an optimistic look into the future, if appropriate.

RESPONDING FAVORABLY TO CLAIMS AND ADJUSTMENT REQUESTS

As anyone in business knows, customers sometimes return merchandise to a company, complain about its services, ask to be compensated, and the like. Such complaints are golden opportunities for companies to build customer loyalty.[2] The most sensible reaction is to assume that the customer's account of the transaction is an honest statement of what happened—unless the same customer repeatedly submits dubious claims, a customer is patently dishonest (returning a dress that has obviously been worn, claiming it's the wrong size), or the dollar amount in dispute is very large. Few

In general, it pays to give customers the benefit of the doubt.

people go to the trouble of requesting an adjustment unless they actually have a problem. Once the complaint is made, however, customers may come to view the original transaction as less important than the events that come after the complaint.[3]

The usual human response to a bad situation is to say, "It wasn't my fault!" However, Campbell's Zoe Coulson must take a different stance, as must all businesspeople. Even when the company's terms of adjustment are generous, a grudging tone can actually increase the customer's dissatisfaction.

To protect your company's image and to regain the customer's goodwill, refer to your company's errors carefully. Don't blame an individual or a specific department, and avoid such lame excuses as "Nobody's perfect" or "Mistakes will happen." Don't promise that problems will never happen again; such guarantees are unrealistic and often beyond your control. Instead, explain your company's efforts to do a good job. In so doing, you imply that the error was an unusual incident.

Imagine that customers who complain to a food company receive the following form letter, which is customized through word processing and individually signed:

Your letter about the Golden Harvest canned fruit you recently purchased has been forwarded to our vice president of operations for review. We're pleased you took the time to write. Your satisfaction is important to us. Since 1906 Golden Harvest has been packaging fine food products. Our workers and inspectors monitor quality carefully, using the most up-to-date technology, but we want to do an even better job. Your letter will help us do just that.

The next time you shop, use the enclosed half-price coupon to pick up a gift-boxed set of Golden Harvest Holiday Spices. This coupon, which will be honored wherever our fine specialty foods are sold, is our way of thanking you for your interest in our products.

This letter exemplifies the following points:

- A form letter like this, which is sent to people with various types of requests or complaints, cannot start with a clear good-news statement, because various customers are seeking different types of good news.
- The letter starts instead with what might be called a "good attitude" statement, which is you-oriented to put the customer at ease.
- At no time does this letter suggest that the customer was mistaken in questioning the quality of the product. On the other hand, the writer does not admit to any defect in the product.
- The middle, explanatory section nicely combines the old and the new: Golden Harvest has been doing business for almost 90 years, but its equipment is thoroughly modern. This explanation of the company's quality controls may restore the reader's confidence in the product.
- The letter closes with some resale and sales promotion made personal by the use of *you* and *your*.

You may send form letters in response to claims, but word them carefully so that they are appropriate in a variety of circumstances.

A claim letter written as a personal answer to a unique situation would start with a clear statement of the good news: the settling of the claim according to the customer's request. Look at this letter:

In just a few days, you'll receive a new factory-tested electronic metric scale to replace the one you returned. Thanks for giving us the opportunity to back up our claim of total buyer satisfaction.

Our goal for the past 104 years has been to provide precise and reliable measuring devices that meet the most exacting standards. Throughout our manufacturing process, every scale must meet stringent factory tests for accuracy and durability. Technicians in our test laboratories have been alerted to your experience, however, so that we can maintain the high ratings we have been given by all major professional journals.

We appreciate your interest in our products, Dr. Clark. Please continue telling us how we may supply your needs for dependable measuring devices.

To review the tasks involved in this type of business message, see this chapter's Checklist for Favorable Responses to Claims and Adjustment Requests.

HANDLING ROUTINE CREDIT REQUESTS

These days much of our economy runs on credit. Consumers often carry a wallet full of plastic credit cards, and businesses of all sizes operate more smoothly because they can pay for their purchases over time. Because credit is so common, most credit requests are routine, as are credit approvals and credit references.

State credit terms factually and in terms of the benefits of having credit.

Approving Credit

Letters approving credit are good-news messages and the first step in what may be a decades-long business relationship. So open your letter with the main idea.

In the middle section, include a reasonably full statement of the credit arrangements: the upper limit of the account, dates that bills are sent, possible arrangements for partial monthly payments, discounts for prompt payments, interest charges for unpaid balances, and due dates. State the terms positively and objectively, not negatively or in an authoritarian manner:

Instead of This	***Write This***
Your credit balance cannot exceed $5,000.	With our standard credit account, you can order up to $5,000 worth of fine merchandise.
We expect your payment within 30 days of receipt of our statement.	Payment is due 30 days after you receive our statement.

As president of Colonial Mortgage Company in Montgomery, Alabama, R. J. Wynn understands that credit is affected by economic and legislative changes on both the national and international levels. But credit also depends on clarity, so Wynn advises that every credit transaction be meticulously handled and spelled out in the clearest terms.

Because the letter approving credit is considered a legal document, check the wording for accuracy, completeness, and clarity.

The final section of the letter provides resale information and sales promotion highlighting the benefits of buying from you. The following letter was written both to approve credit and to bring in customers:

Welcome aboard! Here's your new Ship-to-Shore credit card, which will make shopping at Conrad's even easier than before. Now you can make credit purchases up to a total of $1,000.

The good-news opening gets right to the point.

CHECKLIST FOR FAVORABLE RESPONSES TO CLAIMS AND ADJUSTMENT REQUESTS

A. Initial Statement of the Good News or Main Idea
1. State immediately your willingness to honor the reader's claim.
2. Accept your reader's account as entirely accurate unless good business reasons demand a different interpretation of some points.
3. Adopt a tone of consideration and courtesy; avoid being defensive, recriminatory, or condescending.
4. Thank the reader for taking the time to write.

B. Middle, Informational Section
1. Minimize or, if possible, omit any disagreements with your reader's interpretation of events.
2. Maintain a supportive tone through such phrases as "Thank you for," "May we ask," "Please let us know," and "We are glad to work with you."
3. Apologize only under extreme circumstances; then do so crisply and without an overly apologetic tone.
4. Admit your firm's faults carefully.
   a. Avoid blaming any particular person or office.
   b. Avoid implying general company inefficiency.
   c. Avoid blaming probability ("Mistakes will happen").
   d. Avoid making unrealistic promises about the future.
   e. Remind the reader of your firm's quality controls.
5. Handle carefully the customer's role in producing the problem.
   a. If appropriate, honor the claim in full but without negative comment.
   b. If appropriate, provide an objective, nonvindictive, impersonal explanation.

C. Warm, Courteous Close
1. Clarify any necessary actions that your reader must take.
2. Remind the reader of how you have honored the claim.
3. Avoid negative information.
4. Encourage the customer to look favorably on your company and/or the product in question (resale information).
5. Encourage the customer to continue buying other goods from you (sales promotion), but avoid seeming greedy.

With a Ship-to-Shore card in your wallet, you can enjoy storewide shopping. If you prefer, you can phone in orders to 834-2230 for delivery within two days. A statement mailed on the tenth of each month will list all credit purchases made within the period and the amount due. When you pay the entire balance by the due date, no interest is charged. Otherwise, you may pay as little as 10% of the balance or $20, whichever is greater. A monthly interest charge of 1-1/2% of the outstanding balance will be added to your next statement.

Do visit Conrad's today. You'll find that every department is overflowing with the latest merchandise for your whole family. From gourmet foods to casual clothing to appliances for land and sea, this is your one-stop shopping center. Also, remember our free delivery service. Even if you're berthed in the city docks, we'll deliver your purchases to your door.

An objective statement of the terms constitutes a legal contract. Positive, you-oriented wording avoids an authoritarian tone.

The courteous close provides resale for the store and sales promotion noting a range of customer benefits.

CHECKLIST FOR CREDIT APPROVALS

A. Initial Statement of the Good News or Main Idea
1. Cheerfully tell the reader that he or she now has approved credit with your firm.
2. Tell the reader, with brief resale, that he or she will soon be enjoying the use of any goods that were ordered with the request. Specify the date and method of shipment and other purchase details.
3. Establish a tone of mutual warmth and trust.

B. Middle, Informational Section
1. Explain the conditions under which credit was granted.
2. Include or attach a full explanation of your firm's credit policies and expectations of payment.
3. Stress the advantages of prompt payment in a way that assumes your reader will take advantage of them ("When you pay your account in full within ten days . . .").
4. Include legally required disclosure statements.
5. Inform or remind the reader of the general benefits of doing business with your firm (resale).
   - a. Tell the consumer about free parking, mail and phone shopping, personalized shopping services, your home-decorating bureau, bridal consultants, restaurants, child care, gift wrap-ping, free deliveries, special discounts or purchase privileges, and other benefits, if your firm offers them.
   - b. If the customer is a retailer or wholesaler, tell about nearby warehouses, factory representatives, quantity discounts, free window or counter displays, national advertising support, ads for local newspapers and other media, repair services, manuals, factory guarantees, prompt and speedy deliveries, toll-free phone number, research department, and other benefits, if your firm offers them.
6. Inform or remind the reader of a special sale, discount, or promotion (sales promotion).
7. Avoid exaggerations or flamboyant language that might make this section of your letter read like an advertisement.

C. Warm, Courteous Close
1. Summarize the reasons the reader will enjoy doing business with your firm.
2. Use the "you" attitude, and avoid clichés.
3. Invite the reader to a special sale or the like or provide resale information to motivate him or her to use the new account.

See this chapter's Checklist for Credit Approvals to quickly review the tasks involved in this type of message.

Providing Credit References

When responding to an inquiry about someone's creditworthiness,

- Make sure the request is legitimate
- Limit yourself to factual statements

The great majority of credit applications are checked electronically: Computer terminals at many stores connect directly with databanks maintained by national credit-reporting agencies. Generally, the data are fed to the inquiring business without any recommendation.

At times, however, one businessperson will request a credit rating directly from another. If you're answering an inquiry about someone's creditworthiness, your first responsibility is to make sure the inquiry is legitimate. You're being asked to provide confidential information; do so only if it is requested by a stable business.

As you write a credit reference, remember that the decision to approve credit isn't yours; that's up to the company that has been asked to extend the credit. So no matter how strong your opinion of the applicant may be, limit yourself to factual statements. If you don't, you may end up in court.

Conveying Positive Information About People

Professors, supervisors, and managers are often asked to write letters recommending students or employees for jobs, and nearly anyone may be asked to recommend acquaintances for awards, membership in organizations, and other honors. Such letters may take the direct approach when the recommendation is generally positive. Employers use the same type of organizational plan when telling job applicants the good news—that they got the job.

Recommendation Letters

A letter of recommendation has an important goal: to convince readers that the person being recommended has the characteristics required for the job or other benefit. So it's important that it contain all the relevant details:

- The full name of the candidate
- The job or benefit the candidate is seeking
- Whether the writer is answering a request or taking the initiative
- The nature of the relationship between the writer and the candidate
- Facts relevant to the position or benefit sought
- The writer's overall evaluation of the candidate's suitability for the job or benefit sought

A recommendation letter is usually confidential; that is, it's mailed directly to the person or committee who requested it and is not shown to the candidate. However, recent litigation has made it advisable in some situations to prepare a carefully worded letter that satisfies both parties.

A recommendation letter presenting negatives may be carefully worded to satisfy both the candidate and the person or company requesting information.

Oddly enough, the most difficult recommendation letters to write are those for truly outstanding candidates. Your audience will have trouble believing uninterrupted praise for someone's talents and accomplishments. So illustrate your general points with a specific example or two that point up the candidate's abilities, and discuss the candidate's abilities in relation to the "competition."

Two devices for convincing the reader when the candidate is outstanding:
- *Use examples*
- *Use comparisons with the "competition"*

Most candidates aren't perfect, however. Omitting reference to a candidate's shortcomings may be justified, especially if the shortcomings are irrelevant to the demands of the job. Even so, you have an obligation to your audience, to your own conscience, and even to the better-qualified candidate who's relying on honest references to refer to any shortcoming that is serious and related to job performance.

The danger in writing a critical letter is that you might engage in libel—that is, make a false and malicious written statement that injures the candidate's reputation. It may be unethical and illegal to omit negative information from a recommendation if that information is truthful and relevant. So if you must refer to a possible shortcoming, you can best protect yourself by sticking to the facts and placing your criticism in the context of a generally favorable recommendation, as in the following example:

A serious shortcoming cannot be ignored, but beware of being libelous:
- *Include only relevant, factual information*
- *Avoid value judgments*
- *Balance criticisms with favorable points*

Your new business magazine sounds grand, and I am pleased to support Clark Stone's application to write the "Focus" column spotlighting specific businesses across the country and around the world.

The candidate's full name and the main point are clearly stated.

Over the past three years, Clark and I have worked together on several book projects--all on business topics. I have always been impressed with his writing ability, and he has a unique talent for translating even dry, technical material into clear prose that is both interesting and enthusiastic. His own excitement, even wonder, comes through in his writing, and even though his thoroughness can increase the pressure on him to meet deadlines, the results are always informative and a pleasure to read.

The duration and nature of the relationship are specified to give weight to the evaluation. A possible weakness related to the position is embedded in the discussion of good qualities without resort to overly negative terms.

Clark's enthusiasm and writing talents would certainly benefit any business magazine, and his experience could prove crucial to the type of magazine you're planning. If you wish to discuss Clark's skills further, please call me at (203) 764-8893 any weekday between 8:00 a.m. and 5:00 p.m.

A supportive, personal summary of the writer's evaluation provides a good close. The phone number and invitation to discuss the candidacy further constitute another helpful touch.

In this letter the writer avoids the risk of libel by supporting the statements with facts and by steering clear of vague, critical judgments.

You can also avoid trouble by asking yourself the following questions before mailing a recommendation letter:

- Does the person receiving this frank, personal information have a legitimate right to the information?
- Does all the information I have presented relate directly to the job or other benefit being sought?
- Have I put the candidate's case as strongly as I honestly can?
- Have I avoided overstating the candidate's abilities or otherwise misleading the reader?
- Have I based all my statements on firsthand knowledge or provable facts?

Good News About Employment

Finding suitable job applicants and then selecting the right person are tasks fraught with hard choices and considerable anxiety. In contrast, writing a letter to the successful applicant is a pleasure. Most of the time, such a letter is eagerly awaited, so the direct approach is appropriate:

After interviewing a number of qualified applicants for the position of executive secretary to Cynthia Hargrove, our vice president of marketing, we have selected you. Welcome to Southwest Specialties, Inc.!

We would like you to report for work on July 24 so that the person who currently has the job can spend a week showing you around. You will be paid a monthly salary of $1,800 and will receive the standard benefits package described during the interview process.

Please plan to arrive at 8:30 a.m. on the 24th; ask for me at the reception desk. We will spend an hour or so filling out the necessary forms and going over company employment policies. Then I'll introduce you to the people in the marketing department--and your new career with Southwest Specialties will be under way!

This letter takes a friendly, welcoming tone, and it explains the necessary details: job title, starting date, salary, and benefits. The last paragraph, with its explanation of the first day's routine, helps allay the bewilderment and uncertainty that might afflict the new employee.

Although letters like these are pleasant to write, they constitute a legal job offer. You and your company may be held to any promises you make. So attorneys sometimes recommend stating salary as a monthly amount and keeping the timing of performance evaluations and raises vague; you want to avoid implying that the newly hired employee will be kept on, no matter what, for a whole year or until the next scheduled evaluation.[4]

> A letter telling someone that she or he got the job is a legal document, so make sure all statements are accurate.

WRITING DIRECTIVES AND INSTRUCTIONS

Directives are memos that tell employees *what* to do. Instructions tell people inside and outside the company *how* to do something and may take the form of memos, letters, or even booklets. Directives and instructions are both considered routine messages because readers are assumed to be willing to comply.

> Directives tell employees what to do; instructions tell readers how to do something.

The goal in writing directives and instructions is to make the point so obvious and the steps so self-explanatory that readers won't have to ask for additional help. Directives and instructions are especially important within companies: Faulty internal directives and bungled instructions are expensive and inefficient. The following directive does a good job of explaining what employees are expected to do:

Please send me employee vacation schedules for the third quarter, July through September, no later than June 16.

Note that we have pushed back the deadline for submitting the schedules by two weeks. This change is made possible by the new computerized personnel system. The new deadline should give your line workers more time to firm up their vacation plans.

Use the attached form, which has also been simplified, for reporting third-quarter vacation schedules.

This directive is brief and to the point. Drawn-out explanations are unnecessary because readers are expected simply to follow through on a well-established procedure. Yet it also covers all the bases, answering these questions: Who? What? Where? When? Why? How?

Instructions need to answer the same questions, but they differ from directives in the amount of explanation they provide. Zoe Coulson of Campbell might write a simple three-sentence directive to employees to tell them of a change in the policies regarding employee scholarships. However, a detailed set of instructions would be more appropriate to explain the procedure for applying for a scholarship.

The key with instructions is to take nothing for granted. Assuming that readers know nothing about the process you're describing is better than risking confusion and

Figure 9.2
Instructions for Writing Instructions

HOW TO WRITE INSTRUCTIONS

When you need to explain in writing how to do something, a set of instructions is your best choice. By enumerating the steps, you make it easy for readers to perform the process in the correct sequence. Your goal is to provide a clear, self-sufficient explanation so that readers can perform the task independently.

<u>Equipment Needed:</u> Writing materials

<u>Preparing to Write Useful Instructions</u>
1. Perform the task yourself, or ask experts to demonstrate it or describe it to you in detail.
2. Analyze prospective readers' familiarity with the process so that you can write instructions at their level of understanding.

<u>Making Your Instructions Clear</u>
1. Include four elements as needed: an introduction, a list of equipment and materials, a description of the steps involved in the process, and a conclusion.
2. Explain in the opening why the process is important and how it relates to a larger purpose.
3. Divide the process into short, simple steps, presented in order of occurrence.
4. Present the steps in a numbered list, or present them in paragraph format, making plentiful use of words indicating time or sequence, such as <u>first</u> and <u>then</u>.
5. If the process involves more than ten steps, divide them into groups or stages identified with headings.
6. Phrase each step as a command ("Do this" instead of "You should do this"); use active verbs ("Look for these signs" instead of "Be alert for these signs"); use precise, specific terms ("three" instead of "several").
7. When appropriate, indicate how readers may tell whether a step has been performed correctly and how one step may influence another. Supply warnings when performing a step incorrectly could result in damage or injury, but limit the number of warnings so that readers do not underestimate their importance.
8. Include diagrams of complicated devices, and refer to them in the appropriate steps.
9. Summarize the importance of the process and the expected results in the conclusion.

<u>Testing Your Instructions</u>
1. Review the instructions to be sure they are clear and complete. Also judge whether you have provided too much detail.
2. Ask someone else to read the instructions and tell you whether they make sense and are easy to follow.

As vice president of brand marketing for all beauty products, gifts, and jewelry at Avon Products, Joyce Roché is responsible for the introduction of more than 500 new products each year. Well aware of the power of the media, Roché urges you to communicate a clear product message by including information your readers will be interested in.

possible damage or harm by overlooking some basic information. Figure 9.2 is a set of instructions for writing instructions.

CONVEYING GOOD NEWS ABOUT PRODUCTS AND OPERATIONS

It's good business to spread the word about such positive developments as the opening of new facilities, the appointment of a new executive, the introduction of new products or new customer services, or the sponsorship of community events. Imagine that So-Good Foods has successfully introduced to the stores it serves a new line of vegetable chips (carrot, turnip, and yam chips, not the same old potato chips). To maintain its position on supermarket shelves, So-Good decides to offer a new discount program to stores that buy large quantities of its vegetable chips. It supplements the personal visits of its sales force with a good-news message describing the new program to existing customers. The letter begins by trumpeting the news, fills in the details of the discount program in the middle, and closes with a bit of resale information and a confident prediction of a profitable business relationship.

When the audience for a good-news message is large and scattered, however, it's usually easier to communicate through the mass media. When McDonald's opened its first restaurant in Moscow, it sent announcements to newspapers, magazines, radio stations, and TV networks. The specialized documents used to convey such information to the media are called **news releases.** Written to match the style of the medium they are intended for, news releases are typed on plain $8\frac{1}{2}$-by-11-inch paper or on special letterhead—not on regular letterhead—and they're double-spaced for print media or triple-spaced for electronic media. Figure 9.3 illustrates the correct format.

Specially formatted news releases convey good news to the media, which in turn disseminate it to the public.

Figure 9.3
News Release Format

CRUISE NEWS
Carnival Cruise Lines
3655 N.W. 87th Avenue
Miami, FL 33178-2428
(305) 599-2600, Ext. 776
1-800-327-7373, Ext. 776

CONTACT: Tim Gallagher
Jennifer de la Cruz

FOR IMMEDIATE RELEASE

**CARNIVAL CRUISE LINES CONTRACTS FOR
WORLD'S LARGEST CRUISE SHIP**

MIAMI (01/11/93) -- Carnival Cruise Lines, Inc. (NYSE: CCL) announced it has signed a contract with the Italian shipyard Fincantieri Cantieri Navali Italiani S.p.A. for the construction of the largest passenger cruise ship ever built. Approximately 95,000-gross-registered-tons, the vessel will feature 1,300-plus cabins. The per berth price of the new ship will be competitive with Carnival's other current new ship constructions. Delivery is scheduled for late 1996. Citibank N.A. served as financial advisor to both Carnival and Fincantieri in this transaction.

"We are extremely impressed with Fincantieri's present work on the three new ships for our subsidiary Holland America Line," said Micky Arison, chairman and CEO for Carnival Cruise Lines. "The first of these, the MS Statendam, has just been delivered and already is being described in early media reports as one of the most elegant and beautiful ships ever built," he said.

Added Corrado Antonini, managing director, Fincantieri, "The Fincantieri organization is very excited to be continuing our relationship with Carnival and to be a part of this historic new project."

Carnival is the world's largest cruise line based on number of passengers carried. Together with its affiliated cruise lines, Holland America Line, Windstar Cruises and Seabourn Cruise Line, it operates 18 ships in the Caribbean, Alaska and other worldwide destinations. Carnival has contracted for the construction of three 2,600-passenger ships, the Sensation, Fascination and Imagination, which are scheduled for delivery in 1993, 1994 and 1995, respectively. It also has contracted to construct three new ships for Holland America Line. The first of these, the Statendam, has been delivered and is scheduled to begin service late this month, with the Maasdam and Ryndam to be delivered in late 1993 and 1994, respectively.

###

The Fun Ships Sensations • Ecstasy • Fantasy • Celebration • Jubilee • Holiday • Tropicale • Festivale • Carnivale • Mardi Gras

The company name, address, and phone number are noted at the top, along with the names of people who can provide more information.

Provide your own suggestion for a title, or leave two inches here so that the editor can insert a headline.

Most news is released immediately.

This release for a newspaper starts with a dateline and a summary (who, what, where, when, why) of the rest of the story.

The content of this news release follows the customary pattern for a good-news message: good news, followed by details and a positive close. However, it avoids explicit references to any reader, displaying the "you" attitude by presenting information presumed to be of interest to all readers. In addition to issuing written news releases, many large companies hold news conferences or create their own videotapes, which are sent to TV networks.

Writing Goodwill Messages

Business isn't all business. To a great extent, it's an opportunity to forge personal relationships. You can enhance your relationships with customers and other businesspeople by sending friendly, unexpected notes with no direct business purpose. Goodwill messages like these have a positive effect on business, because people prefer to deal with organizations that are warm and human and interested in more than just money.

Such goodwill messages might be considered manipulative and thus unethical unless you make every attempt to be sincere, honest, and truthful. Without sincerity, skillful writing is nothing more than clever, revealing the writer as interested only in personal gain and not in benefiting customers or fellow workers. One way to come across as sincere is to avoid exaggeration. What do you think a reader's reaction would be to these two sentences?

We were overjoyed to learn of your promotion.

Congratulations on your promotion.

Most likely, your audience wouldn't quite believe that anyone (except perhaps a relative or very close friend) would be "overjoyed." On the other hand, readers will accept your simple congratulations—a human, understandable intention.

To demonstrate your sincerity, back up any compliments with specific points:

Instead Of This	*Write This*
Words cannot express my appreciation for the great job you did. Thanks. No one could have done it better. You're terrific! You've made the whole firm sit up and take notice, and we are ecstatic to have you working here.	Thanks for taking charge of the meeting in my absence. You did an excellent job. With just an hour's notice, you managed to pull the legal and public relations departments together so that we could present a united front in the negotiations. Your dedication and communication abilities have been noted and are truly appreciated.

Note also the difference in the words used in these two examples. Your reader would probably believe the more restrained praise to be more sincere. Offering help in a goodwill message is fine, but promise only what you can and will provide. Avoid giving even the impression of an offer of help where none is intended.

Although goodwill messages have little to do with business transactions, they might include some sales information if you have the opportunity to be of particular service or want to remind the reader of your company's product. However, any sales message

---

Marginal notes:

Goodwill is the positive feeling that encourages people to maintain a business relationship.

Make sure your compliments are grounded in reality.

Offer help only when you are able and willing to provide it.

If a sales pitch ever appears in a goodwill message, make it only the slightest hint.

should be subdued and secondary to the helpful, thoughtful message. In the following example, the dealer succeeds in seeming more interested in the relationship with the reader than in a possible sale:

Congratulations on reeling in the big one at the Grainger County fishing contest! The second we saw the newspaper picture of you holding that beauty in one hand and our Fish-Pro collapsible rod in the other, we felt button-popping proud.

Now that you're a local fishing expert, Lou, you might want to check out our other Fish-Pro equipment. At least come by sometime and let us shake your hand. Maybe we can talk you into telling us about your big catch.

The reader of this letter will not feel a great deal of pressure to buy but will feel that the dealer took special notice of his accomplishments. If you add a sales pitch, make sure that it takes a backseat to your goodwill message. Honesty and sincerity must come across above all else.

Congratulations

One prime opportunity for sending congratulations is news of a significant business achievement—for example, being promoted or attaining an important civic position. Note how the sample congratulatory note in Figure 9.4 moves swiftly to the subject, the good news. It gives reasons for expecting success and avoids such extravagances as "Only you can do the job!"

Highlights in people's personal lives—weddings and births, graduations, success in nonbusiness competitions—are another reason for sending congratulations. You may congratulate business acquaintances on their achievements or on their spouse's or children's achievements. You may also take note of personal events, even if you don't know the reader well. Of course, if you're already friendly with the reader, you can get away with a personal tone.

Some alert companies develop a mailing list of potential customers by assigning an employee to clip newspaper announcements of births, engagements, weddings, and graduations. They then introduce themselves by sending out a form letter that might read like this:

Congratulations!

We thought you might like this extra copy of your picture and wedding announcement from the <u>Evening Herald</u>.

It's a pleasure to send it to you. Please accept our good wishes for your happiness.

In this case, the company's letterhead and address are enough of a sales pitch. This simple message has a natural, friendly tone, even though the sender has never met the recipient.

Messages of Appreciation

An important managerial quality is the ability to see employees (and other business associates) as individuals and to recognize their contributions. People often value praise

Hal Riney's creativity has produced memorable TV advertising for Saturn, Perrier, and Swanson. Riney is president of Hal Riney and Partners in San Francisco, and he thinks too few people take goodwill seriously. Preferring scenes that are tender and sympathetic rather than loud and aggressive, he believes in spending the time it takes to build goodwill.

Taking note of significant events in someone's personal life helps cement the business relationship.

A message of appreciation documents a person's contributions.

Figure 9.4
Letter Congratulating a Business Acquaintance

The point of writing comes first.

The reason for congratulating the reader is expressed early and concisely.

Additional detail fleshes out the letter and clarifies the writer's purpose.

The letter ends with a personalized expression of confidence.

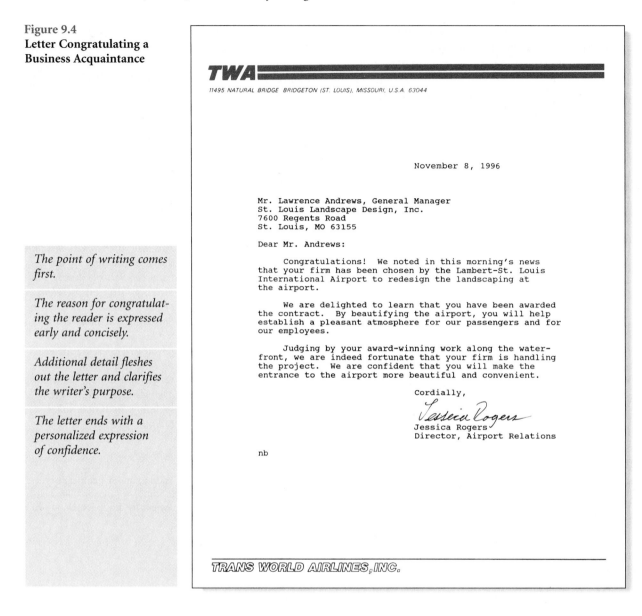

TWA

11495 NATURAL BRIDGE BRIDGETON (ST. LOUIS), MISSOURI, U.S.A. 63044

November 8, 1996

Mr. Lawrence Andrews, General Manager
St. Louis Landscape Design, Inc.
7600 Regents Road
St. Louis, MO 63155

Dear Mr. Andrews:

Congratulations! We noted in this morning's news that your firm has been chosen by the Lambert-St. Louis International Airport to redesign the landscaping at the airport.

We are delighted to learn that you have been awarded the contract. By beautifying the airport, you will help establish a pleasant atmosphere for our passengers and for our employees.

Judging by your award-winning work along the waterfront, we are indeed fortunate that your firm is handling the project. We are confident that you will make the entrance to the airport more beautiful and convenient.

Cordially,

Jessica Rogers

Jessica Rogers
Director, Airport Relations

nb

TRANS WORLD AIRLINES, INC.

more highly than monetary rewards. A message of appreciation may also become an important part of an employee's personnel file:

Thanks a million for programming the computer for the fulfillment department. I suppose only those of us close to this task can really appreciate the size and complexity of the job you did in such a short time. Even during a time when your own workload was unusually heavy, you managed to develop a series of programs that will significantly improve our ability to handle the work of our department.

Always remember, Kathy, that your time and talents are truly appreciated. We view your accomplishment as outstanding!

c: Human Resources Department

With its references to specific qualities and deeds, this note may provide support for future pay increases and promotions.

Suppliers also like to know that you value some exceptional product or the service you received. Long-term support deserves recognition too. Your praise doesn't just make the supplier feel good; it also encourages further excellence. The brief message that follows expresses gratitude and reveals the happy result:

Anyone who does you or your organization a special favor should receive written thanks.

Thank you for the quick service.

You got me that power pack in time for the 8:00 a.m. flight, and the customer was in service by noon!

Thanks again, especially to Brian McKee in your customer service department, for making us both look good.

When you write a message of appreciation to a supplier, try to mention specifically the person or people you want to praise. Your expression of goodwill might net the employee some future benefit. In any case, your message honors the company that the individual represents.

Be sure to thank guest speakers at meetings, even if they've been paid an honorarium or travel expenses—and surely if they have not. They may have spent hours gathering and organizing material for an informative and interesting presentation, so reward their hard work. Messages of appreciation are also appropriate for acknowledging money donations to campaigns or causes. They usually include a few details about the success of the campaign or how the funds are being used so that the donors will feel good about having contributed.

Condolences

In times of serious trouble and deep sadness, written condolences and expressions of sympathy leave their mark. Granted, this type of message is difficult to write, but don't let the difficulty of the task keep you from responding promptly. Those who have experienced a health problem, the death of a loved one, or a business misfortune like to know that they're not alone.

Begin condolences with a brief statement of sympathy, such as "I was deeply sorry to hear of your loss." In the middle, mention the good qualities or the positive contributions made by the deceased. State what the person or business meant to you. In closing, you can offer your condolences and your best wishes. One considerate way to end this type of message is to say something that will give the reader a little lift, such as a reference to a brighter future. A supervisor sent the following condolence letter to the husband (whom she does not know) of a deceased employee:

The news of Georgia's accidental death was a great shock. Please accept my sincere sympathy.

For many years, I enjoyed working with Georgia, as did her other friends and co-workers. She was a woman of integrity, ability, wit, and kindness. We will miss her greatly.

Here are a few general suggestions for writing condolence messages:[5]

In condolence messages, try to find a middle path between being superficial and causing additional distress.

- *Keep reminiscences brief.* Recount a memory or an anecdote (even a humorous one), but don't dwell on the details of the loss, lest you add to the reader's anguish.

CHECKLIST FOR GOODWILL MESSAGES

A. Planning Goodwill Messages
1. Choose the appropriate type of goodwill message for your purpose.
   a. Offer congratulations to make the reader feel noticed.
   b. Express praise or thanks to show your appreciation for good performance.
   c. Offer condolences to show appreciation for the deceased or the person suffering a loss.
   d. Send greetings to put a positive business image before the reader.
2. Be prompt in sending out goodwill messages so that they lose none of their impact.
3. Send a written goodwill message rather than a telephone message, because a written message can be savored more than once. Keep in mind that a telephone message is better than none at all.

B. Format
1. Use the format most appropriate to the occasion.
   a. Use letter format for condolences and for any other goodwill message sent to outsiders or mailed to an employee's home.
   b. Use memo format for any goodwill messages sent through interoffice mail, except for condolences.
   c. Use a preprinted greeting card for condolences (with a brief handwritten message added) or for seasonal greetings.

2. Handwrite condolences (and replies to handwritten invitations); otherwise, type the goodwill message.
3. Use special stationery, if available.
4. For added impact, present congratulations in a folder with a clipping or photo commemorating the special event.

C. Opening
1. State the most important idea first to focus the reader's attention.
2. Incorporate a friendly statement that builds goodwill, right at the beginning.
3. Focus on the good qualities of the person or situation.

D. Middle
1. Provide sufficient details, even in a short message, to justify the opening statement.
2. Express personalized details in sincere, not gushy, language.
3. Be warm but concise.
4. Make the reader, not the writer, the focus of all comments.

E. Close
1. Use a positive or forward-looking statement.
2. Restate the important idea, when appropriate.

- *Write in your own words.* Write as if you were speaking privately to the person. Don't quote "poetic" passages or use stilted or formal phrases. If the loss is a death, refer to it as such rather than as "passing away" or "departing."
- *Be tactful.* Mention your shock and dismay, but keep in mind that the bereaved and distressed loved ones take little comfort in such lines as "Richard was too young to die" or "Starting all over again will be so difficult." Try to strike a balance between superficial expressions of sympathy and heartrending references to a happier past and a possibly bleak future.
- *Take special care.* Be sure to spell names correctly and to be accurate in your facts.
- *Write about special qualities of the deceased.* You may have to rely on reputation to do this, but let the grieving person know the value of his or her loved one.
- *Write about special qualities of the bereaved person.* A pat on the back helps a bereaved family member feel more confident about handling things during such a traumatic time.

Above all, don't let the fear of saying something wrong keep you from saying anything at all. (The tasks involved in this type of business message may be reviewed in this chapter's Checklist for Goodwill Messages.)

On the Job

SOLVING A COMMUNICATION DILEMMA AT CAMPBELL SOUP COMPANY

You would have to search far and wide to find a person more qualified for her job than Zoe Coulson, Campbell Soup's vice president for consumer affairs. In addition to her many years of experience in dealing with consumers, she is a recognized expert in package design, she is the author of the *Good Housekeeping Illustrated Cookbook,* and she counts among her credits past roles as advertising specialist, food editor, member of the board of directors of the Food and Drug Law Institute, and director of the Good Housekeeping Institute. In short, she knows consumers and the food business inside and out, and she knows how to communicate.

Few companies need Coulson's expertise more than Campbell Soup does. During the 1980s, Campbell tried to compensate for two decades of sluggish product innovation by introducing hundreds of new products and branching out into new product areas and new markets. Some of these efforts produced winners, but many products were rushed to market without adequate input from consumers. These expensive flops and the aggressive diversification plans put a big strain on the company's finances and were partly responsible for the former CEO's resignation.

However, by 1990 the company began to refocus on its core businesses (soups, frozen foods, and baked goods) and was paying a lot more attention to consumer tastes and trends. To better meet the diverse needs of consumers across the United States and in other countries, Campbell began varying its recipes according to the needs of particular regions. Now, for instance, consumers in the Southwest can enjoy a spicier blend of Campbell's nacho cheese soup/sauce than consumers elsewhere in the country do. Campbell's profits have improved dramatically, moving above $6 billion and continuing to climb, if somewhat slowly.

Not surprisingly, Zoe Coulson plays a major role in Campbell's efforts to better meet the needs of its millions of customers worldwide. Whether she's responding to dissatisfied customers or answering simple requests for information, Coulson gives Campbell plenty of input. Two of her major concerns, for instance, have been reducing the salt and fat content of Campbell's soups and improving product labeling. As Campbell moves into the next century, Coulson will be communicating with consumers and employees to make sure the giant food producer keeps sales and profits cooking.

Your Mission: You have joined Campbell's consumer marketing staff. As an assistant to Zoe Coulson, you are responsible for handling correspondence with both consumers and Campbell employees. Your objective is to improve the flow of communication between the public and the company so that Campbell can respond quickly and knowledgeably to changing consumer needs. Choose the best alternatives for re-

sponding to the situations described below, and be prepared to explain why your choice is best:

1. Coulson has received a letter from a Mrs. Felton who, although pleased that Campbell offers a line of Special Request reduced-sodium soups, would like to see more flavors added. Which of the following is the best opening paragraph for your reply?
   a. The Campbell Soup Company was founded at the turn of the century by a chemist named J. T. Dorrance, who invented condensed soup and sold it in a 10-ounce can for a dime. He was a conservative man and a stickler for quality. His only son, Jack Dorrance, followed his father into the business and had a similar management philosophy. As chairman of the company, he used to pinch the tomatoes and taste the carrots occasionally to be sure that the folks in the factory were maintaining high standards. Only 12 days before he died at the age of 70 in April 1989, Jack Dorrance was at the Campbell test kitchen in Camden, New Jersey, sampling new soups. He was especially interested in the low-salt line and would be pleased to know that it appeals to you.
   b. Thank you for your enthusiastic letter about Campbell's Special Request soups. We are delighted that you enjoy the flavors currently available, and we are working hard to add new varieties to the line.
   c. Good news! Our world-renowned staff of food technologists is busy in the test kitchen at this very moment, experimenting with additional low-sodium recipes for Special Request soups. Hang on to your bowl, Mrs. Felton, more flavors are on the way!

2. Which of the following versions is preferable for the middle section of the letter to Mrs. Felton?
   a. You can expect to see several exciting new Special Request soups on your supermarket shelf within the next year. Before the new flavors make their debut, however, they must undergo further testing in our kitchens and in selected markets across the country. We want to be sure our soups satisfy consumer expectations.

   While you're waiting for the new flavors of Special Request, you might like to try some of Campbell's other products designed especially for people like you who are concerned about health and nutrition. I'm enclosing coupons that entitle you to sample both Pepperidge Farm Five-Star

Fibre bread and Le Menu Light Style frozen dinners "on the house." We hope you enjoy them.

b. We are sorry that the number of Special Request flavors is limited at this time. Because of the complexities of testing flavors both in the Campbell kitchens and in test markets around the country, we are a bit behind schedule in releasing new varieties. However, several new flavors should be available by the end of the year, if all goes according to plan.

In the meantime, please accept these coupons; they can be redeemed for two other fine Campbell products designed for the health-conscious consumer.

c. Additional flavors of Special Request reduced-sodium soups are currently in formulation. They will arrive on supermarket shelves soon. In the meantime, why not enjoy some of Campbell's other fine products designed for the health-conscious consumer? The enclosed coupons will allow you to sample Le Menu Light Style frozen dinners and Pepperidge Farm Five-Star Fibre bread at our expense.

3. Campbell has received a letter from the American Heart Association asking for information on the fat and sodium content of Campbell's products. Your department has developed a brochure that provides the necessary data, and you plan to send it to the association. Which of the following cover letters should you send along with the brochure?

a. Please consult the enclosed brochure for the answers to your questions regarding the composition of Campbell's products. The brochure provides detailed information on the sodium and fat content of all Campbell's products, which include such well-known brands as V8, Pepperidge Farm, Swanson's, Mrs. Paul's, and Le Menu, as well as Campbell's Soups.

b. Thanks for your interest in Campbell's products. We are concerned about nutrition and health issues and are trying to reduce the salts and fats in our products. At the same time, we are striving to retain the taste that consumers have come to expect from Campbell. In general, we feel very good about the nutritional value of our products and think that after you read the enclosed brochure, you will too.

c. Thank you for your interest in Campbell's Soup. The enclosed brochure provides the information you requested about the fat and sodium content of our products. Over the past ten years, we have introduced a number of reduced-sodium and low-fat products designed specifically for consumers on restricted diets. Additionally, we have reformulated many of our regular products to re-

duce the salt and fat content. We have also revised our product labels so that information on sodium and fat content is readily apparent to health-conscious consumers. If you have any questions about any of our products, please contact our consumer information specialists at 1-800-227-9876.

4. Campbell has received a letter from a disgruntled consumer, Mr. Max Edwards, who was disappointed with his last can of Golden Classic beef soup with potatoes and mushrooms. It appears that the can contained an abundance of potatoes, little beef, and few mushrooms. You have been asked to reply to Mr. Edwards. Which of the following drafts is best?

a. We are extremely sorry that you did not like your last can of Golden Classic beef soup with potatoes and mushrooms. Although we do our very best to ensure that all our products are of the highest quality, occasionally our quality-control department slips up and a can of soup comes out a bit short on one ingredient or another. Apparently you happened to buy just such a can--one with relatively few mushrooms, not much beef, and too many potatoes. The odds against that ever happening to you again are probably a million to one. To prove it, here's a coupon that entitles you to a free can of Golden Classic soup. You may pick any flavor you like, but why not give the beef with potatoes and mushrooms another try? We bet it will meet your standards this time around.

b. You are right, Mr. Edwards, to expect the highest quality from Campbell's Golden Classic soups. And you are right to complain when your expectations are not met. Our goal is to provide the best, and when we fall short of that goal, we want to know about it so that we can correct the problem.

And that is exactly what we have done. In response to your complaint, our quality-control department is reexamining its testing procedures to ensure that all future cans of Golden Classic soup have an even blend of ingredients. Why not see for yourself by taking the enclosed coupon to your supermarket and redeeming it for a free can of Golden Classic soup? If you choose beef with potatoes and mushrooms, you can count on getting plenty of beef and mushrooms this time.

c. Campbell's Golden Classic soups are a premium product at a premium price. Our quality-control procedures for this line have been carefully devised to ensure that every can of soup has a uniform distribution of ingredients. As you can imagine, your complaint came as quite a surprise to us, given the care that we take with our products. We suspect that the uneven distribution of ingredients was just a fluke, but our quality-control department is looking into the matter to ensure that the alleged problem does not recur. We would like you to give our Golden Classic soup another try. We are confident that you will be satisfied, so we are enclosing a coupon that entitles you to a free can. If you are not completely happy with it, please call me at 1-800-227-9876.

5. Zoe Coulson was recently named one of corporate America's 100 most promising women executives by a nationwide business magazine. As her administrative assistant, you have been asked to draft a press release to the local newspapers announcing the good news. Here is your first draft. How can it be improved?

For many years, the Campbell Soup Company has been a leader in equal employment opportunities for women and minorities. Campbell is proud of its reputation for nurturing outstanding female and minority employees. Given the company's commitment to affirmative action, it is gratifying to announce that Ms. Zoe Coulson, Campbell Soup Company's vice president of consumer affairs, has been selected as one of corporate America's 100 top women executives.

Ms. Coulson has been with Campbell since 1981. Before joining Campbell, she was the director of the Good Housekeeping Institute. She holds an M.B.A. degree from the Harvard Business School.

In her capacity as Campbell's in-house consumer advocate, Ms. Coulson has been instrumental in reducing the sodium and fat content of Campbell's products. She has also worked to ensure that all product labels are clear and "user friendly."

a. Omit the initial portion of the press release, down to the section that reads "Ms. Zoe Coulson, Campbell Soup Company's vice president of consumer affairs, has been selected one of corporate America's 100 top women executives." Move the third paragraph up so that it follows this sentence and becomes part of the first paragraph. Complete the press release with the second paragraph, describing Coulson's experience.

b. Add several paragraphs that describe Campbell's products.

c. Rework the press release so that it is more of a personality profile of Zoe Coulson. Add information about her personal life, her hobbies, her management style, and her career progress. Include several direct quotes from Ms. Coulson to illustrate her reaction to the honor.[6]

Questions for Discussion

1. As a local retailer, would you take the time to reply to requests for information and action when no potential sale is involved? Explain.

2. Your company's error has cost an important business customer a new client—you know it, and your customer knows it. Do you apologize, or do you refer to the incident in a positive light without admitting any responsibility?

3. Your customer is clearly at fault and lying. Will you disallow her claim? Why or why not?

4. You've been asked to write a letter of recommendation for an employee who is disabled and uses a wheelchair. The disability has no effect on the employee's ability to do the job, and you feel confident about writing the best recommendation possible. Nevertheless, you know the prospective company, and its facilities aren't well suited to wheelchair access. Do you mention the employee's disability in your letter?

5. Since news releases are published as news items, is it okay to mention the benefits of your company's products, or would that be unethical?

6. Why should resale and sales promotion be subdued (if included at all) in goodwill messages?

Documents for Analysis

Read the following letters; then (1) analyze the strengths and weaknesses of each sentence and (2) revise each letter so that it follows this chapter's guidelines.

DOCUMENT 9.A

After receiving your shipment of returned books, we checked our records to see why we had sent them to you in the first place. Our records show that you were late in returning your card indicating that you did not want the selections. As you know, we will automatically send you the month's new books unless you specifically ask not to receive them by our clearly stated deadline. This policy enables us to see that our subscribers have access to the newest books as soon as possible.

However, you are in luck. Because we value your membership in the Read-a-Lot Club, we are crediting your account for $29.18--the full price of the books that you returned!

In the future, please try to return your reply card more promptly so that you won't face the inconvenience of returning the books. In any case, we want to express our thanks for your long-term patronage of the Read-a-Lot Club. We think you will want next month's selection, which is a murder mystery by John D. MacDonald.

DOCUMENT 9.B

Please accept our apologies for the delay in repairing your video game, which is being shipped under separate cover.

Let me explain what happened: Four Star Games, the manufacturer of your video game system, had expanded its production facilities to capitalize on the boom in video game sales that occurred in the early 1980s. When the market for such games declined, the firm was unable to meet the payments on its bank loans. The firm went bankrupt early this year, and we bought the assets. We also acquired the liabilities, which included all repairs under warranties.

Your broken game was just one of many that fell in our lap, so to speak. As you can imagine, it took us a while to sort out what was happening--hence the delay in repairing your video game.

In the future we will be handling any further repairs covered by warranties through a new dealer network, created through the combination of Four Star's best dealers and our own existing dealers. If you have any further problems with the game, please contact one of these dealers for repairs.

Thanks for your patience. Again, we apologize for the delay. Incidentally, I am enclosing a brochure showing some of our exciting new products.

DOCUMENT 9.C

I was really glad to hear that you were promoted to vice president of research and development at ChemCo. I know that you have wanted that job for years, and I can imagine how happy you must be now that you have finally achieved your goal. Before you break out the champagne, however, take a hard look at what you're getting into.

As you know, I received an important promotion myself last year. Let me tell you, it's not all a bed of roses up here in the executive suite. I've been working 12 and 15 hours a day since I became general manager of the Wingate plant. My wife and children hardly recognize me anymore, and my former friends in the company act like they're afraid of me. As they say, it's lonely at the top. If you find yourself wishing you could undo it all, give me a call. Maybe we can run away and join the circus together.

Cases

WRITING POSITIVE REPLIES

1. Thank you, Japan: Letter from Xerox acknowledging an order Xerox has done it: Not only has it regained some of the low-cost copy machine market lost to Japanese manufacturers in the early 1970s (when Xerox's copier patents expired), but it's now selling its copy machines to Japanese companies. Xerox's success is the result of a slow rebuilding process, in which the company took great pains to increase its market share by dramatically improving the quality of its products. In a process Xerox calls "competitive benchmarking," company executives visited and studied the methods of firms known for excellence in certain areas of manufacturing or distribution, such as L. L. Bean and Toyota.

To develop Xerox model 5100, the copier that has begun to crack the Japanese market, Xerox engineers spent more than four years in research and development, inviting engineers from the company's Japanese joint-venture partner, Fuji Xerox Company, to participate in the process. Chief Engineer Daniel W. Cholish and other executives traveled to Japan to meet with potential customers. After surmounting the barriers of language and culture, Xerox officials learned that Japanese companies need copiers that can reproduce *kanji* (fine, handwritten Japanese characters) on the lightweight, oversized papers frequently used in Japan. The instructions, of course, must be printed in Japanese.

So far, it looks as if all Xerox's efforts are paying off. In 1989 the company won the Malcolm Baldrige National Quality Award, and in Japan the Xerox 5100 is selling well among companies like Tokyu Corporation (nucleus of a huge multinational conglomerate) and Tokyo Electric Power Company (which provides a third of Japan's total electric power). In fact, as a communication specialist at company headquarters in Stamford, Connecticut, you've been asked to develop an appropriate letter of acknowledgment that can be forwarded overseas to each new Japanese customer.

Your Task: Write the form letter that acknowledges an order for the new Xerox 5100. The letter will be personalized with individual company names. Be sure to use this opportunity to reinforce your sales message.[7]

2. Blazing white: Letter to *Maclean's* magazine describing new TCF paper

Now that scientists have revealed the serious environmental impact of the chlorine bleaching traditionally used to create white paper, paper companies are facing some potentially costly changes in their manufacturing techniques. Research indicates that unless a company installs secondary waste-treatment facilities, the chlorine process releases highly toxic by-products (dioxins) into the environment, fouling water supplies and accumulating in both ocean and freshwater fish that humans might consume.

Most countries are considering legislation to limit or ban the use of chlorine in paper and other industries. Many paper companies have already tried producing "totally chlorine free" (TCF) paper, but industry executives complain that they just can't sell the brownish-colored TCF paper. Nobody wants to read brown magazines or mail, they argue, and the TCF paper costs buyers up to 20 percent more than ordinary white paper.

Peter Sweeney, a marketing official at Cross Pointe Paper in Minnesota, isn't worried about the controversy. His company (a division of Pentair) recently developed a new line of paper made by combining TCF paper with recycled materials. Not only is it shining white, but the paper costs a mere 5 percent more than standard chlorine-bleached products. If new legislation forces a change in paper manufacturing, Cross Pointe is in a good position to lead the industry. Although the company hasn't done much advertising, requests are steadily coming in from publishers and environmental groups for more information on the new product line. Even *Maclean's*, Canada's weekly newsmagazine, has sent a request for samples.

Your Task: As a sales representative, you handle the requests for information passed on from Sweeney's department. Address a letter to Sarah Oliver, Purchasing Agent, *Maclean's* magazine (Maclean Hunter, Ltd., 777 Bay Street, Toronto, Ontario M5W 1A7, Canada), describing the new paper and providing samples and a price list for the big Canadian pub-

lisher. If it likes your product, *Maclean's* could become one of Cross Pointe's most important accounts.[8]

3. Calming fear at Eli Lilly: Reply to a woman whose grandmother took DES—a "wonder drug" disaster

When it first became available in 1947, DES (diethylstilbestrol) was hailed as a miracle drug. Thousands of pregnant women in the midst of the postwar "baby boom" eagerly ingested the new synthetic hormone. They had been told by their doctors that it would prevent premature labor and even "build bigger and stronger babies." Then tragedy struck.

By 1971 the drug was definitely linked to clear-cell adenocarcinoma, and its use was restricted by the U.S. Food and Drug Administration. The rare form of cancer was turning up not in the women who took the drug but in their daughters. At the time this tragic link was discovered, your employer, Eli Lilly, produced 75 percent of the country's supply of DES.

For nine years before releasing the drug, Eli Lilly tested it extensively. Independent researchers concluded that it would save babies who might not otherwise be carried to term, with no harm to the mother or the unborn child. Not until years later did officials at your company learn with the rest of the world that 1 out of every 1,000 DES daughters would develop clear-cell cancer. Many of these daughters have sued the companies that produced the DES their mothers took (one damage award alone cost your company $12.2 million).

Although no scientific evidence has so far indicated that DES is passed down genetically to the *third* generation, public concern is growing. Dr. Ruthann Giusti of the National Cancer Institute has issued a statement that, despite the lack of proof of a genetic linkage, there is an *indirect* link between the drug and third-generation babies who suffer serious disabilities caused at birth by their mothers' cervical and uterine abnormalities, which are suspected to have been caused by the DES that their own mothers ingested during pregnancy. (This statistical conclusion has not yet been confirmed by clinical research.)

On your desk is a letter from Kimberly Horton, whose grandmother took DES. Her mother had a hysterectomy at age 29 as a result of cervical cancer, then had a benign lump removed from her breast, and later lost both ovaries and Fallopian tubes when an ovarian cyst ruptured. She never suffered from the clear-cell adenocarcinoma attributed to DES. Kimberly, now 25, says she has already had one miscarriage, and doctors tell her that she, too, suffers from reproductive abnormalities. Her letter is a poignant, fearful plea: "Please tell me everything you know about the effects of DES on third-generation women. Will I suffer from cancer like my mother because my grandmother took the drug your company produced? Although my mother did not have miscarriages, I understand other DES daughters have—is this why I lost my baby?"

Your Task: As a company spokesperson, you've been asked to write a reassuring response to Kimberly (Box 116,

Williamstown, MA 01267). At hand is a previous company statement, cold and factual: "The third-generation claims now being asserted by a few plaintiffs' attorneys allege injuries resulting from premature births and do not involve claims of genetic damage or defect due to DES exposure." Kimberly mentioned in her letter that she was not born prematurely.[9]

RESPONDING FAVORABLY TO CLAIMS AND ADJUSTMENT REQUESTS

4. Play it again: Letter from Listen 2 Books promising free repair At Listen 2 Books, the only books for sale are on audiotape or compact disc. They've become increasingly popular with people on the go who feel they don't have time to read the old-fashioned way. Most customers spend lots of time in their cars and limos, and the tape or disc player can provide information they need to keep up with trends, brush up on skills, or simply relax and enjoy a good story.

Business has been booming, but this morning you received a fax from an angry customer. Albert Mossberger is furious— and he's an important local citizen and regular customer. Apparently he'd put in an early order via fax and waited months for the release of an audiotape version of *Ben & Jerry's: The Inside Scoop* by Fred "Chico" Lager, read by actor Joseph Campanella. The book was a favorite topic in business circles, and Mossberger was counting on listening to it as he made a long commute via limo to an out-of-town business meeting. But when he put the first tape into the machine, it jammed and scrambled.

When you show the fax to your boss, store owner Joe Andahazy, he shrugs. "No problem. Tell him to messenger it over and we'll fix or replace both cassettes for free. But don't just call him—put it in writing."

Soon after he opened the audio-only store, Andahazy learned how to fix malfunctioning audiotapes and get them back on the shelves rather than returning them to manufacturers—especially the best-sellers that customers might seek elsewhere. Andahazy figures he's saved thousands of dollars by taking this hands-on approach, and his calm and quick response has always helped him reassure disgruntled customers.

Your Task: Compose the letter you'll fax to Mr. Albert Mossberger, Executive Director of the Alliance for Business Promotion, 423 Truxton Circle, Washington, DC 20013. Taking your cue from Andahazy, try to reflect a positive and confident attitude to maintain the customer's goodwill. Give him an option: He can send the audio book now by messenger and get it back today, or you'll pick it up tomorrow and return it the next day.[10]

5. Silicon Valley Bank chips in: Letter granting a line of credit to Knights Technology As a credit officer at Silicon Valley Bank, you've talked to plenty of entrepreneurs— American, French, Hungarian, and Iranian. These days the typical loan customers are from China, Taiwan, and Hong Kong. They're securing investment capital from both over-

seas and domestic sources to start companies that manufacture everything from data-storage disks to pen-based computers. These Asian-owned U.S. companies are challenging foreign-dominated markets (such as those for computer monitors), and more than a dozen are already publicly traded. Meanwhile, the new owners are developing important business links with the Far East while providing jobs for Silicon Valley.

Silicon Valley Bank views this development in the local economy as a healthy situation for everyone. That's why you are going to approve an unsecured $50,000 line of credit for Knights Technology. Founded by Dr. Shao-Hung "Gerry" Liu, the company manufactures computer chip–testing equipment, and your credit approval will help it balance operating expenses against cash flow. After analyzing the financial statements provided by Dr. Liu, you conclude that Knights Technology appears to have done quite well in its first three years in business. Since Silicon Valley Bank built its own foundation on the entrepreneurial spirit of people like Dr. Liu, you're happy to count his company among your customers.

Your Task: Write a letter to Dr. Shao-Hung Liu, President, Knights Technology, Inc. (3506 Bassett St., Santa Clara, CA 95054), granting his request for the $50,000 line of credit. Your letter will formally welcome the company as a new customer. All the appropriate loan documentation will be signed and exchanged at a meeting in your office, which you suggest for Thursday, April 23.[11]

CONVEYING POSITIVE INFORMATION ABOUT PEOPLE

6. On a course for Harvard: Reply to a request for a recommendation letter After working for several years for Zoe Coulson in Campbell Soup Company's department of consumer affairs (see this chapter's On-the-Job simulation), one of your co-workers, Angela Cavanaugh, has decided to apply for admission to the Harvard Business School's M.B.A. program. She has asked Coulson, a Harvard graduate, to write a letter of recommendation for her. Here are the facts about Angela Cavanaugh:

1. She has an undergraduate degree in journalism from the University of Iowa, where she was an honors student.
2. She joined Campbell directly after graduating and has worked for the firm for the past five years.
3. Her primary responsibility has been to answer letters from consumers; she has done an outstanding job.
4. Her most noteworthy achievement has been to analyze a year's worth of incoming mail, categorize the letters by type and frequency, and create a series of standardized replies. The department now uses Cavanaugh's form letters to handle approximately 75 percent of its mail.
5. Although Cavanaugh has outstanding work habits and is an excellent writer, she lacks confidence as a speaker. Her reluctance to present her ideas orally has prevented her from advancing more rapidly at Campbell. This could be

a problem for her at Harvard Business School, where skill in classroom discussion influences a student's chances of success.

Your Task: Because you have worked closely with Cavanaugh, Zoe Coulson has asked you to draft the letter, which Coulson will sign.[12]

7. Bon voyage! Letter offering an overseas position with International Discount Telecommunications Although the competition among AT&T, Sprint, and MCI has lowered long-distance rates in the United States, most other countries have state-owned phone monopolies. Even though it costs only about $5 to call Italy from the United States, a comparable call from Italy to the United States runs around $18. So Howard Jonas set out to devise a way for people located overseas to use U.S. phone lines for their international calls. Within a few months, an innovative business service was born: International Discount Telecommunications.

For $250 a month, the service offers overseas customers two phone lines and a black box. The customer calls the company, lets the phone ring once, and hangs up. The equipment in the black box is programmed to call back with the second line connected to a U.S.-based long-distance carrier. Then with that dial tone, the overseas customer can call anywhere in the world, saving about 75 percent of what the call would have cost using a state-owned phone system. The service is also considerably cheaper than the international dialing packages offered directly by U.S. carriers to customers traveling abroad.

Now Jonas's challenge is to sell his service to companies and individuals throughout the world. Even though a patent is pending for his black box, it's only a matter of time before competitors duplicate it. Another problem is that some customers are afraid of offending the telephone monopolies in the countries where they do business and thus losing their regular service. Jonas needs some top-notch sales reps to convince the telecommunications managers at these companies that the savings are worth the risk. He's hired you as personnel director for International Discount Telecommunications, headquartered in the Bronx. Your top priority is to recruit the best sales staff you can find.

One of those individuals is Jorge Banuelos, who has worked both in the United States and in Europe as an overseas sales rep for office equipment. You like him personally, and his qualifications are excellent, as is his sales record.

Your Task: Write to Jorge Banuelos (12 Fifth Ave., Apt. C, New York, NY 10010) and offer him the job, which will require a lot of overseas travel.[13]

WRITING DIRECTIVES AND INSTRUCTIONS

8. No, No, No: Policy memo to "60 Minutes" producers "Hard Copy" does it, "A Current Affair" does it, and the number of syndicated TV news tabloids willing to pay sources for information seems to be multiplying exponentially. As ratings soar and tabloid TV shows proliferate, so does competition for information from people plugged into a hot topic (such as a disgruntled Michael Jackson employee, a Tonya Harding relative, or an O. J. Simpson pal). In some circles, money might buy the lead story of the week.

You've been a "60 Minutes" assistant producer on Don Hewitt's team for one week—a dream job you earned after years of work, starting as an audience seater for Oprah, moving up to production assistant, and then getting a job as assistant producer for Paramount's "Hard Copy." Now you're learning that things are done differently here at "60 Minutes" (and other network-produced newsmagazine shows). You just spoke with an informant who phoned to offer "60 Minutes" the inside scoop of the decade—for a price. You took the offer straight to Hewitt, longtime executive producer of "60 Minutes." You were expecting praise, but Hewitt was not pleased.

Fuming, he stressed that "60 Minutes" hadn't gained its reputation by throwing money around to win ratings. It goes against journalistic ethics. He pointed out that hard investigative work goes into every story and that team effort brings out the facts, exposes the truth—not some cooked-up story concocted by a greedy, money-hungry, disgruntled ex-employee!

After a glaring silence, Hewitt relaxed a bit. "Okay, you're new. You've been working for someone else. But now you know where we stand. The answer is no, no, no."

Your Task: You're not the first producer wanting to buy into a breaking story, and Hewitt decides it's time to put his policy in writing. Hewitt also decides that you should write the memo for him. (Penance, you wonder?) Translate Hewitt's message into an appropriate memo for issuing a company directive.[14]

CONVEYING GOOD NEWS ABOUT PRODUCTS AND OPERATIONS

9. Light and fast: Memo announcing a new product at Ford Imagine a car that weighs 400 pounds less than normal. Would it be more fuel-efficient? Yes, say Ford Motor engineers. So to test the proposition of mass-producing lightweight automobiles (which also happen to be completely rust free and recyclable), the company is releasing 20 prototype all-aluminum Mercury Sables to be test-driven by Ford suppliers.

Ford's newest autos aren't the first all-aluminum cars. Both Audi and Honda produce an aluminum model, but they're top-of-the line, high-performance automobiles retailing at around $70,000. That's because (1) aluminum is more expensive than steel (about $1.35 per pound of sheet aluminum, compared to 36 cents per pound of sheet steel) and (2) it's more difficult to weld (which boosts labor costs). Nevertheless, Ford has invested $30 million in aluminum research during the past two years, and the company believes it can produce 300,000 to 400,000 competitively priced family sedans per year, retailing at around $17,000.

Competitors are skeptical. Ford is understandably quiet about its manufacturing technique, but part of the process involves using the same part-stamping techniques used for steel autos, with high-strength adhesive replacing much of the labor-intensive welding requirements. Eventually, says William Stuef, manager of advanced vehicle systems engineering, Ford will rely entirely on the adhesives—making the only drawback to using aluminum the high cost of the raw material.

One of Ford's primary reasons for betting on aluminum is that, if successful, an all-aluminum automobile will be easily adaptable to electric-car technology. Losing four hundred pounds would make a big difference for cars with lower-powered electric motors. Also, carmakers are expecting federal legislation by the year 2003 that will mandate 32-miles-per-gallon standards. Aluminum could be Ford's "ace in the hole."

Your Task: CEO Alex Trotman has directed you, manager of corporate communications, to write a memo to Ford employees worldwide, announcing the good news about the release of the test models and Ford's plans for the future of aluminum cars. You'll be communicating with employees in such diverse locations as the United States, Europe, Asia, and Latin America, so keep it simple.[15]

10. Job security: Memo announcing Dell Computer's overseas expansion When 19-year-old Michael Dell launched Dell Computer Corporation in 1984, he undoubtedly had high hopes, but he might not have expected his company to post $3 billion in sales just ten years later. Dell was the first to offer mail-order computers built to customers' specifications and delivered quickly, with thorough follow-up service.

Even so, Dell faced challenges in the early 1990s, and new company managers were brought in to help implement more sophisticated management and numerous cost-cutting measures. The new managers systematized and reduced inventory, cut suppliers from 140 to 80, trimmed freight carriers from 21 to 3, and reduced materials costs by 10 to 15 percent. As a result, Dell now has the option of passing on its savings to customers (increasing market share), to shareholders (improving net profits), or to both. Even company critics must admit that Michael Dell is not only surviving but thriving once again as the leader of the mail-order computer business.

Not too surprising, then, was Dell's recent decision to expand its manufacturing plant in Limerick, Ireland, the company's only full-production site outside the United States. As vice president of overseas operations, you know how rapidly European sales have grown in the last few months. The plant in Ireland will need an additional 140,000 square feet and 400 new employees to meet the demand. You're also helping the company search for a new manufacturing site in Asia, and Dell is developing plans to move its desktop, portable, and advanced computers into the retail marketplace for the first time, both in the United States and overseas.

The recent improvements in company performance should boost Dell's stock values, which had fallen significantly before the changes. In fact, with such sweeping changes and all the cost-cutting measures, Dell's overseas employees had begun to worry about the direction of the company and the security of their jobs. Now you're happy to be able to reassure them at last.

Your Task: Send a memo to all overseas employees announcing the good news about Dell's improved prospects and plans for expansion.[16]

WRITING GOODWILL MESSAGES

11. Congratulations: Memo to Columbia Pictures' youngest president You were happy to hear that Lisa Henson has been appointed Columbia Pictures' president of production (the first woman to hold that position). You got to know Henson when you both worked for one of her early mentors: Lucy Fisher, executive vice president of worldwide theatrical production for Warner Bros. Although you soon left to produce films for Columbia, Henson stayed on at Warner Bros., rising through the ranks to become an executive vice president herself.

Henson's reputation grew as she worked on films such as *Lethal Weapon, Batman, New Jack City, Free Willy,* and *Fearless.* You always enjoyed her quick wit. She is very smart but easy to work with. The daughter of Muppet creator Jim Henson and a Harvard graduate who literally grew up in marketing meetings and film studios, Henson could easily have been a snob. But she loves lowbrow comedy as much as anyone. In fact, while studying ancient Greek and folk mythology at Harvard, she blazed an early trail with her comedic skills as the first woman to become president of *The Harvard Lampoon.*

Terrific background for a studio executive, you think, and as a film producer for Columbia, you're looking forward to working under Henson's reign.

Your Task: Jot a memo of sincere congratulations to Henson. Your paths haven't crossed since those early days, ten years ago, when you were both working for Warner Bros., but make sure your memo doesn't sound like an attempt to butter up the new boss.[17]

12. Brave example: Letter of appreciation to a former Bear Stearns colleague Economic advisers aren't often thought of as media superstars, but Larry Kudlow came closer than anyone you know. He had built a highly visible career as a chief economist at Bear Stearns, where you first met him. Kudlow quickly moved into political circles and in the early 1980s became an adviser to former President Ronald Reagan. Then he returned to Bear Stearns to become one of the firm's most-talked-about economists. He had become so recognizable that he even appeared in a series of Cadillac ads.

Yesterday you were shocked to see your former Bear Stearns colleague on the front page of the business section in

The New York Times. His photograph took up nearly a third of a page beneath the blaring headline "A Wall St. Star's Agonizing Confession." In the interview, Kudlow explained how his high-pressure job and high-voltage political activities might have contributed to a pattern of alcohol and drug abuse that he'd managed to keep hidden—until about a year ago.

According to the article, Kudlow sought help for his problem at that time, with the quiet support of the firm's top managers. He says he's been sober ever since, but when he missed a Bear Stearns speaking engagement he subsequently resigned from the firm "by mutual agreement." Although Kudlow's resignation was widely publicized, no one mentioned his substance abuse problems.

Your former colleague now works as an economics editor for *National Review* magazine and says he is going with the truth. He's had success in overcoming his drinking and drug problems, and he hopes his example may help others among the "one in ten Americans" who suffer from alcohol or drug abuse.

Your Task: You admire what Kudlow is doing—a brave move for a man whose public image has always been such a crucial factor in his business and personal success. Write him a brief note of appreciation for his personal courage and honesty (*National Review,* Inc., 150 E. 35th Street, New York, NY 10016). His example may indeed inspire others.[18]

10

Chapter

After studying this chapter, you will be able to

Choose correctly between indirect and direct approaches to a bad-news message

Establish the proper tone from the beginning of your message

Use neutral lead-ins to put your audience in an accepting mood

Present bad news in a reasonable and understandable way

Write messages that motivate your audience to take constructive action

Close messages so that your audience is willing to continue a business relationship with your firm

WRITING BAD-NEWS MESSAGES

On the Job

FACING A COMMUNICATION DILEMMA AT CREATIVE ASSOCIATES

Working for Peanuts

When he was a little boy growing up during the 1920s in St. Paul, Minnesota, "Sparky" Schulz loved to read the comic strips. His deepest ambition was to become a cartoonist. After serving in the Army in World War II, he worked as an art instructor for a correspondence school and sent stacks of comic strips to magazines and syndicates. In 1950 he got lucky. United Feature Syndicate picked up Charles Schulz's *Peanuts*—and Lucy, Charlie Brown, Linus, Snoopy, and the rest of the gang became part of U.S. culture. Today, the Peanuts characters appear in 2,100 newspapers around the world, as well as on toys, greeting cards, lunch pails, music boxes, toothbrushes, T-shirts, cookie jars, paper cups, refrigerator magnets . . .

Unlike many other cartoonists, who employ assistants to fill in backgrounds and do the lettering on their comic strips, Charles Schulz personally creates each installment of *Peanuts.* He also draws for the thousands of licensed products that represent the Peanuts gang. Nothing bears the "Peanuts stamp" without Schulz's personal approval. He is determined to protect the strip from being cheapened by association with second-rate merchandise.

Of course, thousands of applicants would like to become Peanuts vendors, so just responding to all those people is a full-time job. And dozens of other requests must be dealt with on a daily basis. If you were a member of Schulz's business organization, Creative Associates, how would you say no to people in a way that maintains goodwill?[1]

ORGANIZING BAD-NEWS MESSAGES

Even if you're not as famous as Charles Schulz, it's important for you to realize that some people interpret being rejected as a personal failure; being turned down for a job or for credit, or even being rejected in less sensitive areas, usually complicates people's lives. Admittedly, business decisions should not be made solely to avoid hurting someone's feelings, but mixing bad news with consideration for your reader's needs helps your audience understand that the unfavorable decision is based on a business judgment, not on a personal one.

As with direct requests and routine, good-news, and goodwill messages, bad-news messages are best communicated across cultures by using the tone, organization, and other cultural conventions that your audience expects. Only then can you avoid the inappropriate or even offensive approaches that could jeopardize your business relationship.[2] For example, in Latin countries people consider it discourteous and impolite to take negative messages to the boss, so they try to avoid doing so whenever possible. People in Germany tend to be more direct with bad news, but in Japan bad news can be presented so positively that a U.S. businessperson may not detect it at all.[3]

When you need to communicate bad news to a U.S. audience that has minimal cultural differences, consider tone and arrangement. Your tone contributes to your message's effectiveness by supporting three specific goals:

- Helping your audience understand that your bad-news message represents a firm decision
- Helping your audience understand that under the circumstances, your decision was fair and reasonable
- Helping your audience remain well disposed toward your business and possibly toward you

A Charles Schulz Peanuts *cartoon*

With the right tone, you can make an unwelcome point while preserving your audience's ego. One key is to make liberal use of the "you" attitude, for example, by pointing out how your decision might actually further your audience's goals. Another key is to convey concern by looking for the best in your audience; assume your audience is interested in being fair, even when they are at fault. Finally, you can ease disappointment by using positive words rather than negative ones. Just be sure that your positive tone doesn't hide the bad news behind difficult language.[4] You want to convey the bad news, not cover it up.

How you arrange the main idea and supporting data can also ease the audience's disappointment. The two basic strategies described in Chapter 6 are (1) the indirect plan, which presents supporting data before the main idea and (2) the direct plan, which presents the main idea before the supporting data.

In a bad-news message, the "you" attitude translates into

- Emphasizing the audience's goals instead of your own
- Looking for the best in your audience
- Using positive rather than negative phrasing

Indirect Plan

The indirect plan is actually a familiar approach. You've probably used it many times to say something in a roundabout way to avoid upsetting another person. Instead of beginning a business message with a blunt no, which might keep your audience from

Use the indirect plan or the direct plan, depending on the audience's needs.

Not only is Mae C. Jemison an astronaut (the first African American woman to travel in space), she's also a physician, a chemical engineer, and founder of the Jemison Group (a company that researches, develops, and markets advanced technologies). When communicating bad news, says Jemison, show that you understand your audience's needs, but don't undermine your message with apologies.

reading or listening to your reasons, use the indirect plan to ease your audience into the part of your message that demonstrates how you're fair-minded and eager to do business on some other terms.

The indirect plan consists of four parts: (1) a buffer; (2) reasons supporting the negative decision; (3) a clear, diplomatic statement of the negative decision; and (4) a helpful, friendly, and positive close. By presenting the reasons for your decision before the bad news itself, you gradually prepare the audience for disappointment. In most cases, this approach is more appropriate than an abrupt statement of the bad news.

Buffer

The first step in using the indirect plan is to put the audience in an accepting mood by making a neutral, noncontroversial statement closely related to the point of the message, also called a **buffer.** If you wanted to tell another supervisor that you can't spare anyone from your customer service staff for a temporary assignment to the order fulfillment department, you might begin your memo with a sentence like this: "Customer service is one of our major concerns at National Investments. In addition, this department shares your goal of processing orders quickly and efficiently." If possible, base the buffer on statements made by the person you're responding to. Using an unrelated buffer makes you seem to be "beating around the bush"; you appear unethical, so you lose your audience's respect.

A buffer is a neutral lead-in to bad news.

Also, when composing your buffer, avoid giving the impression that good news will follow. Building up the audience at the beginning only makes the subsequent letdown even more painful. Imagine your reaction if you were to get a letter from Schulz's Creative Associates with this opening: "Your résumé indicates that you would be well suited as a vendor for our Peanuts characters." Now compare that opening with this: "Your résumé shows very clearly why you are interested in becoming a vendor for our Peanuts characters." The second opening emphasizes the applicant's favorable interpretation of her or his qualifications rather than the company's evaluation, so it's less misleading while still being positive.

Here are some other things to avoid when writing a buffer:

Use a buffer that is
- Neutral
- Relevant
- Not misleading
- Assertive
- Succinct

- *Avoid saying no.* An audience encountering the unpleasant news right at the beginning will react negatively to the rest of the message, no matter how reasonable and well phrased it is.
- *Avoid using a know-it-all tone.* When you use phrases such as "you should be aware that," the audience will expect your lecture to lead to a negative response and will therefore become resistant to the rest of your message.
- *Avoid wordy and irrelevant phrases and sentences.* Sentences such as "We have received your letter," "This letter is in reply to your request," and "We are writing in response to your request" are irrelevant. You make better use of the space by referring directly to the subject of the letter.
- *Avoid apologizing.* An apology weakens your explanation of the unfavorable decision.
- *Avoid writing a buffer that is too long.* The point is to identify briefly something that both you and the audience are interested in and agree on before proceeding in a businesslike way.

Table 10.1 shows types of buffers you could use to open a bad-news message tactfully.

After you've composed a buffer, evaluate it by asking yourself four questions: Is it pleasant? Is it relevant? Is it neutral, saying neither yes nor no? Does it provide for a smooth transition to the reasons that follow? If you can answer yes to every question, you may proceed confidently to the next section of your message.

Table 10.1 **TYPES OF BUFFERS**	
Buffer	**Example**
Agreement: Find a point on which you and the reader share similar views.	We both know how hard it is to make a profit in this industry.
Appreciation: Express sincere thanks for receiving something.	Your check for $127.17 arrived yesterday. Thank you.
Cooperation: Convey your willingness to help in any way you realistically can.	Employee Services is here to smooth the way for those who work to achieve the company's goals.
Fairness: Assure the reader that you've carefully examined and considered the problem, or mention an appropriate action that has already been taken.	For the past week, we have carefully monitored those using the photocopier to see whether we can detect any pattern of use to explain its frequent breakdowns.
Good news: Start with the part of your message that is favorable.	A replacement knob for your range is on its way, shipped February 10 via UPS.
Praise: Find an attribute or achievement to compliment.	Your résumé shows an admirable breadth of experience, which should serve you well as you progress in your career.
Resale: Favorably discuss the product or company related to the subject of the letter.	With their heavy-duty, full-suspension hardware and fine veneers, the desks and file cabinets in our Montclair line have become a hit with value-conscious professionals.
Understanding: Demonstrate that you understand the reader's goals and needs.	So that you can more easily find the typewriter with the features you need, we are enclosing a brochure that describes all the Olsen typewriters currently available.

Some critics believe that using a buffer is manipulative, dishonest, and thus unethical. In fact, buffers are unethical only if they're insincere. Breaking bad news with kindness and courtesy is the human way. Consideration for the feelings of others is never dishonest, and that consideration helps your audience accept your message.

Reasons

If you've done a good job of composing the buffer, the reasons will follow naturally. Cover the more positive points first; then move on to the less positive ones. Provide enough detail for the audience to understand your reasons, but be concise; a long, roundabout explanation may make your audience impatient.

It is important to explain *why* you have reached your decision before you explain *what* that decision is. If you present your reasons effectively, they will help convince audience members that your decision is justified, fair, and logical. However, someone who realizes you are saying no before he or she understands why may either quit paying attention altogether or be set to rebut the reasons when they're finally given.

Present reasons to show that your decision is reasonable and fair.

When giving your reasons, be tactful by highlighting the benefits of the decision to the audience, instead of focusing on the company. For example, when saying no to a credit request, show how your decision will keep the person from becoming overextended financially. Facts and figures are often helpful in convincing members of your audience that you're acting in their best interest.

Focus on how the audience might benefit from your negative message.

As you explain your reasons, don't try to cushion bad news by hiding behind company policy. If Creative Associates were to say "Company policy forbids our hiring anyone for this position who does not have two years' public relations experience," the applicant might infer that the company hasn't considered the person on her or his own merits. Although skilled and sympathetic communicators may sometimes quote company policy, they also briefly explain it so that the audience can try to meet the requirements at a later time.

Don't apologize when giving your reasons. Apologies are appropriate only when someone in your company has made a severe mistake or done something terribly wrong. If no one in the company is at fault, an apology gives the wrong impression.

The tone of the language you use to explain your reasons greatly influences your audience's reception of the bad news that follows. So avoid negative, counterproductive words like these:

broken	dissatisfied	regret
cannot understand	error	shocked
damage	fault	unfortunately
delay	inconvenience	wrong

Sometimes the "you" attitude is best observed by avoiding the word you.

Furthermore, don't adopt an accusing tone. Protect the audience's pride by using language that conveys respect. Use third-person, impersonal, passive language to explain your audience's mistakes in an inoffensive way. Say "The appliance won't work after being immersed in water" instead of "You shouldn't have immersed the appliance in water." In this case, the "you" attitude is better observed by avoiding the word *you*.

When refusing the application of a management trainee, a tactfully worded letter might give these reasons for the decision not to hire:

Well-written reasons are
- Detailed
- Tactful
- Individualized
- Unapologetic
- Positive

Because these management trainee positions are quite challenging, our human relations department has researched the qualifications needed to succeed in them. The findings show that the two most important qualifications are a bachelor's degree in business administration and two years' supervisory experience.

This paragraph does a good job of stating the reasons for the refusal:

- It provides enough detail to make the reason for the refusal logically acceptable.
- It implies that the applicant is better off avoiding a program in which she or he would probably fail, given the background of others who would be working alongside her.
- It doesn't rest solely on company policy. A relevant policy exists but is presented as logical rather than rigid.
- It offers no apology for the decision.
- It avoids negative personal expressions ("You do not meet our requirements").

Jane Bryant Quinn is a financial columnist for Newsweek. *She points out that companies can paint an overall positive picture and then use phrases such as "subject to," "except for," and "despite the" to moderate the impact of bad news.*

Although specific reasons help the audience accept bad news, reasons cannot always be given. When reasons involve confidential, excessively complicated, or purely negative information or when the reasons benefit only you or your firm (such as enhancing the company's profits), don't include them. Move directly to the next section.

The Bad News
When the bad news is a logical outcome of the reasons that come before it, the audience is psychologically prepared to receive it. However, the audience may still react emotionally if the bad news is handled carelessly. Here are some methods for de-emphasizing the bad news:

- Minimize the space or time devoted to it.
- Subordinate it in a complex or compound sentence ("My department is already shorthanded, so I'll need all my staff for at least the next two months").
- Embed it in the middle of a paragraph.

To make bad news less painful,

- De-emphasize the bad news visually and grammatically
- Use a conditional statement
- Tell what you did do, not what you didn't do

Two other techniques are especially useful for saying no as clearly but painlessly as possible. First, using a conditional (*if* or *when*) statement implies the audience could possibly have received or might someday receive a favorable answer: "When you have more managerial experience, you are welcome to reapply." A statement like this could motivate applicants to improve their qualifications.

The other technique is to tell the audience what you did do, can do, or will do rather than what you did not do, cannot do, or won't do. Say "We sell exclusively through retailers, and the one nearest you that carries our merchandise is . . ." rather than "We are unable to serve you, so please call your nearest dealer." Here's the same principle applied to the letter rejecting the job applicant: "The five positions currently open have been staffed with people whose qualifications match those uncovered in our research." A statement like this need not be followed by the explicit news that you won't be hiring the reader. By focusing on the positive and only implying the bad news, you soften the blow. Of course, when implying bad news, be sure your audience understands the message—including the bad news.

However, it would not be ethical to overemphasize the positive. So if an implied message might leave doubt, state your decision in direct terms. Just be sure to avoid blunt statements that are likely to cause pain and anger. The following phrases are particularly likely to offend:

When writing a bad-news message, avoid negative wording and personal language.

I must refuse	we must deny	we cannot allow
I am unable to	we cannot afford to	much as I would like to
you must understand	we must reject	we must turn down

Use impersonal, positive language instead so that you don't undermine the audience's feelings of self-worth. Your goal is for the audience not only to accept your unfavorable decision but also to pay attention to the end of your message.

Positive Close

After giving the bad news, your job is to end the message on a more upbeat note. You might propose an attainable solution to the audience's problem: "The human resources department has offered to bring in temporary workers when I need them, and they would probably consider doing the same for you." In a message to a customer or potential customer, an off-the-subject ending that includes resale information or sales promotion is also appropriate. If you've asked someone to decide between alternatives or to take some action, make sure she or he knows what to do, when to do it, and how to do it with ease. Whatever type of close you choose, follow these guidelines:

An upbeat, positive close

- Builds goodwill
- Offers a suggestion for action
- Provides a look toward the future

- Don't refer to or repeat the bad news.
- Don't apologize for the decision or reveal any doubt that the reasons will be accepted (avoid statements such as "I trust our decision is satisfactory").
- Don't urge additional communication (avoid saying anything like "If you have further questions, please write") unless you're really willing to discuss your decision further.
- Don't anticipate problems (avoid statements such as "Should you have further problems, please let us know").

*B*EHIND THE SCENES AT AMERICA WEST
Navigating Bad News

How do you tell 14,000 employees that their company has just filed for reorganization in federal bankruptcy court—especially after many of them already saw it in the morning paper or on television? This was the task facing Daphne Dicino, senior director of corporate communications at America West Airlines. Months of negotiations between the Phoenix-based airline and its creditors suddenly collapsed, and the airline had to file for reorganization under Chapter 11 of the U.S. Bankruptcy Code. Unfortunately for Dicino, America West was legally obligated to notify the public immediately, even before employees—many of whom learned about the filing from the press instead of from their own company.

"That was unfortunate and, I suspect, terrifying for our employees," says Dicino. "They were filled with anxiety about their jobs and were under a lot of pressure from the press and the public." Because practically every employee had daily contact with the public—and the press—how they represented the airline was important.

So it was crucial for top management to effectively explain the bad news to employees. If the communication was mishandled, employee morale would decline, possibly affecting customer service and ultimately revenues—which were more necessary than ever. However, if the bad news was related properly, employees would pull together to help save the airline.

The communication process began when Chairman Edward Beauvais, President Michael Conway, and Dicino spent hours that first night writing a letter to employees. Dicino decided to use an indirect approach. Top management needed to break the bad news in a manner that would explain the situation forthrightly while encouraging employee morale. Using a direct approach was considered too risky.

Dicino's letter to employees opened with a factual buffer intended to present a neutral message. The letter explained that the 14 largest U.S. airlines, not just America West, had lost money for three consecutive quarters—$5 billion in total. The industrywide slump was the result of two side effects of the Persian Gulf

As senior vice president of human resources for Metropolitan Life Insurance, Catherine Rein supports the direct method for bad news when you want to maintain a position of strength. Cutting a program can bother those responsible for it, explains Rein, but well-made decisions must prevail.

- Don't include clichés that are insincere in view of the bad news (avoid saying "If we can be of any help, please contact us").
- Don't reveal any doubt that you will keep the person as a customer (avoid phrases such as "We hope you will continue to do business with us").

In the case of the applicant for the management trainee position, you could observe these rules by writing a close like this:

```
Many companies seek other qualifications in management trainees, so I
urge you to continue your job search.  You'll certainly find an opening in
which your skills and aspirations match the job requirements exactly.
```

Keep in mind that the close is the last thing the audience has to remember you by. Try to make the memory a positive one.

Direct Plan

A bad-news message organized on the direct plan would start with a clear statement of the bad news, proceed to the reasons for the decision, and end with a courteous close. Stating the bad news at the beginning has two potential advantages: (1) It makes a shorter message possible, and (2) the audience needs less time to reach the main idea of the message, the bad news itself.

war: Fuel prices were shooting up, and people were flying less because they feared terrorism. The drain on cash reserves at America West forced the airline into the reorganization filing.

With the reasons for the bad news presented, the letter went on to explain that reorganization "did not mean that America West had failed or was going out of business." The letter stressed the importance of the airline's employees, and it emphasized a "business-as-usual" approach. The letter emphasized that employees would be paid as usual and that all benefits were safe. Employees were told about the necessity for pulling together, and the letter ended with a message of reassurance: "This is without question an extremely difficult decision for all of us. However, we will ultimately be viewed as survivors." Attached to the letter was a fact sheet of questions and answers, addressing issues that customers would most likely bring up, so that employees would be prepared.

In addition to the initial letter, Dicino realized that continued open communication with employees would be necessary to keep morale high. Employees' questions, management's answers, updates of reorganization proceedings, and legal definitions and explanations were communicated through the in-house monthly magazine, newsletters, and in-depth executive reports.

Dicino's goal was to do more than merely inform; she had to maintain employees' self-esteem in the face of incredible pressures. One message was stressed through all the communication vehicles: The airline's reorganization filing was no one's fault. "The key was to display our confidence in the employees," Dicino says. "So we sent a clear message that the product itself had been proven successful, particularly because the employees had done their jobs so well." Indeed, as the company worked to secure new financing and emerge from the protection of bankruptcy court, employees worked to maintain customer loyalty, and the number of passengers actually increased.

Apply Your Knowledge

1. How would you write a letter explaining to employees the following decisions: (a) To cut costs throughout the airline, salaries will be frozen by 10 percent (top managers have already cut their own salaries); (b) To cut costs, service to six cities (including New York City) will be discontinued.

2. Should the indirect approach be used every time bad news has to be given to employees? Can employee morale be maintained using the direct approach? Please explain your answers.

Although the indirect approach is preferable in most bad-news messages, you may sometimes want to move right to the point. Memos are often organized so that the bad news comes before the reasons. In fact, some managers expect all internal correspondence to be brief and direct, regardless of whether the message is positive or negative. Remember, however, that a tactful tone, a focus on reasons, and a courteous close will help make any bad-news message easier to accept.

Routine bad-news messages to other companies often follow the direct plan, especially if they relay decisions that have little or no personal impact. Moreover, you'll sometimes know from prior experience that someone prefers the bad news first in any message. The direct plan is also appropriate when you want to present an image of firmness and strength; for example, the last message in a collection series, just before the matter is turned over to an attorney, usually gets right to the point.

Use the direct plan when
- Your boss prefers that internal messages come right to the point
- The message has little personal impact
- You want to make your point emphatically

CONVEYING BAD NEWS ABOUT ORDERS

For several reasons, businesses must sometimes convey bad news concerning orders. When writing to a would-be customer, you have three basic goals:

The basic goal of a bad-news letter about orders is to protect or make a sale.

- To work toward an eventual sale along the lines of the original order
- To keep instructions or additional information as clear as possible
- To maintain an optimistic, confident tone so that your reader won't lose interest

Use the indirect plan when telling a customer that you cannot ship the entire order immediately.

When you must back-order for a customer, you have one of two types of bad news to convey: (1) you're able to send only part of the order, or (2) you're able to send none of the order. When sending only part of the order, you actually have both good news and bad news. In such situations, the indirect plan works very well. The buffer contains the good news that part of the order is en route, along with a resale reminder of the product's attractiveness. After the buffer come the reasons the remainder of the shipment has been delayed. A strong close encourages a favorable attitude toward the total transaction. For a customer whose order for a tapestry cushion and matching notecards can be only partly filled, your letter might read like the one in Figure 10.1.

Had you been unable to send the customer any portion of this order, you would still have used the indirect approach. However, because you would have had no good

Figure 10.1
Letter Advising of a Back Order

The buffer conveys the good news and confirms the wisdom of the customer's choice.

The reason for the bad news shows that the notecards are popular and therefore a good choice.

The bad news itself is implied by telling the reader what is being done, not what cannot be done.

The positive close includes sales promotion material.

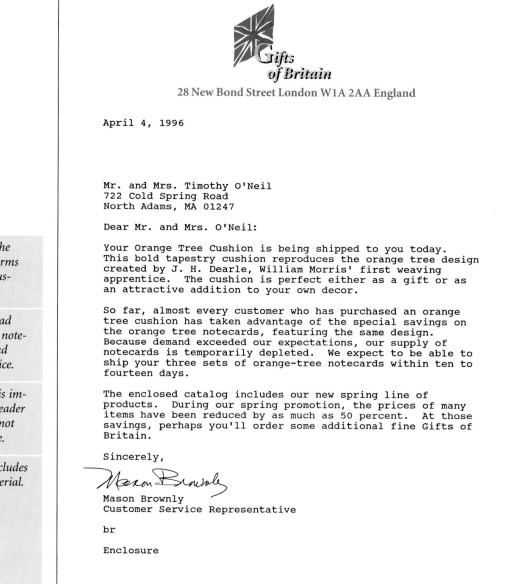

Gifts of Britain

28 New Bond Street London W1A 2AA England

April 4, 1996

Mr. and Mrs. Timothy O'Neil
722 Cold Spring Road
North Adams, MA 01247

Dear Mr. and Mrs. O'Neil:

Your Orange Tree Cushion is being shipped to you today. This bold tapestry cushion reproduces the orange tree design created by J. H. Dearle, William Morris' first weaving apprentice. The cushion is perfect either as a gift or as an attractive addition to your own decor.

So far, almost every customer who has purchased an orange tree cushion has taken advantage of the special savings on the orange tree notecards, featuring the same design. Because demand exceeded our expectations, our supply of notecards is temporarily depleted. We expect to be able to ship your three sets of orange-tree notecards within ten to fourteen days.

The enclosed catalog includes our new spring line of products. During our spring promotion, the prices of many items have been reduced by as much as 50 percent. At those savings, perhaps you'll order some additional fine Gifts of Britain.

Sincerely,

Mason Brownly
Customer Service Representative

br

Enclosure

news to give, your buffer would only have confirmed the sale, and the explanation section would have stated your reason for not filling the order promptly.

A customer will occasionally request something that you no longer sell or that is no longer produced. If you're sure the customer will approve a substitute product, you may go ahead and send it. When in doubt, however, first send a letter that "sells" the substitute product and gives the customer simple directions for ordering it. In either case, be careful to avoid calling the second product a *substitute* because the term carries a negative connotation and detracts from your sales information. Instead, say that you now stock the second product exclusively.

Say a customer has ordered a drill that is no longer manufactured. Because of problems with the original drill, the motor has been upgraded. As a result, the price of the drill has increased from $24.95 to $31.95. So you write a letter to persuade your audience to buy the more expensive drill:

> Use the indirect plan to notify a customer that you must send a substitute, especially when the replacement is more expensive than the original item.

Alpha-Omega, manufacturer of the Mini-Max drill you ordered, is committed to your satisfaction with every product it makes.

> *The buffer includes resale information on the manufacturer.*

For this reason, Alpha-Omega conducts extensive testing. Results for the 1/4-inch Mini-Max with the 1/8-horsepower motor show that although it can drill through 2 inches of wood or 1/4 inch of metal, thicker materials put a severe strain on the motor. Alpha-Omega knows that household jobs come in all sizes and shapes, so it now makes a more powerful 1/4-inch drill with a 3/8-horsepower motor. The new Mini-Max can cut through materials twice as thick as those the former model could handle.

> *The reasons for the bad news are explained in terms of the customer's needs.*

Even with its superior capabilities, the new Mini-Max costs only about 30 percent more than the discontinued model. Using this more powerful drill, you can be confident that even heavy-duty jobs will cause no overheating.

> *The bad news is stated positively. The writer emphasizes the product the firm carries rather than the one it does not.*

You can be using your new heavy-duty drill by this time next week if you just check the YES box on the enclosed form, tuck the form into the postage-paid envelope with $7, and mail it today. Your new, worry-free Mini-Max will be on its way to you at once.

> *The close asks the reader to authorize shipment of the substitute item, makes action easy, and reinforces the benefits described earlier.*

Occasionally, you won't be able to fill an order either in part or with a substitute. In this case, your job is to say no and yet be as helpful as possible. One good way to maintain your audience's confidence in you and your company is to mention another source where the requested product might be obtained. For a brief reminder of the

> Use the indirect plan to say that you cannot fill an order at all.

CHECKLIST FOR BAD NEWS ABOUT ORDERS

A. Overall Strategy

1. Use the indirect plan in most cases.
2. Use the direct plan when the situation is routine (between employees of the same company), when the reader is not emotionally involved in the message, or when you know that the reader would prefer the bad news first.

B. Buffer

1. Express appreciation for the specific order.
2. Extend a welcome to a new customer.
3. Avoid flashy, attention-getting devices or phrasing.
4. Avoid negative words (*won't, can't, unable to*).
5. Avoid expressions of pleasure in receiving the order.
6. Use resale information on the ordered merchandise to build the customer's confidence in her or his choice (except for unfillable orders).

C. Reasons

1. Emphasize what the firm is doing rather than what it isn't doing, what it does have rather than what it lacks.
2. Avoid apologies.
3. Avoid expressions of sorrow or regret.
4. Handle back orders carefully.
   a. Specify shipping dates.
   b. Avoid negative phrases, such as *cannot send.*
   c. Explain why the item is out of stock, such as high popularity or exceptional demand, that may stimulate the customer's desire for the item.
   d. Reinforce the customer's confidence with resale (for consumers: personal attention, credit, repair services, free delivery, special discounts, telephone shopping, and other services; for dealers: free counter and window displays, ad-

tasks involved in these messages, see this chapter's Checklist for Bad News About Orders.

COMMUNICATING NEGATIVE ANSWERS AND INFORMATION

The businessperson who tries to say yes to everyone probably won't win many promotions or stay in business for long. Occasionally, your response to inquiries must simply be no. Imagine what Charles Schulz's schedule would be like if he were to say yes to everyone asking him to give a speech. It's a mark of your skill as a communicator to be able to say no clearly yet not cut yourself off from future dealings with the other person.

Use the direct plan when your negative answer or information will have little personal impact; use the indirect plan in more sensitive situations.

Depending on your relationship with the reader, you could use either the direct plan or the indirect plan in these situations. If the reader is unlikely to be deeply disappointed, use the direct plan. Otherwise, use a buffer that expresses appreciation for being thought of, assures the reader of your attention to the request, compliments the reader, or indicates your understanding of the reader's needs. Continue with the reasons for the bad news and the bad news itself, couched in terms that show how the reader's problem can be solved and what you can do to help. Then close with a statement of interest, encouragement, or goodwill. You can demonstrate your sincerity, and minimize the reader's hostility or disappointment, by promptly fulfilling any promises you make.

Providing Bad News About Products

When you must provide bad news about a product, the situation and the reader will dictate whether to use the direct or indirect plan. If you were writing to tell your com-

vertising materials, sales manuals, factory guarantees, and nearby warehousing).

■ e. Refer to sales promotion material, if desirable.

5. Explain substitutions in detail.

■ a. Introduce the benefits of the substitute before the bad news that the ordered item is unavailable.

■ b. Avoid the word *substitute* because of its negative connotation.

■ c. Describe enough reader benefits to justify any higher price.

6. Explain why orders can't be filled.

■ a. Explain in positive terms the way you market your products (such as through authorized dealers, who may provide personal service, faster delivery, shipping at little or no cost, credit, adjustment and repair services, the opportunity to see goods before buying).

■ b. Name alternate sources, with addresses, telephone numbers, and positive statements about them.

■ c. Stress the benefits to the customer of dealing with other sources.

7. Avoid hiding behind company policy.

D. The Bad News

1. State the bad news as positively and as clearly as possible.

2. Stress the reader benefit.

E. Positive, Friendly, Helpful Close

1. Remind the reader of how his or her needs are being met, if appropriate.

2. Explain the desired reader action as clearly and simply as possible.

3. Use resale information to clinch the sale.

4. Make reader action as easy as possible.

5. Adopt a tone that shows you remain in control of the situation and will continue to give customers' orders personal attention.

---

pany's bookkeeping department about increasing product prices, you'd use the direct plan. The reader would have to make some arithmetical adjustments when the increases are put into effect but presumably won't be emotionally involved in the matter. However, you would probably use the indirect plan to convey the same information to the sales department. A change that weakens your products' competitive edge threatens sales representatives' incomes and possibly their jobs.

The memo in Figure 10.2 was written to tell one company's sales department of a 10 percent across-the-board price increase. The middle section of this memo presents an honest statement of the bad news. The effect of the bad news is diminished by the credible rationale that precedes it, by the avoidance of any overt statement that commissions may get smaller, and by the upbeat close.

Consider the direct or indirect plan for telling the reader bad news about a product.

Denying Cooperation with Routine Requests

When people ask you for information or want you to do something but you can't honor the request, you may answer with either the direct plan or the indirect plan. Say that someone has asked your company to participate in a research project concerning sales promotion. However, the company has a policy against disseminating any information about projected sales figures. If you were the researcher, how would you react to the following letter?

Consider the direct or indirect plan to tell someone you cannot do what has been requested.

This letter is to inform you that Blodgett Corporation has no interest in taking part in your Sales Management Techniques research project. In fact, our company has a policy that prohibits dissemination of any projected sales figures.

Thank you for your interest in our organization. If we can help you in any other way, please let us know.

Figure 10.2
Memo Providing Bad
News About Products

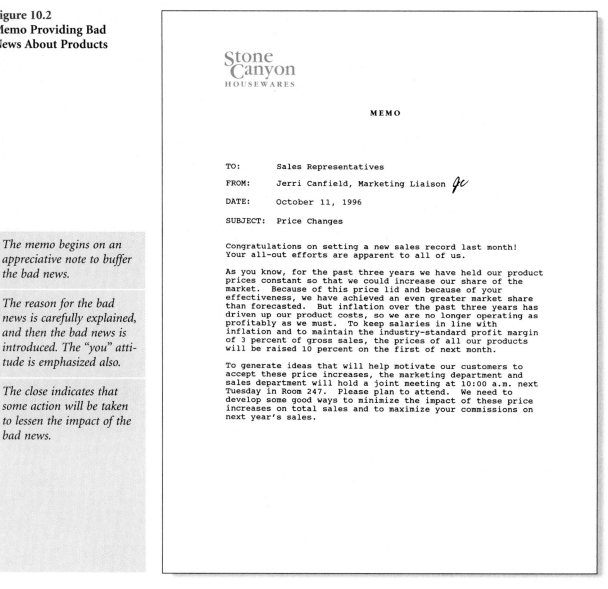

Stone
Canyon
HOUSEWARES

M E M O

TO: Sales Representatives

FROM: Jerri Canfield, Marketing Liaison *JC*

DATE: October 11, 1996

SUBJECT: Price Changes

Congratulations on setting a new sales record last month!
Your all-out efforts are apparent to all of us.

As you know, for the past three years we have held our product
prices constant so that we could increase our share of the
market. Because of this price lid and because of your
effectiveness, we have achieved an even greater market share
than forecasted. But inflation over the past three years has
driven up our product costs, so we are no longer operating as
profitably as we must. To keep salaries in line with
inflation and to maintain the industry-standard profit margin
of 3 percent of gross sales, the prices of all our products
will be raised 10 percent on the first of next month.

To generate ideas that will help motivate our customers to
accept these price increases, the marketing department and
sales department will hold a joint meeting at 10:00 a.m. next
Tuesday in Room 247. Please plan to attend. We need to
develop some good ways to minimize the impact of these price
increases on total sales and to maximize your commissions on
next year's sales.

The memo begins on an appreciative note to buffer the bad news.

The reason for the bad news is carefully explained, and then the bad news is introduced. The "you" attitude is emphasized also.

The close indicates that some action will be taken to lessen the impact of the bad news.

This message would offend most readers, for several reasons:

- The direct plan is used, even though the reader is outside the company and may be emotionally involved in the response.
- The words "This letter is to inform you" are stodgy and condescending.
- The tone of the first paragraph is unnecessarily negative and abrupt.
- The phrase "has no interest in taking part" implies that the research is unimportant.
- The writer hides behind company policy, a policy that the reader may find questionable.
- Clichés in the final paragraph undercut any personal, friendly impact that the letter might have had.
- The offer to help is an unpleasant irony, given the writer's unwillingness to help in this instance.

Wording, tone, and format conspire to make a letter either offensive or acceptable. The letter that follows conveys the same negative message as the previous letter without sounding offensive:

Your upcoming research project sounds fascinating. Thanks for thinking of Blodgett Corporation as a possible contributor.	*The buffer is supportive and appreciative.*
Each year we receive a number of requests for help in various studies. Although we would like to assist everyone who asks, we've had to set up guidelines for deciding which requests we can honor. Many competitors and shareholders would like to get an advance look at some of the figures that researchers request. That's why our sales and earnings projections must be kept within corporate headquarters until they are publicly announced through press releases.	*Without falling back on references to "company policy," the reason for the policy is fully explained. The bad news is implied, not stated explicitly.*
Ms. Dalle, we would like to help you in another way. If you can use sales and earnings data from a previous period, which are shown in the enclosed annual report, please do. Best of luck with your study.	*The close is friendly, positive, and helpful.*

Meredith Layer is senior vice president for public responsibility at American Express Company. Known as responsive and flexible, Layer has still had to present her share of bad-news messages because some requests must simply be refused. However, Layer believes that tact and careful wording can help readers accept bad news.

Declining Requests for Favors

The plan to use when saying no to a requested favor depends on your relationship with the reader. Say the president of the local chamber of commerce asks you to speak at a luncheon five weeks away, but you're scheduled for a business trip at that time. If you don't know the president well, you'd probably use the indirect plan:

Consider the direct or indirect plan to turn down a request for a favor.

The chamber of commerce has accomplished many worthwhile projects, and I've always admired the local organization. Thank you for asking me to speak at your luncheon meeting next month.	*The buffer recaps the request and demonstrates respect.*
As you know, I'm a sales representative for Midland Grain Cooperative, and I do quite a bit of traveling. In fact, I'm scheduled to be in Dubuque on the day you asked me to speak.	*The reason for declining implies the bad news itself.*
Can you suggest an alternate date? Any Thursday during April would be fine for me. The opportunity to speak to your members would be most rewarding.	*The close suggests an alternate plan.*

If you were writing a similar letter to a close friend instead of an acquaintance or a stranger, you could use the direct plan:

Dave, I won't be able to speak at the chamber of commerce luncheon next month. As you know, I'm on the road about half the time, and the middle of next month puts me in Dubuque.

But I'm not always on the road! Keep me in mind; I'll be in town every Thursday during April. With you at the helm, the chamber of commerce is finally making a difference here. I'll be glad to contribute what I can.

This letter gets right to the point but still uses some blow-softening techniques: It compliments the person and organization making the request and looks toward future opportunities for cooperation.

REFUSING ADJUSTMENT OF CLAIMS AND COMPLAINTS

Use the indirect plan in most cases of refusing to make an adjustment.

In almost every instance, a customer who requests an adjustment is emotionally involved; therefore, the indirect plan is generally used for a reply. Your job as a writer is to avoid accepting responsibility for the unfortunate situation and yet avoid blaming or accusing the customer. To steer clear of these pitfalls, pay special attention to the tone of your letter. Keep in mind that a tactful, courteous letter can build goodwill while denying the claim.

Say you work for a sportswear company. A customer who bought one of your swimsuits a month and a half ago has returned it to you because a seam has split. In a pleasant letter, she asks for a refund of the purchase price. Your negative response might read like this:

I agree. You have every right to expect high quality and a comfortable, lasting fit in the Fun 'n' Sun swimsuit you selected.

The buffer covers a point that reader and writer agree on.

Because sunshine and chlorine rapidly destroy the fabric of any swimsuit, few manufacturers are willing to take responsibility for wear-related problems. Nevertheless, we feel that the customer comes first. That's why a tag is attached to every Fun 'n' Sun swimsuit explaining our guarantee. We're always happy to refund every penny if the customer returns a suit within 30 days of purchase for reasons other than a change in taste or fit.

The reason puts the company's policy in a favorable light. The bad news, stated indirectly, tactfully puts some of the responsibility on the customer's shoulders.

We do want to help. So that you can continue enjoying your swimsuit, we've reinforced the inside seams with flexible cloth tape. The seams should now hold through many, many wearings. Inspect them carefully.

A positive alternate action should help soothe the customer.

CHECKLIST FOR REFUSALS TO MAKE ADJUSTMENTS

A. Buffer
1. Use a topic of mutual agreement or a neutral topic to start, but keep to the subject of the letter.
2. Indicate your full understanding of the nature of the complaint.
3. Avoid all areas of disagreement.
4. Avoid any hint of your final decision.
5. Keep the buffer brief and to the point.
6. Maintain a confident, positive, supportive tone.

B. Reasons
1. Provide an accurate, factual account of the transaction.
2. Offer enough detail to show the logic of your position.
3. Emphasize ways in which the product should have been handled (or the contract followed).
4. Word the explanation so that the reader can anticipate the refusal.
5. Avoid relying on unexplained company policy.
6. Avoid accusing or preaching (*you should have*).
7. Do not blame or scold the reader.
8. Do not make the reader appear or feel stupid.
9. Inject a brief resale note after the explanation, if desirable.

C. The Bad News
1. Make the refusal clear by tactful wording, or possibly imply it.
2. Avoid any hint that your decision is less than final.
3. Avoid words like *reject* and *claim*.
4. Make a counterproposal for a compromise settlement or partial adjustment (if desirable) in a willing not begrudging tone, in a spirit of honest cooperation, and without making it sound like a penalty.
5. Include a resale note for the company or for the product.
6. Emphasize a desire for a good relationship in the future.
7. Extend an offer to replace the product or provide a replacement part at the regular price.

D. Positive, Friendly, Helpful Close
1. Eliminate any reference to your refusal.
2. Avoid any apology.
3. Eliminate words suggesting uncertainty.
4. Refer to enclosed sales material.
5. Make any suggested action easy to comply with.

Please inspect the new Hampton House catalog I'm enclosing. You'll find a full line of quality fashions, including a delightful variety of festive swim coverups. You'll also find an entry form for our big $2,000 Designer Wardrobe Giveaway. Fill it in and rush it back today, and you could be the lucky winner!

The close blends sales promotion with acknowledgment of the customer's interests.

When refusing to adjust a claim, avoid language that might have a negative impact on the reader. Instead, demonstrate that you understand and have considered the complaint. Then, even if the claim is unreasonable, rationally explain why you are refusing the request (but don't apologize or rely on company policy). End the letter on a respectful and action-oriented note. This chapter's Checklist for Refusals to Make Adjustments reminds you of the tasks involved in such messages.

Although you may be tempted to respond to something particularly outrageous by calling the person responsible a crook, a swindler, or an incompetent, resist. If you don't, you could be sued for **defamation,** a false statement that tends to damage someone's character or reputation. (Written defamation is called *libel;* spoken defamation is called *slander.*) By this definition, someone suing for defamation would have to prove

When refusing to make an adjustment,
- Demonstrate understanding of the complaint
- Explain your refusal
- Suggest alternative action

(1) that the statement is false, (2) that the language is injurious to the person's reputation, and (3) that the statement has been "published."

If you can prove that your accusations are true, then you haven't defamed the person. The courts are likely to give you the benefit of the doubt because our society believes ordinary business communication should not be hampered by fear of lawsuits. However, beware the irate letter intended to let off steam: If the message has no necessary business purpose and is expressed in abusive language that hints of malice, you'll lose the case. To avoid being accused of defamation, follow these guidelines:

- Avoid using any kind of abusive language or terms that could be considered defamatory.
- Provide accurate information and stick to the facts.
- Never let anger or malice motivate your messages.
- Consult your company's legal department or an attorney whenever you think a message might have legal consequences.
- Communicate honestly, and make sure what you are saying is what you believe to be true.

REFUSING TO EXTEND CREDIT

Use the indirect plan when turning down a credit applicant.

Credit is refused for a variety of reasons, all involving sensitive personal or legal considerations. When denying credit to an applicant with a proven record of delinquent payments or to an applicant with an unstable background, you would probably be justified in offering little hope for future credit approval. You could be more encouraging to other types of applicants. You most certainly would like their current cash business, and you may want their future credit business. The following letter refuses credit for the present but points to the possibility of extending credit later:

Your request for a charge account at Talton's Clothiers tells us something important: You enjoy the rewards of owning a smart, up-to-the-minute wardrobe.

The buffer expresses understanding and offers some subtle resale on the company.

Year after year, value-minded customers like you return to Talton's because of our low prices. How do we do it? We buy our entire inventory of fine men's clothing on a cash basis so that we can get manufacturers' discounts and avoid interest charges. You benefit because we can offer you superb quality at some of the lowest prices in the clothing industry.

So that we can continue to deal with suppliers on a cash basis and to offer you low prices, customer credit applications are approved only when the applicant makes at least $20,000 yearly and has lived in the area for one year or more. As soon as you meet these criteria, we will be glad to reconsider your application.

The reasons for the refusal are explained in some detail.

The actual refusal is stated in positive terms, and the criteria are stated explicitly.

In the meantime, Mr. O'Neill, I want to show you how much we value your business. Enclosed is a certificate that entitles you to a 10 percent discount on any purchase from our Stagg Shoppe. Also, be sure to take advantage of our big storewide sale on August 25 and 26. You'll find some tremendous bargains in every department!

The letter closes gracefully with some sales promotion.

The writer of this letter has taken pains to make the reader feel welcome and realize that his business is appreciated.

Denials of business credit, as opposed to denials of individual credit, are less personally sensitive but more financially significant. Businesses have failed because major suppliers have suspended credit at inconvenient times. When refusing to grant business credit, explain your reasons as factually and impersonally as possible (perhaps the firm's latest financial statements don't meet your criteria or its credit rating has fallen below an acceptable minimum), and explain the steps that must be taken to restore credit. Emphasize the benefits of continued dealings on a cash basis until the firm's creditworthiness has been established or restored. You might also offer discounts for cash purchases or assistance in cooperative merchandising to reduce the firm's inventory and increase its cash flow. Third-party loans are another possibility you might suggest.

> In a letter denying credit to a business
> - Be more factual and less personal than in a letter to an individual
> - Suggest ways to continue doing business

Whether dealing with business customers or consumers, companies that deny credit exercise good judgment to avoid legal action. A faulty decision may unfairly damage a person's reputation, which in turn may provoke a lawsuit and other bad publicity for the company. Handling credit denials over the phone instead of in writing is no guarantee of avoiding trouble; companies that refuse credit orally still proceed with caution. For a reminder of the tasks involved in this type of message, see this chapter's Checklist for Credit Refusals.

> Be aware that credit is a legally sensitive subject.

CONVEYING UNFAVORABLE NEWS ABOUT PEOPLE

From time to time, most managers must convey bad news about people. Letters to prospective employers may be written in direct order. Letters to job applicants and employees, on the other hand, are written in indirect order, because the reader will most certainly be emotionally involved.

> Use the indirect plan when giving someone bad news about his or her own job; use the direct plan when giving bad news about someone else's job.

Refusing to Write Recommendation Letters

With all the legal hazards involved in writing recommendation letters, it's no wonder that some former employers are refusing to write them—especially for people whose job performance has been, on balance, unsatisfactory. Prospective employers don't usually have a personal stake in the response, so letters refusing to provide a recommendation may be brief and direct:

> In letters informing prospective employers that you will not provide a recommendation, be direct, brief, and factual (to avoid legal pitfalls).

Anthony Wright did work at German Auto Repair as a mechanic from June 1993 through April 1994. In light of current legalities, however, we cannot comment on the job performance of people who no longer work here; I'm sure you understand the dilemma. Good luck in your hiring process.

> In letters telling job applicants that you will not write a recommendation, use the utmost tact.

CHECKLIST FOR CREDIT REFUSALS

A. Buffer
1. Introduce a topic that is relevant and that both you and the reader can agree on.
2. Eliminate apologies and negative-sounding words.
3. Phrase the buffer to avoid misleading the reader.
4. Limit the length of the buffer.
5. Express appreciation for the credit request.
6. Introduce resale information.

B. Reasons
1. Check the lead-in from the buffer for smoothness.
2. Make a transition from the favorable to the unfavorable message.
3. Make a transition from the general to the specific.
4. Avoid a condescending lecture about how credit is earned.
5. Avoid relying on unexplained company policy.
6. Stress the benefits of not being overextended.
7. Encourage a later credit application, if future approval is realistic.
8. Phrase reasons in terms of experience with others.
9. Present reasons for the refusal carefully.
   - a. Clearly state the reasons if the reader will accept them.
   - b. Explain your general credit criteria.
   - c. Refer to a credit-reporting agency you have used.
   - d. Use *insufficient information* as a reason only if this is the case.
   - e. To avoid the risk of legal action, omit reasons entirely for extraordinarily sensitive or combative readers or when evidence is unusually negative or involves behavioral flaws.
10. Remind the reader of the benefits of cash purchases.

C. The Bad News
1. Make the refusal clear to the reader.
2. Offer only honest encouragement about considering the credit application at a later date.
3. Avoid negative words, such as *must decline*.
4. Suggest positive alternatives, such as cash and layaway purchases.
5. Handle refusals of business credit differently.
   - a. Recommend cash purchases for small, frequent orders.
   - b. Describe cash discounts (include figures).
   - c. Suggest a reduction of inventory so that the business can strengthen its credit rating.
   - d. Offer promotional and marketing aid.
   - e. Suggest a later review of the credit application, if future approval is realistic.

D. Positive, Friendly, Helpful Close
1. Avoid business clichés, apologies, and words of regret.
2. Suggest actions the reader might take.
3. Encourage the reader to look toward the future, when the application may be approved.
4. Include sales promotion material only if the customer would not be offended.

Letters to the applicants themselves are another matter. Any refusal to cooperate may seem to be a personal slight and a threat to the applicant's future. The only way to avoid ill feelings is to handle the applicant gently:

You have had an interesting year since you left Imperial Bottling. Thank you for bringing me up-to-date.

Your decision to pursue a new line of work seems well thought out, and the classes you have taken should help you get a job. Your instructors at the community college would have more relevant knowledge of your ability to perform the type of job you're applying for, so I suggest you ask them for recommendations. Good luck to you in your future endeavors.

By using positive comments about the reader's recent activities, an implied refusal, a suggested alternative, and a polite close, this letter deftly and tactfully avoids hurting the reader's feelings.

Rejecting Job Applications

It's also hard to tell job applicants tactfully that you aren't going to offer them employment. A rejection letter need not be long, however. After all, the applicant wants to know only one thing: Did I land the job? This brief message conveys the information clearly and with some consideration for the applicant's feelings:

> Congratulations on your fine undergraduate accounting education. Your record of academic achievement is impressive.
>
> Because 35 well-qualified people applied for the position, the selection process was very difficult. After much analysis, we settled on a person who has worked three years for a public accounting firm in Chicago.
>
> Thank you for letting us review your résumé. A person with your qualifications should be able to find just the right position.

The letter implies that the applicant might have been selected if he or she had matched the qualifications of the successful candidate—in other words, the rejection was "nothing personal."

In a letter turning down a job applicant, treat the reader with respect; by applying for a job, he or she has complimented your company.

Giving Negative Performance Reviews

A performance review is a manager's formal or informal evaluation of an employee. Almost always, even if the employee's performance has been disappointing, a performance review mentions some good points. Then, however, managers must clearly and tactfully state how the employee is failing to meet the responsibilities of the job. If the performance review is to have a positive effect, managers must also suggest ways that the employee can improve.[5] For example, instead of telling Joe Worthington only that he damaged some expensive machinery, suggest that he take a refresher course in the correct operation of that machinery. The goal is to leave the impression that you want the employee to succeed.

In performance reviews, say what's right as well as what's wrong, and explain how the employee can improve performance.

Be aware that employee performance reviews can play an important role in lawsuits. It's difficult to criticize employees face-to-face, and it's just as hard to include criticism in written performance evaluations. Nevertheless, if you fire an employee for incompetence and the performance evaluations are all positive, the employee can sue your company, maintaining you had no cause to terminate employment.[6] Also, your company could be sued for negligence if an injury is caused by an employee who received a negative evaluation but received no corrective action (such as retraining).[7] So as difficult as it may be, make sure your performance evaluations are well balanced and honest.

Terminating Employment

Because ill will might result from treating laid-off employees callously or carelessly, make every effort to protect each employee's ego. When writing a termination letter,

CHECKLIST FOR UNFAVORABLE NEWS ABOUT PEOPLE

A. Buffer
1. Identify the applicant or employee clearly when writing to a third party.
2. Express the reasons for writing—clearly, completely, and objectively.
3. Avoid insincere expressions of regret.
4. Avoid impersonal business clichés.

B. Reasons
1. Include only factual information.
2. Avoid negative personal judgments.
3. Word negative job-related messages carefully to avoid legal difficulties.
   - a. Avoid terms with legal definitions (*slanderous, criminal*).
   - b. Avoid negative terms with imprecise definitions (*lazy, sloppy*).
   - c. Embed negative comments in favorable or semifavorable passages, if possible.
   - d. Avoid generalities, and explain the limits of your observations about the applicant's or employee's shortcomings.
   - e. Eliminate secondhand information.
   - f. Stress the confidentiality of your letter.
4. For letters refusing to supply a recommendation to job seekers, suggest another avenue for getting a recommendation.
5. For rejection letters, emphasize the positive qualities of the person hired rather than the shortcomings of the rejected applicant.
6. For performance reviews, describe the employee's limitations and suggest methods for improving performance.

C. The Bad News
1. Understate negative decisions.
2. Imply negative decisions whenever possible.
3. Avoid words like *reject* and *claim.*
4. Make a counterproposal for a compromise settlement or partial adjustment (if desirable) in a willing—not begrudging—tone, in a spirit of honest cooperation, and without making it sound like a penalty.
5. Include a resale note for the company or product.
6. Emphasize a desire for a good relationship in the future.
7. Extend an offer to replace the product or provide a replacement part at the regular price.

D. Positive, Friendly, Helpful Close
1. For refusals to supply recommendations and for rejection letters, extend good wishes.
2. For performance reviews, express a willingness to help further.
3. For termination letters, make suggestions for finding another job, if appropriate.

Carefully word a termination letter to avoid creating undue ill will and grounds for legal action.

you have three goals to keep in mind:

1. To present the reasons for this difficult action
2. To avoid statements that might involve the company in legal action
3. To leave the relationship between the terminated employee and the firm as favorable as possible

For both legal and personal reasons, present specific reasons for asking the employee to leave.[8] Make sure that all your reasons are accurate and verifiable. Avoid words that are open to interpretation, such as *untidy* and *difficult.* Make sure the employee leaves with feelings that are as positive as the circumstances allow. You can do this by telling the truth about the termination and by helping as much as you can to make the employee's transition as smooth as possible.[9] To review the sorts of tasks involved in this type of message, see this chapter's Checklist for Unfavorable News About People.

On the Job

SOLVING A COMMUNICATION DILEMMA AT CREATIVE ASSOCIATES

When he first started drawing his comic strip, licensing was the last thing on Charles Schulz's mind. His primary goal was—and still is—to do a good job on the daily strip. As he says, "I just wanted to draw something that was really good and was different." On the other hand, he realized that cartooning was a business and that he could make a lot of money—not an unattractive prospect.

The licensing of *Peanuts* began modestly in 1952 with the publication of the first paperback collection of reprinted strips. New books followed every year—over a hundred have been published so far. Snoopy dolls appeared; then in 1960, Hallmark applied for a license to create a line of Peanuts greeting cards. CBS produced the first *Peanuts* TV special in 1965. The Peanuts characters are now over 40, and through the years, literally thousands of licensed products have come along. Informed sources estimate that the annual retail sales of Peanuts products run about $1 billion. His six-person organization, known as Creative Associates, handles his business affairs, which have become increasingly complicated, including the burden of responding to licensing requests.

Schulz (who still goes by the nickname "Sparky") and his staff work together in a modest stone-and-wood building at the end of Snoopy Lane in Santa Rosa, California. They get lots of letters—fan letters, invitations, requests for information and contributions, and inquiries about licenses. Every letter is answered, and often the answer must be no.

Your Mission: You're on the Creative Associates staff. Your job is to respond to requests of all sorts—requests for information, licensing arrangements, donations, personal appearances by Mr. Schulz, employment, advice from Lucy . . . For the assignments outlined below, choose the best solutions, and be prepared to explain why your choice is best:

1. You have received a letter from the American Association of Retired Persons (AARP) asking Mr. Schulz to give a speech on creativity in older people at the association's annual convention. Schulz doesn't feel that he can spare the time to prepare a speech or attend the convention. In addition to doing his usual work on the daily comic strip, he's preparing a TV special, which is due to be completed at about the same time as the AARP convention. He has asked you to decline the invitation. Which of the following paragraphs is the best choice for the first paragraph of your reply?
   a. I'm very sorry, but I will be unable to appear at your convention. Much as I respect AARP, my workload is such that I cannot spare the time to prepare a speech or attend the convention.

   b. Creativity in older people is an intriguing topic for the keynote speech at the AARP annual convention. I'm flattered that you are interested in my views on the subject and appreciate your invitation to appear as guest speaker.

   c. I am deeply honored by your kind invitation to appear as guest speaker at the American Association of Retired Persons' annual convention in Atlantic City. Addressing your group--an admirable organization, which I personally support-- would be a privilege.

2. Which version is best for presenting Schulz's reasons for declining the AARP invitation?
   a. Much as I would like to oblige you, I'm sorry to say that I must decline your invitation for a couple of reasons. For one thing, I'm overburdened with work. And also, I haven't been feeling too well the last few years.

   b. Since my heart surgery in 1981, I have made it a policy to limit my speaking engagements to one or two appearances per year. I find that if I allow myself to say yes to too many things, my energy level sinks and my work suffers. Accordingly, I must decline your kind invitation.

   c. I believe that creativity can be cultivated at any age and that it enriches our lives immeasurably, regardless of whether we are 7 or 70. But as I approach retirement age myself, I recognize that my creative energy depends increasingly on my physical condition. If I take on too many projects, my work suffers. Currently, I have about all I can handle doing the daily comic strip and preparing for a TV special to be aired on April 25.

3. Which version is best for the closing of Schulz's reply to AARP?
   a. Again, thank you for thinking of me. I'm sorry that I cannot help you out on this occasion. Perhaps I can speak to your group next year.

   b. Are you planning to pursue the topic of creativity by holding informal workshops on the subject during your convention? If so, I have some videotapes on how to draw cartoons that I would be happy to lend you. They might provide an interesting supplement for a seminar. Please contact me at (707) 435-0192 if you would like more information about the tapes.

   c. If you cannot find another keynote speaker or if you run into a cancellation at the last minute, give me a call. There's always a chance that I might complete the script for the TV special early. If that happens, perhaps I could squeeze in an appearance at the AARP convention.

4. Mr. Schulz is working on the drawings and script for a new Charlie Brown TV special, but he is behind schedule. He had planned to submit the first half of the material to CBS on February 15, but he now estimates that it will not be ready until the end of the month. He is late because he decided to change a portion of the story line that wasn't working out. He thinks the new version will be much better. Although Schulz knows that the slippage is inconvenient for CBS, he thinks the damage can be controlled. He expects to catch up with the schedule and complete the entire script on March 15, as planned. The second half of the material should go very quickly now that he's on the right track. Which of the following letters should Schulz send to CBS?

a. I've just had a fresh idea about how to handle the conflict between Charlie Brown and Lucy in "The Fourth of July" TV special. As usual, Lucy will set Charlie up for a fall, and as usual, he will succumb. But this time, I have a special twist that should please all Charlie's supporters.

I'm reworking some of the early drawings to accommodate the changes, and I'm making good progress. You can expect to see the first half of the material by February 28. When you read the script, I think you'll agree that the revisions are worth the extra trouble.

Now that I'm on the right track, the work should move along quickly. I plan to deliver the second half of the material on March 15, as we originally planned. This promises to be our best Charlie Brown special ever.

b. I've been having second thoughts about the plot for the Charlie Brown TV special. As we originally sketched out the script, the conflict between Lucy and Charlie Brown was too predictable. The problem has been gnawing at me for the past few weeks, but last night I finally had a breakthrough. I've come up with a fresh plot twist that should please all Charlie's supporters.

Unfortunately, though, I'm going to have to redo quite a few of the drawings to accommodate the new plot line. I think I can finish the revisions in a couple of weeks. You can expect to receive the first half of the material by February 28, which is two weeks later than we originally planned.

I know the delay will hold up the animation crew, and I apologize for the inconvenience. But I do think the changes are worth waiting for, and I'm sure you'll agree when you see the results.

Although I hate to make any promises, I'm reasonably confident that I can complete the entire project by March 15, the original due date. Now that I'm on the right track, the rest of the work should proceed quite quickly.

c. I've got some good news and some bad news. First the good news. I've just had a terrific new idea for freshening up the plot of our Charlie Brown TV special.

Now the bad news: It will take me an extra two weeks to redo some of the early drawings. That means you will not be able to begin animating the first half of the script on February 15 as we originally planned. I think you'd better reschedule the animation crew for the 28th.

If it's any consolation, I think I can make up the lost time on the second half of the script. Now that I'm on the right track, the rest of the work should move faster than the Cannonball Express. I plan to submit the final installment by March 15, right on time.

5. Creative Associates has received a letter from Pet Products, a manufacturer of specialty items for dogs and cats. The firm's product line includes food bowls, grooming equipment, leashes, chew toys, and pet beds. The president, Gerald Adams, would like to add doghouses to the list. He envisions a white house with a red roof, just like Snoopy's, and he wants to top it off with a three-dimensional Snoopy roof ornament. He is writing to ask whether he can license Snoopy's image for this purpose. Mr. Schulz agrees that the doghouse is a cute idea, but he has some doubts about Pet Products. In checking on the firm's financial condition, he has discovered that Pet Products is deeply in debt and has failed to keep up the payments on its bank loans. Under the circumstances, Schulz prefers to say no, at least for the time being. He has asked you to draft a letter to that effect. Which of the following versions is the best?

a. Thank you for your interest in licensing Snoopy for your doghouse. The design sounds very appealing.

We have developed several guidelines to help us evaluate the many licensing applications that we receive. Our number-one priority is product quality. We want the Peanuts characters to be associated with only the best merchandise. On this score, Pet Products appears to make the grade.

We are also concerned with market potential. Because we limit the number of licenses we sign, we like to be certain that the ones we select will give us "the most bang for our buck." On this score, we have some doubts about the Pet Products proposal. We feel that the market for doghouses is too small to provide significant sales and profit potential.

Another important criterion is the financial position of the licensee. We prefer to do business with firms that are operating on a sound financial footing. Unfortunately, Pet Products does not appear to be in this position at the moment.

Adding it all up, we have decided to turn down your application for a license at this time. We would be willing to reconsider your proposal at a future time, provided that you get your finances in order.

b. We've screened thousands of licensing applications over the years, but yours is the first for a doghouse. Your design is both original and appealing, and Snoopy would be flattered that you value his image.

Mr. Schulz likes to provide personal input on all the products that bear the Peanuts stamp. Since his time for working with licensees is limited, he accepts only a small percentage of the licensing applications that he receives. One of the things he takes into account is the financial strength of the potential licensee. After running a routine credit check on you with TRW Credit Services, he has decided to defer a decision on your licensing application until your financial position improves.

Launching the Snoopy doghouse might be difficult given your current capital constraints.

We wish you the best of luck with your business and hope that you will contact us again when you are in a better position to add new products to your line.

c. What a cute idea! We've seen proposals for just about everything, but you're the first to think of a Snoopy doghouse. We can just picture the famous pooch perched on the red roof.

As you might expect, Mr. Schulz limits the number of licensing proposals he accepts. His first concern is to ensure that the Peanuts gang is associated with only the very finest merchandise-- a criterion that Pet Products clearly meets. His second priority is to earn a significant profit. In this regard, he looks at such factors as market size and the financial resources of the licensee, preferring to do business with firms having a strong capital base.

We believe that the Snoopy doghouse could be a successful product, once your financial position improves. We look forward to hearing from you at a later date.[10]

Questions for Discussion

1. You have to tell a local restaurant owner that your plans have changed and you're canceling the 90-person banquet scheduled for next month. Do you need to use a buffer? Why or why not?
2. Why is it important to end your bad-news message on a positive note?
3. How do you decide whether to use the direct or the indirect approach in bad-news messages?
4. If the purpose of your letter is to convey bad news, should you take the time to suggest alternatives to your reader? Why or why not?
5. Company policy is to refuse refunds on merchandise after 30 days. An important customer has written to request a refund on a purchase made 31 days ago, or he'll take his business elsewhere. How do you respond?
6. If you were writing a bad-news letter to someone you no longer wished to do business with, would you still close on a helpful, friendly, positive note? Explain.

Documents for Analysis

Read the following documents; then (1) analyze the strengths and weaknesses of each sentence and (2) revise each document so that it follows this chapter's guidelines.

DOCUMENT 10.A
We have included with this letter a list of videotapes, films, slides, and other material that you may wish to order on the subjects of business mathematics and economics. Also included is a price list for these materials plus some other books you may wish to order.

Per your request, we are sorry to tell you that we cannot ship to you free examination copies of the books you requested as a result of reading a review in the Business Education Journal. The books, Business Mathematics Made Easy and Economics Made Easy, are well written in spite of being about a subject most people find difficult. The cost of printing and publishing these supplementary textbooks is getting higher every year, so I'm sure you can understand the reason for our not complying with your request for free examination copies.

We must request prompt payment for these books. The cost is $5.95 each plus $1.00 per book for postage and handling. These books would make good additions to your college's bookstore, even if you don't require them in your classes, because they are helpful supplements to the primary textbooks your students are probably using now. Your students could use the extra help, we're sure. Let us know whether you decide to buy these books or not; the price is going up, so let us know soon.

DOCUMENT 10.B

Yes, in the past, we always did provide free setup for parties using our Grand Ballroom. We have found, however, that parties vary greatly in size. Table settings also vary, depending on the menu to be served.

Therefore, tell everyone in your department that the banquet department will no longer provide free setup.

When working with customers to plan their events, please add a $1 setup charge for each person in the party. That fee will cover arrangement of tables and chairs, table draping and place setting, bar setup, and setup of microphone and podium, if needed. This policy takes effect immediately for any events for which contracts have not already been signed. If any customers have a problem with the new policy, please have them call me.

DOCUMENT 10.C

We'd like to express our thanks for your letter of about six weeks ago. However, we regret to inform you that your claim for an adjustment on the Model XL dictation unit has been denied. Careful inspection by our engineering staff confirmed our original supposition that the unit has been damaged by improper treatment, either by user or by carrier.

Are you aware of the possibility that the Model XL dictation unit could have been dropped or abused by your employees? If this has not happened, you may file a claim against the carrier. It is more than likely that the unit was damaged in transit, because according to you, the unit has never worked properly and because we are clearly not at fault.

Our charges for repairing the unit will be $50 to cover labor costs; the parts will be replaced at no charge under the terms of our 90-day warranty. Please remit payment to us promptly.

We hope to see your representative at our sale, which will be held soon. Pertinent facts appear in the promotional literature that is enclosed.

Cases

CONVEYING BAD NEWS ABOUT ORDERS

1. Please try again: Letter from Ultra-Light Touring Shop about a confused order Manufacturer Chuck Harris is one of the most innovative guys you know. Not content with just talking about the need to recycle, to save the environment, and to use energy-saving transportation methods (you know—walking, bicycling, taking the bus), Harris has invested his creativity in a unique business. And he's doing quite well! You're glad of that, because six months ago you started working for the Ultra-Light Touring Shop in Gambier, Ohio, filling the orders that are pouring in from around the world.

What exactly does Harris manufacture? Bicycle mirrors, the kind that clip to a bike helmet or to a pair of eyeglasses so that riders can see what's coming up behind or beside them. These nifty little octagonal mirrors (about $1\frac{1}{2}$ inches in diameter) are made completely from recycled materials. The bent shaft is crafted from old stainless steel bicycle spokes,

covered with plastic tubing reclaimed from coat hangers and other sources. From Ohio roadsides, Harris collects aluminum and plastic litter that he uses for the mirror backs (the aluminum is embossed with a bicycle image and then coated with clear or green plastic). He shapes and polishes the glass mirrors on a pedal-powered grinder to save fuel. Furthermore, he ships them out in used, custom-shrunk plastic soda bottles.

Maybe it's everything Harris puts into the product that makes it so popular, or maybe the mirrors are just very practical. Whatever the secret, your shop has been swamped with orders from bicycling enthusiasts all over the map, ever since *Garbage* magazine ran an item about Harris's mirrors in its "Keepers" column.

Now you're looking at an order from Harold Lightwater in Reading, England, and you just can't fill it. He got the prices right ($18.00 for two mirrors, $10.00 for one, and $1.50 shipping charge per order). He included an international money order for $19.50 and a shipping address. But he didn't specify whether he wants the mirrors to clip onto eyeglasses or helmets. Maybe he wants one of each?

Lightwater also neglected to mention the embossed design. Normally, you'd ship the standard bicycle design, but since you're going to have to write to Lightwater, you might as well remind him that Harris will emboss the mirror backs with any design a customer requests.

Your Task: Draft a bad-news letter informing Harold Lightwater (11 Moor Copse Close, Reading RG6 2NA, United Kingdom) that you can't ship his order until he clarifies his preferences.[11]

2. More to come: Letter explaining delay of Tesla videotapes Membership is expanding so rapidly at the nonprofit International Tesla Society that volunteers at the organization's headquarters and museum in Colorado Springs can hardly keep up with the daily mail. Many of the letters are orders for the rare books, diaries, patents, videotapes, audiotapes, and T-shirts advertised in the Society's Museum Bookstore Catalog.

Inventor Nikola Tesla, who emigrated from Yugoslavia to the United States in 1884, was responsible for the alternating-current electrical system now used worldwide (which replaced Edison's direct-current system). Called a "genius," a "mental giant," and "a man ahead of his time," Tesla also holds the patent for radio technology (although Guglielmo Marconi got the credit), and he invented a host of other devices that dazzled turn-of-the-century society: remote-controlled submarines, magnetic resonators, and lightning-generating "Tesla coils." For a time, Tesla was so well known he even appeared on the cover of *Time* magazine. Then, for reasons biographers still debate, the world forgot about him.

Now people are catching up with many of Tesla's ideas—and the thousands of unexploited patents he left behind. Industrial and amateur inventors alike are developing working models from his drawings and notes for new concepts that may, like A/C electrical power, revolutionize today's technology. That's why the International Tesla Society hosts an annual symposium at which inventors can demonstrate what they've built and attend lectures on the most esoteric aspects of Tesla research. People from many countries attend; others order videotapes of the lectures and workshops.

Last year's symposium was so popular that you've depleted your supply of videotape copies for 17 of the 29 master tapes (with an all-volunteer operation, no one rushed out to duplicate the missing tapes). Now you've received a letter from a German engineer ordering the complete set. He included $495 in U.S. funds, plus $12.50 for overseas shipping, and as a Tesla Society member, he's expecting the usual "same-day shipping." It's going to take about two weeks to get copies of the 17 missing tapes.

Your Task: Write to Josef Mandelheim, Sonnenstrasse 4, 86669 Erlingshofen, Germany, explaining the back-order situation. With your letter, send the 12 lecture videotapes you have on hand.[12]

COMMUNICATING NEGATIVE ANSWERS AND INFORMATION

3. No time for talking: Memo from Trident Aquaculture Farming the ocean? You thought it was a crazy idea when you first heard of Trident Aquaculture, but you went for an interview anyway, offering your skills as an office manager. You changed your mind after winding up as administrative assistant for Michael D. Willinsky, president of the company and a skilled biologist and fish farmer who helped create the most innovative and promising sea-farming cage ever tested in the open ocean.

After trials in the blustery, icy seas off Nova Scotia and in New York's frozen St. Lawrence River, Willinsky's research team proved that their unique cage design—measuring about 41 feet in diameter and based on Buckminster Fuller's geodesic dome—could survive 80- to 110-mph winds, 6- to 12-foot waves, strong currents, and fast-moving ice floes. Thanks to regular hand feeding and protection from predators, the Arctic charr salmon raised inside the Nova Scotia dome matured in a record 18 months (wild Arctic charr mature in 6 to 8 years).

Seaside communities are desperate for economic alternatives to the traditional fishing industry, now that overfishing, pollution, and coastal development have depleted the world's natural fish supply. About 70,000 U.S. and Canadian fishers lost their livelihood in 1993, when several major Atlantic fishing areas were closed to commercial fishing because of severe depletion. Yet the demand for fish products has increased. Willinsky's prototype sea dome promises to provide a sustainable supply of fresh- or saltwater fish, renewing economic activity in coastal areas and providing new jobs for people in the fishing industry.

One result is that Willinsky has become a popular speaker among government and industry leaders. Your boss has to divide his time between pursuing research and development, promoting aquaculture, and managing his company. Next month he travels to Hawaii to speak at an international conference on ocean farming, sponsored by the United Nations Food and Agriculture Organization. Willinsky's U.S. research partner, Michael A. Champ, wants Willinsky to appear at a joint speaking engagement for the New Bedford, Massachusetts, chamber of commerce. Unfortunately, the date falls during Willinsky's week in Hawaii.

Your Task: Willinsky has asked you to fax Champ. Write the informal memo to Michael A. Champ, President, Environmental Systems Development Company (at 1-703-899-7326 in Falls Church, Virginia) and suggest an alternative date.[13]

4. Save the wave: Refusal to remove a large sign from Julian Surf & Sport Ever since she bolted it to the front of her tiny sporting-goods store, Marcia Hegranes has heard more than an earful of controversy over the bright blue, 14-foot, carved wooden wave cascading its message around the shop's door: "Surf's Up in Julian." Apparently, the old California mining community wasn't ready for the blond grandmother's business style. The town is buzzing with people who think the wave clashes with Julian's rustic image as a mountain tourist stop famous for its history and its fresh apple pie. Even though Hegranes's 300-square-foot shop is tucked into the base of an old Depression-era water tower, they say the sign is too contemporary; the wave must go. Hegranes has also heard these demands echoed by city and county officials.

Last summer Marcia Hegranes hired you to help out because the shop had become so popular. Grandmother or not, she has a great rapport with local teenagers. Many of them are transplants from the surf-conscious coastal zone, having moved to Julian when their parents sought out the slow-paced, woodsy atmosphere that makes the town so popular with tourists. Now the kids feel stuck, living a mile above sea level and an hour's drive from their beloved Pacific waves. For them, the irreverent wave is a symbol—just like the half-eaten apple core on the shop's window with its defiant proclamation "Dedicated to the Hard-Core."

Speaking for the city, Julian Architectural Review Board member Richard Zerbe says that the sign disrupts the historical character of Julian, which is modeled after area photographs dating from 1870 to 1930. He explains that the board has issued carefully developed architectural guidelines for the Julian Historical District, which encompasses the town's commercial area. As chief of zoning code enforcement for San Diego county, Sue Gray believes the wave sign is simply too big. Furthermore, Hegranes failed to go through the proper permit process for signage, so Gray has notified Hegranes that she must remove the wave within two months.

Together, you and Hegranes have decided to fight for the wave. After all, the sculpted wave is more than a sign; it's a work of art. On that basis, you think you might be able to persuade officials to let it stand. You've received dozens of letters of support: "As parents of a teenager, we wholeheartedly support Hegranes's shop, the wave artwork, and her kindnesses to young people. The kids are watching," wrote one couple. "Why does every store have to look the same?" asked another supporter. "If all the buildings here were really historically accurate, we'd all be doing business under sheets of corrugated tin."

Your Task: Write a letter stating the intention of Julian Surf & Sport to keep the wave in place as a sculptural work of art. Provide ample reasoning to back up your position. Address the letter to Sue Gray, Chief of San Diego Zoning Code Enforcement (1222 1st Ave., San Diego, CA 92101) and to the Julian Architectural Review Board (1836 Main, Julian, CA 92036).[14]

5. Sorry, Dad: Memo denying a First Boston employee's request for paternity leave It's a touchy subject, but so far First Boston Corporation has not formalized its policy with regard to paid child-care leave—which used to be known as maternity leave. Company executives are operating on a case-by-case basis, considering each employee's circumstances and making a decision based on that individual's job duties, performance, and other intangible factors (such as an executive's gut feeling about the situation).

As a manager in the information systems division, you have received a request from one of the men under your supervision for three months' paid leave commencing with the birth of his second child, due in about six weeks. Jon Golding cites in his favor the recent paid child-care leave granted to a female supervisor under similar circumstances. "Surely First Boston is required by law to administer this benefit equally between both men and women," his memo concludes. You're not sure about that, since you've never received such a request from a man, so you ask the vice president of human resources. She informs you that First Boston has no such policy of equal treatment. In fact, men who request paid paternity leave are routinely denied.

All your subsequent efforts to convince upper management that Mr. Golding's request has merit are unsuccessful. You learn that First Boston is working on a more equitable policy (especially since Congress passed the family-leave bill, which mandates unpaid leave for both men and women). However, such a change won't occur in time for the birth of Mr. Golding's second child.

Your Task: Write a tactful memo to Jon Golding refusing his request for paid paternity leave.[15]

REFUSING ADJUSTMENT OF CLAIMS AND COMPLAINTS

6. Your monkey, your choice: Letter from an exotic pet dealer refusing a damage claim As a well-known exotic animal dealer in the Cincinnati area, your boss, Roger Duncan, has dealt with his share of customers experiencing buyer's regret. Despite his warnings, many of them still buy exotic pets for the wrong reasons. When Melissa Carpenter bought Binky, the red-tailed guenon monkey, she begged Mr. Duncan to reduce his price to $10,000 because she had "fallen in love with Binky's soulful eyes and adorable button nose." Now she wants to return poor Binky, and you have never seen your boss so angry.

"Listen to this!" fumes Mr. Duncan as he reads Carpenter's letter:

```
While I was at work, I locked your monkey in his own
room--which I equipped with his own color TV (with
cable) and which I spent days wallpapering with ani-
mal pictures.  Then last night your monkey somehow
unlocked the door, ripped out my telephone, opened the
refrigerator, smashed eggs all over my kitchen and my
new Persian carpet, broke 14 of the china dishes my
mother gave me when I got married, and squeezed
toothpaste all over the Louis XIV settee I inherited
from my grandmother!
```

"Not only does she demand that I take poor Binky back after she's abused him through her ignorance and neglect," snapped Mr. Duncan, "but she wants me to pay $150,000 in damages for her apartment and her state of mind."

Your boss is so upset that you decide to write Ms. Carpenter yourself.

Your Task: Write to Melissa Carpenter (876 Newton Ave., Cincinnati, OH 45202) and include a copy of her contract. It clearly states Roger Duncan's policy: refunds only if animals are returned in good health, and absolutely no warranty against damages. Each pet comes with specific care instructions, including warnings about certain idiosyncrasies that could cause problems in the wrong environment.

Despite the fact that Binky has probably been traumatized by his experiences, Mr. Duncan has generously agreed to accept his return, refunding Ms. Carpenter's $10,000. However, he will not accept liability for any loss of property or any claims of mental duress on the part of Ms. Carpenter.[16]

7. Of course they're ugly: Letter from boutique refusing claim over "unsightly" Doc Martens As manager of the trendy Na-Na boutique in Santa Monica, you've sold so many pairs of "Doc Martens"—the clunky, street-combat boots made by Dr. Marten—that your buyer can barely keep them in stock. Even your employees wear them because they're easy on the feet. They cater to comfort first and fashion—not at all.

Ugly as Doc Martens are, you can't remember receiving a single customer complaint about the comfy boots until you received this unusual letter from Susan Stone of Ventura:

Several months ago I purchased a pair of burgundy Doc Martens with black laces, after one of your salespeople convinced me that they're the most comfortable boots around. They look cool with both short and long skirts and with jeans. Then a week ago I got a job as a waitress at the Eggshell Café. After two days of eight-hour shifts, I figured I'd wear my Doc Martens and save what was left of my feet. I got fired. I argued with the manager, pointing out that she lets the girls wear whatever they want--miniskirts or leather or tank tops--but she said, "You're out of here." Why? Customer complaints about my "unsightly footwear."

I was misled by your salesperson, who told me that Doc Martens can be worn anywhere in Los Angeles. I think I'm entitled to a full refund of the $116 that I paid for the boots, plus $1,200 compensation (a month's wages and tips) for losing my job over them.

Ms. Stone says she bought the boots "several months ago," so a full refund is out of the question. Also, because waitress dress codes in Los Angeles are liberal, you suspect that Stone's manager used the boots as an excuse to fire an employee who simply wasn't capable—particularly when she had been on the job for only two days. (It's unfortunate, but you know

that some managers have difficulty telling fired employees the whole truth.) Ms. Stone makes no mention of being given a second chance to improve her wardrobe choice, which convinces you that she was actually fired for other reasons. In any case, the claim for job-loss compensation seems extreme for a shoe retailer, and you're not about to pay it. The boutique's owner agrees.

Your Task: Write a letter to Susan Stone (235 W. Alameda, #42, Ventura, CA 93001) refusing her refund request and her claim for job-loss compensation. As a goodwill gesture, invite her to visit the store for a 20 percent discount on any of the other popular footwear the boutique sells.[17]

8. Many happy returns: Letter from Cliffs Notes refusing a claim in a complicated transaction Like most other publishers, Cliffs Notes of Lincoln, Nebraska, gives full credit to any bookstore that returns unsold copies of its publications, provided that they are received in salable condition within six months of their original shipment to the bookstore. The bookstore pays postage. Even though most large publishers have return rates of 30 to 50 percent, only about 6 percent of Cliffs Notes' 222 titles are returned.

Still, today's mail includes a large return from the University of Wyoming Bookstore (Laramie, WY 82071) containing the following:

21 copies, *Macbeth*

6 copies, *The Scarlet Letter*

12 copies, *Crime and Punishment*

5 copies, *Hamlet*

All the Cliffs Notes sell for a retail (or list) price of $3.95. Cliffs gives the bookstores a 40 percent discount off the list price.

The cover note from the University of Wyoming Bookstore indicates that 23 copies of *Macbeth* have been sent, but you count only 21. The carton has sustained some damage, but nothing appears to have spilled out. Five of the booklets are worn to the extent that they cannot be resold. One copy of *Crime and Punishment* is water-stained and cannot be resold. One copy of *The Scarlet Letter* was damaged in shipping, from a combination of careless packing and rough handling in transit.

The shipment also includes 4 copies of *A Tale of Two Cities*, published by Monarch Notes, a competitor of Cliffs Notes'. Obviously, the company does not owe the bookstore anything for these booklets.

As a customer service representative for Cliffs Notes, you have decided to return the 4 copies of *A Tale of Two Cities* to the university bookstore (and charge them $2.20 for postage), to return the unsalable copies to them with an explanation, and to tell them that they shipped you only 21 copies, not 23 copies, of *Macbeth*.

Your Task: Figure out where things stand and write a letter explaining your decision.[18]

REFUSING TO EXTEND CREDIT

9. Risky business: Memo explaining credit refusal by Digital Equipment One of the hardest parts of your job as a credit manager for Digital Equipment's direct sales division (DEC Direct) is turning down credit applications. Individual customers usually buy computer peripherals and components through your 800 number using their bank credit cards, but businesses often prefer to establish a long-term credit arrangement with Digital. Your office reviews financial statements, researches credit reports, and makes the final decisions.

On your desk is an application from Designs Unlimited, a small art-consulting firm in Prescott, Arizona. The firm is owned by a husband-and-wife team, JoAnn and Richard Brockmeier, who work with hospitals, corporations, and professionals. They offer a variety of art-consulting services (including the selection, purchase or commission, framing, and installation of original artwork) as well as security and maintenance consultations to help institutions manage their expensive art collections. It's a wonderful concept, and you wish the Brockmeiers well—but you can't open a credit account for them just yet. They've been in business for only two months, they have virtually no credit rating, and they have not yet built up their business to an income level that meets your established criteria (in fact, they have only one major client so far).

You hate to disappoint your corporate sales representative, Angel Darosa, who was so enthusiastic about the Brockmeiers when he brought the application to you. They want to purchase a DEC Colorwriter 1000 to produce presentation graphics for potential customers. The ability to print documents in full color would certainly enhance an art-consulting business, but the Brockmeiers will have to pay the $3,999 purchase price up front. You can't approve their application for credit until their business is on more solid ground.

Your Task: Write a memo to Angel Darosa explaining the refusal. You might want to suggest that the Brockmeiers use a personal bank credit card for the purchase, and you (and Darosa) definitely want to encourage their future dealings with Digital.[19]

10. No more advances: Memo outlining Banc One policy against IRS refund loans A few years ago, Banc One in Columbus, Ohio, joined a number of banking institutions in offering its customers "IRS refund loans." These loans allowed customers to borrow against their income tax refunds before actually receiving them. As part of the loan agreement, the Internal Revenue Service would send refunds directly to the bank to pay off the loans.

To get such a loan, customers had to file electronic tax returns, making use of newly implemented IRS technology. Once the computerized return was filed, the IRS responded with immediate confirmation of any refund due the taxpayer, and the bank made its loan based on the IRS-verified amount—which would later be repaid directly to the bank. It seemed a foolproof system until an IRS programming error started creating problems with tax returns from all over the country.

The first year the problem emerged, the IRS was forced to apologize for errors that added up to $3 million in mistakenly confirmed refunds. Banc One lost some money on uncollected loans, but not much. The second year, IRS errors during one 17-day period, January 10 to January 27, totaled nearly $40 million, so Banc One cashed out of the IRS refund loan business. Too risky, bank executives decided. If the IRS confirmed a refund that wasn't forthcoming, the bank could be left with an unsecured balance due that the customer might not be able to pay. Collection costs alone could cause the once-secure loans to become highly unprofitable for the bank.

Although news reports have quoted IRS officials stating that the computer glitch has been corrected, Banc One executives remain firm in their decision to suspend the refund loan program. The only exceptions will be made under special circumstances involving long-term customers who have exemplary credit records and with whom the bank has had prior lending experience, so even if the IRS should err in confirming the refund amount, the bank could feel confident that the customer would be able to repay the loan. The bank's advertisements no longer promote the refund loans, but bank officers are expecting to receive numerous requests from customers wanting to borrow against their tax refunds during the first few months of next year.

Your Task: As communications director, you have been asked to issue a memo to all branch managers and credit officers, informing them of the bank's new policy.[20]

CONVEYING UNFAVORABLE NEWS ABOUT PEOPLE

11. Career moves: Refusal to write a letter of recommendation Tom Terwilliger worked in the office at Opal Pools and Patios for four months, under your supervision (you're office manager). On the basis of what he told you he could do, you started him off as a word processor. His keyboard skills were inadequate for the job, however, and you transferred him to logging in accounts receivable, where he performed almost adequately. Because he assured you that his "really long suit" was customer relations, you moved him to what you aggrandize as the complaint department. After he spent three weeks making angry customers even angrier, you were convinced that no place in your office was appropriate for the talents of Mr. Terwilliger. Five weeks ago, you encouraged him to resign before being formally fired.

Today's mail brings a request from Mr. Terwilliger for you to write a letter recommending him for a sales position with a florist shop. You have no knowledge one way or the other of Mr. Terwilliger's sales abilities, but you do know him to be an incompetent word processor, a careless bookkeeper, and an insensitive customer service representative. Someone is more likely to deserve the sales job than Mr. Terwilliger is. You decide that you have done enough favors for Mr. Terwilliger for one lifetime and plan to refuse his request.

Your Task: Write to Mr. Terwilliger (now living with his parents at 2344 Bob-O-Link Rd., Pineville, SC 29468), indicating that you have chosen not to write a letter recommending him for the sales job.

12. Bad news for 80: Form letter to unsuccessful candidates for a high-level job The Dean's Selection Committee screened 85 applications for the position of dean of arts and sciences at your campus. After two rounds of eliminations, the top 5 candidates were invited to "airport interviews," where the committee managed to meet with each candidate for an hour. Then the top 3 candidates were invited to the campus to meet with students, faculty, and administrators.

The committee recommended to the university president that the job be given to Constance Pappas, who has a doctorate in American studies and has been chairperson of the history department at Minneapolis Metropolitan College for the past three years. The president agreed, and Dr. Pappas accepted the offer.

One final task remains before the work of the Dean's Selection Committee is finished: Letters must be sent to the 84 unsuccessful candidates. The 4 who reached the "airport interview" stage will receive personal letters from the chairperson of the committee. Your job, as secretary of the committee, is to draft the form letter that will be sent to the other 80 applicants.

Your Task: Draft a letter of 100 to 200 words. All copies will be individually addressed to the recipients but will carry identical messages.

After studying this chapter, you will be able to

Strengthen your persuasive messages with an appropriate appeal

Gain credibility by supporting your persuasive message with relevant facts

Use attention, interest, desire, and action (the AIDA plan) to organize persuasive messages

Write a message persuading your audience to take action or grant you an adjustment

Design a sales letter around selling points and benefits

Apply the techniques of persuasion to prompt your audience to pay an overdue bill

WRITING PERSUASIVE MESSAGES

*O*n the Job

FACING A COMMUNICATION DILEMMA
AT UNITED NEGRO COLLEGE FUND
Raising Dollars for Diplomas

William H. Gray III was facing the challenge of a lifetime. He left a 13-year career in the U.S. Congress (including a stint as House majority whip), to join the nonprofit United Negro College Fund (UNCF). As president and CEO, he had three years in which to persuade individuals and corporations to donate $250 million to the fund's new program, Campaign 2000. Philanthropist Walter Annenberg started things off by pledging a gift of $50 million, but it was up to Gray and his team to raise the remaining $200 million.

The money raised during this drive would serve as an endowment base for UNCF's members, 41 private colleges and universities that have historically been dedicated to higher education for African Americans. Although UNCF was already raising more than $50 million every year (through contributions, grants, scholarships, and other donations), Campaign 2000 was the most ambitious fund-raising drive the organization had ever mounted. If successful, campaign 2000 would enable UNCF's members to educate twice as many African American students as before.

The percentage of African American students enrolled in college was dropping, a trend that was expected to continue through the 1990s as tuition costs climbed. At the same time, battles over both minority scholarships and public funding for private institutions that serve minorities were raising concerns about future funding from these sources. This combination of higher tuition and uncertain funding was clouding the future of African American higher education.

William Gray realized that persuading individuals, charitable foundations, and companies to open their wallets would take careful planning. If you were on his team, how would you convince your audience to donate money to UNCF's Campaign 2000? What sort of persuasive messages would you send? How would you organize these messages? What would you do to get your audience's attention?[1]

Motivating with Persuasive Messages

William H. Gray understands that, much more than simply asking somebody to do something, *persuasion* is an attempt to change an audience's attitudes, beliefs, or actions.[2] Although the word has been associated with dishonest and unethical practices, such as coaxing, urging, and sometimes even tricking people into buying a product or taking an action they neither want nor need, the business meaning of **persuasion** is influencing an audience by informing them and aiding their understanding—the audience is free to choose.[3] Ethical businesspeople inform customers of the benefits of a product or an action so that customers can recognize how well that product or action will fill a need they truly have. Your consideration of customer needs is more than ethical; it's the proper use of persuasion. Also, it's more likely to evoke the desired response from your customers and colleagues.

United Negro College Fund

Persuasive messages aim to influence audiences who are inclined to resist. So they depend heavily on strategic planning. Before you begin to write a persuasive message, ask yourself what you're writing about, who you're writing to, and what you want to happen as a result. The best persuasive messages are closely connected to your audience's existing desires and interests.[4] When analyzing your audience, take into account their cultural expectations and practices so that you don't undermine your persuasive message by using an inappropriate appeal or by organizing your message in a way that seems unfamiliar or uncomfortable. When you're addressing an audience in Canada or in the United States and when cultural differences are minimal, you can consider four strategic elements: (1) needs and appeals, (2) emotion and logic, (3) credibility, and (4) semantics.

> Persuasion is the process of changing people's attitudes or influencing their actions.

> Three questions to ask before you begin to write a persuasive message:
> - What are you writing about?
> - Who are you writing to?
> - What do you want to happen as a result?

Needs and Appeals

One of the most effective motivational approaches is offering to satisfy your audience's needs. Of course, people have many needs, but some researchers believe that certain needs have priority and that the most basic needs (such as safety and security) must be met before a person will seek to fulfill higher-level needs (such as esteem and status). Imagine that you supervise someone who consistently arrives late for work. Once you've analyzed the need motivating him to arrive late, you can craft an appeal (a "hook") that will interest him in your message about changing his behavior.

> People are motivated by needs.

Because everyone's needs differ, people respond differently to any given message. Not everyone is interested in economy, for instance, or fair play. As a matter of fact, some people's innermost needs make appeals to status and greed much more effective. To accommodate these individual differences, analyze the members of your audience and then construct a message that appeals to their needs.

> Choose appeals according to your audience's needs.

Emotion and Logic

When people's needs are not being met, they're likely to respond emotionally. For example, a person who lacks a feeling of self-worth is likely to be sensitive to the tone of respect in a message. A collection letter to such a person carefully avoids any hint that the person might be considered dishonorable. The danger is that the person will become upset and not pay attention to your message. Not even the best-crafted, most reasonable message will persuade someone who is emotionally unable to accept it.

> Emotional reactions may result when an audience's needs are overlooked.

Although emotional issues can be a pitfall for persuasive messages, you can actually call on human emotion, as long as your **emotional appeal** is subtle.[5] You can make use of the emotion surrounding certain words. *Freedom*, for instance, brings forth strong feelings, as do words such as *success, prestige, credit record, savings, free, value,*

> Emotion and logic together are more powerful than either alone.

Mary Kay Ash, founder of Mary Kay Cosmetics, uses every imaginable form of communication (from hand-written memos to training manuals, videocassettes, and gala award shows) to motivate and manage the 100,000 salespeople in her company.

and *comfort.* Using words like these puts the audience in a certain frame of mind and helps them accept your message.

Also, emotion works with logic in a unique way: People need to find rational support for an attitude they've already embraced emotionally. To help satisfy this need, a **logical appeal** calls on human reason. To get the best results, companies and organizations like UNCF use both emotional and logical appeals when writing their persuasive messages.

Credibility

Your **credibility** is your capability of being believed because you're reliable and worthy of confidence. For you to persuade skeptical or hostile audience members, they must believe that you know what you're talking about and that you're not trying to mislead them. Without such credibility, your efforts to persuade will seem manipulative.

One of the best ways to gain credibility is to support your message with facts. Testimonials, documents, guarantees, statistics, research results, and the like all provide seemingly objective evidence for what you have to say, so they make your message more credible. The more specific and relevant your proof, the better. It also helps to name your sources, especially if they're respected by your audience. Other ways of gaining credibility include the following:

Enhance your credibility by supplying evidence that is objective and specific.

- *Being enthusiastic.* Your excitement about the subject of your message can infect your audience.
- *Being objective.* Your understanding of and willingness to acknowledge all sides of an issue help you present fair and logical arguments in your persuasive message.
- *Being sincere.* Your honesty, genuineness, good faith, and truthfulness help you focus on your audience's needs.

Express personal traits that enhance credibility through your approach and writing style.

- *Being an expert.* Your knowledge of your message's subject area (or even of some other area) helps you give your audience the quality information necessary to make a decision.
- *Having good intentions.* Your willingness to keep your audience's best interests at heart helps you create persuasive messages that are ethical.
- *Being trustworthy.* Your honesty and dependability help you earn your audience's respect.
- *Establishing common ground.* Your beliefs, attitudes, and background experiences that are like those of your audience help them identify with you.

Semantics

Semantics is concerned with the meaning of words and other symbols.

How do you let an audience know that you're enthusiastic and trustworthy? An outright claim that you have these traits is sure to raise suspicion. However, **semantics** (the meaning of words and other symbols) can do much of the job for you. The words you choose to state your message say much more than their dictionary definitions. For instance, *useful, beneficial,* and *advantageous* may be considered synonyms. Yet these three words are not interchangeable:

> She suggested a useful compromise. (The compromise allowed the parties to get to work.)
> She suggested a beneficial compromise. (The compromise not only resolved the conflict but also had a positive effect, perhaps for both parties.)
> She suggested an advantageous compromise. (The compromise benefited her or her company more than it benefited the other party.)

Another way semantics can affect persuasive messages is in the variety of meanings that people attribute to certain words. Abstractions are subject to interpretation because they refer to things that people cannot experience with their senses. So use abstractions to enhance the emotional content of a persuasive message. You may be able to sell more flags by appealing to your audience's patriotism (which may be interpreted in many ways) than by describing the color and size of the flags. You may have better luck collecting an overdue bill by mentioning honesty and fair play than by repeating the sum owed and the date it was due. However, be sure to include the details along with the abstractions; the very fact that you're using abstract words leaves room for misinterpretation.

> Abstractions are most persuasive when combined with details.

ORGANIZING PERSUASIVE MESSAGES

Persuasion requires the indirect approach. One specialized version is the AIDA plan, which has four phases: (1) attention, (2) interest, (3) desire, and (4) action.

> The AIDA plan:
> - Attention
> - Interest
> - Desire
> - Action

In the attention phase, you convince the audience right at the beginning that you have something useful or interesting to say. The audience wants to know "What's in this message for me?" Try to tell them without making extravagant claims or threats and without bringing up irrelevant points:

> You've mentioned several times in the past two weeks that constructing an employee schedule has become increasingly difficult. Let me share an idea that could substantially reduce the time you spend making and revising schedules.

In the interest phase, you explain how your message relates to the audience. Continuing the theme you started with, you paint a more detailed picture with words. Your goal is to get the audience thinking "This is an interesting idea. Could it possibly solve my problems?"

> Inc. magazine ran an article in the July 2 issue about a scheduling concept called flextime. It gives employees leeway to schedule their own work, within certain guidelines. Two companies profiled in the article were having problems (as we have been) with late arrivals, long lunches, early departures, and too many "sick days." They found it nearly impossible to set up a schedule everyone would adhere to. However, once these companies instituted flextime, their problems practically disappeared.

This interest section ties together a factual description and the benefits of instituting the program. Also, the benefits relate specifically to the attention phase that precedes this paragraph. Even though the flextime system might help improve employee morale, that benefit is secondary to the main interest of the intended audience (to reduce the frustration of devising useless schedules) and is therefore not mentioned.

In the desire phase of a persuasive message, you back up claims and thereby increase your audience's willingness to take the action that you'll suggest in the next section. Whatever you use to prove your claim, make sure the evidence is directly relevant to your point:

> One of the people interviewed in the article, the head of manufacturing for a $10 million company, said: "I seemed to be spending all my time making schedules and then tearing them up. Now I let my employees figure out

In his attempts to regain market share from the Japanese, Black & Decker's CEO, Nolan Archibald, used persuasive messages to transform an entire corporate culture, recapture customers with his vision, and recruit the talent he needed. To persuade others to adopt your point of view, says Archibald, present your case as though you were on the other side and needed to be convinced yourself.

their own schedules. I have more time to oversee the work that's being done and to track the quality of the products we ship." This company had a flextime program in full operation within three months of deciding to start it. Attached is a copy of an article about the factors to consider before going to flextime and the three steps involved in instituting it.

This example draws attention to the evidence and suggests the lessons that may be drawn from it.

In the action phase, you suggest the action you want your audience to take. All persuasive messages end with a section that urges specific action, but the ending is more than a statement such as "Institute this program as soon as possible" or "Send me a refund." In fact, this section offers a good opportunity for one last reminder of the main benefit the audience will realize from taking the action you want:

Let's meet early next week (Monday, 3:00 p.m.?) to see how we might implement a flextime schedule. With a little bit of extra effort now, you could soon be concentrating on something more important than scheduling.

The secret of the action phase is to make the action easy. In a sales letter, you might ask readers to call a toll-free number for more information. You might ask your audience to fill out an enclosed order form, and UNCF's William Gray might use a preaddressed, postpaid envelope for donations or pledges.

WRITING PERSUASIVE REQUESTS FOR ACTION

Many persuasive messages are written to solicit funds, favors, information, or cooperation. In an organization, persuasive techniques are often required to get someone to change policies or procedures, to spend money on new equipment and services, to promote a person, or to protect turf.[6] Persuasive letters to outsiders might solicit donations or ask for some other type of help.

As UNCF's William Gray knows well, an external persuasive message is one of the most difficult persuasive tasks you could undertake. First, people are busy, so they're reluctant to do something new; it takes time and offers no guarantee of any reward in return. Second, competing requests are plentiful. In fact, the public relations departments of many large corporations receive so many requests for donations to worthy causes that they must sometimes resort to lotteries to decide which to support.

Why do people respond to requests for action on an issue that is more important to you than to them? If you're lucky, they may believe in the project or cause that you're writing about. Even so, you must convince them that your request will give them some benefit, perhaps an intangible benefit down the road or a chance to make a meaningful contribution. Also, especially in the case of requests for professional favors or information, people may believe that they are obliged to "pay their dues" by helping others.

When making a persuasive request, therefore, take special care to highlight direct and indirect benefits. Direct benefits might include a reduced workload for a supervisor who institutes flextime or a premium for someone who responds to a survey. Indirect benefits might include better employee morale or the prestige of giving free workshops to small businesses.

The attention-getting device at the beginning of a persuasive request for action usually shows the reader that you know something about his or her concerns and that you have some reason for making such a request. In this type of persuasive message,

---

Margin notes:

Close a persuasive message with an action ending that suggests a specific step the audience may take.

End by

- Describing precisely what you would like to happen
- Restating how the audience will benefit by acting as you wish
- Making action easy

Three problems with requests for action:

- They frequently offer nothing tangible in return.
- They take time that could be used for something else.
- There are so many competing requests.

A former teacher, Lane Nemeth founded Discovery Toys, a company that markets educational toys through home demonstration parties. Whether you're wooing investors, negotiating a loan, or ordering inventory, advises Nemeth, let your readers know you understand their concerns.

more than in most others, a flattering comment about the reader is acceptable, especially if it is sincere. The body of the letter or memo covers what you know about the problem you're trying to solve with the reader's help: the facts and figures, the benefits of helping, your experience in attacking the problem. The goal is to give you and your request credibility, to make the reader believe that helping you will indeed help solve a significant problem. Once you've demonstrated that your message is relevant to your reader, you can request some specific action. Take a look at the request in Figure 11.1. Be aware, however, that a persuasive memo is somewhat more subdued than a letter to an outsider might be.

The most important thing to remember when preparing a persuasive request for action is to keep your request within bounds. Nothing is so distressing as a request so general, all-encompassing, or inconsiderate that it seems impossible to grant, no matter how worthy the cause. Also, be careful not to doom your request to failure by asking your reader to do all your work for you: to provide information that you were too

Make only reasonable requests.

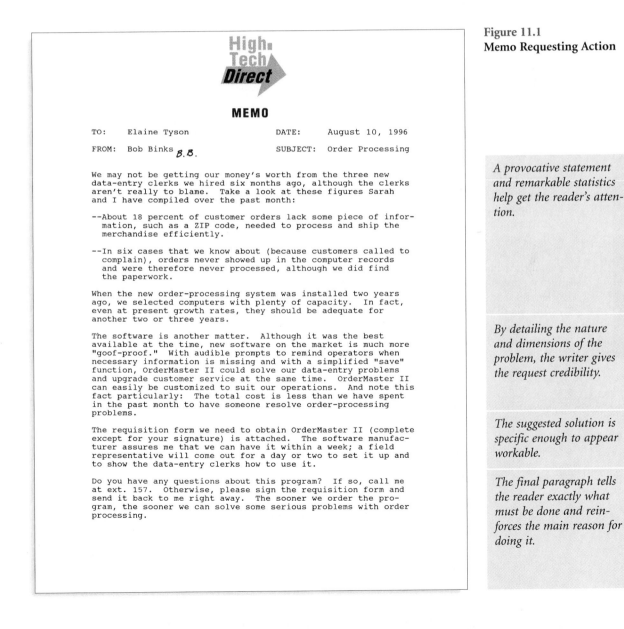

Figure 11.1
Memo Requesting Action

A provocative statement and remarkable statistics help get the reader's attention.

By detailing the nature and dimensions of the problem, the writer gives the request credibility.

The suggested solution is specific enough to appear workable.

The final paragraph tells the reader exactly what must be done and reinforces the main reason for doing it.

CHECKLIST FOR PERSUASIVE REQUESTS FOR ACTION

A. Attention

1. Demonstrate that you understand the audience's concerns.
2. Introduce a direct or indirect benefit that can be developed as a central selling point.
3. Craft statements so that they don't sound like high-pressure sales tactics or bribes.
4. Use an effective opening: a statement the audience will agree with, a sincere compliment, a frank admission that you need the audience's help, a description of the problem, one or two rhetorical questions, a summary of what is being done or has been done to solve a problem.

B. Interest and Desire

1. Early in the body of the message, state your reason for writing.
   - a. Mention the main audience benefit before the actual request.
   - b. Thoroughly explain your reason for asking the favor.
2. Include all necessary descriptions: physical characteristics, project value, and so forth.
3. Include all facts and figures necessary to convince readers that their contribution will be enjoyable, easy, important, and of personal benefit (as much as is true and possible).
   - a. In a request for cooperation, explain the problem, facts, suggestions, other participants' roles, and the audience's part.
   - b. In a request for a donation, explain the problem, past and current attempts to remedy it, future plans, your organization's involvement, and projected costs, along with suggestions about how the audience can help.
   - c. Describe the possible direct benefits.
   - d. Describe the possible indirect benefits.
4. Anticipate and answer possible objections.
   - a. Ignore objections if they're unimportant, if they might not occur to the audience, or if you can focus on positive facts instead.
   - b. Discuss objections (usually) about half or two-thirds the way through the body of the document.
   - c. Acknowledge objections calmly; then overcome them by focusing on more important and more positive factors.
   - d. Turn objections into an advantage by looking at them from another viewpoint or by explaining the facts of the situation more clearly.
5. Introduce any enclosures after you have finished the key message, with an emphasis on what to do with them or what information they offer.

C. Action

1. Confidently ask for the audience's cooperation.
2. Make the desired action clear and easy.
3. Stress the positive results of action.
4. Include the due date for a response (if necessary), and (if possible) tie it in with audience benefits such as adequate time for ordering supplies, prominent billing on a program or donor list, and so forth.
5. Replace negative or tentative statements ("If you can donate anything, . . .") with positive, confident statements ("To make your contribution, just return . . .").
6. As a last audience-benefit plug, tie the last sentence to an appeal or a statement featured in the opening paragraph (if appropriate).

lazy to seek, to spend time saving you from embarrassment or inconvenience, or to provide total financial support for a cause that nobody else is supporting. To review the tasks involved in such messages, see this chapter's Checklist for Persuasive Requests for Action.

WRITING SALES LETTERS

By and large, sales letters are written by specialized and highly skilled professionals. The letters come in letter-size or larger envelopes, with brochures or without. The common denominator is their attempt to motivate people to spend money or patronize an organization.

Knowing the laws that govern sales letters can help you avoid serious legal problems. For example, sales letters are considered binding contracts in many states. So avoid even implying offers or promises that you can't deliver.

Making a false statement in a sales letter is fraud if the recipient can prove (1) that your intent was to deceive, (2) that you made the statement regarding a fact rather than an opinion or a speculation, (3) that the recipient was justified in relying on the statement, and (4) that the recipient was damaged by it (in a legal sense). Misrepresenting the price, quality, or performance of a product in a sales letter is fraud, and so is a testimonial by a person misrepresented to be an expert.

Using a person's name, photograph, or other identity in a sales letter without permission constitutes invasion of privacy—with some exceptions. Using a photo of the members of a local softball team in a chamber of commerce mailer may be perfectly legal if team members are public figures in the community and if using the photo doesn't falsely imply their endorsement. On the other hand, using a photo of your governor, without consent, on a letter about the profits to be made in worm farming could be deemed an invasion of privacy.

Legal problems can also result from publicizing a person's private life in a sales letter. Stating that the president of a local bank (mentioned by name) served six months in prison for income tax evasion is a potentially damaging fact that may be considered an invasion of privacy. You can also risk a suit by publicizing another person's past-due debts or by publishing without consent another person's medical records, X rays, or photograph.

When trying to influence people's actions, knowledge of the law is crucial. However, merely avoiding what is illegal may not always be enough. To maintain the highest standards of business ethics, make every attempt to persuade without manipulating. Choose words that won't be misinterpreted when de-emphasizing negatives. Be sure you don't distort the truth, and show consideration for the audience by adopting the "you" attitude with honest concern for the needs and interests of your current and potential customers.

Sandra Gordon is vice president of communications for the National Easter Seal Society, a nonprofit agency. Each year more than a million people receive Easter Seal services, which requires both money and volunteers. Gordon advises that letters soliciting donations, whether of time or of funds, must give donors reasons to respond— benefits besides helping those who receive services.

Planning Sales Letters

The three steps involved in planning a sales letter are similar to those involved in planning any other persuasive message: (1) determine the main idea (in sales letters, it revolves around a selling point and related benefits), (2) define the audience, and (3) choose the approach and format.

Determining Selling Points and Benefits

Selling points are the most attractive features of a product; consumer benefits are the particular advantages that buyers will realize from those features. One selling point of a personal computer might be its numeric keypad. The consumer benefit of this selling point is that the user doesn't need a separate calculator or the skill to type numbers on the regular keyboard.

Obviously, you can't write about selling points or benefits without a thorough understanding of your subject. The first step in writing any sales letter is to take a good look at the product. Ask yourself (or someone else, if necessary) everything you think a potential buyer might want to know about it. For example, if you're supposed to write a sales letter for a wholesale bakery, you might want to get a full listing of the types of bread the bakery sells and find out whether the breads are prepared in any particular way, say, without preservatives or with only whole-grain wheat. Also investigate prices and discounts, delivery schedules, packaging, and the availability of special display materials.

Know your products' selling points, but talk about their benefits to consumers.

Start with a thorough knowledge of the product.

Think about how the product's features can help potential buyers; then concentrate on the most appealing benefits.

Once you have a complete file on the product, think of how its features can help potential buyers. When selling bread to a retailer, you might want to focus on the wholesale prices (and hence the markup the retailer can impose) and the convenience of being able to call in orders for next-day delivery. However, if you were selling the same bread to consumers, you might want to focus on the ingredients included in the bread. Whatever the case, focus on relatively few product benefits and determine which are most appealing so that you can direct your audience's attention to them. Ultimately, you'll single out one benefit, which will become the hallmark of your campaign.

Defining the Audience

The most persuasive sales letters are written to appeal to a specific audience.

In order to define benefits, you've already started with a general idea of your audience. However, you can learn a great deal more about them. For example, the bakery's pool of potential customers includes grocery stores, convenience markets, delicatessens, and so on, each with its own special needs. Bread retailers may also be divided on the basis of geographic location; rye bread, for instance, may sell much better in large cities and on the East Coast than in rural areas. The specific location of the retailer and the characteristics of the people who shop there would also be of interest.

Marketers seek to define consumers in terms of
- Demographics: age, gender, occupation, income, and education
- Psychographics: personality, attitudes, and lifestyle

When analyzing an audience of individual consumers, marketers refer to **demographics** (the age, gender, occupation, income, education, and other quantifiable characteristics of people who buy products) and **psychographics** (the psychological characteristics of potential buyers, such as personality, attitudes, and lifestyle).

Form a mental picture of the product's typical buyer; then relate selling points and benefits to that picture.

After collecting data about your audience, try to form a mental image of the typical buyer of the product you wish to sell. The point of this exercise is to help you formulate an idea of the central concerns of potential buyers. Then you can check the selling points and benefits you've already come up with against your audience's actual characteristics.

Choosing the Format and Approach

Once you know what you need to say and who you want to say it to, decide how you're going to say it. Will you send just a letter, or will you include brochures, samples, response cards, and the like? Will the letter be printed with an additional color or special symbols or logos? How many pages will it run? You'll also need to decide whether to conduct a multistage campaign, with several mailings and some sort of telephone or in-person follow-up, or rely on a single, hard-hitting mailing.

The more difficult the selling job, the more elaborate the campaign.

All these decisions depend on the audience you're trying to reach—their characteristics, their likely acceptance of or resistance to your message—and what you're trying to get them to do. Generally speaking, expensive items and hard-to-accept propositions call for a more elaborate campaign than low-cost products and simple actions.

Composing Sales Letters

Sales letters are prepared according to the AIDA plan used for any persuasive message—that is, they start with an attention-getting device, move to whet the reader's interest and desire, and end with a specific call to action. Special techniques give them added impact. Figure 11.2 is a typical example employing some of these techniques.

Getting Attention

A number of tried-and-true attention-getting devices are used in sales letters for a wide variety of products.

Take a look at these attention-getting devices commonly used in sales letters:

- *A piece of genuine news.* "In the past 60 days, auto manufacturers' inventories have shrunk by 12 percent."
- *A personal appeal to the reader's emotions and values.* "The only thing worse than paying taxes is paying taxes when you don't have to."

Figure 11.2
Letter Selling a Product

```
                AUTO CARE CENTRE
            MOWBRY'S
            1401 Smith Street
            Winnepeg, Manitoba
            R3C 1J6


                                        October 3, 1996


    Dear Friend:

        Before you know it, the thermometer is going to be
    stuck on "Brrr."  Yes, Old Man Winter is on his way,
    bringing some tough times for your automobile.

        Don't wait for signs of trouble.  Come in and give your
    auto the cold-weather servicing it needs, right now!  By
    having your automobile winterized now, you'll not only
    protect its trade-in value but also enjoy that great feeling
    of security every time you and your family back out of the
    driveway.  You'll know your auto is going to get you where
    you have to go.

        To make sure your whole family is protected, our expert
    service facilities are ready and waiting.  Factory-trained
    mechanics, up-to-the-minute equipment, the latest tools,
    genuine parts--all are ready to make sure your automobile
    performs at its best.

        Do make a point to drive in during the next day or two.
    Let us give your auto a complete inspection, from fender to
    fender.  Then you'll know what's needed to make sure it runs
    right, even on the coldest days.  Remember, a checkup now
    can easily save you much time and hundreds of dollars later,
    when the really cold weather arrives.

        Drive in today or tomorrow and hand the enclosed card
    of introduction to one of our attendants for a 10-percent
    discount, which is good for the next ten days.  The atten-
    dant will see that you get special, personal attention.

        Don't put off your auto's winter checkup.  It pays in
    every way to act now and beat the cold!

                                Sincerely,

                                Glen Mowbry
                                Glen Mowbry
                                Manager
```

A single selling point is emphasized: the service center's specialized cold-weather servicing.

The benefits of the major feature have both a logical appeal (higher trade-in value) and an emotional appeal (family safety).

The emphasis on quality prepares the reader to pay more for these services.

The reader's intelligence and desire to save time and money are the basis of this appeal.

The special time-limited offer should induce quick action.

- *The most attractive feature plus the associated benefit.* "New control device ends problems with employee pilferage!"
- *An intriguing number.* "Here are three great secrets of the world's most-loved entertainers."
- *A sample of the product.* "Here's your free sample of the new Romalite packing sheet."
- *A concrete illustration with story appeal.* "In 1985 Earl Colbert set out to find a better way to process credit applications. After ten years of trial and error, he finally developed a procedure so simple but thorough that he was cited for service to the industry by the American Creditors Association."
- *A specific trait shared by the audience.* "Busy executives need another complicated 'timesaving' device like they need a hole in the head!"
- *A provocative question.* "Are you tired of watching inflation eat away at your hard-earned profits?"

BEHIND THE SCENES WITH JOHN KEIL
The Case of the Rat's Guillotine

John M. Keil has over 20 years in advertising. His work includes creating ads for Toyota, Life Savers, and L'Eggs, as well as doing the TV voice of McGruff, the (Take a Bite Out of) Crime Dog. He approaches every persuasive challenge with six questions: (1) What is my single most important objective? (2) Who is my audience? (3) What reaction do I want from my message (what do I want my audience to do)? (4) What is the principal thought I wish the audience to be left with? (5) What is there about the message I'm sending that will help the audience believe the principal thought (what is the "because" statement)? (6) What's happening in the marketplace (what perceptions do people have) that might influence my ability to persuade people to my objective?

Keil's approach helps him develop a persuasive presentation for a common household product: a new high-quality spring-type rat trap. It has a long-lasting oak base, a strong steel spring, a "wicket," and an exclusive release mechanism that can be put on "safety" until the trap is baited and then put in the ready position with the tip of a pencil. Its advantages are that it will last longer than the average rat trap because of its quality materials, it's extremely efficient and thus more humane because of the strong spring, and it's less accident prone because of the safety feature. Its disadvantage is that it costs more than other rat traps. We also know that rats congregate in urban areas and along waterfronts, dislike cold weather, and have insatiable appetites.

Now consider Keil's persuasion strategy point for point:

1. *The objective.* We could hope that members of our audience would buy our rat trap rather than using poison. Or we could hope that they would pay more money for ours because it's more efficient and lasts longer than other spring-type traps, or that they would buy ours because of the safety features. These are all laudable objectives, but if we use all of them, we will be forced into a three-headed message. Let's narrow our choices.

    Better than poison? People who use poison want

- *A challenge.* "Don't waste another day wondering how you're going to become the success you've always wanted to be!"
- *A solution to a problem.* "Tired of arctic air rushing through the cracks around your windows? Stay warm and save energy with StormSeal Weatherstripping."

A look at your own mail will show you how many products these few techniques can be applied to.

Even so, not all attention-getting devices are equally effective. The best is the one that makes the audience read the rest of the letter. Look closely at the three examples below. Which seems most interesting to you?

Choose an attention-getter that encourages the reader to read more.

How would you like straight A's this semester?

Get straight A's this semester!

Now you can get straight A's this semester, with . . .

If you're like most people, you'll find the first option the most enticing. The question invites your response—and, by no mistake, a positive response designed to encourage you to read on. The second option is fairly interesting too, but its commanding tone may make you wary of the claim. The third option is acceptable, but it certainly con-

nothing to do with baiting and setting traps. They are not our audience. By saying "Use our trap rather than poison," we are heading in the wrong direction. Efficiency? Research tells us that most people believe there's very little difference in the efficiency of rat traps. One or two seconds gained by our product is not important. Long-lasting? Who likes to think of needing rat traps that last a lifetime?

That leaves us the safety feature. Ask people what they don't like about rat traps. Odds are that 9 out of 10 will say: "I hate to set them. I'm scared stiff one is going to go off and de-finger me." So our persuasive objective might read: "We want our audience to buy our rat trap rather than the competition's because of the safety feature."

2. *The audience.* We want to address apartment house owners and managers, food store owners, restaurant owners and managers, and people who live near or on waterfronts. Our audience statement might read: "The message is directed to all people who are particularly susceptible to rodent problems."

3. *The reaction.* As stated in the objective, we want our audience to buy our rat trap.

4. *The core idea.* We've arrived at it through our deduction. The safety feature becomes the one outstanding difference between our product and the competition's. So, "The principal thought that we'd like to leave with our audience is that our rat trap is safer to use than any other."

5. *The "because" section.* Here, we prove our point: "It's safer to use than any other because it has an exclusive release mechanism that can be put on *safety* while you set it and bait it."

6. *Influences and perceptions.* What influences might affect the persuasive message? We know rats don't like cold weather. That means their presence in houses, stores, and so on, will increase as cold weather arrives. This is the type of circumstance that might influence our ability to persuade people that our objective is correct.

Apply Your Knowledge

1. Select a memorable direct-mail piece you or someone in your household has received recently. Does the letter reflect Keil's six-point prescription for persuasive presentations? Comment on each question the letter does and does not address.

2. How would the presence or absence of visuals influence your comments on the direct-mail package just discussed? What sorts of visual aids would be useful for each of Keil's six questions?

veys no sense of excitement, and its quick introduction of the product may lead you to a snap decision against reading further.

Sales letters prepared by professionals also use a variety of formats to get your attention, including personalized salutations, special sizes or styles of type, underlining, color, indentions, and so on. Whatever special techniques are used, the best attention-getter for a sales letter is a hook that gets the reader thinking about the needs your product might be able to help fill.

Emphasizing the Central Selling Point

Say your company's alarm device is relatively inexpensive, durable, and tamperproof. Although these are all attractive features, you want to focus on only one. Ask what the competition has to offer, what most distinguishes your product, and what most concerns potential buyers. The answers to these three questions will help you select the **central selling point,** the single point around which to build your sales message. Make this point a feature of your letter, in the heading or within the first paragraph, and make it stand out through typography, design, or high-impact writing.[7]

To determine your product's central selling point, ask:

- What does the competition offer?
- What is special about my product?
- What are potential buyers really looking for?

Highlighting Benefits

Determining the central selling point will help you define the benefits to potential buyers. Perhaps your company's alarm device has been built mainly to overcome the inadequacies of the competition in resisting tampering by would-be burglars. This fea-

Selling points + "you" attitude = benefits.

ture is your central selling point; the benefits of this feature are that burglars won't be able to break in so easily and therefore burglaries will be reduced. You'll want to mention this benefit repeatedly, in words and pictures (if possible), near the beginning and the end of your letter. You might get attention by using a news item to stress this benefit: "Burglaries of businesses in our county have increased 7.7 percent over the past year; police department officials cite burglars' increasing sophistication and familiarity with conventional alarm devices." You might pose a provocative question: "Worried about the reliability of your current alarm system in repelling today's sophisticated burglars?"

In the rest of the letter, continue to stress this theme but also weave in references to other benefits: "You can get this worry-free protection for much less than you might think." Also, "The same technology that makes it difficult for burglars to crack your alarm system makes the device durable, even when it must be exposed to the elements." Remember, sales letters reflect the "you" attitude through references to benefits, so always try to phrase the selling points in terms of what such features will do for potential customers.

Using Action Terms

To give force to a message,
- Use action terms
- Use colorful verbs and adjectives

Active words, which give force to any business message, are especially important in sales letters. Compare the following:

Instead of This	*Write This*
The NuForm desk chair is designed to support your lower back and relieve pressure on your legs.	The NuForm desk chair supports your lower back and relieves pressure on your legs.

The second version says the same thing in fewer words and puts more emphasis on what the chair does for the user ("supports") than on the intentions of the design team ("is designed to support").

In general, use colorful verbs and adjectives that convey a dynamic image. Be careful, however, not to overdo it: "Your factory floors will sparkle like diamonds" is hard to believe and may prevent your audience from believing the rest of your message.

Talking About Price

You can prepare readers for your product's price by subtle choice and arrangement of words.

The price customers will pay for a product depends on the prices of similar products, the general state of the economy, and the psychology of the buyer. Price is therefore a complicated issue and often a sensitive one.

Whether the price of your product is highlighted or downplayed, prepare the reader for it. Such words as *luxurious* and *economical* provide unmistakable clues about how your price compares with that of competitors, and they help the reader accept the price when you finally state it. If your price is relatively high, definitely stress the features and benefits that justify it. If the price is low, you may wish to compare the features of your product with those of the competition, either directly or indirectly. In either case, if the price you eventually mention is a surprise to the reader, you've made a mistake that will be hard to overcome. Here's an example of a sales letter offering a product at a bargain price:

All the Features of Name-Brand Pantyhose at Half the Price!

If the price is an attractive feature, emphasize it by displaying it prominently.

Why pay for fancy packaging or that little tag with a famous name on it when you can enjoy cotton lining, reinforced toes, and matchless durability for only $1.99?

In this example the price falls right at the end of the paragraph, where it stands out. In addition, the price issue is featured in a bold headline. This technique may even be used as the opening of a letter if the price is the most important feature and the audience for the letter is value-conscious.

If price is not a major selling point, you can handle it in several ways. You could leave out the price altogether or mention it only in an accompanying brochure. You could de-emphasize the price by putting the actual figures in the middle of a paragraph close to the end of your sales letter, well after you've presented the benefits and selling points. The same paragraph might include a discussion of related topics, such as credit terms, special offers, and volume discounts. Mentioning favorable money matters before the actual price also reduces its impact.

To de-emphasize price
- Bury actual figures in the middle of a paragraph near the end
- Mention benefits and favorable money matters before the actual price
- Break a quantity price into units
- Compare the price with the cost of some other product or activity

> Only 100 prints of this exclusive, limited-edition lithograph will be created. On June 1, they will be made available to the general public, but you can reserve one now for only $350, the special advance reservation price. Simply rush the enclosed reservation card back today so that your order is in before the June 1 publication date.

Emphasis on the rarity of the edition signals value and thus prepares the reader for the big-ticket price that follows. The actual price, buried in the middle of a sentence, is tied in with another reminder of the exclusivity of the offer.

The pros use two other techniques for minimizing price. One is to break a quantity price into units. Instead of saying that a case of wine costs $144, you might say that each bottle costs $12. The other is to compare your product's price with the cost of some other product or activity: "The cost of owning your own spa is less than you'd pay for a health club membership." Your aim is to make the cost seem as small and affordable as possible, thereby eliminating price as a possible objection.

Supporting Your Claims

You can't assume that people will believe what you say about your product just because it's in writing. You'll have to prove your claims, especially if your product is complicated, expensive, or representative of some unusual approach.

Support for your claims may take several forms. Samples and brochures, often with photographs, may be enclosed in the sales package and referred to in the letter. The letter also describes or typographically highlights examples of how the product has benefited others, includes testimonials (actual quotations) from satisfied customers, or cites statistics from scientific studies of the product's performance. Guarantees of exchange or return privileges, which may also be woven into the letter or set off in a special way, indicate that you have faith in the product and are willing to back it up.

Types of support for product claims:
- Samples
- Brochures
- Examples
- Testimonials
- Statistics
- Guarantees

It's almost impossible to provide too much support. Try to anticipate every question your audience may want to ask. Put yourself in your audience's place so that you can ask, and answer, all the what-ifs.[8]

Motivating Action

The overriding purpose of a sales letter is to get the reader to do something. Many companies selling consumer products through the mail simply ask for a check—in other words, an immediate decision to buy. On the other hand, companies selling big-ticket and more complex items frequently ask for just a small step toward the final buying decision, such as sending for more information or authorizing a call by a sales representative.

Try to persuade readers to take action, whatever it is, right away. Convince them that they must act now, perhaps to guarantee a specific delivery date. If there's no par-

Aim to get the reader to act as soon as possible.

ticular reason to act quickly, many sales letters offer discounts for orders placed by a certain date or prizes or special offers to, say, the first 500 people to respond. Others suggest that purchases be charged to a credit card or paid off over time. Still others offer a free trial, an unconditional guarantee, or a no-strings-attached request card for information, all in an effort to overcome readers' natural inertia.

Packaging Sales Letters

Sales letters don't often stand alone. They're one part of a campaign to market a product or an idea, and they're often part of a **direct-mail package,** a collection of selling materials that is mailed directly to consumers.

Direct-Mail Elements

Direct-mail packages traditionally have five elements, all coordinated to reinforce the central selling point.

Traditionally, a direct-mail package has five elements: (1) outer envelope telegraphing a sales message, (2) multipage sales letter, (3) brochure (usually in color), (4) order blank, and (5) postage-paid return envelope. A postage-paid order card sometimes takes the place of the order blank and return envelope. Other elements are sometimes included, such as samples or small gifts, catalogs, invitations, coupons, plastic "credit cards," and a short folded note "for those who have decided not to buy at this time." All these pieces emphasize the same theme and are written in the same style and tone. Of course, the information in all elements is consistent without merely repeating the same message.

One alternative to the traditional package is a self-mailer, a single piece of cleverly folded paper that both conveys a message to the reader and carries the order back to the original sender. Another format is the simulated telegram or invitation, which may entice recipients into reading the message.

Personalization of sales letters is not always cost-effective.

Very often, personalized letters are more effective than those addressed to, say, "Occupant" or "Office Manager." However, people have become accustomed to personalization, and it's expensive. So before using it, determine whether the cost is justified by test-mailing letters with and without personalized messages.

In sales letters, use visual emphasis to keep the reader's attention.

Advertising professionals seem to agree that a longer letter is more effective than a short one because it provides plenty of room for the specific information that will persuade a reader to accept your message. Most sales letters are four pages long. However, because very few recipients have the patience to read all of a long letter, attention-getting devices such as underlining, indenting, and colored type are used to help readers find the points of greatest interest. Enclosures give necessary details about the product too.

Mailing Lists

Direct mail is an effective means of reaching a specialized audience.

Direct mail is especially useful for organizations trying to reach special groups of people. Perhaps you're trying to market expensive exercise equipment. Although exercise and fitness have become important to large segments of the public, television and magazine advertising scatters the message to many people who may not be interested in exercise or may not be willing to spend much money for it. The secret is to find the people who would definitely be interested in hearing about your product.

A key to direct-mail success is to choose the right kind of mailing list.

Fortunately, you can rent, buy, or create **mailing lists,** names and addresses of people who buy certain products, subscribe to certain magazines, belong to certain organizations, and so on. Three types of direct-mail lists exist:

- *House lists* are compiled from the rolls of previous customers and even those who have inquired about the company's product. This is often the best type of list because the people on it tend to be receptive to the company (assuming it has cultivated their goodwill).

- *Compiled lists* are taken from easily obtained sources of data and may include lists of automobile owners, new-house purchasers, business owners, union members, and so forth. Compiled lists provide many names but are often too general to target interested parties. Selling exercise equipment by mailing promotional literature to every name in the telephone book wouldn't be cost-effective. However, literature about tax-preparation services might well be sent to every name in the phone book.
- *Mail-response lists* are like house lists, except that they come from other companies and contain the names of people who have responded to direct mail in the past. Direct competitors don't usually trade mail-response lists. However, list brokers often accumulate competitors' lists and make them available temporarily or for a certain number of mailings.

Direct-mail lists can also be purchased or rented. Check under "Mailing Lists" in the yellow pages, or consult one of the major sources for locating lists. For example, *Direct Mail List Rates & Data,* published by Standard Rate and Data Service, describes the Columbia Record & Tape Club (Columbia House), which has 1,135,745 active members and rents their names out for $60 per thousand. Columbia's list can be subdivided by listening preference (country and western, jazz, and so forth), by ZIP code, by state, or by any one of a host of other factors. (See this chapter's Checklist for Sales Letters as a reminder of the tasks involved in these messages.)

Writing Collection Messages

The causes of overdue accounts are as varied as the individuals and companies they represent. A bill may truly be lost in the mail or misfiled. A few people mistakenly borrow more than they can possibly repay. Some have an unforeseen difficulty that makes timely repayment a problem. Still others are irresponsible about paying bills, dissatisfied with their purchase, or temporarily negligent. Luckily for the writers of collection letters, most individuals and businesses value their good name and credit rating and respond quickly to reminders and inquiries.

> People have many reasons for not paying bills; give debtors the benefit of the doubt as long as reasonably possible.

The Collection Context

One key to success in collecting is remembering that collection is a process, not just a single demand.[9] The purpose of the collection process is to maintain goodwill while collecting what is owed. Your decisions about how to achieve these twin goals depend on (1) the amount of money owed, the time elapsed, the nature of the credit agreement, and the creditor's attitude; (2) the debtor's values, feelings of self-esteem, and attitudes toward financial responsibility; and (3) the debtor's ability to solve the problem and withstand external and internal pressures.

Collection is a sensitive issue; it's also closely governed by federal and state laws. The Fair Debt Collection Practices Act of 1978 outlines a number of restrictions on collection procedures. The following practices are prohibited:

> Your dual goal in sending collection messages:
> - Collect what is owed
> - Maintain goodwill

- Falsely implying that a lawsuit has been filed
- Contacting the debtor's employer or relatives about the debt
- Communicating to other persons that the person is in debt
- Harassing the debtor (although definitions of harassment may vary)
- Using abusive or obscene language
- Using defamatory language (such as calling the person a *deadbeat* or a *crook*)
- Intentionally causing mental distress

CHECKLIST FOR SALES LETTERS

A. Planning the Direct-Mail Package
1. Determine the specific purpose of the mailing.
2. Define the selling points and the consumer benefits.
3. Analyze the audience, using demographic and psychographic information if available.
4. Choose the approach and format.
   - a. Determine the appeal, remembering that the most potent appeals relate to making money, saving money, saving time, or avoiding effort.
   - b. Write a sales letter that is long enough to present all necessary information.
   - c. Use short paragraphs, underlining, handwritten notes, bullets, color, and so on, to make the letter visually appealing.
   - d. Include several enclosures to improve response.
   - e. Enclose or offer a free sample to demonstrate your product.
   - f. Telegraph your main appeal on the envelope.
5. Pretest every element of your package.

B. Attention
1. Design a positive opening that awakens in the reader a favorable association with the product.
2. Promise a benefit to the reader.
3. Write an opening that is appropriate, fresh, honest, interesting, specific, and relevant to the central selling point.
4. Keep the first paragraph short, preferably two to five lines, sometimes only one.
5. Design an attention-getting opening that uses any of the following techniques: significant fact about the product, solution to a problem, special offer or gift, testimonial, stimulation of the senses or emotions, reference to current events, action picture, startling fact, agreeable assertion, comparison, event or fact in the reader's life, problem the reader may face, quotation.

C. Interest
1. State information clearly, vividly, and persuasively, and relate it to the reader's concerns.
2. Develop the central selling point.
3. Feature the product in two ways: physical description and consumer benefits.
   - a. Interweave benefits with a physical description, or place benefits first.
   - b. Describe the objective details of the product: size, shape, color, scent, sound, texture.
   - c. Through psychological appeals, present the sensation, satisfaction, or pleasure your reader will

---

- Threatening violence
- Communicating by postcard (not confidential enough)
- Sending anonymous C.O.D. communications
- Misrepresenting the legal status of the debt
- Communicating in such a way as to make the receiver physically ill
- Giving false impressions, such as labeling the envelope "Tax Information"
- Misrepresenting the message as a government or court document

To protect people from unreasonable persecution and harassment by debt collectors, the law also delineates when you may contact a debtor, how many times you may call, and what information you must provide to the debtor (timely responses, accurate records, and understandable documents). However, that doesn't mean you can't be tough in collection letters. As long as what you state is true and lawful, it can't be construed as harassment or misrepresentation.

Ironically, the more your audience agrees with the justice of your claim, the more likely they are to react defensively. The true deadbeat expects to be dunned and has little reaction to requests for payment. A normally conscientious customer, on the other hand, is embarrassed about such a slip. In such an emotional state, the customer may resort, consciously or unconsciously, to blaming you for the problem, procrastinating, avoiding the situation altogether, or reacting aggressively. Your job is to neutralize those feelings by using **positive appeals,** by accentuating the benefits of

A debtor's response is likely to be emotional, especially when the debtor is usually conscientious, so use tact.

Positive appeals are usually more effective than negative ones.

gain, translating the product or service into the fulfillment of needs and desires.

d. Blend cold facts with warm feelings.

D. Desire

1. Enlist one or more appeals to support the central selling point.
   a. Provide one paragraph of desire-creating material in a one-page letter with descriptive brochure; provide several paragraphs if the letter itself is two or more pages long, with or without an enclosed brochure.
   b. Emphasize reader use and benefits.
   c. If the product is valued mainly because of its appearance, describe its physical details.
   d. If the product is machinery or technical equipment, describe its sturdiness of construction, fine crafting, and other technical details in terms that help readers visualize themselves using it.
   e. Include technical sketches and meaningful pictures, charts, and graphs, if necessary.
2. Anticipate and answer the reader's questions.
3. Use an appropriate form of proof.
   a. Include facts about users' experience with the product, including verifiable reports and statistics from users.
   b. Provide names (with permission only) of other satisfied buyers and users.

c. Present unexaggerated testimonials from persons or firms that are users of the product and whose judgment the reader respects.
   d. Provide the results of performance tests by recognized experts, testing laboratories, or authoritative agencies.
   e. Offer a free trial.
   f. Offer a guarantee.
   g. Refer to samples if they are included.
4. Note any enclosures in conjunction with a selling point.

E. Action

1. State clearly the action you desire.
2. Provide specific details on how to order the product or specific information on how to reach your place of business.
3. Make action easy through the use of a mail-back reply card, preaddressed envelope, phone number, or promise of a follow-up call or visit.
4. Offer a special inducement to act: time limit, special price for a limited time, premium for acting before a certain date, free gift for buying, free trial, no obligation to buy but more information or a suggested demonstration, easy payments with no money down, credit card.
5. Supply a final consumer-benefit plug.
6. Include a postscript conveying an important sales point (if desired for emphasis).

complying with your request for payment. Here are a few examples of positive appeals:

- *Sense of pride.* "A good credit rating is something to be proud of. Send in your payment today, and your credit standing with us will remain unblemished."
- *Need to belong.* "We want you back in the fold. Send us your payment today, and we will continue uninterrupted service."
- *Sense of fair play.* "We special-ordered your tools when you needed them. You know you can depend on us. We also depend on you to send in your payment today."
- *Need to follow rules.* "We supplied you with the products you required. You agreed to pay for them. Please send your payment in the return envelope."
- *Recognition of mutual effort.* "If you're having budget problems, why not let us help? After all, our business is to help people solve their financial needs. Please let us know the reason for the delay so that we can suggest a solution to the problem."
- *Need for closure.* "You agreed to make your payments according to the schedule we worked out together. If you send us your check today, the matter will be settled and your credit protected."

If positive appeals fail, you may have to consider a **negative appeal,** which stresses the unpleasant consequences of not acting rather than the benefits of acting. Of course, using abusive or threatening language and harassing your customer is ineffective and

If positive appeals fail, you may need to point out the actions legally available to you.

illegal. Persuasion is the opposite of force, so continue to use a polite and businesslike tone as you point out some of the actions legally available to you:

- Reporting the delinquent customer to a central credit agency
- Repossessing the purchased item
- Demanding the surrender of collateral put up to secure the loan
- Turning the account over to a collection agency
- Engaging the services of a lawyer and taking the matter to court

Indirect negative consequences, such as embarrassment and inconvenience, are also associated with these actions.

Don't forget that your real aim is to persuade the customer to make the payment. So your best approach is to try to maintain the customer's goodwill.

The Collection Series

In a well-managed company, past-due accounts are flagged early (often by computer), and simple reminders (often form letters) are sent out immediately. As the past-due period lengthens, a series of collection letters reflecting the increasing seriousness of the problem is sent to the customer at predetermined intervals.

The typical collection series includes a notification, a reminder, an inquiry, an urgent notice, and an ultimatum. Usually, only the first step or two is required for a simple oversight or temporary problem on the part of a debtor who normally pays bills. Further steps are usually reserved for those who deliberately refuse to accept responsibility for a debt. At these later stages the customer's past credit and buying history, the amount of money owed, and the customer's overall credit rating determine the content and style of collection messages.

Notification

Most creditors send bills to customers on a regular schedule, depending on the terms of the credit agreement. Typically, this standard notification is a form letter or statement, often computerized, stating clearly the amount due, the date due, the penalties for late payment, and the total amount remaining to be paid. The standardized form, far from being an insult to the recipient, indicates the creditor's trust that all will go according to plan.

Reminder

If payment has not been received within a few days after the due date, most creditors send out a reminder. Again, a standardized letter is reassuring. A reminder notice is written under the assumption that some minor problem has delayed payment—in other words, that the customer has every intention of paying and needs only to be reminded. The tone is not too serious:

As of October 1, we still hadn't received your September payment of $197.26. Has the payment been overlooked? Please check your records.

Using a different strategy, some companies send out a copy of the unpaid bill at this stage, with a handwritten note or preprinted stamp or sticker indicating that payment has not yet been received.

Inquiry

As frustrating as it may be to send out a reminder and still get no response, don't assume that your customer plans to ignore the debt, especially if the customer has paid

Steps in the collection series:

- Notification
- Reminder
- Inquiry
- Urgent notice
- Ultimatum

The standardized notification is a sign of trust.

The reminder notice, which still assumes only a minor problem, may be a standardized form or an informal message.

The inquiry

- *Assumes that something unusual is preventing payment*
- *Is personalized*
- *Avoids any suggestion of customer dissatisfaction*

bills promptly in the past. So avoid accusations in your inquiry message. However, the time has passed for assuming that the delay is merely an oversight, so you may assume that some unusual circumstance is preventing payment:

Because you're a valued customer who's been conscientious about paying bills on time, Ms. Jablonski, I'm wondering why we haven't received your September payment of $197.26. Is there a problem we should know about? Please send us your payment right away or phone me at 555-4495 to discuss your situation. We want to help you fulfill your obligations.

Personalization at this stage is appropriate because you're asking your customer to work out an individualized solution. The letter also avoids any suggestion that the customer might be dissatisfied with the purchase. Instead, it emphasizes the reader's obligation to communicate about the problem and the creditor's willingness to discuss it. Including the writer's name and number helps motivate a response at this stage.

Urgent Notice

This stage represents a significant escalation. Convey your desire to collect the overdue payment immediately and your willingness to get serious, but avoid any overt threats. To communicate a sense of urgency, you might resort to a letter signed by a top official in the company or to a negative appeal. However, an urgent notice still leaves an opening for the debtor to make a payment without losing face:

An urgent notice
- Might be signed by a top company official
- Might indicate the negative consequences of noncompliance
- Should leave an opening for payment without loss of face

I was very surprised this morning when your file reached my desk with a big tag marked OVERDUE. Usually, I receive customer files only when a serious problem has cropped up.

An attention-getter focuses on the unusual circumstances leading to this letter.

Opening your file, I found the following facts: Your order for five cases of Panza serving trays was shipped six months ago. Yet we still haven't received the $232.70 due. You're in business too, Mr. Rosen, so you must realize that this debt needs to be paid at once. If you had a customer this far behind, you'd be equally concerned.

The recipient is reminded of the order. Personalization and an attempt to emphasize common ground may motivate the reader to respond.

Please see that a check for $232.70 is mailed to us at once. If you need to work out an alternate plan for payment, call me now at (712) 693-7300.

The preferred action is spelled out; an option is also suggested in case of serious trouble.

Sincerely,

The signature of a ranking official lends weight to the message.

Artis Knight
Vice President

A well-written urgent notice has a good chance of persuading customers who still view themselves as responsible and trustworthy. At this stage a telephone call backing up your written message may also get a promise to pay. However, the irresponsible debtor is unlikely to be swayed by anything less than an ultimatum.

CHECKLIST FOR COLLECTION MESSAGES

A. Effective Collections

1. Reflect in your message the fact that you are communicating with a person, not with an account number.
2. Employ a tactful, courteous "you" attitude, coupled with firmness and patience.
3. Assume that the customer honestly wants to pay as agreed.
4. Balance your two main goals—collecting the money and retaining the customer's goodwill—because too much emphasis on one reduces the chance of achieving the other.
5. Keep communication between collector and debtor open.
6. Focus on only one appeal in each letter.
   a. Use positive appeals—cooperation, fair play, and pride—if possible.
   b. Use negative appeals—self-interest and fear—after positive appeals have failed.
7. Avoid giving the debtor any reason for not paying you ("Your company has had a lot of problems this year, but . . .").
8. Take the debtor's past behavior into account when deciding on the timing of collection messages.
   a. Allow generous time intervals for a customer with a good credit record.
   b. Shorten intervals for a customer who has earned the reputation of being slow.
9. Regardless of the stage in the collection procedure, clarify the amount due and the account number.
10. Include an easy-action envelope, postpaid, for every stage.

B. Collection Stages

1. At every stage, make it easy for the debtor to respond.
   a. Clarify the account number and the amount due.
   b. Include an easy-action envelope, postpaid.
2. Send out an initial notification.
   a. Provide details on how much is owed, when it's due, where it should be sent, and what happens if it isn't paid on time.
   b. Use a standard, impersonal format to avoid implying that anything is out of the ordinary.
3. In the reminder stage, provide a routine, direct request to jog the customer's memory.
   a. Present the main question or subject first, then explain (when necessary), and follow up with a request for action.
   b. Assume the payment is delinquent because of customer oversight.
   c. Subordinate sales material or humorous gimmicks to the main goal: collecting the debt.
   d. Include a duplicate copy of the original bill, perhaps stamped "Reminder" or "Past Due," with a short note (usually a form) specifying

---

Ultimatum

An ultimatum

- Should state the exact consequences of nonpayment
- Must avoid any hint of defamation or harassment
- Need not take a personal, helpful tone

Some people's finances are in such disorder that you won't get their attention until this stage. However, don't send an ultimatum unless you intend to back it up and are well supported by company policy. Even then, maintain a polite, businesslike manner and avoid defaming or harassing the debtor.

By itemizing the precise consequences of not paying the bill, you can encourage debtors to reevaluate their priorities. You're no longer interested in hearing why it has taken them so long to respond; you're interested in putting your claim at the top of their list. The tone of the ultimatum need not be as personal or individualized as the inquiry or urgent notice. At this stage, you're in a position of justified authority and should no longer be willing to return to an earlier stage of communication and negotiation:

> On September 2, 1994, we shipped a standard assortment of consumer publications to City News (invoice number CN3-0014). Your application for credit was approved because of the credit references you supplied. Under our usual terms, we sent a statement for $757.93, due October 3. Although we were concerned when we didn't receive payment by that date, we assumed there was some oversight. After all, you had a history of paying debts promptly.

the amount, due date, late charge, and account number.

4. In the inquiry stage, provide a personalized message with an inside address and a salutation with the customer's name.

a. Assume that something unusual has happened and that for some reason unknown to you the customer cannot or does not want to pay.

b. Employ a positive tone.

c. Avoid suggesting that reader dissatisfaction with your goods or services might be responsible for the late payment.

d. Demonstrate a genuine willingness to help.

e. Attract attention in the first paragraph with a reader-benefit theme: something beneficial, pleasant, interesting, or important to the reader.

f. Include facts, figures, or reasons the customer will benefit by doing as requested.

g. Leave the reader with alternatives that allow her or him to recover from the transaction with dignity intact.

h. Provide for easy action.

5. In an urgent notice, convey the seriousness of the situation.

a. Assume that the customer must pay.

b. Phrase the letter to retain the customer's goodwill and future business (although probably for cash), if possible.

c. Employ the strongest appeal—fear—by mentioning the unfortunate consequences of collection enforcement.

d. Tell the customer that you would prefer not to take this drastic action, but (because of obligations to credit-reporting agencies and company procedures) you must do so unless the debtor pays or explains.

e. Tell the customer that by not paying, she or he is likely to lose credit privileges, goods or services not paid for, additional money or property, reputation, and self-respect.

f. Employ urgent language.

g. Insist on immediate payment, and set a date by which you must receive it.

h. To protect yourself from legal problems, state facts correctly, make no malicious or defamatory accusations, and send messages in sealed envelopes that are addressed to the debtor personally.

i. Offset the negativity of an appeal to fear with at least one positive appeal, to give the debtor a chance to avoid the drastic action and extra costs.

j. Arrange for the letter to be signed by a higher executive, such as a vice president or even the president (if desirable).

6. In an ultimatum, you may resort to a bad-news message.

a. Make the action request firm, and be definite about the amount to be sent and the place to send it.

b. Be polite, businesslike, and impersonal.

c. Put into effect any actions that you have stated you will take.

Over the past three months, we've tried repeatedly to get you to send a check for $757.93. So far, we have had only your oral agreement to pay. Ms. Park in our credit department phoned you, as you'll recall. At that time, you assured her a check would be mailed to us at once.

No longer can we accept such assurances. If we don't receive payment in full within the next five days, we will have to turn your account over to a collection agency.

To save embarrassment and a black mark on your permanent credit record, do mail your check today.

This letter outlines the steps that have already been taken, implying that the drastic action to come is the logical follow-up. Although earlier collection messages were based on persuasion, this one is essentially a bad-news letter. (As a reminder of the tasks involved in the collection series, see this chapter's Checklist for Collection Messages.)

If a letter like this doesn't yield results, the only remaining remedy is actually to begin legal collection procedures. As a final courtesy, you may wish to send the debtor a notice of the action you're about to take. By maintaining until the bitter end your respect for the customer, you may still salvage some goodwill.

On the Job

SOLVING A COMMUNICATION DILEMMA AT UNITED NEGRO COLLEGE FUND

In more than 50 years of operation, the UNCF has raised a total of almost $1 billion and sent more than 250,000 students through college. With Campaign 2000, William H. Gray and his team at UNCF wanted to raise enough money to double the number of students that member colleges could afford to educate. The goal of this fund-raising program was to raise $250 million in three years.

The son of a man who had served as president of two African American colleges in the 1940s, Gray could envision the generations of students who would graduate from college because contributors to the United Negro College Fund had provided the support needed to build a better future. He knew that the key to success would be persuasive communication. "An organization must have a strong message to communicate," Gray pointed out. "You must be able to explain your cause and what makes it different from other philanthropic causes. You should also have a history of doing good work."

Five decades of good work gave UNCF the credibility that is so important in persuasive messages. Through a compelling combination of emotional and logical appeals, UNCF requested a donation to Campaign 2000. Communicators reached out to potential donors using direct mail, telephone solicitations, advertising, and special events.

As the weeks and months passed, donations and pledges for future contributions started to arrive. More than half the money came from foundations and major corporations such as NationsBank, EDS, American Airlines, Frito-Lay, Texas Instruments, Wal-Mart, Coca-Cola, Dow Jones, J. C. Penney, and Exxon. Individual donors also gave generously. For example, Michael Bolton donated his time to give a concert that raised $135,000 for Campaign 2000 in 1993.

By 1994, with Annenberg's $50 million pledge, Gray and his staff had raised more than $200 million, and he was confident that effective communication would enable the UNCF to raise the remaining $50 million by 1995. UNCF was nearing its fund-raising goal, and Gray never missed a beat putting the money to work providing endowment, scholarships, improved facilities, and other necessities for the 41 member institutions.

Your Mission: As William Gray's executive assistant, you are responsible for drafting correspondence to businesses about their involvement with the United Negro College Fund. Use your knowledge of persuasive messages to choose the *best* alternative in each of the following situations. Be prepared to explain why your choice is best.

1. Gray wants to reduce the amount of money spent renting office space for UNCF personnel who work with colleges around the country. He would like companies to donate a small section of their facilities for use as UNCF local offices. You have been asked to draft a form letter that will be signed by Gray and sent to large companies in ten cities where UNCF currently maintains offices. These companies have made contributions to UNCF in the past, so they're familiar with your work. Which of the following versions is the best attention-getter for this letter?

   a. No, this is not another letter asking for a cash contribution. We know that you've been generous with your donations in the past, and we appreciate your help. Instead of asking for money, we're looking for a valuable resource you may be able to share with us: a few hundred square feet of unused office space.

   b. Don't let that unused office space go to waste month after month! Space that sits idle doesn't help you. Let the United Negro College Fund take idle space off your hands. We're looking for office space in [city]. If you let us have any office space you're not using, you'll be giving us a chance to continue our work with member colleges and students in your area.

   c. Did you know that the United Negro College Fund is seeking donated office space in your area? Even a few hundred square feet of empty space will help. We don't care whether the offices have purple walls, torn carpeting, or windows overlooking the local recycling plant. Our workers will be so busy helping hundreds of African American college students in [city] get a good education that they'll never notice.

   d. If you could put your empty office space to productive use--and earn a charitable contribution at the same time--wouldn't you be interested? Donate some of your unused space to the United Negro College Fund, and you'll gain a tax break as well as the satisfaction of providing additional help to the hundreds of African American students who attend member colleges in your area.

2. Which of the following versions is the most compelling interest and desire section for your letter?

   a. Let's face it, everyone is looking for ways to reduce costs these days. We can cut our costs if you help. We need donated office space. We're not looking for a palace; our field representatives can work productively in as little as 400 square feet of office space. Please take a moment right now to look over your facilities and decide how much empty space you want to donate to our worthy cause.

b. You may know of one large office, two smaller offices, or even a portion of an open work area that you no longer use. Just 400 square feet would allow our field representatives to work more closely with local member colleges and students. We will adapt any empty office space, regardless of its location, at no cost to (name of company). Of course, we will pay for all insurance and moving costs as well as for utilities and other expenses connected with using the donated space.

Donating space you no longer need or use will cost you nothing. We'll even prepare all the paperwork you need to support a charitable tax deduction. But you'll get more than just a tax break. You'll also get the satisfaction of helping African American students get a good college education.

c. The United Negro College Fund's local representatives can work productively in as little as 400 square feet of empty office space. So please look around. Check every nook and cranny in your facility. See whether you have a large, empty office or two smaller empty offices. Even a portion of an open work area that you no longer use may be suitable.

Your donation of empty office space--regardless of the location in [city]--will help the United Negro College Fund. You can be proud of this donation, which will help us serve member colleges and universities in your area. Help us educate the next generation of leaders by donating your unused office space today.

d. The United Negro College Fund needs your help. Any office space--as little as 400 square feet--will help us put local representatives near member colleges and the students they serve. Please take a moment to see whether you have one large office, two smaller offices, or a portion of an open work area that you no longer use.

If you donate this empty space, we'll take care of all the other details. So you get a tax break, and we get free office space. We both benefit, but the people who will benefit most from this arrangement are the African American students who attend our member colleges in your area.

3. Which of the following versions would be the best action section for your letter?
   a. Your donation of unused office space will make a real difference to the United Negro College Fund and to the colleges and students we serve. If you have any questions about donating office space or about the tax consequences, please call me toll free at (800) 555-0334. I'd be happy to discuss

the details with you. Because the leases for all current facilities expire at the end of this year, we are interested in arranging for new office space no later than October 15.
   b. Your donation of free office space for our local representatives would be much appreciated. If you have space that you are willing to donate, call me immediately toll free at (800) 555-0334. I will be ready to answer any questions about donating space or the tax consequences. Please respond by October 15 if possible.
   c. If you can donate unused office space, you will help the United Negro College Fund as well as your company. If you are willing to donate space, please take a moment to call me toll free at (800) 555-0334. I will try to answer any questions you may have about donating space or the tax consequences. Please do your best to call before October 15, because the leases for all current facilities expire at the end of the year.
   d. If you have any questions about donating office space or the tax consequences, please call me toll free at (800) 555-0334. I would be happy to discuss the details with you. The first company in [city] that offers appropriate space will be entitled to the tax break that this donation can provide, so be sure to call as soon as possible.

4. Like many charitable organizations, the UNCF prepares television commercials about its work and asks stations to air them without charge, as a public service. The advertising agency is putting the finishing touches on a new commercial to spotlight Campaign 2000. Gray has asked you to compose a letter requesting television station managers around the United States to air the new UNCF commercial for free at least once a week during the next two months. Which of the following appeals to the audience would be the most effective in such a letter?
   a. An entirely emotional appeal stressing the need of the students and the satisfaction of helping a worthy cause.
   b. An entirely logical appeal stressing that the commercials can be aired whenever the station has commercial time that hasn't been sold to another advertiser, which means the station won't lose money.
   c. A combination of emotional and logical appeals, stressing both the satisfaction of helping a worthy cause and the rational reasoning behind airing the commercial whenever the station has unsold commercial time.
   d. A combination of emotional and logical appeals, stressing the need for giving commercial airtime generously so that UNCF receives the support it needs to send African American students to college and the importance of donating commercial time at the best hours of the day so that this worthy cause can be brought to the attention of all viewers.

5. As you compose this letter to television station managers, you need to think about ways of establishing credibility

with your audience. Which of the following ideas would be the best way to support your main idea?

a. Write enthusiastically, peppering the letter with a lot of excitement about the opportunity of airing commercials on this popular station.

b. Demonstrate your knowledge of television by using industry jargon throughout the letter.

c. Stress that both UNCF and television station management share similar beliefs about and attitudes toward the need for providing higher education for African American students.

d. Stress your sincerity and genuine interest in providing higher education for African American students.[10]

Questions for Discussion

1. When you must persuade your audience to take some action, are you being manipulative and unethical? Explain.
2. As a manager, how many of your daily tasks require persuasion? List as many as you can think of.
3. Are emotional appeals ethical? Why or why not?
4. Is it honest to use a hook before presenting your request? Explain.

5. Why is it important to maintain goodwill in your collection letter?
6. For over a year, you've tried repeatedly, without success, to collect $6,000 from a client who is able to pay but simply refuses. You're writing one last letter before turning the matter over to your attorney. What sorts of things can you say in your letter? What things should you avoid saying?

Documents for Analysis

Read Document 11.A; then (1) analyze the strengths and weaknesses of each sentence and (2) revise the document so that it follows this chapter's guidelines.

DOCUMENT 11.A

We have developed a revolutionary new fertilizer that can easily be applied to lawns to keep them green and weed free during the summer months with a minimum of effort. For just pennies, our trained experts will make weekly applications (in liquid form) of our fantastic fertilizer that kills weeds and strengthens the fibers of the roots. It works in both shady and sunny areas and particularly well in your climate zone!

Green-Gro works in any kind of climate and should not harm pets or birds. All you have to do is water your lawn and keep the grass cut, and we will do all the rest to ensure that you have a green lawn for the entire season! We look forward to having your business, and we trust that you'll want to purchase many of our other excellent lawn products.

Please fill out the enclosed coupon and avail yourself of the "early-bird discount" of 25 percent off the prices we regularly charge.

DOCUMENT 11.B

Find a direct-mail package containing a letter. Bring the package to class, along with answers to the following questions:

1. Who is the intended audience?
2. What are the demographic and psychographic characteristics of the intended audience?
3. What is the purpose of the direct-mail package? Has it been designed to obtain a sales lead, make a mail-order sale, obtain a charitable contribution, or do something else?
4. What kind of letter is included? Is it fully printed, printed with computer fill-in, or fully computer typed? Is the letter personalized? If so, how many times?
5. Did the writer use the AIDA plan? If not, explain how the letter is organized.
6. What needs are being appealed to?
7. What emotional appeals and logical arguments are given in the letter?
8. How many and what kinds of enclosures (supporting pieces such as brochures and order cards) are used?
9. What has been done to encourage you to open the envelope?
10. Is the message in the letter and on the supporting pieces believable? Would the letter sell the product to you?
11. What selling points and consumer benefits are offered?
12. Is an unusual format used? Are eye-catching graphics used?

Cases

WRITING PERSUASIVE REQUESTS FOR ACTION

1. Shape up: Letter offering wellness incentives at Johnson & Johnson As a human resources specialist at Johnson & Johnson, you've identified a costly problem related to employee health. Every time a worker calls in sick or comes to the office feeling lousy and unable to perform well, productivity slides and the company loses money—not just a little money but thousands of dollars each year.

To put a lid on the high cost of employee illness, Johnson & Johnson has decided against building another gymnasium or adding more low-cholesterol foods to the cafeteria menu (earlier tactics that haven't paid off so well). Its "Live for Life" wellness campaign offers incentives for achieving and maintaining good health. Even if the program ends up costing the company several hundred dollars per employee, your calculations indicate that it could save millions of dollars per year through reduced absenteeism and fewer health claims.

The Live for Life program targets several major contributors to poor health and accidents: smoking, drinking, lack of exercise, stress, high blood pressure, high cholesterol, excess weight, and neglecting to use automobile seat belts. Instead of rewarding results (which can be temporary), the company will reward the process, thus encouraging employees to develop new habits that should keep them healthier, happier, and more productive over the long term.

For example, every employee who exercises an average of four hours per week for a month will earn 30 Live for Life dollars—play money exchangeable for merchandise like sweatshirts, sweatsocks, or health club memberships. A blood pressure or cholesterol check is worth 5 Live for Life dollars, and a talk with the children about drug and alcohol abuse is worth 10. Always wearing a seat belt when driving or riding in a car brings a reward of 25 Live for Life dollars. For all nonsmokers, Johnson & Johnson will reduce employees' health insurance co-payment rates by 5 percent.

To implement the reward system, the company plans to accept all claims employees make about their wellness efforts. After all, getting people to think about health may get them to do something about it.

Your Task: Write a letter introducing Live for Life and persuading workers to participate in the new wellness campaign.[11]

2. Charity begins with breakfast: Memo urging Kellogg's U.S. division to adopt a new marketing approach From your vantage point as a marketing executive at the Kellogg company's headquarters in Battle Creek, Michigan, your Canadian colleagues have just come up with a whopper of an idea for launching a new product without costly advertising or market testing. Kellogg Canada has linked Nutrific (a cereal that flopped in the United States) with a philanthropic campaign to raise funds for cancer research. For every box of the wheat-flake cereal sold, Kellogg Canada donates 50 cents to the Canadian Cancer Society and the Canadian Breast Cancer Foundation. The sales target is 1.2 million boxes, which would raise more than half a million dollars for breast cancer education and research.

What intrigues you about Kellogg Canada's approach is not only the new formula for the cereal (wheat instead of barley) but also the cost-effective way Nutrific is being introduced to the Canadian market. In addition to saving the usual up-front promotional investment, Kellogg Canada is not paying any fees to the handful of retailers who control the Canadian supermarket industry (known as listing allowances in Canada and slotting fees in the United States). Instead, the new brand appears in supermarkets in special promotional displays announcing the breast cancer fund-raising link. Best of all, the campaign appeals to the concerns of women, your major buyers. Launching a new cereal this way is saving Kellogg Canada millions of dollars.

You want to try a similar campaign in the United States on a three-month trial basis: If Nutrific sells well, the Canadians will announce their intention to keep producing the brand. If not, the company's investment will have been minimal, and two worthy charities will have received much-needed support. Your idea is to develop a new cereal specifically for a promotion to raise funds for the American Cancer Society (as opposed to Kellogg's traditional practice of linking promotions to its classic brands).

Your Task: Draft a memo persuading your superiors to adopt Kellogg Canada's marketing campaign in the United States.[12]

3. Avon calling—again: Memo urging improved relations with sales representatives Avon Products built its business on personalized, door-to-door cosmetics sales, immortalizing the image of the "Avon Lady" who came calling with her catalog and her samples in an era when many women had the luxury of staying at home. Over the past two decades, a succession of top managers has tried to help the direct-sales company keep up with the social changes that are eroding sales to its major customers: women. The company has survived, but many sales representatives were lost as corporate survival strategies cut into the reps' commissions and benefits.

The "Avon Ladies" were bypassed altogether by a $34 million direct-mail advertising campaign promoting toll-free numbers for direct Avon purchases. Management reduced the value of the trips, prizes, and commissions Avon's reps could earn. Then the company eliminated the top sellers' awards of birthday gifts and porcelain statuettes of the first Avon Lady (Mrs. P. F. E. Albee). The sales force was in an uproar. Many Avon representatives simply stopped selling, and that had an impact on Avon's bottom line. By working 14-hour days at the kitchen table, some top representatives have brought in as much as $500,000 each in gross annual sales. It's not unusual for a representative to sell some $33,000 worth of cosmetics every year.

Now Christina A. Gold, formerly head of Avon's Canadian division, is the first woman to be appointed division head for the United States, Canada, and Puerto Rico (representing about 40 percent of the $4 billion company). One of Gold's primary tasks is to reenergize Avon's sales force. She plans to restore the 10 to 50 percent commissions, to reinstate all the prizes and benefits (including the "Mrs. Albees"), and to put the "heart and soul" back into the corporate culture. She also wants this year's "Avon Representative Day" celebrated with style and is asking managers to handwrite personalized thank-you notes to every representative.

Your Task: As Gold's assistant, you've been asked to write a memo, for her signature, urging U.S., Canadian, and Puerto Rican district managers to get back to treating local sales representatives like the special assets they are. Most important, your memo must convince managers to handwrite their thank-you notes for delivery before March 19.[13]

4. Thanks-A-Bunch: Letter asking for continued funding At Thanks-A-Bunch flower shop in Chula Vista, California, former psychiatric patients can learn the skills—and regain the confidence—to reenter the workaday world. In a little over a dozen years, more than 400 people have successfully "graduated" from the innovative program. Once day-treatment patients suffering from hallucinations, these individuals are now functioning normally, thanks to the right psychotropic drugs rectifying certain chemical imbalances. However, functioning normally and rejoining society are sometimes two different matters. That's where Thanks-A-Bunch can help.

At the flower shop, the former patients become trainees, handling all the tasks necessary to operate the retail business. They assemble flowers, truck them to delivery sites, and handle cash sales. The trainees earn minimum wages—but the chance to work in a "safe environment" (where no one pushes too hard or demands too much) is priceless. "They won't get fired if they screw up," explains program director Nina Garcia.

Unfortunately, support from local businesses, who buy most of the shop's flower arrangements, isn't enough to pay for the costly program, so the shop depends on additional funding from San Diego County Mental Health Services (CMHS). Now, even though Thanks-A-Bunch has been used as a model for developing other rehabilitation centers throughout the county (breakfast cafés, furniture stores, ceramics shops, and bakeries), it's being threatened by county budget cuts. Garcia has received news that Thanks-A-Bunch may be targeted for elimination as the county board of su-

pervisors weighs alternatives for stretching dwindling government funds.

Your Task: Garcia spotted the business communication course you listed on your résumé and has asked you, her assistant, to write a strong letter to Collins Munns, regional director for San Diego County Mental Health Services (1700 Pacific Highway, San Diego, CA 92186). You must convince him that Thanks-A-Bunch deserves to survive the impending budget cuts.[14]

5. Safety first: Memo pressing for a new security system at Hertz After all the headlines about tourists who got lost in unsavory neighborhoods while driving rental cars and wound up being robbed—or worse—your customers at Hertz Rent A Car are pretty jittery. Police say thieves target vacationers because they're likely to be carrying large sums of money or valuables. Driving a rental car is like waving a big flag that says "tourist." To help solve the problem, some states have stopped issuing distinctive license plates for rental cars, but as vice president at Hertz international headquarters, you realize that's not enough to calm your customers and ensure their safety. An executive group has already met to discuss the problem, and you've been looking into the latest developments in auto security.

Nynex has just developed a new security system that combines cellular telephone technology with the navigational aid offered by the Pentagon's Global Positioning System satellite network. For Hertz, it could work like this: A driver uses the cellular phone to call a Hertz service operator, making voice contact while a small transmitter sends a signal to the Hertz office indicating the car's location—accurate to within a few feet. The Hertz operator's computer matches the car signal with radio signals transmitted from the Pentagon satellites and, through triangulation, the computer pinpoints exactly where the driver is located. The car's position appears on a computerized map so detailed that the Hertz operator can advise customers about speed limits, one-way streets, and nearby services such as automated teller machines, 24-hour pharmacies, and convenience markets.

Nynex plans eventually to market the navigation and security system to the general public (with its own offices providing the operator service), but the current system seems ideal for the rental car industry. In fact, you're not the first to discover it. Your source at Nynex says Avis has already run a successful trial on 30 cars based at New York's La Guardia Airport.

Your Task: Write a memo to your executive colleagues, describing the new Nynex system and urging a trial run.[15]

6. We hate it: Letter demanding removal of Health Club Television from New York's Vertical Club When you finally shelled out for a membership at the Vertical Club, the priciest gym in Manhattan, the only thought on your mind was its testimony to your financial success—and the chance that you might bump into Brooke Shields one day. Now you're staring at something you never dreamed could happen to such a classy place.

Across from your Stairmaster, an evil glow disrupts your rhythm with its relentless flicker. Obnoxious voices hawking yogurt and soap are booming from the ugly box, with a few brief interludes in which well-known sports celebrities are interviewd by unknown reporters. Yes—it's a television screen, right here in your upscale, color-coordinated, sweat-smelling environs, blaring out the Health Club Television Network (HCTN). It has no knobs, no remote control, no way for you or any of your fellow exercisers to shut the darn thing off. You'd heard these things were coming to doctors' waiting rooms and to supermarket checkout lines, and now it's here in your exclusive heatlh club.

Everyone at the Vertical Club is complaining about the 24-hour channel. To smooth things over, management tried circulating a polite memo advising all members that the installation of the television sets (two in each room) was a test-run for the new satellite service. According to the memo, HCTN claims that 80 percent of consumers love the idea of being able to watch TV while they exercise, and the sets were free, installed by HCTN as a "bonus" for Vertical Club members. The memo made no mention of the fact that 30 percent of the channel's programming consists of commercials, sold to advertisers at a high rate because viewers are virtually captive. Rather than calming the rumbling in the locker room, the memo made members angrier. You and the rest of the Thursday afternoon regulars had no trouble gathering 400 signatures on a petition demanding that the sets be removed.

Members plan to send a cover letter echoing the petition's demands to top management at Bally's Health & Tennis Corporation, which owns the Vertical Club. A copy of both petition and letter will also go to executives at the Health Club Television Network. Moreover, every advertiser spotted on the channel will receive a copy of the petition, with a special letter informing them that club members are boycotting their products. In addition, your group of regulars hopes to catch the media's interest with a press release headed "Vertical Club Members Held Captive." (Fortunately, the whole campaign is being funded by the Vertical Club's wealthy membership; your efforts won't stop until the television screens are history. It has become a matter of principle among you.)

Your Task: Impressed by your offhand remark that the Vertical Club was becoming "a commercial police state," your fellow regulars have decided you're the right person to formulate the letter to Bally's Health & Tennis Corporation, demanding removal of the TV sets. The address is 7755 Center Avenue, Huntington Beach, CA 92647.[16]

7. The real "Doc Hollywood" stands up: Letter urging lower fees Down in the swampy, piney regions of southern Georgia, folks who could never before afford a doctor's care are being treated by a network of practitioners who have de-

cided that helping people is more important than making $180,000 a year.

One young graduate, Dr. James Hotz, became the subject of a film, *Doc Hollywood*, starring Michael J. Fox. The cardiologist-to-be had agreed to spend two years in urban Athens, Georgia, before going off to earn his fortune. While en route, Hotz and his wife were literally hijacked by car and driven 200 miles south to rural Leesburg. The townspeople were desperate for a doctor; like many small towns in the area, they hadn't had one for over a decade. The entire community turned out to cajole Hotz with a home-cooked chicken dinner. He stayed.

Eventually, Hotz brought in eight other doctors and set up a revolutionary system for providing low-cost (sometimes free) health care for indigent patients: Doctors in three counties agree to keep their fees about 25 percent lower than normal, and Phoebe-Putney Memorial Hospital in Albany treats patients whether they can pay or not (all of Hotz's doctors serve on the board of directors). The founder of Coca-Cola, who owns a nearby plantation, built a $1 million medical clinic for Hotz, and most specialists have agreed to perform for free such costly procedures as bypass surgery or cancer therapy when patients can't afford them.

To help defray the cost of the free services, Hotz applies for federal grant monies. He also gets $250,000 worth of free drugs through special programs set up by drug companies. Most important to area residents, however, is the fact that doctors are actually available—for both rich and poor.

You met Dr. Hotz recently while visiting relatives in nearby Putney. He's a genius at marshaling support for his style of people-friendly medicine, and when he heard you were a business student, he put you right to work. It seems a new doctor has moved into the Albany area and is charging fees better suited to big-city practices. The newcomer, Dr. Albert Reed, hasn't yet discovered that doctors in Hotz's loose network won't be referring patients to him or that the only hospital in the area (Phoebe-Putney) won't let him work there unless he adopts the team spirit that has made health care in southern Georgia affordable for one and all.

Your Task: Dr. Hotz wants you to compose a letter to Dr. Reed, 25 Franklin Rd., Newton, GA 31770, explaining the situation and persuading him to lower his fees.[17]

8. Welcome to capitalism: Memo persuading General Electric's Hungarian managers to think "quality" When General Electric purchased a controlling share of Tungsram in Budapest, Hungary, the U.S. manufacturer underestimated the effect of 40 years of communism on the factory's 18,000 employees. *Profit* had become an evil word to them.

As executive vice president of GE Lighting in Cleveland, you've just received a fax from David Gadra, one of your managers sent to establish Tungsram's first information systems department. Gadra is introducing 500 new computer terminals and a retraining program for Tungsram employees, but he's having trouble teaching Hungarian managers to think like capitalists.

When asked to brainstorm about a problem, the managers are terrific at relating the details of what went wrong, including a thorough analysis of the current situation. However, they never speak up with proposed solutions; under the communist system, creative thinking and initiative were discouraged. He's also having trouble explaining the need for producing quality products. Hungarian workers are used to standing in line for hours for the basic necessities of life, and they are grateful to find goods of any quality.

Gadra asks you for a memo of support and encouragement from GE's U.S. division to present at an upcoming "Business Made Easy" seminar. He thinks such a memo might spark enthusiasm for quality-mindedness. The Hungarians are eager to adapt to capitalism but are thoroughly baffled by the way GE conducts business. His seminar will encourage employees "to win, not just to exist" and to feel free to express their ideas and opinions, even if they aren't complimentary. He'll discuss the concepts of reward for effort, quality, innovation, and enthusiasm, with personal and corporate pride as a major benefit and profit as the ultimate goal. Gadra wants to make it clear to workers that the company's strength will mean future pay raises and possibly new jobs for family and community. One of his greatest challenges will be to overcome the Hungarians' skepticism, another carryover from years of false promises.

Your Task: Write a persuasive memo reinforcing the points Gadra mentions and emphasizing the need for quality. Address your remarks to all Tungsram employees.[18]

WRITING SALES LETTERS

9. Pepsi Max: Sales letter announcing a new product Diet sodas have always been sluggish sellers in foreign markets. Outside the United States, men have traditionally rejected diet sodas as wimpy drinks made for women, dieters, or sick people. But PepsiCo has developed a new strategy: Pepsi Max.

The new diet soda uses a combination of aspartame and acesulfame-K (a new sugar substitute not yet approved for U.S. distribution) to achieve a sweeter, stronger flavor than traditional diet drinks have. Moreover, the advertising campaign for Pepsi Max will feature images of brash young men doing things like snowboarding off mountain cliffs, with the slogan "Live Life to the Max." Even the name was chosen because of its "bold masculinity."

At PepsiCo's headquarters in Purchase, New York, Chris Sinclair (head of PepsiCo's international food and beverage division) and Mark Blecher (international marketing director) believe the new diet soda will open up an entirely new market by appealing to young men (age 16–29) outside the United States. Test marketing in the United Kingdom has already indicated that more men than women bought the new soda and that sales of Pepsi's other products held steady. That means Pepsi Max really did bring in new male customers, just

as Blecher and Sinclair had hoped. Pepsi already faces some competition: Coca-Cola has launched Tab X-Tra in Norway. So the company plans to make Pepsi Max available in all overseas markets by the end of the year. Blecher turns to you, his assistant, and hands you a news release.

"Here are the basic facts," Blecher says. "I think you'll find everything you need to put together a sales letter we can send to our retailers in Europe, the South Pacific, Asia, and Latin America. Just get it started," Blecher adds. "We'll worry about separate versions later."

Your Task: Write a basic sales letter that can be adapted for different cultures and translations.[19]

10. All natural: Letter promoting crystal Deodorant Stones of America When Larry Morris, owner of Deodorant Stones of America (DSA), first walked into your advertising office and placed what looked like a large piece of rock salt in your hand, proclaiming that this product could make Arrid, Dial, Ban, and all the others obsolete, all you could do was stare at the thing. You couldn't imagine how this clear, hard rock could keep anyone's underarms sweet-smelling. In the first place, what were you supposed to do with it? Wear it around your neck? You looked at Morris with a skeptical squint—was this some new "crystal healing" device?

But Morris smiled patiently and sat down to explain his new product. The only ingredients are mineral salts, used for centuries in Thailand to get rid of body odors by destroying the skin bacteria that cause the unpleasant smells. The stones contain no perfumes, preservatives, oils, emulsifiers, alcohol, propellants, or harsh chemicals. The naturally occurring minerals (potassium, alum, ammonium, barium, calcium, iron, magnesium, manganese, phosphorus, silicon, sodium, strontium, and titanium) are crystallized over a period of several months, then hand-shaped and smoothed for rubbing over the skin. When either the skin or stone is wet, an invisible layer of the mineral salts stick to the skin but won't stain clothing or clog pores. Morris says the minerals kill odor-causing bacteria so thoroughly that the stones are 300 percent more effective than conventional chemical deodorants.

DSA now sells about 7 million stones annually, in 50 states and 7 countries, under several brand names: Fresh Foot (Foot Deodorant Stone), The Jock's Rock (World Class Deodorant), Nature's Crystal (Body Deodorant), Thai Deodorant Stone, and Pure & Natural (push-up sticks and spray). Morris wants to expand, and he's hired you to write an all-purpose sales letter directed to both consumers and retailers.

Your Task: You've tried the stone and signed the contract. You especially liked the facts that it gave off absolutely no odor at all and worked for a full 24 hours. Write the sales letter for one or all of the product names listed above.[20]

11. Power pioneers: Sales letter touting ONSI's fuel cells If you can turn water (H_2O) into hydrogen and oxygen by running an electrical current through it (electrolysis), can you produce an electrical current by combining hydrogen and oxygen? A British lawyer, Sir William Robert Grove, proved in 1839 that it could be done, producing the world's first electricity-generating "fuel cell." However, until now, no one could produce a commercially viable version of Grove's invention.

The simple device is somewhat like a battery, producing an electrical current through an electrochemical reaction. However, it's also like a combustion or turbine engine, continuing to operate as long as it's supplied with fuel (some form of hydrogen and oxygen). Best of all, the fuel cell's only by-product emissions are water, heat, and if certain fuels are used, carbon dioxide.

Analysts predict that two decades from now fuel cells will account for 15 percent of growth in the global power-producing industry. So far, ONSI Corporation is the only company to reach the marketplace with fuel cells that can be used for large-scale power generation. Since you signed on several months ago as a marketing representative, ONSI has sold 57 of its 200-kilowatt fuel cells to hospitals, hotels, office buildings, and research centers in the United States, Europe, and Asia. Southern California Gas Company is using ten of them, cutting their energy costs by 5 to 40 percent annually.

ONSI's phosphoric-acid cells are rated 85 percent efficient if, in addition to the electrical current, the heat they generate is captured to produce hot water. The unit is about 12 feet tall by 24 feet long and costs $600,000—twice the price of a gas turbine generator of comparable power output. However, it's highly reliable, producing enough electricity to power a 30-unit apartment building. Moreover, it emits less than one-hundredth of the nitrogen oxide pollutants and only 75 percent of the carbon dioxide produced by a fossil-fuel power plant. Such emissions more than meet the pollution-control standards mandated by many governments—a bonus that makes the cells attractive despite their high price tag.

Your Task: Write a brief introductory sales letter touting the benefits of fuel cells for large institutions. Plan to enclose a separate brochure with detailed technical information about ONSI's phosphoric-acid fuel cells.[21]

12. Did you forget?: Polite reminder from Schneider Trucking With its sophisticated use of information technology, Schneider Trucking in Green Bay, Wisconsin, has been outperforming its competitors by increasing business by 20 percent every year. Plenty of investors want to buy a share of Schneider Trucking, now that they've seen what can happen when you successfully pair state-of-the-art computer technology with skilled drivers (whose CB radios were long ago replaced by laptop computers linked to the company via satellite). But CEO Don Schneider isn't interested in selling the company his father built from a single truck.

However, he is interested in keeping up with accounts receivable. The top-drawer computer system that tracks drivers' traveling speeds, hours on the road, exact locations, and estimated arrival times not only assigns them new loads based on a correlation of this computer data with customers' requirements but also keeps excellent track of the company's billing system. With a 9,000-truck fleet and some $1.25 billion in revenue to manage, there's no room for sloppy collections.

That's one reason your department (accounts receivable) is constantly striving to improve customer relations. Periodically, staff members are asked to come up with better form letters that will maintain customer goodwill and also prod sluggish accounts. Your supervisor has just asked you to take another look at the company's standard reminder letter, which is usually sent 33 days after an invoice is mailed (3 days after the payment is due).

Your Task: Your supervisor is right; the letter is a little too abrasive. Write a new form letter reminding customers of their overdue bill.[22]

13. Please pay: Inquiry from Noonan Design about Sidewalk Sergeant billing Marilyn Noonan's little boys, Conor, Ryley, Charlie, and Patrick (ages 3 through 8) loved to play in the cul-de-sac outside the family home. But their mother worried about the cars that came screeching down the La Jolla street. "Children believe that cars can stop instantly," Noonan explains, adding that traffic accidents are the number-one cause of death for children her sons' ages.

Of necessity, Noonan invented a mother's helper: Sidewalk Sergeant, a bright orange traffic safety cone with the bold letters "Children Playing" beneath a cartoon of a police officer blowing a whistle and holding his hand up in a halt signal. She put them up as a warning sign to drivers around the children's play area. Inevitably, other parents saw the cones, and before long Noonan was taking orders and searching for a manufacturer. Now her company, Noonan Design, is selling the Sidewalk Sergeant to both large and small toy retailers. However, one of the smaller retailers is giving Noonan some trouble.

"Can you help me with this?" she greets you one Thursday morning, the day you usually spend at Noonan Design as a freelance bookkeeper. She hands you a file on More Toys, a new account in Muncie, Indiana, for which credit was approved. They bought 50 of the 28-inch cones (which retail for $25) and 25 of the 18-inch cones ($13 retail). The first invoice went out 120 days ago, but the small retailer hasn't sent a dime. As you go over the paperwork, you see that with a 40 percent wholesale discount, the company owes $945 for the cones plus $159.75 for shipping and insurance.

Your Task: Since no one from Noonan Design has contacted More Toys yet, you suggest the "polite inquiry" approach—followed by stronger communications if necessary. Draft the first letter to show Noonan what you mean. Address it to her original contact: Bruce Vinchot, Manager, More Toys, 1473 Sedalia Avenue, Muncie, IN 47305.[23]

14. Last chance: Ultimatum from Rancho San Diego Vision Care Center You don't know why Jennifer Buzzell stopped sending monthly payments—she had always been so conscientious. During her last office visit with Dr. Barbara Bytomski at Rancho San Diego Vision Care Center, Ms. Buzzell received her new contact lenses and signed a written promise for you (the office manager) stating that she would pay her total bill of $485 in monthly payments of $35 each.

For six months, she sent the payments as agreed. Then, for the next five months, you received no money from Ms. Buzzell, despite regular bills and several letters from you. Three weeks ago, you tried a phone call but reached only an answering machine. You left a message asking Ms. Buzzell to contact you immediately, and you have received no response at all. Although it's standard office procedure to turn all nonpaying accounts over to a collection agency after six months, you want to try sending one more letter.

Your Task: Write one last letter to Jennifer Buzzell, 2385 Charles Street, La Mesa, CA 91941.[24]

Planning Short Reports · Organizing Short Reports · Making Reports and Proposals Readable

REPORTS AND

ports · Defining the Problem · Outlining Issues for Investigation · Preparing the Work Plan

PROPOSALS

search · Analyzing and Interpreting Data · Preparing the Final Outline · Report Production

Chapter 12
Writing Short Reports

Chapter 13
Planning Long Reports

Chapter 14
Writing Long Reports

After studying this chapter, you will be able to

Identify the qualities of good business reports and proposals

Choose the proper format and length for your report

Decide when to use direct versus indirect order

Organize informational and analytical reports

Establish an appropriate degree of formality in a report

Use headings, lists, transitions, openings, and summaries to guide readers through the report

WRITING SHORT REPORTS

On the Job

FACING A COMMUNICATION DILEMMA AT FEDERAL EXPRESS

Delivering On Time, Every Time

Imagine collecting, transporting, and delivering more than 1.5 million letters and packages every day. Now imagine that every one of these parcels absolutely, positively has to arrive at its destination when expected. That's the standard against which Federal Express managers—and customers—measure performance. Living up to this exacting standard, day in and day out, presents founder and CEO Frederick W. Smith and his entire management team with a variety of communication challenges.

When Federal Express began operation in 1973, its services covered 22 U.S. cities. Today it delivers throughout the United States and to 186 countries around the world. It also has a growing business managing international parts and parcel distribution for global companies such as National Semiconductor (which makes computer chips) and Laura Ashley (which designs and retails fashions and home furnishings). So that it can deliver on time, every time, Federal Express employs more than 90,000 people, operates nearly 500 airplanes, and maintains a fleet of 28,000 trucks and vans.

However, keeping packages in motion and customers happy is only part of the challenge. Federal Express must also battle a host of rivals, including United Parcel Service (UPS), the U.S. Postal Service, Airborne Express, DHL International, and other delivery companies. Competition is fierce, and Federal Express can't afford to let down its guard for an instant. For example, Federal Express uses teams (made up of employees from billing, quality control, and other departments) to find and fix problems that cross departmental boundaries (such as incorrect bills and lost packages).

In short, Smith and his management team have their work cut out for them. Monitoring and controlling the Federal Express operation, training new employees, making a host of decisions—all these activities require the communication of timely, accurate information. To keep the business running smoothly, maintain satisfied customers, and hold competitors at bay, Federal Express managers receive and prepare reports of all kinds. How can Smith and his managers use reports for internal communication? How can writers make their reports readable? What makes one report better than another?[1]

WHAT MAKES A GOOD REPORT

Business reports are like bridges spanning time and space. Organizations such as Federal Express use them to provide a formal, verifiable link among people, places, and times. Some reports are needed for internal communication; others are vehicles for corresponding with outsiders. Some are required as a permanent record; others are needed to solve an immediate problem or to answer a passing question. Many move upward through the chain of command to help managers monitor the various units in the organization; some move downward to explain management decisions to lower-level employees responsible for day-to-day operations.

Federal Express

Reports are essentially a management tool. Even the most capable managers must often rely on other people to observe events or collect information for them. Like Frederick Smith, managers are usually too far away to oversee everything themselves, and they don't have enough time. In addition, they often lack the specialized background required to research and evaluate certain subjects. So reports are usually for management or on its behalf.

You may be surprised at the variety of documents that qualify as reports. The word *report* covers everything from preprinted forms to brief, informal letters and memos to formal three-volume manuscripts. Some reports are even delivered orally, as Chapter 18 explains. In general, however, when businesspeople speak of **reports,** they are thinking of written, factual accounts that objectively communicate information about some aspect of the business. Although business reports serve hundreds of purposes, six basic uses are common (see Table 12.1).

The goal in developing a report is to make the information as clear and convenient as possible. Because time is precious, you tell your readers what they need to know— no more, no less—and you present your information in a way that's geared to their needs. Although reports vary widely in purpose and often in the audience they're written for, all good reports have at least three things in common: (1) The information is accurate, (2) the content shows the writer's good judgment, and (3) the format, style, and organization respond to the reader's needs.

Make business reports as concise as possible.

Accuracy

The first thing a business report writer must learn is how to tell the truth. If Frederick Smith received information that was inaccurate or incomplete, any decisions he based on it would be bad ones. As a result, Federal Express would suffer and so would Smith's reputation. Unfortunately, telling the truth is not always a simple matter. We all see reality a little differently and describe it in a unique way. The following guidelines help limit the distortions introduced by differences in perception:

To ensure accuracy,
- Check the facts
- Reduce distortion

Table 12.1   **THE SIX MOST COMMON USES OF REPORTS**

Purpose of Report	*Common Examples*	*Preparation and Distribution*	*Features*
To monitor and control operations	Plans, operating reports, personal activity reports	Internal reports move upward on a recurring basis; external reports go to selected audiences.	**Format:** Standard memo or preprinted form **Style:** Telegraphic **Organization:** Topical **Order:** Direct
To implement policies and procedures	Lasting guidelines, position papers	Internal reports move downward on a nonrecurring basis.	**Format:** Matches policies and procedures manual **Style:** Fully developed text **Organization:** Topical **Order:** Direct
To comply with regulatory requirements	Reports for IRS, SEC, EEOC, Revenue Canada, Canadian Human Rights Commission, and other industry regulators	External reports are sent on a recurring basis.	**Format:** Standardized; perhaps preprinted form **Style:** Skeletal **Organization:** To follow reader's instructions **Order:** Direct
To obtain new business or funding	Sales proposals	External reports are sent on a nonrecurring basis.	**Format:** Letter or manuscript **Style:** Fully developed text **Organization:** Problem-solution **Order:** Commonly direct
To document client work	Interim progress reports, final reports	External reports are sent on a nonrecurring basis.	**Format:** Letter or manuscript **Style:** Fully developed text **Organization:** Around sequential steps or key findings **Order:** Usually direct
To guide decisions	Research reports, justification reports, troubleshooting reports	Internal reports move upward on a nonrecurring basis.	**Format:** Memo or manuscript **Style:** Fully developed text **Organization:** Around conclusions or logical arguments **Order:** Direct or indirect

- *Describe facts or events in concrete terms.* It's better to say "Sales have increased from $400,000 to $435,000 in the past two months" rather than "Sales have skyrocketed." Indicate quantities whenever you can. Be specific.
- *Report all the relevant facts.* Regardless of whether these facts will support your theories or please your readers, they are included. Omitting the details that undermine your position might be convenient, but it isn't accurate. Readers will be misled if you hesitate to be the bearer of bad news and leave out unpleasant information.
- *Put the facts in perspective.* If you tell readers "The value of the stock has doubled in three weeks," you are giving only a partial picture. They will have a much clearer understanding if you say "The value of the stock has doubled in three weeks, rising

from $2 to $4 per share on the rumor of a potential merger." Taken out of context, even the most concrete facts can be misleading.

- *Give plenty of evidence for your conclusions.* You can't expect readers to fully understand your conclusions unless you offer substantial supporting evidence. Statements like "We have to reorganize the sales force or we're bound to lose market share" may or may not be true. Readers have no way of knowing unless you provide enough data to support your claim.
- *Present only objective evidence and verifiable conclusions.* Of course, your facts and figures must be checked, and your sources must be reliable. In addition, try to avoid drawing conclusions from too little information. Just because one sales rep reports that customers are dissatisfied with your product doesn't mean that all customers are dissatisfied. Also, don't assume that a preceding event is the cause of what follows. The fact that sales declined right after you switched advertising agencies doesn't necessarily mean that the new agency is to blame. Other factors may be responsible, such as the general state of the economy.
- *Keep your personal biases in check.* Even if you have strong feelings about the subject of your report, try to keep those feelings from influencing your choice of words. Don't say "Locating a plant in Kraymore is a terrible idea. The people there are mostly students, they'd rather play than work, and they don't have the ability to operate our machines." Such language not only offends but also obscures the facts and provokes emotional responses.

Good Judgment

Some things simply don't belong in a report, whether or not they are true. You can harm both yourself and your employer by being indiscreet. Of course, it's unethical to cover up any wrongdoing. In addition, be prepared to back up in a court of law whatever you write. Business documents are frequently used as evidence in legal proceedings.

Do not include anything in a report that might jeopardize you or your organization.

Also be aware that managers have distinct preferences when it comes to reports. They particularly dislike personal gripes, criticism, alibis, attempts to blame someone else, incomplete or sugarcoated data, unsolicited opinions, and attempts to bypass the manager when distributing the document. On the other hand, they like five things:[2]

Keep "politics" out of your reports; provide a clear, direct accounting of the facts.

- Getting the main idea at the beginning of the report
- Seeing the facts
- Receiving the whole story
- Reading language they can understand
- Learning something that will make their jobs easier

It's fair to say that all readers, not just managers, will appreciate your attention to these points.

Regardless of what type of report you're preparing, try to keep the likes and dislikes of your readers in mind. As you make decisions about the content, the needs of your audience are your main concern, so exercise your best judgment when trying to meet those needs.

Responsive Format, Style, and Organization

Before you write, decide (1) whether to use letter, memo, or manuscript format (see Appendix B for details); (2) whether to group the ideas one way or another; and (3) whether to employ a formal or an informal style. All these decisions revolve around

Select a format, a style, and an organization that reflect the reader's needs.

*B*EHIND THE SCENES AT THE SAN DIEGO ZOO
Even Tapirs Leave a Paper Trail

When zoo curator Rick Barongi flew to Panama to rescue six wild Baird's tapirs, he probably wasn't thinking about the report he'd have to write at the end of his adventure. Left to starve at the ranch of deposed dictator Manuel Noriega, the long-nosed mammals (distant relatives of horses and rhinos) were in the care of people who regard these endangered animals as creatures to be hunted for food.

Barongi made four trips to Noriega's government-seized estate, and for the last one, he organized an international team of zoo experts to accompany him. They saved five of the tapirs, and they helped educate local officials about the special care needed by such endangered animals in captivity.

After braving touchy politics, hair-raising traffic, and tropical heat (not to mention the razor-sharp canine teeth of unhappy 300-pound tapirs), Barongi returned home to his regular job as children's zoo director at the San Diego Zoo, and he promptly turned out an eight-page activity report on "The Panama Tapir Project." Writing reports is as much a part of Barongi's working life as making sure the baby monkeys that live in the nursery beneath his office are diapered and fed properly by their keepers. As director of the children's zoo, he's responsible for a million-dollar budget, a staff of 20 keepers, and a collection of domestic and exotic animals larger than many entire zoos. To manage both people and animals successfully, Barongi writes a lot of memo and letter reports.

Barongi explains that when obtaining new animals for the children's zoo, he usually sends a memo report to all departments affected by the animals' arrival. For example, when he acquired a colony of naked mole rats,

---

the reader's needs. When thinking about these issues, ask yourself the following questions and tailor the report accordingly:

When making decisions about the format, style, and organization of a report, consider its

- Origin
- Subject
- Timing
- Distribution
- Purpose
- Probable reception

- *Who initiated the report?* **Voluntary reports,** which are prepared on your own initiative, require more detail and support than **authorized reports,** which are prepared at the request of another person. When writing a voluntary report, you give more background on the subject and explain your purpose more carefully.
- *What subject does the report cover?* The subject of a business report affects its vocabulary and format. For example, audit reports (which verify an accountant's inspection of a firm's financial records) contain a lot of numbers, often in the form of tables. Reports from the legal department (perhaps on the company's patents) contain many legal terms. When you and your readers are familiar with the subject and share the same background, you don't need to define terms or explain basic concepts.
- *When is the report prepared?* **Routine reports** are submitted on a recurring basis (daily, weekly, monthly, quarterly, annually) and require less introductory and transitional material than do **special reports,** nonrecurring reports that deal with unique situations. Routine reports are often prepared on preprinted forms or using computerized formats (either of which the writer simply fills in), or they're simply organized in a standard way.
- *Where is the report being sent?* **Internal reports** (used within the organization) are generally less formal than **external reports** (sent to people outside the organization). Many internal reports, especially those under ten pages, are written in memo format. External reports, on the other hand, may be in letter format (if they are no longer than five pages) or in manuscript format (if they exceed five pages).
- *Why is the report being prepared?* **Informational reports** focus on facts; **analytical reports** include analysis, interpretation, conclusions, and recommendations.

"a bizarre rodent from Africa," Barongi's superiors were concerned about the cost of building the rodents' new exhibit/home. So Barongi's first memo report about these animals was written to justify that cost. Later, he organized information about the rats in a direct format for subsequent short reports to the zoo's veterinary hospital (reserving space for the mole rats' month-long quarantine) and to the public relations and photography departments (initiating publicity about the new residents). Barongi says he strives to keep such reports "really short—I don't want to be redundant." If people are interested, they'll call him for more background information.

But some of Barongi's reports require more thoroughness. His dream is to revamp and expand the children's section of San Diego's huge zoo, making it an interactive, state-of-the-art conservation learning experience that will be set in a simulated rain forest. Barongi is currently preparing a justification report to persuade the zoo's board of directors to raise funds for the project. He wants this preliminary report to be "short, colorful, and eye-catching," but he also wants to include enough supporting data to make the project seem feasible, exciting, and essential to the zoo's future.

The short report will draw on months of brainstorming by a zoo task force, set up by Barongi to plan a "children's zoo for the twenty-first century." It will be about ten pages, with watercolor illustrations to convey a feeling of the lush, tropical setting that Barongi and his colleagues envision. To save everyone's time, he will use the direct approach, opening with a plan for the zoo that will serve as an interactive learning center "not just for children, but for all age groups."

Apply Your Knowledge

1. If you were proposing a major renovation of a museum or a zoo exhibit area, would you use a direct approach or an indirect approach? Why?

2. How would Barongi's proposal for the new children's zoo differ if the idea had actually originated with the board of directors?

Informational reports are usually organized around subtopics; analytical reports are generally organized to highlight conclusions, recommendations, or reasons.

- *How receptive is the reader?* When the reader is likely to agree with the content of the report, the material is presented in direct order, starting with the main idea (key findings, conclusions, recommendations). If the reader may have reservations about the report, the material is presented in indirect order, starting with the details and leading to the main idea.

As you can see, the origin, subject, timing, distribution, purpose, and probable reception of a report have quite an impact on its format, style, and organization.

P LANNING SHORT REPORTS

When planning short reports, be sure to follow the report-writing customs your audience expects. The guidelines discussed here are for addressing U.S. and Canadian audiences having minimal cultural differences. In addition to your audience, also consider your purpose and subject matter. All three elements influence the format and length of your report, as well as its basic structure.

Deciding on Format and Length

Decisions about the format and length of your report may be made for you by the person who requests the document. If you are preparing a periodic status report, for example, you'll probably follow a standard pattern that enables the reader to quickly compare results from one reporting period to the next. Generally speaking, the more routine the report, the less flexibility you have in deciding on format and length.

Before writing complicated decisions, Supreme Court Justice Sandra Day O'Connor devotes considerable time to organizing her thoughts and developing a logical order for her arguments and opinions. She maintains that time spent in planning is never wasted.

When you do have some leeway about these issues, your decisions are based on your readers' needs. As Frederick Smith can attest, your goal is to tell members of your audience what they need to know in a format that's easy for them to use. When selecting a format for your report, you have four options:

You may present a report in one of four formats.

- *Preprinted form.* Basically for "fill-in-the-blank" reports, preprinted forms are relatively short (five or fewer pages) and deal with routine information, often mainly numerical. Use this format when it's requested by the person authorizing the report.
- *Letter.* For reports of five or fewer pages that are directed to outsiders, letter reports include all the normal parts of a letter, and they may also have headings, footnotes, tables, and figures.
- *Memo.* The most common format for short (fewer than ten pages) informal reports distributed within an organization, memos have headings at the top: *To, From, Date,* and *Subject.* In addition, like longer reports, memo reports often have internal headings and sometimes visual aids. Memos exceeding ten pages are sometimes referred to as memo reports to distinguish them from their shorter cousins. They also begin with the standard memo headings.
- *Manuscript.* For a formal approach, manuscripts range from a few pages to several hundred pages. As their length increases, reports in manuscript format require more elements both before the text of the report (prefatory parts) and after the text (supplementary parts). Chapter 14 explains these elements and includes a checklist for preparing formal reports.

Length depends on
- Subject
- Purpose
- Your relationship with the readers

The length of your report obviously depends on your subject and purpose, but it's also affected by your relationship with the readers. If they are relative strangers, if they are skeptical or hostile, or if the material is nonroutine or controversial, you usually have to explain your points in greater detail. Thus you end up with a longer document. You can afford to be brief if you are on familiar terms with your readers, if they are likely to agree with you, or if the information is routine or uncomplicated. Generally speaking, short reports are more common in business than long ones; you'll probably write many more 5-page memos than 250-page formal reports.

Establishing a Basic Structure

In addition to deciding on format and length, you have to decide on the basic structure of your report. This problem involves three issues:

Choice of structure involves three decisions:
- What to say?
- Direct or indirect order?
- Topical or logical organization?

- What information will you include? Will you cover all the facts at your disposal or eliminate some of the data?
- What psychological approach is best with your particular readers? Will you use direct order and lead off with the main idea (a summary of key findings, conclusions, or recommendations)? Or will you use indirect order and lay out the facts to gradually build toward the main idea?
- What method of subdivision will make your material both clear and convincing? Will you use a topical organization based on order of importance, sequence, chronology, location, spatial relationships, or categories? Or will you organize your ideas around logical arguments?

Key Points to Cover

If Frederick Smith asked you to write a report on the current status of Federal Express, what ideas would you include? When deciding on the content of your report, the first step is to put yourself in the audience's position. What major questions do you think

Your report should answer the audience's key questions.

your audience has about the subject? Your objective is to answer all those questions in the order that makes the most sense.

Your audience usually has one main question of greatest importance: "Why are we losing money?" "Is this a good investment?" "What will our sales and profits be over the next six months?" "What is the progress to date on the work assigned?" Whether it's one of these or another, define the main question as precisely as possible before formulating your answer. The main question is usually the reason you've been asked to write the report, and once you've defined it, you can sketch a general answer, based on the information available. Your answer, like the question, should be broad.

The next step is to determine what additional questions your audience is likely to ask based on your answer to the main question. Your answers to these questions will raise additional questions. As the chain of questions and answers is forged, the points multiply and become increasingly specific, as Figure 12.1 illustrates. When you've identified and answered all your audience's probable questions, you have defined the content of your report or presentation. The process is akin to outlining.

The question-and-answer chain clarifies the main idea of the report (your answer to the main question) and establishes the flow of ideas from the general to the specific. All effective reports and presentations are constructed this way, with a mix of broad concepts and specific details. When the mix is right, the message works: Members of the audience grasp both the general meaning and the practical implications of the ideas.

> Pursue the chain of questions and answers from the general to the specific.

Business communication tends to be concerned with details: facts, figures, and hard data. Routine, recurring messages are especially heavy on details; analytical, problem-solving messages are heavier on generalizations. In either case, the trick is to draw conclusions and generalizations out of all the information and relate them to your audience's needs. For every piece of information that you're tempted to include, ask why the audience needs it and how it relates to the main question.

Direct Versus Indirect Order

As Chapter 6 explains, audience attitude is the basis for decisions about organization. When the audience is considered either receptive or open-minded, use the direct approach: Emphasize your key findings, conclusions, and recommendations. This approach is most common for business reports because it enables readers to get the main

> The direct approach gives readers the main idea first, saving time and making the report easier to understand.

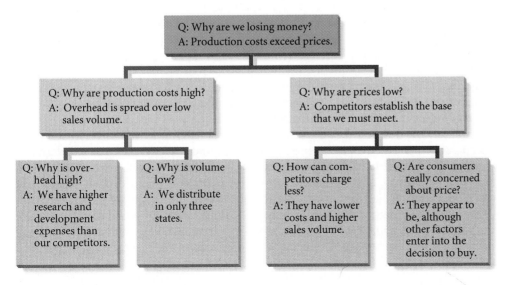

Figure 12.1
A Typical Question-and-Answer Chain

idea of the report at the outset, which saves time and makes the rest of the report easier to follow. For those who have questions or want more information, later parts of the report provide complete findings and supporting details. In addition to being more convenient for readers, the direct approach generally produces a more forceful report. You sound sure of yourself when you state your conclusions confidently at the outset.

However, confidence may sometimes be misconstrued as arrogance. If you're a junior member of a status-conscious organization or if your audience is skeptical or hostile, you may want to use indirect order—introducing the complete findings and supporting details before the conclusions and recommendations, which come last. The indirect approach gives you a chance to prove your points and gradually overcome your audience's reservations. By deferring the conclusions and recommendations, you imply that you have weighed the evidence objectively without prejudging the facts. You also imply that you're subordinating your judgment to that of the audience, whose members are capable of drawing their own conclusions when they have access to all the facts.

Although the indirect approach has its advantages, some report readers will always be in a hurry to get to "the answer," flipping immediately to the recommendations and defeating your purpose. For this reason, consider length when deciding whether to use direct or indirect order. Generally speaking, the longer the message, the less effective an indirect approach is likely to be. Furthermore, an indirect argument is harder to follow than a direct argument. In business, because both the direct and indirect approaches have merit, people often combine them, revealing their conclusions and recommendations as they go along, rather than putting them either first or last.

> *The indirect approach withholds the main idea until later in the report, helping overcome resistance.*

*O*RGANIZING SHORT REPORTS

Regardless of whether you use the direct or indirect approach in your report, you must still deal with the question of how your ideas will be subdivided and developed. The key is to decide first whether the purpose of the report is to provide chiefly information or analysis. From there, you can choose an organizational plan that suits your topic and goals.

Organizing Informational Memos and Reports

> *The purpose of informational reports is to explain.*

Informational reports have one basic purpose: explaining something in straightforward terms. They have hundreds of uses in business, including reports for monitoring and controlling operations, statements of policies and procedures, reports on the organization's compliance with government requirements, personal activity reports, and reports documenting client work.

> *Make clarity your main objective in informational reports.*

When writing informational reports, you don't usually have to worry too much about reader reaction. Because readers will presumably respond unemotionally to your material, you can present it in the most direct fashion possible. What you do need to be concerned about in informational reports is reader comprehension. The information must be presented logically and accurately so that readers will understand exactly what you mean and be able to use the information in a practical way.

When structuring an informational report, you can let the nature of whatever you're describing serve as the point of departure. For example, if you're reporting on the company's sales, you might present results for the country as a whole and then for each of the various geographic regions. If you're describing a machine, each component can correspond to a part of your report. If you're describing an event, you can approach the discussion chronologically, and if you're explaining how to do something, you can describe the steps in the process.

Some informational reports (especially compliance reports to government regulators and internal reports prepared on preprinted forms) are organized according to instructions supplied by the person requesting the information. In addition, many proposals conform to an outline specified in the request for proposal issued by the client (which might include a statement of the problem, some background, the scope of the work, any restrictions, the sources and methods used, a work schedule, the qualifications of personnel, a description of facilities, any anticipated costs, and the expected results).

Informational reports take many forms. The following two examples give you an idea of the typical organization and tone.

Even as successful as they've been with such movies as Flashdance, Beverly Hills Cop, *and* Top Gun, *Hollywood producers Don Simpson and Jerry Bruckheimer are emphatic about keeping costs in line. Their spending decisions are based on expense reports they receive daily. In such reports, insist Simpson and Bruckheimer, the information must be both accessible and accurate.*

Interim Progress Report

Interim progress reports give customers an idea of the work that has been accomplished to date. These reports naturally vary in length, depending on the period covered and the complexity of the contract. They are often keyed to the work plan that was established at the beginning of the contract. The writer tells the customer what tasks have been accomplished, identifies problems, and outlines future steps. Important findings are summarized. These reports are written for outsiders and are submitted over the life of the contract. As many as five or six progress reports are followed by a final report.

The style of such progress reports is more formal than that of internal reports. Progress reports need less attention to introductions and transitions than final reports, which are lasting records covering the contract. Interim progress reports are often written in letter format, and they tend to be brief. (Final reports are generally longer and often in manuscript format.)

When writing interim reports, be honest about problems as well as accomplishments. In fact, the bad news is probably more important than the good news, because problems require action whereas good news often does not. Use direct order, emphasizing what has been accomplished during the reporting period. Main headings correspond to the tasks performed. In the ending, outline plans for the coming period. For final reports, focus on results rather than progress.

The interim progress report excerpted in Figure 12.2 was prepared by Jill Rivers, vice president of engineering at Seabold. Rivers has this to say about progress reports: "Most of our projects require at least two kinds of documentation. The first kind, monthly letter reports, are fairly routine status reports that begin with a summary of events, followed by a discussion of any problems we're having. There's often an updated schedule as well. These reports range in length from 20 to 50 pages, and their contents are spelled out in the contract.

"The second kind of documentation we provide is to support major client review meetings. We usually have three of these meetings for each project, at the beginning, middle, and end of the contract. During these reviews key members of our team give overviews of their portion of the work. We use transparencies as a communication tool at the meetings, but we generally provide a large written report as well, which the customer can study at leisure."

Personal Activity Report

A personal activity report calls for an individual's description of what occurred during a conference, a convention, a trip, or other activity. It's intended to inform management of any important information or decisions that emerged during the activity.

Interim progress reports are nonrecurring reports that keep customers informed about the work that has been performed to date.

Progress reports must expose any problems that exist.

Personal activity reports are often in the form of brief memos and describe the facts and decisions that emerge during conventions, trips, and business meetings.

Figure 12.2
**Sample Interim Progress
Report (excerpt)**

SEABOLD ENGINEERING, INC.
5680 Ventura Boulevard
Los Angeles, CA 91601-2416

July 17, 1996

Mr. Jack Constable, City Manager
City of Santa Luisa Beach
2863 Calverra Street
Santa Luisa Beach, CA 92600

Dear Mr. Constable:

This report covers the work performed by Seabold Engineering on jetties
for Santa Luisa Beach from May 1 to June 31 under the terms of contract SLB-659-X15.

BACKGROUND RESEARCH

Historical analysis of the beach erosion problem is under way. The
Seabold project team has studied records dating back ten years to determine changes over time in the coastline of Santa Luisa Beach. In addition, city records and private property deeds for parcels along the coast
have been analyzed. Lifeguards and local residents have been interviewed, as well as oceanographers from the Scripps Institution of Ocean-
ography in La Jolla, California. The team has also reviewed newspaper
accounts describing coastal storms, inland development, and efforts to
halt sand erosion at Santa Luisa Beach.

Particular attention has been given to interviews with city officials responsible for previous efforts to deal with the erosion problem. Both
Carlos Zamora and Richard Barta of the city manager's office have been
extremely helpful in describing the effects of the Longard tube and the
transportation of sand from inland river beds.

OCEANOGRAPHIC RESEARCH

The project team is conducting oceanographic experiments to test the
direction and intensity of currents and tides and their effects on

Personal activity reports are ordinarily written in memo format. Because they're
nonrecurring documents, they require more of an introduction than interim progress
reports. They're often organized chronologically, but some are organized around topics that reflect the reader's interests.

Figure 12.3 gives an example of a personal activity report organized by topic. It is
a conference report prepared by Chris Bowers, who is on the staff of a large housing-
development company. Says Bowers, "My boss sent me to the Manufactured Housing
Convention to find out whether we might be able to use factory-built houses to reduce our development costs. Because I knew my boss was mainly interested in learning about various kinds of factory-built housing, I went to the seminars that covered
the four main types. When I wrote my conference report, I devoted a section to each
one."

Figure 12.3
Sample Personal Activity Report

MEMO

TO: Gary Boone
FROM: Chris Bowers   *C.B.*
DATE: October 23, 1996
SUBJECT: Manufactured Housing Convention

My trip to the Manufactured Housing Convention, held October 16-20 in Miami, was extremely interesting. One clear point was made repeatedly by many speakers: Factory-built homes have the potential to transform the housing industry. By 1999, 37 percent of all new homes will be manufactured away from the development site, freeing the developer to concentrate on site acquisition, preparation, and marketing. The four main types of manufactured housing discussed at the convention are described below.

MOBILE HOMES

Design improvements and price advantages are both swelling demand for mobile homes. The new models are spacious and attractive--hard to distinguish from conventional site-built homes. In fact, more so-called mobile homes are never relocated once they are in place at their first site. With proper landscaping, they create an impression that is far better than the unattractive trailer camps of the 1940s. The attached brochures will give you an idea of how some of the new models look.

Sales of new mobile homes are growing at an annual rate of 6 percent and will reach 500,000 units per year by 1999. Currently, almost 50 percent of all new single-family homes priced at less than $80,000 are mobile homes. Buyers range from first-time homeowners to middle-income retirees.

MODULAR HOUSING

The main difference between modular and mobile homes is that modular homes must be trucked to their site, whereas mobile homes can be towed on their own chassis. Sales of new modular homes are increasing 7 percent per year and should total 120,000 units by 1999.

PANELIZED HOUSING

Panelized housing is assembled at the development site from large factory-built components, such as walls, floors, and roofs. The developer has the option of using the components in various configurations. Shipments are increasing at an annual rate of 8 percent and will reach 175,000 units by 1999.

PRECUT HOUSING

People who want to build their own homes or act as their own general contractor can now buy precut but unassembled components packaged in kit form. This market has traditionally been dominated by mail-order firms featuring log cabins, geodesic domes, and A-frames, but a few manufacturers are currently trying to gear their packages to the development market. Sales are beginning to pick up. Shipments are growing by 6 percent annually and will reach 42,000 units by 1999.

Organizing Analytical Reports

Analytical reports differ from informational reports in their purpose and thus in their organization. Informational reports are mainly intended to educate readers. Analytical reports are designed to persuade readers to accept certain conclusions or recommendations; they include justification reports, research reports, client proposals, and troubleshooting reports. In informational reports, the information alone is the focus of attention. In analytical reports, the information plays a supporting role. The facts are a means to an end rather than an end in themselves.

Analytical reports are generally written to respond to special circumstances. They go by various names, but no matter what you call them, they all have one thing in common: They are designed to guide the reader toward a decision. Suppose you wanted

The purpose of an analytical report is to convince the reader that the conclusions and recommendations developed in the text are valid.

to convince Frederick Smith that new employees need more intense training. You would write an analytical report.

Regardless of which type of analytical report you're writing, organize your ideas so that they will convince readers of the soundness of your thinking. Your choice of a specific approach is based on your estimate of the readers' probable reactions: direct if you think they are likely to agree with you, indirect if you think they will resist your message. If you use the direct approach, you can base the structure of the report on your conclusions and recommendations, using them as the main points of your outline. If you use an indirect approach, your organization can reflect the thinking process that will lead readers to your conclusions.

Justification Report

Justification reports are internal proposals used to persuade top management to approve an investment or a project. The justification report shown in Figure 12.4 pro-

Figure 12.4
Sample Justification Report

MEMO

TO: Marshall Boswell, Plant Manager

FROM: Raymond Verdugo, Manufacturing Engineering RV

DATE: August 4, 1996

SUBJECT: Expansion of facial tissue production capacity

The steady increase in facial tissue sales is making it more difficult to keep our inventory levels where they should be for efficient distribution. Our back-order situation has become worse in recent months, and the marketing department is complaining about it. The new plant won't be ready until next March, so we can't expect any relief for at least ten months.

I've studied the product flow on our three facial tissue lines, and I believe we can increase capacity 22 percent by taking two short-term measures that do not require a significant investment:

1. Speed up cut-off machine on #1 line to eliminate bottleneck.
2. Eliminate the green, pine-scented tissue product.

SPEED UP #1 CUT-OFF MACHINE

The bottleneck on #1 line is the old Evans cut-off machine. This unit runs at a speed of only 200 packs per minute. The rest of the #1 line can handle 300 packs per minute, as can line #2.

I propose to speed up the Evans machine by installing a 20-horsepower motor to replace the old 15-horsepower motor, by thickening the transfer bolts, and by replacing two cams. Stress analysis shows that the machine can then safely be run at 300 packs per minute. This change will give us 50 percent more output on line #1 at a cost of roughly $6,500 and one day's lost production.

ELIMINATE GREEN, PINE-SCENTED TISSUE

Eliminating the green, pine-scented tissue is a sensitive subject. I'm aware of your running battle with marketing on this, but I'd like to urge you to try once again to get them to kill this product. When we run it on line #3, we can operate at only 120 packs per minute because the tissue is weakened by the dye and pine perfume. The other colored tissues run on line #3 are capable of 200 packs per minute.

The green pine product constitutes only 4 percent of total tissue sales and, by marketing's own data, sells well only in Maine and northern Minnesota. I have to believe that those customers would buy one of our other colors if we pulled the green pine off the market. If you can swing this, I estimate that we can get another 9 percent out of line #3.

SUMMARY

I recommend the following steps:

1. Speed up #1 line cut-off machine; capital cost = $6,500; output increases from 200 to 300 packs/minute.
2. Eliminate green pine product on #3 line; cost = zero; output increases from 120 to 200 packs/minute.

vides a good example of the direct approach. It was written by Raymond Verdugo, director of manufacturing engineering at a paper products company in New Jersey. Verdugo was asked by top management to suggest ways to increase the company's production of facial tissue without making a heavy investment. Says Verdugo: "I must have looked at a dozen ways we could increase our output. When I wrote up the results, I thought about discussing all the options I'd evaluated, but then it occurred to me that management wasn't really interested in the ideas that wouldn't work. So I just talked about the two things we could do to increase capacity."

Note in Figure 12.4 how Verdugo uses recommendations to organize his discussion. This structure is extremely efficient because it focuses the reader's attention on what needs to be done. You can use a similar approach when you're asked to analyze a problem or an opportunity and draw conclusions, rather than provide recommendations. In such situations, the main headings of the report correspond to your conclusions rather than your recommendations.

New Business Proposal to an Outside Client

Proposals to outside clients are attempts to get products, plans, or projects accepted by outside businesses or government clients. The letter in Figure 12.5 also takes a relatively direct approach, but instead of being organized around conclusions or recommendations, it's organized around the statement of a problem and its solution—a common approach in proposals. This proposal was prepared by Lia Chung, who works for the Communication Skills Institute, an organization that trains businesspeople to write and speak more effectively.

This particular proposal was submitted to Arnold Hastings, the director of training and development for a rapidly growing management consulting firm that advises small to midsize companies on organizational issues. When writing the proposal, Chung was relatively sure of a positive response. As she says: "This particular proposal was pretty short because I knew that the prospective client would be receptive. We had already discussed the need for such a program and I had outlined our qualifications. The proposal was basically a follow-up to that conversation. However, some of the proposals I write are considerably longer and contain more background on why a program is needed, what the alternatives are, and why a particular choice is best.

"Regardless of their length, all of my proposals have one thing in common: They offer to solve a problem for a specific price. Every time I write one, I follow the same basic formula: (1) Here's the problem, (2) here's the solution, and (3) here's what it will cost."

Troubleshooting Report

Whenever a problem exists, someone must investigate it and propose a solution. A troubleshooting report is a decision-oriented document prepared for submission to top management. When you want your readers to concentrate on *why* your ideas make sense, your best bet is to let your logical arguments provide the structure for your report. The main points in your outline correspond to the reasons that underlie your conclusions and recommendations. You support each of these reasons with the evidence you have collected during your analysis.

Gary Johansen, executive assistant to the president of a diversified company, was asked to prepare a report analyzing the performance of the restaurant division. He was also asked to recommend what to do with it: continue the current course, sell off the chain, or remodel existing facilities and build new restaurants.

But Gary had a problem: "I knew that whatever I recommended would alienate somebody. My difficulties were compounded by the nature of the problem. I could have made a good case for any of the three options. But as an objective, neutral, and

Liz Claiborne attributes the success of her clothing designs to the reports prepared by her marketing department: reports that analyze sales figures, define women's roles and issues, identify trends, and communicate recommendations that can be translated into fashions. When writing such analytical reports, it is important to use the facts in a convincing way.

Proposals for obtaining new business typically define a problem and describe the proposed solution.

By using reasons as the main divisions in your outline, you can gradually build a case for your conclusions and recommendations.

Figure 12.5
Sample New Business
Proposal to an Outside
Client

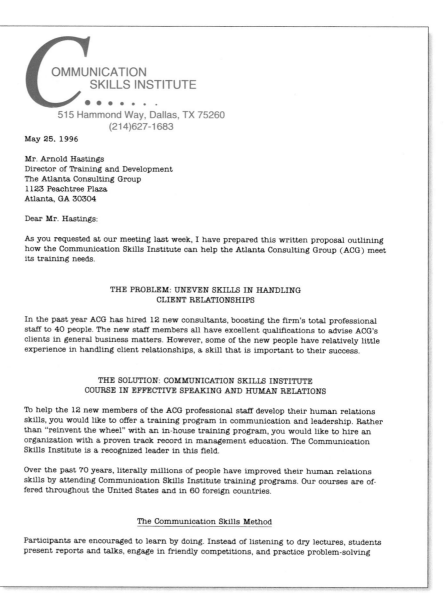

COMMUNICATION
SKILLS INSTITUTE

515 Hammond Way, Dallas, TX 75260
(214)627-1683

May 25, 1996

Mr. Arnold Hastings
Director of Training and Development
The Atlanta Consulting Group
1123 Peachtree Plaza
Atlanta, GA 30304

Dear Mr. Hastings:

As you requested at our meeting last week, I have prepared this written proposal outlining how the Communication Skills Institute can help the Atlanta Consulting Group (ACG) meet its training needs.

THE PROBLEM: UNEVEN SKILLS IN HANDLING
CLIENT RELATIONSHIPS

In the past year ACG has hired 12 new consultants, boosting the firm's total professional staff to 40 people. The new staff members all have excellent qualifications to advise ACG's clients in general business matters. However, some of the new people have relatively little experience in handling client relationships, a skill that is important to their success.

THE SOLUTION: COMMUNICATION SKILLS INSTITUTE
COURSE IN EFFECTIVE SPEAKING AND HUMAN RELATIONS

To help the 12 new members of the ACG professional staff develop their human relations skills, you would like to offer a training program in communication and leadership. Rather than "reinvent the wheel" with an in-house training program, you would like to hire an organization with a proven track record in management education. The Communication Skills Institute is a recognized leader in this field.

Over the past 70 years, literally millions of people have improved their human relations skills by attending Communication Skills Institute training programs. Our courses are offered throughout the United States and in 60 foreign countries.

The Communication Skills Method

Participants are encouraged to learn by doing. Instead of listening to dry lectures, students present reports and talks, engage in friendly competitions, and practice problem-solving

unbiased observer, I gradually came to a conclusion of my own: that we should sell some of the restaurants and use the proceeds to offset the cost of remodeling the remaining locations and adding new outlets. When writing my report, I decided that my strategy would be to build a case for this course of action by gradually presenting the various reasons that had emerged from my analysis of the options."

Figure 12.6 is a copy of Gary's report. His introduction does not reveal his position. Instead of summarizing his recommendations, he begins by discussing the report's purpose and scope, the background of the study, and his methods of research. In the body, he presents the facts in an objective tone, without revealing his own point of view. He saves his recommendations for the fourth section, where he finally adds up all the reasons.

Figure 12.5
(concluded)

and decision-making techniques. Applying the lessons in class reinforces the learning process and gives students constructive feedback from instructors.

Anticipated Results of the Program

The Communication Skills course in effective speaking and human relations is ideally suited to the needs of your consulting staff. This course is designed to enhance communication skills and help people develop their leadership potential. Your consultants will be taught how to get better results from meetings and how to gain the cooperation of clients. During the course, the participants will study and practice various techniques to improve their business and personal relationships. They will learn how to handle responsibility, work under pressure, and motivate themselves and others. At the conclusion of the program, they will be more confident and effective in their work.

Instructor's Qualifications

Communication Skills instructors are carefully chosen and well trained. Each is a successful professional with experience directly related to the course. To ensure that the courses are uniform in quality, all instructors undergo a rigorous training program and use the same proven methods and course materials. Your course would be taught by Melissa Steinberg, who has been a Communication Skills instructor for five years. She has a master's degree in psychology from New York University.

Course Scheduling and Costs

The Communication Skills course in effective speaking and human relations consists of 14 sessions, which last approximately 3-1/2 hours each. Classes will be held at your offices on Monday mornings from 9:00 to 12:30 for 14 consecutive weeks. The cost for 12 students will be $9,000.

CONCLUSION

If you have any questions about the course, I would be happy to answer them. You can reach me at my office during working hours by calling (555) 555-8976. I look forward to working with you on this interesting assignment.

Sincerely,

Lia Chung

Ms. Lia Chung
Director

Organizing an analytical report around a list of reasons that collectively support your main conclusions or recommendations is a natural approach to take. Many problems are solved this way, and readers tend to accept the gradual accumulation of evidence, even though they may question one or two points.

However, not every problem or reporting situation can be handled with this organizational plan. Some analytical reports are organized to highlight the pros and cons of a decision; others might be structured to compare two or more alternatives against a set of criteria. The best organizational approach in any given situation depends on the nature of the facts at your disposal. Essentially, you choose a structure that matches the reasoning process you used to solve the problem. The objective is to focus your reader's attention on the rationale for your conclusions and recommendations.

Figure 12.6
Sample Troubleshooting
Report

MEMO

TO: Alton Sanders, President
FROM: Gary Johansen, Executive Assistant to the President   G.J.
DATE: March 27, 1996
SUBJECT: Possibilities for the Restaurant Division

INTRODUCTION

This report was authorized by President Alton Sanders on January 11, 1996. Its purpose is to analyze the performance of our restaurant division and to recommend a course of action. The analysis does not include institutional food-service operations.

The first Gateway restaurant was opened over 25 years ago in Falls Church, Virginia. Initially, the chain consisted of moderately priced cafeteria-style restaurants located in the suburbs of Washington, D.C. Encouraged by the success of these operations, Gateway management gradually expanded the chain into surrounding states, moving first into the Middle Atlantic and New England areas, then into the Southeast. As the chain grew, the cafeteria format was modified. Although some sites still feature a self-serve buffet, most of the restaurants now provide table service and a complete breakfast, lunch, and dinner menu.

Historically, the restaurant division has been one of Gateway's strongest operations, providing approximately 20 percent of the corporation's sales and 26 percent of its profits for much of the past decade. However, in the past two years, the restaurant division's sales and profits have fallen below expectations. In an attempt to determine why, management has decided to take a closer look at the division's recent performance in light of trends in the restaurant industry as a whole. These issues are examined in the following sections. A final section analyzes the alternatives available to management and presents recommendations for the future.

In preparing this report, the study team analyzed internal data and reviewed published information pertaining to the restaurant industry. The team also analyzed demographic data furnished by the business development agencies of the 21 states in which Gateway restaurants are located. In addition, the team has interviewed over 50 restaurant owners and managers, politicians, civic leaders, and real estate professionals and has surveyed some 1,500 Gateway restaurant patrons.

RECENT PERFORMANCE OF THE RESTAURANT DIVISION

By historical standards, the restaurant division shows signs of slowing down. Instead of growing at the customary rate of 8 to 10 percent each year, the division's sales and profits have edged up by only 3 percent for the past two years (Figure 1). Despite this leveling off, restaurant operations still account for approximately 25 percent of the corporation's business (Figure 2). Restaurant division sales in the most recent fiscal year totaled $44 million, and profits were $3.9 million.

A closer look at the division's financial results suggests that two internal factors are involved in the restaurant division's relatively slow growth:

--In years past, the growth in sales and profits was fueled by the addition of new restaurants to the chain. However, in the past two years, only three new restaurants have been opened. This record is less than half the average annual rate of openings throughout the 1970s and most of the 1980s (Figure 3).

--Performance has been uneven. Sales have declined in the Middle Atlantic and New England states, where facilities are aging, but sales have increased in the Southeast, where most of the newer restaurants are located (Figure 4).

*M*AKING REPORTS AND PROPOSALS READABLE

When the time comes to write your report, you face the challenge of finding the most effective way to communicate your message to an audience. Decisions about formality and structure affect the way your message will be received and understood by readers.

Figure 12.6
(continued)

2

These facts suggest that the leveling off in the restaurant division's growth is at least partially attributable to a lack of investment in the chain's facilities rather than to a fundamental weakness in the chain itself. In fact, a survey of Gateway patrons underscores the restaurants' continued popularity. Offering moderate prices in a pleasant, family-oriented environment still has broad appeal. (See Appendix A.)

TRENDS IN THE RESTAURANT INDUSTRY

Although Gateway's restaurant division appears to be fundamentally sound, the flattening of its growth curve reflects a slowdown in the restaurant industry as a whole. The rate of sales growth for full-service restaurants has fallen from 5 percent in the early 1980s to roughly 1.1 percent today (Figure 5).[1]

Many analysts contend that this slowing growth reflects a subtle shift in consumer behavior. In the 1970s and 1980s, as more women joined the workforce, eating out became increasingly common, and restaurants sprang up to satisfy demand. In the past few years, however, the number of meals eaten in restaurants seems to have reached a plateau. Many people would rather pop a "gourmet" frozen dinner into the microwave and watch a movie on the VCR than pay restaurant prices.

Whatever the reasons, the leveling out of demand has left too many restaurants vying for too few patrons, a situation that spells trouble for many participants in the industry. Typically, when an industry has excess capacity, a shakeout period occurs; weaker companies fail and only the strong survive. Once the shakeout ends, the survivors generally enjoy a period of higher sales and profits.

If the restaurant industry follows the usual pattern, the small, independent restaurants will be most likely to fail. Larger chains can be expected to weather the shakeout because of their superior financial strength. Ultimately, the survivors will be the restaurants with the best locations and the most appealing combinations of food, price, atmosphere, and service.[2]

If a shakeout does occur, our restaurant division should be in a strong position, particularly in the Southeast. The division's facilities in this region are relatively new, and they are located in rapidly growing, affluent suburbs (Figure 6). Furthermore, Gateway patrons in the Southeast are particularly loyal, typically dining at a Gateway restaurant at least twice a month (Appendix A).

ANALYSIS OF ALTERNATIVES

Management is considering three alternatives for the restaurant division:
- Continue to operate the existing restaurants, but minimize the capital reinvested in the business.
- Sell off the chain.
- Upgrade the chain by remodeling older facilities and adding new sites.

The first alternative is certainly viable. Although sales and profits have leveled off, the restaurant division is still a major source of earnings. One could argue that by maintaining the status quo, Gateway can generate approximately $4 million per year in cash to reinvest in other businesses with higher growth potential. On the other hand, without additional investment the restaurant division is likely to experience a further erosion as its aging facilities become less and less appealing to patrons.

1. Steve Whitelaw, "Trends in the Restaurant Industry," speech delivered at the 1987 Western Restaurant Convention and Exposition, Los Angeles, California.
2. Conrad Hammond, "Recipes for Success in Restaurant Management," Restaurant News, December 1988, 24.

(*continued on next page*)

Choosing the Proper Degree of Formality

The issue of formality is closely related to considerations of format, length, and organization. If you know your readers reasonably well and if your memo or report is likely to meet with their approval, you can generally adopt an informal tone. In other words, you can speak to readers in the first person, referring to yourself as *I* and to your read-

Write informal reports in a personal style, using the pronouns *I* and *you*.

**Figure 12.6
(concluded)**

3

The alternative of selling off the division is somewhat more appealing from a financial standpoint. Instead of gradually pulling cash out of the restaurant operation until the business deteriorates, Gateway could sell its holdings immediately while the business is still performing well. The restaurant operation has a market value of approximately $40 million, a sum that would go a long way toward funding management's diversification program. But selling the operation would mean the loss of about a quarter of our sales and profits. Unless management can immediately acquire a business of similar size, this loss would have a severe impact.

The third alternative is to expand and upgrade the restaurant operation in an effort to restore its historical growth pattern. According to division management, such a program would require an investment of approximately $22 million over the next three years for remodeling 20 of the older restaurants and adding 9 new sites (Figure 7). This expansion could result in a 10 percent annual growth in sales and a 12 percent annual growth in profits over the next five years (Figure 8).

The key stumbling block to this alternative is the required allocation of $22 million in investment capital. In the company's most recent strategic plan, management committed itself to a program of diversification into new, higher-growth businesses. The lion's share of the firm's investment funds is being channeled into new areas, leaving very little for shoring up existing operations.

One possible solution would be to sell off several of the restaurant division's existing sites, then use the money to refurbish other locations and add new restaurants to the chain. Discussions with real estate professionals suggest that a number of Gateway's older restaurants are located on land that has appreciated greatly in value. Many of these sites were purchased in the early 1970s, when land values were considerably lower than they are today. These same sites tend to be Gateway's oldest, least attractive restaurants, where sales have slipped most dramatically. As Figure 9 illustrates, by selling off 7 of the chain's 80 restaurants, Gateway could raise approximately $12.6 million, which is over half the amount required to fund the remodeling and expansion program. The remaining $9.4 million could be obtained by reinvesting the division's annual earnings for three years. Although selling the 7 sites would initially reduce the division's sales and earnings, over a five-year period the loss would be more than offset by gains from new and remodeled locations (Figure 10).

SUMMARY

The restaurant division appears to be fundamentally sound. The fall-off in its sales and earnings growth is due largely to a reduction in the cash being reinvested in the business. Although the restaurant industry as a whole is maturing, strong chains like Gateway can expect to achieve continued growth in sales and profits as weaker operations fall by the wayside. By selling off some of its older, less appealing sites and using the cash to refurbish and expand the chain, the restaurant division can resume its historic growth pattern and continue to play a major role in the corporation.

ers as *you.* This informal, personal approach is often used in brief memo or letter reports, although there are many exceptions.

Longer reports dealing with controversial or complex information are traditionally handled in a more formal vein, particularly if the audience is a group of outsiders. You achieve this formal tone by using the impersonal style, eliminating all references to *you* and *I* (including *we, us,* and *our*). Borrowed from journalism, the style stresses the reporter's objectivity. However, avoiding personal pronouns may lead to overuse of such phrases as *there is* and *it is,* which are not only dull but also wordy.

Being formal means putting your readers at a distance and establishing an objective, businesslike relationship.

Even so, formality is more than a matter of personal pronouns; it's a question of your relationship with your audience. When you write in a formal style, you impose a certain distance between you and your readers. You remain businesslike, unemotional, and objective. You use no jokes, no similes or metaphors, and very few colorful adjectives or adverbs. You eliminate your own subjective opinions and perceptions and retain only the objective facts.

The formal style does not guarantee objectivity, however. When determining the fairness of a report, the selection of facts is far more important than the way they are phrased. If you omit crucial evidence, you are not being objective, even though you are using an impersonal style. In addition, you can easily destroy objectivity by exaggerating and by using overblown language: "The catastrophic collapse in sales, precipitated by cutthroat pricing on the part of predatory and unscrupulous rivals, has jeopardized the very survival of the once-soaring hot-air balloon division." This sentence has no personal references, but its objectivity is highly questionable.

Despite such drawbacks, the impersonal style is a well-entrenched tradition. Many readers are uncomfortable with informality in a report. They associate the personal tone with sloppy thinking, a lack of objectivity, and excessive familiarity. You can often tell what tone is appropriate for your readers by looking at other reports of a similar type in your company. If all the other reports on file are impersonal, adopt the same tone yourself, unless you're confident that your readers prefer a more personal style. Most organizations, for whatever reasons, expect an unobtrusive, impersonal writing style for business reports.

> Although the impersonal style has disadvantages, use it if your readers expect it.

For an example of the short but formal report, take another look at Figure 12.6. Because Johansen was dealing with an important and controversial issue, he wanted to give his report a formal tone. To achieve this effect, he used the third person and a manuscript format rather than a memo format. Although the text is only four pages long, the report also has several figures (not shown here), which add to the formality. The final copy includes a cover page and a table of contents that lists the figures as well as the major headings.

Developing Structural Clues

As you begin to write, remember that readers have no concept of how the various pieces of your report relate to one another. Because you have done the work and outlined the report, you have a sense of its wholeness, and you can see how each page fits into the overall structure. But readers see the report one page at a time. As you begin to write, your job is to give readers a preview or road map of the report's structure so that they can see how the parts of your argument relate to one another.

In a short report, readers are in little danger of getting lost. As the length of a report increases, however, so do the opportunities for readers to become confused and to lose track of the relationship among ideas. If you want readers to understand and accept your message, you must prevent this confusion. Four tools are particularly useful for giving readers a sense of the overall structure of your document and for keeping them on track as they read: the opening, headings and lists, smooth transitions, and the ending.

The Opening
A good opening accomplishes at least three things:

- Introduces the subject of the report
- Indicates why the subject is important
- Gives readers a preview of the main ideas and the order in which they'll be covered

In the opening, tell readers what to expect and orient them toward your organizational plan.

If you fail to provide readers with these clues to the structure of your report, they will read aimlessly and miss important points, much like drivers trying to find their way through a strange city without a map.

If your audience is skeptical, the opening should downplay the controversial aspects of your message while providing the necessary framework for understanding your report. Here's a good example of an indirect opening, taken from the introduction of a controversial memo on why a new line of luggage has failed to sell well. The writer's ultimate goal is to recommend a shift in marketing strategy.

The performance of the Venturer line can be improved. In the two years since its introduction, this product line has achieved a sales volume lower than we expected, resulting in a drain on the company's overall earnings. The purpose of this report is to review the luggage-buying habits of consumers in all markets where the Venturer line is sold so that we can determine where to put our marketing emphasis.

This paragraph quickly introduces the subject of the document (disappointing sales), tells why the problem is important (drain on earnings), and indicates the main points to be addressed in the body of the report (review of markets where the Venturer line is sold), without revealing what the conclusions and recommendations will be.

Headings and Lists

Use headings to give readers the gist of your report.

Phrase all same-level headings within a section in parallel terms.

A **heading** is a brief title at the start of a section within a report, alerting readers to the content of the section that follows. Headings are useful markers for clarifying the framework of a report. They visually indicate shifts from one idea to the next, and when both subheadings and headings are used, they help readers see the relationship between subordinate and main ideas. In addition, busy readers can quickly understand the gist of a document simply by scanning the headings.

Headings within a given section that are of the same level of importance are phrased in parallel form. In other words, if one heading begins with a verb, all same-level headings in that section will begin with verbs. If one is a noun phrase, all are noun phrases. Putting comparable ideas in similar terms tells readers that the ideas are related. The only exception might be such descriptive headings as "Introduction" at the beginning of a report and "Conclusions" and "Recommendations" at the end. Many companies specify a format for headings. If yours does, use that format. Otherwise, you can use the scheme shown in Figure 12.7.

A **list** is a series of words, names, or items arranged in a specific order. Setting off important ideas in a list provides an additional structural clue. Lists can show the sequence of ideas or visually heighten their impact. Like headings, list items should be phrased in parallel form.

Transitions

Such phrases as *to continue the analysis, on the other hand,* and *an additional concept* are another type of structural clue. These are examples of **transitions,** words and phrases that tie ideas together within a report and keep readers moving along the right track. Here is a list of some words and phrases frequently used to provide continuity between parts of sentences and paragraphs:

Additional detail   moreover, furthermore, in addition, besides, first, second, third, finally

As director of the Red Cross's risk-management division, Gregory L. Daniels gets reports generated by a computerized information system. However, it is his own communication style—his ability to articulate difficult concepts to a diverse audience—that has led to his success. One key to clarity, says Gregory, is to strengthen the connections among your ideas by using good transitions.

Figure 12.7
Heading Formats for Reports

<u>TITLE</u>

The title is centered at the top of the page, underlined, and typed in capital letters. When the title runs to more than one line, the lines should usually be double-spaced and arranged as an inverted pyramid (longer line on the top).

FIRST-LEVEL HEADING

A first-level heading should indicate what the following section is about, perhaps by describing the subdivisions. All first-level headings should be grammatically parallel, with the possible exception of such headings as "Introduction," "Conclusions," and "Recommendations." Some text should appear between every two headings, regardless of their levels.

<u>Second-Level Heading</u>

Like first-level headings, second-level headings should indicate what the following material is about. All second-level headings within a section should be grammatically parallel. Never use only one second-level heading under a first-level heading. (The same is true for every other level of heading.)

Third-Level Heading

A third-level heading should be worded to reflect the content of the material that follows. All third-level headings beneath a second-level heading should be grammatically parallel.

<u>Fourth-Level Heading</u>. Like all the other levels of heading, fourth-level headings should reflect the subject that will be developed. All fourth-level headings within a subsection should be parallel.

   <u>Fifth-level headings</u> are generally the lowest level of heading used. However, you can indicate further breakdowns in your ideas by using a list:

1. <u>The first item in a list</u>. You may indent the entire item in block format to set it off visually. Numbers are optional.
2. <u>The second item in a list</u>. All lists should have at least two items. An introductory phrase or sentence may be underlined for emphasis, as shown here.

Causal relationship	therefore, because, accordingly, thus, consequently, hence, as a result, so
Comparison	similarly, here again, likewise, in comparison, still
Contrast	yet, conversely, whereas, nevertheless, on the other hand, however, but, nonetheless
Condition	though, if
Illustration	for example, in particular, in this case, for instance
Time sequence	formerly, after, when, meanwhile, sometimes
Intensification	indeed, in fact, in any event
Summary	in brief, in short, to sum up
Repetition	that is, in other words, as has been stated

Use transitions consisting of a single word, a few words, or a whole paragraph to provide additional structural clues.

CHECKLIST FOR SHORT INFORMAL REPORTS

A. Format
1. For brief external reports, use letter format, including a title or a subject line (after the reader's address) that clearly states the subject of the document.
2. For brief internal reports, use memo or manuscript format.
3. Present all short informal reports with appropriate format and elements.
   - a. Single-space the text.
   - b. Double-space between paragraphs.
   - c. Use headings where helpful, but try not to use more than three levels of headings.
   - d. Call attention to significant information by setting it off visually with lists or indention.
   - e. Include visual aids to emphasize and clarify the text.

B. Opening
1. For short, routine memos, use the subject line of the memo form and the first sentence or two of the text as the introduction.
2. For all other short reports, cover topics in the introduction such as purpose, scope, background, restrictions in conducting the study, sources of information, methods of research, and organization of the report.
3. If using direct order, place conclusions and recommendations in the opening.

C. Body (Findings and Supporting Details)
1. Use direct order for informational reports to receptive readers, developing ideas around subtopics (for example, chronologically, geographically, categorically).

Although transitional words and phrases are useful, they are not sufficient in themselves to overcome poor organization. Your goal is to put your ideas in a strong framework and then use transitions to link them together even more strongly.

In longer reports, transitions that link major sections or chapters are often complete paragraphs that serve as mini-introductions to the next section. These paragraphs can also serve as summaries of the ideas presented in the section just ending. Here's an example:

Given the nature of this problem, the alternatives are limited. As the following section indicates, we can stop making the product, improve it, or continue with the current model. Each of these alternatives has advantages and disadvantages. The following section discusses the pros and cons of each of the three alternatives.

The Ending

Reemphasize your main ideas in the ending.

Research shows that the **ending,** the final section of a report, leaves a strong and lasting impression. Use the ending to emphasize the main objective of your message. In a report written in direct order, you may want to remind readers once again of your key points, conclusions, or recommendations. If your report is written in indirect order, end with a summary of key points (except in short memos). In analytical reports, end with conclusions and recommendations as well as key points. In general, the ending ties up all the pieces and reminds readers how those pieces fit together. It provides a final opportunity to emphasize the wholeness of your message. For a quick refresher in what's required for this sort of message, see this chapter's Checklist for Short, Informal Reports.

2. Use direct order for analytical reports to receptive readers, developing points around conclusions or recommendations.
3. Use indirect order for analytical reports to skeptical or hostile readers, developing points around logical arguments.
4. Use an appropriate writing style.
   a. Use an informal style (*I* and *you*) for letter and memo reports, unless company custom calls for more formality.
   b. Use an impersonal style for more formal short reports in manuscript form.
5. Give each paragraph a topic sentence.
6. Link paragraphs by using transitional words and phrases.
7. Strive for readability by using short sentences, concrete words, and terminology that is appropriate for your readers.
8. Be accurate, thorough, and impartial when presenting the material.
9. Avoid including irrelevant and unnecessary details.
10. Include documentation for all material quoted or paraphrased from secondary sources, using consistent format.

D. Ending
1. In informational reports, summarize major findings at the end, if you wish.
2. Summarize points in the same order in which they appear in the text.
3. In analytical reports using indirect order, list conclusions and recommendations at the end.
4. Be certain that conclusions and recommendations follow logically from facts you have presented in the text.
5. Consider using a list format for emphasis.
6. Avoid introducing new material in the summary, conclusions, or recommendations.

*O*n the Job

SOLVING A COMMUNICATION DILEMMA AT FEDERAL EXPRESS

Entrepreneur Frederick Smith was sure that his new transportation network would increase Federal Express's efficiency and decrease the cost of moving packages from state to state. He wanted to fly packages from around the country to a central hub in Memphis, where they would be sorted and flown to their final destinations. To raise money for this venture, Smith used business reports, and they have remained important through the years as he and his managers have built Federal Express into a global business with $8 billion in annual revenues.

For example, because of Federal Express's heavy orientation toward satisfying customers, the company has a strong emphasis on training. Because training costs money, reports are used to justify training expenditures. One of those expenditures might be for video equipment to support the company's interactive video training program. Of course, before managers buy video equipment, these items are thoroughly and objectively investigated and analyzed. Then managers can read through special, nonrecurring reports, study the justification for each major purchase, and weigh the pros and cons.

Reports are also important to the company's internal auditors, who are charged with studying how the company controls its finances, operations, and legal compliance. Internal auditors visit the departments they are assigned to examine,

conduct their investigations, and then write reports to communicate their findings and any ideas for improvement. The analytical reports that Federal Express's auditors prepare contain recommendations as well as conclusions.

The human resources and internal audit departments are only two of the many Federal Express departments that prepare and receive reports. As Frederick Smith and his managers strive against competitors, try to satisfy customers, and keep the business running smoothly, business reports are sure to continue to play a key role at Federal Express.

Your Mission: You have recently joined Federal Express as Frederick Smith's administrative assistant. Your job is to help him with a variety of special projects. During an average week, he might ask you to handle three or four assignments and then report back to him in writing. In each of the following situations, choose the best communication alternative from among those listed, and be prepared to explain why your choice is best.
1. To keep tabs on the industry, Smith has asked you to research the delivery guarantees and services offered by Federal Express's top three competitors. How should you introduce your report? Choose the best introduction from the four that follow.

a. Recognizing that Federal Express no longer has the overnight delivery business to itself, management has decided to examine the effect of delivery guarantees and services offered by other companies. Specifically, management wants to review two issues:

1. What delivery guarantees and services are offered by the top three competitors?

2. How can Federal Express use its own delivery guarantee and services to compete more effectively?

The following pages present the results of a two-week study of these questions.

b. Major changes are occurring in the overnight delivery business. Since UPS instituted its 10:30 a.m. on-time guarantee, most other carriers have adopted midmorning delivery guarantees as a way of meeting this competitive challenge. Such guarantees are important to customers who need documents and packages delivered as early in the day as possible. At the same time, the number of customers interested in saving money by choosing later delivery has been growing. For these customers, timely delivery is less important than cost-efficiency, prompting several competitors to introduce nonpriority delivery services.

Given the importance of delivery guarantees for time-sensitive customers and the need for less-costly alternatives to retain other customers, Federal Express can compete more effectively if it (1) publicizes its dependable, 100 percent on-time priority delivery guarantee more heavily and (2) introduces additional nonpriority delivery services for cost-sensitive customers. These conclusions are examined in detail in the following pages.

c. I am happy to report that Federal Express is still ahead of all competitors. However, I have to point out that our rivals are doing everything they can to keep up the pressure. The two-week study of competitors' delivery services that I recently conducted shows that UPS and others offer a variety of delivery guarantees that directly compete with our own offerings.

Let me stress that as much as 40 percent of Federal Express's revenues come from priority (10:30 a.m.) delivery services. Although this is obviously an important service, I want to emphasize that more and more customers are interested in saving money by ordering nonpriority delivery. Because of this trend, I want to present two recommendations that Federal Express might pursue.

d. Since Federal Express was founded more than 20 years ago, it has provided timely overnight delivery to customers who can't afford to wait for urgent documents or packages. On the first night of service, Federal Express handled just eight packages; today, the company handles more than 1.5 million packages every day. Although the volume of shipments has grown dramatically, the need for on-time delivery remains the same.

At the request of senior management, an examination of the delivery guarantees offered by competitors was conducted. The following pages present the findings of this study, which addressed the following questions:

1. What delivery guarantees and services do competitors offer?

2. How do Federal Express's services compare?

3. What challenges and opportunities do such delivery guarantees represent?

2. Smith has asked you to provide a brief overview of UPS, Airborne Express, and DHL Worldwide Express, all of which are important Federal Express competitors. This overview will be handed out at a stockholders' meeting in Memphis. Because stockholders are likely to know very little about the competition, Smith has asked you to write a brief informational memo on the subject. He wants you to cover the following points for each competitor: (1) annual sales, (2) number of employees, (3) names of top executives, and (4) main services. You have to write this immediately, so you'll just have to use whatever facts you can find. Which of the following versions is preferable?

a. The three companies in question, UPS, Airborne Express, and DHL Worldwide Express, are a mixed bag in terms of size. Their sales range from $11 billion (UPS) to under $2 billion (for DHL and Airborne Express).

Similarly, the number of employees varies from competitor to competitor. Airborne employs about 9,000 people, DHL employs about 20,000, and UPS employs more than 100,000.

Kent C. Nelson rose through the ranks to become the CEO of UPS. Patrick Foley was chairman of Hyatt Hotels and Braniff Airlines before joining DHL as CEO in 1988. Airborne is headed by CEO Robert Cline.

All four competitors offer domestic and international delivery. Although DHL offers delivery throughout the United States, it is better known for international delivery to 160 countries. In fact, the company handles more than 50 million international shipments every year. In contrast, only about one quarter of Airborne's deliveries are to overseas destinations. UPS went worldwide in 1985.

b. Federal Express's $8 billion in annual sales puts the company closer to the sales figures of UPS than to those of DHL Worldwide or Airborne Express. Similarly, Federal Express has more than 90,000 employees, which puts it closer in size to UPS than to either of the smaller rivals.

Federal Express's founder, Frederick Smith, has been CEO since he began the company more than 20 years ago. Kent C. Nelson is CEO of UPS, Patrick Foley is CEO of DHL, and Robert Cline is CEO of Airborne. All three competitors serve customers around the world as well as around the United States.

c. Here's the lowdown on the poor hapless souls that Federal Express will mow down in the next year:

-- UPS is the top dog of delivery services. It has annual sales of $11 billion and employs something like 100,000 people. Kent C. Nelson is the top banana here. We know that UPS delivers around the world, but we don't know how many countries it serves or how many packages it sends around the globe every year.

-- Airborne Express is teeny compared with UPS and Federal Express. Its sales are puny----just a little over $1 billion or so--and only 9,000 people work for the company. A lot less than half of Airborne's deliveries go to international destinations. Robert Cline is the head honcho.

-- DHL Worldwide's Patrick Foley has the arduous task of being CEO and competing with Federal Express's vastly superior services. Like Airborne, DHL's annual sales of less than $2 billion are anemic when compared with UPS and Federal Express. But it does have 20,000 workers toiling away at domestic and international deliveries.

d. Here are the annual sales, number of employees, names of top executives, and international presence of three of our competitors:

-- UPS is our largest competitor, with $11 billion in annual sales (compared to our own $8 billion in annual sales). UPS employs more than 100,000. The CEO is Kent C. Nelson. Since 1985, UPS has offered both domestic and international delivery service, but we don't have data on the number of global deliveries or the number of countries served.

-- DHL Worldwide has annual sales under $2 billion, and the number of employees is 20,000. CEO Patrick Foley was chairman of Hyatt Hotels and Braniff Airlines before joining DHL in 1988. Although DHL offers delivery throughout the United States, it is better known for international delivery to 160 countries. The company handles more than 50 million international shipments every year.

-- Airborne Express also has annual sales under $2 billion, and the company employs 9,000 people. Robert Cline is Airborne's CEO. Like the other three competitors, Airborne offers both domestic and international delivery, but only about one quarter of its deliveries are to overseas destinations.

3. Smith wants to celebrate Federal Express's twenty-fifth anniversary by creating a special advertising insert on the company's history. He wants to distribute this insert inside the April issue of a national business magazine. The magazine's publisher is excited about the concept and has asked Smith to send her "something in writing." Smith asks you to draft the proposal, which should be no more than ten pages long. Which of the following outlines should you use?

a. Version one:
   I. An overview of Federal Express's history
      A. How company was founded
      B. Overview of company services
      C. Overview of markets served
      D. Overview of transportation operations
   II. The Federal Express magazine insert
      A. Historic events to be included
      B. Employees to be interviewed
      C. Customers to be discussed
      D. Production schedule
   III. Pros and cons of Federal Express magazine insert
      A. Pros: Make money for magazine, draw new customers for Federal Express
      B. Cons: Costs, questionable audience interest

b. Version two:
   I. Introduction: Overview of the Federal Express special insert
      A. Purpose
      B. Content
      C. Timing
   II. Description of the insert
      A. Text
         1. Message from CEO
         2. History of Federal Express
         3. Interviews with employees
         4. Customer testimonials
      B. Advertising
         1. Inside front and back covers
         2. Color spreads
         3. Congratulatory ads placed by customers
   III. Next steps
   IV. Summary

c. Version three:
   Who: Federal Express
   What: Special magazine insert
   When: Inserted in April issue
   Where: Coordinated by magazine's editors

Why: To celebrate Federal Express's anniversary

How: Overview of content, production
responsibilities, and schedule

d. Version four:

   I. Introduction: The rationale for producing a magazine insert promoting Federal Express
   A. Insert would make money for magazine
   B. Insert would boost morale of Federal Express employees
   C. Insert would attract new customers

   II. Insert description
   A. Interview with founder Frederick Smith
   B. Interviews with employees
   C. Description of historic moments
   D. Interviews with customers
   E. Advertisements

   III. Production plan
   A. Project organization
   B. Timing and sequence of steps
   C. Federal Express's responsibilities
   D. Magazine's responsibilities

   IV. Detailed schedule
   V. Summary of benefits and responsibilities

4. Smith has asked you to think about ways of attracting new customers that need Federal Express's expertise in managing international parts and parcel distribution. You have talked with executives at Laura Ashley and National Semiconductor, two current customers, and discovered that they are most concerned about the time needed to process orders and deliver parts to stores or factories. Federal Express can cut the delivery time from as much as 21 days to as little as 4 days after ordering. You believe that an advertising campaign featuring testimonials from these two satisfied customers will give Federal Express a tremendous advantage over other competitors, who haven't yet developed a track record with large global companies. As a relatively junior person at Federal Express, you are a little apprehensive about suggesting your idea. You don't want to seem presumptuous, but on the other hand you think your idea is good. You have decided to raise the issue with Smith. Which of the following approaches is preferable?

a. Instead of writing a report, arrange a meeting to discuss your ideas with Smith, the advertising manager, and an executive from the company's advertising agency. This allows you to address the issues and ideas firsthand in an informal setting.

b. You write the following short report:

You recently asked me to give some thought to how Federal Express might attract new customers for its international parts distribution business. I decided to sound out two of our largest customers to get a feel for why they hired us to handle this operation. Interestingly, they didn't choose Federal Express because they wanted to reduce their shipping costs. Rather, they were interested

in reducing the time needed to process and ship orders to stores and factories.

Many companies are in the same situation as Laura Ashley and National Semiconductor. They're not looking for the carrier with the lowest prices, they're looking for the carrier with the proven ability to process orders and get shipments to their destinations as quickly as possible. Instead of waiting as long as 21 days for shipments to reach their destination, these companies can promise delivery in 4 days.

Clearly, our track record with Laura Ashley and National Semiconductor is the key to capturing the attention of other global companies. After all, how many competitors can show they have the ability to cut as much as 17 days off the time needed to process and deliver an order? Of course, companies might be skeptical if we made this claim on our own, but they would be more likely to accept it if our customers told their own stories. That's why Federal Express should ask executives from Laura Ashley and National Semiconductor to offer testimonials in an advertising campaign.

c. You write the following short report:

In response to your request, I have investigated ways in which Federal Express might attract new customers for its international parts distribution business. In conducting this investigation, I have talked with executives at two of our largest customers, Laura Ashley and National Semiconductor, and discussed the situation with our advertising manager and our advertising agency. All agreed that companies are interested in more than merely saving money on international shipments.

Typically, a global company has to keep a lot of parts or materials on hand and be ready to ship these whenever a store or factory places an order. As soon as an order arrives, the company packages the parts and ships it out. The store or factory doesn't want to wait a long time because it, in turn, has to keep a lot of money tied up in parts to be sure it doesn't run out before the new shipment arrives. Thus, if the company can cut the time between ordering and delivery, it will save its stores or factories a lot of money and, at the same time, build a lot of customer loyalty.

As a result, shipping costs are less important than the need to process orders and get shipments to their destinations as quickly as possible. Instead of delivery in 21 days, these companies can promise deliveries in 4 days. If we can show global companies how to do this, we will attract many more customers.

d. You write the following short report:

This report was authorized by Frederick W. Smith on May 7. Its purpose is to analyze ways of attracting more customers to Federal Express's international parts distribution business.

Laura Ashley and National Semiconductor are two large, global companies that use our international parts distribution service. Both companies are pleased with our ability to cut the time between ordering and parts delivery. Both are willing to give testimonials to that effect.

These testimonials will help attract new customers if they are used in newspaper, magazine, and television advertising. A company is more likely to believe a satisfied customer than someone who works for Federal Express. If the advertising department and the advertising agency start working on this idea today, it could be implemented within two months.[3]

Questions for Discussion

1. If a report is pushing toward a specific recommendation, should the writer include information that might support a different recommendation? Why or why not?
2. What would you do if your boss asked you to alter or destroy a report that might be used as evidence in legal proceedings?
3. How do you explain the fact that so many kinds of documents qualify as reports? What makes them all reports?
4. What are the advantages and disadvantages of the direct and the indirect approaches?
5. Why do some companies require an impersonal tone in their reports? What are the advantages and disadvantages of such a tone?
6. How can a writer help readers understand the structure of a report?

Exercises

1. Team up with a classmate to research one of the following topics. Working together, plan an analytical report focusing on your conclusions. Write out the main idea, and draft an informative outline with first- and second-level headings.
   a. Trends in SAT scores for high school students in your town, city, or state
   b. The number of businesses that are formed and that fail in your local area
   c. Fluctuations in the number of students enrolled in your college each semester
2. Select one of the following topics and plan an analytical report focusing on your recommendations. Develop the main idea, and draft an informative outline with first- and second-level headings.
   a. How to reduce the amount of electricity consumed by your college
   b. How to prepare your home for a weather problem (hurricane or snowstorm)
   c. How to reduce the cost of car insurance
3. Obtain the annual report of any public corporation. Read through the management report made by the president, chief executive officer, or chairperson. Outline this report and indicate whether it's in direct or indirect order. Why do you think the direct or indirect order was chosen? Does the opening explain the report's structure and indicate the importance of the information? How well does the ending pull all the details together?
4. Team up with a classmate to practice writing informative openings. For the analytical report you outlined in exercise 2, draft an opening that tells what the report covers, explains why the subject is important, and previews the main ideas and the order in which ideas will be presented. Swap with your teammate and critique each other's opening section. Does each give sufficient clues to the structure of the report? How can these openings be improved?
5. Team up with a classmate to practice writing emphatic and informative endings. For the analytical report you outlined in exercise 2, draft an ending that includes conclusions, recommendations, and key points. Swap with your teammate and compare each ending with the Checklist for Short Informal Reports. How well does each ending communicate the main points and the overall message? How can these endings be improved?
6. Attend the next meeting of the college's student government and take notes on what occurs. Then write a brief (two-page) personal activity report on that meeting, using the memo format. Think about what your audience, the other students in your business communication class, will want to know about the issues discussed and conclusions reached during that meeting. What key question should you answer in this report?

Cases

1. My progress to date: Progress report on your academic career As you know, the bureaucratic process involved in getting a degree or certificate is nearly as challenging as any course you could take.

Your Task: Prepare a progress report detailing the steps you've taken toward completing your graduation or certification requirements. After examining the requirements listed in your college catalog, indicate a realistic schedule for completing those that remain. In addition to course requirements, include such steps as completing the residency requirement, filing necessary papers, and paying necessary fees. Use letter format for your report, and address it to anyone who is helping or encouraging you through school.

2. Gavel to gavel: Personal report of a meeting Meetings, conferences, and conventions abound in the academic world, and you have probably attended your share.

Your Task: Prepare a report on a meeting, convention, or conference that you have recently attended. Use memo format, and direct the report to other students in your field who were not able to attend.

3. Expanding operations: Justification report for business expansion Consider a job that you now hold or have held in the past. Imagine an expansion of the company's business, possibly the addition of a new product line or new services (for example, adding brake repairs to a shop that currently only replaces mufflers).

Your Task: Develop a budget for the enlarged operation, considering personnel, equipment, space, and possibly inventory. Next write a report explaining your concept, describing the major budget items, and briefly predicting the future benefits that this expansion will bring. Write your report in memo format to the owner or manager of the business.

4. Selling something special: Proposal to a business Pick a company or business that you know something about. Now think of a customized item or service that you believe the business needs. Examples might be a specially designed piece of equipment, a workshop for employees on improving their communication skills, a program for curtailing shoplifting, a catering service to a company's construction site, or a customized word-processing system, to name just a few possibilities.

Your Task: Write a proposal to the owners or managers of this business. Convince them that they need the product

you're selling. Include a statement of the problem, purpose (benefits), scope (areas in which your product will help the business), methods and procedures, work plan and schedule, your qualifications, projected costs, and any other pertinent information. Use letter format.

5. Restaurant review: Report on a restaurant's food and operations Visit any restaurant, possibly your school cafeteria. The workers and fellow customers will assume that you are an ordinary customer, but you are really a spy for the owner.

Your Task: After your visit write a short memo to the owner, explaining (a) what you did and what you observed, (b) any violations of policy that you observed, and (c) your recommendations for improvement. The first part of your report (what you did and what you observed) will be the longest. Include a description of the premises, inside and out. Tell how long the various steps of ordering and receiving your meal took. Describe the service and food thoroughly. You are interested in both the good and bad aspects of the establishment's decor, service, and food. For the second section (violations of policy), use some common sense. If all the servers but one have their hair covered, you may assume that policy requires hair to be covered; a dirty window or restroom obviously violates policy. The last section (recommendations for improvement) involves professional judgment. What management actions will improve the restaurant?

6. Pumping up gasoline sales: Report on suggested advertising approaches Gasoline advertising is heating up in Brazil, where Esso, Shell, Atlantic-Arco, Texaco, and Ipiranga compete with Petrobras, the state-owned monopoly. All are in a race to increase their share of Brazil's 5-billion-liter gasoline products market. However, Brazilian drivers know that Petrobras actually produces and refines the gasoline that everyone of its competitors sells. What differentiates one brand from another are the additives the oil companies put into their individual formulations. Esso's advertising in Brazil is handled by the ad agency J. Walter Thompson. Knowing that rivals put a variety of ingredients into their formulations, the agency recommends that Esso use a new advertising approach: Alert drivers to the differences among brands and warn them to look closely at the quality of the gasoline they use.

Your Task: As the J. Walter Thompson manager assigned to the Esso account, draft a one-page memo to Esso's managers in which you justify your agency's recommendation. Use your contact's first name, Don, and your own first name in the memo heading. Explain why you believe Esso should adopt this new advertising approach, discuss the main benefit you see in using this approach, and summarize your position.[4]

7. Preparing for the worst: Report on crisis management When the anonymous call came in, Campbell Soup officials refused to take any chances. The caller claimed to have put poison in Campbell's tomato juice cans at a New England supermarket. The company quickly decided to yank the product from 84 area stores. Even though the call turned out to be a hoax, Campbell Soup believes it's best to be prepared for the worst. Moreover, an important part of any crisis management plan is the way company officials tell the public about the situation.

Your Task: You're a public relations consultant with special expertise in crisis management. You've been asked to recommend how and when Campbell Soup should reveal any threats and the steps that have been taken in response. In addition, you want to suggest ways of reassuring consumers that Campbell Soup products are pure and completely safe. Draft the outline for an impersonal but informal analytical report

to CEO David W. Johnson that includes your recommendations and the justifications for those recommendations. Be sure the headings you choose show what your report will cover, including the need for action, the benefits to be achieved, the list of recommendations (without details), and a summary.[5]

8. Fishing for more revenue: Report for a nonprofit organization The Historic Fishing Village of Puget Sound has asked you to determine why revenues have been lower than expected and to suggest how to improve revenues. You've found two probable causes for the low revenue: (1) unusually bad weather during prime tourism periods and (2) shoddy, inexpensive merchandise in the gift shop.

Your Task: Draft a two-page troubleshooting report to present to the nonprofit organization's trustees. Make up whatever details you need about the merchandise and about ways to improve revenues. Bear in mind that the trustees originally approved the purchase of merchandise for the gift shop, so you'll want to use objective language to avoid offending them.

After studying this chapter, you will be able to

Define the problem to be solved by studying and outlining the issues to be analyzed

Identify and outline the issues that have to be analyzed during your study

Prepare a work plan for conducting the investigation, planning the necessary steps, estimating their timing, and deciding on the sources of information required

Organize the research phase of the investigation, including the identification of secondary and primary sources of data

Draw sound conclusions and develop practical recommendations

Develop a final outline and visual aid plan for the report

PLANNING LONG REPORTS

n the Job

FACING A COMMUNICATION DILEMMA
AT HARLEY-DAVIDSON

Staying on the Road to Higher Sales

When Japanese companies began selling heavyweight motorcycles in the United States in the early 1970s, Harley-Davidson remained calm. The Milwaukee company controlled 99.7 percent of the market and saw no reason to panic. After all, if your customers love your product so much that they tattoo your logo on their chests, can't you count on their loyalty?

The company was mistaken. The Harley was no longer the superb machine it once had been. It leaked oil, vibrated wildly, and broke down frequently. Harley's older customers patiently rebuilt their motorcycles, but younger riders were not so forgiving. Increasing numbers of them chose the trouble-free, smooth-riding imports, and Harley's U.S. market share eventually tumbled to 23 percent.

During the 1980s, Harley decided to open the throttle on quality production. The company changed its design and manufacturing systems to stress quality and reliability, and it carefully controlled the number of motorcycles produced so that their quality could be maintained. This turnaround reestablished Harley's worldwide reputation for superior quality. Customers liked the new motorcycles, and sales began to climb. By the early 1990s, Harley's biggest problem was making enough motorcycles to keep up with soaring demand in the United States and abroad.

Satisfying customers is still a top priority for Harley's CEO Richard F. Teerlink. He and all Harley managers realize that to stay in the fast lane, they need careful research and analysis of issues ranging from product design to inventory control to customer needs. If you were in charge of writing reports on these issues, how would you go about planning them? What steps would you take to define each problem, conduct the research, and analyze the data necessary for such reports?[1]

*F*IVE STEPS IN PLANNING REPORTS

Whether you're employed by Harley-Davidson or by another business, you usually have some work to do before you begin to write a report. Even if you're preparing a strictly informational report that does nothing more than transmit facts, you must still gather those facts and arrange them in a convenient format. Before putting a single word on the page, follow the series of steps that form the foundation of any report:

Harley-Davidson

1. Define the problem and the purpose
2. Outline the issues for investigation
3. Prepare a work plan
4. Conduct research
5. Analyze and interpret data, draw conclusions, and develop recommendations

The relative importance of these five steps depends on the type of assignment. Because informational reports contain facts alone, they may require very little in the way of conclusions and recommendations. On the other hand, because analytical reports include conclusions and recommendations, they require all five steps.

*D*EFINING THE PROBLEM

Your first step is to write a **problem statement,** a statement that defines the problem your report will cover. This problem may be either negative or positive; it may deal with filling a need (How this company would benefit from child-care facilities) or answering a question (Why have sales been shrinking so dramatically?). The *problem* your report covers is merely the matter you intend to deal with, whether you're gathering information, supporting a decision, or actually solving an existing problem. However, be careful not to confuse a simple topic (campus parking) with a problem (the lack of enough campus parking). A clear problem statement helps you decide what information is needed to complete your report.

Say you've been asked to study the extent of drug and alcohol abuse by assembly-line workers in your company's main plant and make a factual report on what's happening. Before conducting your investigation, you decide on a few boundaries for your report. For example, are you going to study the source and distribution of drugs and alcohol in the plant, or are you going to disregard the question of where these substances come from? What time period are you going to cover? This month? The past 12 months? The past 5 years? Your answers to these and similar questions establish the extent of your investigation and, ultimately, the content of your report.

If you're writing an analytical report that interprets facts and draws conclusions about them, you generally shape your investigation by the way you define the problem to be solved. For example, assume that you've also been asked to *analyze* the alcohol and drug abuse problem, not just report the facts. Do you try to determine why plant workers are using these substances and try to recommend ways to keep them from doing so? Or do you try to determine the impact of drug and alcohol abuse on

The first step in writing a report is to narrow the focus of your investigation.

Ted Koppel is anchor of ABC's Nightline. *He points out that you don't have to become an expert on every subject you undertake, but he urges you to learn enough about the subject you are investigating to pose intelligent questions.*

productivity and product quality, recommending measures to make up for their effects? In other words, exactly what is the problem to be solved? The way you define the problem establishes the framework for your investigation.

Asking the Right Questions

Often, the problem is defined for you by the person who authorizes the report. When this is the case, talk about the objectives of the report before you begin your investigation—to ensure that you understand exactly what is required. Ask questions such as the following:

- What needs to be determined? (What is the problem?)
- Why is the issue important?
- Who is involved in the situation?
- Where is the trouble actually located?
- When did it start?
- How did the situation originate?

Not all these questions apply in every situation, but asking them helps you clarify the boundaries of your investigation. You can then draft a written statement of the problem you're investigating, which will help you stay on track as you proceed.[2] In the case of your informational report on substance abuse, your problem statement might be defined this way:

> What is the extent of alcohol and drug abuse among employees at the main plant?

If you're writing an analytical report, your problem statement might be slightly broader:

> What is the extent of alcohol and drug abuse among employees at the main plant, and how does this abuse affect productivity and product quality?

This problem statement goes beyond the problem you defined for your informational report. That's because your analytical report is expected to look at the facts and also draw conclusions about the impact on plant operations.

Developing the Statement of Purpose

Prepare a written statement of your purpose; then review it with the person who authorized the study.

A study's purpose may be stated as an infinitive.

Once you've asked some preliminary questions, you should develop a clear **statement of purpose,** which defines the objective of your report. In contrast to the problem statement, which defines only what you're going to investigate, the statement of purpose defines what the report will accomplish.[3]

The most useful way to phrase your purpose is to begin with an infinitive phrase. In the case of an informational report on substance abuse, you might state your purpose by saying:

> *Purpose:* To summarize the extent of substance abuse among factory employees.

However, for your analytical report on substance abuse, your statement of purpose might be:

> *Purpose:* To analyze the effects of employee substance abuse on productivity and product quality and to recommend ways of counteracting these effects.

Using an infinitive phrase (*to* plus a verb) encourages you to take control and decide where you're going before you begin. When you choose such a phrase—*to inform, to confirm, to analyze, to persuade, to recommend*—you pin down your general goal in preparing the report. At the same time, be sure to define the benefit (the information or the recommended action) your reader will gain from reading your report. The more specific your purpose, the more useful it will be as a guide to planning and writing the report.

Before you proceed, it's important to anticipate how your audience will react. Double-check your statement of purpose with the person who authorized the report. When the authorizer sees the purpose written down in black and white, he or she may decide to redirect the study toward other areas. Your audience's reaction dictates all the decisions you'll make about content, structure, outline, and so forth. So make sure your efforts are audience-centered.

OUTLINING ISSUES FOR INVESTIGATION

Once you've defined the problem and established the purpose of the study, you're ready for the second step in planning reports: outlining the issues you'll be investigating. To organize your effort, break the problem into a series of specific questions—a process sometimes called **problem factoring.** Chances are, you already use this approach subconsciously when facing a problem. When your car won't start, what do you do? You look at the various **hypotheses,** or tentative explanations that can be investigated— the battery is dead, you're out of gas, the ignition system is broken—checking one hypothesis at a time until you find the cause. Subdividing the problem like this helps you cover every important aspect.

Consultant Jim Lowry faced a complex problem when he was asked to research and write a report for the U.S. Department of Commerce (DOC) about how to stimulate minority business development.[4] To investigate this problem, Lowry and his associates broke it down into a series of questions (see Figure 13.1).

"We began with a general question," says Lowry. "Why have government programs had such limited success in fostering minority-owned businesses, and how can they be improved? We then divided that question into three subquestions: Are the programs flawed? Is program administration at fault? How can programs be improved?

The second step in report writing is to outline the issues you plan to study.

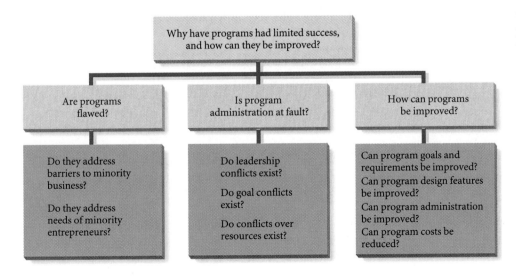

Figure 13.1
How Lowry & Associates Factored Its Problem

"Looking at the area of program design, we speculated that the government's programs have had limited success for a very basic reason: They have not provided the right kind of help to the right people. This hypothesis naturally led us to some more questions: What kind of help do minorities need in order to create and operate successful businesses? What specific barriers need to be removed for them to enter the economic mainstream? What are their general social and economic problems? And what are their specific business problems? We went through a similar thought process to come up with some specific questions about program administration."

Once Lowry had determined what was wrong with the DOC's program, he could address the third subquestion: How can programs be improved? He had to decide what the new programs ought to accomplish, how they should be designed, who should administer them, and what they would cost.

The process of outlining the issues enabled Lowry and his colleagues to solve a problem methodically, just as outlining a report enables you to write in a systematic way. It's worth noting, however, that the outline you use in an investigation may differ from the outline you use in the resulting report. Solving the problem is one thing; selling the solution is another. During your investigation, you might analyze five possible causes of a problem and discover that only two causes are relevant. In your report, you probably wouldn't even introduce the three unrelated causes.

Developing a Logical Structure

Because any subject can be factored in many ways, your job is to choose the most logical method, the one that makes the most sense. Start by looking carefully at the purpose of your study. Informational assignments are structured differently from analytical assignments, and many assignments require both information and analysis. Therefore, be careful to discern the overall purpose of the study. If your general goal is to provide background information that someone else will interpret, an informational outline is appropriate overall, even though subsections of the study may require some analysis to emphasize important facts. If the purpose of your study is to scrutinize the data and generate your own conclusions and recommendations, use an analytical outline overall, even though your opinions will obviously be based on facts. You may use a variety of structural schemes in problem solving, as long as you avoid errors in logic.

Informational and analytical studies are factored differently.

Informational Assignments

Studies that lead to factual reports with very little analysis or interpretation are generally factored on the basis of subtopics dealing with specific subjects. These subtopics can be arranged in various ways:

Studies that emphasize the discovery and reporting of facts may be factored by subtopic.

- *In order of importance.* Say you're reviewing five product lines. You might organize your study in order of sales for each product line, beginning with the line that produces the most revenue and proceeding to the one that produces the least revenue.
- *Sequentially.* If you're studying a process, present your information step by step— 1, 2, 3, and so on.
- *Chronologically.* When investigating a chain of events, organize the study according to what happened in January, what happened in February, and so on.
- *Spatially.* If you're studying a physical object, study it left to right, top to bottom, or outside to inside.
- *Geographically.* If location is important, factor your study geographically.
- *Categorically.* If you're asked to review several distinct aspects of a subject, look at one category at a time, such as sales, profit, cost, or investment.

These methods of subdivision are commonly used in the preparation of such informational reports as monitor/control reports, policies and procedures, compliance reports, and interim progress reports.

Analytical Assignments

Studies that result in reports containing analyses, conclusions, and recommendations are generally categorized by a problem-solving method. Hypotheses and relative merits are the two most common structural approaches of this type. When the problem is to discover causes, predict results, or find a solution to a problem, one natural way to proceed is to formulate hypothetical explanations. Say that your problem is to determine why your company is having trouble hiring secretaries. You would factor this problem by speculating about the reasons; then you would collect information to confirm or disprove each reason. Your outline of the major issues might look something like this:

Studies that focus on problem solving may be factored on the basis of hypotheses; those that focus on the evaluation of alternatives may be factored on relative merits.

Why are we having trouble hiring secretaries?

I. Salaries are too low.
   A. What do we pay our secretaries?
   B. What do comparable companies pay their secretaries?
   C. How important is pay in influencing secretaries' job choices?
II. Our location is poor.
   A. Are we accessible by public transportation and major roads?
   B. Is the area physically attractive?
   C. Are housing costs affordable?
   D. Is crime a problem?
III. The supply of secretaries is diminishing.
   A. How many secretaries were available five years ago as opposed to now?
   B. What was the demand for secretaries five years ago as opposed to now?

When the problem is to evaluate how well various alternatives meet your criteria, the natural way to subdivide your analysis is to focus on the criteria. For example, if the problem is to decide where new dealerships should be located, you might factor the investigation along the following lines:

Where should we locate a new dealership?

I. Construction costs
   A. Location A
   B. Location B
   C. Location C
II. Labor availability
   A. Location A
   B. Location B
   C. Location C
III. Transportation facilities
   A. Location A
   B. Location B
   C. Location C

Another way of using relative merits is to identify the alternatives first and then analyze how well each alternative meets your criteria.

Following the Rules of Division

Follow the rules of division to ensure that your study will be organized in a logical, systematic way.

Dividing something physical, such as a pie, is much easier than dividing something intangible, such as an idea. How do you know that the pieces of an idea are cut in the right size, shape, and number? Over the centuries, scholars have developed a concise set of rules for dividing an idea into components:

- *Divide a topic into at least two parts.* A topic cannot be divided into only one part. For example, if you wanted to divide a topic such as "Alternatives for Improving Division Profits," you wouldn't look only at increasing sales. You would need at least one other subtopic, such as reducing production costs or decreasing employee absenteeism. If you were interested only in increasing sales, then that would be your topic, which you would probably divide into at least two subtopics.
- *Choose a significant, useful basis or guiding principle for the division.* For example, you could subdivide production problems into two groups: problems that arise when the machines are turned off and problems that occur when the machines are turned on. However, this basis for breaking down the subject would not be of much use to anyone. A better choice might be dividing the subject into problems caused by human error versus problems caused by machine failure.
- *When subdividing a whole into its parts, restrict yourself to one basis at a time.* If you switch from one basis to another, you get a mixed classification, which can confuse your analysis. Say you're subdividing your study of the market for toothpaste according to sales of fluoride versus nonfluoride brands. You would upset the investigation by adding another category to your analysis (say, sales of toothpaste in Alabama). If you are dealing with a long, complex subject, you will no doubt have to use several bases of division before you complete your work, but the shift from one basis to another must be made at a logical point, that is, after you have completed your study of a particular issue. For example, after you have looked at sales of fluoride versus nonfluoride toothpaste, you might want to look at toothpaste sales by geographic location or socioeconomic group.
- *Make certain that each group is separate and distinct.* The groups must be mutually exclusive, or you will end up talking about the same item under two or more headings. For example, subdividing a population into males, females, and teenagers wouldn't make any sense, because the categories overlap.
- *Be thorough when listing all the components of a whole.* For example, it would be misleading to subdivide an engine into parts without mentioning the pistons. An important part of the whole would be missing, and the resulting picture of the engine would be wrong.

If you follow these rules, your investigation will be logical, systematic, and complete.

Preparing a Preliminary Outline

Organize your study by preparing a detailed preliminary outline.

As you go through the factoring process, you may want to use an outline format to represent your ideas (see Figure 13.2). In some cases, such as writing a short, informal report in memo format, a few notes on a piece of paper are enough to guide you. But a preliminary outline gives you a convenient frame of reference for your investigation, and a detailed outline is definitely worth the effort when

- You are one of several people working on an assignment
- Your investigation will be extensive and will involve many sources and many types of data

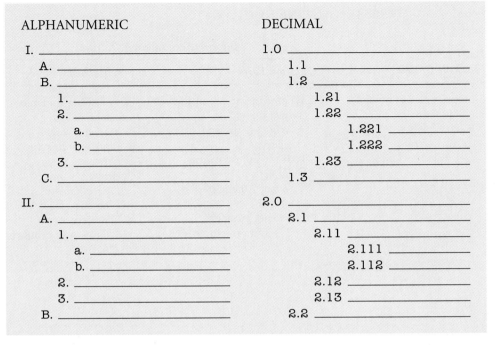

Figure 13.2
Two Common Outline Formats

- You know from past experience that the person who requested the study will revise the assignment during the course of your investigation (and you want to keep track of the changes)

Two widely used systems of outlining, the alphanumeric system and the decimal system, are illustrated in Figure 13.2. Both are perfectly acceptable, but some companies traditionally favor one method over the other. You usually write the headings at each level of your outline in the same grammatical form. In other words, if item I uses a verb, then items II, III, and IV also use verbs. This parallel construction enables readers to see that the ideas are related, of similar importance, and on the same level of generality. It makes the outline a more useful tool for establishing the table of contents and headings in your final report, and it is considered the correct format by most of the people who might review your outline.

> Use the same grammatical form for each group of items in your outline.

When writing the outline, you also choose between descriptive (topical) and informative (talking) headings. Descriptive headings label the subject that will be discussed, whereas informative headings (in either question or summary form) suggest more about the meaning of the issues (see Table 13.1). Although outlines with informative headings take a little longer to write, they are generally more useful in guiding your work, especially if written in terms of the questions you plan to answer during the study. In addition, they have the advantage of being easier for others to review. If other people are going to comment on your outline, they may not have a very clear idea of what you mean by the descriptive heading "Advertising." But they'll get the main idea if you use the informative heading "Cuts in Ad Budget May Explain Sales Decline."

> Informative outlines are generally more helpful than descriptive outlines.

Remember that at this point you're only developing a preliminary outline to guide your investigation. Later on, when you have completed your research and are preparing a final outline or a table of contents for the report, you may want to switch from a working outline to an outline that summarizes your findings.

	Table 13.1	TYPES OF OUTLINE HEADINGS	

	Informative (Talking) Outline	
Descriptive (Topical) Outline	*Question Form*	*Summary Form*

I. Industry characteristics
  A. Annual sales
  B. Profitability
  C. Growth rate
    1. Sales
    2. Profit
	I. What is the nature of the industry?
	  A. What are the annual sales?
	  B. Is the industry profitable?
	  C. What is the pattern of growth?
	    1. Sales growth?
	    2. Profit growth?
		I. Flour milling is mature industry.
		  A. Market is large.
		  B. Profit margins are narrow.
		  C. Growth is modest.
		    1. Sales growth averages less than 3 percent a year.
		    2. Growth in profits is flat.

P REPARING THE WORK PLAN

The third step in report writing is the work plan.

Your third step in planning reports is to establish a work plan based on your preliminary outline. If you're preparing this plan for yourself, it can be relatively informal: a simple list of the steps you plan to take, an estimate of their sequence and timing, and a list of the sources of information you plan to use. If you're conducting a lengthy, formal study, however, the work plan will be quite detailed because it will guide the performance of many tasks over a span of time. Moreover, most proposals require a detailed work plan, which becomes the basis of a contract if the proposal is accepted. A formal work plan might include the following items (especially the first two):

- Problem statement
- Statement of purpose
- Discussion of the sequence of tasks to be accomplished (indicating sources of information, required experiments or observations, and any restrictions on time, money, or available data)
- Description of the end products that will result from the investigation (such as reports, plans, operating improvements, or tangible products)
- Review of project assignments, schedules, and resource requirements (indicating who will be responsible for what, when tasks will be completed, and how much the investigation will cost)

Some work plans also include a tentative outline of the report. Figure 13.3 is an example of a work plan for a study of whether to launch a company newsletter.

C ONDUCTING THE RESEARCH

The value of your report depends on the quality of the information it's based on. Your fourth step in planning reports is to gather that information, and it's important to begin by getting organized. If you're working alone on a project, getting organized may

Over the years, Connie Chung has worked long hours on both NBC and CBS news programs. Her days are always full: meeting with network executives and affiliates, holding briefing sessions with researchers, interviewing subjects, planning story lineups for upcoming programs, taping news broadcasts, and more. To coordinate the efforts of everyone involved in producing a news program, says Chung, a detailed work plan is essential.

Figure 13.3
**Sample Work Plan for a
Formal Study**

Statement of the Problem
The rapid growth of our company over the past five years has reduced the sense of community among our staff. People no longer
feel like part of an intimate organization where they matter as
individuals.

Purpose and Scope of Work
The purpose of this study is to determine whether a company newsletter would help rebuild employee identification with the organization. The study will evaluate the impact of newsletters in other companies and attempt to identify features that might be desirable in our
own newsletter. Such variables as length, frequency of distribution,
types of articles, and graphic design will be considered. Costs will be
estimated for several approaches. In addition, the study will analyze
the personnel and procedures required to produce a newsletter.

Sources and Methods of Data Collection
Sample newsletters will be collected from 50 companies similar to
ours in size, growth rate, and types of employees. The editors will be
asked to comment on the impact of their publications on employee
morale. Our own employees will be surveyed to determine their interest in a newsletter and their preferences for specific features. Production procedures and costs will be analyzed through conversations
with newsletter editors and possible printers.

Preliminary Outline
    I. Do newsletters affect morale?
       A. Do people read them?
       B. How do employees benefit?
       C. How does the company benefit?
   II. What are the features of good newsletters?
       A. How long are they?
       B. What do they contain?
       C. How often are they published?
       D. How are they designed?
  III. How should a newsletter be produced?
       A. Should it be written, edited, and printed internally?
       B. Should it be written internally and printed outside?
       C. Should it be totally produced outside?
  IV. What would a newsletter cost?
       A. What would the personnel costs be?
       B. What would the materials costs be?
       C. What would outside services cost?
   V. Should we publish a company newsletter?
  VI. If so, what approach should we take?

Work Plan

Collect and analyze newsletters	Sept. 01-14
Interview editors by phone	Sept. 16-20
Survey employees	Sept. 14-28
Develop sample newsletter	Sept. 28-Oct. 05
Develop cost estimates	Oct. 07-10
Prepare report	Oct. 10-24
Submit final report	Oct. 25

The fourth step in report writing is to conduct the research by consulting primary (firsthand) and secondary (secondhand) sources.

mean nothing more than setting up a file and checking out a few books and periodicals from the nearest library. However, if you're part of a team, you'll have to work out each person's assignment and coordinate activities. Your work plan will be a big help during this research effort.

The work plan contains a list of the primary and secondary sources you'll consult. As the name implies, primary sources provide firsthand information; secondary sources are secondhand reports. Most business problems call for a mix of both secondary and primary sources. You are likely to find, however, that much of what you need to know has never been collected. For example, you probably wouldn't locate much existing information on what Harley-Davidson dealerships should look like. Reliance on primary sources is one of the main differences between business reports and school reports. Even so, business report writers begin by researching secondary sources.

Reviewing Secondary Sources

Conduct secondary research by locating information that has already been collected, usually in the form of books, periodicals, and reports.

Although you may plan to rely heavily on primary sources, you are wise to begin your study with a thorough review of the information that has already been collected. By searching the literature, you're protected against the embarrassment of failing to report something that is common knowledge. You also save yourself the trouble of conducting a study that has already been done. Once you gain a feel for the structure of the subject, you can decide what additional research will be required.

Depending on your subject, you may find useful information in general reference works, popular publications, and government documents. In addition, each field of business has a handful of specialized references that are considered indispensable. You will quickly come to know these sources once you've joined a particular industry. And don't overlook internal sources. Often, the most useful references are company reports and memos. Also check company brochures, newsletters, and annual reports to shareholders.

If you're working for a large organization with a company library, you may have direct access to a professional librarian who can help you identify and obtain other useful materials. If not, look for the nearest public or university library, and ask the librarians there for help. Reference librarians are trained to know where to find just about everything, and many of them are pleased to help people pursue obscure information.

When it comes to choosing your references, be selective. Avoid dated or biased material. If possible, check on the author's qualifications and the reputation of the publisher.

The amount of library research you do depends on the subject you're studying and the purpose of your investigation. In most cases, when you find yourself reading essentially the same things over and over again, move out of the library and on to the next phase of your work. Remember that in business, time is money. Your objective is to be as accurate and as thorough as possible but within a reasonable length of time.

Regardless of the amount of research you do, retain complete and accurate notes on the sources of all the material you collect, using one of the systems explained in Appendix B, "Documentation of Report Sources." Documenting your sources through footnotes, endnotes, or some similar system lends credibility to your report.

Collecting Primary Data

When the information you need is unavailable from secondary sources, you'll collect and interpret the data yourself by doing primary research. You must go out into the real world to gather information through your own efforts. The four main ways to collect primary data are by examining documents, observing things, surveying people, and conducting experiments.

Conduct primary research by collecting basic information yourself.

Documents

In business, a great deal of information is filed away for future reference. Your own company's files may provide you with accurate, factual historical records that you cannot obtain any other way. Business documents that qualify as primary data include sales reports prepared by field representatives, balance sheets, income statements, policy statements, correspondence with customers and suppliers, contracts, and logbooks. Many government and legal documents are primary sources as well, because they represent a decision made by those present at some official proceeding.

Documentary evidence and historical records are sources of primary data.

A single document may be both a secondary source and a primary source. For example, when citing summaries of financial and operations data from an annual report, you're using the report as a secondary source. That same report would be considered a primary source if you were analyzing its design features or comparing it with annual reports from other years or other companies.

Observations

Informal observations are a rather common source of primary data in business. All you have to do is use your five senses, especially your eyes and ears, to gather information. Many reports, for instance, are based on the writer's visiting a facility to observe operations.

Observation applies your five senses and your judgment to the investigation.

More objective information can be gathered through formal observations, which give observers a structure for noting what they see, thus minimizing opportunities for interpretation. For example, if you were trying to find out how teenagers react to various video arcade games, you might send researchers to a number of arcades to observe what goes on. Your results would be more useful if your observers were armed with a specific list of things to watch for. That way, you could compare the results from arcade to arcade and reach relatively objective conclusions.

In general, observation is a useful technique when you're studying objects, physical activities, processes, the environment, or human behavior. It does, however, have one major drawback: The value of the observation depends on the reliability of the observer. Many people have a tendency to see what they want to see or to interpret events in light of their own experience. However, if the observer is trustworthy and has proper instructions, observation can provide valuable insights that would be difficult to obtain with other methods.

Steve Jobs co-founded Apple Computer, and his current company is NeXT, where he is now deeply involved in software development. Jobs sees an added dimension to researching what customers want: technology. He cautions that customers are unable to foresee what technology can do, so in addition to asking customers what they want, it's important to acquaint them with what's possible.

Surveys

Often the best way to obtain answers to your questions is to ask people who have relevant experience and opinions. Such surveys include everything from a single interview to the distribution of thousands of questionnaires.

When you need specialized information that hasn't been recorded anywhere, you may want to conduct a personal interview with an expert, which is the simplest form of survey. Many experts come from the ranks of your own organization: people from other departments who have specialized knowledge, your predecessor in the job, and "old-timers" who've seen it all. On occasion, you may also want to talk with outsiders who have some special expertise. Doing an interview may seem an easy way to get information, but you must prepare carefully. (See Chapter 17 for tips on interviewing people.) You don't want to waste anyone's time, and you want your efforts to be productive.

A formal survey is a way of finding out what a cross-section of people think about something.

Two important research criteria:
- Reliability—when the same results would be obtained if the research were repeated
- Validity—when research measures what it is intended to measure

Although they have the same purpose, interviews are quite different from formal, large-scale surveys in which a sample population answers a series of carefully tested questions. A formal survey requires a number of important decisions:

- Should you use face-to-face interviews, phone calls, or printed questionnaires?
- How many individuals should you contact to get results that are *reliable* (that is, the results would be reproduced if the same study were repeated), and who should those people be (what sample is an accurate reflection of the population)?
- What specific questions should you ask in order to get a *valid* picture (a true reflection of the group's feelings on the subject)?

Your answers to these questions will have a profound effect on the results of your survey.

Having seen rival preelection polls that come up with conflicting projections of who's going to win, you may wonder whether it makes sense to rely on survey results at all. You'll want to use survey results, but only if you understand the nature of surveys. For one thing, surveys reveal only what people think about something at a specific moment. For another, pollsters ask various people different questions in different ways and, not surprisingly, get different answers. Just because surveys produce varying results does not mean that they are a poor form of research. Of course, conducting a reliable, valid survey is not easy to do. Generally speaking, it helps to have the advice of a specialist.

Developing an effective questionnaire requires care and skill.

One of the most critical elements of a survey is the questionnaire. To develop one, begin by making a list of the points you're trying to determine. Then break these points into specific questions, choosing an appropriate type of question for each point (see Figure 13.4 for some variations). The following guidelines will help you produce valid results:

- Provide clear instructions so that respondents know exactly how to fill out the questionnaire.
- Keep the questionnaire short and easy to answer. People are more likely to respond if they can complete the questionnaire within 10 or 15 minutes, so ask only those questions relevant to your research, and don't ask questions that require too much work on the respondent's part. People aren't willing to dig up the answers to questions like "What was your monthly rate of water consumption in 1995?"
- Formulate questions that provide easily tabulated or analyzed answers. Numbers and facts are easier to deal with than opinions are. Nevertheless, you may be able to elicit countable opinions with multiple-choice questions, or you might group open-ended opinions into a limited number of categories.
- Avoid questions that lead to a particular answer; they bias your survey. For example, Harley-Davidson would gain little useful information by asking customers "Do you prefer that our dealerships stay open on Sundays for your convenience?" The question obviously calls for a yes answer. A less biased question would be "What day of the week are you most likely to visit one of our dealerships?"
- Ask only one thing at a time. When you pose a compound question like "Do you read books and magazines regularly?" you don't allow for the respondent who reads one but not the other.
- Avoid questions having vague or abstract words. Instead of asking "Are you frequently troubled by colds?" ask "How many colds did you have in the past 12 months?"

Figure 13.4
Types of Survey Questions

Question Type	Example
OPEN-ENDED	How would you describe the flavor of this ice cream?
EITHER-OR	Do you think this ice cream is too rich? _____ Yes _____ No
MULTIPLE CHOICE	Which description best fits the taste of this ice cream? (Choose only one.) a. Delicious b. Too fruity c. Too sweet d. Too intensely flavored e. Bland f. Stale
SCALE	Please make an X on the scale to indicate how you perceive the texture of this ice cream. ⟵ ———————————————————— ⟶ Too light Light Creamy Too creamy
CHECKLIST	Which flavors of ice cream have you had in the past 12 months? (Check all that apply.) _____ Vanilla _____ Chocolate _____ Strawberry _____ Chocolate chip _____ Coffee
RANKING	Rank these flavors in order of your preference, from 1 (most preferred) to 5 (least preferred): _____ Vanilla _____ Cherry _____ Maple nut _____ Chocolate ripple _____ Coconut
SHORT-ANSWER QUESTIONS	In the past month, how many times did you buy ice cream in the supermarket? _____ In the past month, how many times did you buy ice cream in ice cream shops? _____

- Pretest the questionnaire on a sample group to identify questions that are subject to misinterpretation.
- Include a few questions that rephrase earlier questions, as a cross-check on the validity of the responses.

If you're mailing your questionnaire, as opposed to administering it in person, include a persuasive cover letter that explains why you're conducting the research. Try to convince the person that her or his response is important to you. If possible, offer to share the results with the respondent. Include a preaddressed envelope with prepaid postage so that the respondent won't have to find an envelope or pay the postage to return the questionnaire to you. However, remember that even under the best of circumstances, you may not get more than a 10 to 20 percent response.

AIDS research is one technical field in which experiments are common. For example, Dr. Jonas Salk is attacking AIDS with the same confidence that helped him develop his polio vaccine in 1955. Salk's killed-virus vaccine is currently being tested in a long process of experiments on humans.

The fifth step in report writing is to analyze your results by calculating statistics, drawing reasonable conclusions, and if appropriate, developing a set of recommendations.

The same set of data can be used to produce three kinds of averages: mean, median, and mode.

Experiments

Although some general business questions justify the need for experiments, their use is far more common in technical fields. That's because an experiment requires extensive manipulation of various factors, which is often expensive and may even be unethical when people are one of the factors involved. Nevertheless, experiments do have their place. For example, if you want to find out whether a change in lighting levels increases the productivity of the pattern cutters in your dressmaking business, the most objective approach is to conduct an experiment using two groups of cutters: one working under existing conditions and the other working under the new lighting.

When conducting an experiment, you have to be careful to control those factors (called variables) you are *not* testing. For the results to be valid in the lighting experiment, the only difference in the environments of the two groups should be the lighting, and there should be no differences between the groups themselves. Otherwise, discrepancies in productivity could be attributed to such factors as age differences or experience on the job. It's even possible that introducing any change into the pattern cutters' environment, whether lighting or something else entirely, might be enough to increase productivity.

ANALYZING AND INTERPRETING DATA

Once you've completed your research, you're ready for the fifth step in planning reports: analyzing and interpreting your findings. The analytical process is essentially a search for relationships among the facts and bits of evidence you've compiled. By looking at the data from various viewpoints, you attempt to detect patterns that will enable you to answer the questions outlined in your work plan. Your mind begins to fit pieces together and to form tentative conclusions. As your analysis proceeds, you either verify or reject these conclusions because your mind is constantly filtering, sorting, and combining ideas.

Calculating Statistics

Much of the information you compile during the research phase will be in numerical form. Assuming that it has been collected carefully, this factual data is precise, measurable, and objective—and therefore credible. However, statistical information in its raw state is of little practical value. It must be manipulated so that you and your readers can interpret its significance.

Averages

One useful way of looking at data is to find the **average,** which is a single number that represents a group of numbers. Consider the data presented in Figure 13.5, the sales booked by a group of nine salespeople over one week. To analyze this information, you could calculate the average, but which average? Depending on how you plan to use the data, you would choose the mean, the median, or the mode.

The most commonly used average is the *mean,* or the sum of all the items in the group divided by the number of items in the group. The mean is useful when you want to compare one item or individual with the group. In the example, the mean is $7,000. If you were the sales manager, you might well be interested in knowing that Wimper's sales were average; that Wilson, Green, and Carrick had below-average sales; and that Keeble, Kemble, O'Toole, Mannix, and Caruso were above average. One problem with using the mean, however, is that it can give you a false picture if one of the numbers is extreme. Let's say that Caruso's sales for the week were $27,000. The mean would then be $9,000, and eight of the nine salespeople would be "below average."

The *median* is the "middle of the road" average.[5] In a numerical ranking like the one shown in Figure 13.5, the median is the number right in the middle of the list: $7,500. The median is useful when one (or a few) of the numbers is extreme. For example, even if Caruso's sales were $27,000, the median would still be $7,500.

The *mode* is the "fashionable" average, the pattern followed most often, the case you're most likely to come across.[6] It's the best average for answering a question like "What is the usual amount?" For example, if you wanted to know what level of sales was most common, you would answer with the mode, which is $8,500. Like the median, the mode is not affected by extreme values. It's much easier to find than the median, however, when you have a large number of items or individuals.

While you're analyzing averages, you should also consider the range, or the spread, of a series of numbers. The fact that, in the example, sales per person ranged from $3,000 to $9,000 may raise the question of why there is such a wide gap between Wilson's and Caruso's performances. A range tells you the context in which the averages were calculated and demonstrates what values are possible.

Figure 13.5
Three Types of Averages: Mean, Median, and Mode

Sales-person	Sales	
Wilson	$ 3,000	
Green	5,000	
Carrick	6,000	
Wimper	7,000	Mean
Keeble	7,500	Median
Kemble	8,500	
O'Toole	8,500	Mode
Mannix	8,500	
Caruso	9,000	
Total	$63,000	

Trends

If you were overseeing the work of Wilson, Caruso, and the rest, you might be tempted to make some important personnel decisions on the basis of the week's sales figures. But you would be a lot smarter to compare them with sales figures from other weeks, looking for a **trend,** a steady upward or downward movement in a pattern of events taking place over time. You could begin to see which salespeople were consistently above average and which were consistently below. You could also see whether sales for the group as a whole were increasing, declining, or remaining steady and whether there were any seasonal fluctuations in the sales pattern. This type of analysis, known as trend analysis, is common in business. By looking at data over a period of time, you can detect patterns and relationships that will help you answer important questions.

Trend analysis involves an examination of data over time so that patterns and relationships can be detected.

Correlations

Once you've identified a trend, you should look for the cause. Say that Caruso consistently produces the most sales. You would undoubtedly be curious about the secret of her success. Does she call on her customers more often? Is she a more persuasive person? Does she have larger accounts or a bigger sales territory? Is she simply more experienced than the others?

To answer these questions, you could look for a **correlation,** a statistical relationship between two or more variables. In this case, a correlation would be a consistent relationship between each person's sales and other variables, such as average account size or years of selling experience. For example, if salespeople with the largest accounts consistently produced higher sales, you might assume that these two factors were correlated, or related in a predictable way. Thus you might conclude that Caruso's success was due, at least in part, to the average size of her accounts. However, your conclusion might be wrong. Correlations are useful evidence, but they do not prove a cause-and-effect relationship. Caruso's success might well be the result of several other factors. To know for sure, you would have to collect more evidence.

A correlation is a statistical relationship between two or more variables.

Drawing Conclusions

Regardless of how much evidence you amass, at some point in every analysis you move beyond hard facts, which can be objectively measured and verified. When you reach that point, you begin to formulate a **conclusion,** which is a logical interpretation of what the facts in your report mean. You then step into the realm of assumptions and value judgments that have been formed by your own experience. Nothing is inher-

Conclusions may be based on a combination of facts, value judgments, and assumptions.

ently wrong with assumptions and value judgments; very few decisions are made on the basis of facts alone. Nevertheless, you must understand the extent to which conclusions may be based on subjective factors.

Imagine that, as sales manager, you have gathered these facts:

- Sales in New England are three times as high as sales in the Southeast.
- The two regions are roughly equal in the size and number of potential accounts.
- Both regions have the same number and type of salespeople, who have all been trained in the same selling techniques.
- In the past three years, six of the eight salespeople in the Southeast have requested a transfer.
- Sales in the Southeast have declined by 5 percent over the past three years.
- The current manager of the Southeast region has been there for three years.

With additional investigation, using scientific research and statistical analysis, you might come up with an objective, indisputable conclusion about the cause of these facts.

In the fast-paced world of business, however, you're far more likely to seek a quicker, more subjective conclusion. Again, nothing is inherently wrong with this type of decision making. In fact, skill at making subjective decisions is often highly valued. But you should be aware of the possible pitfalls.

Your own personal values may affect your thought process. For example, you may believe that the difference in sales between the two regions is unacceptable. Another person, with different values, might be willing to accept the discrepancy. In analyzing the facts, you might assume that something within your control is responsible for the disparity, even though it's possible that some unknown characteristics of buyers or competing products are responsible. Nevertheless, to the extent that your value judgments and assumptions correspond to the facts, you can draw a sound conclusion.

In this case, after applying a subjective thought process to objective evidence, you may well conclude that the current manager of the Southeast region is associated with the sales problem. You're probably right, although you might want more evidence to confirm your hunch before you recommend any action.

But what if you don't have enough hard facts to go on? Or what if the facts are inconclusive or inconsistent? In either case, subjectivity becomes more of a factor. For example, a decision to hire one candidate rather than another is largely a matter of personal judgment. In situations of this type, testing your logic is particularly important. Try to be as objective as possible; be aware of possible biases that aren't justified by the circumstances. Diminish subjectivity by establishing criteria and measuring each candidate against the same standards.

Check the logic that underlies your conclusions.

If you're working as part of a team, you have the benefit of being able to discuss your conclusions with co-workers, so values and assumptions come into focus. Even so, don't expect everyone to agree all the time. Some business decisions are fuzzy; the "right" answers aren't always clear. Often the best bet is to accept the consensus position rather than fight for a conclusion that others won't accept and therefore won't implement with enthusiasm. Then, once the decision has been made, stick with it unless conditions change significantly.

The best conclusion is often the one that gains the most support.

Developing Recommendations

Concluding that the sales manager of the Southeast region is somehow associated with low sales is one thing. Deciding what to do about it and then recommending a solution is something else. Recommendations are inappropriate in a report when you're not expected to supply them, so be sure you know the difference between conclusions and recommendations. A conclusion is an opinion or interpretation of what the facts mean; a **recommendation** suggests what ought to be done about the facts. Here's an example of the difference:

Conclusions are opinions or interpretations; recommendations are suggestions for action.

Conclusion

I conclude that, on the basis of its track record and current price, this company is an attractive buy.

Recommendation

I recommend that we write a letter to the president offering to buy the company at a 10 percent premium over the market value of its stock.

When you have been asked to take the final step and translate your conclusions into recommendations, be sure to make the relationship between them clear.

You might also want to test the soundness of your recommendations against the following criteria:

- The recommendations must offer real advantages to the organization.
- The recommendations must be financially and politically feasible.
- Specific plans must be developed for dealing with roadblocks that might impede implementation of the recommendations.
- The risks associated with the recommendations must be acceptable.
- The picture of what happens next (of who will do what) must be clear.

Consider whether your recommendations are practical and acceptable to your readers; they are the people who have to make the recommendations work. Also be certain that you've adequately described the steps that come next. Don't leave your readers scratching their heads and saying, "This all sounds good, but what do I do on Monday morning?"

Good recommendations are
- Practical
- Acceptable to readers
- Explained in enough detail so that readers can take action

P*REPARING THE FINAL OUTLINE*

Once you've completed your research and analysis, you can prepare the final outline of the report. Sometimes you can use the preliminary outline that guided your research as a final blueprint for the report. More often, however, you have to rework it to take into account your purpose, your audience's probable reactions, and the things you learned during your study. As already mentioned, informational reports are generally organized around topics suggested by the information itself, such as steps in a process, divisions of a company, or results in various geographical areas. Analytical reports, on the other hand, are organized around conclusions or recommendations if the audience is receptive, and around problem-solving approaches if the audience is skeptical or hostile. The placement of conclusions and recommendations depends on the audience's probable response. Put them up front if you expect a positive reaction, toward the end if you anticipate resistance.

The final outline is phrased so that the points on the outline can serve as the headings that appear in the report. Bear in mind that the phrasing of the headings will affect the tone of the report. If you want a hard-hitting, direct tone, use informative phrasing. If you prefer an objective, indirect tone, use descriptive phrasing. Be sure to use parallel construction when wording the points on the outline.

Once you have an outline in mind, you can begin to identify which points can and should be illustrated with visual aids—tables, graphs, schematic drawings, or pho-

The final outline of the report should be geared to your purpose and the audience's probable reaction.

Visual aid: illustration in tabular, graphic, schematic, or pictorial form

BEHIND THE SCENES AT GANNETT COMPANY
Getting the Scoop on a Media Giant

Sheila J. Gibbons is director of public affairs for Gannett Company, the nation's largest newspaper publisher. Gannett owns 118 newspapers, including *USA Today,* as well as 10 television stations and 16 radio stations. In the course of a year, Gibbons's department compiles and publishes a half-dozen in-depth reports for higher management.

"We're working on one right now," says Gibbons, "a 'white paper' analyzing media coverage of Gannett. Management wants a 'big-picture' assessment of how the outside world looks at us. The various newspapers, electronic media, and magazines are all being reviewed—everything that has appeared about us in the last 12 months."

When planning the report, Gibbons considers issues such as (1) how Gannett is perceived by the public and (2) how those perceptions are affected by Gannett's being both a large corporation and a media company. Says Gibbons: "First, we don't know a lot about the public perception of Gannett. Many see us as *USA Today,* so if you mention *USA Today* and Gannett, people connect them. But if you mention Gannett alone, they don't necessarily connect it with *USA Today.* We want to know

what implications this has for Gannett. Second, attitudes about large corporations tend to shift back and forth between positive and negative, and people tend to vary how much or how little they trust the media. Because our company is both large and media-concerned, we are curious about how all these factors affect public perceptions of Gannett."

"So far, we're only in the information-gathering stage," points out Gibbons, who has taken an unusual approach to the research for this report. "I've given part of that assignment to our college intern. She is reviewing data, looking for themes and a consistency of views. She is not 'of Gannett,' so she won't be biased by our philosophy and corporate culture. Another staff member is looking into the impact of image campaigns that have been launched by other large corporations."

Whenever she works with college interns or with new staff members, Gibbons asks them first to review files and old reports and to take note of the various forms such communication has taken in the past. "That's the best way to learn how the company communicates," says Gibbons. In other words, get to know your subject through background reading.

The shape of the final report is beginning to emerge.

---

tographs. (See Chapter 14 for more detail on visual aids.) Ask yourself whether there is some way to visually dramatize the key elements of your message. You might approach the problem as though you were writing a picture book or making a movie. Think of each main point on your outline as a separate scene. Your job is to think of a "picture," a chart or graph, that will communicate that point to the audience.

Then take your analysis a step further. Undoubtedly, some of the supporting items on your outline involve the presentation of detailed facts and figures. This sort of information may be confusing and tedious when presented in paragraph form. Often the best approach is to display this information in a table, which arrays the data in a convenient format. You might want to use flow charts, drawings, or photographs to clarify physical relationships or procedures.

When planning the illustrations for your report or presentation, aim to achieve a reasonable balance between the verbal and the visual. The ideal blend depends on the nature of the subject. Some topics are more graphic than others and require more visual aids. Just remember that illustrating every point dilutes the effectiveness of all your visual aids. In a written report, particularly, too many visuals can be a problem. If readers are told in every paragraph or two to consult a table or chart, they are likely to lose the thread of the argument you are trying to make. Furthermore, readers tend to assume that the amount of space allocated to a topic indicates its relative importance. If you use visual aids to illustrate a minor point, you may be sending a misleading message about its significance.

Use visual aids to simplify, clarify, and emphasize important information.

Gibbons says she'll "use a cover to make it stand out from routine paperwork, followed by a title page and an executive summary written as an inverted pyramid. In all, there will be about ten pages of text, normal for our long reports. Any illustrations will go in the appendix. I'll probably not do a bibliography for this particular report. First, we're looking at everything that's been written or said about us in a one-year period, so any bibliography will be extensive. Second, the intended audience will be looking for a short assessment of an important issue. My job is to simplify the complexities. The language will be kept simple to encourage readership, and the report will be concise and tightly written to benefit the time-pressured executives who will receive it. One other thing: there will be no typos."

This report, like others Gibbons prepares, will go to her boss, the vice president of public affairs and government relations, and from there to selected Gannett executives. Although this particular report will be unusual, Gibbons expects all members of the management committee to read it and give her a response.

"All our reports are analytical reports. Each has a portion that leads to recommendations for further action." Small-group conferences (usually four or five people) meet to hash over the findings and recommendations, and Gibbons gets feedback from them. "In this case, there will no doubt be a lot of discussion," Gibbons speculates. "The conference will address whether there is anything we should do to improve the way others see us,

report on us, and so forth." The result may well be additional projects for Gibbons's department during the coming year.

Apply Your Knowledge

1. Sheila Gibbons points out that one of the biggest worries for anyone doing long reports is that the report may not see the "light of day." List the circumstances that might lead to a long report's being tabled before it can be read. If you're responsible for the preparation of such a report, what could you do to prevent the circumstances you've listed?

2. If you were the intern Sheila Gibbons assigned to research how other media report on Gannett, how would you define the scope of your task? How many examples of each of the media—newspapers, electronic media, magazines—would you include? For instance, among television stations, would you cover only the major networks? All nationally available cable channels? Or some combination of these? How would you decide the combination? Answer similar questions for newspapers and magazines. Would you recommend that Gibbons report the findings by media group? By broad theme? By issues uncovered? Why?

On the Job

SOLVING A COMMUNICATION DILEMMA AT HARLEY-DAVIDSON

Harley-Davidson had regained its reputation for building dependable motorcycles, but higher demand had created a new dilemma for CEO Richard Teerlink: how to increase production and boost sales without sacrificing quality. Teerlink refused to risk disappointing Harley customers by compromising quality for quantity. To keep Harley on track toward higher sales, he and his management team needed to collect and analyze mountains of information, much of it in the form of reports.

One key to Harley's stunning turnaround was its revamped manufacturing process. After analyzing information on Honda's manufacturing processes, the Harley staff installed a system of inventory management known as just-in-time (JIT). Similar systems have propelled some of the world's leading manufacturers to success. Among other things, JIT lowers the number of parts and supplies held in waiting, which allowed Harley to funnel more money into re-

search to improve product quality and speed up the manufacturing process.

JIT forced Harley to change everything from its purchasing practices to the layout of its factories. Harley forged cooperative relationships with a select group of suppliers who could deliver high-quality parts on time. In turn, this allowed the company to cut costs and increase quality.

Because Harley now uses fewer suppliers, it can place larger orders that qualify for bulk discounts. Also, Harley's design and production teams can work more closely with a smaller number of suppliers to ensure the quality of parts and supplies.

By redesigning its production machinery and creating more standardized parts for multiple bike models, Harley can now build individual models in smaller batches that allow more frequent product upgrades and boost quality by limiting defects to fewer parts. Reports help Harley management stay informed about the details they need to keep this lean-and-mean manufacturing process running smoothly.

Thanks to the emphasis on quality rather than quantity, Harley's share of the U.S. heavyweight motorcycle market is up to 64 percent, well ahead of second-place Honda. As it expands its production capacity, Harley is eager to gain additional market share in Europe, Japan, and Australia. Not only has the company beaten back competition from Japanese firms, it's also demonstrated that a U.S. firm can be a low-cost, high-quality producer. Teerlink and his managers are unlikely to forget that careful collection and analysis of key business data can help any company stay on the road to success.

Your Mission: Since 1986 Harley-Davidson's sales have more than quadrupled, and earnings have also accelerated. Even so, Richard Teerlink doesn't want the company to grow complacent and forget how intense the competition is today. He is particularly interested in continuing to improve customer service at Harley dealerships around the world. As his executive assistant, you've been asked to plan a report that will outline ways to increase customer satisfaction by improving customer service. You'll need to conduct the necessary research, analyze the findings, and present your recommendations. From the following, choose the best responses, and be prepared to explain why your choices are best.

1. Which of the following represents the most appropriate statement of purpose for this study?
   a. The purpose of this study is to identify any customer service problems in Harley-Davidson's worldwide dealer network.
   b. This study answers the following question: "What improvements in customer service can our dealers make in order to increase overall customer satisfaction?"
   c. This study identifies those dealers in the world-wide network who are most responsible for poor customer satisfaction.
   d. This study identifies steps that dealers should take to change customer service practices.

2. You have tentatively identified the following factors for analysis:

   I. To improve customer service, we need to hire more salespeople.
      A. Compute competitors' employee-to-sales ratio.
      B. Compute our employee-to-sales ratio.
   II. To improve customer service, we need to hire better salespeople.
      A. Assess skill level of competitors' salespeople.
      B. Assess skill level of our salespeople.
   III. To improve customer service, we need to retrain our salespeople.
      A. Review competitors' training programs.
      B. Review our training programs.

   IV. To improve customer service, we need to compensate and motivate our people differently.
      A. Assess competitors' compensation levels and motivational techniques.
      B. Assess our compensation levels and motivational techniques.

   Should you proceed with the investigation based on this preliminary outline, or should you consider other approaches to factoring the problem?
   a. Proceed with this outline.
   b. Do not proceed. Factor the problem by asking customers how they perceive Harley's current customer service efforts. In addition, ask dealers what they think they should be doing differently.
   c. Do not proceed. Factor the problem by considering what successful car dealers do in terms of customer service.
   d. Do not proceed. Factor the problem by considering what the rest of the company, aside from the dealers, could be doing to improve customer service.

3. Which of the following work plans is the best option for guiding your study of ways to improve customer service?
   a. Version one

   > Statement of Problem: As part of Harley-Davidson's continuing efforts to offer the most attractive heavyweight motorcycles in the world, Richard Teerlink wants to improve customer service at the dealer level. The challenge here is to identify service improvements that are meaningful and valuable to the customer without being too expensive or time consuming.
   >
   > Purpose and Scope of Work: The purpose of this study is to identify ways to increase customer satisfaction by improving customer service at our dealerships worldwide. A four-member study team, composed of the vice president of marketing and three dealers, has been appointed to prepare a written service-improvement plan. To accomplish this objective, this study will survey customers to learn what changes they'd like to see in terms of customer service. The team will analyze these potential improvements in terms of cost and time requirements and then design new service procedures that dealers can use to better satisfy customers.
   >
   > Sources and Methods of Data Collection and Analysis: The study team will assess current dealer efforts by (1) querying dealership employees regarding their customer service, (2) observing employees in action dealing with customers, (3) surveying current Harley owners regarding their purchase experiences, and (4) surveying

visitors to dealerships who decide not to purchase Harleys (by intercepting a sample of these people as they leave the dealerships). The team will also visit competitive dealerships to determine firsthand how they treat customers, and the team will mail questionnaires to a sample of registered motorcycle owners and classify the results by brand name. Once all these data have been collected, the team will analyze them to determine where buyers and potential buyers consider customer service to be lacking. Finally, the team will design procedures to meet their expectations.

Schedule:

Query dealer employees	Jan 10-Jan 20
Observe employees in action	Jan 21-Jan 30
Survey current Harley owners	Jan 15-Feb 15
Survey nonbuyers at dealerships	Jan 20-Jan 30
Visit competitive dealerships	Jan 31-Feb 15
Conduct mail survey of registered owners	Jan 15-Feb 15
Analyze data	Feb 15-Mar 1
Draft new procedures	Mar 2-Mar 15
Prepare final report	Mar 16-Mar 25
Present to management/ dealer committee	Mar 28

b. Version two

Statement of Problem: Harley's dealerships need to get on the ball in terms of customer service, and we need to tell them what to do in order to fix their customer service shortcomings.

Purpose and Scope of Work: This report will address how we plan to solve the problem. We'll design new customer service procedures and prepare a written report that dealers can learn from.

Sources and Methods of Data Collection: We plan to employ the usual methods of collecting data, including direct observation and surveys.

Schedule:

Collect data	Jan 10-Feb 15
Analyze data	Feb 15-Mar 1
Draft new procedures	Mar 2-Mar 15
Prepare final report	Mar 16-Mar 25
Present to management/ dealer committee	Mar 28

c. Version three

Task 1--Query dealer employees: We will interview a sampling of dealership employees to find out what steps they take to ensure customer satisfaction. Dates: Jan 10-Jan 20

Task 2--Observe employees in action: We will observe a sampling of dealership employees as they work with potential buyers and current owners, in order to learn firsthand what steps employees typically take. Dates: Jan 21-Jan 30

Task 3--Survey current Harley owners: Using a sample of names from Harley's database of current owners, we'll ask owners how they felt about the purchase process when they bought their bikes and how they feel they've been treated since then. We'll also ask them to suggest steps we could take to improve service. Dates: Jan 15-Feb 15

Task 4--Survey nonbuyers at dealerships: While we are observing dealership employees, we will also approach people who visit dealerships but leave without making a purchase. In the parking lot, we'll go through a quick survey, asking them what they think about Harley's customer service policies and practices and whether these had any bearing on their decisions not to purchase a Harley. Dates: Jan 20-Jan 30

Task 5--Visit competitive dealerships: Under the guise of shoppers looking for new motorcycles, we will visit a selection of competitive dealerships to discover how they treat customers and whether they offer any special services that Harley doesn't. Dates: Jan 31-Feb 15

Task 6--Conduct mail survey of registered owners: Using vehicle registration files from several states around the country, we will survey a sampling of motorcycle owners (of all brands). We will then sort the answers by brand of bike owned to see which dealers are offering which services. Dates: Jan 15-Feb 15

Task 7--Analyze data: Once we've collected all these data, we'll analyze them to identify (1) services that customers would like to see Harley dealers offer, (2) services offered by competitors that aren't offered by Harley dealers, and (3) services currently offered by Harley dealers that may not be all that important to customers. Dates: Feb 15-Mar 1

Task 8--Draft new procedures: From the data we've analyzed, we'll select new services that should be considered by Harley dealers. We'll also assess the time and money burdens that these services are likely to present, so that dealers can see whether each new service will yield a positive return on investment. Dates: Mar 2-Mar 15

Task 9--Prepare final report: This is essentially a documentation task, during which we'll describe our work, make our recommendations, and prepare a formal report. Dates: Mar 16-Mar 25

Task 10--Present to management/dealer committee: We'll summarize our findings and recommendations and make the full report available to dealers at the quarterly meeting. Date: Mar 28

d. Version four

Problem: To identify meaningful customer service improvements that can be implemented by Harley dealers.

Data Collection: Use direct observation and surveys to gather details about customer service at Harley dealers and at competing dealers. Have the study team survey current Harley owners, talk with people who visited Harley dealerships but did not buy, and send a questionnaire to registered motorcycle owners.

Schedule:
Step 1: Data collection. Work will begin on January 10 and end on February 15.
Step 2: Data analysis. Work will start on February 15 and end on March 1.
Step 3: Drafting new procedures. Work will start on March 2 and end on March 15.
Step 4: Preparation of the final report. Work will start on March 16 and end on March 25.
Step 5: Presentation of the final report. The report will be presented to management and to the dealer committee on March 28.

4. You're working on the questionnaire to send to current Harley-Davidson owners. One of the questions concerns the amount of information the salesperson shared with the customer. You want to make sure customers get all the information they need to make a good decision, but you don't want them to get overloaded with technical details.

Which of the following questions would do the best job of gathering this bit of information?

a. Were you overloaded with technical information when you spoke with a Harley-Davidson salesperson?
   _____ Yes
   _____ No
b. Did you receive enough information to make a smart purchase decision?
   _____ Yes
   _____ No
c. When you purchased a Harley, did the salesperson give you too little information, too much information, or just the right amount?
   _____ Too little
   _____ Too much
   _____ Just the right amount
d. Which of the following best describes how you felt about the amount of information you were given at the Harley dealership when you purchased your bike?
   _____ I think I did not receive enough information.
   _____ I am convinced that I did not receive enough information.
   _____ I didn't need any information from the salesperson; I knew what I wanted.
   _____ I think I received too much information.
   _____ I am convinced that I received too much information.

5. Assume that your survey results indicate that BMW motorcycle dealers rank highest in terms of customers' satisfaction with the treatment they received while buying motorcycles. Which of the following conclusions can you safely draw from this piece of data?
a. Harley needs to improve its customer service.
b. BMW sells the most motorcycles in the regions of the country covered by the survey.
c. Because BMW is not one of the world's leading motorcycle manufacturers, customer service is not very important.
d. None of the above.[7]

Questions for Discussion

1. Why are informational assignments factored differently from analytical assignments?
2. Why is the outline for a study likely to differ from the outline used for the report on that study?
3. If you were in charge of a study, would you instruct your assistants to restrict their research, or would you prefer that they exhaust all possible sources of information? Explain your answer.
4. What are the advantages and disadvantages of primary research using documents, observations, surveys, and experiments?
5. After an exhaustive study of an important problem, what would you do if you came to a conclusion that you knew your company's management would reject?
6. What is the difference between conclusions and recommendations?

Exercises

1. State the purpose of a report written to address each question below. Then break the problem down, and indicate whether subtopics, hypotheses, or relative merits would be the basis for an outline.
   a. Which of two careers would be best for you?
   b. What should be considered when renting an apartment?
   c. How should you go about starting a small business?
   d. How should convenience stores protect themselves against robberies?
   e. What computer printer would be the best for you to buy?

2. The following statements of purpose indicate how problems have been broken down. Critique each subdivision for violations of the rules of division.
   a. This report will analyze the pros and cons of advertising our hardware store in each of the major local media: radio, newspapers, and yellow pages.
   b. This report will analyze the major market segments in the Pacific Northwest for our line of raincoats: teenagers, yuppies, baby boomers, affluent over-50s, and senior citizens.
   c. This report focuses on the seven main categories of products carried in our chain of music stores: keyboards, stringed instruments, beginning band instruments, professional band instruments, sheet music, and accessories.
   d. This report analyzes inventory methods, distribution channels, point-of-purchase advertising, and product pricing for our line of suntan lotions, hand creams, and beauty soaps.

3. The college administration has asked you to head a student committee that will look into how the bookstore can ease the long lines during the first two weeks of every term, when students need to buy books. Select two other students to serve on your committee and help plan a feasibility study and an analytical report showing your recommendations. As a first step, your committee should prepare a brief memo to the administration covering the following points:
   a. Draft the problem statement and the statement of purpose.
   b. Identify two or three likely alternatives to be investigated.
   c. Determine clear criteria for selecting among the options.
   d. Identify the primary and secondary sources of information to be used in the study.

4. Your four-person accounting business specializes in going directly to clients' places of business. Your clients appreciate this personal attention, and you benefit from the availability of material on the premises, material your clients might not remember to bring to your central office. Your policy has been for each accountant to log business mileage and then to be reimbursed 25 cents per mile. Now accountants with large cars complain that they should be receiving more than the fixed rate. They argue that the large cars aid the company's image but 25 cents per mile is inadequate reimbursement. "Do you want us all to show up in old wrecks?" they ask.

   Thus you are considering leasing or purchasing four company cars. Before deciding, however, you want to compare the cost of the three options: (a) maintaining the present system (possibly with some minor adjustments), (b) leasing four cars, or (c) purchasing four cars. If you provide the cars, accountants will use them only for company business and for commuting to and from work.

   Factor the problem in the form of an outline. To begin, list eight or ten factual questions that must be answered before you can seriously address the problem.

5. As the new manager at The Gap clothing store located in your local mall, you've been assigned to research and write a factual report about the day-to-day variations in store sales throughout a typical week. What's the most logical way to factor this problem and structure your informational report? Indicate the subtopics you might use in your report.

6. The baking business is highly competitive, but you are succeeding with the small Philadelphia bakery turned over to you by your father. You produce an attractive line of sweet cookies, the type children point to in the supermarket and their mothers buy because of the low price. Your secret is to employ people who are certified "economically disadvantaged" and who have been unemployed for over two years. The federal government gives you tax credits for these workers, and you have found that they are very conscientious.

   In a trade journal, you read about a small, fully operational bakery outside Trenton, New Jersey. It is for immediate sale at a modest price (because of the owner's failing health). One of your workers has been with you for six years and understands your system; she could manage this bakery if you bought it. What you don't know is whether there is any demand for your product in Trenton or what the extent of the local competition is. You are also concerned about the bakery itself: its size, the age and condition of its equipment, and its location. Given your fairly modest budget for activities outside the normal sweep of your business, what types of primary research might you conduct to examine the feasibility of extending operations into Trenton? What specific questions would you like answered?

7. You have parlayed promises ("You'll get 3 percent of the gross"), a little luck, your contagious faith, and a lot of goodwill into an almost-completed motion picture, the story of a group of unknown musicians finding work and making a reputation in a difficult world. You have captured vibrant vignettes, both painful and happy, along with considerable footage of successful and less-successful gigs. The work is almost done. Some of your friends leave the first complete screening saying that the 132-minute movie is simply too long; others (including you) can't imagine any more editing cuts. You decide to test the movie on a regular audience, members of which will be asked to complete a questionnaire that may or may not lead to additional editing. You obtain permission from a local theater manager to show your film at 4:30 and 8:15 P.M., straddling his scheduled presentation. Design a questionnaire that can solicit valid answers.

8. Go to the library and look through back issues of *Inc., Mademoiselle, Cosmopolitan,* or other magazines in which reader views are requested through survey questionnaires. Select and analyze one such questionnaire.
   a. What is the purpose of the questionnaire?
   b. Classify the questions in the survey. Are all the questions of the same type? Do any rephrase earlier questions as a cross-check on the responses?
   c. Do any questions seem vague or abstract? If so, how would you reword these to improve them?
   d. Do any questions seem biased? How would you reword these questions to remove the bias?
   e. Are the instructions clear enough to guide respondents through the survey? What improvements can you suggest?

9. Prepare a list of ten questions about a current political issue or a class of consumer products. Then interview five randomly chosen people over the telephone. To obtain the five interviews, you will probably need to make more than twice that number of calls. Tabulate your results, and write a one- or two-page summary of your findings.

10. Visit a supermarket or fast-food outlet during a busy time in its operation, and observe customers passing through one checklist line for half an hour. You are interested in the gender and approximate age of the customers, the size and composition of the groups they're in, and the size of their purchases. Before your investigation, you need to prepare a sheet that will help you collect data systematically. Afterward, draft a brief narrative and a statistical report of your findings for your instructor. You should be able to answer these three questions: Do men or women make larger purchases? Does the age of the customer help predict the size of the purchase? How many purchases can this checkout counter handle in 30 minutes?

WRITING LONG REPORTS

After studying this chapter, you will be able to

Describe how organizations produce formal reports and proposals

Prepare all the necessary parts of a formal report

Select and prepare visual aids to support the text of your report

Assemble all the parts of a formal report in the proper order and use an appropriate format

Prepare and assemble all the parts of a formal proposal

Critique formal reports prepared by someone else

On the Job

FACING A COMMUNICATION DILEMMA AT PENN STATE

What's the Score?

Common sense would tell you that a good football team is an asset to any college town, but it takes more than common sense to figure out exactly how much a team is worth in dollars and cents. Take the Nittany Lions of Pennsylvania State University, for example—a good, strong team with a solid record of wins. Under the direction of head football coach Joe Paterno, the Lions consistently pack the college stadium with fans for Saturday afternoon home games.

How much do you suppose those fans contribute to the economy of State College, Pennsylvania? Would you believe $500,000 for each game? $1 million? $2 million? $3 million? More? Rodney A. Erickson, director of Penn State's Center for Regional Business Analysis, decided to find out. He wanted to document just exactly how important the Nittany Lions are to local businesses.

If you were reporting on the subject, how would you approach the task? Would the report be a formal one? Would you include a table of contents? An executive summary? A letter of transmittal? Just what sorts of components are included in formal reports?[1]

REPORT PRODUCTION

Experienced business communicators such as Rodney Erickson realize that planning formal reports and proposals, conducting the necessary research, organizing the ideas, developing the visual aids, and drafting the text are demanding and time-consuming

Penn State University

tasks. They also know that the process doesn't end there. After careful editing and rewriting, you still need to produce a polished final version.

How the final version is actually produced depends on the nature of the organization. If you work for an organization that produces many reports and proposals, the preparation process is likely to involve the interaction of a number of people. You and other members of a study team may subdivide the writing job (sometimes called *collaborative writing*). Working from a jointly developed outline, each of you may draft a section of the text and then delegate final preparation of the report to the company editor, the secretarial staff, and the art department. You won't be involved in the finer points of formatting, such as setting up a title page or positioning page numbers properly. The support staff will handle these tasks, using the approved company format. Your role will be to review their work and be sure it reflects the proper professionalism. On the other hand, if you work for a small business with a limited staff, you may compose and keyboard the entire report yourself, handling everything from outline to final version.

Personal computers can automatically handle many of the mechanical aspects of report preparation.

How you produce your report also depends on the equipment you have available. If you draft the report on a personal computer, using a word-processing program and perhaps a computer graphics package, you can easily incorporate editorial changes and reviewer comments. In addition, you can let the computer handle such mechanical chores as setting margins, adding footnotes, numbering pages, and checking your spelling and readability. Without a computer, the preparation process may take longer. You may have to retype the entire document in order to make changes, and each page must be formatted separately.

Be sure to schedule enough time to turn out a document that looks professional.

Regardless of precisely how the final product is produced, be sure to allocate enough time for a thorough job. Be realistic about what you expect from the support staff. Secretaries can type only about eight pages an hour; editors may spend 10 to 15 minutes on a single page; graphic artists may spend an hour or more preparing just one chart. In addition, every person who reviews the draft of the report will need time to read it and to recommend changes that are time consuming to incorporate.

Once you've completed a major report and sent it to your audience, you'll naturally expect a positive response, and quite often you'll get one—but not always. You may get halfhearted praise or no action on your conclusions and recommendations. Even worse, you may get some serious criticism. Try to learn from these experiences. Of course, sometimes you won't get any response at all, which is frustrating. If you haven't heard from your readers within a week or two, you might want to ask politely whether the report arrived. In hopes of stimulating a response, you could also offer to answer their questions or provide them with additional information.

Regardless of how the final report is produced, it will be up to you to make sure that all the necessary components are included. Depending on the length and formality of your report, various prefatory and supplementary parts may be necessary. The more formal your report, the more components you'll include.

COMPONENTS OF A FORMAL REPORT

When Penn State's Rodney Erickson assembles the final version of his report on the economic impact of college football, he will include many components not usually found in informal reports. Formal reports differ from informal ones in both format and tone. Manuscript format and an impersonal tone convey an impression of professionalism. But a formal report can be either short (fewer than ten pages) or long (ten pages or more). It can be informational or analytical, direct or indirect. It may

A formal report conveys the impression that the subject is important.

be directed to readers inside or outside the organization. What sets it apart from other reports is its polish.

The components listed in Figure 14.1 fall into three categories, depending on where they are found in a report: prefatory parts, text of the report, and supplementary parts. The prefatory parts of a short report usually include only a title page, a letter of transmittal combined with a synopsis, and a table of contents; usually no supplementary parts are included. (In very short formal reports, the table of contents and letter of transmittal are omitted too.) Long reports often include all the components listed. This chapter's sample formal report illustrates how all the parts fit together.

> The three basic divisions of a formal report:
> - Prefatory parts
> - Text
> - Supplementary parts

Prefatory Parts

Although the prefatory parts are placed before the text of the report, you may not want to write them until after you have written the text. Many of these parts—such as the table of contents, list of illustrations, and synopsis—are easier to prepare after the text is complete because they directly reflect the contents. Other parts can be prepared at almost any time.

> Prefatory parts may be written after the text has been completed.

Cover

Many companies have standard covers for reports, made of heavy paper and imprinted with the company's name and logo. Report titles are either printed on these covers or attached with gummed labels. If a company does not have standard covers, you can usually find something suitable in a good stationery store. Look for a cover that can be labeled with the title of the report, the writer's name (optional), and the submission date (also optional).

Think carefully about the title before you put it on the cover. A business report is not a mystery story, so give your readers all the information they need: the who, what, where, when, why, and how of the subject. At the same time, try to be reasonably concise. You don't want to intimidate your audience with a title that is too long, awkward, or unwieldy. One approach is to use a subtitle: "Opportunities for Improving Market Share in the Athletic Shoe Department: Customer Attitudes Toward Marshall's Athletic Footwear, December 1996." You can reduce the length of your title by eliminating phrases like *A report of, A study of,* and *A survey of.*

> Put a title on the cover that is informative but not too long.

PREFATORY PARTS	TEXT OF THE REPORT	SUPPLEMENTARY PARTS
Cover	Introduction	Appendixes
Title fly	Body	Bibliography
Title page	Summary	Index
Letter of authorization	Conclusions	
Letter of acceptance	Recommendations	
Letter of transmittal	Notes	
Table of contents		
List of illustrations		
Synopsis or executive summary		

**Figure 14.1
Parts of a Formal Report**

BEHIND THE SCENES AT THE ROCKY MOUNTAIN INSTITUTE
Energy Efficiency—Getting the Word to the World

The Rocky Mountain Institute (RMI) has plans to save the world's resources. Its primary tool? Words. The nonprofit environmental think tank expends most of its own energy convincing governments, corporations, utilities, architects, and anyone else who will listen that "it's cheaper to save energy than to waste it." To get this message to the world, RMI's 40 researchers produce thousands of pages of written reports each year for some 200 clients in over 32 countries. Many of these reports are highly technical, but the institute's founders, Amory and Hunter Lovins, like to present them in witty, straightforward language that anyone can understand. They've even invented words when necessary—like *negawatt*, a measure of electricity *saved*.

Amory, a child prodigy who became a Harvard and Oxford scholar, built his reputation as an energy wizard in the mid-1970s, when his book *Soft Energy Paths* correctly predicted that economic growth could be accompanied by lowered energy consumption. Hunter, RMI's president and executive director, is an attorney-turned-activist who rides rodeo and dirt bikes in her spare time. For years the married couple traveled the world as energy-efficiency consultants, but in 1982 they settled in Snowmass, Colorado, in a state-of-the-art, environmentally sound building that serves as home and office for RMI's research team.

The institute's programs are in five areas: energy efficiency, water usage, economic renewal of rural areas, sustainable agriculture, and global security through more efficient resource use and distribution. "What we do concerns policy," Hunter explains. "We do very little hardware testing, invention, or fiddling around." Instead, staffers may use the telephone to contact officials who have successfully implemented efficiency programs. The researchers ask what worked and what didn't, how much it cost, what roadblocks were overcome, and where to obtain any equipment that was used. This information may be combined with hardware evaluations, supply sources, and implementation recommendations in reports as long as 600 pages; Hunter calls them "tomes as big as a Manhattan phone book."

Other reports are smaller and friendlier and wind up in the hands of consumers (such as the popular softcover *Practical Home Energy Savings*). However, most begin as commissions from such company clients as

Title Fly and Title Page

The title page usually includes four blocks of information.

The **title fly** is a plain sheet of paper with only the title of the report on it. You don't really need one, but it adds a touch of formality to a report. The **title page** includes four blocks of information, as shown in the sample report later in this chapter: (1) the title of the report; (2) the name, title, and address of the person, group, or organization that authorized the report (which is usually the intended audience); (3) the name, title, and address of the person, group, or organization that prepared the report; and (4) the date on which the report was submitted. The title page can serve as the cover if the report is relatively short and is intended solely for internal use.

Letter of Authorization and Letter of Acceptance

A letter of authorization usually follows the direct-request plan.

If you received written authorization to prepare the report or proposal, you may want to include that letter or memo (or a copy of the request for proposal) in your report. The **letter of authorization** (or *memo of authorization*) is a document requesting that a report be prepared. It normally follows the direct-request plan described in Chapter 8, and it typically specifies the problem, scope, time and money restrictions, special instructions, and due date.

Use the good-news plan for a letter of acceptance.

The **letter of acceptance** (or *memo of acceptance*) acknowledges the assignment to conduct the study and to prepare the report. Following the good-news plan, the acceptance confirms time and money restrictions and other pertinent details. This document is rarely included in a report.

Pacific Gas & Electric, General Motors, and the World Bank.

Hunter admits that organizing such lengthy reports can be challenging. She must often rewrite early drafts to make sure readers can follow the flow of what she calls "the argument." When the U.S. Environmental Protection Agency (EPA) commissioned a 100-page report from RMI to serve as a manual for local water utilities, "they were interested in what water-efficiency measures existed and how to implement them," says Hunter. The first draft, written by a junior staff member, wandered a bit, so Hunter reshaped it. "I try in the introduction to set up a structure of argument that is signposted along the way. For example, I'll say, 'In almost every instance it will be more cost-effective for you to save water than to try to bring in new supplies, and this is true because of the following six reasons.' Then I have six subheads or chapters, depending on the amount of material. I try to prove the argument at each step along the way, and then I sum it all up." For the EPA report, Hunter stressed RMI's recommendations throughout the body, then briefly reinforced them in a "Final Note."

Of course, organization wasn't the only problem. Hunter also had to revise the document six times in response to comments from various EPA officials. Some of their comments were helpful, Hunter remembers, "but one guy scrawled in big red letters all the way across the page, 'Where's the beef?' That wasn't very useful. On the other hand, he was a senior guy at EPA, so we had to figure out what he meant by that. That took a lot of phone calls."

More than a year and plenty of headaches later, the "Water Efficiency" report was accepted and printed. It's rich with case studies, and it includes a table of contents, a formal introduction, brief overviews introducing each section, 172 footnotes, 7 appendixes, 9 figures, and 5 tables. There's no bibliography or index, but an appendix lists over a hundred names and addresses of water-efficiency contacts. Because the institute retained the right to distribute the booklet, "Water Efficiency" has now become part of RMI's save-the-world toolbox.

Apply Your Knowledge

1. Hunter Lovins says that executive summaries often omit important information that executives need. What steps would you take to avoid this problem?

2. Amory Lovins has written a groundbreaking treatise proving that plutonium waste from nuclear power reactors can be used to develop nuclear weapons. How would you arrange this material for a report to be distributed among government policy makers in countries that might fund nuclear power programs in developing nations?

Letter of Transmittal

The **letter of transmittal** (or *memo of transmittal*) conveys your report to your audience. (In a book, this section is called the preface.) The letter of transmittal says what you'd say if you were handing the report directly to the person who authorized it, so the style is less formal than the rest of the report: For example, the letter would use personal pronouns (*you, I, we*) and conversational language.

Generally, the transmittal letter appears right before the table of contents. However, if your report is quite formal, with wide distribution, you may want to include the letter of transmittal only in selected copies, making certain comments to a specific audience. Say you're recommending that two departments be merged, which will displace one of the department heads. In your report, you might not want to recommend either person for the remaining position, especially if both department heads will receive a copy of it. Rather, you might want to discuss the issue privately in a letter of transmittal to top management.

The letter of transmittal follows the routine and good-news plans described in Chapter 9. Begin with the main idea, officially conveying the report to the readers and summarizing its purpose. Typically, such a letter begins with a statement like "Here is the report you asked me to prepare on . . ." The rest includes information about the scope of the report, the methods used to complete the study, and the limitations that became apparent. In the middle section of the letter, you may also highlight important points or sections of the report, make comments on side issues, give suggestions

Use a less formal style for the letter of transmittal than for the report itself.

The most famous long report was written by Federal Express founder Frederick Smith. It detailed the then-revolutionary idea of air express delivery and persuaded investors to fund him. Smith believes that your reports reflect on you. If the report looks good, you look good. A messy report may not even get read.

for follow-up studies, and transmit any information that will help readers better understand and use the report. If the report does not have a synopsis, you can use the letter of transmittal to summarize the major findings, conclusions, and recommendations. You may also wish to acknowledge any help given by others. The concluding paragraph of the transmittal letter should be a note of thanks for having been given the report assignment, an expression of willingness to discuss the report, and an offer to assist with future projects.

Table of Contents

The table of contents indicates in outline form the coverage, sequence, and relative importance of the information in the report. In fact, the headings used in the text of the report are the basis of the table of contents. However, depending on the length and complexity of the report, the contents page may show only the top two or three levels of headings, sometimes only first-level headings. Excluding some levels of headings may frustrate readers who want to know where to find every subject you cover, but simplification of the table of contents also helps readers focus on the major points.

The table of contents is prepared after the other parts of the report have been typed so that the beginning page numbers for each heading can be shown. The headings are worded exactly as they are in the text of the report. Also listed on the contents page are the prefatory parts (only those that follow the contents page) and the supplementary parts. If you have four or fewer visual aids, you may wish to list them in the table of contents too; if you have more than four visual aids, you should list them separately in a list of illustrations.

List of Illustrations

For simplicity's sake, some reports refer to all visual aids as illustrations or exhibits. In other reports, as in the sample report in this chapter, tables are labeled separately from all other types of visual aids, which are called figures. Regardless of the system used to label visual aids, the list of illustrations gives their titles and page numbers.

Put the list of illustrations on a separate page if it won't all fit on one page with the table of contents; start the list of figures and the list of tables on separate pages if they won't both fit on one page.

If there is enough space on a single page, type the list of illustrations directly beneath the table of contents. Otherwise, type it on a separate page following the contents page. When tables and figures are numbered separately, they are also listed separately. Both lists can be typed on the same page if they fit; otherwise, start each list on a separate page.

Synopsis or Executive Summary

Provide an overview of the report in a synopsis or an executive summary.

A **synopsis** is a brief overview (one page or less) of a report's most important points, designed to give readers a quick preview of the contents. It's often included in long informational reports dealing with technical, professional, or academic subjects and can also be called an *abstract*. Because it is a concise representation of the whole report, it may be distributed separately to a wide audience. Interested readers can then opt to order a copy of the entire report.

An informative synopsis summarizes the main ideas; a descriptive synopsis states what the report is about.

The phrasing of a synopsis can be either informative or descriptive, depending on whether the report is in direct or indirect order. An informative synopsis presents the main points of the report in the order in which they appear in the text. In contrast, a descriptive synopsis simply tells what the report is about and is only moderately more detailed than the table of contents; the actual findings of the report are omitted. Here are examples of statements from each type:

Informative Synopsis: Sales of superpremium ice cream make up 11 percent of the total ice cream market.

Descriptive Synopsis: This report contains information about superpremium ice cream and its share of the market.

The way you handle a synopsis reflects the approach you use in the text. If you're using an indirect approach in your report, you're better off with a descriptive synopsis. An informative synopsis, with its focus on conclusions and key points, may be too confrontational if you have a skeptical audience. You don't want to spoil the effect by providing a controversial beginning.

Many business report writers prefer to include an executive summary instead of a synopsis. A synopsis is essentially a prose table of contents that outlines the main points of the report. An **executive summary** is a fully developed "mini" version of the report itself, intended for readers who lack the time or motivation to study the complete text. As a consequence, an executive summary is more comprehensive than a synopsis, generally about 10 percent of the document length.

Unlike a synopsis, an executive summary may contain headings, well-developed transitions, and visual aids. It should be organized in the same way as the report, using a direct or indirect approach, depending on the audience's receptivity. In analytical reports, enough evidence should be provided in the executive summary to make a convincing case for the conclusions and recommendations. After reading the summary, the executive should know the essentials and be in a position to make a decision. Later, when time permits, he or she may read certain parts of the report to obtain additional detail.

Many reports do not require either a synopsis or an executive summary. Generally speaking, length is the determining factor. Most reports of fewer than 10 pages either omit one or combine it with the letter of transmittal. However, if your report is over 30 pages long, you should probably include either a synopsis or an executive summary as a convenience for readers. Which one you'll provide depends on the traditions of your organization.

Text of the Report

Chapters 12 and 13 tell you a good deal about how to write the text of a report. But apart from deciding on the fundamental issues of content and organization, you will also make decisions about the design and layout of the report. You can use a variety of techniques to present your material effectively. Many organizations have format guidelines that make your decisions easier, but the goal is always to focus the reader's attention on major points and on the flow of ideas.

Headings are the most powerful format tool available to you. Each heading should give clues to the material that follows. By skimming along from heading to heading, readers should be able to pick up the structure or outline of your report. This process is easier if the headings are phrased and typed in a consistent way (see Figure 12.7 in Chapter 12).

To highlight the headings, you can use typographical distinctions such as all capital letters, initial capitals, underlining, italics, and boldface print. Be sure that you use these signals consistently so that the hierarchy among the headings is visually apparent. You can also emphasize the headings by allowing extra white space between them and the text. In fact, in longer reports, you should call attention to the major breaks in thought by beginning each main section or chapter on a separate page. In shorter reports, the sections or chapters may run continuously, with only first-level headings separating the major divisions.

Visual aids are also useful tools for calling attention to key points and helping readers grasp the flow of ideas. By depicting important information visually, you capture the attention of readers who are leafing through the report. Eye-catching graphics dramatize the high points of the message, and informative captions explain their meaning.

Debi Coleman is head of worldwide manufacturing for Apple Computer. She oversees the modernization of plants and manufacturing processes, and many of her decisions are based on reports. If the reports are well researched, accurate, and clear, says Coleman, the risks involved in decision making are reduced, resulting in better decisions.

An introduction has a number of functions and covers a wide variety of topics.

It is also a good idea to preview key points at the beginning of each major section or chapter and to sum them up at the end. In other words, readers benefit when you

1. Tell them what you're going to tell them
2. Tell them
3. Tell them what you told them

When accomplished without being overly redundant, this strategy keeps readers positioned and reinforces the substance of your message.

Introduction

The introduction to a report serves a number of important functions:

- Putting the report in a broader context by tying it to a problem or an assignment
- Telling readers the report's purpose
- Previewing the report's contents and organization
- Establishing the tone of the report and the writer's relationship with the audience

The length of the introduction depends on the length of the report. If you're writing a relatively brief report, the introduction may be only a paragraph or two and may not be labeled with a heading of any kind. On the other hand, the introduction to a major formal report may extend to several pages and can be identified as a separate section by the first-level heading "Introduction." Here's a list of topics that are generally covered in an introduction:

- *Authorization.* When, how, and by whom the report was authorized; who wrote it; and when it was submitted. This material is especially important when no letter of transmittal is included.
- *Problem/purpose.* The reason for the report's existence and what is to be accomplished as a result of the report's being written. (You might also subtly indicate which audience your report is addressing by saying something like "This report will help engineers determine whether . . .")
- *Scope.* What is and what isn't going to be covered in the report. The scope indicates the report's size and complexity.
- *Background.* The historic conditions or factors that have led up to the report. This section enables readers to understand how the problem developed and what has been done about it so far.
- *Sources and methods.* The secondary sources of information used and the primary sources such as interviews, surveys, experiments, and observations. This section tells readers what sources were used, how the sample was selected, how the questionnaire was constructed (a sample questionnaire and cover letter are usually included in the appendix), what follow-up procedures were used, and the like. It provides enough detail to give readers confidence in the work and to convince them that the sources and methods were satisfactory.
- *Definitions.* A brief introductory statement leading into a column of terms used in the report and their definitions. The terms may be unfamiliar but essential to understanding the report (such as *duopsony:* "a market situation in which two rival buyers determine the demand for a product"), or the terms may be familiar expressions used in a specific way (such as *business education* used exclusively to mean "the education of business teachers"). Terms may be defined in other places as well: in the body, as the terms are used; in explanatory footnotes; or in a glossary, an alphabetical listing of terms placed at the end of the report.

- *Limitations.* Factors affecting the quality of the report, such as a budget too small to do all the work that should have been done, an inadequate amount of time to do all the research desired, an unreliability or unavailability of data, or other conditions beyond your control. This is the place to mention doubts about any aspect of the report. Although candor may lead readers to question the results, it will also enable them to assess the results more accurately and will help maintain the integrity of the report. However, limitations are no excuse for conducting a poor study or writing a bad report.
- *Report organization.* The organization of the report (what topics are covered and when), along with a rationale for following this plan. This section is a road map that helps readers understand what comes next and why.

Some of these items may be combined in the introduction; some may not be included at all. Make your decision about what to include by figuring out what kind of information will help your readers understand and accept the report.

Also give some thought to how the introduction relates to the prefatory parts of the report. In longer reports, you may have a letter of transmittal, a synopsis or an executive summary, and an introduction, all of which cover essentially the same ground. To avoid redundancy, you may need to juggle the various sections. If the letter of transmittal and synopsis are fairly detailed, for example, you might want the introduction to be relatively brief. However, remember that some people may barely glance at the prefatory parts; thus the introduction should be detailed enough to provide an adequate preview of the report. If you need to repeat information that has already been covered in one of the prefatory parts, simply use different wording.

Body

The body of the report follows the introduction. It consists of the major sections or chapters (with various levels of headings) that present, analyze, and interpret the material gathered as part of your investigation. These chapters contain the "proof," the detailed information necessary to support your conclusions and recommendations.

One of the decisions to make when writing the body of your report is how much detail to include. Your decision depends on the nature of your information, the purpose of the report, and the preferences of your audience. Some situations call for detailed coverage; others lend themselves to shorter treatment. In general, provide only enough detail in the body to support your conclusions and recommendations; if needed, put additional detail in tables, charts, and appendixes.

Another decision to make is whether to put your conclusions in the body, in a separate section, or in both. If the conclusions seem to flow naturally from the evidence, you'll almost inevitably cover them in the body. However, if you want to give your conclusions added emphasis, you may include a separate section to summarize them. Having a separate section is particularly appropriate in longer reports; the reader may lose track of the conclusions if they're given only in the body.

Summary, Conclusions, and Recommendations

The final section of text in a report tells readers "what you told them." In a short report, this final wrap-up may be only a paragraph or two, but a long report generally has separate sections labeled "Summary," "Conclusions," and "Recommendations." Here's how the three differ:

- *Summary.* The key findings of your report, paraphrased from the body and stated or listed in the order in which they appear in the body.
- *Conclusions.* The writer's analysis of what the findings mean. These are the answers to the questions that led to the report.

Linda J. Wachner is CEO of lingerie maker Warnaco and is often called on to make decisions based on reports. But if a report makes a recommendation and lacks the detail to support it, the recommendation is useless. Likewise, a recommendation buried in too much detail may be too difficult to uncover. Wachner advises balancing the amount of detail to complement the subject and its complexity.

Summaries, conclusions, and recommendations serve different purposes.

- *Recommendations.* Opinions, based on reason and logic, about the course of action that should be taken. These should come directly from and be supported by the findings and conclusions.

If the report is organized in direct order, the summary, conclusions, and recommendations are presented before the body and are reviewed only briefly at the end. If the report is organized in indirect order, these sections are presented for the first time at the end and are covered there in detail.

Some report writers combine the conclusions and recommendations under one heading. It is often difficult to present a conclusion without implying a recommendation. Whether you combine them or not, if you have several conclusions and recommendations, you may want to number and list them. An appropriate lead-in sentence for the list of conclusions is "The findings of this study lead to the following conclusions." A statement that could be used for the list of recommendations is "Based on the conclusions of this study, the following recommendations are made." Present no new findings in either the conclusions or the recommendations section.

In action-oriented reports, put all the recommendations in a separate section and spell out precisely what should happen next.

In reports that are intended to lead to action, the recommendations section is particularly important; it spells out exactly what should happen next. It brings all the action items together in one place and gives the details about who should do what, where, when, and how. Readers may agree with everything you say in your report but still fail to take any action if you're vague about what should happen next. Readers must understand what's expected of them and must have some appreciation of the difficulties that are likely to arise. A timetable and specific assignments are helpful because concrete plans have a way of commanding action.

Notes

Give credit where credit is due.

When writing the text of your report, you decide how to acknowledge your sources. You have an ethical and legal obligation to give other people credit for their work. When you use someone else's research, it is unfair, and also illegal, to pass it off as your own. **Plagiarism** occurs when one person misappropriates without permission or acknowledgment any ideas, facts, words, or structures that were reported or originated by others.[2] In general, you're flirting with plagiarism when your business documents fail to alert your audience that you have

- Repeated someone else's information word for word
- Paraphrased another's material too closely
- Lifted a series of phrases and put them together with your own words
- Borrowed a unique term that originated elsewhere

In the college environment, putting your name on a term paper written by another student would be considered plagiarism. In the business world, however, drafting documents on behalf of your supervisor is a legitimate part of your job in most organizations. Putting a supervisor's name on your business report would rarely be seen as plagiarism.

In general, using quotation marks when quoting from a source—and then citing the original source—enables you to properly credit the person whose words you're using. It also tells your audience where to look if they want more information. Similarly, even if you paraphrase from a source, it's important to indicate who originated the information you're using. Although your company may have more specific guidelines, here are a few general tips on how to handle situations that commonly arise:

- *Repeating information from another company document.* If you reuse information that has appeared in other company documents, your audience may believe that you've independently verified the repeated material and eliminated any errors that were in the original report. To avoid such misunderstandings, it's best to mention where the material appeared earlier. That way, your readers can check the source for further details.

- *Using the same sources as another document.* Consulting someone else's sources for further information is perfectly acceptable. Plagiarism deals with the way information is reported or analyzed, not with whether you can access the sources used by someone else. When you approach cited sources to get the same information yourself, you're being absolutely ethical.
- *Repeating information protected by copyright.* If you repeat information from books, published articles, songs, and other copyrighted materials, be sure to avoid infringing on the originators' legal rights. Even when you document your sources, you may find that your use of outside information has inadvertently violated copyright laws. Although ideas can't be copyrighted, words, illustrations, graphs, maps, cartoons, poetry, and other creative expressions of ideas can be legally protected against unauthorized use by others. To be safe, talk to your company's attorney before you repeat information or reprint artwork that is protected by copyright.

At the very least, people lose respect for someone who has been caught plagiarizing the words of another. At worst, plagiarism in business documents can lead to more serious consequences: loss of funding, loss of employment, monetary damages, and so forth. Consider how you would feel if you saw your words used without proper credit. On the other hand, you would probably be flattered if a business report mentioned your work and cited you as the source. So to avoid even the most unintentional plagiarism, the best approach in most cases is to acknowledge the contributions of others by citing sources carefully and completely.

Of course, even though acknowledging your sources enhances the credibility of your report and demonstrates that you have thoroughly researched the topic, you want to cite your sources in a way that doesn't make your report read like an academic treatise. No one wants to drag along from footnote to footnote. Handle your source references as conveniently and as inconspicuously as possible (see Appendix B for some alternatives). One approach, especially for internal reports, is simply to mention a source in the text:

According to Dr. Lewis Morgan of Northwestern Hospital, hip replacement operations account for 7 percent of all surgery performed on women aged 65 and over.

If your report will be distributed to outsiders, however, you should include additional information on where you obtained the data.

Visual Aids

In his report about the impact of college football on the local economy, Rodney Erickson can complement his text by including tables, bar charts, pie charts, organization charts, maps, or other visual aids. When illustrating the text of any report, you face the problem of choosing the specific form that best suits your message. Moreover, good business ethics demand you choose a form of visual aid that will not mislead your audience.

Tables

When you have to present detailed, specific information, choose a **table**, a systematic arrangement of data in columns and rows. Tables are ideal when the audience needs

Use tables to help your audience understand detailed information.

Figure 14.2
Parts of a Table

	TABLE 1 Title			
	Multicolumn Head		Single-Column Head*	Single-Column Head
Stub head	Subhead	Subhead		
Line head	XXX	XXX	XX	XX
Line head				
Subhead	XX	XXX	XX	XX
Subhead	XX	XXX	X	XX
Totals	XXX	XXX	XX	XX

Source: (in the same format as a text footnote; see Component Chapter B)
*Footnote (for explanation of elements in the table; a superscript number or small letter may be used instead of an asterisk or other symbol)

all the facts and the information would be either difficult or tedious to handle in the main text.

Most tables contain the same standard parts, which are illustrated in Figure 14.2. What makes a table a table is the grid that allows you to find the point where two factors intersect. Every table must therefore include vertical columns and horizontal lines, with useful headings along the top and side. Tables that are projected onto a screen for use in oral presentations should be limited to three column heads and six line heads; tables presented on paper may include from one or two heads to a dozen or more. If the table has too many columns to fit comfortably between the margins of the page, turn the paper horizontally and insert it in the report with the top toward the binding.

Although formal tables set apart from the text are necessary for conveying complex information, some data can be presented more simply within the text. The table becomes, in essence, a part of the paragraph, typed in tabular format. These "text tables" are usually introduced with a sentence that leads directly into the tabulated information. Here's an example:

The farm population has declined steadily since 1960, but the average size of a farm has increased:

Year	Farm Population (in millions)	Average Farm Size (in acres)
1960	15.6	297
1970	9.7	374
1980	6.0	429
1990	5.2	435

The flow of people away from farming seems likely to continue, but many experts believe that farm size will stabilize at around current acreages.

In setting up a numerical table, be sure to identify the units in which amounts are given: dollars, percentages, price per ton, or whatever. All items in a column should be expressed in the same units.

Tabular information can be introduced within the text without a formal title.

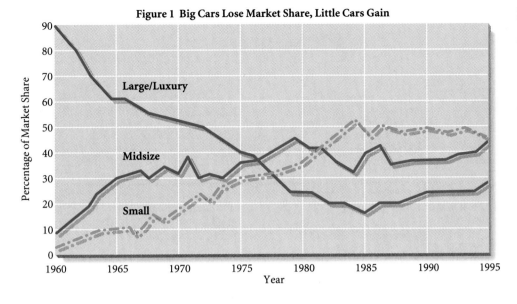

Figure 1 Big Cars Lose Market Share, Little Cars Gain

Figure 14.3
Line Chart Plotting Three Lines

Line and Surface Charts

A **line chart** illustrates trends over time or plots the interaction of two variables. In line charts showing trends, the vertical axis shows amount, and the horizontal axis shows time or quantity being measured. Ordinarily, both scales begin at zero and proceed in equal increments. However, if the data are plotted far above zero, the vertical axis can be broken to show that some of the increments have been left out.

A simple line chart may be arranged in many ways. One of the most common is to plot several lines on the same chart for comparative purposes, as shown in Figure 14.3. If at all possible, use no more than three lines on any given chart, particularly if the lines cross.

A **surface chart** is a form of line chart with a cumulative effect; all the lines add up to the top line, which represents the total (see Figure 14.4). This form of chart is useful when you want to illustrate changes in the composition of something over time.

Use line charts
- To indicate changes over time
- To plot the interaction of two variables

A surface chart is a kind of line chart showing cumulative effect.

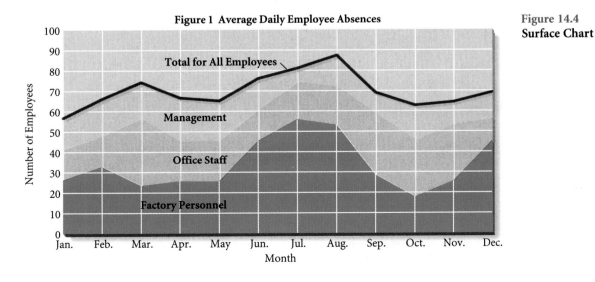

Figure 1 Average Daily Employee Absences

Figure 14.4
Surface Chart

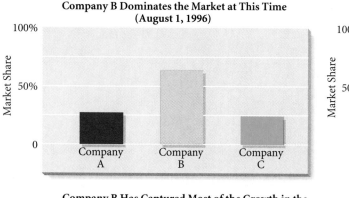

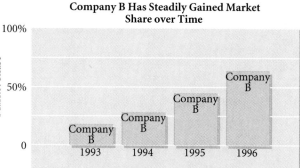

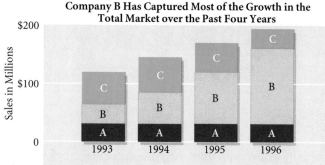

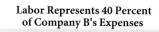

Figure 14.5
The Versatile Bar Chart

When preparing this type of chart, put the most important segment against the baseline, and limit the number of strata to four or five.

Bar Charts

Bar charts are useful in many situations and take a variety of forms.

A **bar chart** is a chart in which amounts are visually portrayed by the height or length of rectangular bars. Bar charts are almost as common in business reports as line charts are, and in some ways they are more versatile. As Figure 14.5 illustrates, they are particularly valuable when you want to

- Compare the size of several items at one time
- Show changes in one item over time
- Indicate the composition of several items over time
- Show the relative size of components of a whole

You can be creative with bar charts in many ways. You can align the bars either vertically or horizontally and double the bars for comparisons. You can even use bar charts to show both positive and negative quantities.

Pie Charts

Use pie charts to show the relative sizes of the parts of a whole.

Another type of chart you see frequently in business reports is the **pie chart,** in which numbers are represented as slices of a complete circle, or pie. Although they are somewhat less versatile than either line or bar charts, pie charts are nevertheless a valuable item in your inventory of visual aids. Nothing is better for showing the composition of a whole than a pie chart (see Figure 14.6).

When composing a pie chart, try to limit the number of slices in the pie to no more than seven. Otherwise, the chart looks cluttered and is difficult to label. If necessary,

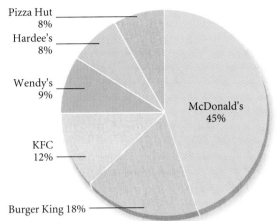

Percentage of Sales Among the Six Leading Restaurant Chains

Pizza Hut 8%
Hardee's 8%
Wendy's 9%
KFC 12%
McDonald's 45%
Burger King 18%

Figure 14.6
Pie Chart

lump the smallest pieces together in a "miscellaneous" category. Ideally, the largest or most important slice of the pie, the segment you want to emphasize, is placed at the 12 o'clock position; the rest are arranged clockwise either in order of size or in some other logical progression. You might want to shade the segment that is of the greatest interest to your readers or use color to distinguish the various pieces. In any case, be sure to label all the segments and to indicate their value in either percentages or units of measure so that your readers will be able to judge the value of the wedges. The segments must add up to 100 percent.

Organization Charts and Flowcharts

If you need to show physical or conceptual relationships rather than numerical ones, you might want to use an organization chart or a flowchart. **Organization charts,** as the name implies, illustrate the positions, units, or functions of an organization and the way they interrelate. An organization's normal communication channels are almost impossible to describe without a chart like the one in Figure 14.7. **Flowcharts**

Use organization charts to depict the interrelationships among the parts of an organization.

Use flowcharts
- To show a series of steps from beginning to end
- To show relationships

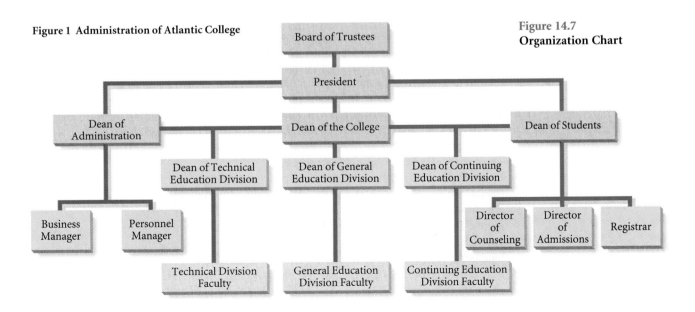

Figure 1 Administration of Atlantic College

Board of Trustees
President
Dean of Administration
Dean of the College
Dean of Students
Dean of Technical Education Division
Dean of General Education Division
Dean of Continuing Education Division
Business Manager
Personnel Manager
Director of Counseling
Director of Admissions
Registrar
Technical Division Faculty
General Education Division Faculty
Continuing Education Division Faculty

Figure 14.7
Organization Chart

Figure 1 Flow of Clients Through Health Center

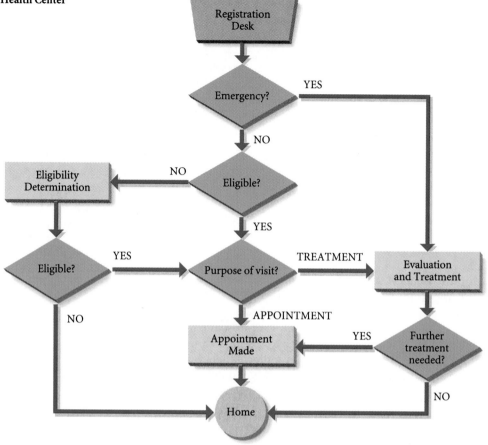

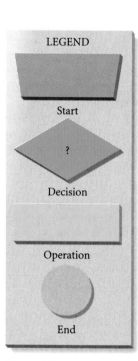

Figure 14.8
Flowchart

illustrate a sequence of events from start to finish. They are indispensable when illustrating processes, procedures, and relationships. The various elements in the process may be represented by pictorial symbols or geometric shapes, as in Figure 14.8.

Maps

Use maps
- To represent statistics by geographic area
- To show locational relationships

For certain applications, maps are ideal. One of the most common uses is to show concentrations of something by geographic area. In your own reports, you might use maps to show regional differences in such variables as your company's sales of a product. Or you might indicate proposed plant sites and their proximity to sources of supply or key markets. Most office supply stores carry blank maps of the United States, various U.S. regions, and other areas around the world. You can illustrate these maps to suit your needs, using dots, shading, labels, numbers, and symbols.

Drawings, Diagrams, and Photographs

Business reports occasionally use drawings, diagrams, and photographs, although these tend to be less common than some of the other visual aids. Drawings and diagrams are most often used in technical reports to show how something looks or operates. Figure 14.9, for example, is from an article explaining how satellite communications aid cellular phone users. Although this diagram was professionally prepared, even a hand-drawn sketch is better than words alone for giving your audience a clear idea of how an item looks or how it can be used. In industries such as engineering and architecture, computer-aided design systems are capable of producing detailed diagrams and drawings. In addition, a variety of widely available programs for use on micro-computers provide a file of symbols and pictures of various types that can be used (sparingly) to add a decorative touch to reports and presentations.

Photographs have always been popular in business documents such as catalogs and annual reports, where their visual appeal is used to capture the interest of readers. As the technology for reproducing photographs improves and becomes less expensive, even analytical business reports for internal use are beginning to have more pho-tographs in them. Nothing can demonstrate the exact appearance of a new facility, a piece of property or equipment, or a new product the way a photograph can.

Incorporation of Visual Aids in the Text

Every visual aid you use should be clearly referred to by number in the text of your report. Some report writers refer to all visual aids as exhibits and number them con-secutively throughout the report; many others number tables and figures separately (everything that isn't a table is regarded as a figure). In a very long report with num-bered chapters (as in this book), visual aids may have a double number, consisting of the chapter number and an individual number separated by a period or a hyphen.

A reference to a visual aid precedes the piece itself so that readers are not confronted with visual aids whose significance they can't yet understand. The reference helps read-ers understand why the table or chart is important. The following selection from a re-port on the market for motorcycles shows how the connection can be made:

In-text references tell readers why the illustration is impor-tant.

Figure 1 shows the financial history of the motorcycle division over the past five years, with sales broken into four categories. Total sales were steady over this period, but the mix of sales by category changed dramatically.

Figure 14.9
Diagram

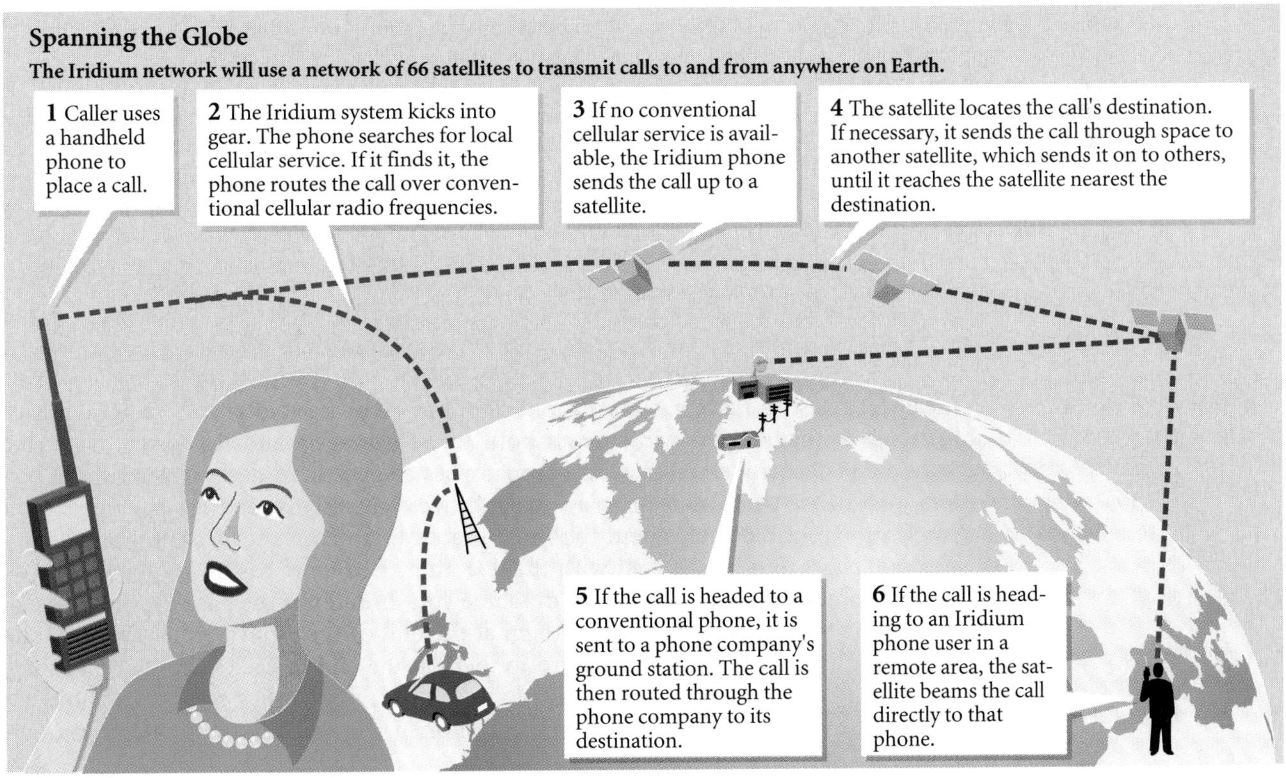

Spanning the Globe

The Iridium network will use a network of 66 satellites to transmit calls to and from anywhere on Earth.

1 Caller uses a handheld phone to place a call.

2 The Iridium system kicks into gear. The phone searches for local cellular service. If it finds it, the phone routes the call over conven-tional cellular radio frequencies.

3 If no conventional cellular service is avail-able, the Iridium phone sends the call up to a satellite.

4 The satellite locates the call's destination. If necessary, it sends the call through space to another satellite, which sends it on to others, until it reaches the satellite nearest the destination.

5 If the call is headed to a conventional phone, it is sent to a phone company's ground station. The call is then routed through the phone company to its destination.

6 If the call is head-ing to an Iridium phone user in a remote area, the sat-ellite beams the call directly to that phone.

REPORT WRITER'S NOTEBOOK
Creating Colorful Visual Aids with Computers

More and more people are learning to use graphics software to create striking and attractive visual aids. No matter which type of software you use, your design is likely to look more professional than a graphic drawn by hand. Once you've designed your visual, you can also use your computer and software to plan the colors.

You know from your own experience that color helps make a point more effectively than black and white. However, there's more to using color than simply picking ones that appeal to you. To choose an effective color scheme, ask yourself these questions:

- *What colors will best convey the effect I want?* As a general rule, bright, solid colors are more pleasing to the eye and easier to distinguish than pastel or patterned colors. Yellow, blue, and green are usually good choices, but the possibilities are numerous. Just keep in mind that too many colors may overwhelm the message. Use color as an accent: bright color for emphasis and darker or lighter colors for background information. Color can also visually connect related points or set apart points that represent significant change.

- *Are these colors appropriate for my message, purpose, and audience?* Liking red is not a good reason for using it in all your graphic designs. It's too "hot" for some people and conveys the wrong message in some instances. For example, using red to show profits in an annual report might confuse readers because they're likely to associate it with "red ink," or losses. Also remember that people in other cultures will make color associations that differ from yours.

- *Is my audience familiar with these colors?* Unless your aim is to shake up your audience, avoid uncommon colors or unusual combinations. In general, conventional colors are best for conventional audiences. However, young or trendy audiences probably won't be jarred by unfamiliar colors.

- *Can I improve the effect by changing any of the colors?* When you have the opportunity to use more than one color, choose those that contrast. Colors without contrast blend together and obscure the message. At the same time, be careful to use vivid or highly saturated colors sparingly.

Of course, your color choices may be limited or dictated in certain situations. Some organizations specify the exact color or combination to be used on company logos and other official symbols or illustrations. At other times you'll be free to decide on any combination of colors that works best for the visual aid you're preparing. That's when you'll find graphics software especially useful.

Depending on the capabilities of your software and your computer monitor, you can try out various colors and combinations and see the results immediately. Even the most basic program offers three colors. More sophisticated programs can give you thousands or even millions of color and shading choices.

To start, select a background color from the program's "palette" of available colors. Then choose a dominant color to set the tone for the overall color scheme. Continue adding colors as necessary, until you find the combination that works best. Because you can test many colors and combinations with a quick click of the

---

Put a visual aid as close as possible to its in-text reference to help readers understand the illustration's relevance.

Ideally, it's best to place each visual aid right beside or right after the paragraph it illustrates so that readers can consult both the explanation and the visual aid at the same time. Of course, unless your company has a specialized desktop publishing system, you'll have trouble creating layouts with artwork and text on the same page. With conventional office equipment, the most practical approach is to put visual aids on separate pages and mesh them with the text after the report has been typed.

This solution raises the question of where you should put the pages with the visual aids. Some writers prefer to cluster them at the end of the report, either as a separate section or as an appendix. Others group them at the end of each chapter. Still others prefer to place them as close as possible to the paragraphs they refer to. Although a case can be made for each approach, the best one is generally to place the pages of vi-

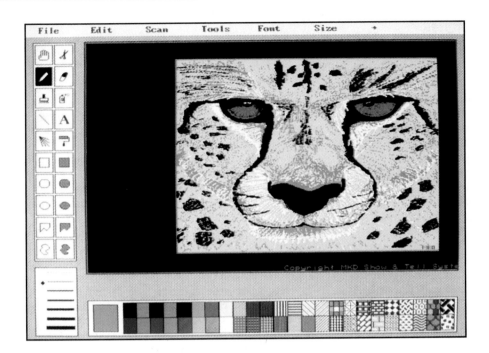

mouse, you can come to a final decision more quickly (and with less effort) than if you had to do it without the software.

Once you've decided on colors, you can print out a hard copy or an acetate transparency using a color printer or color plotter. You can also create full-color slides using a film recorder, or you can simply project the colorful image from your computer screen through an overhead projector to a large viewing screen.

1. Would you use green or red to shade a visual aid showing the geographic areas where your firm does business? Would you use green or red to shade the areas where your firm does not do business? Why?

2. How can you use color in a line chart to help your audience differentiate between current and projected sales? Between expected and actual sales? Explain your answers.

sual aids right after the pages containing references to them. This arrangement encourages readers to look at the visual aids when you want them to and in the context you have prepared.

Supplementary Parts

The supplementary parts follow the text of the report and include the appendix(es), bibliography, and index. They are more common in long reports than in short ones.

An **appendix** is a supplementary part that contains materials related to the report but not included in the text because they are too lengthy, too bulky, or not directly relevant. Sample questionnaires and cover letters, sample forms, computer printouts,

Include in an appendix those materials that are

- Bulky or lengthy
- Not directly relevant to the text

(Text continues on page 357)

REPORT WRITER'S NOTEBOOK
Analyzing a Formal Report: An In-Depth Critique

The report presented in the following pages was prepared by Andy O'Toole, an analyst in the cost accounting department of TriTech Industries, a medium-size company headquartered in San Francisco. TriTech's main product is optical character recognition equipment, which is used by the U.S. Postal Service for sorting mail. O'Toole's job is to help analyze the company's costs. He has this to say about the background of his report:

"For the past three or four years, TriTech has been on a roll. Our A-12 optical character reader was a real breakthrough, and the post office grabbed up as many as we could make. Our sales and profits kept climbing, and morale was fantastic. Everybody seemed to think that the good times would last forever. Unfortunately, everybody was wrong. When the Postal Service announced that it was 'postponing' all new-equipment purchases because of cuts in its budget, we woke up to the fact that we are essentially a one-product company with one customer. At that point management started scrambling around looking for ways to cut costs until we can diversify our business a bit.

"The vice president of administration, Jean Alexander, asked me to help identify cost-cutting opportunities in the travel and entertainment area. On the basis of her personal observations, she felt that TriTech was overly generous in its travel policies and that we might be able to save a significant amount by controlling these costs more carefully. My investigation confirmed her suspicion.

"I was reasonably confident that my report would be well received. I've worked with Ms. Alexander before and know what she likes: plenty of facts, clearly stated conclusions, and specific recommendations for what should be done next. I also knew that my report would be passed on to other TriTech executives, so I wanted to create a good impression. I wanted the report to be accurate and thorough, visually appealing, readable, and appropriate in tone."

When writing the analytical report that follows, O'Toole used an organization based on conclusions and recommendations, presented in direct order. The first two sections of the report correspond to O'Toole's two main conclusions: that TriTech's travel and entertainment costs are too high and that cuts are essential. The third section presents recommendations for achieving better control over travel and entertainment expenses. As you review the report, analyze both the mechanical aspects and the way O'Toole presents his ideas. Be prepared to discuss the way the various components convey and reinforce the main message.

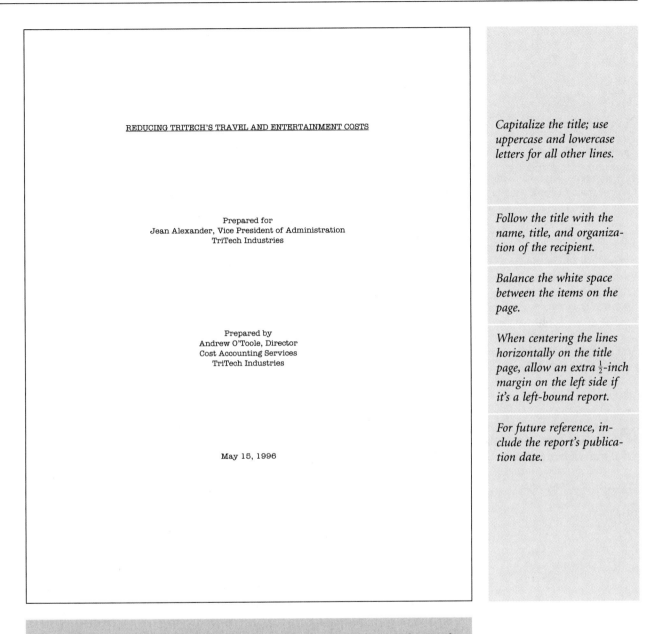

REDUCING TRITECH'S TRAVEL AND ENTERTAINMENT COSTS

Prepared for
Jean Alexander, Vice President of Administration
TriTech Industries

Prepared by
Andrew O'Toole, Director
Cost Accounting Services
TriTech Industries

May 15, 1996

Capitalize the title; use uppercase and lowercase letters for all other lines.

Follow the title with the name, title, and organization of the recipient.

Balance the white space between the items on the page.

When centering the lines horizontally on the title page, allow an extra $\frac{1}{2}$-inch margin on the left side if it's a left-bound report.

For future reference, include the report's publication date.

The "how to" tone of this title is appropriate for an action-oriented report that emphasizes recommendations. A more neutral title, such as "An Analysis of TriTech's Travel and Entertainment Costs," would be more suitable for an informational report.

Use memo format for transmitting internal reports, letter format for transmitting external reports.

Present the main conclusion or recommendation right away if you expect a positive response.

Use an informal, conversational style for the letter or memo of transmittal.

Acknowledge any help that you have received.

Close with thanks, an offer to discuss results, and an offer to assist with future projects, if appropriate.

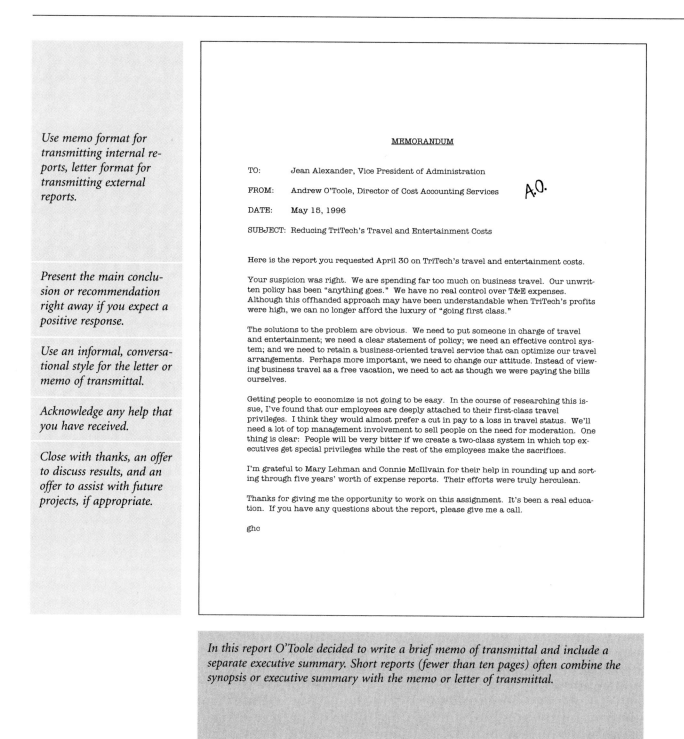

MEMORANDUM

TO: Jean Alexander, Vice President of Administration

FROM: Andrew O'Toole, Director of Cost Accounting Services   A.O.

DATE: May 15, 1996

SUBJECT: Reducing TriTech's Travel and Entertainment Costs

Here is the report you requested April 30 on TriTech's travel and entertainment costs.

Your suspicion was right. We are spending far too much on business travel. Our unwritten policy has been "anything goes." We have no real control over T&E expenses. Although this offhanded approach may have been understandable when TriTech's profits were high, we can no longer afford the luxury of "going first class."

The solutions to the problem are obvious. We need to put someone in charge of travel and entertainment; we need a clear statement of policy; we need an effective control system; and we need to retain a business-oriented travel service that can optimize our travel arrangements. Perhaps more important, we need to change our attitude. Instead of viewing business travel as a free vacation, we need to act as though we were paying the bills ourselves.

Getting people to economize is not going to be easy. In the course of researching this issue, I've found that our employees are deeply attached to their first-class travel privileges. I think they would almost prefer a cut in pay to a loss in travel status. We'll need a lot of top management involvement to sell people on the need for moderation. One thing is clear: People will be very bitter if we create a two-class system in which top executives get special privileges while the rest of the employees make the sacrifices.

I'm grateful to Mary Lehman and Connie McIllvain for their help in rounding up and sorting through five years' worth of expense reports. Their efforts were truly herculean.

Thanks for giving me the opportunity to work on this assignment. It's been a real education. If you have any questions about the report, please give me a call.

ghc

In this report O'Toole decided to write a brief memo of transmittal and include a separate executive summary. Short reports (fewer than ten pages) often combine the synopsis or executive summary with the memo or letter of transmittal.

CONTENTS

	Page
Executive Summary	v
Introduction	1
Purpose, Scope, and Limitations	1
Sources and Methods	1
Report Organization	2
The High Cost of Travel and Entertainment	2
$10 Million per Year Spent on Travel and Entertainment	2
TriTech's Budget Exceeds Competitors'	3
Spending Has Been Encouraged	4
Growing Impact on the Bottom Line	4
Lower Profits Underscore Need for Change	5
Air Fares Are Rising	5
Methods for Reducing Travel and Entertainment Costs	6
Three Ways to Trim Expenses	6
The Impact of Reforms	9
Conclusions and Recommendations	10
Notes	11
Bibliography	12

iii

Word the headings exactly as they appear in the text.

Extend spaced periods (leaders) from the end of the heading to the page number. (For spaced periods, strike the space bar and the period alternately.) Align the periods under one another.

Type only the page numbers where sections begin; align the last digits of the page numbers.

O'Toole included only first- and second-level headings in his table of contents, even though the report contains third-level headings. He prefers a shorter table of contents that focuses attention on the main divisions of thought. He used informative titles, which are appropriate for a report to a receptive audience.

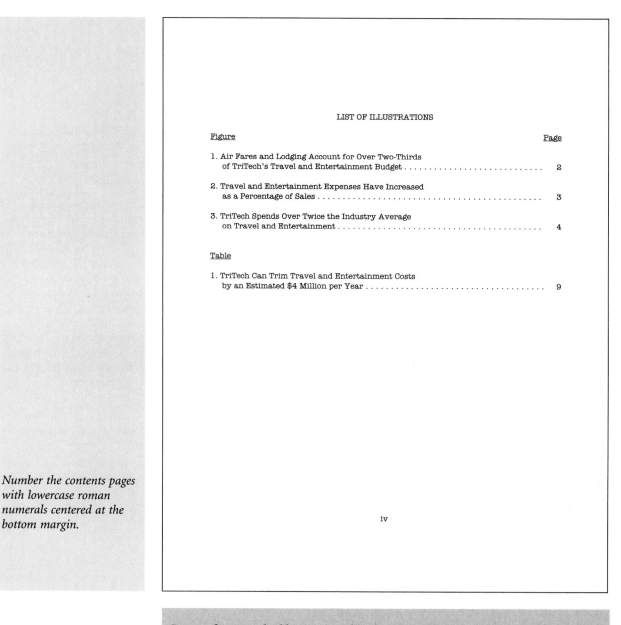

LIST OF ILLUSTRATIONS

Figure   Page

1. Air Fares and Lodging Account for Over Two-Thirds
   of TriTech's Travel and Entertainment Budget   2

2. Travel and Entertainment Expenses Have Increased
   as a Percentage of Sales   3

3. TriTech Spends Over Twice the Industry Average
   on Travel and Entertainment   4

Table

1. TriTech Can Trim Travel and Entertainment Costs
   by an Estimated $4 Million per Year   9

iv

Number the contents pages with lowercase roman numerals centered at the bottom margin.

Because figures and tables were numbered separately in the text, O'Toole listed them separately here. If all were labeled as exhibits, a single list of illustrations would have been appropriate.

EXECUTIVE SUMMARY

This report analyzes TriTech's travel and entertainment (T&E) costs and presents recommendations for reducing those costs.

Travel and Entertainment Costs Are Too High

Travel and entertainment is a large and growing expense category for TriTech Industries. The company currently spends about $10 million per year on business travel, and costs are increasing by 7 percent annually. Company employees make some 5,000 trips each year at an average cost per trip of $2,000. Air fares are the biggest expense, followed by hotels, meals, and rental cars.

The nature of TriTech's business does require extensive travel, but the company's costs appear to be excessive. Every year TriTech spends twice as much on T&E for each professional employee as its main competitors do. Although the location of the company's facilities may partly explain this discrepancy, the main reason for TriTech's high costs is the firm's philosophy and managerial style. TriTech encourages employees to go first class and pays relatively little attention to travel costs.

Cuts Are Essential

Although TriTech has traditionally been casual about travel and entertainment expenses, management now recognizes the need to gain more control over this element of costs. The company is currently entering a period of declining profits, prompting management to look for every opportunity to reduce spending. At the same time, rising air fares are making travel and entertainment expenses more important to the bottom line.

TriTech Can Save $4 Million per Year

Fortunately, TriTech has a number of excellent opportunities for reducing its travel and entertainment costs. Savings of up to $4 million per year should be achievable, judging by the experience of other companies. The first priority should be to hire a director of travel and entertainment to assume overall responsibility for T&E spending. This individual should establish a written travel and entertainment policy and create a budgeting

v

Begin by stating the purpose of the report.

Present the points in the executive summary in the same order as they appear in the report. Use subheadings that summarize the content of the main sections of the report without repeating those that appear in the text.

Type the synopsis or executive summary in the same manner as the text of the report. Single-space if the report is single-spaced, and use the same format in both the executive summary and the text for margins, paragraph indentions, and headings.

O'Toole decided to include an executive summary because his report was aimed at a mixed audience. He knew that some readers would be interested in the details of his report and some would prefer to focus on the big picture. The executive summary was aimed at the latter group. O'Toole wanted to give these readers enough information to make a decision without burdening them with the task of reading the entire report.

The hard-hitting tone of this executive summary is appropriate for a receptive audience. A more neutral approach would be better for hostile or skeptical readers.

and cost-control system. The director should also retain a nationwide travel agency to handle our reservations.

At the same time, TriTech should make employees aware of the need for moderation in travel and entertainment spending. People should be encouraged to forgo any unnecessary travel and to economize on airline tickets, hotels, meals, rental cars, and other expenses.

In addition to economizing on an individual basis, TriTech should look for ways to reduce costs by negotiating preferential rates with travel providers. Once retained, a travel agency should be able to accomplish this.

These changes, although necessary, are likely to hurt morale, at least in the short term. Management will need to make a determined effort to explain the rationale for reduced spending. By exercising moderation in their own travel arrangements, TriTech executives can set a good example and help make the changes more acceptable to other employees.

vi

Number the pages of the executive summary with lowercase roman numerals centered about 1 inch from the bottom of the page.

This executive summary is written in an impersonal style, which adds to the formality of the report. Some writers prefer a more personal approach. Generally speaking, you should gear your choice of style to your relationship with the readers. O'Toole chose the formal approach because several members of his audience were considerably higher up in the organization. He did not want to sound too familiar. In addition, he wanted the executive summary and the text to be compatible, and his company prefers the impersonal style for formal reports.

REDUCING TRITECH'S TRAVEL AND ENTERTAINMENT COSTS

INTRODUCTION

TriTech Industries has traditionally encouraged a significant amount of business travel, in the belief that it is an effective way of conducting operations. To compensate employees for the stress and inconvenience of frequent trips, management has authorized generous travel and entertainment allowances. This philosophy has undoubtedly been good for morale, but the company has paid a price. Last year TriTech spent $10 million on T&E, $5 million more than it spent on research and development.

This year the cost of travel and entertainment will have a bigger impact on profits, owing to changes in airline fares. The timing of these changes is unfortunate because the company anticipates that profits will be relatively weak for a variety of other reasons. In light of these profit pressures, Ms. Jane Alexander, Vice President of Administration, has asked the accounting department to take a closer look at the T&E budget.

Purpose, Scope, and Limitations

The purpose of this report is to analyze the travel and entertainment budget, evaluate the impact of recent changes in air fares, and suggest ways to tighten management's control over travel and entertainment expenses.

Although the report outlines a number of steps that could reduce TriTech's expenses, the precise financial impact of these measures is difficult to project. The estimates presented in the report provide a "best guess" view of what TriTech can expect to save. Until the company actually implements these steps, however, there is no way of knowing how much the travel and entertainment budget can be reduced.

Sources and Methods

In preparing this report, the accounting department analyzed internal expense reports for the past five years to determine how much TriTech spends on travel and entertainment. These figures were then compared with statistics on similar companies in the electronic equipment industry, obtained through industry association data, annual reports, and magazine articles. In addition, the accounting department screened magazine and newspaper articles to determine how other companies are coping with the high cost of business travel.

1

Center the title of the report on the first page of the text, 2 inches (2½ inches if top-bound) from the top of the page.

Begin the introduction by establishing the need for action.

Single-spacing the report can create a formal, finished look; however, double-spacing can make a long report easier to read.

Mentioning sources and methods increases the credibility of a report and gives readers a complete picture of the study's background.

Use the arabic numeral 1 for the first page of the report; center the number about 1 inch from the bot-

In a brief introduction like this one, some writers would omit the subheadings within the introduction and rely on topic sentences and on transitional words and phrases to indicate that they are discussing such subjects as the purpose, scope, and limitations of the study. O'Toole decided to use headings because they help readers scan the document. Also, to conserve space, O'Toole used single spacing and 1-inch side margins.

Using arabic numerals, number the second and succeeding pages of the text in the upper-right-hand corner where the top and right-hand margins meet.

2

Report Organization

This report reviews the size and composition of TriTech's travel and entertainment expenses, analyzes trends in air fare pricing, and recommends steps for reducing the travel and entertainment budget.

THE HIGH COST OF TRAVEL AND ENTERTAINMENT

Although many companies view travel and entertainment (T&E) as an "incidental" cost of doing business, the dollars add up. Last year U.S. industry paid an estimated $90 billion for travel and entertainment.[1] At TriTech Industries the bill for air fares, hotels, rental cars, restaurants, and entertainment totaled $10 million. The company's travel and entertainment budget has increased by 12 percent per year for the past five years. By industry standards TriTech's budget is on the high side.[2] This is largely because management has a generous policy on travel benefits.

$10 Million per Year
Spent on Travel and Entertainment

TriTech Industries' annual budget for travel and entertainment is only 8 percent of sales. Because this is a relatively small expense category compared with such things as salaries and commissions, it is tempting to dismiss travel and entertainment costs as insignificant. However, T&E is TriTech's third-largest controllable expense, directly behind salaries and data processing.

Last year TriTech personnel made about 5,000 trips at an average cost per trip of $2,000. The typical trip involved a round-trip flight of 3,000 miles, meals and hotel accommodations for three days, and a rental car. Roughly 80 percent of the trips were made by 20 percent of the staff. Top management and sales personnel were the most frequent travelers, averaging 18 trips per year.

Figure 1 illustrates how the travel and entertainment budget is spent. The largest categories are air fares and lodging, which together account for $7 out of every $10 that

Figure 1
Air Fares and Lodging Account
for Over Two-Thirds of TriTech's
Travel and Entertainment Budget

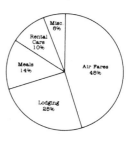

Placement of visual aids titles should be consistent throughout a report. This sample report, however, shows all options for placement: above, below, or beside the visual aid.

O'Toole opened the first main section of the body with a topic sentence that introduced an important fact about the subject of the section. Then he oriented the reader to the three major points developed in the section. He put his data in perspective by comparing growth in travel and entertainment expenses with growth in sales. After all, if sales were also increasing by 12 percent a year, an increase of 12 percent in travel and entertainment expenses might be acceptable.

3

employees spend on travel and entertainment. This spending has been relatively steady for the past five years and is consistent with the distribution of expenses experienced by other companies.

Although the composition of the travel and entertainment budget has been consistent, its size has not. As Figure 2 shows, expenditures for travel and entertainment have increased by about 12 percent per year for the past five years, roughly twice the rate of the company's growth in sales. This rate of growth makes travel and entertainment TriTech's fastest-growing expense item.

Figure 2
Travel and Entertainment
Expenses Have Increased as
a Percentage of Sales

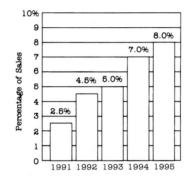

TriTech's Budget Exceeds Competitors'

There are many reasons TriTech has a high travel and entertainment budget. TriTech's main customer is the U.S. Postal Service. The company's mode of selling requires frequent face-to-face contact with the customer, yet corporate headquarters is located on the West Coast, some 2,600 miles from Washington, D.C. Furthermore, TriTech's manufacturing operations are widely scattered; facilities are located in San Francisco, Detroit, Boston, and Dallas. To coordinate these operations, corporate management and division personnel must make frequent trips to and from company headquarters.

Although much of TriTech's travel budget is justified, the company spends considerably more on travel and entertainment than its competitors do, as Figure 3 indicates. Data supplied by the International Association of Electronics indicates that the typical company in our industry spends approximately $1,900 per month per professional employee on travel and entertainment.[3] TriTech's per capita travel costs for professional employees are running $4,000 per month.

Introduce visual aids before they appear, and indicate what readers should notice about the data.

Number the visual aids consecutively, and refer to them in the text by their numbers. If your report is a book-length document, you may number the visual aids by chapter: Figure 4-2, for example, would be the second figure in the fourth chapter.

O'Toole originally drew this bar chart as a line chart, showing both sales and T&E expenses in absolute dollars. However, the comparison was difficult to interpret because sales were so much greater than T&E expenses. The vertical axis stretched from $0 to $125 million. Switching to a bar chart expressed in percentage terms made the main idea much easier to grasp.

Place the visual aid as close as possible to the point it illustrates.

Give each visual aid a title that clearly indicates what it is about.

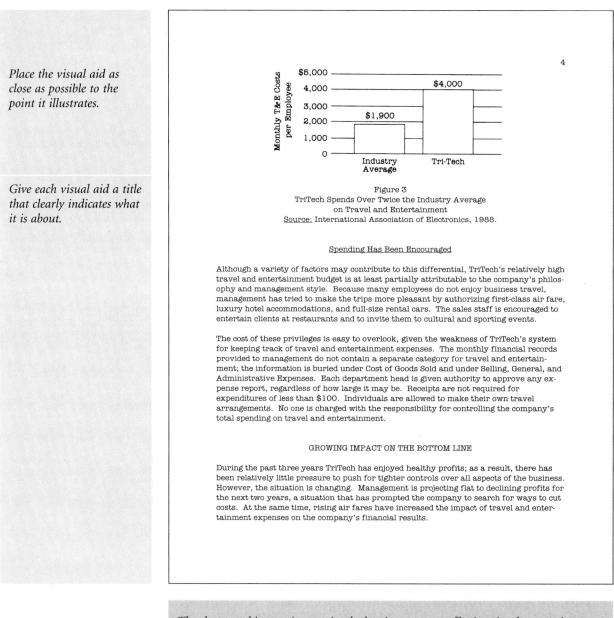

Figure 3
TriTech Spends Over Twice the Industry Average
on Travel and Entertainment
Source: International Association of Electronics, 1988.

Spending Has Been Encouraged

Although a variety of factors may contribute to this differential, TriTech's relatively high travel and entertainment budget is at least partially attributable to the company's philosophy and management style. Because many employees do not enjoy business travel, management has tried to make the trips more pleasant by authorizing first-class air fare, luxury hotel accommodations, and full-size rental cars. The sales staff is encouraged to entertain clients at restaurants and to invite them to cultural and sporting events.

The cost of these privileges is easy to overlook, given the weakness of TriTech's system for keeping track of travel and entertainment expenses. The monthly financial records provided to management do not contain a separate category for travel and entertainment; the information is buried under Cost of Goods Sold and under Selling, General, and Administrative Expenses. Each department head is given authority to approve any expense report, regardless of how large it may be. Receipts are not required for expenditures of less than $100. Individuals are allowed to make their own travel arrangements. No one is charged with the responsibility for controlling the company's total spending on travel and entertainment.

GROWING IMPACT ON THE BOTTOM LINE

During the past three years TriTech has enjoyed healthy profits; as a result, there has been relatively little pressure to push for tighter controls over all aspects of the business. However, the situation is changing. Management is projecting flat to declining profits for the next two years, a situation that has prompted the company to search for ways to cut costs. At the same time, rising air fares have increased the impact of travel and entertainment expenses on the company's financial results.

The chart on this page is very simple, but it creates an effective visual comparison. O'Toole included just enough data to make his point.

5

Lower Profits Underscore Need for Change

The next two years promise to be difficult for TriTech Industries. After several years of steady increases in spending, the U.S. Postal Service is tightening procurement policies for automated mail-handling equipment. Funding for TriTech's main product, the A-12 optical character reader, has been canceled. As a consequence, sales are expected to decline by 15 percent. Although TriTech is negotiating several promising research and development contracts with nongovernment clients, management does not foresee any major procurements for the next two to three years.

At the same time, TriTech is facing cost increases on several fronts. The new production facility now under construction in Salt Lake City, Utah, is behind schedule and over budget. Labor contracts with union workers in Boston and Dallas expire within the next six months, and management anticipates that significant salary and benefits concessions may be necessary to avoid strikes. Moreover, marketing and advertising costs are expected to increase as TriTech attempts to strengthen these activities to better cope with competitive pressures. Given the expected decline in revenues and increase in costs, management projects that profits will fall by 12 percent in the coming fiscal year.

Air Fares Are Rising

Over the next 8 to 12 months, rising air fares can be expected to inflate TriTech's travel and entertainment costs. The recent round of mergers in the airline industry has reduced competition among carriers, thereby reducing the companies' incentives to cut ticket prices. Currently, 94 percent of all air traffic in the United States is controlled by just eight airlines, up from 80 percent in 1976 when the airline industry was decontrolled.[4] The decline in competition is expected to lead to higher air fares, particularly for business travelers. According to industry analysts, the airline price wars that followed deregulation are a thing of the past. Any future fare reductions will be aimed at narrow market segments, such as families taking summer vacations. Meanwhile, business travelers who pay full fare will face price increases of up to 15 percent on some routes.[5]

Several factors apart from the reduction in competition are pushing fares up. Perhaps the most significant factor is the increasing sophistication of the airlines' pricing strategies. For example, airlines used to discount unfilled seats in the moments before flights departed, on the theory that low-fare passengers were better than none at all. Now, though, travelers who arrive at the gate just before departure are likely to pay full fare. The reason: Airlines discovered that most late arrivals were so desperate to get on the plane they would willingly pay almost any price.[6]

The tendency toward increasing fares also reflects the airlines' increasing costs. Higher fuel costs are probably the most important short-term factor, but labor costs are also beginning to rise, as are landing fees, passenger meals, advertising expenses, and debt-

Informative headings focus readers' attention on the main points of the report. Thus they are most appropriate when the report is in direct order and is aimed at a receptive audience. Descriptive headings are more effective when a report is in indirect order and the readers are less receptive.

Documenting the facts adds weight to O'Toole's argument.

Because air fares represent TriTech's biggest T&E expense, O'Toole included a subsection that deals with the possible impact of trends in the airline industry. Air fares are rising, so it is especially important to gain more control over employees' air travel arrangements.

6

service costs. Furthermore, the airlines are committed to buying some $95 billion worth of new equipment within the next several years.[7]

Given the fact that air fares account for 45 percent of TriTech's T&E budget, the trend toward higher ticket prices will have serious consequences on the company's expenses unless management takes action to control these costs.

METHODS FOR REDUCING
TRAVEL AND ENTERTAINMENT COSTS

By implementing a number of reforms, management can expect to reduce TriTech's travel and entertainment budget by as much as 40 percent. However, these measures are likely to be unpopular with employees. To gain acceptance for the changes, management will need to sell employees on the need for moderation in travel and entertainment allowances.

Three Ways to Trim Expenses

By researching what other companies are doing to curb travel and entertainment expenses, the accounting department has identified three prominent opportunities that should enable TriTech to save about $4 million annually in travel-related costs.

Institute Tighter Spending Controls

A single individual should be appointed to spearhead the effort to gain control of the travel and entertainment budget. The individual should be familiar with the travel industry and should be well versed in both accounting and data processing. He or she should report to the vice president of administration and should be given the title of director of travel and entertainment. The director's first priorities should be to establish a written travel and entertainment policy and to implement a system for controlling travel and entertainment costs.

TriTech currently has no written policy on travel and entertainment, despite the fact that 73 percent of all firms have such policies.[8] Creating a policy would clarify management's position and serve as a vehicle for communicating the need for moderation. At a minimum, the policy should include the following provisions:

*All travel and entertainment should be strictly related to business and should be approved in advance.
*Instead of going first class, employees should make a reasonable effort to economize on air fares, hotels, rental cars, and meals.

Pointing out both the benefits and risks of taking action gives recommendations an objective flavor.

The indented list format calls attention to important points and adds visual interest. You can also use visual aids, headings, and direct quotations to break up large, solid blocks of print.

O'Toole created a forceful tone by using action verbs in the third-level subheadings of this section. This approach is appropriate to the nature of the study and the attitude of the audience. However, in a status-conscious organization, the imperative verbs might sound a bit too presumptuous coming from a junior member of the staff.

7

The travel and entertainment policy should apply equally to employees at all levels in the organization. No special benefits should be allowed for top executives.

To implement the new policy, TriTech will need to create a system for controlling travel and entertainment expenses. Each department should prepare an annual T&E budget as part of its operating plan. These budgets should be presented in detail so that management can evaluate how travel and entertainment dollars will be spent and recommend appropriate cuts.

To help management monitor performance relative to these budgets, the director of travel should prepare monthly financial statements showing actual travel and entertainment expenditures by department. The system for capturing this information should be computerized and should be capable of identifying individuals who consistently exceed approved spending levels. The recommended average should range between $1,500 and $2,500 per month for each professional employee, depending on the individual's role in the company. Because they make frequent trips, sales and top management personnel can be expected to have relatively high travel expenses.

The director of travel should also be responsible for retaining a business-oriented travel service that will schedule all employee business trips and look for the best travel deals, particularly in air fares. In addition to centralizing TriTech's reservation and ticketing activities, the agency will negotiate reduced group rates with hotels and rental car agencies. The agency selected should have offices nationwide so that all TriTech facilities can channel their reservations through the same company. By consolidating its travel planning in this way, TriTech can increase its control over costs and achieve economies of scale.

<u>Reduce Unnecessary Travel and Entertainment</u>

One of the easiest ways to reduce expenses is to reduce the amount of traveling and entertaining that occurs. An analysis of last year's expenditures suggests that as much as 30 percent of TriTech's travel and entertainment is discretionary. The professional staff spent $1.7 million attending seminars and conferences last year. Although some of these gatherings are undoubtedly beneficial, the company could save money by sending fewer representatives to each function and by eliminating some of the less valuable seminars.

Similarly, TriTech could economize on trips between headquarters and divisions by reducing the frequency of such visits and by sending fewer people on each trip. Although there is often no substitute for face-to-face meetings, management could try to resolve more internal issues through telephone contacts and written communication.

TriTech can also reduce spending by urging employees to economize. Instead of flying first class, employees can fly tourist class or take advantage of discount fares. Instead of taking clients to dinner, TriTech personnel can hold breakfast meetings, which tend to

When including recommendations in a report, specify the steps required to implement them.

O'Toole decided to single-space his report to save space; however, double-spacing can make the text of a long report somewhat easier to read, and it provides more space for readers to write comments.

The use of an example adds credibility and makes the discussion more interesting.

Pointing up the difficulties demonstrates that you have considered all the angles and builds readers' confidence in your judgment.

8

be less costly. Rather than ordering a $20 bottle of wine, employees can select a less expensive bottle or dispense with alcohol entirely. People can book rooms at moderately priced hotels and drive smaller rental cars. In general, employees should be urged to spend the company's money as though it were their own.

Obtain Lowest Rates from Travel Providers

Apart from urging individual employees to economize, TriTech can also save money by searching for the lowest available air fares, hotel rates, and rental car fees. Currently, few TriTech employees have the time or specialized knowledge to seek out travel bargains. When they need to travel, they make the most convenient and most comfortable arrangements. However, if TriTech contracts with a professional travel service, the company will have access to professionals who can be more efficient in obtaining the lower rates from travel providers.

Judging by the experience of other companies, TriTech may be able to trim as much as 30 to 40 percent from the travel budget by looking for bargains in air fares and negotiating group rates with hotels and rental car companies.[9] By guaranteeing to provide selected hotels with a certain amount of business, Weston Computer was able to achieve a 20 percent reduction in its hotel expenses. Now, instead of choosing between 40 or 50 hotels in a city like Chicago, Weston employees stay at one of the 6 or 7 hotels where the company has negotiated a corporate rate.[10] TriTech should be able to achieve similar economies by analyzing its travel patterns, identifying frequently visited locations, and selecting a few hotels that are willing to reduce rates in exchange for guaranteed business. At the same time, the company should be able to save up to 40 percent on rental car charges by negotiating a corporate rate.

The possibilities for economizing are promising, but it's worth noting that making the best arrangements is a complicated undertaking, requiring many trade-offs. The airlines currently offer 4 million air fares, and on any given day, as many as 1 million of them might change in some way.[11] When booking a particular reservation, the travel agent might have to choose between 20 or 25 options with varying prices and provisions. The best fares might not always be the lowest. Indirect flights are often less expensive than direct flights, but they take longer and may end up costing more in lost work time. Similarly, the cheapest tickets may have to be booked 30 days in advance, often an impossibility in business travel. Also, discount tickets may be nonrefundable, which is a real negative if the trip has to be canceled at the last minute. TriTech is currently not equipped to make these and other trade-offs. However, by employing a business-oriented travel service, the company will have access to computerized systems that can optimize its choices.

Notice how O'Toole made the transition from section to section. The first sentence under the heading on this page refers to the subject of the previous paragraph and signals a shift in thought.

9

The Impact of Reforms

By implementing tighter controls, reducing unnecessary expenses, and negotiating more favorable rates, TriTech Industries should be able to reduce its travel and entertainment budget significantly. As Table 1 illustrates, the combined savings should be in the neighborhood of $4 million, although the precise figures are somewhat difficult to project. Reductions in air fares and hotel accommodations are the most important source of savings, accounting for about $2.3 million.

Table 1
TriTech Can Trim Travel and Entertainment Costs
by an Estimated $4 Million per Year

Source of Savings	Amount Saved
More efficient scheduling and selection of airline reservations	$1,400,400
Preferred rates on hotels	900,000
Fewer trips to conferences	700,000
Reduction in interdivisional travel	425,000
Reduced rates on rental cars	375,000
More economical choices by individuals	200,000
TOTAL SAVINGS	$4,000,000

Source: Accounting department estimates based on internal data and experience of other companies.

To achieve the economies outlined in the table, TriTech will incur expenses associated with hiring a director of travel and implementing a travel and entertainment cost-control system. These costs are projected at $60,000: $55,000 per year in salary and benefits for the new employee and a one-time expense of $5,000 associated with the cost-control system. The cost of retaining a full-service travel agency will be negligible because agencies receive a commission from travel providers rather than a fee from clients.

The measures required to achieve these savings are likely to be unpopular with employees. TriTech personnel are accustomed to generous travel and entertainment allowances, and they are likely to resent having these privileges curtailed. To alleviate their disappointment, management should make a determined effort to explain why the changes are necessary. The director of corporate communication should be asked to develop a multifaceted campaign that will communicate the importance of curtailing travel and entertainment costs. In addition, management should set a positive example by adhering strictly to the new policies. To maintain morale, the limitations should apply equally to employees at all levels in the organization.

The use of informative titles for illustrations is consistent with the way headings are handled and is appropriate for a report to a receptive audience. The use of complete sentences helps readers focus immediately on the point of the illustrations.

Even though estimated savings may be difficult to project, including dollar figures helps management envision the impact of your suggestions.

The table on this page puts O'Toole's recommendations in perspective. Notice how he called attention in the text to the most important sources of savings and also spelled out the costs required to achieve these results.

Use a descriptive heading for the last section of the text. In informational reports, this section is generally called "Summary"; in analytical reports, it is called "Conclusions" or "Conclusions and Recommendations."

Emphasize the recommendations by presenting them in list format, if possible.

Do not introduce new facts in this section of the text.

10

CONCLUSIONS AND RECOMMENDATIONS

TriTech Industries is currently spending $10 million per year on travel and entertainment. Although much of this spending is justified, the company's costs appear to be high relative to competitors', mainly because TriTech has been generous with its travel benefits.

TriTech's liberal approach to travel and entertainment was understandable during years of high profitability; however, the company is facing the prospect of declining profits for the next several years. Management is therefore motivated to cut costs in all areas of the business. Reducing T&E spending is particularly important because the impact of these costs on the bottom line will increase as a result of fare increases in the airline industry.

TriTech should be able to reduce travel and entertainment costs by about 40 percent by taking three important steps:

1. Institute tighter spending controls. Management should hire a director of travel and entertainment who will assume overall responsibility for T&E activities. Within the next six months, this individual should develop a written travel policy, institute a T&E budgeting and cost-control system, and retain a professional, business-oriented travel agency that will optimize arrangements with travel providers.

2. Reduce unnecessary travel and entertainment. TriTech should encourage employees to economize on travel and entertainment spending. Management can accomplish this by authorizing fewer trips and by urging employees to be more conservative in their spending.

3. Obtain lowest rates from travel providers. TriTech should also focus on obtaining the best rates on airline tickets, hotel rooms, and rental cars. By channeling all arrangements through a professional travel agency, the company can optimize its choices and gain clout in negotiating preferred rates.

Because these measures may be unpopular with employees, management should make a concerted effort to explain the importance of reducing travel costs. The director of corporate communication should be given responsibility for developing a plan to communicate the need for employee cooperation.

Because O'Toole organized his report around conclusions and recommendations, readers have already been introduced to them. Thus he summarizes his conclusions in the first two paragraphs. A simple list is enough to remind readers of the three main recommendations. In a longer report he might have divided the section into subsections, labeled "Conclusions" and "Recommendations," to distinguish between the two. If the report had been organized around logical arguments, this would have been the readers' first exposure to the conclusions and recommendations, and O'Toole would have needed to develop them more fully.

NOTES

1. Jeffrey Lang, "Rx for Controlling Travel Costs," <u>Management Review</u>, June 1993, 59-63.

2. Damon W. Dayton, "What to Do When the Sky Is Not the Limit," <u>Management Accounting</u>, June 1991, 33.

3. <u>Analysis of Costs in the Electronics Industry</u> (Washington, D.C.: International Association of Electronics, 1990), 23.

4. "Tracking Travel Costs," <u>Small Business Reports</u>, March 1993, 5.

5. Barry Gillespie, "Automated Travel Reimbursement Form," <u>CPA Journal</u>, July 1993, 66.

6. "Tracking Travel Costs," 5.

7. "Cutting Costs While Flying Frequently," <u>Accountancy</u>, June 1993, 55.

8. Lang, "Rx for Controlling Travel Costs," 61.

9. Daniel Green, "Clipped Wings for High Flyers," <u>Financial Times</u>, 5 July 1993, 1.

10. Milton D. Gallanos, Dylan Betts, and Lawton Crawford, "Corporate T&E Expenditures: A Plan for Regaining Control," <u>Journal of Managerial Accounting</u>, October 1990, 139-145.

11. "Airline Regulation: The War in the Skies," <u>Economist</u>, 14 August 1993, 66, 71.

11

To simplify the typing process, most writers prefer to place all source notes together at the end of the text. (See Appendix B for details on handling documentation.)

O'Toole decided this major supplementary part should allow a 2-inch top margin.

List references alphabetically by the author's last name or, when the author is unknown, by the title of the reference. (See Appendix B for additional details on preparing bibliographies.)

BIBLIOGRAPHY

"Airline Regulation: The War in the Skies." <u>Economist</u>, 14 August 1993, 66, 71.

<u>Analysis of Costs in the Electronics Industry</u>. Washington, D.C.: International Association of Electronics, 1990.

"Cutting Costs While Flying Frequently." <u>Accountancy</u>, June 1993, 55.

Dayton, Damon W. "What to Do When the Sky Is Not the Limit." <u>Management Accounting</u>, June 1991, 33-36.

Gallanos, Milton D., Dylan Betts, and Lawton Crawford. "Corporate T&E Expenditures: A Plan for Regaining Control." <u>Journal of Managerial Accounting</u>, October 1990, 139-145.

Gillespie, Barry. "Automated Travel Reimbursement Form." <u>CPA Journal</u>, July 1993, 66.

Green, Daniel. "Clipped Wings for High Flyers. " <u>Financial Times</u>, 5 July 1993, 1.

Lang, Jeffrey. "Rx for Controlling Travel Costs." <u>Management Review</u>, June 1993, 59-63.

"Tracking Travel Costs." <u>Small Business Reports</u>, March 1993, 5.

12

O'Toole's bibliography is a reading list of sources cited in the notes. Some report writers use the bibliography to list additional sources.

and statistical formulas are frequently included in appendixes. A glossary of terms may be either an appendix or a separate supplementary part. Finally, as mentioned, visual aids may be included in an appendix, particularly if they are tangential to the report.

Each type of material deserves a separate appendix. Identify the appendixes by labeling them, for example, "Appendix A: Questionnaire," "Appendix B: Computer Printout of Raw Data," and the like. All appendixes should be mentioned in the text and listed in the table of contents.

A **bibliography** is a list of sources consulted when preparing the report. The construction of a bibliography is shown in this chapter's sample report and in Appendix B.

An **index** is an alphabetical list of names, places, and subjects mentioned in the report with the page numbers on which they occur, as in the index for this book. An index is rarely included in unpublished reports.

List your secondary sources in the bibliography.

COMPONENTS OF A FORMAL PROPOSAL

As mentioned in Chapter 12, certain analytical reports are called proposals; these include bids to perform work under a contract and pleas for financial support from outsiders. Such bids and pleas are nearly always formal. The goal is to impress the potential client or supporter with your professionalism, and this goal is best achieved through a structured, deliberate approach.

Formal proposals contain many of the same components as other formal reports (see Figure 14.10). The difference lies mostly in the text, although a few of the prefatory parts are also different. With the exception of an occasional appendix, most proposals have few supplementary parts.

Prefatory Parts

The cover, title fly, title page, table of contents, and list of illustrations are handled just as they are in other formal reports. However, some prefatory parts are quite different:

- *Copy of the RFP.* Instead of having a letter of authorization, a formal proposal may have a copy of the **request for proposal (RFP),** which is a letter or memo soliciting a proposal or bid for a particular project. The RFP is issued by the client to whom the proposal is being submitted and outlines what the proposal should cover. If

Use a copy of the request for proposal in place of the letter of authorization.

Figure 14.10
Parts of a Formal Proposal

PREFATORY PARTS	TEXT OF THE PROPOSAL	SUPPLEMENTARY PARTS
Cover	Introduction	Appendixes
Title fly	Body	
Title page	Summary	
Letter of transmittal		
Table of contents		
List of illustrations		
Synopsis or executive summary		

the RFP includes detailed specifications, it may be too long to bind into the proposal; in that case, you may want to include only the introductory portion of the RFP. Another option is to omit the RFP and simply refer to it in your letter of transmittal.

- *Letter of transmittal.* The way you handle the letter of transmittal depends on whether the proposal is solicited or unsolicited. If the proposal is solicited, the transmittal letter follows the pattern for good-news messages, highlighting those aspects of your proposal that may give you a competitive advantage. If the proposal is unsolicited, the transmittal letter takes on added importance; in fact, it may be all the client reads. The letter must persuade the reader that you have something worthwhile to offer, something that justifies the time required to read the entire proposal. The transmittal letter for an unsolicited proposal follows the pattern for persuasive messages (see Chapter 11).

- *Synopsis or executive summary.* Although you may include a synopsis or an executive summary for your reader's convenience if your proposal is quite long, these components are somewhat less useful in a formal proposal than they are in other formal reports. If your proposal is unsolicited, your transmittal letter will already have caught the reader's interest, making a synopsis or an executive summary pointless. It may also be pointless if your proposal is solicited, because the reader is already committed to studying the text to find out how you propose to satisfy the terms of a contract. The introduction to a solicited proposal provides an adequate preview of the contents.

Marginal note: Use the good-news pattern for the letter of transmittal if the proposal is solicited; use the persuasive plan if the proposal is unsolicited.

Marginal note: Most proposals do not require a synopsis or an executive summary.

Text of the Proposal

The text of a proposal performs two essential functions: It persuades the client to award you a contract (or financial support), and it spells out the terms of that contract (or what will be done with the funds). The trick is to sell the client on your ideas without making promises that will haunt you later. If the proposal is unsolicited, you have some latitude in arranging the text. However, the organization of a solicited proposal is governed by the request for proposal. Most RFPs spell out precisely what you should cover and in what order so that all bids will be similar in form. This uniformity enables the client to evaluate the competing proposals in a systematic way. In fact, in many organizations, a team of evaluators splits up the proposals so that each member can look at a different section. For example, an engineer might review the technical portions of all the proposals submitted, and an accountant might review the cost estimates.

Marginal note: A proposal is both a selling tool and a contractual commitment.

Marginal note: Follow the instructions presented in the RFP.

Introduction

The introduction orients readers to the rest of the proposal. It identifies your organization and your purpose, and it outlines the remainder of the text. If the proposal is solicited, the introduction refers to the RFP; if not, it mentions any factors that led you to submit the bid. For example, you might refer to previous conversations you've had with the client or mention mutual acquaintances. Subheadings for proposals often include the following:

Marginal note: In the introduction, establish the need for action and summarize the key benefits of your proposal.

- *Background or statement of the problem.* Briefly reviews the client's situation, worded to establish the need for action.
- *Overview of approach.* Highlights your key selling points and their benefits, showing how your proposal will solve the client's problem. The heading for this section

might also be "Preliminary Analysis" or some other heading that will identify this section as a summary of your solution to the problem.

- *Scope.* States the boundaries of the study, what you will and will not do. This brief section might also be labeled "Delimitations."
- *Report organization.* Orients the reader to the remainder of the proposal and calls attention to the major divisions of thought.

Body

The heart of the proposal is the body, which generally has the same purpose as the body of other reports. In a proposal, however, the body must cover some specific types of information:

As chairman of the board of Computer Associates International, Charles B. Wang must often make fast decisions on proposals. A clear purpose stated concisely saves time and promotes understanding, advises Wang, and that allows your reader to make the right decision.

- *Proposed approach.* Might also be titled "Technical Proposal," "Research Design," "Issues for Analysis," or "Work Statement." Regardless of the heading, this section is a description of what you have to offer: your concept, product, or service. For example, if you are proposing to develop a new airplane, you might describe your preliminary design, using drawings or calculations to demonstrate the soundness of your solution. To persuade the client that your proposal has merit, focus on the strengths of your product in relation to the client's needs. Point out any advantages that you have over your competitors. For example, you might describe how the unique wing design of your plane provides superior fuel economy, a particularly important feature specified in the client's request for proposal.
- *Work plan.* Describes how you will accomplish the work that must be done (necessary unless you are proposing to provide a standard, off-the-shelf item). For each phase of the work plan, you describe the steps you will take, their timing, the methods or resources you will use, and the person or persons who will be responsible. Indicate any critical dates when portions of the work will be completed. If your proposal is accepted, the work plan will become contractually binding. Any slippage in the schedule you propose may jeopardize the contract or cost your organization a considerable amount of money. Therefore, be careful when preparing this section of the proposal. Don't promise to deliver more than you can realistically achieve within a given period.

Use the work plan to describe the tasks to be completed under the terms of the contract.

- *Statement of qualifications.* Describes your organization's experience, personnel, and facilities in relation to the client's needs. If you work for a large organization that frequently submits proposals, you can usually borrow much of this section intact from previous proposals. However, be sure to tailor any of this boilerplate material to suit the situation. The qualifications section can be an important selling point, and it deserves to be handled carefully.

In the qualifications section, demonstrate that you have the personnel, facilities, and experience to do a competent job.

- *Costs.* Typically has few words and many numbers but can make or break the proposal. If your price is out of line, the client will probably reject your bid. However, before you deliver with a low bid, remember that you'll have to live with the price you quote in the proposal. It's rarely advantageous to win a contract if you're doomed to lose money on the job. Because it's often difficult to estimate costs on experimental projects, the client will be looking for evidence that your cost proposal is realistic. Break down and itemize the costs in detail so that the client can see how you got your numbers: so much for labor, so much for materials, so much for overhead.

The more detailed your cost proposal, the more credible your estimates.

In a formal proposal, it pays to be as thorough and accurate as possible. Carefully selected detail enhances your credibility. So does successful completion of any task you promise to perform.

CHECKLIST FOR FORMAL REPORTS AND PROPOSALS

A. Quality of the Research

1. Define the problem clearly.
2. State the purpose of the document.
3. Identify all relevant issues.
4. Accumulate evidence pertaining to each issue.
5. Check evidence for accuracy, currency, and reliability.
6. Justify your conclusions by the evidence.
   - a. Do not omit or distort evidence in order to support your point of view.
   - b. Identify and justify all assumptions.

B. Preparation of Reports and Proposals

1. Choose a format and length that are appropriate to your audience and the subject.
2. Prepare a sturdy, attractive cover.
   - a. Label the cover clearly with the title of the document.
   - b. Use a title that tells the audience exactly what the document is about.
3. Provide all necessary information on the title page.
   - a. Include the full title of the document.
   - b. Include the name, title, and affiliation of the recipient.
   - c. Give the name, title, and affiliation of the author.
   - d. Provide the date of submission.
   - e. Balance the information in blocks on the page.
4. Include a copy of the letter of authorization or request for proposal, if appropriate.
5. Prepare a letter or memo of transmittal.
   - a. Use memo format for internal documents.
   - b. Use letter format for external documents.
   - c. Include the transmittal letter in only some copies if it contains sensitive or personal information suitable for some but not all readers.
   - d. Place the transmittal letter right before the table of contents.
   - e. Use the good-news plan for solicited proposals and other reports; use the persuasive plan for unsolicited proposals.
   - f. Word the letter to "convey" the document officially to the readers; refer to the authorization; and discuss the purpose, scope, background, sources and methods, and limitations.
   - g. Mention any special points that warrant readers' attention.
   - h. If you use direct order, summarize conclusions and recommendations (unless they are included in a synopsis).
   - i. Acknowledge all those who were especially helpful in preparing the document.
   - j. Close with thanks, offer to be of further assistance, and suggest future projects, if appropriate.
6. Prepare the table of contents.
   - a. Include all first-level headings (and all second-level headings or perhaps all second- and third-level headings).
   - b. Give the page number of each heading.
   - c. Word all headings as they appear in the text.
   - d. Include the synopsis (if there is one) and supplementary parts in the table of contents.
   - e. Number the table of contents and all prefatory pages with lowercase roman numerals centered at the bottom of the page.
7. Prepare a list of illustrations if you have four visual aids or more.
   - a. Put the list in the same format as the table of contents.
   - b. Identify visual aids either directly beneath the table of contents or on a separate page under the heading "List of Illustrations."
8. Develop a synopsis or an executive summary if the document is long and formal.
   - a. Tailor the synopsis or executive summary to the document's length and tone.
   - b. Condense the main points of the document, using either the informative approach or the descriptive approach, according to the guidelines in this chapter.
   - c. Present the points in the synopsis in the same order as they appear in the document. Remember that an executive summary can deviate from the order of the points made in the report.

Summary

You may want to include a summary or conclusion section; it is your last opportunity to convince the reader to accept your proposal. Summarize the merits of your approach, reemphasize why you and your firm are the ones to do it, and stress what the

9. Prepare the introduction to the text.

   a. Leave a 2-inch margin at the top of the page, and center the title of the document.

   b. In a long document (ten pages or more), type the first-level heading "Introduction" three lines below the title.

   c. In a short document (fewer than ten pages), begin typing three lines below the title of the report or proposal without the heading "Introduction."

   d. Discuss the authorization (unless it's covered in the letter of transmittal), purpose, scope, background, sources and methods, definitions, limitations, and text organization.

10. Prepare the body of the document.

   a. Carefully select the structural scheme (see Chapter 13).

   b. Use either a personal or an impersonal tone consistently.

   c. Use either a past or a present time perspective consistently.

   d. Follow a consistent format in typing headings of different levels, using a company format guide, a sample proposal or report, or the format in this textbook as a model (see Appendix A)

   e. Express comparable (same-level) headings in any given section in parallel grammatical form.

   f. Group ideas into logical categories.

   g. Tie sections together with transitional words, sentences, and paragraphs.

   h. Give ideas of equal importance roughly equal space.

   i. Avoid overly technical, pretentious, or vague language.

   j. Develop each paragraph around a topic sentence.

   k. Make sure all ideas in each paragraph are related.

   l. Double-space if longer than ten pages.

   m. For documents bound on the left, number all pages with arabic numerals in the upper right-hand corner (except for the first page, on which the number is centered 1 inch from the bottom); for top-bound documents, number all pages with arabic numerals centered 1 inch from the bottom.

11. Incorporate visual aids into the text.

   a. Number visual aids consecutively throughout the text, numbering tables and figures (other visual aids) separately if that style is preferred.

   b. Develop explicit titles for all visual aids except in-text tables.

   c. Refer to each visual aid in the text, and emphasize the significance of the data.

   d. Place visual aids as soon after their textual explanations as possible, or group them at the ends of chapters or at the end of the document for easy reference.

12. Conclude the text of reports and proposals with a summary and, if appropriate, conclusions and recommendations.

   a. In a summary, recap the findings and explanations already presented.

   b. Place conclusions and recommendations in their order of logic or importance, preferably in list format.

   c. To induce action, explain in the recommendations section who should do what, where, when, and how.

   d. If appropriate, point up the benefits of action, to leave readers with the motivation to follow recommendations.

13. Document all material quoted or paraphrased from secondary sources, using a consistent format (see Appendix B).

14. Include appendixes at the end of the document to provide useful and detailed information that is of interest to some but not all readers.

   a. Give each appendix a title, such as "Questionnaire" or "Names and Addresses of Survey Participants."

   b. If there is more than one appendix, number or letter them consecutively in the order they're referred to in the text.

   c. Type appendixes in a format consistent with the text of the report or proposal.

15. Include a bibliography if it seems that readers would benefit or the document would gain credibility.

   a. Type the bibliography on a separate page headed "Bibliography" or "Sources."

   b. Alphabetize bibliography entries.

   c. Use a consistent format for the bibliography (see Appendix B).

benefits will be. The section should be relatively brief, assertive, and confident. You can review this and other components in this chapter's Checklist for Formal Reports and Proposals.

On the Job

SOLVING A COMMUNICATION DILEMMA AT PENN STATE

When Rodney Erickson set out to assess the impact of football on State College's economy, he assumed he would come up with a pretty big number, but he didn't know *how* big. After surveying some 1,974 season ticket holders, he discovered—to his amazement—that the average home game is worth almost $3 million in extra revenue to local businesses. Adding the ripple effect of those dollars flowing through the economy, Erickson calculates that the seven-game home season enriches the town to the tune of $40.3 million per year. That boils down to roughly $1,300 for each of the community's 30,000 permanent residents.

In fact, the economic impact of football on State College may be even bigger than Erickson's figures indicate. His study excluded spending by local fans and spending associated with the annual Blue and White preseason scrimmage, which draws a big crowd. He looked only at the 54,000 fans who come from outside the immediate area to see each of the seven regular-season home games. Those fans travel an average of 186 miles to attend the games and spend approximately $54 apiece while they're in town.

How do these fans spend their money? First, there are hotel bills. All the local hotels and motels enforce a two-day minimum stay on football weekends, and most of them jack up their room rates by 20 to 40 percent, depending on the quality of the competing team. Many of the hotels also stage special events—dances, musical performances, and the like—which boost their revenues still further.

Meals, of course, are another expense. The Sub Shop on Beaver Street is a popular source of provisions for tailgate picnics. The Sub Shop's owner, Ralph Petrino, figures that on a football Saturday, he sells 480 subs, twice the normal number. Business also generally doubles at fancier spots like the Tavern Restaurant, where, after one Penn State–Notre Dame game, the chef prepared a record-breaking 792 meals, 50 to 60 percent more than his usual Saturday night quota.

As you might expect, shopping also picks up. Football fans flock to the Lions Pride, a store that stocks 500 to 700 Penn State items ranging from sweatshirts to telephone cords decorated with Nittany Lions. According to Jim Styer, the store's manager: "On a football Saturday, you're talking at least triple normal business. At least. It's wall to wall in here. Front to back. Side to side. Everything goes. They clean us out." And it's not just souvenirs that sell. The jewelry stores and dress shops also do plenty of business, since some of the folks who come along for the weekend prefer to spend Saturday shopping rather than watching the football game.

Gasoline is another item that pumps faster on football weekends. Cars clog every road leading into town, and the University Park Airport is crammed with private airplanes. Sometimes as many as 60 planes crowd into the little airport,

and most of them slurp up a tank of fuel before departing. Add it all up, and it makes a big difference to a small town like State College. As Rodney Erickson says, "It's a pretty amazing phenomenon."

Your Mission: You are an aide to Rodney Erickson at Penn State's Center for Regional Business Analysis. He has asked you to help finalize his report about the economic impact of college football on the local economy. For each of the following situations, choose the best solution, and be prepared to explain your choice.

1. The text of Erickson's report is 15 pages long. Which of the following prefatory parts should he include?
   a. Cover
   b. Title fly
   c. Title page
   d. Letter of authorization
   e. Letter of acceptance
   f. Letter/memo of transmittal
   g. Table of contents
   h. List of illustrations
   i. Synopsis or executive summary

2. Erickson has decided to send a copy of the report to the chamber of commerce, the president of the alumni association, head football coach Joe Paterno, and several members of Penn State's administration. He has asked you to draft a letter of transmittal. How should you proceed?
   a. Using the good-news organizational plan, develop a brief form letter that can be sent to all the recipients.
   b. Using the good-news plan, develop a form letter but customize the first paragraph so that it is slanted specifically to each of the recipients.
   c. Since each recipient has different interests and needs, write a separate letter for each and use the most appropriate organizational plan, given your objective in each case.

3. Erickson has asked you to draft the introductory section of the text. Which of the following versions is superior?
   a. Version one

INTRODUCTION

State College is a town of 30,000 located in the rolling hills of central Pennsylvania. Since 1871 the community has been a "college town." During the school year, 34,000 students swell the local population, providing an important boost to the economy. The magnitude of that boost is especially great during football season, when the Nittany Lions draw big crowds to Beaver Stadium.

This report, prepared by the Pennsylvania State Center for Regional Business Analysis, attempts to quantify the economic impact of the Lions' seven home games on the local business community. The information is intended to provide perspective on the importance of football to the city and the university.

The analysis deals specifically with the impact of out-of-town fans who travel 25 miles or more to attend the regular-season home games. The figures presented in the report do not reflect spending by students or local fans who attend the games, nor do they reflect spending associated with preseason scrimmages. The information presented in the report is based on a mail survey of 1,974 season ticket holders who live at least 25 miles away from State College, 86 percent of whom responded.

The report opens with an overview of the impact of football on the local economy and then reviews the impact of spending for various types of goods and services: hotels and motels, restaurants, retailing, personal services, and other businesses. The final section summarizes the data.

b. Version two

INTRODUCTION

This report attempts to calculate how much college football is worth to the economy of State College, Pennsylvania. The report was prepared by the Pennsylvania State University's Center for Regional Business Analysis with the objective of providing local businesses, government officials, and university personnel with accurate information on the financial impact of football on the town.

The report is based on the results of a mail survey of 1,974 out-of-town season ticket holders, 86 percent of whom responded. The analysis tends to understate the importance of football to local businesses because the figures do not reflect spending by students and local fans or spending associated with the preseason scrimmage.

As the following pages indicate, local businesses are the big winners when the Nittany Lions take on their rivals at Beaver Stadium. For a typical Saturday afternoon game, some 54,000 out-of-town fans travel to State College and spend an average of $54 apiece while they're here. Over the course of the regular seven-game home season, these fans spend $20.3 million on lodging, food, merchandise, personal services, and miscel-

laneous items. If the ripple effect of this spending is taken into consideration, it is safe to say that the total impact of the football season is $40.3 million, or $5.7 million per game.

c. Version three

INTRODUCTION

If you shudder when football season rolls around and Nittany Lions' fans descend on State College like a plague of locusts, devouring every available parking space, you might want to count your blessings instead of grumbling about the tourists. After surveying some 1,974 out-of-town season ticket holders, the Pennsylvania State University Center for Regional Business Analysis has concluded that college football gives the local community a $40.3 million boost every year. That amounts to $1,300 for every man, woman, and child who lives in State College.

The following pages provide the details on how the fans spend their money, benefitting hotel keepers, restaurateurs, retailers, hairdressers, and even baby-sitters.

4. Erickson has asked your opinion on whether to include in his report (1) a copy of the direct-mail survey that was used to collect the data for the report and (2) a computer printout quantifying the responses to each question. The survey document is two pages long; the computer compilation of results is five pages long. Without the documents, the report has 15 pages. What do you think?
   a. Include both the survey and the computer compilation of responses in the text of the report.
   b. Include a copy of the survey in the text of the report, and put the computer compilation of responses in an appendix.
   c. Describe both the survey and the computer compilation in the text, but put the actual documents in an appendix.
   d. Describe both the survey and the computer compilation in the text, but do not include copies of either document.
   e. Include a copy of the survey in an appendix, but do not include the computer compilation of results.
5. Erickson has compiled the following statistics on spending by the 54,000 nonresident fans who attended the seven Penn State home football games: stadium, $8,283,600; restaurants, $2,693,100; lodging, $2,075,100; retail goods, $1,793,500; private auto, $984,800; clothing and equipment used in stadium, $801,700; bars and nightclubs, $743,200; retail groceries and beverages, $588,100; commercial transportation, $247,800; donations, $105,100; admission fees, $103,400; personal and health, $41,300; baby-sitters, $25,100; equipment rentals, $17,900; and other, $1,944,900—for a total of $20,448,600. What format is best for presenting this information in the report?

a. The figures should be displayed in a table.
b. The figures should be shown in a pie chart.
c. The figures should be shown in a horizontal bar chart.

d. The figures should be shown in a line chart.
e. The figures should be explained in several paragraphs in the text.[3]

Questions for Discussion

1. What are the distinguishing characteristics of a formal report?
2. How should you decide whether to use a synopsis or an executive summary?
3. In what ways might visual aids help people overcome some of the barriers to communication that were discussed in Chapter 2?
4. How does the information shown in flowcharts, organization charts, and diagrams differ from the information shown in line, bar, and pie charts?
5. How do the prefatory parts of a solicited proposal differ from the prefatory parts of an unsolicited proposal?
6. How does the text of a formal proposal differ from the text of other formal reports?

Exercises

1. Present the following information in three separate visual aids: a table, a line chart, and a bar chart.

   Assets of international banks (in billions of dollars):
   1985—47.6; 1986—55.0; 1987—59.8; 1988—46.5;
   1989—34.1; 1990—42.2; 1991—47.6; 1992—45.0;
   1993—44.9; 1994—49.3; 1995—58.3

2. For each of the following types of information, what form of visual aid would you choose?
   a. Data on annual sales for FretCo Guitar Corporation for the past 20 years
   b. Comparison of FretCo Guitar sales, product by product (electric guitars, bass guitars, amplifiers, acoustic guitars), for this year and last year
   c. Explanation of how a FretCo acoustic guitar is manufactured
   d. Comparison of FretCo sales figures to sales figures for three other major guitar makers over the past ten years
3. You're planning a series of visual aids to support your nonprofit organization's written request for a government grant. To be eligible for the grant, you need to demonstrate that (1) the percentage of your annual operating budget devoted to administrative salaries is less than 12 percent, (2) the children your group assists live primarily in urban areas, and (3) your plan for constructing a new community health center is proceeding on schedule. What types of visual aids would you use for each of the three points you need to make? Explain.
4. The pet-food manufacturer you work for is interested in the results of a recent poll of U.S. pet-owning households. Look at the statistics that follow and decide on the most appropriate scale for this chart; then create a line chart of the trends in cat ownership. What conclusions do you draw from the trend you've charted? Draft a paragraph or two discussing the results of this poll and the potential consequences for the pet-food business. Support your conclusions by referring readers to your chart.

   In 1980, 22 million U.S. households owned a cat. In 1985, 24 million households owned a cat. In 1990, 28 million households owned a cat. In 1995, 32 million households owned a cat.

5. In other textbooks or in *U.S. News & World Report, Fortune,* or other news or business magazines, locate an example of four of the following types of visual aids: table, line chart, surface chart, bar chart, pie chart, flowchart, organization chart. Bring these samples to class and discuss the effectiveness of each. Is the information presented in a convenient format? Do you believe the effect to be honest? Is the visual aid clear, readable, meaningful? Is it properly introduced and discussed in the text? As an alternative to class discussion, write a one-paragraph evaluation of the strong and weak points of each visual aid.
6. As a market researcher for a statewide bank, you're examining home ownership and rental patterns among single-person households in various age groups. You're particularly interested in pinpointing when these households tend to switch from renting to owning a home. Using the following information, prepare a bar graph comparing the number of owners with the number of renters in each age category. Be sure to label your graph and include combined totals for owners and renters ("total households"). Then prepare a pie chart showing the proportion of owners and renters in the one age group you believe holds the most promise for mortgage loans. Write a sentence that prepares your bank's management for the information they will see in the pie chart.

Age of Group	Owners (in 000s)	Renters (in 000s)		Age of Group	Owners (in 000s)	Renters (in 000s)
18–24	143	1,208		45–54	824	1,207
25–29	454	1,796		55–64	1,697	1,348
30–34	596	1,326		65–75	2,513	1,655
35–44	816	1,545		75 +	2,344	1,767

Cases

SHORT FORMAL REPORTS

1. Selling overseas: Report on the prospects for marketing a product in another country Select (a) a product and (b) a country. The product might be a novelty item that you own (an inexpensive but accurate watch or clock, a desk organizer, or a coin bank). The country should be one that you are not now familiar with. Imagine that you're with the international sales department of the company that manufactures and sells the novelty item and that you're proposing to make it available in the country you have selected.

The first step is to learn as much as possible about the country in which you plan to market the product. Check almanacs and encyclopedias for the most recent information, paying particular attention to descriptions of the social life of the inhabitants and their economic conditions. If your library carries *Yearbook of International Trade Statistics, Monthly Bulletin of Statistics,* or *Trade Statistics* (all put out by the United Nations), you may want to consult them. In addition, check the card catalog and recent periodical indexes for sources of additional information. Look for (among other matters) cultural traditions that would encourage or discourage use of the product.

Your Task: Write a short report that describes the product you plan to market abroad, briefly describes the country you have selected, indicates the types of people in this country who would find the product attractive, explains how the product would be transported into the country (or possibly manufactured there if materials and labor are available), recommends a location for a regional sales center, and suggests how the product should be sold. Your report is to be submitted to the chief operating officer of the company, whose name you can either make up or find in a corporate directory. The report should include your conclusions (how the product will do in this new environment) and your recommendations for marketing (steps the company should take immediately and those it should develop later).

2. Rating some textbooks: Report comparing textbook readability Gather the textbooks you're reading this term (if you have fewer than six, include some from previous terms to total at least six).

- Rank the books in order of the difficulty you are having in understanding them (number 1 is the most difficult).
- Rank the books by how much you enjoy reading them (number 1 is the least enjoyable).
- Rank the books by how well you are doing in the courses that they cover (number 1 is the book for the course that you're having the most trouble with). If several books are used for the same course, assign them the same rank.
- Determine the Fog Index for the prose in each book (see Chapter 7 for an explanation).

Your Task: Write a short formal report that (a) is directed toward college professors, (b) summarizes the relationship between the textbooks' scores on the Fog Index and your own evaluations of the textbooks, (c) displays your results graphically, (d) describes the methods you used and any special problems you encountered (did one contain poetry or works by many authors?), (e) compares the Fog Index with your grade level, and (f) evaluates and explains the use of the Fog Index as a measure of readability.

3. A park inspection: Report on the condition of public facilities As an employee of the city, you have been assigned to inspect some of its parks.

Your Task: Visit a city park, and report back to your supervisor (Ben Willis, Commissioner of Parks) on the use and condition of the park that you have inspected. Your report should include at least the following information: the date and time of your inspection, a general description of the park and its facilities, an indication of who (if anyone) was on duty at the time of your inspection, an estimate of the number of people using the park at the time of your inspection, a breakdown by age and activity of these people, conclusions about the general use and condition of the park, recommendations for making the park more useful or attractive, and a statement of any problems more significant than ordinary day-to-day maintenance (such as inadequate parking or inadequate facilities).

Show in your report that you have inspected the park carefully. Check the bolts in the swings (for rust, wear, or inadequate lubrication), and make other observations necessary for a conscientious inspection. Write factually. A serious inspector would write "The swing area was littered with 12 empty soda cans," not "The swing area was filthy."

LONG FORMAL REPORTS REQUIRING ADDITIONAL RESEARCH

4. Equipment purchase: Report on competitive product features Say that your office or home needs some new equipment. Choose one of the following, and figure out which brand and model would be the best buy.

a. Typewriter
b. Calculator
c. Telephone answering machine
d. Home security system
e. Photocopier
f. Microcomputer
g. Word-processing software
h. Dictation equipment

Your Task: Write a long formal report comparing the features of available alternatives, and make your recommendation clear.

5. Is there any justice?: Report critiquing legislation Plenty of people complain about their state legislators, but few are specific about their complaints. Here's your chance.

Your Task: Write a long formal report about a law that you believe should not have been enacted or should be enacted. Be objective. Write the report using specific facts to support your beliefs. Reach conclusions and offer your recommendation at the end of the report. As a final step, send a copy of the report to an appropriate state official or legislator.

6. Group effort: Report on a large-scale topic The following topics may be too big for any one person, yet they need to be investigated:

a. A demographic profile (age, gender, socioeconomic status, residence, employment, educational background, and the like) of the students at your college or university
b. The best part-time employment opportunities in your community
c. The best of two or three health clubs or gyms in your community
d. Actions that can be taken in your community or state to combat alcohol (or other drug) abuse
e. Improvements that could be made in the food service at your college or university
f. Your college's or university's image in the community and ways to improve it
g. Your community's strengths and weaknesses in attracting new businesses

Your Task: Because these topics require considerable research, your instructor may wish to form groups to work on each. If your group writes a report on the first topic, summarize your findings at the end of the report. For all the other topics, reach conclusions and make recommendations in the report.

FORMAL PROPOSALS

7. A new kind of campus "party": Proposal to hold a promotional event at colleges Marketers of all kinds have their eyes on college students. Besides being consumers of a wide variety of products, students seem to have discretionary funds for everything from stereo equipment to cosmetics to snack foods. The problem for marketers is reaching their targets—college students are notoriously difficult for advertisers to get to.

A new approach that is meeting with some success is the product festival. College Fest, a two-day event held at a Massachusetts convention center, drew some 19,000 students from 50 Boston-area colleges, each of whom paid a $5 admission fee. While rock bands played, 150 companies ranging from Guess? to Revlon to Toyota pushed their products via contests, free samples, and such activities as mechanical-bull rides and complimentary manicures. Most of the companies were enthusiastic, since the festival allowed target consumers to interact directly with their products and even make purchases on the spot.

Your employer, MarketSource Corporation, based in Cranbury, New Jersey, is also engaged in college "party marketing," but on a smaller scale. MarketSource's Campus Fest is held directly on college campuses, where 20 to 25 companies set up their booths under a giant tent. Exhibitors are encouraged to provide activities and displays that contribute to the festival atmosphere. So far, Campus Fest has been held at more than 60 universities all over the United States.

Your Task: Write a proposal that can be sent to colleges and universities where MarketSource would like to hold Campus Fests. Use your imagination to provide details about such things as the benefits to the university, the types of companies that will participate, and the activities the companies will sponsor.[4]

8. When is a program not a program? Proposal to produce a television infomercial If you have cable television, you already know something about "infomercials." As you flip through the channels, you can't help noticing these half-hour "programs" that extol the benefits of products ranging from baldness cures to exercise equipment to car wax. Many of the ads are in a talk-show format and feature celebrities such as John Ritter and Cathy Lee Crosby talking with people who have used the product and want to share their success stories. Other infomercials focus primarily on product demonstrations (the infomercial industry gave one of its first "awards" to a program demonstrating the versatility of the Jet Stream Oven).

This form of "direct-response television" has proliferated because the ads are relatively inexpensive to produce and cable airtime often comes cheap. Whereas producing a 30-second network commercial might cost $200,000, a marketer can get by with as little as $150,000 to produce a 30-minute infomercial. In addition, placing the spots can cost in the hundreds or thousands of dollars instead of the ten thousands or hundred thousands.

You've recently joined the staff of American Telecast, one of the three major producers of infomercials. With annual revenues of $150 million, American Telecast's claims to fame include the highly successful Richard Simmons weight-loss-plan "long-form marketing program." Your boss has handed you a magazine ad for Audio-Forum, a company that sells audio cassettes that teach people how to speak foreign languages, how to play the piano or read music, how to improve their vocabulary or their speech, and even how to touch-type. "This looks like the kind of product we could really run with in an infomercial—especially the foreign-language stuff," your boss says. She wants you to come up with an unsolicited proposal that will entice Audio-Forum into entering the infomercial game.

You look through the company's highly detailed ad, which you remember seeing in a variety of magazines. The portion of the ad devoted to language learning tapes says, "Learn to speak a foreign language fluently on your own and at your own pace" and goes on to give the course's credentials (developed for the U.S. State Department for diplomatic personnel who need to learn a language quickly), describe what each course consists of, and list the languages available. Both an order form and a toll-free number are provided. You remember reading somewhere that Audio-Forum has been quite successful with its magazine direct-marketing approach.

Your Task: Write a proposal to Audio-Forum, 96 Broad St., Guilford, CT 06437, indicating American Telecast's desire to produce an infomercial for Audio-Forum's language learning tapes. Use your imagination to fill in any additional details.[5]

V

a Résumé · Writing an Application Letter · Writing Other Types of Employment Messages

EMPLOYMENT

wing With Potential Employers · Following Up After the Interview · Employment Messages

MESSAGES

oyers · Following Up After the Interview · Thinking About Your Career · Writing a Résumé

Chapter 15
Writing Résumés and Application Letters

Chapter 16
Interviewing for Employment and Following Up

15
Chapter

After studying this chapter, you will be able to

Plan your job search

Choose the appropriate format and style for your résumé

Tailor the contents of your résumé to focus on your strengths without distorting the facts

Select the appropriate organizational plan for your résumé

Write an application letter that gets you an interview

Write job-inquiry letters, fill out application forms, and write application follow-up letters

WRITING RÉSUMÉS AND APPLICATION LETTERS

On the Job

FACING A COMMUNICATION DILEMMA AT PINKERTON

Keeping a Private Eye on Hiring

When you screen more than a million job applicants every year, you're sure to gain an in-depth knowledge of employment messages. That's the kind of expertise Pinkerton has developed. As the first private security and investigations agency in the United States, Pinkerton screens job applicants for clients as well as for its own operations, and the company takes pride in matching the right person to the right job.

Chairman and CEO Thomas W. Wathen and his team of professionals faced an important challenge when Pinkerton was hired to provide security officers for the Academy Awards in Los Angeles. Mounted by the Academy of Motion Picture Arts and Sciences, the Academy Awards has become a magnet for the news media as well as for adoring fans anxious to get close to their favorite stars. Security officers would protect the celebrities, maintain order among the spectators, and prevent any problems that might disrupt an event seen by hundreds of millions of television viewers around the world. Many people would jump at the chance to work at such a glittery event, but not everyone is qualified to do the job.

What qualities does Wathen look for in a job applicant? How does he evaluate the résumés and application letters that land on his desk? What constitutes a good résumé? A good application letter? If you were Wathen, what steps would you take to screen job candidates?[1]

Thinking About Your Career

As Pinkerton's Wathen will tell you, getting the job that's right for you takes more than sending out a few letters and signing up with the college placement office. Planning and research are important if you are to find a company that suits you. So before you limit your employment search to a particular industry or job specialty, analyze what you have to offer and what you hope to get from your work. Only then can you identify the employers most likely to want you and those you'll be happiest with.

Pinkerton

What Do You Have to Offer?

Think about your marketable skills. First, jot down ten achievements you're proud of—learning to ski, taking a prizewinning photo, tutoring a child, editing the school paper. Analyze each of these achievements, and you'll begin to recognize a pattern of skills that are valuable to potential employers.

Second, look at your educational preparation, work experience, and extracurricular activities. What kinds of jobs are you qualified to do based on your knowledge and experience? What have you learned from participating in volunteer work or class projects that could benefit you on the job? Have you held any offices, won any awards or scholarships, or mastered a second language?

What you have to offer:
- Functional skills
- Education and experience
- Personality traits

Third, take stock of your personal characteristics to determine the type of job you'll do best. Are you aggressive, a born leader? Or would you rather follow? Are you outgoing, articulate, great with people? Or do you prefer working alone? Make a list of what you believe are your four or five most important qualities. Ask a relative or friend to rate your traits as well. If you're having trouble figuring out your interests and capabilities, consult your college placement office or career guidance center for advice.

What Do You Want to Do?

Knowing what you *can* do is one thing. Knowing what you *want* to do is another. Don't lose sight of your own values. Discover the things that will bring you satisfaction and happiness on the job.

Decide What You'd Like to Do Every Day

Talk to people in various occupations. You might contact relatives, local businesses, or former graduates (through your school's alumni relations office). After making a few phone calls, you'll know a lot more.

Envision the ideal "day at the office." What would you enjoy doing every day?

Read about various occupations. Your college library or placement office might be a good place to start. One of the liveliest books aimed at college students is Lisa Birnbach's *Going to Work,* which describes various jobs from test-driving cars for Ford to selling cosmetics at Bloomingdale's. Another useful source is the 13-volume *Career Information Center* encyclopedia of jobs and careers, which is arranged by industry and describes each job title as to the nature of the work, entry requirements, application procedures, advancement possibilities, working conditions, earnings, and benefits.

Also consider more general factors, such as how much independence you want on the job, how much variety you like, and whether you prefer to work with products, machines, people, ideas, figures, or some combination thereof. Do you like physical work, mental work, or a mix? Constant change or a predictable role?

Establish Some Specific Compensation Targets

What do you hope to earn in your first year on the job? What kind of pay increase do you expect each year? What's your ultimate earnings goal? Would you be comfortable

How much do you want to earn, and how high do you hope to climb?

with a job that paid on commission, or do you prefer a steady paycheck? What occupations offer the kind of money you're looking for? Are these occupations realistic for someone with your qualifications? Are you willing to settle for less money in order to do something you really love?

Consider where you'd like to start, where you want to go from there, and the ultimate position you'd like to attain. How soon after joining the company would you like to receive your first promotion? Your next one? What additional training or preparation will you need to achieve these goals?

Consider the Type of Environment You Prefer

What type of industry and organization do you want to work for?

Think in broad terms about the size and type of operation that appeals to you. Do you like the idea of working for a small, entrepreneurial operation, or would you prefer to be part of a large company? How do you feel about profit-making versus non-profit organizations? Are you attracted to service businesses or manufacturing operations? What types of products appeal to you? Do you want regular, predictable hours, or do you thrive on flexible, varied hours? Would you enjoy a seasonally varied job like education (which may give you summers off) or retailing (with its selling cycles)?

Think about location. Would you like to work in a city, a suburb, or a small town? In an industrial area or an uptown setting? Do you favor a particular part of the country? Does working in another country appeal to you? Do you like working indoors or outdoors?

Consider facilities. Is it important to you to work in an attractive place, or will simple, functional quarters suffice? Do you need a quiet office to work effectively, or can you concentrate in a noisy, open setting? Would you prefer to work at the company's headquarters or in a small field office? Do such amenities as an in-house gym or handball court matter to you? Is access to public transportation or freeways important?

What type of corporate culture best suits you?

Perhaps the most important environmental factor is the corporate culture. Would you be happy in a well-defined hierarchy, where roles and reporting relationships are clear, or would you prefer a less-structured situation? What qualities do you want in a boss? Are you looking for a paternalistic organization or one that fosters individualism? Do you like a competitive environment or one that rewards teamwork?

Where Do You Find Employment Information?

Find out where the job opportunities are.

Once you know what you have to offer and what you want, you can start finding an employer to match. If you haven't already committed yourself to any particular career field, first find out where the job opportunities are. Which industries are strong? Which parts of the country are booming, and which specific job categories offer the best prospects for the future?

Whether your major is business, biology, or philosophy, start your search for information by keeping abreast of business and financial news. Subscribe to a major newspaper and scan the business pages every day. Watch television programs that focus on business, such as "Wall Street Week," and read the business articles in popular magazines such as *Time* and *Newsweek*. You might even subscribe to a business magazine such as *Fortune, Business Week,* or *Forbes.*

You can obtain information about the future for specific jobs in *The Dictionary of Occupational Titles* (U.S. Employment Service), *Occupational Outlook Handbook* (U.S. Bureau of Labor Statistics), and the employment publications of Science Research Associates. For an analysis of major industries, see the annual Market Data and Directory issue of *Industrial Marketing* and Standard & Poor's industry surveys.

Study professional and trade journals in the career fields that interest you. Also, talk to people in these fields; for names of the most prominent, consult *Standard & Poor's*

Register of Corporations, Directors and Executives. You can find recent books about the fields you're considering by checking *Books in Print* at your library. You may be able to network with executives in your field by participating in student business organizations, especially those with ties to real-world organizations such as the American Marketing Association or the American Management Association.

Once you've identified a promising industry and a career field, compile a list of specific organizations that appeal to you. Consult directories of employers, such as *The College Placement Annual* and *Career: The Annual Guide to Business Opportunities* (other directories are listed in Chapter 16). Write to the organizations on your list and ask for their most recent annual report and any descriptive brochures or newsletters they've published. If possible, visit some of the organizations on your list, contact their human resources departments, or talk with key employees.

Ads for specific job openings appear in local and major newspapers. Also check the trade and professional journals in career fields that interest you; *Ulrich's International Periodicals Directory* lists these publications (and is available at the library). In addition, don't forget to check the job listings at your college placement office and state employment bureaus.

Now you know what skills you have to offer, what you want from a job, and where to look for potential employers. You're ready to contact employers, but how do you let them know that you have skills to offer and are available? You send them your résumé.

> Of the organizations that interest you, find out which ones need your skills.

Writing a Résumé

A **résumé** is a structured, written summary of a person's education, employment background, and job qualifications. A résumé is a form of advertising, designed to help you get an interview. This interview may serve any number of purposes, for example, getting a job, getting a promotion, obtaining membership in a professional organization, or becoming a member of a nonprofit board. As in all forms of advertising, your objective is to call attention to your best features and to downplay your disadvantages, without distorting or misrepresenting the facts.[2] You arrange these facts according to your purpose.

Executives like Pinkerton's Thomas Wathen believe a good résumé shows that a candidate (1) thinks in terms of results, (2) knows how to get things done, (3) is well rounded, (4) shows signs of progress, (5) has personal standards of excellence, (6) is flexible and willing to try new things, and (7) possesses strong communication skills. As you put your résumé together, think about how the format, style, and content help you convey these seven qualities.

> Your résumé is a structured, written summary of your educational and employment background, and it shows your qualifications for a job.

> A résumé is designed to get you an interview.

Controlling the Format and Style

Quick—you've got less than 30 seconds to make a good impression. That's the amount of time a typical recruiter devotes to each résumé before tossing it into either the "maybe" or the "reject" pile.[3] If your résumé doesn't *look* sharp, chances are nobody will read it carefully enough to judge your qualifications.

It's important to use a clean typeface on high-grade, letter-size bond paper (in white, off-white, light ivory, or other light earth tone). Be sure your application letter and envelope are on matching-colored stationery. Leave ample margins all around, and be sure any corrections are unnoticeable. Avoid italic typefaces, which can be difficult to read. If you have reservations about the quality of your typewriter or printer (dot matrix printing is not suitable for most résumés), you might want to turn your résumé over to a professional service. To make copies, use offset printing or photocopying.

> The key characteristics of a good résumé are
> - Neatness
> - Simplicity
> - Accuracy
> - Honesty

Martina L. Bradford is vice president of external affairs at AT&T, overseeing one of the largest and most profitable regions of the United States. Bradford targeted the high-growth company as a potential employer only after studying the industry thoroughly. She advises that you analyze where your skills fit in best and target your efforts toward that company.

In terms of layout, your objective is to make the information easy to grasp.[4] Break up the text by using headings that call attention to various aspects of your background, such as your work experience and education. Underline or capitalize key points, or set them off in the left margin. Use indented lists to itemize your most important qualifications. Leave plenty of white space, even if doing so forces you to use two pages rather than one. Sometimes it's useful to use a specialized computer program to help format and organize your résumé.

Pay attention to mechanics. Check the headings and itemized lists to make sure they're grammatically parallel. Be sure your grammar, spelling, and punctuation are correct. Because your résumé has only seconds to make an impression, keep your writing style simple and direct. Instead of whole sentences, use short, crisp phrases starting with action verbs. You might say, "Coached a Little League team to the regional play-offs" or "Supervised a fast-food restaurant and four employees."

As a rule of thumb, try to write a one-page résumé. If you have a great deal of experience and are applying for a higher-level position, you may wish to prepare a somewhat longer résumé. The important thing is to give yourself enough space to present a persuasive but accurate portrait of your skills and accomplishments.

Tailoring the Contents

Most potential employers expect to see certain items in any résumé. The bare essentials are name and address, academic credentials, and employment history. Otherwise, make sure your résumé emphasizes your strongest, most impressive qualifications. Think in terms of an image or a theme you'd like to project. Are you academically gifted? Are you a campus leader? A well-rounded person? A creative genius? A technical wizard? If you know what you have to sell, you can shape the elements of your résumé accordingly. Don't exaggerate, and don't alter the past or claim skills you don't have, but don't dwell on negatives, either. By focusing on your strengths, you can convey the desired impression without distorting the facts.

Name and Address

The opening section shows at a glance
- Who you are
- How to reach you

The first thing an employer needs to know is who you are and where you can be reached: your name, address, and phone number. If you have an address and phone number at school and another at home, you may include both. At the same time, if you have a work phone and a home phone, list both and indicate which is which. Many résumé headings are nothing more than the name and address centered at the top of the page. You really have little need to include the word *Résumé,* but if you have a specific job in mind, you could use a heading that indicates that fact:

Qualifications of Craig R. Crisp for Insurance Sales Representative

Résumé Sheet of Mary Menendez, an Experienced Retail Fashion Buyer

Public Relations Background of Bradley R. (Brad) Howard

Susan Lee Selwyn's Qualifications
for the Position of Teaching Assistant
in the Dade County School District

Profile of Michael de Vito for Entertainment Management

Whatever heading you use, make sure the reader can tell in an instant who you are and how to communicate with you.

Career Objective or Summary of Qualifications

Experts disagree about stating a career objective on your résumé. Some argue that your objective will be obvious from your qualifications. They also point out that stating a career objective is counterproductive (especially if you would like to be considered for a variety of openings) because it labels you as being interested in only one thing. Other experts point out that employers will undoubtedly try to categorize you anyway, so you might as well be sure they attach the right label. If you decide to state your objective, be as specific as possible about what you want to do:

> *Stating your objective or summarizing your qualifications helps the recruiter categorize you.*

    Human Resources Management, requiring international experience

    Advertising assistant, with print media emphasis

If you have two types of qualifications (such as a certificate in secretarial science and two years' experience in retail sales), prepare two separate résumés, each with a different objective. If your immediate objective differs from your ultimate one, combine the two in a single statement:

    A marketing position with an opportunity for eventual managerial status

    Proposal writer, with the ultimate goal of becoming a contracts
    administrator

As an alternative to stating your objective, you might want to summarize your qualifications in a brief statement that highlights your strongest points, particularly if you have had a good deal of varied experience. Use a short, simple phrase:

    Summary of qualifications: Ten years of experience in commission selling

    Hospital administrator responsible for 350-bed facility

Education

If you're still in school, your education is probably your strongest selling point. So present your educational background in depth, choosing facts that support your "theme." Give this section a heading, such as "Education," "Professional College Training," or "Academic Preparation." Then starting with the school you most recently attended, list for each school the name and location, the term of your enrollment (in months and years), your major and minor fields of study, significant skills and abilities you've developed in your course work, and the degree(s) or certificate(s) you have earned. Showcase your qualifications by listing courses that have directly equipped you for the job sought, and indicate any scholarships, awards, or academic honors you have received.

In addition, include in your education section any off-campus training sponsored by business, industry, or government. Mention any relevant seminars or workshops you've attended, as well as the certificates or other documents you have received. Include high school or military training only if your achievements are pertinent to your career goals. Whether you list your grades depends on the job you want and the quality of your grades. If you choose to show a grade point average for your total program or your major, be sure to mention the scale if a 5-point scale is used rather than a 4-point scale.

Education is usually given less emphasis in a résumé after you've worked in your chosen field for a year or more. If work experience is your strongest qualification, save the section on education for later in the résumé and provide less detail.

William A. Schreyer is chairman and CEO of Merrill Lynch & Company. He urges you to stress summer employment, extracurricular activities, honors, scholarships, and other accomplishments. He says that job offers go to those who make the most persuasive presentation of their qualifications—don't just list what you did, show how well you did it.

BEHIND THE SCENES AT MOBIL CORPORATION
How to Write a Résumé with the Winning Edge

Henry Halaiko is manager of recruiting operations for Mobil Corporation, and he's a busy person: Year round, he coordinates Mobil's college relations and recruiting. During a recruiting cycle, he provides a strategic framework for the company's interaction with campuses. "I work with the office of Career Planning and Placement," says Halaiko. "In December I reserve space at next fall's on-campus recruiting. In September, we post our openings, list our requirements, and describe the work locations. Interested students submit résumés to the placement office, which forwards them to Mobil for consideration. At Mobil, the line managers who posted the openings screen the résumés. Then we write to those students who match our needs, and we set up an on-campus interview for October or November. The placement office notifies those students we decide not to schedule for an interview. The managers who screened the résumés conduct the on-campus interviews. Finally, when mutual interest extends beyond the initial interview, an on-site day of from four to six interviews is scheduled. These fall interviews result in hiring people who will report to work after graduation. The whole process, from initial campus interview to an accepted job offer, shouldn't take more than 60 days."

Mobil typically gets (from all sources) around 30,000 résumés a year to review. One large university, for example, forwarded 1,651 résumés in response to Mobil's posting. Of these, 253 students were interviewed. On average, 1 in 12 of those interviewed is offered a position, a total each year of 700 to 800 students hired. "Seventy-five percent of our new hires are from the campus pro-gram," says Halaiko. "We promote largely from within, so there's little room for outside hiring beyond entry-level positions. But because everyone who submits a résumé is a potential employee—not to mention a customer, a stockholder, and an influence on others—the company is sensitive even to unsolicited résumés. Each one is reviewed, answered, and filed for future consideration."

The obvious question is, How do I make myself stand out in such a crowd? "This is not a science," Halaiko says. "We're looking for whole people. I go through a résumé looking for personal standards of excellence in the classroom, at work, and in extracurricular activities; for flexibility, a willingness to try new things; and for strong oral and written communication skills, regardless of major. It's to your advantage not only to list your job responsibilities but also to list your accomplishments and achievements as well. Give some indication of your level of success. Most candidates will say something like 'I worked in the toy department, replenishing inventory, closing the books.' What I'm looking for is someone who adds, 'I was responsible for increasing sales by 12 percent during such-and-such a promotion.' This conveys to me that he or she is interested in performance and takes pride in accomplishment. People who describe themselves in this way want to do things better, more effectively. The same is true of extracurricular activities. Don't just say 'I was on the team or in the fraternity.' Add that you accomplished certain objectives in those roles."

Should you stress your grade point average? "We aren't one of those companies that take the posture that

Work Experience

Like the education section, the discussion of your work experience focuses on your overall theme. Tailor your description to highlight the relationship between your previous responsibilities and your target field. Call attention to the skills you've developed and the progression from jobs of lesser to greater responsibility.

When describing your work experience, you'll usually list your jobs in chronological order, with the current or last one first. Include any part-time, summer, or intern positions even if the jobs have no relation to your present career objective. Employers will see that you have the ability to get and hold a job, which is an important qualification in itself. If you have worked your way through school, say so. Employers interpret this as a sign of character.

In each listing, include the name and location of the employer. Then, if the reader is unlikely to recognize the organization, briefly describe what it does. When you want

we won't consider anyone below, say, a 3.5 GPA. We certainly look for academic excellence, and 2.8 is more or less a threshold because so many students fall above that level. But we look beyond that to roundedness. Did you carry a 3.0 but work full-time to pay for your education? Was your 2.9 earned in a tough course schedule? Have your grades progressed?"

What role do letters have in this process? Usually, submitting a résumé to the placement office is the appropriate response to a posting. "But even this early," Halaiko adds, "we welcome a cover letter in several situations. If you have a low GPA but feel it does not adequately reflect who you are, if you took courses outside your major (which is a real plus), if your résumé doesn't show how you used your time (that you were going from a part-time job to class, then to an extracurricular activity, then home to care for a family), write to tell me. It shows you have a high capacity for work and learning. We're interested in people who have enthusiasm for work."

Once the interview process has begun, several letters are called for. First, acknowledge the letter inviting you to the first interview and confirm your interest. After the interview, write the interviewer a personalized follow-up letter, focusing on something that was specifically discussed in the interview.

As a package, your letters and résumé should convey a sincere interest in the work described in the posting. Tailor your résumé to that particular position. "You'd probably not be considered if we posted an opening for a job in technical marketing or sales and your résumé said you were seeking a career in design engineering. Don't misrepresent what your real interests are just to get an interview," Halaiko points out. "That wastes your time and mine."

Are there any other no-no's? "If there's a classic error on a résumé, it's the one-page résumé with a half or a third of the page devoted to references. What that shows me is, you haven't done much."

In the end, says Halaiko, "there's no better feeling than having successfully recruited the candidate everyone was after but for whom the Mobil opportunity offered the best match of interests and needs." As an applicant, you can have the same feeling about completing a job search.

Apply Your Knowledge

1. After the deadline for responding to posted job opportunities, you learned that Mobil Corporation will be recruiting at your school to fill a vacancy for which you'd be perfect. On-campus interviews are to be held in three weeks. What strategies would you employ to try to bring your interest and qualifications to the attention of Halaiko and the Mobil managers who will be conducting the initial interviews? How will you address the fact that you "missed the posting deadline"?

2. Take a copy of your résumé. (If you don't yet have a résumé, this can be your first step toward creating one.) Highlight each duty or responsibility you've listed for each job you've held. On a separate sheet of paper, list those duties down the right-hand side. To the left of each one, write out the kind of performance statement Halaiko referred to in his toy department example. For each duty/responsibility, select your performance/result that best illustrates your ability. When you're finished, review the list. Does it reveal anything new about your career interests? Does it change your "feeling" for what you are really good at? In what situations will your résumé stand out from the pack? Incorporate the achievement statements into your résumé.

---

to keep the name of your present employer confidential, identify the firm by industry only ("a large film-processing laboratory"), or use the name but request confidentiality in the application letter or in an underlined note ("Résumé submitted in confidence") at the top or bottom of the résumé. If an organization's name or location has since changed, state the present name or location and then "formerly . . ."

Before or after each job listing, state your functional title, such as "clerk typist" or "salesperson." If you were a dishwasher, say so. Don't try to make your role seem more important by glamorizing your job title, functions, or achievements. Also state how long you worked on each job, from month/year to month/year. Use the phrase "to present" to denote current employment. If a job was part-time, say so.

Be honest about the positions you've held, the companies you've worked for, and your dates of employment. You'll be courting trouble if you list jobs you never held, claim to have worked for a firm when you didn't, or change dates to cover up a gap

The work experience section lists all the related jobs you've had:

- Name and location of employer
- What the organization does (if not clear from its name)
- Your functional title
- How long you worked there
- Your duties and responsibilities
- Your significant achievements or contributions

in unemployment. More employers are checking candidates' backgrounds, so inaccuracies are likely to be exposed sooner or later.

Devote the most space to the jobs that relate to your target position. If you were personally responsible for something significant, be sure to mention it ("Devised a new collection system that accelerated payment of overdue receivables"). Facts about your accomplishments are the most important information you can give a prospective employer, so quantify your accomplishments whenever possible ("Designed a new ad that increased sales by 9 percent").

Quantify your accomplishments whenever possible.

Relevant Skills

You may also want to include a section that describes other aspects of your background that pertain to your career objective. If you were applying for a position with a multinational organization, you would mention your command of another language or your travel experience. Other skills you might mention include the ability to operate a computer, word processor, or other equipment. In fact, you might entitle a special section "Computer Skills" or "Language Skills" and place it near your "Education" or "Work Experience" sections.

Include miscellaneous facts that relate to your career objective:
- *Command of other languages*
- *Computer expertise*
- *Date you can start working*
- *Availability of references*

If your academic transcripts, samples of your work, or letters of recommendation might increase your chances of getting the job, insert a line at the end of your résumé offering to supply these on request. If your college placement office keeps these items on file for you, you can say "References and supporting documents available from . . ."; be sure to include the exact address of the placement office. Many potential employers prefer to have actual references on the résumé. As a convenience for the prospective employer, you may also list the month and, if you know it, the day you will be available to start work.

Activities and Achievements

Your résumé also describes any volunteer activities that demonstrate your abilities. List projects that required leadership, organization, teamwork, and cooperation. Emphasize career-related activities such as "member of the Student Marketing Association," list skills you learned in these activities, and explain how these skills relate to the job you're applying for. Include speaking, writing, or tutoring experience, participation in athletics or creative projects, experience gained during internships, fund-raising or community service activities, and offices held in academic or professional organizations. (However, mention of political or religious organizations may be a red flag to someone with different views, so use your judgment.) Note any awards you have received. Again, quantify your achievements with numbers wherever possible. Instead of saying that you addressed various student groups, state how many and the approximate audience sizes. If your activities have been extensive, you may want to group them into divisions like these: "College Activities," "Community Service," "Professional Associations," "Seminars and Workshops," and "Speaking Activities." An alternative is to divide them into two categories: "Service Activities" and "Achievements, Awards, and Honors."

Nonpaid activities may provide evidence of work-related skills.

Personal Data

To differentiate your résumé, you might want to mention your hobbies, travel experiences, or personal characteristics, particularly if they suggest qualities that relate to your career goals. This section helps present you as a well-rounded person, and it can be used to spark conversation during an interview.[5] However, civil rights laws prohibit employers from discriminating on the basis of gender, marital or family status, age (although only those 40 to 70 are protected), race, color, religion, national origin, or physical or mental disability. So be sure to exclude any items that could encourage discrimination.

Provide only the personal data that will help you get the job.

If military service is relevant to the position you are seeking, you may list it in this section (or under "Education" or "Work Experience"). List the date of induction, the branch of service, where you served, the highest rank you achieved, any accomplishments related to your career goals, and the date you were discharged.

Choosing the Best Organizational Plan

Although you may want to include a little information in all categories, emphasize the information that has a bearing on your career objective and minimize or exclude any that is irrelevant or counterproductive. You do this by adopting an organizational plan—chronological, functional, or targeted—that focuses attention on your strongest points. The "right" choice depends on your background and goals as Table 15.1 illustrates.

> Select an organizational pattern that focuses attention on your strengths.

The Chronological Résumé

The most traditional type of résumé is the **chronological résumé,** in which a person's employment history is listed sequentially in reverse order, starting with the most recent experience. When you organize your résumé chronologically, the "Work Experience" section dominates the résumé and is placed in the most prominent slot, immediately after your name, address, and objective. You develop this section by listing your jobs in reverse order, beginning with the most recent position and working

> Most recruiters prefer the chronological plan—a historical summary of your education and work experience.

Table 15.1   HOW TO CHOOSE AN ORGANIZATIONAL PLAN FOR YOUR RÉSUMÉ

Type of Résumé	When to Use	When Not to Use
Chronological: Lists work experience or education in reverse chronological order; describes responsibilities and accomplishments associated with each job or educational experience	Your last employer is well known and highly respected. You plan to continue along your established career path. Your job history shows progressively more responsible positions. You are applying to a traditional organization.	You have changed jobs frequently. You are changing your career goals. You have not progressed in your career. You have been away from the job market for some time. You are applying for your first job.
Functional: Lists functional experience separately from employment history	You want to emphasize capabilities not used in recent jobs. You are changing careers. You are entering the job market for the first time or are reentering after an absence. Your past career progression has been disappointing. You have held a variety of unrelated jobs. Your work has been of a freelance or temporary nature.	You want to emphasize your career progress. You have performed a limited number of functions. Your most recent employers are well known and prestigious. You are applying to a traditional organization.
Targeted: Lists capabilities and accomplishments pertaining to a specific job; briefly lists work experience in a separate section	You are clear about your job target. You have several career objectives and want a separate résumé for each. You want to emphasize capabilities that you may not have performed for a regular employer.	You want to use one résumé for several applications. You are not clear about your capabilities or accomplishments. You are just starting your career and have little experience.

backward toward earlier jobs. Under each listing you describe your responsibilities and accomplishments, giving the most space to the most recent positions. If you are just graduating from college, you can vary the chronological plan by putting your educational qualifications before your experience, thereby focusing attention on your academic credentials.

The chronological approach is the most common way to organize a résumé, and many employers prefer it. Robert Nesbit, a vice president with Korn/Ferry International, speaks for many recruiters: "Unless you have a really compelling reason, don't use any but the standard chronological format. Your résumé should not read like a treasure map, full of minute clues to the whereabouts of your jobs and experience. I want to be able to grasp quickly where a candidate has worked, how long, and in what capacities."[6]

The chronological approach is especially appropriate if you have a strong employment history and are aiming for a job that builds on your current career path. This is the case for Roberto Cortez, whose résumé appears in Figure 15.1. Cortez calls atten-

Figure 15.1
Chronological Résumé

The applicant emphasizes his achievements by using bulleted lists.

The chronological organization highlights the applicant's impressive career progress.

The applicant's special qualifications are presented as personal data.

```
                              ROBERTO CORTEZ
                5687 Crosswoods Drive, Falls Church, Virginia 22044
                   Home: (703) 987-0086     Office: (703) 549-6624


        OBJECTIVE

           Accounting management position requiring a knowledge of
           international finance

        EXPERIENCE

           STAFF ACCOUNTANT/FINANCIAL ANALYST
           Inter-American Imports       Alexandria, VA
           April 1992 to present

           •  Prepare general accounting reports for wholesale giftware
              importer with annual sales of $15 million
           •  Audit all financial transactions between headquarters and
              suppliers in 12 Latin American countries
           •  Created a computerized model to adjust accounts for
              fluctuations in currency exchange rates
           •  Negotiated joint venture agreements with major suppliers in
              Mexico and Columbia

           STAFF ACCOUNTANT
           Monsanto Agricultural Chemicals      Mexico City, Mexico
           October 1988 to March 1992

           •  Handled budgeting, billing, and credit processing functions for
              the Mexico City branch
           •  Audited travel and entertainment expenses for Monsanto's
              30-member Latin American sales force
           •  Assisted in launching an on-line computer system (IBM)

        EDUCATION

           GEORGE MASON UNIVERSITY      Fairfax, Virginia
           M.B.A. with emphasis on international business
           1992-1995

           UNIVERSIDAD NACIONAL AUTÓNOMA DE MEXICO      Mexico City, Mexico
           B.B.A., Accounting
           1984-1988

        PERSONAL DATA

           Born and raised in Mexico City; became U.S. citizen in 1994
           Fluent in Spanish and German
           Traveled extensively in Latin America


                          References Available on Request
                           Résumé Submitted in Confidence
```

tion to his most recent achievements by setting them off in list format with bullets. The section titled "Personal Data" emphasizes his international background and fluency in Spanish, which are important qualifications for the position he desires.

The Functional Résumé

In a **functional résumé,** you organize your résumé around a list of skills and accomplishments and then identify your employers and academic experience in subordinate sections. This pattern stresses individual areas of competence, and it's useful for people who are just entering the job market, for those who want to redirect their careers, or for those who have little continuous career-related experience.

A functional résumé focuses attention on your areas of competence.

Figure 15.2 illustrates how a recent graduate used the functional approach to showcase her qualifications for a career in retailing. Glenda St. Johns knows a good deal about retailing from course work and field experience. As a result, she was able to organize her résumé in a way that demonstrates her ability to handle a retailing position.

Figure 15.2
Functional Résumé

```
                          Glenda St. Johns

Home Address:                          School Address:

   457 Mountain View Road                 1254 Main Street, #7
   Clear Lake, Iowa 50428                 Council Bluffs, Iowa 51501
   (515) 633-5971                         (712) 438-5254

       OBJECTIVE:  Retailing position that utilizes my experience

RELEVANT SKILLS

Personal Selling/Retailing:
• Led housewares department in the fewest transaction mistakes while
  cashiering and balancing register receipts
• Created end-cap and shelf displays for special housewares promotions
• Sold the most benefit tickets during college fund-raising drive for
  local community center
Public Interaction:
• Commended by housewares manager for resolving customer complaints
  amicably
• Performed in summer theater productions in Clear Lake, Iowa
Managing:
• Trained part-time housewares employees in cash register operation and
  customer service
• Reworked housewares employee schedules as assistant manager
• Organized summer activities for children 6-12 years old for city of
  Clear Lake, Iowa--including reading programs, sports activities, and
  field trips

EDUCATION

Iowa Western Community College, September 1993-June 1996
A.A. retailing mid-management (3.81 GPA on 4.0 scale)

In addition to required retailing, buying, marketing, and merchandising
courses, completed electives in visual merchandising, business information
systems, principles of management, and business mathematics

WORK EXPERIENCE

• Assistant manager, housewares at Jefferson's Department Store during
  off-campus work experience program, Council Bluffs, Iowa (Winter
  1995-Spring 1996)
• Salesclerk, housewares at Jefferson's Department Store during off-campus
  work experience program, Council Bluffs, Iowa (Winter 1994-Spring 1995)
• Assistant director, Summer Recreation Program, Clear Lake, Iowa
  (Summer, 1994)

PERSONAL DATA

Willing to relocate

REFERENCES AND SUPPORTING DOCUMENTS

Available from Placement Office, Iowa Western Community College, Council
Bluffs, Iowa 51501
```

Because she is a recent graduate, the applicant describes her relevant skills first.

The use of action verbs and specific facts enhances this résumé's effectiveness.

The applicant's course work and field experience are related to relevant skills.

The Targeted Résumé

A targeted résumé shows how you qualify for a specific job.

A **targeted résumé** is organized to focus attention on what you can do for a particular employer in a particular position. Immediately after stating your career objective, you list any related capabilities. This list is followed by a list of your achievements, which provide evidence of your capabilities. Employers and schools are listed in subordinate sections.

Targeted résumés are a good choice for people who have a clear idea of what they want to do and who can demonstrate their ability in the targeted area. This approach was effective for Erica Vorkamp, whose résumé appears in Figure 15.3. Instead of using a chronological pattern, which would have focused attention on her lack of recent work experience, she uses a targeted approach that emphasizes her ability to organize

Figure 15.3
Targeted Résumé

The capabilities and achievements all relate to the specific job target, giving a very selective picture of the candidate's abilities.

This work history has little bearing on the candidate's job target, but she felt that recruiters would want to see evidence that she has held a paying position.

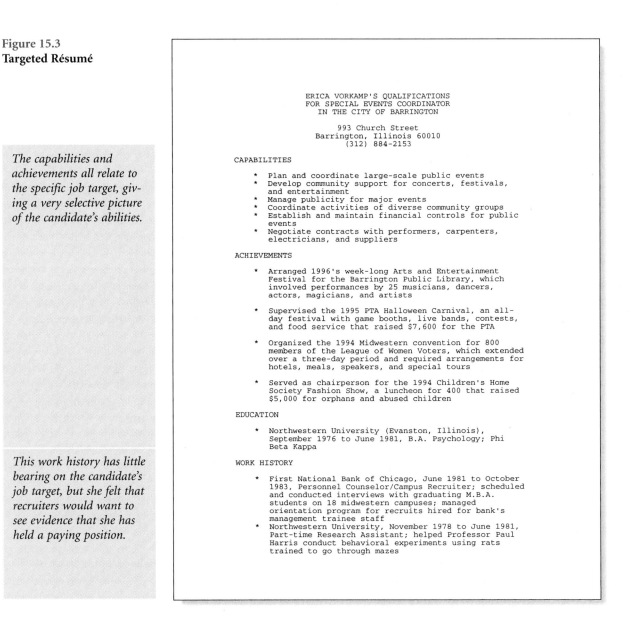

```
                    ERICA VORKAMP'S QUALIFICATIONS
                    FOR SPECIAL EVENTS COORDINATOR
                       IN THE CITY OF BARRINGTON

                          993 Church Street
                       Barrington, Illinois 60010
                          (312) 884-2153

CAPABILITIES

      *  Plan and coordinate large-scale public events
      *  Develop community support for concerts, festivals,
         and entertainment
      *  Manage publicity for major events
      *  Coordinate activities of diverse community groups
      *  Establish and maintain financial controls for public
         events
      *  Negotiate contracts with performers, carpenters,
         electricians, and suppliers

ACHIEVEMENTS

      *  Arranged 1996's week-long Arts and Entertainment
         Festival for the Barrington Public Library, which
         involved performances by 25 musicians, dancers,
         actors, magicians, and artists

      *  Supervised the 1995 PTA Halloween Carnival, an all-
         day festival with game booths, live bands, contests,
         and food service that raised $7,600 for the PTA

      *  Organized the 1994 Midwestern convention for 800
         members of the League of Women Voters, which extended
         over a three-day period and required arrangements for
         hotels, meals, speakers, and special tours

      *  Served as chairperson for the 1994 Children's Home
         Society Fashion Show, a luncheon for 400 that raised
         $5,000 for orphans and abused children

EDUCATION

      *  Northwestern University (Evanston, Illinois),
         September 1976 to June 1981, B.A. Psychology; Phi
         Beta Kappa

WORK HISTORY

      *  First National Bank of Chicago, June 1981 to October
         1983, Personnel Counselor/Campus Recruiter; scheduled
         and conducted interviews with graduating M.B.A.
         students on 18 midwestern campuses; managed
         orientation program for recruits hired for bank's
         management trainee staff
      *  Northwestern University, November 1978 to June 1981,
         Part-time Research Assistant; helped Professor Paul
         Harris conduct behavioral experiments using rats
         trained to go through mazes
```

special events. A targeted résumé is also appropriate when you want to emphasize abilities that you may not have performed for a regular employer.

Writing the Perfect Résumé

Regardless of what organizational plan you follow, the key to writing the "perfect" résumé is to put yourself in the reader's position. Think about what the prospective employer needs, and then tailor your résumé accordingly.

People like Pinkerton's Thomas Wathen read thousands of résumés every year and complain about the following common résumé problems:

- *Too long.* The résumé is not concise, relevant, and to the point.
- *Too short or sketchy.* The résumé does not give enough information for a proper evaluation of the applicant.
- *Hard to read.* A lack of "white space" and of such devices as indentions and underlining makes the reader's job more difficult.
- *Wordy.* Descriptions are verbose, with numerous words used for what could be said more simply.
- *Too slick.* The résumé appears to have been written by someone other than the applicant, which raises the question of whether the qualifications have been exaggerated.
- *Amateurish.* The applicant appears to have little understanding of the business world or of the particular industry, as revealed by including the wrong information or presenting it awkwardly.
- *Poorly reproduced.* The print is faint and difficult to read.
- *Misspelled and ungrammatical throughout.* Recruiters conclude that candidates who make these kinds of mistakes don't have good verbal skills, which are important on the job.
- *Lacking a career objective.* The résumé fails to identify the applicant's job preferences and career goals.
- *Boastful.* The overconfident tone makes the reader wonder whether the applicant's self-evaluation is realistic.
- *Dishonest.* The applicant claims to have expertise or work experience that he or she does not possess.
- *Gimmicky.* The words, structure, decoration, or material used in the résumé depart so far from the usual as to make the résumé ineffective.

Guard against making these mistakes in your own résumé, and compare your final version with the suggestions in this chapter's Checklist for Résumés. Also, update your résumé continuously. You'll need it whether you're applying for membership in a professional organization, working toward a promotion, or changing employers. People used to spend the majority of a career with one company. However, today the average person beginning a job in the United States will probably work in ten or more jobs for five or more employers before retiring.[7] So keeping your résumé updated is a good idea.

If you're like most job seekers, your résumé won't be the only one employers receive, so you'll want to attract your audience's attention. Moreover, you'll want to tailor your application to each employer as specifically as possible. So in addition to adapting your résumé to each company, you'll include a cover letter (or application letter) that projects your theme and explains what you can do for that specific organization.

The "perfect" résumé responds to the reader's needs and preferences and avoids some common faults.

Within a year of becoming president of Godfather's Pizza, Herman Cain returned the floundering chain to profitability. Now principal owner (following a leveraged buyout), Cain says his success springs from his love of the restaurant business. Simple ambition isn't enough to succeed in any business, he advises, so send résumés to companies whose business you have a real passion for.

CHECKLIST FOR RÉSUMÉS

A. Contents and Style
1. Prepare the résumé before the application letter to summarize the facts the letter will be based on.
2. Present the strongest qualifications first.
3. Use short noun phrases and action verbs, not whole sentences.
4. Use facts, not opinions.
5. Avoid excessive use of personal pronouns.
6. Omit the date of preparation.
7. Omit mention of your desired salary, work schedule, or vacation schedule.

B. Contact Information
1. Use a title or your name and address as a heading.
2. List your name, address, area code, and telephone number—for both school or work and home, if appropriate.

C. Career Objective and Skills Summary (optional)
1. Be as specific as possible about what you want to do.
   - a. State a broad and flexible goal to increase the scope of your job prospects.
   - b. Prepare two different résumés if you can do two unrelated types of work.
2. Summarize your key qualifications.

3. State the month and, if you know it, the day on which you will be available to start work.

D. Education
1. List all relevant schooling and training since high school, with the most recent first.
   - a. List the name and location of every postsecondary school you have attended, with the dates you entered and left and the degrees or certificates you obtained.
   - b. Indicate your major (and minor) fields in college work.
   - c. State the numerical base of your grade point average, overall or in your major, if your average is impressive enough to list.
2. List relevant required or elective courses in descending order of importance.
3. List any other related educational or training experiences, such as job-related seminars or workshops attended and certificates obtained.

E. Work Experience
1. List all relevant work experience, including paid employment and volunteer work.
2. List full-time and part-time jobs, with the most recent one first.

WRITING AN APPLICATION LETTER

Follow the AIDA plan when writing your application letter: attention, interest, desire, action.

Like your résumé, your application letter is a form of advertising, and it's organized like a persuasive message. You need to stimulate the reader's interest before showing how you can satisfy the organization's needs. Adopt a style that projects confidence; you can't hope to sell a potential employer on your merits unless you truly believe in them yourself and sound as though you do.

However, this approach isn't appropriate for job seekers in every culture. If you're applying for a job abroad or want to work with a subsidiary of an organization based in another country, you may need to adjust your tone. For instance, blatant self-promotion is considered bad form in some cultures. Other cultures stress group performance over individual contributions. Because of these cultural variations, do some research before you draft your letter.

Let your letter reflect your personal style. Be yourself, but be businesslike too; avoid sounding cute. Don't use slang or a gimmicky layout. The only time to be unusually creative in content or format is when the job you're seeking requires imagination, such as a position in advertising. In most cases you'll use a typewriter or letter-quality printer

a. State the month/year when you started and left each job.

b. Provide the name and location of the firm that employed you.

c. List your job title and describe your functions briefly.

d. Note on-the-job accomplishments, such as an award or a suggestion that saved the organization time or money.

F. Activities, Honors, and Achievements

1. List all relevant unpaid activities, including offices and leadership positions; significant awards or scholarships not listed elsewhere; projects you have undertaken that show an ability to work with others; and writing or speaking activities, publications, and roles in academic or professional organizations.

2. In most circumstances, exclude mention of religious or political affiliations.

G. Other Relevant Facts

1. List other information, such as your typing speed or your proficiency in languages other than English.

2. Mention your ability to operate any machines, equipment, or computer software used in the job.

H. Personal Data

1. Omit personal details that could be regarded negatively or be used to discriminate against you.

2. Omit or downplay references to age if it could suggest inexperience or approaching retirement.

3. Describe military service (branch of service, where you served, rank attained, and the dates of induction and discharge) here or, if relevant, under "Education" or "Work Experience."

4. List job-related interests and hobbies, especially those indicating stamina, strength, sociability, or other qualities that are desirable in the position you seek.

I. References

1. Offer to supply the names of references on request.

a. Supply names of academic, employment, and professional associates—but not names of relatives.

b. Provide a name, a title, an address, and a telephone number for each reference.

c. List no name as a reference until you have that person's permission to do so.

2. Exclude your present employer if you do not want the firm to know you are seeking another position, or add "Résumé submitted in confidence" at the top or bottom of the résumé.

to produce your application letter, but in some countries, including France, recruiters prefer handwritten letters.

Finally, showing that you know something about the organization can pay off. Imagine yourself in the recruiter's situation: How can you demonstrate that your background and talents will solve a particular problem or fill a need? By using a "you" attitude and showing you've done some homework, you'll capture the reader's attention and convey your desire to join the organization. The more you can learn about the organization, the better you'll be able to write about how your qualifications fit its needs.[8] In addition, prove you've done your homework by finding out the name, title, and department of the person you're writing to. Reaching and addressing the right person is the most effective way to gain attention. So be sure to avoid phrases such as "To Whom It May Concern" or "Dear Sir."

Writing the Opening Paragraph

A **solicited application letter** is one sent in response to an announced job opening. An **unsolicited letter,** also known as a *prospecting letter,* is one sent to an organization

You write a solicited application letter in response to an announced job opening.

385

You write an unsolicited application letter to an organization that has not announced a job opening.

that has not announced an opening. When you send a solicited letter, you usually know in advance what qualifications the organization is seeking. However, you also have more competition because hundreds of other job seekers will have seen the listing and may be sending applications. In some respects, therefore, an unsolicited application letter stands a better chance of being read and of receiving individualized attention.

Whether your application letter is solicited or unsolicited, your qualifications are presented similarly. The main difference is in the opening paragraph. In a solicited letter, no special attention-getting effort is needed because you have been invited to apply. However, the unsolicited letter starts by capturing the reader's attention and interest.

Getting Attention

The opening of an unsolicited application letter captures attention and raises the reader's interest.

One way to spark attention in the opening paragraph is to show how your strongest work skills could benefit the organization. A 20-year-old secretary with $1\frac{1}{2}$ years of college might begin like this:

When you need a secretary in your export division who can take shorthand at 125 words a minute and transcribe notes at 70--in English, Spanish, or Portuguese--call me.

Here's another attention-getter. It describes your understanding of the job's requirements and then shows how well your qualifications fit the job:

Your annual report states that Pinkerton runs training programs about workforce diversity for managers and employees. The difficulties involved in running such programs can be significant, as I learned while tutoring inner-city high school students last summer. My 12 pupils were enrolled in vocational training programs and came from an eclectic mix of ethnic and racial backgrounds. The one thing they had in common was the lack of familiarity with the typical employer's expectations. To help them learn the "rules of the game," I developed exercises that cast them in various roles: boss, customer, new recruit, and co-worker. Of the 12 students, 10 have subsequently found full-time jobs and have called or written to tell me how much they gained from the workshop.

Mentioning the name of a person known to and highly regarded by the reader is bound to capture some attention:

When Janice McHugh of your franchise sales division spoke to our business communication class last week, she said you often need promising new marketing graduates at this time of year.

References to publicized company activities, achievements, changes, or new procedures can also be used to gain attention:

Today's issue of the <u>Detroit News</u> reports that you may need the expertise of computer programmers versed in robotics when your Lansing tire plant automates this spring.

Another type of attention-getting opening uses a question to demonstrate an understanding of the organization's needs:

Can your fast-growing market research division use an interviewer with 1-1/2 years of field survey experience, a B.A. in public relations, and a real desire to succeed? If so, please consider me for the position.

A catchphrase opening can also capture attention, especially if the job sought requires ingenuity and imagination:

Grande monde--whether said in French, Italian, or Arabic, it still means "high society." As an interior designer for your Beverly Hills showroom, not only could I serve and sell to your high-society clientele, I could do it in all these languages. I speak, read, and write them fluently.

In contrast, a solicited letter written in response to a job advertisement usually opens by identifying the publication in which the ad ran; then it describes what the applicant has to offer:

Your ad in the April issue of Travel & Leisure for a cruise-line social director caught my eye. My eight years of experience as a social director in the travel industry would allow me to serve your new Caribbean cruise division well.

All these openings demonstrate the "you" attitude, and many indicate how the applicant can serve the employer.

Clarifying Your Reason for Writing

The opening paragraph of your application letter also states your reason for writing: You are applying for a job, so the opening paragraph should identify the desired job or job area:

Please consider my application for an entry-level position in technical writing.

Your firm advertised a fleet sales position in the Baltimore Sun (March 23, 1995). Having had 16 months of new-car sales experience, I'm applying for that position.

Another way to state your reason for writing is to use a title at the opening of your letter:

Subject: Application for bookkeeper position

After this clear signal, your first paragraph can focus on getting attention and indicating how hiring you may benefit the organization.

Summarizing Your Key Selling Points

The middle section of your application letter presents your strongest selling points in terms of their potential benefit to the organization, thereby creating interest in you and a desire to interview you. If your selling points have already been mentioned in the opening, don't repeat them. Simply give supporting evidence. Otherwise, spell out your key qualifications, together with some convincing evidence of your ability to perform.

Oprah Winfrey has a humanistic approach to running her company, Harpo Productions. She's known to be demanding of her 135 employees, but she's also generous. Winfrey reminds applicants to get attention by emphasizing how they can help the employer. And don't be afraid to be yourself, she says.

Start a solicited application letter by mentioning how you found out about the open position.

The middle section of an application letter

- Summarizes your relevant qualifications
- Emphasizes your accomplishments
- Suggests desirable personal qualities
- Justifies salary requirements
- Refers to your résumé

To avoid a cluttered application letter, mention only the qualifications that indicate you can do the job. Show how your studies and your work experience have prepared you for that job, or tell the reader about how you grew up in the business. Be careful not to repeat the facts presented in your résumé; simply interpret those facts for the reader:

> Experience in customer relations and college courses in public relations have taught me how to handle the problem-solving tasks that arise in a leading retail clothing firm like yours. Such important tasks include identifying and resolving customer complaints, writing letters that build good customer relations, and above all, promoting the organization's positive image.

When writing a solicited letter responding to a help-wanted advertisement, discuss each requirement specified in the ad. If you are deficient in any of these requirements, stress other solid selling points to help strengthen your overall presentation.

Stating that you have all the necessary requirements for the job is rarely enough to convince the reader, so back up assertions of your ability by presenting evidence of it. Cite one or two of your key qualifications; then show how you have effectively put them to use.

Instead of This	*Write This*
I completed three college courses in business communication, earning an A in each course, and have worked for the past year at Imperial Construction.	Using the skills gained from three semesters of college training in business communication, I developed a collection system for Imperial Construction that reduced its 1994 bad-debt losses by 3.7 percent, or $9,902, over those of 1993. The new collection letters offered discount incentives for speedy payment rather than timeworn terminology.

This section of the letter also presents evidence of a few significant job-related qualities. The following paragraph demonstrates that the applicant is diligent and hardworking:

> While attending college full-time, I trained 3 hours a day with the varsity track team. Additionally, I worked part-time during the school year and up to 60 hours a week each summer in order to be totally self-supporting while in college. I can offer your organization the same level of effort and perseverance.

Other relevant qualities worth noting include the abilities to learn quickly, to handle responsibility, and to get along with people.

Another matter to bring up in this section is your salary requirements—but only if the organization has asked you to state them. The best strategy, unless you know approximately what the job pays, is to suggest a salary range or to indicate that the salary is negotiable or open. You might also consult the latest government "Area Wage Survey" at the library; this document presents salary ranges for various job classifications and geographic areas. If you do state a target salary, tie your request to the benefits you would provide the organization, much as you would handle price in a sales letter:

For the past two years, I have been helping a company similar to yours organize its database. I would therefore like to receive a salary in the same range (the mid-20s) for helping your company set up a more efficient customer database.

Toward the end of this section, refer the reader to your résumé. You may do so by citing a specific fact or general point covered in the résumé.

As you can see in the attached résumé, I have been working part-time for a local publisher since my sophomore year.

Writing the Closing Paragraph

The final paragraph of your application letter has two important functions: to ask the reader for a specific action and to make a reply easy. In almost all cases, the action you should ask for is an interview. Don't demand it, however; try to sound natural and appreciative. Offer to come to the employer's office at a convenient time or, if the firm is some distance away, to meet with its nearest representative. Make the request easy to fulfill by stating your phone number and the best time to reach you. Refer again to your strongest selling point and, if desired, your date of availability:

Close by asking for an interview and making the interview easy to arrange.

After you have reviewed my qualifications, could we discuss the possibility of putting my marketing skills to work for your company? Because I will be on spring break the week of March 8, I would like to arrange a time to talk then. You can reach me by calling (901) 235-6311 during the day or (901) 529-2873 any evening after 5:00.

An alternative approach is to ask for an interview and then offer to get in touch with the reader to arrange a time for it, rather than requesting a reply. Whichever approach you use, mail your application letter and résumé promptly, especially if they have been solicited.

Writing the Perfect Application Letter

The "perfect" application letter, like the "perfect" résumé, accomplishes one thing: It gets you an interview. It conforms to no particular model because it's a reflection of your special strengths. Nevertheless, an application letter should contain the basic components.

In Figure 15.4, an unsolicited letter for a retail clerk position, the applicant gains attention by spelling out the skills and qualities a retail manager would value. The letter in Figure 15.5, written in response to a help-wanted ad, highlights the applicant's chief qualifications. Compare your own letters with the tasks in this chapter's Checklist for Application Letters.

Figure 15.4
Sample Unsolicited Application Letter

457 Mountain View Road
Clear Lake, Iowa 50428
June 16, 1996

Ms. Patricia Downings, Store Manager
Wal-Mart
840 South Oak
Iowa Falls, Iowa 50126

Dear Ms. Downings:

You want retail clerks and managers who are accurate,
enthusiastic, and experienced. You want someone who cares
about customer service, who understands merchandising, and
who can work with others to get the job done. When you're
ready to hire a manager trainee or a clerk who is willing to
work toward promotion, please consider me for the job.

Working as clerk and then as assistant department manager in
a large department store has taught me how challenging a
career in retailing can be. Moreover, my A.A. degree in
retailing (including work in such courses as retailing,
marketing, and business information systems) will provide
your store with a well-rounded associate. Most important, I
can offer Wal-Mart's Iowa Falls store more than my two
years' of study and field experience. You'll find that I'm
interested in every facet of retailing, eager to take on
responsibility, and willing to continue learning throughout
my career. Please look over my résumé to see how my skills
can benefit your store.

I understand that Wal-Mart prefers to promote its managers
from within the company, and I would be pleased to start out
with an entry-level position until I gain the necessary
experience. Do you have any associate positions opening up
soon? Could we discuss my qualifications? I will phone you
early next Wednesday to see whether we can arrange a meeting
at your convenience.

Sincerely,

Glenda St. Johns

Glenda St. Johns

Enclosure

The applicant gains attention in the first paragraph.

The applicant points out personal qualities that aren't specifically stated in her résumé.

Knowledge of the company's policy toward promotions is sure to interest the reader.

Even though the last paragraph uses the word I, *the concern and the focus of the letter are clearly centered on the audience with a "you" attitude.*

WRITING OTHER TYPES OF EMPLOYMENT MESSAGES

In your search for a job, you may prepare three other types of written messages: job-inquiry letters, application forms, and application follow-up letters.

Writing Job-Inquiry Letters

Use a job-inquiry letter to request an application form, which is a standardized data sheet that simplifies comparison of applicants' credentials.

Some organizations will not consider you for a position until you have filled out and submitted an **application form,** a standardized data sheet that simplifies comparison of applicants' qualifications. The inquiry letter is mailed to request such a form. To increase your chances of getting the form, include enough information about yourself in the letter to show that you have at least some of the requirements for the position you are seeking:

Figure 15.5
**Sample Solicited
Application Letter**

2893 Jack Pine Road
Chapel Hill, NC 27514
February 2, 1996

Ms. Angela Clair
Director of Administration
Cummings and Welbane, Inc.
770 Campus Point Drive
Chapel Hill, NC 27514

Dear Ms. Clair:

Your advertisement in the January 31 issue of the <u>Chapel Hill Post</u> attracted my attention because I believe that I have the "proven skills" you are looking for in an administrative assistant. In addition to having previous experience in a variety of office settings, I am familiar with the computer system that you use in your office.

The opening states the reason for writing and links the writer's experience to stated qualifications.

I recently completed a three-course sequence at Hamilton College on operation of the Beta computer system. I learned how to apply this technology to speed up letter-writing and report-writing tasks. A workshop on "Writing and Editing with the Beta Processor" gave me experience with other valuable applications.

As a result of this training, I am able to compose many types of finished documents, including sales letters, financial reports, and presentation slides.

These specialized skills have proven valuable in my work for the past eight months as assistant to the chief nutritionist at the University of North Carolina campus cafeteria. As my résumé indicates, my duties include drafting letters, typing finished correspondence, and handling phone calls. I'm particularly proud of the order-confirmation system I designed, which has sharply reduced the problem of late shipments and depleted inventories.

By discussing how his specific skills apply to the job sought, the applicant shows that he understands the job's responsibilities.

Because "proven skills" are best explained in person, I would appreciate an interview with you. Please phone me any afternoon between 3 and 5 p.m. at (919) 220-6139 to let me know the day and time most convenient for you.

In closing, the writer asks for an interview and facilitates action.

Sincerely,

Ken Sawyer

Kenneth Sawyer

Enclosure

Please send me an application form for work as an interior designer in your home furnishings department. For my certificate in design, I took courses in retail merchandising and customer relations. I have also had part-time sales experience at Capwell's department store.

Instead of writing a letter of this kind, you may want to drop in at the office you're applying to. You probably won't get a chance to talk to anyone other than the receptionist or a personnel assistant, but you can pick up the form, get an impression of the organization, and demonstrate your initiative and energy.

Filling Out Application Forms

Some organizations require an application form instead of a résumé, and many require both an application form and a résumé. When filling out an application form,

Your care in filling out application forms suggests to the employer that you will be thorough and careful in your work.

CHECKLIST FOR APPLICATION LETTERS

A. Attention (Opening Paragraph)

1. Open the letter by capturing the reader's attention in a businesslike way.

   a. *Summary opening.* Present your strongest, most relevant qualifications, with an explanation of how they can benefit the organization.

   b. *Name opening.* Mention the name of a person who is well known to the reader and who has suggested that you apply for the job.

   c. *Source opening.* When responding to a job ad, identify the publication in which the ad appeared and briefly describe how you meet each requirement stated in the ad.

   d. *Question opening.* Pose an attention-getting question that shows you understand an organization's problem, need, or goal and have a genuine desire to help solve or meet it.

   e. *News opening.* Cite a publicized organizational achievement, contemplated change, or new procedure or product; then link it to your desire to work for the organization.

   f. *Personalized opening.* Present one of your relevant interests, mention previous experience with the organization, or cite your present position or status as a means of leading into a discussion of why you want to work for the organization.

   g. *Creative opening.* Demonstrate your flair and imagination with colorful phrasing, especially if the job requires these qualities.

2. State that you are applying for a job, and identify the position or the type of work you seek.

B. Interest and Desire, or Evidence of Qualifications (Next Several Paragraphs)

1. Present your key qualifications for the job, highlighting what is on your résumé: job-related edu-

---

try to be thorough and accurate, because the organization will use this as a convenient one-page source for information about your qualifications. Be sure to have your résumé with you to remind you of important information. If you can't remember something and have no record of it, provide the closest estimate possible. If the form calls for information that you cannot provide because you have no background in it—such as military experience—write "Not applicable." When filling out applications on the premises, use a pen (unless specifically requested to use a pencil). If you're allowed to take the application form with you, use a typewriter to fill it out.

Application forms rarely seem to provide the right amount of space or to ask the right kinds of questions to reflect one's skills and abilities accurately. Swallow your frustration, however, and show your cooperation by doing your best to fill out the form completely. If you get an interview, you'll have an opportunity to fill in the gaps. You might also ask the person who gives you the form if you may submit a résumé and an application letter as well.

Writing Application Follow-Ups

Use a follow-up letter to let the employer know you're still interested in the job.

If your application letter and résumé fail to bring a response within a month or so, follow up with a second letter to keep your file active. This follow-up letter also gives you a chance to update your original application with any recent job-related information:

> Since applying to you on May 3 for an executive secretary position, I have completed a course in office management at South River Community College. I received straight A's in the course. My typing speed has also increased to 75 words per minute.

cation and training; relevant work experience; and related activities, interests, and qualities.

2. Adopt a mature and businesslike tone.
   a. Eliminate boasting and exaggeration.
   b. Back up your claims of ability by citing specific achievements in educational and work settings (or in outside activities).
   c. Demonstrate a knowledge of the organization and a desire to join it by citing its operations or trends in the industry.
3. Link your education, experience, and personal qualities to the job requirements.
   a. Relate aspects of your training or work experience to those of the target position.
   b. Outline your educational preparation for the job.
   c. Provide proof that you learn quickly, are a hard worker, can handle responsibility, and/or get along well with others.
   d. Present ample evidence of the personal qualities and the work attitudes that are desirable for job performance.

   e. If asked to state salary requirements, provide current salary or a desired salary range, and link it to the benefits of hiring you.
4. Refer the reader to the enclosed résumé.

C. Action (Closing Paragraph)
1. Request an interview at the reader's convenience.
2. Request a screening interview with the nearest regional representative, if company headquarters is some distance away.
3. State your phone number (with area code) and the best time to reach you, to make the request for an interview easy to comply with, or mention a time when you will be calling to set up an interview.
4. Express appreciation for an opportunity to have an interview.
5. Repeat your strongest qualification, to help reinforce the claim that you have something to offer the organization.

Please keep my application in your active file, and let me know when you need a skilled executive secretary.

Even if you've received a letter acknowledging your application and saying that it will be kept on file, don't hesitate to send a follow-up letter three months later to show that you are still interested:

Three months have elapsed since I applied to you for an underwriting position, but I want to let you know that I am still very interested in joining your company.

I recently completed a four-week temporary work assignment at a large local insurance agency. I learned several new verification techniques and gained experience in using the on-line computer system. This experience could increase my value to your underwriting department.

Please keep my application in your active file, and let me know when a position opens for a capable underwriter.

Unless you state otherwise, the human resources office is likely to assume that you've already found a job and are no longer interested in the organization. In addition, organizations' requirements change. Sending a letter like this demonstrates that you are sincerely interested in working for the organization, that you are persistent in pursuing your goals, and that you continue upgrading your skills to make yourself a better employee—and it might just get you an interview.

On the Job

SOLVING A COMMUNICATION DILEMMA AT PINKERTON

Safeguarding hundreds of famous personalities and thousands of enthusiastic fans—as well as many members of the media—isn't an everyday kind of job. That's why the Academy of Motion Picture Arts and Sciences hired Pinkerton. The security company, founded by Allan Pinkerton in 1850, made its name with such exploits as tracking Butch Cassidy and the Sundance Kid and protecting Abraham Lincoln before his inauguration. Thomas Wathen bought Pinkerton in 1987 and built it into a worldwide network encompassing 220 offices, 46,000 employees, and $772 million in annual revenue.

When he accepted the assignment to provide security for the Academy Awards, Wathen knew that Pinkerton would have to screen potential job seekers and pick only those individuals who had the experience, attitude, and talent to perform well in this unique and demanding situation. These security officers would also need excellent communication skills to interact with the public and handle the sort of "Hollywood egos" that attend this type of function.

Pinkerton followed the same five-step approach to screening, evaluating, and selecting employees that it uses whether filling internal openings or helping clients evaluate job candidates. In the first step, each candidate fills out a job application and sits through an initial interview with Pinkerton personnel. Only candidates whose qualifications meet Pinkerton's job requirements move to the second step. Next, prospective employees fill out questionnaires measuring attitudes toward honesty and willingness to follow company rules.

Again, only people who meet Pinkerton's standards advance. In the third step, candidates participate in a ten-minute interview session conducted over the telephone by a computerized voice system. They answer roughly 100 questions about job stability, career goals, work ethic, enthusiasm, and other aspects of their work history by pushing buttons on the telephone keypad—one button for *yes,* another for *no,* and a third for *uncertain.*

Just a few minutes after each candidate hangs up the phone, Pinkerton personnel can call the computer center and get the results. This information helps the staff members pinpoint topics to be addressed in the fourth step of the process, an in-depth personal interview.

At least 30 percent of the applicants are weeded out by this point. In the fifth step, Pinkerton investigators check the backgrounds of those candidates who have completed the personal interview successfully. Once they have the results of the investigation, Pinkerton personnel are able to decide which candidates to hire for the Academy Awards ceremony.

Your Mission: As a member of Pinkerton's human resources department, you regularly review résumés that arrive unin-

vited. You're particularly on the lookout for recent college graduates who might be good candidates for management training positions in Pinkerton's new security operations for General Motors, which span the United States, Canada, and Mexico. Give Thomas Wathen your best advice regarding the following applicants, and be prepared to explain your recommendations.

1. You have received résumés from four people. Based only on the career objectives listed, which one of the candidates will you consider hiring as a management trainee?
   a. Career Objective: An entry-level management position in a large company
   b. Career Objective: To invest my management talent and business savvy and shepherd a business toward explosive growth
   c. Career Objective: A management position in which a degree in business administration and experience in managing personnel will be particularly useful
   d. Career Objective: To learn all I can about personnel management in an exciting environment with a company whose reputation is outstanding

2. On the basis of only the education sections of another four résumés, which of the following candidates would you recommend to Wathen?
   a. EDUCATION
      Morehouse College, Atlanta, GA, 1991-1995.
      Received B.A. degree with a major in Business Administration and a minor in Finance. Graduated with a 3.65 grade point average. Played varsity football and basketball. Worked 15 hours per week in the library. Coordinated the local student chapter of the American Management Association. Member of Alpha Phi Alpha social fraternity.
   b. Education: I attended Wayne State University in Detroit, Michigan, for two years and then transferred to the University of Michigan at Ann Arbor, where I completed my studies. My major was economics, but I also took many business management courses, including employee motivation, leadership, history of management theory, and organizational behavior. I selected courses based on the professors' reputation for excellence, and I received mostly A's and B's. Unlike many college students, I viewed the acquisition of knowledge--rather than career preparation--as my primary goal. I believe I have received a well-rounded education that has prepared me to approach management situations as problem-solving exercises.

c. ACADEMIC PREPARATION

University of Connecticut, Storrs, CT. Graduated with a B.A. degree in 1994. Majored in Physical Education. Minored in Business Administration. Graduated with a 2.85 average.

d. Education: North Texas State University and University of Texas at Tyler. Received B.A. and M.B.A. degrees. I majored in business as an undergraduate and concentrated in manufacturing management during my M.B.A. program. Received a special $2,500 scholarship offered by Rotary International recognizing academic achievement in business courses. I also won the MEGA award in 1992. Dean's list.

3. Which of the following four candidates would you recommend, based only on the experience sections?

a. RELATED WORK EXPERIENCE

McDonald's, Peoria, IL, 1989-1990. Part-time cook. Worked 15 hours per week while attending high school. Prepared hamburgers, chicken bits, and french fries. Received employee-of-the-month award for outstanding work habits.

University Grill, Ames, IA, 1990-1993. Part-time cook. Worked 20 hours per week while attending college. Prepared hot and cold sandwiches. Helped manager purchase ingredients. Trained new kitchen workers. Prepared work schedules for kitchen staff.

b. RELATED EXPERIENCE

Although I have never held a full-time job, I have worked part-time and during summer vacations throughout my high school and college years. During my freshman and sophomore years in high school, I bagged groceries at the A&P store three afternoons a week. The work was not terribly challenging, but I liked the customers and the other employees. During my junior and senior years, I worked at the YMCA as an after-school counselor for elementary school children. The kids were really sweet, and I still get letters from some of them. During summer vacations while I was in college, I did construction work for a local home builder. The job paid well, and I also learned a lot about carpentry. The guys I worked with were a mixed bag who expanded my vocabulary and knowledge of the world. I also worked part-time in college in the student cafeteria, where I scooped food onto plates. This did not require much talent, but it taught me a lot about how people behave when standing in line. I also learned quite a bit about life from my boss, Sam "The Man" Benson, who has been managing the student cafeteria for 25 years.

c. PREVIOUS WORK EXPERIENCE

The Broadway Department Store, Sherman Oaks, CA, Summers, 1991-1994. Sales Consultant, Furniture Department. I interacted with a diverse group of customers, including suburban matrons, teenagers, career women, and professional couples. I endeavored to satisfy their individual needs and make their shopping experience memorable, efficient, and enjoyable. Under the direction of the sales manager, I helped prepare employee schedules and fill out departmental reports. I also helped manage the inventory, worked the cash register, and handled a variety of special orders and customer complaints with courtesy and aplomb. During the 1994 annual storewide sale, I sold more merchandise than any other salesperson in the entire furniture department.

d. EXPERIENCE RELATED TO MANAGEMENT

Belle Fleur, GA, Civilian Member of Public Safety Committee, January-December 1993.

-- Organized and promoted a lecture series on vacation safety and home security for the residents of Belle Fleur, GA; recruited and trained 7 committee members to help plan and produce the lectures; persuaded local businesses to finance the program; designed, printed, and distributed fliers; wrote and distributed press releases; attracted an average of 120 people to each of three lectures

-- Developed a questionnaire to determine local residents' home security needs; directed the efforts of 10 volunteers working on the survey; prepared written report for city council and delivered oral summary of findings at town meeting; helped persuade city to fund new home security program

-- Initiated the Business Security Forum as an annual meeting at which local business leaders could meet to discuss safety and security issues; created promotional flyers for the first forum; convinced 19 business owners to fund a business security survey; arranged press coverage of the first forum

4. You've received the following résumé. What action will you take?

Maria Martin
1124 2nd S.W.
Rhinelander, WI 54501
(715) 369-0098

Career Objective: To build a management career in a growing U.S. company

Summary of Qualifications: As a student at the University of Wisconsin in Madison, carried out various assignments that have required skills related to a career in management. For example:

Planning Skills. As president of the university's foreign affairs forum, organized six lectures and workshops featuring 36 speakers from 16 foreign countries within a nine-month period. Identified and recruited the speakers, handled their travel arrangements, and scheduled the facilities.

Interpersonal Skills. As chairman of the parade committee for homecoming weekend, worked with the city of Madison to obtain approval, permits, and traffic control for the parade. Also encouraged local organizations such as the Lion's Club, the Kiwanis Club, and the Boy Scouts to participate in the parade. Coordinated the efforts of the 15 fraternities and 18 sororities that entered floats in the parade. Recruited 12 marching bands from surrounding communities and coordinated their efforts with the university's marching band. Also arranged for local auto dealers to provide cars for the ten homecoming queen candidates.

Communication Skills. Wrote over 25 essays and term papers dealing with academic topics. Received an A on all but two of these papers. As a senior, wrote a 20-page analysis of the paper products industry, interviewing the five top executives at the Rhinelander paper company. Received an A+ on this paper.

a. Definitely recommend that Wathen take a look at this outstanding candidate.

b. Turn down the candidate. She doesn't give enough information about when she attended college, what she majored in, or where she has worked.

c. Call the candidate on the phone and ask for more information. If she sounds promising, send her an application form that requests more specific information about her academic background and employment history.

d. Consider the candidate's qualifications relative to those of other applicants. Recommend her if you do not have three or four other applicants with more directly relevant qualifications.

5. Which of the following applicants would you recommend to Wathen, based on the application letters shown below?

a. Please consider me as a candidate for employment with Pinkerton. I am particularly interested in a job in security management.

As a devoted fan of mysteries and detective stories, I think I can make a real contribution to your organization. I have an M.B.A. degree in management from the University of Michigan. I wrote my graduate thesis on industrial espionage in the computer industry, and I believe I have a good understanding of security issues. In fact, while I was a student, I gained first-hand experience as a night security guard at Ann Arbor Cinema.

I'd be delighted to share my security ideas with you when I'm in California during spring break, March 21-April 5. I will call next week to arrange a specific appointment to talk with someone, preferably a member of your security department.

b. Reading about Allan Pinkerton's role in saving President Lincoln from an assassination plot gave me goose bumps. I was also surprised to learn that Pinkerton's founder crusaded against slavery. It would be an honor and a privilege to work for a company with such a proud heritage.

If you are currently looking for management trainees, please consider me as a candidate. As my résumé indicates, I have a bachelor's degree in business administration from Bishop College. I believe that my sports background might be useful to you in field operations, as well.

c. A recent newspaper article indicated that Pinkerton has contracted to provide security services to General Motors in North America. If you are actively recruiting bilingual candidates for entry-level management positions in Mexico, please consider my application.

The son of a Mexican immigrant who settled in California in 1949, I am fluent in Spanish and English and comfortable in both the Latin and Anglo communities. I am graduating in May with a bachelor's degree from UCLA, where I majored in business. For the past two summers, I have been a management intern at Tianguis supermarkets, a chain that serves Hispanic-American neighborhoods. In addition, I have worked part-time on weekends and holidays in my family's clothing store. I'm particularly proud of an anti-shoplifting system I devised that reduced theft by 50 percent.

Do you have a representative in California who would be available to tell me more about opportunities at your General Motors operations in Mexico? Please write me at my home address (above) or call me at (213) 998-7698 to schedule an interview.

d. I read with interest a recent newspaper article about Pinkerton's contract to take over General Motors' security operations. Because your company will be responsible for providing security services in Canada, Mexico, and the United States, I am sure you need dependable entry-level managers who are available to relocate wherever you have an appropriate opening. Please consider me a candidate.

I am hardworking and results-oriented. My experiences as a member of the University of

Louisville/Kentucky debate team and a participant in the campus food drive have helped me develop my planning and organizing skills. I know these are key skills for all corporate managers, and I believe that my background has prepared me well for a responsible management job in any company. Also, because I enjoy traveling and meeting new people, I am willing to relocate to work in any office.

I would appreciate a few minutes to discuss my qualifications if you or a member of your staff will be in Kentucky this spring. Please write me at my home address (above) or call me at (502) 555-3029 to arrange a convenient time.[9]

Questions for Discussion

1. Do you think that employers are justified in reacting to a résumé on the basis of its appearance?
2. "A good résumé lists all your talents so that potential employers know how versatile you are." Do you agree or disagree? Explain your answer.
3. As an employer, what would you do to detect résumé inflation, such as misrepresented job qualifications, salaries, and academic credentials?
4. If you were a recruiter, would you prefer one organizational pattern for résumés over the others? If so, which one? Why?
5. Stating your career objective might limit your opportunities by labeling you too narrowly. Not stating your career objective, however, might lead an employer to categorize you incorrectly. Which outcome is riskier? Do summaries of qualifications overcome such drawbacks? If so, how?
6. How can you make your letter of application unique without being cute or gimmicky?

Documents for Analysis

Read the following documents; then (1) analyze the strengths or weaknesses of each sentence and (2) revise each document so that it follows this chapter's guidelines.

DOCUMENT 15.A

I'm a motivated, experienced professional who can play a key managerial role in helping you become one of the aggressive and recognized leaders in the shopping center industry. As the accountant for a prestigious real estate development company, I have extensive experience in such vital executive activities as:

-- Administering and controlling accounting systems, reports, and project costs
-- Preparing budgets and cash flow projections
-- Managing and supervising a large accounting staff
-- Interfacing with a variety of highly skilled development professionals

In addition to offering you ten years of hands-on experience, I offer impressive academic and personal credentials, having both an M.B.A. degree and a C.P.A. certificate. My knowledge of computers and my excellent interpersonal communications skills will be of value to you in your negotiations and transactions, in both the long run and the short run.

Although I am extremely interested in your fine company, let me point out that this self-starter will not be available for long. Five of your competitors in the real estate development industry have also received copies of my résumé. It will be advantageous for you to contact me in the immediate future.

DOCUMENT 15.B

Two months ago, I sent you my résumé. As I'm sure you remember, you replied that you had no openings for which I was qualified. But you said you would keep my résumé in your files in case something turned up. I was wondering whether things had changed there, because I'm still looking for a job and would really like to work in Boston. As you know, looking for a permanent job is not a pleasant task (especially if you've been looking as long as I have).

However, I haven't been completely unemployed since I first wrote you. I've taken a variety of odd jobs:

waitress, baby-sitter, door-to-door salesperson. Although none of these positions are in my chosen field of social work, they have increased my understanding of people. I think I have matured considerably in the past two months and would make a better social worker now that I have seen how tough it is to make ends meet when you're making the minimum wage. I'd like to come talk to you about the great things that I can do.

And I have a real commitment to Boston. Because it's one of my favorite cities, I am positive that I would be a real asset to the community.

DOCUMENT 15.C

I saw your ad for a finance major in one of the papers last week, and I'd like to apply for the position. I think I have all the qualifications you're looking for, as you will see when you read my résumé (attached).

Let me tell you a little bit about myself. Since I got my B.A. degree in finance (with honors) three years ago from State, I've been working for a little company in Sorrento Valley that makes magnetic tape heads for computers. My title is financial analyst, and I do most of the things you mentioned in your ad: budgeting, cash forecasting, and computer modeling. The work is interesting, but the company is having some problems, and I'd like to get into a more secure situation. Although I don't know much about your outfit, the fact that you are owned by a large company is reassuring.

I'd be grateful if you'd give me an interview. I know you must get a lot of résumés, and I guess mine is pretty much like all the rest, but I have a nice personality and would work hard. You can reach me most of the time by calling 420-4665. Thanks for taking the time to read this.

Cases

WRITING A RÉSUMÉ AND AN APPLICATION LETTER

1. "Help wanted": Application for a job listed in the classified section Among the jobs listed in today's *New Orleans Sentinel* (500 Canal Street, New Orleans, LA 70130) are the following:

ACCOUNTANT/MANAGER
Supervisor needed for 3-person bookkeeping department. Degree in accounting plus collection experience helpful. L. Cichy, Reynolds Clothiers, 1572 Abundance Dr., New Orleans 70119.

ACTIVIST—MAKE DEMOCRACY WORK
The state's largest consumer lobbying organization has permanent positions (full- or part-time) for energetic individuals with excellent communication skills who are interested in working for social change. Reply Sentinel Drawer 973.

ATTENDANT
For video game room, 4647 Almonaster Ave., New Orleans 70216.

CONVENIENCE FOOD STORE MANAGER
Vacancies for managers and trainees in New Orleans area. We are seeking energetic and knowledgeable individuals who will be responsible for profitable operation of convenience food stores and petroleum product sales. Applicants should possess retail sales or managerial training. Interested candidates mail résumés and salary requirements to Prestige Products, Inc., 444 Sherwood Forest Blvd., Baton Rouge, LA 70815. Equal opportunity employer M/F.

Your Task: Send a résumé and an application letter to one of these potential employers.

2. The goat and the tire: Application letter that shows the writer's creative abilities When Lillian Farmer opened her one-person advertising agency four years ago, it had two small accounts, no name, no office, no reputation. Now all that has changed. Her agency does more than $1 million in annual billings, and it has a name (Notorious, Inc.) and a statewide reputation for placing print and television advertisements that are visible, distinctive, memorable, varied, and compelling.

Her secrets for success are just that—secrets. Lillian Farmer knows how to find the "heart" of the enterprise, the "drama" in the product, and how to bring these intangibles to life through the color of her words and the bite of her graphics. She makes the ordinary memorable by showing it in unusual combinations or from odd angles, and she makes the extraordinary seem comfortably familiar.

Consider the Roadmaster tire draped around the body of a stuffed goat. Almost nobody who saw the ad turned the page without reading the copy, and nobody will ever forget that tire.

Your Task: Apply for a job as copywriter with Notorious, Inc. (674 Pellissippi Parkway, Atlanta, GA 30338). By its own example, your application letter must demonstrate your creative ability to write ad copy that gets results. Your résumé lists the facts of your academic and professional life; your letter gives you the chance to show off your ability.

WRITING OTHER TYPES OF EMPLOYMENT MESSAGES

3. Crashing the last frontier: Letter of inquiry about jobs in Alaska Your friend can't understand why you would want to move to Alaska. So you explain: "What really decided it for me was that I'd never seen the northern lights."

"But what about the bears? The 60-below winters? The permafrost?" asks your friend.

"No problem. Anchorage doesn't get much colder than Buffalo does. It's just windier and wetter. Anyhow, I want to live near Fairbanks, which is near the gold-mining area—and the university is there. Fairbanks has lots of small businesses, like a frontier town in the West about 50 years ago. I think it still has homesteading tracts for people who want to do their own thing."

"Your plans seem a little hasty," your friend warns. "Maybe you should write for information before you just take off. How do you know you could get a job?"

Your Task: Take your friend's advice and write to the Chamber of Commerce, Fairbanks, AK 99701. Ask what types of employment are available to someone with your education and experience, and ask who specifically is hiring year-round employees.

4. Toward Florida employment: Letter to follow up a job application Three weeks ago you applied for the position of sales trainee with Riverland Foods (323 Ted Hines Dr., Tallahassee, FL 32308), sending your résumé and a strong cover letter to Christine Christopoulos, the director of human resources. Given your experience in the food industry and your good academic record, you believe that you have a chance to get the position.

Your application has not been acknowledged yet, so you decide to write a follow-up letter to show your genuine interest in the position. You consider the points the letter might make:

- You're uncertain that your original letter and résumé arrived.
- Since you wrote, you've been named activities editor of the campus newspaper.
- You've been notified that you'll complete the requirements for graduation at the end of this term.
- You've submitted applications to several other firms but would prefer to work at Riverland Foods.

Your Task: Write a follow-up letter to Ms. Christopoulos that will strengthen your application with Riverland Foods.

16

Chapter

After studying this chapter, you will be able to

Describe the dual purpose of the job interview

Explain the steps in the interview process

Identify and adapt to various types of interviews

List the types of questions you are likely to encounter during a job interview

Discuss how to perform well during the three phases of a typical job interview

Write the six most common types of messages required to follow up after an interview

INTERVIEWING FOR EMPLOYMENT AND FOLLOWING UP

On the Job

FACING A COMMUNICATION DILEMMA AT HERMAN MILLER, INC.
How to Tell a Good Dancer Before the Waltz Begins

Looking for a company that cares about people? You might try Herman Miller, a highly successful establishment that manufactures office furniture in Zeeland, Michigan. Founded in 1923 by D. J. DePree, Herman Miller is justifiably famous for its corporate culture. It may be the only company on the Fortune 500 list that actually has a vice president for people. Participation is the name of the game in this organization. Employees at all levels are consulted about important decisions and reap the rewards if the business does well.

When Herman Miller's recruiters interview a job candidate, they look at the person's education and experience, of course, but they also look for something else: the ability to get along with others. If the candidate's personality is outstanding, the company may be willing to overlook a lack of relevant experience. A senior vice president of research was once a high school football coach. The senior vice president of marketing and sales used to be the dean of agriculture at Michigan State. And the vice president for people had planned to become a prison warden but joined Herman Miller instead.

On the surface, these people didn't seem like good candidates for management jobs in the office furniture business, but Herman Miller looked beyond the superficial to see their true potential. The most important quality in a Herman Miller employee is the capacity for teamwork. "To be successful here," says one Herman Miller executive, "you have to know how to dance."

How do you know whether someone is a good dancer before you actually begin the waltz? That's the challenge facing Herman Miller's recruiters when they interview job candidates. The challenge facing candidates is how to prepare for a job interview. What would you do? What can you do during an interview? Is there anything you can do after the interview?[1]

*I*NTERVIEWING WITH POTENTIAL EMPLOYERS

As Herman Miller's recruiters can tell you, the best way to prepare for a job interview is to think carefully about the job itself and to understand that job interviews have a dual purpose. The organization's main objective is to find the best person available for the job. The applicant's main objective is to find the job best suited to his or her goals and capabilities. To help you better understand employment interviews, the following sections discuss the interview process, what employers look for, what applicants need to find out, how to prepare for interviews, and what to do during an interview.

Herman Miller, Inc.

The Interview Process

Various types of organizations approach the recruiting process in various ways. In any case, once you get your foot in the door, you meet with a recruiter during an **employment interview,** a formal meeting during which an employer and an applicant ask questions and exchange information to see whether the applicant and the organization are a good match. As an applicant, you may face a sequence of interviews, varying types of interviews, and sometimes even preemployment testing.

An employment interview is a formal meeting in which employers and applicants ask questions and exchange information to learn more about each other.

The Typical Sequence of Interviews

Most employers conduct two or three interviews before deciding whether to offer a person a job. The first interview, generally held on campus, is the **preliminary screening interview,** which helps employers eliminate (screen out) unqualified applicants from the hiring process. Those candidates who best meet the organization's requirements are invited to visit company offices for further evaluation. Screening interviews are fairly structured, so applicants are often asked roughly the same questions. Many companies use standardized evaluation sheets to "grade" the applicant so that each candidate is measured against the same criteria. Your best approach to a screening interview is to follow the interviewer's lead. Keep your responses short and to the point. However, if an opportunity presents itself, emphasize the "theme" you used when developing your résumé. You want to give the interviewer a way to differentiate you from other candidates, and you want to demonstrate your strengths and qualifications.

The next round of interviews is designed to help the organization narrow the field a little further. Typically, if you're invited to visit a company, you will talk with several people: a member of the human resources department, one or two potential colleagues, and your potential supervisor. You might face a **panel interview,** meeting with several interviewers who ask you questions during a single session. Your best approach during this round of interviews is to show interest in the job, relate your skills and experience to the organization's needs, listen attentively, ask insightful questions, and display enthusiasm.

Most organizations interview an applicant several times before extending a job offer.

Types of Interviews

Companies use a variety of interviewing techniques to evaluate various attributes.

Interviews take various forms, depending on what the recruiter is attempting to discover about the applicant. In the **directed interview,** generally used in screening, the employer controls the interview. Working from a checklist, the interviewer asks you questions in order, staying within a specified time period. Although useful in gathering facts, directed interviews are too structured to measure an applicant's personal qualities.

In contrast, the **open-ended interview** is a less formal, unstructured interview with an open, relaxed format. By posing broad, open-ended questions, the interviewer encourages you to talk freely, perhaps even to divulge more than you should. This type of interview is good for bringing out an applicant's personality. Interviewers also ask behavioral or situational questions to determine how candidates would handle real-life work problems. Some companies interview several candidates simultaneously to see how they interact—whether they smile, support one another's comments, or try to score points at one another's expense.[2] Other companies ask the candidate to participate in a series of simulated exercises, either individually or in a group. Trained observers evaluate the candidates' performance and then advise management on how well each person is likely to handle the challenges normally faced on the job.[3]

Perhaps the most unnerving type of interview is the **stress interview,** designed to see how well a candidate handles stressful situations (an important qualification for certain jobs). During a stress interview you might be asked pointed questions designed to irk or unsettle you. You might be subjected to long periods of silence, criticisms of your appearance, deliberate interruptions, and abrupt or even hostile reactions by the interviewer. Many corporate managers believe that stress interviews are inappropriate and unethical.[4]

Preemployment Testing

Preemployment tests attempt to provide objective, quantitative information about candidates' skills, attitudes, and habits.

Given the high cost of hiring unsuitable employees, more and more companies are turning to preemployment testing to determine whether applicants have the necessary skills and psychological characteristics to handle a particular job. Many employers now require newly hired employees to undergo drug and alcohol testing. Many also administer "honesty" tests, which ask applicants questions designed to bring out their attitudes toward stealing and work habits.

Some employers prefer not to go to the extra expense of administering such tests or believe that educated judgment works just as well. Some applicants question the validity of honesty and drug tests or consider them an invasion of privacy. However, used in conjunction with other evidence, the tests attempt to provide an objective, quantitative measure of applicants' qualifications. To protect candidates' interests, employment tests must meet strict criteria of fairness set forth by the Equal Employment Opportunity Commission.

What Employers Look For

Suitability for the specific job is judged on the basis of

- Academic preparation
- Work experience
- Job-related personality traits

During the interview, you'll be asked to describe your education and previous jobs in more depth so that the interviewer can determine how well your skills match the requirements. In many cases, the interviewer will be seeking someone with the flexibility to apply diverse skills in several areas.[5] In addition, every position requires certain personality traits. A personal interview is vital because a résumé can't show whether a person is lively and outgoing, subdued and low-key, able to take direction, or able to take charge.

Interviewers also try to decide whether the candidate will be compatible with the other people in the organization. Every interviewer approaches this issue a little differently, considering factors such as the following:

- *Physical appearance.* This includes clothing, grooming, posture, eye contact, handshake, facial expressions, and tone of voice.
- *Age.* Job discrimination against middle-aged people is prohibited by law, but if you feel your youth could count against you, you can counteract its influence by emphasizing your experience, dependability, and mature attitudes.
- *Personal background.* To broaden your interests, hobbies, awareness of world events, and so forth, you can read widely, make an effort to meet new people, and participate in discussion groups, seminars, and workshops.
- *Attitudes and personal style.* Interviewers are likely to be impressed by openness, enthusiasm, interest, courtesy, sincerity, willingness to learn, and self-confidence.

Compatibility with the organization is judged on the basis of
- Appearance
- Age
- Personal background
- Attitudes and style

What Applicants Need to Find Out

What things should you find out about the prospective job and employer? By doing a little advance research and asking the right questions during the interview, you can probably find answers to all the following questions and more:

Candidates are responsible for deciding whether the work and the organization are compatible with their goals and values.

- Are these my kind of people?
- Can I do this work?
- Will I enjoy the work?
- Is the job what I want?
- Does the job pay what I'm worth?
- What kind of person would I be working for?
- What sort of future can I expect with this organization?

How to Prepare for a Job Interview

It's perfectly normal to feel a little anxious before an interview. So much depends on it, and you don't know quite what to expect. Don't worry too much; preparation will help you perform well. To prepare for a job interview, do some basic research, think ahead about interview questions, build your confidence, practice your interview style, plan to look your best, and be ready when you arrive.

Do Some Basic Research

Learning about the organization and the job is important because it enables you to review your résumé from the employer's point of view (see Figure 16.1). Consider Microsoft, for example. With a little research, you would discover that the company is moving aggressively into international markets and now operates in 27 countries around the world. You'd also learn that Microsoft is deeply committed to customer service and that it answers more than 26,000 customer phone calls every day.[6] Knowing these facts might help you pinpoint aspects of your background (such as language capabilities and communication skills) that would appeal to Microsoft's recruiters.

Be prepared to relate your qualifications to the organization's needs.

Think Ahead About Questions

Most job interviews are essentially question-and-answer sessions: You answer the interviewer's questions about your background, and you ask questions of your own to

WHERE TO LOOK
- *Annual report:* Summarizes year's operations; mentions products, significant events, names of key personnel
- *In-house magazine or newspaper:* Reveals information about company operations, events, personnel
- *Product brochures and publicity releases:* Provide insight into organization's operations and values (obtain from public relations office)
- *Stock research reports:* Help you assess stability and prospects for growth (obtain from local stockbroker)
- *Business and financial pages of local newspapers:* Contain news items about organizations, current performance figures
- *Periodicals indexes:* Contain descriptive listings of magazine and newspaper articles about organizations (obtain from library)
- *Better Business Bureau and chamber of commerce:* Distribute information about some local organizations
- *Former and current employees:* Have insight into job and work environment
- *College placement office:* Collects information on organizations that recruit and on job qualifications and salaries

WHAT TO FIND OUT
About the Organization
- *Full name:* What the organization is officially known as (for example, 3M is Minnesota Mining & Manufacturing Company)
- *Location:* Where the organization's headquarters, branch offices, and plants are
- *Age:* How long the organization has been in business
- *Products:* What goods and services the organization produces and sells
- *Industry position:* What the organization's current market share, financial position, and profit picture are
- *Earnings:* What the trends in the organization's stock prices and dividends are (if the firm is publicly held)
- *Growth:* What changes in earnings and holdings the organization has experienced in recent years and its prospects for expansion
- *Organization:* What subsidiaries, divisions, and departments make up the whole

About the Job
- *Job title:* What you will be called
- *Job functions:* What the main tasks of the job are
- *Job qualifications:* What knowledge and skills the job requires
- *Career path:* What chances for ready advancement exist
- *Salary range:* What the organization typically offers and what pay is reasonable in this industry and geographic area
- *Travel opportunities:* How often, long, and far you'll be allowed (or required) to travel
- *Relocation opportunities:* Where you might be allowed (or required) to move and how often you might be moved

Figure 16.1
Finding Out About the Organization and the Job

determine whether the job and the organization are right for you. By planning for your interviews, you can handle these exchanges intelligently.

Employers usually gear their interview questions to specific organizational needs, and many change their questions over time. In general, you can expect to be asked about your skills, achievements, and goals; your attitude toward work and school; your relationships with work supervisors, colleagues, and fellow students; and, occasionally, your hobbies and interests. For a look at the types of questions that are often asked, see Figure 16.2. Jot down a brief answer to each one. Then read the answers over until you feel comfortable with each one. You may want to tape-record them and then listen to the tape to make sure they sound clear and convincing. Although practicing your answers will help you feel prepared and confident, you don't want to memorize responses or sound overrehearsed. Another suggestion is to give a list of interview questions to a friend or relative and have that person ask you various questions at random. That way you'll learn to articulate answers while looking at the person as you answer.

The questions you ask in an interview are just as important as the answers you provide. By asking intelligent questions, you can demonstrate your understanding of the organization and steer the discussion into those areas that allow you to present your qualifications to peak advantage. More important, you can get the information you need to evaluate the organization and the job. While recruiters like those at Herman Miller are trying to decide whether you are right for them, you must decide whether Herman Miller or any other company is right for you.

Before the interview, prepare a list of about a dozen questions, using a mix of formats to elicit various types of information. Start with a warm-up question to help break the ice. You might ask a Herman Miller recruiter "What departments usually hire new graduates?" After that, you might build rapport by asking an open-ended question that draws out the recruiter's opinion—for example, "How do you think the current economic environment will affect Herman Miller's ability to expand?" Indirect questions are another approach. You can get useful information and show that you've prepared for the interview with comments such as "I'd really like to know more about Herman Miller's plans for increasing product distribution" or "That recent *Business*

Types of questions to ask during an interview:
- Warm-up
- Open-ended
- Indirect

Figure 16.2
Twenty-Five Common Interview Questions

Questions About College
1. What courses in college did you like most? Why?
2. Do you think your extracurricular activities in college were worth the time you devoted to them? Why or why not?
3. When did you choose your college major? Did you ever change your major? If so, why?
4. Do you feel you did the best scholastic work you are capable of?
5. Which of your college years was the toughest? Why?

Questions About Employers and Jobs
6. What jobs have you held? Why did you leave?
7. What percentage of your college expenses did you earn? How?
8. Why did you choose your particular field of work?
9. What are the disadvantages of your chosen field?
10. Have you served in the military? What rank did you achieve? What jobs did you perform?
11. What do you think about how this industry operates today?
12. Why do you think you would like this particular type of job?

Questions About Personal Attitudes and Preferences
13. Do you prefer to work in any specific geographic location? If so, why?
14. How much money do you hope to be earning in five years? In ten years?
15. What do you think determines a person's progress in a good organization?
16. What personal characteristics do you feel are necessary for success in your chosen field?
17. Tell me a story.
18. Do you like to travel?
19. Do you think grades should be considered by employers? Why or why not?

Questions About Work Habits
20. Do you prefer working with others or by yourself?
21. What type of boss do you prefer?
22. Have you ever had any difficulty getting along with colleagues or supervisors? With other students? With instructors?
23. Would you prefer to work in a large or a small organization? Why?
24. How do you feel about overtime work?
25. What have you done that shows initiative and willingness to work?

Figure 16.3
Fifteen Questions to
Ask the Interviewer

1. What are this job's major responsibilities?
2. What qualities do you want in the person who fills this position?
3. Do you want to know more about my related training?
4. What is the first problem that needs the attention of the person you hire?
5. What are the organization's major strengths? Weaknesses?
6. Who are your organization's major competitors, and what are their strengths and weaknesses?
7. What makes your organization different from others in the industry?
8. What are your organization's major markets?
9. Does the organization have any plans for new products? Acquisitions?
10. What can you tell me about the person I would report to?
11. How would you define your organization's managerial philosophy?
12. What additional training does your organization provide?
13. Do employees have an opportunity to continue their education with help from the organization?
14. Would relocation be required, now or in the future?
15. Why is this job now vacant?

Week article about the company was very interesting." Of course, any questions you ask should be put into your own words so that you don't sound like every other candidate. For a list of other questions you might use as a starting point, see Figure 16.3.

Take your list of questions to the interview on a notepad or clipboard. Don't jot down the interviewer's answers during the meeting, but try to remember the answers and record them afterward. Having a list of questions will probably impress the interviewer with your organization and thoroughness. It will also show that you're there to evaluate the organization and the job as well as to sell yourself.

Bolster Your Confidence

If you feel shy or self-conscious, remember that recruiters are human too.

By overcoming your tendencies to feel self-conscious or nervous during an interview, you can build your confidence and make a better impression. The best way to counteract apprehension is to try to remove its source. You may be shy because you think you have some flaw that will prompt other people to reject you. Bear in mind, however, that you're much more conscious of your limitations than other people are. If some aspect of your appearance or background makes you uneasy, correct it or exercise positive traits to offset it, such as warmth, wit, intelligence, or charm. Instead of dwelling on your weaknesses, focus on your strengths so that you can emphasize them to an interviewer. Make a list of your good points and compare them with what you see as your shortcomings. Remember, all the other candidates for the job are probably just as nervous as you are. In fact, even the interviewer may be nervous.

Polish Your Interview Style

Staging mock interviews with a friend is a good way to hone your style.

Confidence helps you walk into an interview, but you'll walk out without a job if you don't also give the interviewer an impression of poise, good manners, and good judgment. One way to develop an adept style is to stage mock interviews with a friend. After each practice session, have your friend critique your performance, using the list of interview faults shown in Figure 16.4 to identify opportunities for improvement. You can videotape these mock interviews and then evaluate them yourself. Although the taping process can be intimidating, it helps you work out any problems before you begin actual job interviews.

As you stage your mock interviews, pay particular attention to your nonverbal behavior. In the United States, you are more likely to be invited back for a second interview or offered a job if you maintain eye contact, smile frequently, sit in an attentive position, and use frequent hand gestures. These nonverbal signals convince the interviewer that you are alert, assertive, dependable, confident, responsible, and energetic.[7] Of course, some companies based in the United States are owned and managed by people from other cultures. So during your basic research, find out about the company's cultural background and preferences.

Like other forms of nonverbal behavior, the sound of your voice can have a major impact on your success in a job interview.[8] You can work with a tape recorder to overcome voice problems. If you tend to speak too rapidly, practice speaking more slowly. If your voice sounds too loud or too soft, practice adjusting it. Work on eliminating speech mannerisms such as *you know, like,* and *um,* which might make you sound inarticulate. Speak in your natural tone, and try to vary the pitch, rate, and volume of your voice to express enthusiasm and energy. If you speak in a flat, emotionless tone, you convey the impression that you're passive or bored.

Plan to Look Good

When your parents nagged at you to stand up straight, comb your hair, and get rid of your gum, they were right. You can impress an interviewer just by the way you look. The best policy is to dress conservatively. Wear the best-quality businesslike clothing you can, preferably in a dark, solid color. Avoid flamboyant styles, colors, and prints.

Barbara Walters has conducted countless political and celebrity interviews, and she has the reputation of going for emotional revelations. But an employment interview is simply an exchange of information to see whether company and candidate are a good match. According to Walters, a nervous interview that sounds rehearsed is a disaster. You can be focused and still be yourself. Just being asked to an interview should give you more confidence.

1. Has a poor personal appearance
2. Is overbearing, overaggressive, conceited; has a "superiority complex"; seems to "know it all"
3. Is unable to express self clearly; has poor voice, diction, grammar
4. Lacks knowledge or experience
5. Is not prepared for interview
6. Has no real interest in job
7. Lacks planning for career; has no purpose or goals
8. Lacks enthusiasm; is passive and indifferent
9. Lacks confidence and poise; is nervous and ill at ease
10. Shows insufficient evidence of achievement
11. Has failed to participate in extracurricular activities
12. Overemphasizes money; is interested only in the best dollar offer
13. Has poor scholastic record; just got by
14. Is unwilling to start at the bottom; expects too much too soon
15. Makes excuses
16. Is evasive; hedges on unfavorable factors in record
17. Lacks tact
18. Lacks maturity
19. Lacks courtesy; is ill-mannered
20. Condemns past employers
21. Lacks social skills
22. Shows marked dislike for schoolwork
23. Lacks vitality
24. Fails to look interviewer in the eye
25. Has limp, weak handshake

Figure 16.4

Marks Against Applicants (in General Order of Importance)

To look like a winner,
- Dress conservatively
- Be well-groomed
- Smile when appropriate

Good grooming makes any style of clothing look better. Make sure your clothes are clean and unwrinkled, your shoes unscuffed and well shined, your hair neatly styled and combed, your fingernails clean, and your breath fresh. If possible, check your appearance in a mirror before entering the room for the interview. Don't spoil the effect by smoking cigarettes during the interview. Finally, remember that one of the best ways to look good is to smile at appropriate moments.

Be Ready When You Arrive

Be prepared for the interview:
- Take proof of your accomplishments
- Arrive on time
- Wait graciously

For the interview, plan to take a small notebook, a pen, a list of the questions you want to ask, two copies of your résumé protected in a folder, an outline of what you have learned about the organization, and any past correspondence about the position. You may also want to take a small calendar, a transcript of your college grades, a list of references, and if appropriate, samples of your work. Recruiters are impressed by tangible evidence of your job-related accomplishments, such as reports, performance reviews, and certificates of achievement. In an era when many people exaggerate their qualifications, visible proof of your abilities carries a lot of weight.[9]

Be sure you know when and where the interview will be held. The worst way to start any interview is to be late. Check the route you will take, even if it means phoning the interviewer's secretary to ask. Find out how much time it takes to get there; then plan to arrive early. Allow a little extra time just in case you run into a problem on the way.

Once you arrive, relax. You may have to wait a little while, so bring along something to read or do (the less frivolous or controversial, the better). If company literature is available, read it while you wait. In either case, be polite to the interviewer's assistant. If the opportunity presents itself, ask a few questions about the organization or express enthusiasm for the job. Refrain from smoking before the interview (since nonsmokers can smell smoke on the clothing of interviewees), and avoid chewing gum in the waiting room. Anything you do or say while you wait may get back to the interviewer, so make sure your best qualities show from the moment you enter the premises.

How to Be Interviewed

The way to handle the interview itself depends on where you stand in the interview process. If you're being interviewed for the first time, your main objective is often to differentiate yourself from the many other candidates who are also being screened. Say you've signed up to talk on campus with a recruiter, who may talk with 10 or 15 applicants during the course of the day. Without resorting to gimmicks, you need to call attention to one key aspect of your background so that the recruiter can say, "Oh yes, I remember Jones—the one who sold used Toyotas in Detroit." Just be sure the trait you accentuate is relevant to the job in question. In addition, you'll want to be prepared in case an employer such as Herman Miller expects you to demonstrate a particular skill (such as problem solving) during the screening interview.

Ken and Sheryl Dawson own the Houston-based firm Dawson and Dawson Management Consultants. Having worked with major corporations around the world, the Dawsons remind you that the interview is a two-way street: Not only does the company want to be sure you're right for it, you want to be sure the company is right for you.

If you have progressed to the initial selection interview, broaden your sales pitch. Instead of telegraphing the "headline," give the interviewer the whole story. Touch at least briefly on all your strengths, but explain three or four of your best qualifications in depth. At the same time, probe for information that will help you evaluate the position objectively. As important as it is to get an offer, it's also important to learn whether the job is right for you.

If you're asked back for a final visit, your chances of being offered a position are quite good. At this point, you'll talk to a person who has the authority to make an offer and negotiate terms. This individual may already have concluded that you have the right background for the job, so she or he will be concerned with sizing up your personality. In fact, both you and the employer need to find out whether there is a good psychological fit. Be honest about your motivations and values. If the interview goes well, your objective is to clinch the deal on the best possible terms.

Of course, no matter where you are in the interview process, every interview will proceed through three stages: the warm-up, the question-and-answer session, and the close (after which you'll update your interview notes).

The Warm-up

Of the three stages, the warm-up is most important, even though it may account for only a small fraction of the time you spend in the interview. Psychologists say that 50 percent of the interviewer's decision is made within the first 30 to 60 seconds, and another 25 percent is made within 15 minutes. If you get off to a bad start, it's extremely difficult to turn the interview around.[10]

Body language is important at this point. Because you won't have time to say much in the first minute or two, you must sell yourself nonverbally. Begin by using the interviewer's name if you're sure you can pronounce it correctly. If the interviewer extends a hand, respond with a firm but gentle handshake. Then wait until you are asked to be seated. Let the interviewer start the discussion, and listen for cues that tell you what he or she is interested in knowing about you as a potential employee.

The Question-and-Answer Stage

Questions and answers will consume the greatest part of the interview. During this phase, the interviewer will ask you about your qualifications and discuss many of the points mentioned in your résumé. You'll also be asked whether you have any questions of your own.

As questions are asked, tailor your answers to make a favorable impression. Don't limit yourself to yes or no answers. Be sure you pause to think before responding if you're asked a difficult question. Consider the direction of the discussion, and guide it where you wish with your responses.

Another way you can reach your goal is to ask the right questions. If you periodically ask a question or two from the list you've prepared, you'll not only learn something but also demonstrate your interest. It's especially useful to probe for what the company is looking for in its new employees. Once you know that, you can show how you meet the firm's needs. Also try to zero in on any reservations the interviewer might have about you so that you can dispel them.

Paying attention when the interviewer speaks can be as important as giving good answers or asking good questions. Listening makes up about half the time you spend in an interview. For tips on becoming a better listener, read Chapter 17. Be alert to nonverbal communication. The interviewer's facial expressions, eye movements, gestures, and posture may tell you the real meaning of what's being said. If the interviewer says one thing but sends a different message nonverbally, you may want to discount the verbal message. Be especially aware of how your comments are received. Does the interviewer nod in agreement or smile to show approval? If so, you're making progress. If not, you might want to introduce another topic or modify your approach.

Bear in mind that employers cannot legally discriminate against a job candidate on the basis of race, color, gender, age (if 40 to 70), marital status, religion, national origin, or disability. In the course of your interview, you may be asked questions that directly or indirectly touch on these prohibited areas:

Van Carlisle is CEO of FireKing International, maker of fireproof filing cabinets. As such, he tries to perform each task at the optimum level, and he likes working with people who do their homework and who are honest, energetic, and thorough. Carlisle advises applicants to show their own commitment to performance by being well prepared for interviews.

Paying attention to both verbal and nonverbal messages can help you turn the question-and-answer stage to your advantage.

BEHIND THE SCENES AT IBM
Secrets of Winning an Interview

Jim Greenwood is area manager at IBM's National College Recruiting, South, in Atlanta, Georgia. Greenwood, his staff, and IBM managers nationwide work year round arranging career fairs, booking speaking engagements, and responding to inquiries—all to attract the best students for the company. Greenwood also coordinates recruiting activity at 40 campuses. Of the more than 8,000 entry-level people hired by IBM in a recent year, 2,800 were college graduates—75 percent of them from targeted campuses.

Whether at the IBM Information Day or any other career fair, be aware that the interview process begins when you step up to a company representative. "On that first day," says Greenwood, "the managers who want to recruit at a given school are there, so bring a résumé. Seek out managers in the skill group that is of interest to you. Talk with them about your background and interests. Our managers know their requirements, and if there's a match, they will sign you up to be interviewed the next day." That will be your second interview, the 30-minute

job interview many people mistakenly think of as the first interview.

"We do a total assessment," Greenwood says. At the site interview, managers explore technical background and breadth, interests, likes, and dislikes. "We're looking for people who can communicate. When you get into an environment, say a lab or a marketing department, you have to relate to people, sell your ideas, explain how things are to be done."

Greenwood listens for your level of interest. "If you did an internship at Hewlett-Packard, I might say, 'Tell me about your job.' Then I'll ask, 'What did you do? What did you like about it? What didn't you like? What kind of programming did you do? What languages? How proficient are you in those languages? Which do you like the best? Why? Do you like to program? Do you like to write code?'"

Greenwood also listens to the types of questions you ask. "They tell me how well informed you are, what you have done to prepare yourself for the interview, whether you researched us, and whether you know about our

- Your religious affiliation or organizations and lodges you belong to
- Your marital status or former name
- The names or relationships of people you live with
- Your spouse, spouse's employment or salary, dependents, children, or child-care arrangements
- Your height, weight, gender, pregnancy status, or any health conditions or disabilities that are not reasonably related to job performance
- Arrests or criminal convictions that are not related to job performance or that occurred more than seven years ago

How you respond depends on how badly you want the job, how you feel about revealing the information asked for, what you think the interviewer will do with the information, and whether you want to work for a company that asks illegal questions. If you don't want the job, you can tell the interviewer that you think a particular question is illegal and mention that you plan to contact the proper government agency. You can also simply refuse to answer—which, in many cases, will leave an unfavorable impression with the interviewer.[11]

However, if you want the job (and you don't want to leave an unfavorable impression), you can choose a more tactful approach. You might (1) ask how the question relates to your qualifications for the job, (2) explain that the information is personal, (3) respond to what you think is the interviewer's real concern, or (4) answer both the

products and our corporate culture. But don't try to bluff or tell us what you think we want to hear. Ask questions that matter and that make the right impression. Don't ask the interviewer 'What do you do?' That shows a lack of preparation and interest. Instead, ask about the future: 'What technology are you developing? Where's it going?' You should also raise legitimate concerns—the size of a company like IBM, for example. Ask, 'How are you structured? How do I get my ideas across? How do I interact with other departments?'"

Greenwood's goal is for you to leave the interview feeling positive about IBM and knowing when you will learn the outcome. He wants you to feel "that you were given a good, courteous interview." So, what about follow-up? "Don't write for the sake of writing," he says. "But if you want to stress special interests or reinforce skills, or if you feel you blew the interview and want to be reconsidered, write to the department manager."

Regarding that much-discussed situation of needing experience to get a job but needing a job to get experience, Greenwood offers this advice: "Getting experience is important, whether it's work-study, a cooperative education program, or work you did over the summers, maybe a preprofessional internship. Experience helps you focus your academic choices, prepares you for your job search, and lets you sift and sort out what you do

and don't want. That shows in the interview—you have a sharper focus on your wants and needs." To come across well in an interview, you have to stress what experience you have and relate it to what you can do once you're employed.

Apply Your Knowledge

1. You're scheduled for a job interview in your chosen profession. You anticipate that the interviewer will ask you to describe your job-related experience. Although you have no full-time experience, you've held a position in a preprofessional organization and completed an internship in a similar job. To prepare for your interview, write a description of your job-related experience, specifying what experience you have and relating it to what you can do for the employer once you get the job.

2. How would you handle this situation: A company—your first choice both as a career and as a place to work—has offered you a position. However, the starting salary you've been offered is below your expectation and below what you've already been offered by another firm (your third choice as a career and as a workplace). What would you do? Lay out a strategy that you think will get you both the position you most desire and the salary you expect.

question and the concern. Of course, if you answer an unlawful question, you run the risk that your answer may hurt your chances, so think carefully before answering.[12]

When a business can show that the safety of its employees or customers is at stake, it may be allowed to ask questions that would seem discriminatory in another context. Despite this exception, if you believe that an interviewer's questions are unreasonable, unrelated to the job, or designed to elicit information in an attempt to discriminate, you may complain to the Equal Employment Opportunity Commission or to the state agency that regulates fair employment practices. To report discrimination on the basis of age or physical disability, contact the employer's equal opportunity officer or the U.S. Department of Labor. Be prepared to spend a lot of time and effort if you file a complaint—and remember that you may not win.[13]

The Close

Like the opening, the end of the interview is more important than its duration would indicate. In the last few minutes, you need to evaluate how well you've done and correct any misconceptions the interviewer might have.

You can generally tell when the interviewer is trying to conclude the session by watching for verbal and nonverbal cues. The interviewer may ask whether you have any more questions, sum up the discussion, change position, or indicate with a gesture that the interview is over. When you get the signal, respond promptly, but don't rush. Be sure to thank the interviewer for the opportunity and express an interest in

Conclude the interview with courtesy and enthusiasm.

CHECKLIST FOR INTERVIEWS

A. Preparation

1. Determine the requirements and general salary range of the job.
2. Research the organization's history, products, structure, financial standing, and prospects for growth.
3. Determine the interviewer's name, title, and status in the firm.
4. Prepare (but don't overrehearse) answers for the questions you are likely to be asked about your qualifications and achievements, your feelings about work and school, your interests and hobbies.
5. Develop relevant questions to ask, such as what training the organization might offer after employment, what type of management system the firm has, whether its executives are promoted from within, and why the position is vacant.
6. Plan your appearance.
   - a. Dress in a businesslike manner, regardless of the mode of dress preferred within the organization.
   - b. Select conservative, good-quality clothing to wear to the interview.
   - c. Check your clothing to make sure it's clean and wrinkle-free.
   - d. Choose traditional footwear, unscuffed and well shined.
   - e. Wear a minimum of jewelry, but wear a wristwatch to keep track of the time.
   - f. Use fragrances sparingly, and avoid excessive makeup.
   - g. Choose a neat, well-groomed, conventional hairstyle.
   - h. Clean and manicure your fingernails.
   - i. Check your appearance just before going into the interview, if possible.
7. In a briefcase take a list of questions, two copies of your résumé, and samples of your work (if appropriate).
8. Double-check the location and time of the interview.
   - a. Map out the route beforehand, and estimate the time you'll need to get there.
   - b. Plan your arrival for 10 to 15 minutes before the interview.
   - c. Add 10 or 15 more minutes to cover problems that may arise en route.

---

the organization. If you can do so comfortably, try to pin down what will happen next, but don't press for an immediate decision.

If this is your second or third visit to the organization, the interview may culminate with an offer of employment. You have two options: accepting it or requesting time to think it over. The best course is usually to wait. If no job offer is made, the interviewer may not have reached a decision yet, but you may tactfully ask when you can expect to know the decision.

Be realistic in your salary expectations and diplomatic in your negotiations.

If you do receive an offer during the interview, you'll naturally want to discuss salary. However, let the interviewer raise the subject. If asked your salary requirements, say that you would expect to receive the standard salary for the job in question. If you have added qualifications, point them out: "With my 18 months of experience in the field, I would expect to start in the middle of the normal salary range."

If you don't like the offer, you might try to negotiate, provided you're in a good bargaining position and the organization has the flexibility to accommodate you. You'll be in a fairly strong position if your skills are in short supply and you have several other offers. It also helps if you're the favorite candidate and the organization is booming. However, many organizations are relatively rigid in their salary practices, particularly at the entry level. Still, in the United States and some European countries, it is acceptable to ask, "Is there any room for negotiation?"

Even if you can't bargain for more money, you may be able to win some concessions on benefits and perquisites. The value of negotiating can be significant because benefits often cost the employer 25 to 45 percent of your salary. In other words, if you're offered an annual salary of $20,000, you'll ordinarily get an additional $5,000

B. Initial Stages of the Interview

1. Greet the interviewer by name, with a smile and direct eye contact.
2. Offer a firm but not crushing handshake if the interviewer extends a hand.
3. Take a seat only after the interviewer invites you to be seated or has taken his or her own seat.
4. Sit with an erect posture, facing the interviewer.
5. Listen for cues about what the interviewer's questions are trying to reveal about you and your qualifications.
6. Assume a calm and poised attitude.
7. Avoid gum chewing, smoking, and other displays of nervousness.

C. Body of the Interview

1. Display a genuine, not artificial, smile when appropriate.
2. Convey interest and enthusiasm.
3. Listen attentively so that you can give intelligent responses.
4. Make no notes, but remember key points and record them later.
5. Sell the interviewer on hiring you.
   a. Relate your knowledge and skills to the position you are seeking.
   b. Stress your positive qualities and characteristics.
6. Answer questions wisely.
   a. Keep responses brief, clear, and to the point.
   b. Avoid exaggeration, and convey honesty and sincerity.
   c. Avoid slighting references to former employers.
7. Avoid alcoholic drinks if you are interviewed over lunch or dinner.

D. Salary Discussions

1. Put off a discussion of salary until late in the interview, if possible.
2. Let the interviewer initiate the discussion of salary.
3. If asked, state that you would like to receive the standard salary for the position.

E. Closing Stages of the Interview

1. Watch for signs that the interview is about to end.
2. Tactfully ask when you will be advised of the decision on your application.
3. If you're offered the job, either accept or ask for time to consider the offer.
4. Thank the interviewer for meeting with you, with a warm smiler and a handshake.

---

to $9,000 in benefits: life, health, and disability insurance; pension and savings plans; vacation time; or even tuition reimbursement.[14] If you can trade one benefit for another, you may be able to enhance the value of the total package. For example, life insurance may be relatively unimportant to you if you're single, whereas extra vacation time might be very valuable indeed. Don't inquire about benefits, however, until you know you have a job offer.

Interview Notes

If yours is a typical job search, you'll have many interviews before you accept a final offer. For that reason, keeping a notebook or binder of interview notes can be helpful. To refresh your memory of each conversation, as soon as the interview ends, jot down the names and titles of the people you met. Next write down in capsule form the interviewer's answers to your questions. Then briefly evaluate your performance during the interview, listing what you handled well and what you didn't. Going over these notes can help you improve your performance in the future.[15] To review important tips, consult this chapter's Checklist for Interviews.

Keep a written record of your job interviews.

F OLLOWING UP AFTER THE INTERVIEW

Once you've completed your job interview, you'll want to do some follow-up. Touching base with the prospective employer after the interview, either by phone or in writing, shows that you really want the job and are determined to get it. It also brings your name to the interviewer's attention again and reminds him or her that you're waiting to learn the decision. As Herman Miller's recruiters will advise you, following up shows your continued interest in the job.

The two most common forms of follow-up are the thank-you message and the inquiry. These are generally handled by letter, but a phone call is often just as effective, particularly if the employer seems to favor a casual, personal style. The other four types of follow-up messages—request for a time extension, letter of acceptance, letter declining a job offer, and letter of resignation—are sent only in certain cases. These messages are better handled in writing, because it's important to document any official actions relating to your employment. Regardless of your method of communicating, follow the principles outlined in this chapter.

Six types of follow-up messages:
- Thank-you message
- Inquiry
- Request for a time extension
- Letter of acceptance
- Letter declining a job offer
- Letter of resignation

Thank-You Message

Express your thanks within two days after the interview even if you feel you have little chance of getting the job. Acknowledge the interviewer's time and courtesy, and restate the specific job you're applying for. Convey the idea that you continue to be interested. Then ask politely for a decision.

Keep your thank-you message brief (less than five minutes for a phone call, only one page for a letter), and organize it like a routine message. Like all good business messages, it demonstrates the "you" attitude, and it sounds positive without sounding overconfident. You don't want to sound doubtful about your chances of getting the job, but you don't want to sound arrogant or too sure of yourself either.

The following sample thank-you letter shows how to achieve all this in three brief paragraphs:

A note or phone call thanking the interviewer
- *Is organized like a routine message*
- *Closes with a request for a decision or future consideration*

As senior vice president of personnel at Levi Strauss and Company, Donna J. Goya believes that developing people is vital to successful business management. You want to be in a company that cares about people, says Goya. You can show that you care about people by expressing your thanks to the interviewer either by phone or in a letter.

After talking with you yesterday, touring your sets, and watching the television commercials being filmed, I remain very enthusiastic about the possibility of joining your staff as a television/film production assistant. Thank you for taking so much time to show me around and to introduce me to the staff.

During our meeting, I said that I would prefer not to relocate, but I've reconsidered the matter. I would be pleased to relocate wherever you need my skills in set decoration and prop design.

Now that you've explained the details of your operation, I feel quite strongly that I can make a contribution to the productions you are lining up. You can also count on me to be an energetic employee and a positive addition to your crew. I would appreciate your letting me know your decision as soon as possible.

The opening reminds the interviewer of the reasons for meeting and graciously acknowledges the consideration shown to the applicant.

This paragraph indicates the writer's flexibility and commitment to the job if hired. It also reminds the recruiter of special qualifications.

The letter closes on a confident, you-oriented note, ending with a request for a decision.

Figure 16.5
Sample Thank-You Note

```
                              585 Montoya Road
                              Las Cruces, NM 88005
                              January 16, 1996


Ms. Gloria Reynolds, Editor
Las Cruces News
317 N. Almendra Street
Las Cruces, NM 88001

Dear Ms. Reynolds:

     Our conversation on Tuesday about your newspaper's
opening for a food-feature writer was enlightening.  Thank
you for taking time to talk with me about it.

     Your description of the profession makes me feel more
certain than ever that I want to be a newspaper writer.
Following your advice, I am going to enroll in an evening
journalism course soon.

     After I achieve the level of writing skills you sug-
gested, I would deeply appreciate the chance to talk with
you again.

                         Sincerely,

                         *Michael Espinosa*

                         Michael Espinosa
```

The main idea is the expression of thanks for the interviewer's time and information.

The writer specifically refers to points discussed in the interview. Enthusiasm and eagerness to improve skills are qualities that will impress the interviewer.

The letter closes with a specific and cordial request.

Even if the interviewer has said that you are unqualified for the job, a thank-you message like that shown in Figure 16.5 may keep the door open. A letter of this type will probably go into the file for future openings because it demonstrates courtesy and interest.

Inquiry

If you're not advised of the interviewer's decision by the promised date or within two weeks, you might make an inquiry. An inquiry is particularly appropriate if you have received a job offer from a second firm and don't want to accept it before you have an answer from the first. The following inquiry letter follows the general plan for a direct request; the writer assumes that a simple oversight, not outright rejection, is the reason for the delay:

An inquiry about a hiring decision follows the plan for a direct request.

When we talked on April 7 about the fashion coordinator position in your Park Avenue showroom, you said you would let me know your decision before May 1. I would still like the position very much, so I'm eager to know what conclusion you've reached.

The opening paragraph identifies the position and introduces the main idea.

To complicate matters, another firm has now offered me a position and has asked that I reply within the next two weeks.

The reason for the request comes second. The writer tactfully avoids naming the other firm.

Because your company seems to offer a greater challenge, I would appreciate knowing about your decision before Thursday, May 12. If you need more information before then, please let me know.

The courteous request for a specific action comes last, in the context of a clearly stated preference for this organization.

Request for a Time Extension

A request for a time extension follows the plan for a direct request but pays extra attention to easing the reader's disappointment.

If you receive a job offer while other interviews are still pending and you want more time to decide, write to the offering organization and ask for a time extension. Employers understand that candidates often interview with several companies. They want you to be sure you are making the right decision, and most of them are happy to accommodate you with a reasonable extension. Just be sure to preface your request with a friendly opening like the one shown in the following sample letter. Ask for more time, stressing your enthusiasm for the organization. Conclude by allowing for a quick decision if your request for additional time is denied. Ask for a prompt reply confirming the time extension if the organization grants it.

The customer relations position in your snack foods division seems like an exciting challenge and a great opportunity. I'm very pleased that you offered it to me.

The letter begins with a strong statement of interest in the job.

Because of another commitment, I would appreciate your giving me until August 29 to make a decision. Before our interview, I scheduled a follow-up interview with another company. I'm very interested in your organization because of its impressive quality-control procedures and friendly, attractive work environment. However, I do feel obligated to keep my appointment.

The writer stresses professional obligations, not her desire to learn what the other company may offer. Specific reasons for preferring the first job offer help reassure the reader of her sincerity.

If you need my decision immediately, I'll gladly let you know. However, if you can allow me the added time to fulfill the earlier commitment, I'd be grateful. Please let me know right away.

The expression of willingness to yield or compromise conveys continued interest in the position.

This type of letter is, in essence, a direct request. However, because the recipient may be disappointed, be sure to temper your request for an extension with statements indicating your continued interest.

Letter of Acceptance

When you receive a job offer that you want to accept, reply within five days. Begin by accepting the position and expressing thanks. Identify the job you're accepting. In the next paragraph, cover any necessary details. Conclude by saying that you look forward to reporting for work.

> A letter of acceptance follows the good-news plan.

I'm delighted to accept the graphic design position in your advertising department at the salary of $1,575 a month.	*The good-news statement at the beginning confirms the specific terms of the offer.*
Enclosed are the health insurance forms you asked me to complete and sign. I've already given notice to my current employer and will be able to start work on Monday, January 18.	*Miscellaneous details are covered in the middle.*
The prospect of joining your firm is very exciting. Thank you for giving me this opportunity for what I'm sure will be a challenging future.	*The letter closes with another reference to the good news and a look toward the future.*

As always, a good-news letter conveys your enthusiasm and eagerness to cooperate.
Be aware that a job offer and a written acceptance of that offer constitute a legally binding contract for both you and the employer. So before you write an acceptance letter, be sure you want the job.

> Acceptance of a job offer is legally binding.

Letter Declining a Job Offer

After all your interviews, you may find that you need to write a letter declining a job offer. The best approach is to open warmly, state the reasons for refusing the offer, decline the offer explicitly, and close on a pleasant note, expressing gratitude. By taking the time to write a sincere, tactful letter like the one shown here, you leave the door open for future contact:

> A letter declining a job offer follows the bad-news plan.

One of the most interesting interviews I have ever had was the one last month at your Durham textile plant. I'm flattered that you would offer me the computer analyst position that we talked about.	*The opening paragraph is a buffer.*
During my job search, I applied to five highly rated firms like your own, each one a leader in its field. Both your company and another offered me a position. Because my desire to work abroad can more readily be satisfied by the other company, I have accepted that job offer.	*Tactfully phrased reasons for the applicant's unfavorable decision precede the bad news and leave the door open.*

I deeply appreciate the hour you spent talking with me. Thank you again for your consideration and kindness.

A sincere and cordial ending lets the reader down gently.

The bad-news plan is ideally suited to this type of letter.

Letter of Resignation

A letter of resignation also follows the bad-news plan.

If you get a job offer and are presently employed, write a letter of resignation to maintain good relations with your current employer. Your letter of resignation should be addressed to your immediate supervisor. Make it sound positive, regardless of how you feel. Say something favorable about the organization, the people you work with, or what you have learned on the job. Then state your intention to leave and the termination date. It's customary to give employers at least two weeks notice when leaving one job for another.

My sincere thanks to you and to all the other Emblem Corporation employees for helping me learn so much about serving the public these past 11 months. You have given me untold help and encouragement.

An appreciative opening serves as a buffer.

You may recall that when you first interviewed me, my goal was to become a customer relations supervisor. Because that opportunity has been offered to me by another organization, I am submitting my resignation. I regret leaving all of you, but I can't pass up this opportunity.

Reasons stated before the bad news itself and tactful phrasing help keep the relationship friendly, should the writer later want letters of recommendation.

I would like my last day here to be two weeks from today (July 14), but I can arrange to work an additional week if you want me to train a replacement.

An extra paragraph discusses necessary details.

My sincere thanks and best wishes to all of you.

A cordial close tempers any disappointment.

This letter follows the bad-news plan. By sending one like it, you show that you are considerate and mature, and you also help ensure the good feeling that may help you get another job in the future. Compare your messages to the suggestions in this chapter's Checklist for Follow-Up Messages.

CHECKLIST FOR FOLLOW-UP MESSAGES

A. Thank-You Message

1. Thank the interviewer by phone or in writing within two days after the interview.
2. Keep the message to less than five minutes for a phone call or to one page for a letter.
3. In the opening express thanks and identify the job and the time and place of the interview.
4. Use the middle section for supporting details.
   - a. Express your enthusiasm about the organization and the job after the interview.
   - b. Add any new facts that may help your chances.
   - c. Try to undo any negative impressions you may have left during the interview.
5. Use an action ending.
   - a. Offer to submit more data.
   - b. Express confidence that your qualifications will meet the organization's requirements.
   - c. Look forward to a favorable decision.
   - d. Request an opportunity to prove that you can aid the organization's growth or success.

B. Inquiry

1. Phone or write an inquiry if you are not informed of the decision by the promised date, especially if another organization is awaiting your reply to a job offer.
2. Follow the plan for direct requests: main idea, necessary details, specific request.

C. Request for a Time Extension

1. Send this type of letter if you receive a job offer while other interviews are pending and you want more time before making your decision.
2. Open with an expression of warmth.
3. In the middle section explain why you need more time and express your continuing interest in the organization.
4. Conclude by allowing for a quick decision if your request for more time is denied and by asking the interviewer to confirm the time extension if it is granted.

D. Letter Accepting a Job Offer

1. Begin by stating clearly that you accept the offer with pleasure and by identifying the job you are accepting.
2. Fill out the letter with vital details.
3. Conclude with a statement that you look forward to reporting for work.

E. Letter Rejecting a Job Offer

1. Open a letter of rejection warmly.
2. Fill out the letter with an explanation of why you are refusing the offer and an expression of appreciation.
3. End on a sincere, positive note.

F. Letter of Resignation

1. Send a letter of resignation to your current employer as soon as possible.
2. Begin with an appreciative buffer.
3. Fill out the middle section with your reasons for looking for another job and the actual statement that you are leaving.
4. Close cordially.

On the Job

SOLVING A COMMUNICATION DILEMMA AT HERMAN MILLER, INC.

Herman Miller's corporate culture reflects the philosophy of Max DePree, current chairman of the board and son of the firm's founder. DePree bases his management style on his assumptions about human nature. In his view, the idea of motivating people is nonsense. "Employees bring their own motivation," he says. "What people need from work is to be liberated, to be involved, to be accountable, and to reach their potential."

DePree believes that good management consists of establishing an environment in which people can unleash their cre-

ativity. "My goal for Herman Miller is that when people both inside and outside the company look at all of us, they'll say, 'Those folks have a gift of the spirit.'" He wants the organization, like its products, to be a work of art. To carry out his philosophy, DePree created an employee bill of rights, which includes: "The right to be needed, the right to understand, the right to be involved, the right to affect one's own destiny, the right to be accountable, and the right to appeal."

Herman Miller's organizational structure reinforces DePree's philosophy. All company employees are assigned to work teams. The team leader evaluates the workers every six months, and the workers voluntarily evaluate the leader as well. Teams elect representatives to caucuses that meet periodically to discuss operations and problems. Through the team structure, employees have a say in decisions that affect them. They also have a vehicle for dealing with grievances. If a problem isn't resolved by the team supervisor, employees can go directly to the next executive level. In fact, Max DePree himself is available to discuss problems with anyone in the organization.

However, like all good things, Herman Miller's corporate culture has its downside. Teamwork takes time, and an egalitarian approach to decision making can be frustrating if you value efficiency. Although the business environment of the 1990s requires decisive action, it takes a special kind of talent to draw the line between participation and permissiveness. Finding people who appreciate the distinction—and who can operate effectively in this climate—is a real challenge.

To identify people who have the right mix of attitudes, Herman Miller uses what it calls "value-based" interviewing. During an initial job interview, the staffing department probes the candidate's work style, likes, and dislikes by posing "what if" questions. By evaluating how the candidate would handle a variety of scenarios, the recruiter gets a good idea of how well the individual would fit into the company. If the fit seems good, the candidate is invited back for follow-up interviews with members of the department where he or she would be working. During these follow-up interviews, the candidate's functional expertise is evaluated along with his or her psychological makeup. By the end of the interview process, Herman Miller has a good idea of whether the candidate "knows how to dance."

Your Mission: As a member of Herman Miller's staffing department, you screen job candidates and arrange for candidates to interview with members of Herman Miller's professional staff. Your responsibilities include the development of interview questions and evaluation forms for use by company employees involved in the interview process. You also handle all routine correspondence with job candidates. In each of the following situations, choose the best alternative, and be prepared to explain why your choice is best.

1. Herman Miller has decided to establish a management training program for recent college graduates. The training program is designed to groom people for careers in finance, strategic planning, marketing, administration, and general management. To recruit people for the program, the firm will conduct on-campus interviews at several colleges—something it has not generally done. You and the other Herman Miller interviewers will be talking with 30 or 40 applicants on campus. You will have 20 minutes for each interview. Your goal is to identify the candidates who will be invited to come to the office for evaluation interviews. You want the preliminary screening process to be as fair and objective as possible, so how will you approach the task?

   a. Meet with all the Herman Miller interviewers to discuss the characteristics that successful candidates will exhibit. Allow each interviewer to use his or her own approach to identify these characteristics in applicants. Encourage the interviewers to ask whatever questions seem most useful in light of the individual characteristics of each candidate.

   b. Develop a list of 10 to 15 questions that will be posed to all candidates. Instruct the Herman Miller interviewers to stick strictly to the list so that all applicants will respond to the same questions and be evaluated on the same basis.

   c. Develop a written evaluation form for measuring all candidates against criteria such as academic performance, relevant experience, capacity for teamwork, and communication skills. For each criterion, suggest four or five questions that interviewers might use to evaluate the candidate. Instruct the interviewers to cover all the criteria and to fill out the written evaluation form for each applicant immediately after the interview.

   d. Design a questionnaire for candidates to complete prior to their interviews. Then ask the interviewers to outline the ideal answers they would like to see a candidate offer for each item on this questionnaire. These ideal answers give you a standard against which to measure actual candidate answers.

2. During the on-campus screening interviews, you ask several candidates, "Why do you want to work for this organization?" Of the following responses, which would you rank the highest?

   a. "I'd like to work here because I'm interested in the office furniture business. I've always been fascinated by industrial design and the interaction between people and their environment. In addition to studying business, I have taken courses in industrial design and industrial psychology. I also have some personal experience in building furniture. My grandfather is a cabinet maker and an antique restorer, and I have been his apprentice since I was 12 years old. I've paid for college by working as a carpenter during summer vacations."

   b. "I'm an independent person with a lot of internal drive. I do my best work when I'm given a fairly free reign to use my creativity. From what I've read about your corporate culture, I think my working style would fit very well with your management philosophy. I'm also the sort of person who identifies very strongly with my job. For better or worse, I define myself through my affiliation with my employer. I get a great sense of pride from being part of a first-rate operation, and I think Herman Miller is first-rate. I've read about the design awards you've won and about your selection as one of America's most admired companies. The articles say that Herman Miller is a well-managed company. I think I would learn a lot working here, and I think my drive and creativity would be appreciated."

   c. "There are several reasons why I'd like to work for Herman Miller. For one thing, I have family and friends in Zeeland, and I'd like to stay in the area. Also, I have friends who work for Herman Miller, and they both say it's terrific. I've also heard good things about your compensation and benefits."

   d. "My ultimate goal is to start my own company, but first I need to learn more about managing a business. I read in *Fortune* that Herman Miller is one of America's most admired corporations. I think I could learn a lot by joining your management training program and observing your operations."

3. You are preparing questions for the professional staff to use when conducting follow-up interviews at Herman Miller's headquarters. You want a question that will reveal something about the candidates' probable loyalty to the organization. Which of the following questions is the best choice?

   a. If you knew you could be one of the world's most successful people in a single occupation, such as music, politics, medicine, or business, what occupation would you choose? If you knew you had only a 10 percent chance of being so successful, would you still choose the same occupation?

   b. We value loyalty among our employees. Tell me something about yourself that demonstrates your loyalty as a member of an organization.

   c. What would you do if you discovered that a co-worker routinely made personal, unauthorized long-distance phone calls from work?

   d. What other companies are you interviewing with?

4. In concluding an evaluation interview, you ask the candidate, "Do you have any questions?" Which of the following answers would you respond most favorably to?

   a. "No. I can't think of anything. You've been very thorough in describing the job and the company. Thank you for taking the time to talk with me."

   b. "Yes. I have an interview with one of your competitors, Steelcase, next week. How would you sum up the differences between your two firms?"

   c. "Yes. If I were offered a position here, what would my chances be of getting promoted within the next 12 months?"

   d. "Yes. Do you think Herman Miller will be a better or worse company 15 years from now?"

5. You have interviewed four candidates who all seem equally qualified for the management trainee slot. Each of the four candidates follows up in a different way. Which approach creates the most favorable impression?

   a. The first candidate telephones and says: "I wanted to thank you for showing me the facility yesterday and for giving me the chance to present my qualifications. Everything I saw and heard confirms my favorable impression of your organization. I just wanted to know that I'm extremely interested in working for Herman Miller. I think it's a terrific outfit, and I'd love to be part of your team."

   b. The second candidate does not communicate in any way.

   c. The third candidate writes the following letter:

> I'd like to thank you and the other Herman Miller employees for talking with me yesterday. Seeing the facility made me realize how exciting your organization really is. The atmosphere struck me as being extremely open and creative.
>
> During our conversation, you asked me whether I had any previous experience in the furniture business, and I said no. But I neglected to mention that I do have some experience in space planning and office design. Last summer, my father decided to move his six-person law practice to new quarters. He asked me to locate space, negotiate a lease, and oversee any office improvements that needed to be made. I approached the task by talking with the members of the firm about their space and equipment needs, both now and over the next five years. I then visited 15 potential offices and evaluated the pros and cons of each. After selecting the most suitable site, I oversaw such tasks as painting, recarpeting, furniture selection, kitchen improvements, and electrical work. This experience opened my eyes to many of the details of space planning that Herman Miller's clients must encounter.
>
> Thank you again for showing me around. I would sincerely welcome the opportunity to join your organization and believe I could make a valuable contribution.

   d. The fourth candidate writes:

> After seeing Herman Miller in person, I am more convinced than ever that I belong there. My goal is to join your organization and do what I can to make the company even better than it is today.
>
> I think the thing that impresses me most is your team spirit. For a long time, I have felt that companies are the communities of the future. Like the small towns of the past, corporations mold the characters of their members. Without a sense of community, work is merely a means to an end, a way to earn a living. But when an organization is infused with community spirit, work is elevated and attains a spiritually rewarding dimension. The job defines the person, in the best sense. We are what we do.
>
> I want to emphasize my desire to join your organization. Believe me, if you offer me a position, I will take the ball and run with it. I am committed to excellence. Thank you again for sharing your time with me.[16]

Questions for Discussion

1. How can you distinguish yourself from other candidates in a screening interview and still keep your responses short and to the point?
2. What can you do to make a favorable impression when you discover that an open-ended interview has turned into a stress interview?
3. Should applicants ask about preemployment testing during an interview? Explain your answer.

4. Why is it important to distinguish unlawful interview questions from lawful questions?
5. If you want to switch jobs because you can't work with your supervisor, how can you explain this to a prospective employer? Give an example.
6. If you feel you've gotten off to a bad beginning during a preliminary screening, what can you do to try to save the interview?

Documents for Analysis

Read the following documents; then (1) analyze the strengths or weaknesses of each sentence and (2) revise each document so that it follows this chapter's guidelines.

DOCUMENT 16.A

Thank you for the really marvelous opportunity to meet you and your colleagues at Starret Engine Company. I really enjoyed touring your facilities and talking with all the people there. You have quite a crew! Some of the other companies I have visited have been so rigid and uptight that I can't imagine how I would fit in. It's a relief to run into a group of people who seem to enjoy their work as much as all of you do.

I know that you must be looking at many other candidates for this job, and I know that some of them will probably be more experienced than I am. But I do want to emphasize that my two-year hitch in the Navy involved a good deal of engineering work. I don't think I mentioned all my shipboard responsibilities during the interview.

Please give me a call within the next week to let me know your decision. You can usually find me at my dormitory in the evening after dinner (phone: 877-9080).

DOCUMENT 16.B

I have recently received a very attractive job offer from the Warrington Company. But before I let them know one way or another, I would like to consider any offer that your firm may extend. I was quite impressed with your company during my recent interview, and I am still very interested in a career there.

I don't mean to pressure you, but Warrington has asked for my decision within ten days. Could you let me know by Tuesday whether you plan to offer me a position? That would give me enough time to compare the two offers.

DOCUMENT 16.C

I'm writing to say that I must decline your job offer. Another company has made me a more generous offer, and I have decided to accept. However, if things don't work out for me there, I will let you know. I sincerely appreciate your interest in me.

Cases

INTERVIEWING WITH POTENTIAL EMPLOYERS

1. Interviewers and interviewees: Classroom exercise in interviewing Interviewing is clearly an interactive process involving at least two people. So the best way to practice for interviews is to work with others.

Your Task: You and all other members of the class are to write letters of application for a management trainee position requiring a pleasant personality and intelligence but a minimum of specialized education or experience. Sign your letter with a fictitious name that conceals your identity. Next polish (or prepare) a résumé that accurately identifies you and that presents your educational and professional accomplishments.

Three members of the class, who volunteer as interviewers, divide equally among themselves all the anonymously written application letters. Then each interviewer selects for an interview the candidate who seems the most pleasant and convincing in his or her letter. At this time the selected candidates identify themselves and give the interviewers their résumés.

Each interviewer then interviews his or her chosen candidate in front of the class, seeking to understand how the items on the résumé qualify the candidate for the job. At the end of the interviews, the class may decide who gets the job and discuss why this candidate was successful. Then retrieve your letter, sign it with the right name, and submit it to your instructor for credit.

FOLLOWING UP AFTER THE INTERVIEW

2. "Dear Mr. Chacon": Follow-up letter to straighten out a possible confusion You have been interviewed for the position of assistant manager of a retail outlet in the In-a-Minute chain, consisting of company-owned stores that sell groceries, some medications, and petroleum products. The chain is successful, with new outlets opening regularly in Missouri, Kentucky, and Tennessee. You would appreciate a chance to join the firm.

During the interview, Roger Chacon asked you several questions about your academic record. Your answers, you feel, were somewhat scattered and left Mr. Chacon with no clear understanding of the courses you've taken, your proficiency in several key areas, and the date you expect to graduate—matters that he seemed most interested in.

Your Task: Working with your own record, draft a follow-up letter to send to Mr. Chacon with a copy of your college transcript. Describe what you have accomplished in one or two academic areas. Mr. Chacon is with the human resources department at the corporation's headquarters, 99 Litzinger Lane, St. Louis, MO 63124.

3. Journey to Long Island City: Letter accepting a good job offer Today's mail brings you the following letter from Rhonda Frederick, Director of Human Resources, Chesterton Ceramics, 3 Chesterton Place, Long Island City, NY 11101:

We are pleased to offer you the position of chemical technician beginning 60 days from the date of this letter at a monthly salary of $1,650. Please let us know of your acceptance of this position within ten days.

Your work will be given 6-month and 12-month reviews; we offer 4 percent salary increases at these points if the employee's work progress is satisfactory. As was indicated to you in the interview, employee participation in the company pension plan is voluntary during the first full year of employment; after that, participation is required. We will fund your moving expenses up to $850, with 50 percent of this amount sent to you in advance if you desire.

We hope that you will accept this position. Your academic record and experience indicate that you should do well in our laboratories, and you will find that Long Island City provides easy access to Manhattan. We maintain a file of house and apartment listings; if you let me know your housing needs, I will send you whatever information you require.

If you plan to join our pension program during your first year, please let me know so that I can start the paperwork before your arrival.

Enclosed is our check for $232.76, covering your interview expenses.

Your Task: Write a letter accepting the job and answering the questions Ms. Frederick asks.

4. Job hunt: Set of employment-related letters to a single company Where would you like to work? Pick a real or an imagined company, and assume that a month ago you sent your résumé and application letter. Not long afterward, you were invited to come for an interview, which seemed to go very well.

Your Task: Use your imagination to write the following: (a) a thank-you letter for the interview, (b) a note of inquiry, (c) a request for more time to decide, (d) a letter of acceptance, and (e) a letter declining the job offer.

g Orally · Conducting Interviews on the Job · Participating in Small Groups and Meetings

ORAL

To Speak · Developing Formal Speeches and Presentations · Mastering The Art Of Delivery

COMMUNICATION

g Orally · Conducting Interviews on the Job · Participating in Small Groups and Meetings

Chapter 17
Listening, Interviewing, and Conducting Meetings

Chapter 18
Giving Speeches and Oral Presentations

After studying this chapter, you will be able to

Apply the communication process to oral communication

Summarize the skills involved in being an effective listener

Identify nine common types of business interviews

Define four types of interview questions and clarify when to use each type

Describe how groups make decisions

Discuss the preparations and duties necessary for productive meetings

LISTENING, INTERVIEWING, AND CONDUCTING MEETINGS

On the Job

FACING A COMMUNICATION DILEMMA AT ROCKPORT

Convening an Unconventional Meeting

Calling a meeting isn't unusual; executives do it every day. Even so, few executives shut down an entire company to bring everyone to a meeting, but that's exactly what Rockport president John Thorbeck decided to do. Rockport is a footwear subsidiary of Reebok, and except for the handful of people left behind to answer telephones in the company's Marlboro, Massachusetts, headquarters, all 350 managers and employees were asked to gather in a huge room for a two-day meeting.

Many of Thorbeck's top managers questioned the need for halting the daily functions that had built Rockport's annual sales to $300 million. The chief financial officer complained that "a company as large as ours cannot afford to lose two whole shipping days." He was also skeptical about the discussions yielding any concrete results. But Thorbeck believed this meeting was important enough to involve every employee at every level. His objective was nothing less than to increase the company's potential. "I felt that there was so much more we could do, given our profitability and resources," he said. "Our goals were far too modest."

If you were John Thorbeck, how would you use a two-day meeting to elicit input from your employees? What factors of oral communication would you use to get them talking? Would good listening skills be valuable? What would you do to be sure the meeting was productive?[1]

COMMUNICATING ORALLY

Rockport's John Thorbeck knows that speaking and listening are the communication skills we use most. Given a choice, people would rather talk to each other than write to each other. Talking takes less time and needs no composing, typing, rewriting, retyping, duplicating, or distributing.

Rockport

More important, oral communication provides the opportunity for feedback. When people communicate orally, they can ask questions and test their understanding of the message; they can share ideas and work together to solve problems. They can also convey and absorb nonverbal information, which reveals far more than words alone. By communicating with facial expressions, eye contact, tone of voice, gestures, and posture, people can send subtle messages that add another dimension to the spoken words. Oral communication satisfies people's need to be part of the human community and makes them feel good. Talking things over helps people in organizations build morale and establish a group identity.

Oral communication saves time and provides opportunities for feedback and social interaction.

Nonetheless, oral communication also has its dangers. Under most circumstances, oral communication occurs spontaneously. You can't cross out what you just said and start all over. Your most foolish comments will be etched in the other person's memory, regardless of how much you try to explain that you really meant something else entirely. Moreover, if you let your attention wander while someone else is speaking, you miss the point. You either have to muddle along without knowing what the other person said or admit you were daydreaming and ask the person to repeat the comment. One other problem is that oral communication is personal. People tend to confuse your message with you as an individual. They're likely to judge the content of what you say by your appearance and delivery style.

The spontaneous quality of oral communication limits your ability to edit your thoughts.

People often judge the substance of a remark by the speaker's style.

Intercultural barriers can be as much a problem in oral communication as they can be in written communication (see Chapter 2). As always, it's best to know your audience, including any cultural differences they may have. Then communicate your message in the tone, manner, and situation your audience will feel most comfortable with.

Whether you're using the telephone, engaging in a quick conversation with a colleague, participating in a formal interview, or attending a meeting, oral communication is the vehicle you use to get your message across. When communicating orally, try to take advantage of the positive characteristics while minimizing the dangers. To achieve that goal, work on improving two key skills: speaking and listening.

Speaking

Because speaking is such an ingrained activity, we tend to do it without much thought, but that casual approach can be a problem in business. Be more aware of using speech as a tool for accomplishing your objectives in a business context. To do this, break the habit of talking spontaneously, without planning what you're going to say or how you're going to say it. Learn to manage the impression you create by consciously tailoring your remarks and delivery style to suit the situation. Become as aware of the consequences of what you say as you are of the consequences of what you write.

Learn to think before you speak.

With a little effort, you can learn to apply the composition process to oral communication. Before you speak, think about your purpose, your main idea, and your audience. Organize your thoughts in a logical way, decide on a style that suits the occasion, and edit your remarks mentally. As you speak, watch the other person, judging from verbal and nonverbal feedback whether your message is making the desired impression. If not, revise and try again.

Just as various writing assignments call for different writing styles, various situations call for different speaking styles. Your speaking style depends on the level of in-

Adjust your speaking style to suit the situation.

timacy between you and the other person and on the nature of your conversation. When you're talking with a friend, you naturally speak more frankly than when you're talking with your boss or a stranger. When you're talking about a serious subject, you use a serious tone. As you think about which speaking style is appropriate, think too about the nonverbal message you want to convey. People derive less meaning from your words than they do from your facial expressions, vocal characteristics, and body language. The nonverbal message should reinforce your words. Perhaps the most important thing you can do to project yourself more effectively is to remember the "you" attitude, earning other people's attention and goodwill by focusing on them. For example, professionals like Rockport's John Thorbeck elicit opinions from others not only by asking them pointed questions but also by paying attention to their responses.

> Apply the "you" attitude to oral communication.

An important tool of oral communication, the telephone, can extend your reach across town and around the world. However, if your telephone skills are lacking, you may waste valuable time and appear rude.[2] You can minimize your time on the phone while raising your phone productivity by delivering one-way information by fax, jotting down an agenda before making a call, saving social chitchat for the end of a call (in case your conversation is cut short), saving up all the short calls you need to make to one person during a given day and simply making one longer call, sending your message by fax if you can't reach someone by phone, and making sure your assistant has a list of people whose calls you'll accept even if you're in a meeting.[3]

Listening

> The ability to listen is a vital skill in business.

If you're typical, you spend over half your communication time listening.[4] Listening supports effective relationships within the organization, enhances the organization's delivery of products, alerts the organization to the innovations growing from both internal and external forces, and allows the organization to manage the growing diversity both in the workforce and in the customers it serves.[5] An individual with good listening ability is more likely to succeed; good listening enhances performance, leading to raises, promotions, status, and power.[6] However, no one is born with the ability to listen; the skill is learned and improved through practice.[7] Most of us like to think of ourselves as being good listeners, but the average person remembers only about half of what's said during a 10-minute conversation and forgets half of that within 48 hours.[8]

What Happens When You Listen

The process of listening involves five related activities, which most often occur in sequence:[9]

1. *Sensing* is physically hearing the message and taking note of it. This reception can be blocked by interfering noises, impaired hearing, or inattention. Tune out distractions by focusing on the message.
2. *Interpreting* is decoding and absorbing what you hear. As you listen, you assign meaning to the words according to your own values, beliefs, ideas, expectations, roles, needs, and personal history. The speaker's frame of reference may be quite different, so the listener may need to determine what the speaker really means. Increase the accuracy of your interpretation by paying attention to nonverbal cues.
3. *Evaluating* is forming an opinion about the message. Sorting through the speaker's remarks, separating fact from opinion, and evaluating the quality of the evidence require a good deal of effort, particularly if the subject is complex or emotionally charged. Avoid the temptations to dismiss ideas offered by people who are unattractive or abrasive and to embrace ideas offered by people who are charismatic speakers.

When Keith Dunn and his partners started McGuffey's Restaurants, their goals were people oriented—they wanted a restaurant that wouldn't mistreat employees. But it wasn't until Dunn truly began listening to employees that the approach began to work, resulting in increased profits and lowered turnover. Listening is hard, says Dunn, but you have to learn how to do it.

4. *Remembering* is storing a message for future reference. As you listen, retain what you hear by taking notes or making a mental outline of the speaker's key points.
5. *Responding* is acknowledging the message by reacting to the speaker in some fashion. If you're communicating one on one or in a small group, the initial response generally takes the form of verbal feedback. If you're one of many in an audience, your initial response may take the form of applause, laughter, or silence. Later on you may act on what you have heard. Actively provide feedback to help the speaker refine the message.

Listening requires a mix of physical and mental activities and is subject to a mix of physical and mental barriers.

Listening involves five steps: sensing, interpreting, evaluating, remembering, and responding.

To be a good listener, vary the way you listen to suit various situations.

The Three Types of Listening

Various situations call for different listening skills. The three types of listening differ not only in purpose but also in the amount of feedback or interaction that occurs. The goal of **content listening** is to understand and retain information imparted by a speaker. You may ask questions, but basically information flows from the speaker to you. Your job is to identify the key points of the message, so be sure to listen for clues to its structure: previews, transitions, summaries, enumerated points. In your mind create an outline of the speaker's remarks; afterward, silently review what you've learned. You may take notes, but you do this sparingly so that you can concentrate on the key points. It doesn't matter whether you agree or disagree, approve or disapprove—only that you understand.[10]

The goal of **critical listening** is to evaluate the message at several levels: the logic of the argument, strength of the evidence, and validity of the conclusions; the implications of the message for you or your organization; the speaker's intentions and motives; the omission of any important or relevant points. Because absorbing information and evaluating it at the same time is hard, reserve judgment until the speaker has finished. Critical listening generally involves interaction as you try to uncover the speaker's point of view. You are bound to evaluate the speaker's credibility as well. Nonverbal signals such as eye contact and body language are often your best clue.[11]

The goal of **active** or **empathic listening** is to understand the speaker's feelings, needs, and wants so that you can appreciate his or her point of view, regardless of whether you share that perspective. By listening in an active or empathic way, you help the individual vent the emotions that prevent a dispassionate approach to the subject. Avoid the temptation to give advice. Try not to judge the individual's feelings. Just let the other person talk.[12]

All three types of listening can be useful in work-related situations, so it pays to learn how to apply them.

The three forms of listening:
- *Content listening enables you to understand and retain the message.*
- *Critical listening enables you to evaluate the information.*
- *Active listening is used to draw out the other person.*

How to Be a Better Listener

Regardless of whether the situation calls for content, critical, or active listening, you can improve your listening ability by becoming more aware of the habits that distinguish good listeners from bad (see Figure 17.1). In addition, put nonverbal skills to work as you listen: Maintain eye contact, react responsively with head nods or spoken signals, and pay attention to the speaker's body language. You might even test yourself from time to time: When someone is talking, ask yourself whether you're actually listening to the speaker or mentally rehearsing how you'll respond. Above all, try to be open to the information that will lead to higher-quality decisions, and try to accept the feelings that will build understanding and mutual respect. If you do, you'll be well on the way to becoming a good listener—an important quality when conducting business interviews.

Effective listening involves being receptive to both information and feelings.

TO LISTEN EFFECTIVELY	THE BAD LISTENER	THE GOOD LISTENER
1. Find areas of interest	Tunes out dry subjects	Opportunizes; ask "What's in it for me?"
2. Judge content, not delivery	Tunes out if delivery is poor	Judges content; skips over delivery errors
3. Hold your fire	Tends to enter into argument	Doesn't judge until comprehension is complete; interrupts only to clarify
4. Listen for ideas	Listens for facts	Listens for central themes
5. Be flexible	Takes extensive notes using only one system	Takes fewer notes; uses four to five different systems, depending on speaker
6. Work at listening	Shows no energy output; fakes attention	Works hard; exhibits active body state
7. Resist distractions	Is distracted easily	Fights or avoids distractions; tolerates bad habits; knows how to concentrate
8. Exercise your mind	Resists difficult expository material; seeks light, recreational material	Uses heavier material as exercise for the mind
9. Keep your mind open	Reacts to emotional words	Interprets emotional words; does not get hung up on them
10. Capitalize on the fact that thought is faster than speech	Tends to daydream with slow speakers	Challenges, anticipates, mentally summarizes, weighs the evidence; listens between the lines to tone of voice

Figure 17.1
Distinguishing Good Listeners from Bad Listeners

CONDUCTING INTERVIEWS ON THE JOB

Your speaking and listening skills will serve you throughout your career. For example, from the day you apply for your first job until the day you retire, you'll be involved in a wide variety of business **interviews**—planned conversations with a predetermined purpose that involve asking and answering questions. In a typical interview the action is controlled by the interviewer, the person who scheduled the session. This individual poses a series of questions designed to elicit information from the interviewee. Interviews sometimes involve several interviewers or several interviewees, but more often only two people participate. The conversation bounces back and forth from interviewer to interviewee. Although the interviewer guides the conversation, the interviewee may also seek to accomplish a purpose, perhaps to obtain or provide information, to solve a problem, to create goodwill, or to persuade the other person to take action. If the participants establish rapport and stick to the subject at hand, both parties have a chance of achieving their objectives. To help you understand interviews on the job, the following sections discuss how interviews are categorized, how you can plan for them, what sorts of questions you can use, and how you can structure them.

An interview is any planned conversation with a specific purpose involving two or more people.

When both the interviewer and the interviewee achieve their purpose, the interview is a success.

Categorizing Interviews

The various types of interviews call for different communication skills.

The interviewer establishes the style and structure of the session, depending on the purpose of the interview and the relationship between the parties, much as a writer varies the style and structure of a written message to suit the situation. Each situation calls for a slightly different approach, as you can imagine when you try to picture your-self conducting some of these common business interviews:

- *Job interviews.* The job candidate wants to learn about the position and the organi-zation; the employer wants to learn about the applicant's abilities and experience. Both hope to make a good impression and to establish rapport. Initial job inter-views are usually fairly formal and structured, but later interviews may be relatively spontaneous as the interviewer explores the candidate's responses.

- *Information interviews.* The interviewer seeks facts that bear on a decision or con-tribute to basic understanding. Information flows mainly in one direction: One per-son asks a list of questions that must be covered and listens to the answers supplied by the other person.

- *Persuasive interviews.* One person tells another about a new idea, product, or ser-vice and explains why the other should act on the recommendation. Persuasive in-terviews are often associated with, but are certainly not limited to, selling. The per-suader asks about the other person's needs and shows how the product or concept is able to meet those needs. Thus persuasive interviews require skill in drawing out and listening to others as well as the ability to impart information.

- *Exit interviews.* The interviewer tries to understand why the interviewee is leaving the organization or transferring to another department or division. A departing em-ployee can often provide insight into whether the business is being handled effi-ciently or whether things could be improved. The interviewer tends to ask all the questions while the interviewee provides answers. Encouraging the employee to fo-cus on events and processes rather than on personal gripes will elicit more useful information for the organization.

- *Evaluation interviews.* A supervisor periodically gives an employee feedback on his or her performance. The supervisor and the employee discuss progress toward pre-determined standards or goals and evaluate areas that require improvement. They may also discuss goals for the coming year, as well as the employee's longer-term as-pirations and general concerns.

- *Counseling interviews.* A supervisor talks with an employee about personal problems that are interfering with work performance. The interviewer is concerned with the welfare of both the employee and the organization. The goal is to establish the facts, convey the company's concern, and steer the person toward a source of help. (Only a trained professional should offer advice on such problems as substance abuse, mar-ital tension, and financial trouble.)

- *Conflict-resolution interviews.* Two competing people or groups of people (such as Smith versus Jones, day shift versus night shift, General Motors versus the United Auto Workers) explore their problems and attitudes. The goal is to bring the two parties closer together, cause adjustments in perceptions and attitudes, and create a more productive climate.

- *Disciplinary interviews.* A supervisor tries to correct the behavior of an employee who has ignored the organization's rules and regulations. The interviewer tries to get the employee to see the reason for the rules and to agree to comply. The inter-viewer also reviews the facts and explores the person's attitude. Because of the emo-tional reaction that is likely, neutral observations are more effective than critical comments.

- *Termination interviews.* A supervisor informs an employee of the reasons for the ter-mination. The interviewer tries to avoid involving the company in legal action and tries to maintain as positive a relationship as possible with the interviewee. To ac-complish these goals, the interviewer gives reasons that are specific, accurate, and verifiable.

As vice president of the home and personal services unit at US West (which provides tele-phone service over a 14-state region), Jerry Johnson is fa-miliar with interviews: talking with employees in the field, listening to customers' ideas, and discussing competitive strategies with upper manage-ment. Whether you're seeking information or providing it, cautions Johnson, listening skills are critical in any interview.

Planning Interviews

Planning an interview is similar to planning any other form of communication. You begin by stating your purpose, analyzing the other person, and formulating your main idea. Then you decide on the length, style, and organization of the interview.

To accomplish their objectives, interviewees develop a communication strategy.

Even as an interviewee, you gain some control over the conversation by anticipating the interviewer's questions and then planning your answers so that the points you want to make will be covered. You can also introduce questions and topics of your own. In addition, by your comments and nonverbal cues, you can affect the relationship between you and the interviewer. Think about your respective roles. What does this person expect from you? Is it to your advantage to confirm those expectations? Will you be more likely to accomplish your objective by being friendly and open or by conveying an impression of professional detachment? Should you allow the interviewer to dominate the exchange, or should you try to take control?

The interviewer assumes the main responsibility for planning the interview.

If you're the interviewer, responsibility for planning the session falls on you. On the simplest level, your job is to schedule the interview and see that it's held in a comfortable and convenient location. Good interviewers are good at collecting information, listening, and probing.[13] So you'll also develop a set of interview questions and decide on their sequence. Having a plan will enable you to conduct the interview more efficiently, even if you find it advantageous to deviate from the plan during the interview.

Interview Questions

The purpose of the interview and the nature of the participants determine the types of questions that are asked. When you plan the interview, bear in mind that you ask questions (1) to get information, (2) to motivate the interviewee to respond honestly and appropriately, and (3) to create a good working relationship with the other person.

Four basic types of interview questions:
- Open-ended questions
- Direct open-ended questions
- Closed-ended questions
- Restatement questions

To obtain both factual information and underlying feelings, you'll probably use various types of questions. **Open-ended questions** invite the interviewee to offer an opinion, not just a yes, no, or one-word answer: "What do you think your company wants most from its suppliers?" You can learn some interesting and unexpected things from open-ended questions, but they diminish your control of the interview. The other person's idea of what's relevant may not coincide with yours, and you may waste some time getting the interview back on track. Use open-ended questions to warm up the interviewee and to look for information when you have plenty of time to conduct the conversation.

To suggest a response, use **direct open-ended questions.** For example, asking "What have you done about . . ." assumes that something has been done and calls for an explanation. With direct open-ended questions you have somewhat more control over the interview, but you still give the other person some freedom in framing a response. You use this form to understand the reasons behind a decision or an event, to better understand a complex issue, or to get a specific conclusion or recommendation from someone.

Closed-ended questions require yes or no answers or call for short responses: "Did you make a reservation for the flight?" "What is your grade-point average: 3.5 to 4.0, 3.0 to 3.5, 2.5 to 3.0, 2.0 to 2.5?" Questions like these produce specific information, save time, require less effort to answer, and eliminate bias and prejudice in answers. The disadvantage is that they limit the respondent's initiative and may prevent important information from being revealed. They're better for gathering information than for prompting an exchange of feelings.

Questions that mirror a respondent's previous answer are called **restatement questions.** They invite the respondent to expand on an answer: "You said you dislike completing travel vouchers. Is that correct?" They also signal the interviewee that you're paying attention. Restatements provide opportunities to clarify points and correct misunderstandings. Use them to pursue a subject further or to encourage the other person to explain a statement. You can also use restatement questions to soothe upset customers or co-workers. By acknowledging the other person's complaint, you gain credibility.

Interview Structure

Good interviews have an opening, a body, and a close. The opening establishes rapport and orients the interviewee to the remainder of the session. You might begin by introducing yourself, asking a few polite questions, and then explaining the purpose and ground rules of the interview. At this point, you may want to clear the use of notes or a tape recorder with the interviewee, especially if the subject is complex or if you plan to quote the interviewee in a written document such as a business report.

> Organize an interview much as you would organize a written message.

The questions in the body of the interview reflect the nature of your relationship with the interviewee. For an informational session, such as a market research interview, you may want to structure the interview and prepare a detailed list of specific questions. This approach enables you to control the interview and use your time efficiently. It also facilitates repeating the interview with other participants. You may even wish to provide the interviewee with a list of questions before the interview, giving the other person a chance to prepare coherent and well-developed answers. On the other hand, if the interview is designed to explore problems or to persuade the interviewee, you may prefer a less-structured approach. You might simply prepare a checklist of general subjects and then let the interview evolve on the basis of the participant's responses.

> Use the opening to set the tone and orient the interviewee.

In the body of the interview, use a mix of question types. One good technique is to use closed-ended questions to pin down specific facts that emerge during an open-ended response. You might follow up an open-ended response by asking "How many people did you contact to get this information?" or "Can we get this product in stock before May 15?"

> Use a mix of question types to give the body of the interview rhythm.

The close of the interview is when you summarize the outcome, preview what comes next, and underscore the rapport that has been established. Restate the interviewee's key points, allowing the person to clarify any misunderstandings or add any other ideas. To signal that the interview is coming to an end, you might lean back in your chair, smile, and use an open, palms-up gesture as you say, "Well, I guess that takes care of all my questions. Would you like to add anything?" If the interviewee has no comments, you might go on to say, "Thank you so much for your help. You've given me all the information I need to finish my report. I should have it completed within two weeks; I'll send you a copy." Then you might rise, shake hands, and approach the door. In parting, you could add a friendly comment to reaffirm your interest in the other person: "I hope you have a nice trip to Yellowstone. I was there when I was a kid, and I've never forgotten the experience."

> Use the close to sum up the interview and leave the interviewee with a cordial feeling.

From a practical standpoint, you need to be certain that your interview outline is about the right length for the time you've scheduled. People can speak at the rate of about 125 to 150 words (roughly one paragraph) per minute. Assuming that you're using a mix of various types of questions, you can probably handle about 20 questions in a half hour (or about the same amount of information that you would cover in a 10- to 12-page single-spaced document). However, you may want to allow more or less time for each question and response, depending on the subject matter and the

> Don't try to cover more questions than you have time for.

CHECKLIST FOR INTERVIEWS ON THE JOB

A. Preparation
1. Decide on the purpose and goals of the interview.
2. Outline your interview based on your goals and the interview category.
   - a. Set a level of formality.
   - b. Choose a structured or unstructured approach.
3. Determine the needs of your interviewee, and gather any necessary background information.
4. Formulate questions as clearly and concisely as possible, and plot their order according to your purpose and the interviewee's needs.
5. Project the outcome of the interview, and develop a plan for accomplishing the goal.
6. Select a time and a site.
7. Inform the interviewee of the nature of the interview and the agenda to be covered.

B. Conduct
1. Be on time for the interview appointment.
2. Remind the interviewee of the purpose and format.
3. Clear the taking of notes or the use of a tape recorder with the interviewee.
4. Use ears and eyes to pick up verbal and nonverbal cues.
5. Follow the stated agenda, but be willing to explore relevant subtopics.
6. At the end of the interview, restate the interviewee's key ideas, reviewing the actions, goals, and tasks that each of you has agreed to.
7. Close the interview on an appreciative note, with thanks to the interviewee for her or his time, interest, and cooperation.

C. Follow-Up
1. Write a thank-you memo or letter that provides the interviewee with a record of the meeting.
2. Provide the assistance that you agreed to during your meeting.
3. Monitor progress by keeping in touch through discussions with your interviewee.

---

complexity of the questions. Bear in mind that open-ended questions take longer to answer than other types do.

When you've concluded the interview, take a few moments to write down your thoughts. If it was an information-gathering session, go over your notes. Fill in any blanks while the interview is fresh in your mind. In addition, you might write a short letter or memo that thanks the interviewee for cooperating, confirms understandings between you, and if appropriate, outlines the next steps. (As a reminder of the tasks involved in interviews, see this chapter's Checklist for Interviews on the Job.)

PARTICIPATING IN SMALL GROUPS AND MEETINGS

Meetings are called to solve problems or share information.

Whereas participating in interviews usually involves two people working one on one, working in small groups and attending meetings involve more people and can be more complicated. As more and more corporations embrace the concept of participative management, involving employees in a company's decision making, the importance of teamwork has increased. Companies are looking for people who can interact successfully in small groups and make useful contributions during meetings.

At their best, meetings can be an extremely useful forum for making key decisions and coordinating the activities of people and departments. Theoretically, the interaction of the participants should lead to good decisions based on the combined intelligence of the group. Whether the meeting is held to solve a problem or to share information, the participants gain a sense of involvement and importance from their attendance. Because they share in the decision, they accept it and are committed to seeing it succeed.

At their worst, meetings are unproductive and frustrating. They waste everyone's time and they're expensive. More important, poor meetings may actually be counter-productive, because they may result in bad decisions. When people are pressured to conform, they abandon their sense of personal responsibility and agree to ill-founded plans. The following sections examine how to understand group dynamics, how to arrange meetings, and how to contribute to a productive meeting.

Understanding Group Dynamics

A meeting is called for some purpose, and this purpose gives form to the meeting. In addition, however, the interactions and processes that take place during a meeting, the **group dynamics,** also affect the outcome. People are assembled to achieve a work-related task, but at the same time, each person has a **hidden agenda,** private motives that affect the group's interaction. Such personal motives either contribute to or de-tract from the group's ability to perform its task. Bear in mind that it would be un-ethical for any group member to make decisions solely on the basis of his or her hid-den agenda.

A meeting's success depends not only on what the goal is but also on how the group approaches the task.

Role-Playing

The roles people play in meetings fall into three categories (see Figure 17.2). Members who assume **self-oriented roles** are motivated mainly to fulfill personal needs, and they tend to be less productive than the other two types. Far more likely to contribute to group goals are those who assume **group-maintenance roles** to help members work well together and those who assume **task-facilitating roles** to help members solve the problem or make the decision.

Each member of a group plays a role that affects the outcome of the group's activities.

To a great extent, the role we assume in a group depends on our status in that group. In most groups a certain amount of "politics" occurs as people try to establish their relative status. One or two people typically emerge as the leaders, but often an un-dercurrent of tension remains as members of the group vie for better positions in the pecking order. These power struggles often get in the way of the real work.

Group members' personal motives may interfere with the group's efforts to accomplish its mission.

Figure 17.2
Roles People Play in Groups

SELF-ORIENTED ROLES	GROUP-MAINTENANCE ROLES	TASK-FACILITATING ROLES
Controlling: dominating others by exhibiting superiority or authority	**Encouraging:** drawing out other members by showing verbal and nonverbal support, praise, or agreement	**Initiating:** getting the group started on a line of inquiry
Withdrawing: retiring from the group either by becoming silent or by refusing to deal with a particular aspect of the group's work	**Harmonizing:** reconciling differences among group members through mediation or by using humor to relieve tension	**Information giving or seeking:** offering (or seeking) information relevant to questions facing the group
Attention seeking: calling attention to oneself and demanding recognition from others	**Compromising:** offering to yield on a point in the interest of reaching a mutually acceptable decision	**Coordinating:** showing relationships among ideas, clarifying issues, summarizing what the group has done
Diverting: focusing group discussion on topics of interest to the individual rather than those relevant to the task		**Procedure setting:** suggesting decision-making procedures that will move the group toward a goal

*B*EHIND THE SCENES AT 3M
The Keys to Masterful Meetings

Virginia Johnson is the manager of 3M's recently established Meeting Management Institute. Among American companies, 3M is known for its role in promoting the importance of effective meetings (as well as for producing such brand names as Scotch cellophane tape and Post-it Notes). The company also produces graphics and presentation equipment, which suggests a natural connection between 3M's products and its emphasis on effective meetings. The company finances research, sponsors seminars, and publishes articles and books on the subject.

"We define a meeting as three or more people gathering for an expected outcome," explains Johnson. But top executives spend 17 hours a week in such gatherings and another 6 hours preparing for them: a total of 38 percent of their typical 61-hour week. So, why call meetings at all? Why not put what has to be said in writing and save everybody some time? Johnson says, "You can't accomplish some things without getting your people together—when you want to provide them direct access to an expert, for example, or show that avenues of communication in the company are open. Meetings here at 3M serve other needs too. They allow us to share information, build teams, brainstorm problems and solutions, reach decisions, and train people. Young companies, especially, and companies in trouble may find meetings indispensable."

To determine whether to hold a meeting, Johnson says she writes "one 25-word sentence stating what I expect people to know, do, and believe after attending. If I can't create that sentence, the need for a meeting isn't apparent." When a meeting is appropriate, she believes that preparation is what makes it successful. "I start by thinking in terms of the agenda. Once it's outlined, I create the visuals that will illustrate the points I want to make.

"Listening is an important skill. Traditionally, you help yourself listen by taking notes. We've found that graphics also help people listen, enabling them to visualize and retain information. That's why I plan my graphics early." Johnson finishes by preparing notes containing her main ideas or key phrases. "I never write a speech," she explains. "Speeches are not meetings. My personal style is to be natural and extemporaneous. My agenda, visuals, and notes help me achieve that tone."

Group Norms

A group that meets regularly develops unwritten rules governing the behavior of the members. To one degree or another, people are expected to conform to these norms. For example, there may be an unspoken agreement that it's okay to be 10 minutes late for meetings but not 15 minutes late. In the context of work, the most productive groups tend to develop norms that are conducive to business.

Some groups are more cohesive than others. When the group has a strong identity, the members all observe the norms religiously. They're upset by any deviation, and individuals feel a great deal of pressure to conform. This sense of group loyalty can be positive: Members generally have a strong commitment to one another, and they're highly motivated to see that the group succeeds. However, such group loyalty can also lead members into **groupthink,** the willingness of individual members to set aside their personal opinions and go along with everyone else, even if everyone else is wrong, simply because belonging to the group is important to them. Because decisions based on groupthink are more a result of group loyalty and conformity than of carefully considered opinion and fact finding, actions and decisions based on groupthink can be considered unethical.

Because they feel pressured to conform, members of a group may agree to unwise decisions.

Group Decision Making

Groups usually reach their decisions in a predictable pattern. The process can be viewed as passing through four phases. In the *orientation phase* group members socialize, es-

"For me, the toughest meeting to run is the creative session. Trying to bring out the child in adults, achieving fantasy and free thinking by breaking down management roles, is very demanding." A meeting to generate new ideas in sales training was Johnson's most recent challenge. "I used what I call a 'brain writing' sheet. I asked the eight managers to write down three things about sales training they'd like to see added or changed. They handed their ideas in and took the sheet of another participant. They read that person's suggestions and wrote down three more. After a few rounds of this, they'd forgotten their jobs and titles and were busy scribbling. Each round triggered new ideas."

Johnson is more alert than most to the conduct of meetings, and as a participant, she has the greatest trouble when there is little or no leadership from the meeting facilitator. "My mind wanders," she admits. "If a leader speaks more than 15 or 20 percent of the time, for example, he or she is not being effective. The role of the facilitator is to help other people get their opinions or questions out and responded to." To get the most out of her attendance, Johnson adopts a listening behavior appropriate to the meeting. "If it's a formal meeting, I'll take notes to help me listen and for later recall. At creative sessions I may have to listen intently or shout out my responses. Either way, I want to be free of the technical aspects of meeting attendance." For Virginia Johnson and 3M, planning, conducting, or attending a

well-run meeting rewards everyone involved. "If it produces that 'expected outcome,' it's a job well done."

Apply Your Knowledge

1. You followed Virginia Johnson's advice. For a meeting on the need to improve office telephone techniques, you created 30 visuals to guide you and eight managers through your agenda. En route to the meeting, the case with your visuals was lost. What steps can you take to carry off a productive meeting anyway?

2. Determine the hourly cost of meetings. Create a grid of six vertical columns with these labels: Salary, 2 (executives), 4, 6, 8, and 10. Down the left side, under salary, label five lines with these annual salaries: $20,000, $40,000, $60,000, $80,000, and $100,000. Do the arithmetic and fill in the grid with how much a 1-hour meeting of each group would cost a company (assuming fifty 40-hour weeks to a year). For example, a 1-hour meeting of four executives earning $80,000 a year costs the company $160. Next, determine the cost of an all-morning (3-hour) meeting involving eight executives: one earning $20,000, three earning $40,000, one earning $60,000, two earning $80,000, and one earning $100,000.

tablish their roles, and agree on their reason for meeting. In the *conflict phase* members begin to discuss their positions on the problem. If group members have been carefully selected to represent a variety of viewpoints and expertise, disagreements are a natural part of this phase. The point is to air all the options and all the pros and cons fully. At the end of this phase, group members begin to settle on a single solution to the problem. In the *emergence phase* members reach a decision. Those who advocated different solutions put aside their objections, either because they're convinced that the majority solution is better or because they recognize that arguing is futile. Finally, in the *reinforcement phase* group feeling is rebuilt and the solution is summarized. Members receive their assignments for carrying out the group's decision and make arrangements for following up on these assignments.[14]

Group decision making passes through four phases: orientation, conflict, emergence, reinforcement.

Arranging the Meeting

By being aware of how small groups of people interact, meeting leaders can take steps to ensure that their meetings are productive. The key to productive meetings is careful planning of purpose, participants, agenda, and location. The trick is to bring the right people together in the right place for just enough time to accomplish your goals.

- *Determining the purpose.* Rockport's John Thorbeck warns that the biggest mistake is when meetings have no specific goal. So before you call one, satisfy yourself that

Before calling a meeting, ask yourself whether it is really needed.

Jennifer C. Smith is assistant vice president of claims at Aetna Life & Casualty. Noted for her ability to interact with top management during meetings, she maintains that the decision-making process can occur more easily if the leader of the group prepares carefully.

Prepare a detailed agenda well in advance of the meeting.

Give attention to the small details that help participants focus on the task at hand.

The meeting leader's duties:

- Pacing the meeting
- Appointing a note taker
- Following the agenda
- Stimulating participation and discussion
- Summarizing the debate
- Reviewing recommendations
- Circulating the minutes

a meeting is truly needed. Generally, the purpose of a meeting is either informational or decision making, although many meetings comprise both purposes. An informational meeting is called so that the participants can share information and, possibly, coordinate actions. This type of meeting may involve individual briefings by each participant or a speech by the leader followed by questions from the attendees. Informational meetings are a valuable form of primary research. So to avoid needless questions and wasted time, it's important to identify in advance the kind of information you're interested in and how you plan to use it. It's also important to identify credible people who are knowledgeable about the topic. Decision-making meetings are mainly concerned with persuasion, analysis, and problem solving. They often include a brainstorming session that is followed by a debate on the alternatives, and they tend to be somewhat less predictable than informational meetings.

- *Selecting the participants.* Try to invite only those whose presence is essential. The number of participants should reflect the purpose of the meeting. If the session is purely informational and one person will be doing most of the talking, you can include a relatively large group. However, if you're trying to solve a problem, develop a plan, or reach a decision, try to limit participation to between 6 and 12 people.[15] However, be sure to include those who can make an important contribution and those who are key decision makers.

- *Setting the agenda.* Although the nature of a meeting may sometimes prevent you from developing a fixed agenda, at least prepare a list of matters to be discussed (see Appendix A). Distribute the agenda to the participants several days before the meeting. The more participants know ahead of time about the purpose of the meeting, the better prepared they'll be to respond to the issues at hand.

- *Preparing the location.* Decide where you'll hold the meeting, and reserve the location. For work sessions, morning meetings are usually more productive than afternoon sessions. If you work for a large organization with technological capabilities, you may want to use teleconferencing or videoconferencing for your meeting. Also consider the seating arrangements. Are rows of chairs suitable, or do you need a conference table? Give some attention to such details as room temperature, lighting, ventilation, acoustics, and refreshments. These things may seem trivial, but they can make or break a meeting.

Contributing to a Productive Meeting

Whether the meeting is conducted electronically or conventionally, its success depends largely on how effective the leader is. If the leader is prepared and has selected the participants carefully, the meeting will generally be productive. Moreover, according to Rockport's Thorbeck, listening skills are especially important to meeting leaders. The leader's ability to listen well facilitates good meetings.

As meeting leader, you're responsible for keeping the ball rolling. Avoid being so domineering that you close off suggestions (people become resentful when they feel their ideas aren't considered carefully). At the same time, don't be so passive that you lose control of the group. If the discussion lags, call on those who haven't been heard from. Pace the presentation and discussion so that you'll have time to complete the agenda. As time begins to run out, interrupt the discussion and summarize what has been accomplished. Another leadership task is either to arrange for someone to record the proceedings or to ask a participant to take notes during the meeting. (Appendix A includes an example of the format for minutes of meetings.)

As leader, you're also expected to follow the agenda; participants have prepared for the meeting on the basis of the announced agenda. However, don't be rigid. Allow enough time for discussion, and give people a chance to raise related issues. If you cut off discussion too quickly or limit the subject too narrowly, no real consensus can emerge.

As the meeting gets under way, you'll discover that some participants are too quiet and others are too talkative. To draw out the shy types, ask for their input on issues that particularly pertain to them. You might say something like, "Roberto, you've done a lot of work in this area. What do you think?" For the overly talkative, simply say that time is limited and others need to be heard from. The best meetings are those in which everyone participates, so don't let one or two people dominate your meeting while others doodle on their notepads. As you move through your agenda, stop at the end of each item, summarize what you understand to be the feelings of the group, and state the important points made during the discussion.

At the conclusion of the meeting, tie up the loose ends. Either summarize the general conclusion of the group or list the suggestions. Wrapping things up ensures that all participants agree on the outcome and gives people a chance to clear up any misunderstandings. Before the meeting breaks up, briefly review who has agreed to do what by what date.

As soon as possible after the meeting, the leader gives all participants a copy of the minutes or notes, showing recommended actions, schedules, and responsibilities. The minutes will remind everyone of what took place and will provide a reference for future actions.

Like leaders, participants have responsibilities during meetings. If you've been included in the group, try to contribute to both the subject of the meeting and the smooth interaction of the participants. Use your listening skills and powers of observation to size up the interpersonal dynamics of the people; then adapt your behavior to help the group achieve its goals. Speak up if you have something useful to say, but don't monopolize the discussion. (To review the tasks that contribute to productive meetings, see this chapter's Checklist for Meetings.)

David Kessler is commissioner of the U.S. Food and Drug Administration. He prepares for meetings by doing his homework, reading through all the material he can find, and preparing detailed questions. During the meeting, says Kessler, good listening is important, but taking part makes the meeting more productive.

CHECKLIST FOR MEETINGS

A. Preparation
1. Determine the meeting's objectives.
2. Work out an agenda that will achieve your objectives.
3. Select participants.
4. Determine the location, and reserve a room.
5. Arrange for light refreshments, if appropriate.
6. Determine whether the lighting, ventilation, acoustics, and temperature of the room are adequate.
7. Determine seating needs: chairs only or table and chairs.

B. Conduct
1. Begin and end the meeting on time.
2. Control the meeting by following the announced agenda.
3. Encourage full participation, and either confront or ignore those who seem to be working at cross-purposes with the group.
4. Sum up decisions, actions, and recommendations as you move through the agenda, and restate main points at the end.

C. Follow-Up
1. Distribute the meeting's notes or minutes on a timely basis.
2. Take the follow-up action agreed to.

On the Job

SOLVING A COMMUNICATION DILEMMA AT ROCKPORT

Many executives shook their heads over John Thorbeck's idea of shutting down the entire Rockport operation so that everyone could attend a two-day meeting. They were even more baffled when they arrived at the cavernous distribution center where the meeting was held. Instead of finding an agenda, a set of reading materials, or a keynote speaker, they were confronted by hundreds of chairs, loosely arranged in a circle. They also found large, blank sheets of paper; a pile of felt-tip markers; several rolls of masking tape; and 12 computers.

Nobody knew quite what to expect when Harrison Owen, a consultant hired by Thorbeck, stepped into the center of the circle and began to talk. Rockport was holding an "open-space meeting," he explained, and what happened during the next two days was up to the participants. The rules were simple: anyone who felt "passionate" about a business-related topic should step forward, announce the topic, write it on one of the sheets of paper, and tack it on the wall. The company's 350 managers and employees would then sign up to discuss the topics that interested them. The employee who initiated a particular idea would be responsible for leading the discussion in his or her group and for recording the minutes of that meeting.

Before leaving the circle, Owen outlined one more rule: "The Law of Two Feet." All discussions were voluntary, he said, so anyone who was bored, not learning anything, or not able to contribute information should simply walk out. Allowing people to leave any group at any time would serve as a safeguard against discussion leaders who acted pompous or self-important.

After Owen made his way out of the circle, the room was silent for a time. In the words of Keith Mathis, director of distribution, "I thought the meeting had ended right there. With so much of the top brass around, I fully expected that no one would write anything down. But one person rose tentatively, then another, and soon it was like ants going to sugar." One employee introduced the topic of compensation policy; another proposed a discussion of office politics; a third wanted to talk about reducing paperwork.

What had begun as a leaderless, agendaless meeting soon turned into a series of smaller meetings, each with a real sense of purpose. More than 60 topics were tacked to the wall, and Rockport personnel eagerly signed up for the groups of their choice. The hottest topics drew 150 people, but even the smallest group had at least 5 participants. After each group met, its leader entered the results and recommendations into one of the 12 computers.

John Thorbeck knew that coming up with ideas was only the first step in releasing the company's potential. The next step was following through to see that the ideas were implemented. Rockport managers didn't have to worry about su-

pervising this part of the process: the energized workforce got busy right after the meeting. All the recorded suggestions were assembled into a book, and many people who had led discussion groups went on to establish committees that put the recommended changes into practice.

Both large and small changes came about as a result of the meeting. Thanks to ideas contributed by people from sales, production, purchasing, and merchandising, the company found a way to cut its purchasing cycle and save $4 million. A security guard suggested a new line of shoes that is expected to bring in $20 million in annual sales. In addition, Rockport installed an E-mail system, hired a training specialist, and published an employee directory.

As effective as it was for Rockport, the open-space meeting isn't appropriate for every situation or every company. For example, an open-space meeting isn't a good way to implement a new word-processing system. It's also unlikely to yield results when top management wants to control the process and the outcome. But it can help when an organization wants to examine such questions as "What should we be doing?" and "How can we feel more involved and alive at work?"

Your Mission: As John Thorbeck's executive assistant, you handle a wide range of assignments that put you in daily contact with managers and employees at all levels of the company. Oral communication skills are vitally important to your success in this key role. Choose the best alternative for handling the following situations, and be prepared to explain why your choice is best:

1. One of the employees who works at the distribution center comes to you with the following complaint: "I told my supervisor that I could do my job better if he would arrange to adjust the lighting over my work area. It's so dark that I can hardly see what I'm doing. I know I could work faster if I could see without squinting and straining my eyes. Now you'd think that with everybody pushing to increase productivity, the supervisor would jump at the chance to boost my output, wouldn't you? But what does he do? He says, 'Hey, try bifocals.' It's a big joke to him. I don't think it's fair that people like me have to be held back by people like him, who are too lazy or too cheap to change the lighting." Which of the following remarks is the best way to begin your reply to the machine operator's complaint?
   a. "It sounds as though you and your supervisor don't see eye to eye on this issue."
   b. "I can see why you're provoked. I'd be annoyed too if somebody treated me that way."
   c. "Maybe your supervisor has a good point. I think you should have your eyes checked and see if that might be the problem."

d. "I'd like to take a look at the situation. Let's go to your workstation right now so I can get a better idea of the lighting conditions there."

2. A benefits expert from the human resources department has asked you to attend a meeting and answer questions about using open-space meetings within departments that have fewer than 20 people. The benefits specialist launches the meeting by summarizing a variety of concerns about how small groups might react to open-space meetings. His comments last about 15 minutes. After responding to these points, you throw the meeting open to additional questions from the group. One employee stands up, crosses his arms in front of his chest, and says, "How do we know that management will allow us enough time to hold this kind of meeting when a department like ours sees the need to address important issues?" The question seems straightforward, but the employee's tone of voice strikes you as being belligerent. His posture is aggressive, and he has a sneer on his face. How would you interpret his question?

a. The employee is implying that management will not allow departmental employees to take time from their regular duties to hold open-space meetings when important issues should be addressed.

b. The employee is simply trying to learn about management's attitude toward future open-space meetings around the company.

c. The employee is implying that Rockport should encourage employees to take time from their regular duties to hold open-space meetings every week or two.

d. The employee wants to know whether future open-space meetings to address important issues will be long or short.

3. John Thorbeck has asked you to explain the electronic mail system to a new manager who will be running the company's accounting department. The manager is expected to exchange E-mail messages about accounting practices with people in other departments and other locations, so you want to be sure that she fully understands the system's details and will be able to use it. Which of the following versions would provide the best structure for this interview?

a. Version one

1. Overview of E-mail and Rockport's reasons for adopting it
2. Feature-by-feature description of the E-mail system
3. Description of accounting department's use of E-mail
4. Problems the manager might encounter in learning the E-mail system
5. Questions the manager might have about the system

b. Version two

1. Do you have any experience with E-mail systems?

2. What advantages and disadvantages do you see in using E-mail to communicate internally?
3. If you were designing an E-mail system, what features would you include?
4. What steps will you take to ensure that the E-mail system is used throughout your department?
5. How will you deal with technical problems that might arise when you use the system?

c. Version three

1. The problem: Employees waste a lot of time waiting for memos to arrive in the interoffice mail.
2. Background: Rockport implemented E-mail to eliminate paper memos.
3. Objectives: To boost productivity and slash the time needed to send and receive messages.
4. Alternatives: Various types of E-mail systems were evaluated (give a description and the pros and cons of each approach).
5. Solution: Give key features of selected system.
6. Next steps: Discuss manager's role in using E-mail in her department.
7. Answer manager's questions.

d. Version four

1. Conclusions: Show how E-mail saves a lot of time and paper.
2. Supporting details: Discuss specific time-saving features of the system, and mention how much paper is saved in a typical week, month, or year.
3. External evidence: Introduce facts about how other companies have used E-mail systems to speed internal communication.
4. Concerns: Bring out specific fears others have expressed about E-mail systems.

4. Some Rockport employees have been pushing the company to adopt a corporate statement of goals. In response, John Thorbeck has decided to call a companywide meeting to discuss goals. Which purpose should Thorbeck focus on during the meeting?

a. Purpose: To find out about competitors' goals and determine whether these are appropriate for Rockport

b. Purpose: To inform employees of his intention to evaluate all employees on the basis of their contributions to corporate goals

c. Purpose: To decide which employees should be asked to come to a meeting about corporate goals

d. Purpose: To reach agreement about Rockport's primary corporate goals

5. During the companywide meeting, you notice that one of the department heads tries repeatedly to dominate the discussion. This manager is one of the company's rising stars whose organizational power and forceful personality command respect and deference. Regardless of what other people say, this manager keeps repeating the same basic comment: The company is doing just fine without a formal statement of goals. Even though the meeting seems to be making progress toward assembling a statement, you can see that Thorbeck is worried that ultimately, the group will agree with this person's position. If you could give Thorbeck one piece of advice, what would you suggest?

a. Adjourn the meeting as soon as possible without reaching any conclusion on the issue; then call another meeting but do not invite the plan's chief critic.
b. Suggest that the company create a special task force to study the issue in more detail.
c. Politely but firmly discourage any further comments from this individual. Encourage other people to voice their opinions. Steer the group toward a compromise less extreme than scrapping the entire idea of a goal statement.
d. Go along with the dominant individual publicly, but try to work behind the scenes later to salvage the plan.[16]

Questions for Discussion

1. Do you feel that you are best at sending written, oral, or nonverbal messages? Why does this particular form of communication appeal to you? When receiving messages, are you best at reading, listening, or interpreting nonverbal cues?
2. What are your major problems as a listener?
3. What are the advantages and disadvantages of the various types of interview questions?
4. How do information-sharing meetings differ from problem-solving or decision-making meetings?
5. How do the goals of various group members affect the ability to achieve group goals?
6. Think of a meeting you have led (or one you have attended). Did the meeting achieve its objectives? What contributed to its success? What could have been done differently to make the meeting more successful?

Exercises

1. As a middle manager, you report to your supervisor monthly in an informative interview. The only problem is, your boss keeps interrupting the interview to accept phone calls, leaving you sitting, staring at the ceiling, until she's finished. Make a list of what, if anything, you can do about her behavior.
2. With a partner, attend the same meeting, and each of you take notes. Compare your notes. What differences are apparent in your perceptions? What in the listening process accounts for those differences? Summarize what you learn in a memo to your instructor.
3. What kinds of questions (open-ended, direct open-ended, closed-ended, restatement) are most likely to be asked by the interviewers in these situations? Explain your answers.
   a. A management consultant evaluating a proposed personnel policy
   b. A job interviewer attempting to solicit additional information from a shy respondent
   c. A supervisor trying to settle a dispute between coworkers
   d. An accountant preparing a client's tax returns
   e. A personnel counselor probing for more information in a sensitive area
4. Read through the following situations, and think about them from the viewpoint of both participants:
   a. A high school debate coach has scheduled an appointment with the school principal in an attempt to obtain $250 to take her debate team to the state finals in Peoria, Illinois. The team is strong, and she feels that it has a good chance of winning some type of award. However, the school activities budget is limited.
   b. A counselor has scheduled an interview with a company employee who has a long, consistent record of excellent work. Recently, however, the employee has been coming to work late and often appears distracted on the job.
   c. As part of the job-evaluation process and in an attempt to have her civil service position upgraded, an employee has submitted a job description of her work. An evaluator from the civil service has scheduled an interview at the job location to discuss the candidate's requested upgrading.

For each participant, what is the general purpose of the interview? What sequence of conversation might best accomplish this purpose? What type of information should be sought or presented?

5. Plan to conduct an informational interview with a professional working in your chosen career area. Plan the tone and structure of the interview, and create a set of interview questions. Using the information you gather, write a summary describing for another student the tasks, pitfalls, and advantages this career entails. (Your reader is a person who plans to enter this career.)

6. Attend a campus meeting (preferably of a preprofessional organization). Evaluate the meeting with regard to (a) the leader's ability to articulate the meeting's goals clearly, (b) the leader's ability to engage members in a meaningful discussion, (c) the group's dynamics, and (d) the group's listening skills. Prepare a memo summarizing your evaluations.

GIVING SPEECHES AND ORAL PRESENTATIONS

After studying this chapter, you will be able to

Categorize speeches and presentations according to their purpose

Analyze the audience for speeches and presentations

Discuss the steps required in planning a speech or presentation

Develop an introduction, a body, and a close for a long formal presentation

Select, design, and use visual aids that are appropriate for various types of speeches and presentations

Deliver your speech or presentation and handle audience questions effectively

On the Job

FACING A COMMUNICATION DILEMMA AT THE KEYS GROUP

Keys's Key

"Acceptance in the community is the key," says Brady Keys. His company—the Keys Group—operates 11 KFC fast-food restaurants in Georgia. With annual sales of more than $7 million, the Keys Group ranks among the most well-respected African American business owners in the country.

When Keys started out in the restaurant business nearly 30 years ago, he realized that good food was only half the battle. Consumers have hundreds of fast-food outlets to choose from, all with similar menus. If you want the public to come to your restaurant rather than going to the one across the street, you have to do something extra.

For Brady Keys, the extra ingredient has been personal charisma. A former all-pro defensive halfback for the Pittsburgh Steelers, Keys has used his forceful personality along with expert speaking skills to inspire both investors and employees and to build a presence in the communities in which he does business. Today, he's a well-known and highly respected member of the business community, but winning acceptance hasn't been a fast or an easy process.

Keys realized that if he wanted to succeed in business, he'd have to gain people's respect. He'd have to persuade bankers to loan him money and big companies to do business with him. He'd have to convince employees to work hard and customers to trust him. But how? If you were Keys, whether you were addressing a large crowd or an audience of one, what would you need to know about preparing, developing, and delivering speeches? Can improving your speaking skills really lead to the success Keys has realized?[1]

PREPARING TO SPEAK

Brady Keys has used his speaking skills effectively because he knows that preparing speeches and oral presentations is much like preparing any other message: You define your purpose, analyze your audience, and develop a plan for presenting your points. However, because speeches and presentations are delivered orally under relatively public circumstances, they require a few special communication techniques.

Defining Your Purpose

Speeches and presentations can be categorized according to their purpose, much as interviews and meetings are. The purpose helps you determine content and style. It also affects the amount of audience participation that occurs:

- *To motivate or entertain.* When you're trying to motivate or entertain your audience, you generally do most of the talking. During your speech the audience plays an essentially passive role, listening to your remarks but providing little direct input in the form of comments or questions. You control the content of the message.
- *To inform or analyze.* When your purpose is to provide information or analyze a situation, you and the audience generally interact somewhat. Basically, a group of people meets to hear the oral equivalent of a written report; then audience members offer comments or ask questions.
- *To persuade or collaborate.* The most interaction occurs when your purpose is to persuade people to take a particular action or to collaborate with them in solving a problem or reaching a decision. You generally begin by providing facts and figures that increase your audience's understanding of the subject; you might also offer arguments in defense of certain conclusions or recommendations. In addition, you invite the audience members to participate by expressing their needs, suggesting solutions, and formulating conclusions and recommendations. Because persuasive and collaborative presentations involve so much audience interaction, you have relatively little control of the material. To be flexible enough to adjust to new input and unexpected reactions, you cannot adhere to a prewritten script. A speech or presentation can often accomplish several of these purposes simultaneously.

Brady Keys, Jr., President, Keys Group

The amount of audience interaction varies from presentation to presentation, depending on your purpose.

Analyzing Your Audience

Once you have your purpose firmly in mind, think about another basic element of your speech or presentation: your audience. This is particularly important because you'll be gearing the style and content of your speech to your audience's needs and interests. First consider the size and composition of the audience. You can easily involve audience members in your presentation when you speak to a relatively small group. With more than 12 people, however, it's difficult to manage the give-and-take that's essential to building a consensus, so your approach may lean more toward telling than asking. In addition, a homogeneous group (made up, say, entirely of young engineers or entirely of East Coast sales representatives) will benefit from a focused speech or presentation; a diverse group requires a more generalized approach, using less technical jargon and presenting a broader picture.

Another important factor is your audience's likely reaction to your speech or presentation. Brady Keys expects different reactions from various audiences, whether it's one banker considering him for a loan or a hundred employees attending a company picnic. So decide whether your audience will be hostile, receptive, or indifferent to

The nature of the audience affects your strategy for achieving your purpose.

Gear the content, organization, and style of your message to the audience's size, background, and attitude.

General H. Norman Schwarzkopf was the military commander of the allied liberation of Kuwait from Iraqi occupation. Now retired, he makes frequent speeches, highlighting his perspective on the Persian Gulf war. A direct and forceful speaker, Schwarzkopf advises you to catch the audience's interest by clearly spelling out your main idea.

your point of view: Do they care about the issues you'll discuss? Also, learn as much as you can about their level of understanding: How much do they already know about your subject? Finally, take a cold, hard look at their relationship with you: Do they already know you? Do they respect your judgment? The answers to these questions will help you decide on the best way to go about planning your speech.

Planning Your Speech or Presentation

Planning an oral message is similar to planning a written message: You develop the main idea, construct an outline, estimate the appropriate length, and decide on the most effective style.

Establishing a Main Idea

Start by focusing on "the big picture." What is the main idea (or theme) that you want to convey to the audience? Look for a one-sentence generalization that links your subject and purpose to the audience's frame of reference, much as an advertising slogan points out how a product can benefit consumers:

Demand for your low-calorie, high-quality frozen foods will increase because of basic social and economic trends.

Reorganizing our data-processing department will lead to better service at a lower cost.

We should build a new plant in Texas to reduce our operating costs and to capitalize on growing demand in the Southwest.

The new health plan gives all our employees more options for coverage.

The main idea shows how the audience can benefit from your message.

Each of these statements puts a particular slant on the subject, one that is positive and directly related to the audience's interests. This sort of "you" attitude helps keep the audience's attention and convinces people that your points are relevant.

Organizing an Outline

With a well-crafted main idea to guide you, you can begin to outline the speech or presentation. Gear the structure to the subject, the purpose, the audience, and the time allotted for your speech or presentation. If you have ten minutes or less to deliver your message, organize your thoughts much as you would a letter or brief memo, using the direct approach if the subject involves routine information or good news and using the indirect approach if the subject involves bad news or persuasion. Figure 18.1 shows the outline of a brief persuasive speech delivered by an art dealer trying to persuade a group of executives to invest in corporate art.

Structure a short speech or presentation like a letter or memo.

Longer speeches and presentations are organized like reports (see Chapter 14 for specific suggestions). If the purpose is to entertain, motivate, or inform, use a direct order imposed naturally by the subject. If the purpose is to analyze, persuade, or collaborate, organize your material around conclusions and recommendations or around a logical argument. Use direct order if the audience is receptive, indirect if you expect resistance. Regardless of the length of your speech or presentation, bear in mind that simplicity of organization is especially useful in oral communication.

Organize longer speeches and presentations like formal reports.

Use a clear, direct organization to accommodate your listeners' limitations.

A carefully prepared outline may be more than just the starting point for composing a speech or presentation. If you plan to deliver your presentation from notes rather than from a written text, your outline will also be your final "script." For this reason

Figure 18.1
Sample Outline for a Brief Speech

WHO OWNS THE VAN GOGH?

Purpose: To convince executives that corporate art is a good investment

I. Introduction: On a cold night in March collectors assembled at Christie's auction gallery in London to bid on Van Gogh's <u>Sunflowers</u>. Within five minutes the price soared to $39.9 million. The buyer? A Japanese insurance company.

II. Corporations are becoming major consumers of art.

    A. Over 1,000 corporations now have art collections.

    B. Companies are motivated by three factors:

        1. Top executives' love of art

        2. Desire to provide public and employees with aesthetic value

        3. Potential for appreciation in the value of the work of art

III. Most corporate collections are conservative.

    A. Corporate collectors tend to avoid the controversial.

    B. The art is generally the work of 20th-century artists.

        1. Moderately priced, compared with Old Masters

        2. In plentiful supply

IV. Several corporate collections have soared in value.

    A. PepsiCo paid $150,000 for a sculpture by Alexander Calder, which is worth $1 million today. [slides]

    B. First Bank Systems, Inc.'s, collection, acquired for $3 million, has doubled in value. [slides]

    C. Sterling Regal's collection of 180 works cost about $2 million and is now worth about $4.5 million. [slides]

    D. Domino's Pizza has invested $7.5 million in its collection, which is currently valued at $12 million. [slides]

V. Conclusion: Investing in art provides both aesthetic and monetary rewards. Corporations are the Medicis of the current art renaissance.

---

the headings on the outline should be complete sentences or lengthy phrases rather than one- or two-word topic headings. Many speakers also include notes that indicate where visual aids will be used. You might want to write out the transitional sentences you'll use to connect main points (see Figure 18.2). Experienced speakers often use a two-column format that separates the "stage directions" from the content.

Of course, you may have to adjust your organization in response to input from the audience, especially if your purpose is to collaborate. You might want to think of several organizational possibilities, based on "what if" assumptions about the audience's reactions. That way, if someone says something that undercuts your planned approach, you can switch smoothly to another one.

Use an outline as your "script," but be prepared to deviate in response to audience feedback.

Slide 1:
    Text
    Overview
	INTRO: Mention Cowboys versus '49ers game—Analogy to company

Slide 2:
    Text
    Highlight 1st main
    point
	I. The company's sales growth has flattened because of weakening demand
	    for cosmetics and our lack of new products.

Slide 3:
    Line chart
    Sales 1980-1992
	A. Consumption of cosmetics has leveled off in the past 3 years.
	    —Working women have more money and less time to spend it.

Slide 4:
    Bar chart
    Shift to cheap brands
	—Recession has dampened demand, prompted shift to cheaper brands.

Slide 5:
    Line chart
    Market share
	B. Our market share has declined.

Slide 6:
    Pie chart
    Sales by outlet, 1990
    vs. 1992
	—Consumers are shifting to new outlets.

Slide 7:
    Table
    Relative shares
	—Competitors have gained share by introducing cheaper lines.

Slide 8:
    Text
    Highlight 2nd point
	Transition: We can regain share if we launch our own inexpensive line.

Figure 18.2
**Sample Outline with Notes
on Delivery**

*The average speaker can deliver
about one paragraph, or 125 to
150 words, in a minute.*

Estimating Length

Time for speeches and presentations is often strictly regulated, so you'll need to tailor your material to the available time. You can use your outline to estimate how long your speech or presentation will take. The average speaker can deliver about 125 to 150 words a minute (or roughly 7,500 to 9,000 words an hour), which corresponds to 20 to 25 double-spaced, typed pages of text. The average paragraph is about 125 to 150 words in length, so most of us can speak at a rate of about one paragraph per minute.

Say you want to make three basic points. In a 10-minute speech, you could take about 2 minutes to explain each of these points, using roughly two paragraphs for each point. If you devoted a minute each to the introduction and the conclusion, you would have 2 minutes left over to interact with the audience. If you had an hour, however, you could spend the first 5 minutes introducing the presentation, establishing rapport with the audience, providing background information, and giving an overview of your topic. In the next 30 to 40 minutes, you could explain each of the three points, spending about 10 to 13 minutes per point (the equivalent of 5 or 6 typewritten pages). Your conclusion might take another 3 to 5 minutes. The remaining 10 to 20 minutes would then be available for responding to questions and comments from the audience.

Which is better, the 10-minute speech or the hour-long presentation? If your speech doesn't have to fit into a specified time slot, the answer depends on your subject, your audience's attitude and knowledge, and the relationship you have with your audience. For a simple, easily accepted message, 10 minutes may be enough. On the other hand, if your subject is complex or your audience is skeptical, you'll probably need more time. Don't squeeze a complex presentation into a period that is too brief, and don't draw out a simple talk any longer than necessary.

> Be sure that your subject, purpose, and organization are compatible with the time available.

Deciding on the Style

Another important element in your planning is the style most suitable to the occasion. Is this a formal speech or presentation in an impressive setting, with professionally developed visual aids? Or is it a casual, roll-up-your-sleeves working session? The size of the audience, the subject, your purpose, your budget, and the time available for preparation all determine the style.

In general, if you're speaking to a relatively small group, you can use a casual approach that encourages audience participation. A small conference room, with the audience seated around a table, may be appropriate. Use simple visual aids. Invite the audience to interject comments. Deliver your remarks in a conversational tone, using notes to jog your memory if necessary.

> Use a casual style for small groups; use a formal style for large groups and important events.

On the other hand, if you're addressing a large audience and the event is an important one, you'll want to establish a more formal atmosphere. Hold the presentation in an auditorium or a convention hall, and seat the audience in rows. Show slides or films to dramatize your message. Ask people to hold their questions until after you've completed your remarks. Use detailed notes or a complete script to guide your delivery.

DEVELOPING FORMAL SPEECHES AND PRESENTATIONS

Developing a major speech or presentation is much like writing a formal report, with one important difference: You need to adjust your technique to an oral communication channel. This is both an opportunity and a challenge.

The opportunity lies in the interaction that's possible between you and the audience. When you speak before a group, you can receive information as well as transmit it. So you can adjust both the content and the delivery of your message as you go along, editing your speech or presentation to make it clearer and more compelling. Instead of simply expressing your ideas, you can draw out the audience's ideas and use them to reach a mutually acceptable conclusion. You can also capitalize on nonverbal signals to convey information to and from your audience.

> How formal speeches and presentations differ from formal reports:
> - More interaction with the audience
> - Use of nonverbal cues to express meaning
> - Less control of content
> - Greater need to help the audience stay on track

The challenge lies in maintaining control and accommodating your audience's limitations. To get the benefits of oral communication, be flexible. The more you plan to interact with your audience, the less control you'll have. Halfway through your presentation an unexpected comment from someone in the audience could force you to shift to a new line of thought, which requires great skill. At the same time, accommodate the limitations of your listeners. To prevent your audience from losing interest or getting lost, use special techniques when developing the various elements of the presentation: the introduction, the body, the close, the question-and-answer period, and the visual aids.

The Introduction

You have a lot to accomplish during the first few minutes of your speech or presentation, including arousing your audience's interest in your topic, establishing your credibility, and preparing the audience for what will follow. That's why developing the introduction often requires a disproportionate amount of your attention.

Arousing Interest

Some subjects are naturally more interesting than others. If you happen to be discussing a matter of profound significance that will personally affect the members of your audience, chances are they'll listen regardless of how you begin. All you really have to do is announce your topic ("Today I'd like to announce the reorganization of the company").

The best approach to dealing with an uninterested audience is to appeal to human nature. Encourage people to take the subject personally. Show them how they'll be affected as individuals. For example, when addressing clerical employees about a pension program, you might plan to start off like this:

> If somebody offered to give you $200,000 in exchange for $5 per week, would you be interested? That's the amount you can expect to collect during your retirement years if you choose to contribute to the voluntary pension plan. During the next two weeks, you will have to decide whether you want to participate. Although for most of you retirement is many years away, this is an important financial decision. During the next 20 minutes, I hope to give you the information you need to make that decision intelligently.

Make sure your introduction matches the tone of your speech or presentation. If the occasion is supposed to be fun, you might begin with something light; but if you'll be talking business to a group of executives, don't waste their time with cute openings. Avoid jokes and personal anecdotes when you plan to discuss a serious problem. If you're developing a routine oral report, don't be overly dramatic. Most of all, try to make your introduction natural. Nothing turns off the average audience faster than a trite, staged beginning.

Building Credibility

One of the chief drawbacks of overblown openings is that they damage the speaker's credibility, and building credibility is probably even more important than arousing interest. A speaker with high credibility is more persuasive than a speaker with low credibility.[2] So when developing a speech, it's important to establish your credentials quickly; people will decide within a few minutes whether you're worth listening to.[3] You want the audience to like you as a person and to respect your opinion.

Establishing credibility is relatively easy if you'll be speaking to a familiar, open-minded audience. The real difficulty comes when you must try to earn the confidence of strangers, especially those predisposed to be skeptical or antagonistic.

One way to handle the problem is to let someone else introduce you. That person can present your credentials so that you won't appear boastful, but make sure the person introducing you doesn't exaggerate your qualifications. If Brady Keys were to address a group of fast-food franchisees on inner-city operations, some of them might bristle at his being billed as the world's only knowledgeable authority on the subject.

If you plan to introduce yourself, keep your comments simple. At the same time, don't be afraid to mention your accomplishments. Your listeners will be curious about

As founder of the consulting firm Success Strategies, Lynda R. Paulson addresses the "people needs" of companies of all sizes. A dynamic speaker, Paulson advises that you establish your credibility early. Everything else depends on it, including your listeners' acceptance of you and their respect for your opinion.

Chapter 18: Giving Speeches and Oral Presentations 451

your qualifications, so plan to tell them briefly who you are and why you're there. Generally speaking, one or two aspects of your background are all you need to mention: your position in an organization, your profession, the name of your company. You might plan to say something like this:

I'm Karen Whitney, a market research analyst with Information Resources Corporation. For the past five years, I've specialized in studying high-technology markets. Your director of engineering, John LaBarre, has asked me to brief you on recent trends in computer-aided design so that you'll have a better idea of how to direct your research-and-development efforts.

Without boasting, explain why you are qualified to speak on the subject.

This speaker establishes credibility by tying her credentials to the purpose of her presentation. By mentioning her company's name, her position, and the name of the audience's boss, she lets her listeners know immediately that she's qualified to tell them something they need to know. She connects her background to their concerns.

Previewing the Presentation

Giving your audience a preview of what's ahead adds to your authority and, more important, helps people understand your message. In an oral presentation, however, the speaker provides the framework. Your introduction will summarize your main idea, identify the supporting points, and indicate the order in which you'll develop those points. Once you've established the framework, you can move into developing the body of your presentation, confident that your audience will understand how the individual facts and figures relate to your main idea.

Let the audience know what lies ahead.

The Body

The bulk of your speech or presentation will be devoted to a discussion of the three or four main points in your outline. Use the same organizational patterns you'd use in a letter, memo, or report, but keep things simple. Your two goals are making sure the structure of your speech or presentation will be clear and making sure your organization will keep your audience's attention.

Limit the body to three or four main points.

Emphasizing Structure

To show how ideas are related in oral presentations, you rely more on words. For the small links between sentences and paragraphs, one or two transitional words will be enough: *therefore, because, in addition, in contrast, moreover, for example, consequently, nevertheless, finally.* To link major sections of the speech or presentation, you'll need complete sentences or paragraphs, such as "Now that we've reviewed the problem, let's take a look at some solutions." Every time you shift topics, stress the connection between ideas. Summarize what's been said; preview what's to come.

Help your audience follow your presentation
- By summarizing as you go along
- By emphasizing the transitions from one idea to the next

The longer the speech or presentation, the more important the transitions become. When you present many ideas, the audience has trouble absorbing them and seeing the relationship among them. Listeners need clear transitions to guide them to the most important points. Furthermore, they need transitions to pick up any ideas they may have missed. If you repeat key ideas in the transitions, you can compensate for lapses in the audience's attention. You might also want to call attention to the transitions by using gestures, changing your tone of voice, or introducing a visual aid.

Holding the Audience's Attention

To communicate your points effectively, you have to maintain the audience's attention. Here are a few helpful tips for creating memorable speeches:

Make a special effort to capture wandering attention.

Roberto Goizueta is chairman and CEO of the Coca-Cola Company. He is a successful speaker, often relating his accomplishments at Coke and what they've taught him. To keep the audience's attention, says Goizueta, be sure you show how your subject applies to your industry and to the work of your listeners.

- *Relate your subject to the audience's needs.* People are interested in things that affect them personally. Present every point in light of the audience's needs and values.
- *Use clear, vivid language.* People become bored quickly when they don't understand the speaker. If your presentation involves abstract ideas, try to show how those abstractions connect with everyday life. Use familiar words, short sentences, and concrete examples.
- *Explain the relationship between your subject and familiar ideas.* By showing how your subject relates to ideas the audience already understands, you give people a way to categorize and remember your points.[4]

You can also hold the audience's interest by introducing variety into your speech or presentation. One useful technique is to plan occasional pauses for questions or comments from the audience. These pauses help you determine whether the audience understands key points before you launch into another section; they also give the audience a chance to switch for a time from listening to participating. Visual aids are another source of both clarification and stimulation. Varying your gestures and tone of voice helps too.

The Close

The close should leave a strong and lasting impression.

The close of a speech or presentation is almost as important as the beginning because audience attention peaks at this point. Plan to devote about 10 percent of the total time to the ending. Begin your conclusion by telling listeners that you're about to finish so that they'll make one final effort to listen intently. Don't be afraid to sound obvious. Plan to say something like "in conclusion" or "to sum it all up." You'll want people to know that you're in the home stretch.

Restating the Main Points

Summarize the main idea, and restate the main points.

Once you've planned how to get everyone's attention, you'll repeat your main idea. Be sure to emphasize what you want the audience to do or think. Then state the key motivating factor. Reinforce your theme by repeating the three or four main supporting points. A few sentences are generally enough to refresh people's memories. Here's how one speaker ended a presentation on the company's executive compensation program:

We can all be proud of the way our company has grown. If we want to continue that growth, however, we will have to adjust our executive compensation program to reflect competitive practices. If we don't, our best people will look for opportunities elsewhere.

In summary, our survey has shown that we need to do four things to improve executive compensation:

-- Increase the overall level of compensation.
-- Install a cash bonus program.
-- Offer a variety of stock-based incentives.
-- Improve our health insurance and pension benefits.

By making these improvements, we can help our company cross the threshold of growth into the major leagues.

This speaker repeats her recommendations and then concludes with a memorable statement that motivates the audience to take action.

Outlining the Next Steps

Some speeches and presentations require the audience to reach a decision or agree to take specific action. In such cases the close provides a clear wrap-up. If the audience has agreed on an issue covered in the presentation, plan to review the consensus in a sentence or two. If not, make the lack of consensus clear by saying something like "We seem to have some fundamental disagreement on this question." Then you'll be ready to suggest a method of resolving the differences.

If you expect any action to occur, you must explain who is responsible for doing what. One effective technique is to list the action items, with an estimated completion date and the name of the person responsible. Plan to present this list in a visual aid that can be seen by the entire audience, and ask each person on the list to agree to accomplish his or her assigned task by the target date. This public commitment to action is the best insurance that something will happen.

Be certain that everyone agrees on the outcome and understands what should happen next.

If the required action is likely to be difficult, make sure everyone understands the problems involved. You don't want people to leave the presentation thinking their tasks will be easy, only to discover later that the jobs are quite demanding. If that happens, they may become discouraged and fail to complete their assignments. You'll want everyone to have a realistic attitude and to be prepared to handle whatever arises. So use the close to alert people to potential difficulties.

Ending on a Positive Note

Make your final remarks enthusiastic and memorable. Even if parts of your speech will be downbeat, try to develop your ending on a positive note. You might stress the benefits of action or express confidence in the listeners' ability to accomplish the work ahead. An alternative is to end with a question or statement that will leave your audience thinking.

Remember that your final words round out the presentation. You'll want to leave the audience with a satisfied feeling, a feeling of completeness. The close is not the place to introduce new ideas or to alter the mood of the presentation. Moreover, although you'll want to close on a positive note, avoid developing a staged finale. Keep it natural.

The Question-and-Answer Period

Along with the introduction, body, and close, include in your speech or presentation an opportunity for questions and answers. Otherwise, you might just as well write a report. If you aren't planning to interact with the audience, you're wasting the chief advantage of an oral format.

Specifics about handling questions from the audience are discussed later in this chapter under the heading "Mastering the Art of Delivery." In general, the important thing to consider when you're developing your speech is the nature and timing of that audience interaction. Responding to questions and comments during the presentation can interrupt the flow of your argument and reduce your control of the situation. If you'll be addressing a large group, particularly a hostile or unknown group, questions can be dangerous. Your best bet in such a case would be to ask people to hold their questions until after you have concluded your remarks. On the other hand, if you'll be working with a small group and will need to draw out their ideas, you'll want to encourage comments from the audience throughout the presentation.

Encourage questions throughout your speech if you are addressing a small group, but ask a large audience to defer questions until later.

The Visual Aids

Most formal speeches and presentations incorporate visual aids. Whether soliciting funds or outlining a company's strategy, Brady Keys uses visual aids to clarify his ideas. From a purely practical standpoint, they are a convenience for the speaker, who can use them as a tool for remembering the details of the message (no small feat in a lengthy presentation); novice speakers also like visual aids because they draw audience attention away from the speaker. More important, visual aids dramatically increase the audience's ability to absorb and remember information.

Visual aids help both the speaker and the audience remember the important points.

Designing and Presenting Visual Aids

Two types of visual aids are used to supplement speeches and presentations. Text visuals consist of words and help the audience follow the flow of ideas. Because text visuals are simplified outlines of your presentation, you can use them to summarize and preview the message and to signal major shifts in thought. On the other hand, graphic visual aids illustrate the main points. They help the audience grasp numerical data and other information that would be hard to follow if presented orally.

Two kinds of visual aids:
- *Text visuals help listeners follow the flow of ideas.*
- *Graphic visuals present and emphasize important facts.*

Simplicity is the key to effectiveness when designing both types of visual aids. Because people can't read and listen at the same time, the visual aids have to be simple enough that the audience can understand them within a moment or two. As a rule, text visuals are more effective when they consist of no more than six lines, with a maximum of six words per line. Produce them in large, clear type, using uppercase and lowercase letters, with extra white space between lines of text. Make sure the type is large enough to be seen from any place in the room. Phrase list items in parallel grammatical form. Use telegraphic wording ("Compensation Soars," for example) without being cryptic ("Compensation"); you are often better off including both a noun and a verb in each item.

Visual aids are counterproductive if the audience can't clearly see or understand them within a few moments.

You can use any of the graphic visuals you might show in a formal report, including line, pie, and bar charts, as well as flowcharts, organization charts, diagrams, maps, drawings, and tables. However, graphic visuals used in oral presentations are simplified versions of those that appear in written documents. Eliminate anything that is not absolutely essential to the message. To help the audience focus immediately on the point of each graphic visual, use headings that state the message in one clear phrase or sentence: "Earnings have increased by 15 percent."

When you present visual aids, you'll want people to have the chance to read what's there, but you'll also want them to listen to your explanation:

- Be sure all members of the audience can see the visual aids.
- Allow the audience time to read a visual aid before you begin your explanation.
- Limit each visual aid to one idea.
- Illustrate only the main points, not the entire presentation.
- Use no visual aids that conflict with your verbal message.
- Paraphrase the text of your visual aid; don't read it word for word.
- When you've finished discussing the point illustrated by the visual aid, remove it from the audience's view.[5]

The visual aids are there to supplement your words—not the other way around.

Selecting the Right Medium

Visual aids for documents are usually limited to paper. For speeches and presentations, however, you have a variety of media to choose from:

Visual aids may be presented in a variety of media.

- *Handouts.* Even in a presentation, you may choose to distribute sheets of paper bearing an agenda, an outline of the program, an abstract, a written report, or supplementary material such as tables, charts, and graphs. Listeners can keep the handout to remind them of the subject and the main ideas of your presentation. In addition, they can refer to it while you're speaking. Handouts work especially well for informal situations in which the audience takes an active role; they often make their own notes on the handouts. However, handouts can be distracting because people are inclined to read the material rather than listen to you, so many speakers distribute handouts after the presentation.
- *Chalkboards and whiteboards.* When you're addressing a small group of people and want to draw out their ideas, use a board to list points as they are mentioned. Because visual aids using this medium are produced on the spot, boards provide flexibility. However, they're too informal for some situations.
- *Flip charts.* Large sheets of paper attached at the top like a tablet can be propped on an easel so that you can flip the pages as you speak. Each chart illustrates or clarifies a point. You might have a few lines from your outline on one, a graph or diagram on another, and so on. By using felt-tip markers of various colors, you can highlight ideas as you go along. Keep it simple: Try to limit each flip-chart page to three or four graphed lines or to five or six points in list format.
- *Overheads.* One of the most common visual aids in business is the overhead transparency, which can be projected on a screen in full daylight. Because you don't have to dim the lights, you don't lose eye contact with your audience. Transparencies are easy to make using a typed original on regular paper, a copying machine, and a page-size sheet of plastic. Opaque projections are similar to transparencies but do not require as much preparation. You could use an opaque projector to show the audience a photograph or an excerpt from a report or manual.
- *Slides.* The content of slides may be text, graphics, or pictures. If you're trying to create a polished, professional atmosphere, you might find this approach worthwhile, particularly if you'll be addressing a crowd and don't mind speaking in a darkened room. However, remember that you may need someone to operate the projector and that you'll need to coordinate the slides with your speech. Take a few minutes before your speech to verify that the equipment works correctly.
- *Computers.* With a special projector, a personal computer can be turned into a large-screen "intelligent chalkboard" that allows you to create and modify your visual aids as the presentation unfolds. If you're discussing financial projections, you can show how a change in sales forecasts will affect profits by typing in a new number. When the presentation is over, you can print out hard copies of the visual aids and distribute them to interested members of the audience. You can also use a computer-generated slide show, which gives you the opportunity to make changes right up to the minute you start speaking. Using this technology, you can incorporate both animation and photos into your presentation.[6]
- *Other visual aids.* In technical or scientific presentations, a sample of a product or material allows the audience to experience your subject directly. Models built to scale are convenient representations of an object. Audiotapes are often used to supplement a slide show or to present a precisely worded and timed message. Filmstrips and movies can capture the audience's attention with color and movement. Television and videotapes are good for showing demonstrations, interviews, and other events. In addition, filmstrips, movies, television, and videotapes can be used as stand-alone vehicles (independent of a speaker) for communicating with dispersed audiences at various times. For example, PepsiCo's CEO, Wayne Calloway, has many of his important presentations videotaped and sends them to all the company's operating divisions to keep employees updated on the business.[7]

BEHIND THE SCENES WITH CHARLES OSGOOD
Speaking Out on Public Speaking

As the star of CBS's *Sunday Morning* television news program and as writer and star of *The Osgood File* on CBS radio, Charles Osgood is in demand as a public speaker. Also noted for his light verse, he travels throughout the country to address clubs, conferences, and professional organizations. He is well qualified, then, to advise you on relating to your audience.

Here's How It Is with Audiences

Speakers sometimes overlook the Golden Rule, I fear.
They go ahead and give a speech that they would hate to hear.

Like them, and they'll like you. Help them, and they'll help you. Enjoy yourself, and they'll enjoy themselves. Be relaxed, and they'll be relaxed. Lead . . . they'll follow.

Fear

The audience won't throw things, you will find with any luck.
But if they do, do not despair, just be prepared to duck.

Your principal enemy is blind, unreasoning fear. You know that the audience is not going to stone you to death, yet your "fight or flight" instincts are triggered.

The adrenaline is pumping. Your mental attitude is that of being attacked by a lion. The last thing you're able to do under these circumstances is relax and speak comfortably to your audience. To put your audience at ease, you have to radiate confidence.

Be Prepared

You don't have to spend weeks preparing. But don't think you can just get up and dazzle everybody by making something up as you go along. Don't confuse worry with preparation. Just because you have been thinking about your speech for a long time and dreading it does not mean that you've been getting ready for it. The more prepared you are, the less worried and the more effective you'll be. Knowing you're going to be effective, you won't worry.

What Are You Going to Say?

If you know there's a lot you've been wanting to say, and forgive me for being a nag,
All that wisdom and wit but you still cannot fit fifty pounds in a twenty-pound bag.

Your audience will come away from your speech with some impression of you and one or two of the main points you'll be talking about. One or two. Not ten. Not

---

Use visual aids to highlight your spoken words, not as a substitute for them.

With all visual aids, the crucial factor is how you use them. Properly integrated into an oral presentation, they can save time, create interest, add variety, make an impression, and illustrate points that are difficult to explain in words alone.

MASTERING THE ART OF DELIVERY

When you've planned all the parts of your presentation and have your visual aids in hand, you're ready to begin practicing your delivery. You have a variety of delivery methods to choose from, some of which are easier to handle than others:

- *Memorizing.* Unless you're a trained actor, avoid memorizing an entire speech, particularly a long one. You're likely to forget your lines. Furthermore, a memorized speech often sounds very stiff and stilted. On the other hand, memorizing a quotation, an opening paragraph, or a few concluding remarks can bolster your confidence and strengthen your delivery.

twenty. You must decide what those one or two ideas are going to be. Covering too much ground is not going to work. What do you want the audience to feel or to think as a result of hearing you? Concentrate on those things. Forget about everything else. Use only those jokes, anecdotes, and so on that help you set up and make those points. If you cannot express in a sentence or two what it is you intend to get across, your speech is not focused well enough.

Don't Read; Try to Sound Spontaneous

Listening to someone read a prepared text is about as exciting as attending a congressional hearing on interstate commerce. Do not read your statement. Make it. If you're speaking to an audience, speak to them. If you're giving a talk, then talk!

The 12-Minute Secret

The standard length of a vaudeville act was 12 minutes. It was believed that no act, other than the headliner, could sustain interest for longer than that. Consider, then: If all those troupers singing and dancing their hearts out, if all those jugglers and magicians, if all those trained dogs and ponies couldn't go on for more than 12 minutes without boring the customers, what makes you think you can?

The Key to Success

The audience is just like you and me, for goodness' sake. So relax and be yourself, and give the audience a break.

Be Real

You will probably not get away with trying to be what you are not. The situation magnifies you. If you are being phony, the audience will spot it a mile away. If you don't think a story is funny, the audience won't laugh at it. If you aren't moved by your information, the audience won't be moved either.

Apply Your Knowledge

1. Select a speech, lecture, or talk you have recently heard that left you disappointed or confused. What advice from Charles Osgood would have improved the speaker's presentation? Make a list of things the speaker could have done.

2. Your regional sales manager stops in your office to tell you there will be a staff meeting in one hour to preview your unit's sales results for the quarter. You are the sales representative in charge of new lines, and you are asked to comment on how the new cookies with a pudding filling are performing. Using Charles Osgood's recommendations as a guide, how would you prepare for the meeting? List ways you can help the audience enjoy themselves, radiate confidence, be prepared, cover the right amount of material, sound spontaneous, avoid boring your audience, relax, and be real. (Remember, you have only an hour to prepare.)

- *Reading.* If you're delivering a technical or complex presentation, you may want to read it. Policy statements by government officials (such as the economists at the Federal Reserve Bank) are sometimes read because the wording may be critical. If you choose to read your speech, practice enough so that you can still maintain eye contact with the audience. Triple-spaced copy, wide margins, and large type help too. You might even want to include stage cues for yourself, such as *pause, raise hands, lower voice*.
- *Speaking from notes.* Making a presentation with the help of an outline, note cards, or visual aids is probably the most effective and easiest delivery mode. You have something to refer to and can still have eye contact and interaction with the audience. If your listeners look puzzled, you can expand on a point or put it another way. (Generally, note cards are preferable to sheets of paper; nervousness is more evident in shaking sheets of paper.)
- *Impromptu speaking.* You might give an impromptu, or unrehearsed, speech in two situations: when you've agreed to speak but have neglected to prepare your remarks or when you're called on to speak unexpectedly. Avoid speaking unprepared unless

Speaking from notes is generally the best way to handle delivery.

you've spoken countless times on the same topic or are an extremely good public speaker. When you're asked to speak "off the cuff," take a moment or two to think through what you're going to say. Then avoid the temptation to ramble.

Regardless of which delivery mode you use, be sure that you're thoroughly familiar with the subject. Knowing what you're talking about is the best way to build your self-confidence. It's also helpful to know how you'll approach preparing for successful speaking, delivering the speech, and handling questions.

Preparing for Successful Speaking

You can build self-confidence by practicing, especially if you haven't had much experience with public speaking. Even if you practice in front of a mirror, try to visualize the room filled with listeners. Put your talk on tape to check the sound of your voice and your timing, phrasing, and emphasis. If possible, rehearse on videotape to see yourself as your audience will. Go over your visual aids and coordinate them with the talk.

Whenever you can, check the location for your presentation in advance. Look at the seating arrangements, and make sure they're appropriate for your needs. If you want the audience to sit at tables, be sure tables are available. Check the room for outlets that may be needed for your projector or microphone. Locate the light switches and dimmers. If you need a flip-chart easel or a chalkboard, be sure it's on hand. Check for chalk, an eraser, extension cords, and any other small but crucial items you might need.

If you're addressing an audience that doesn't speak your language, consider using an interpreter. Of course, anytime you make a speech or presentation to people from other cultures, take into account cultural differences in appearance, mannerisms, and other customs, in addition to adapting the content of your speech. When you're addressing a U.S. or Canadian audience with few cultural differences, follow the specific guidelines in this chapter.

Delivering the Speech

A. Barry Rand is president of the U.S. Marketing Group of the Xerox Corporation. Known as a persuasive and gifted speaker, Rand uses his talents to inspire employees and colleagues. The more familiar you are with your subject, the better, says Rand. Not only will you feel more comfortable during your speech, but your ease will come across as self-confidence.

When it's time to deliver the speech, you may feel a bit of stage fright. Most people do, even professional actors. A good way to overcome your fears is to rehearse until you're thoroughly familiar with your material.[8] Communication professionals have suggested other tips:

- Prepare more material than necessary. Extra knowledge, combined with a genuine interest in the topic, will boost your confidence.
- Think positively about your audience, yourself, and what you have to say. See yourself as polished and professional, and your audience will too.
- Be realistic about stage fright. After all, even experienced speakers admit that they feel butterflies before they address an audience. A little nervous excitement can actually provide the extra lift that will make your presentation sparkle.
- Use the few minutes while you're arranging your materials, before you actually begin speaking, to tell yourself you're on and you're ready.
- Before you begin speaking, take a few deep breaths.
- Have your first sentence memorized and on the tip of your tongue.
- If your throat is dry, drink some water.

- If you feel that you're losing your audience during the speech, don't panic. Try to pull them back by involving them in the action.
- Use your visual aids to maintain and revive audience interest.
- Keep going. Things usually get better, and your audience will silently be wishing you success.

A little stage fright is normal.

Perhaps the best way to overcome stage fright is to concentrate on your message and your audience, not on yourself. When you're busy thinking about your subject and observing the audience's response, you tend to forget your fears. Even so, as you deliver your presentation, try to be aware of the nonverbal signals you're transmitting. To a great degree, your effectiveness will depend on how you look and sound.

As you approach the speaker's podium, breathe deeply, stand up straight, and walk slowly. Face the audience. Adjust the microphone. Count to three slowly; then survey the room. When you find a friendly face, make eye contact and smile. Count to three again; then begin your presentation.[9] Even if you feel nervous inside, this slow, controlled beginning will help you establish rapport.

Don't rush the opening.

Once your speech is under way, be particularly careful to maintain eye contact with the audience. Pick out several people positioned around the room, and shift your gaze from one to another. Doing this will make you appear to be sincere, confident, and trustworthy, and it will help you perceive the impression you're creating.

Use eye contact, posture, gestures, and voice to convey an aura of mastery and to keep your audience's attention.

Your posture is also important in projecting the right image. Stand tall, with your weight on both feet and your shoulders back. Avoid gripping the podium. In fact, you might step out from behind the podium to help the audience feel more comfortable with you and to express your own comfort and confidence in what you're saying. Use your hands to emphasize your remarks with appropriate gestures. At the same time, vary your facial expressions to make the message more dynamic.

Finally, think about the sound of your voice. Studies indicate that people who speak with lower voice tones at a slightly faster than average rate are perceived as being more credible.[10] Speak in a normal, conversational tone but with enough volume so that everyone in the audience can hear you. Try to sound poised and confident, varying your pitch and speaking rate to add emphasis. Don't ramble or use meaningless filler words like *um, you know, okay,* and *like.* Speak clearly and crisply, articulating all the syllables, and sound enthusiastic about what you're saying.

Handling Questions

The key to handling this segment effectively is preparation. Spend time before your speech thinking about the questions that might arise—including abrasive or difficult questions. Then be ready with answers. In fact, some experts recommend that you hold back some dramatic statistics as ammunition for the question-and-answer session.[11] However, bear in mind that circumstances may require some changes in the answers you prepare.

When someone poses a question, focus your attention on that individual. Pay attention to body language and facial expression to help determine what the person really means. Nod your head to acknowledge the question; then repeat it aloud to confirm your understanding and to ensure that the entire audience has heard it. If the question is vague or confusing, ask for clarification. Then give a simple, direct answer. Don't say more than you need to if you want to have enough time to cover all the questions. If giving an adequate answer would take too long, simply say "I'm sorry that we don't have time to get into that issue right now, but if you'll see me after the presentation, I'll be happy to discuss it with you." If you don't know the answer, don't

Keep your answers short and to the point.

CHECKLIST FOR SPEECHES AND ORAL PRESENTATIONS

A. Development of the Speech or Presentation
1. Analyze the audience.
2. Begin with an attention-getter.
3. Preview the main points.
4. Limit the discussion to no more than three or four points.
5. Explain who, what, when, where, why, and how.
6. In longer presentations include previews and summaries of major points as you go along.
7. Close by reviewing your main points and making a memorable statement.

B. Visual Aids
1. Use visual aids to show how things look, work, or relate to one another.
2. Use visual aids to highlight important information and create interest.
3. Select appropriate visual aids.
   - a. Use flip charts, boards, or transparencies for small, informal groups.
   - b. Use slides or films for major occasions and large groups.
4. Limit each visual aid to three or four graphed lines or five or six points.
5. Use short phrases.
6. Use large, readable type.
7. Make sure equipment works.

C. Delivery
1. Establish eye contact.
2. Speak clearly and distinctly.
3. Do not go too fast.
4. Be sure everyone can hear.
5. Speak in your natural style.
6. Stand up straight.
7. Use gestures in a natural, appropriate way.
8. Encourage questions.
   - a. Allow questions during the presentation if the group is small.
   - b. Ask the audience to hold their questions until the end if the group is large or hostile.
9. Respond to questions without getting sidetracked.
10. Maintain control of your feelings in spite of criticism.

Don't let any member of the audience monopolize your attention or turn a question into a debate.

pretend that you do. Instead, say something like "I don't have those figures. I'll get them for you as quickly as possible."

Don't allow one or two people to monopolize the question period. Try to give everyone a chance to participate; call on people from different parts of the room. If the same person keeps angling for attention, say something like "Several other people have questions; I'll get back to you if time permits." If audience members try to turn a question into an opportunity to mount their own soapboxes, it's up to you to maintain control. You might admit that you and the questioner have a difference of opinion and offer to get back to the questioner after you've done more research. Then call on someone else. Another approach is to respond with a brief answer, thus avoiding a lengthy debate or additional questions.[12] Finally, you might thank the person for the question and then remind the questioner that you were looking for specific questions. Don't indulge in put-downs, which may backfire and make the audience more sympathetic to the questioner.

Respond unemotionally to tough questions.

When the time allotted for your presentation is up, call a halt to the question-and-answer session, even if more people want to talk. Prepare the audience for the end by saying "Our time is almost up. Let's have one more question." After you've made your reply, summarize the main idea of the presentation and thank people for their attention. Conclude the same way you opened: by looking around the room and making eye contact. Then gather your notes and leave the podium, shoulders straight, head up. (The Checklist for Speeches and Oral Presentations is a reminder of the tasks involved in these types of oral communication.)

On the Job

SOLVING A COMMUNICATION DILEMMA AT THE KEYS GROUP

When Brady Keys retired from professional football in the late 1960s, he pursued his dream of owning his own business. After noticing how well a friend's restaurant was doing, he decided on a fried-chicken business.

His first hurdle was raising enough money to launch the restaurant. Ten banks said "No thanks," but he finally persuaded his former team to loan him $10,000—enough to open his first All-Pro Fried Chicken store. Within three years, he'd presented himself and his ideas to banks and to the government, convincing them to loan him enough capital to open 35 more outlets in Pittsburgh, New York, and Cleveland. By that time, he was selling a million dollars' worth of fried chicken a year.

He decided it was time to try something new— hamburgers. Keys convinced Burger King to let him try turning around a struggling Burger King franchise in Detroit's inner city. Realizing that something had to spark sales, "we introduced a couple of themes that are now universal in the industry," says Keys. "We found that black people didn't want the Whopper fixed the usual way, so we made it to order." That concept eventually formed the basis for Burger King's successful "Have It Your Way" advertising campaign. Then, as lines began to form for the new customized Whopper, Keys stationed employees at the end of the lines to take orders and cut the waiting time—a practice that has become standard in many fast-food restaurants. These innovations transformed the struggling franchise into the top-selling U.S. Burger King outlet, which Keys eventually sold.

As Keys points out, "You don't get acceptance by going in and saying 'accept me.' You get it by doing worthy activities." For example, Keys has used his position to help other African Americans succeed in franchising: He founded both Burger King's and KFC's Minority Franchise associations; he talked Burger King's management into awarding the construction contract for the company's first inner-city outlet to an African American general contractor; and he convinced management to increase the number of minority people on Burger King's roster of franchisees, employees, and vendors.

After taking over the Burger King franchise, Keys sold his All-Pro Fried Chicken stores and became a KFC franchisee. Most of his new outlets were in Albany, Georgia, where worthy activities became even more important. Gaining acceptance in the predominantly white community was more of a challenge than it had been in either Detroit or Pittsburgh. So, says Keys, "I became a philanthropist, I stressed my athletic background, and we brought in the Harlem Globetrotters as a benefit to the Special Olympics." He also served as chairman of the board of the Albany Civic Center Commission, and he is one of the largest individual contributors to the city's March of Dimes fund.

Keys's abilities to speak, to win friends, and to influence people help him deal with employees too. He believes in giving people a chance to live up to their potential. He promotes from within, and he rewards long-term employees with a piece of the business. In return, his employees are loyal, so his turnover is low—which keeps costs down and service up. His restaurants actually serve as a "business school" for many young people who eventually move on to more challenging careers. In fact, a recent ad campaign featured distinguished former "graduates" of the Brady Keys school of practical experience.

Keys's current projects include real estate development, a video game company, a mining and brokering business, and a movie production company. In the process of selling these ideas, he uses his speaking skills to present his ideas to potential investors, to build goodwill in the communities where he operates, and to motivate his employees.

Your Mission: As a member of the Keys Group's public relations department, you help Brady Keys plan some of the speeches he delivers to employees and to business, professional, and civic groups. For each of the following assignments, choose the best solution and be prepared to explain your choice.

1. Keys has agreed to give a 20-minute talk in Albany, Georgia, to a group of approximately 35 businesspeople who meet for lunch and networking on a monthly basis. The president of the group has suggested that Keys deal with the topic of franchising. Which of the following purposes do you think he should try to accomplish?
   a. To inform the audience about the history of franchising in the United States
   b. To inspire members of the audience to buy a franchise
   c. To entertain the audience with stories about Keys's franchising experiences
   d. To analyze the impact of national franchises on small, independently owned local businesses

2. Keys has been invited to give a ten-minute speech during the graduation ceremonies at a two-year vocational college in Detroit attended by many African American students. Based on his own experience, he expects that many of the minority students will face daunting obstacles as they build their careers. He wants to inspire these students to establish a goal and keep on trying to achieve it, regardless of the problems that arise. He has asked you to give him some ideas for developing the speech. Which of the following main ideas would you recommend to him?
   a. Life is like a football game. If you want to win, you have to know where the end zone is and keep on trying to

get there, even if the other team is bigger and tougher than your team.

b. During the darkest days of World War II, Winston Churchill inspired the English people by telling them that England would "never, never, never, never give up." The English eventually won the war, and you can win too if you remember Churchill's advice.

c. If you can communicate effectively with all types of people, you will eventually succeed in your career.

d. Despite the difficulties that lie ahead, you can triumph over adversity, just like many other African Americans who have overcome tough odds and achieved success. These individuals all shared one trait: perseverance.

3. Keys has asked you to help plan a ten-minute speech that he can give to his KFC employees during the annual summer picnic. He expects up to 1,000 employees to attend. His topic is "the state of the company." His purpose is to inspire employees to keep up the good work. His main idea is that the Keys Group is doing an excellent job in meeting the competition, thanks to the efforts of its workers. What general organizational scheme do you recommend for developing this idea?

a. *Chronological:* Highlights of company performance over the past year and outlook for the future

b. *Geographical:* Performance, problems, and opportunities in each of the 11 KFC outlets

c. *Topical:* Achievements of various types of employees such as store managers, kitchen workers, order takers, maintenance workers, and so on

d. *Comparison and contrast:* KFC versus Boston Chicken and other fast-food competitors

4. Keys is trying to persuade a group of investors to put some money into his new movie production company. He has prepared a presentation that describes the company's goals, activities, and financial prospects. He is currently wrestling with the introduction to the presentation. Which of the following introductions would you recommend?

a. Years ago, when I opened my first restaurant, I knew I had to do something to attract business. So I said to myself, why not try some TV advertising? I was operating on a shoestring, so I decided to write, produce, direct, and star in the commercial myself. If I'd had more money and more sense, I probably wouldn't have taken on the job, but lacking both money and experience, I was willing to try anything. Anyway, once I got started, I discovered that making commercials isn't really all that tricky. All you need is a little money, a little equipment, a little imagination, and a little luck. And bingo! You're in business. I've made a lot of my own commercials since then, and I've thoroughly enjoyed the process.

That's one of the reasons I decided to get into the movie business. I said to myself, "Brady, if making commercials is fun, imagine what a ball you can have making movies." But fun is only one

reason to start a movie production company. My principal motive is making money. And that's what I want to talk to you about today: how you can make money in the movie business.

b. In the last ten years, the number of movie screens in the United States has increased by 50 percent, to nearly 25,000. Those screens are all designed to do one thing: show films. But the major studios cannot possibly provide enough films to fill all these new theaters. As a result, a new breed of independent filmmaker is springing up, and many of them are far more profitable than their larger rivals.

I'd like to talk to you today about how you can participate in this exciting business opportunity. I think you will be intrigued by the potential payoff and the relatively limited risk involved. I'll begin by giving you a little background on the revolution currently under way in the movie industry. Then I'll describe the film production company that I'm forming in partnership with actor Leon Issac Kennedy. After you've heard our strategy and plans, I'll brief you on the returns that you could expect on your investment in my business.

c. When's the last time you went to the movies? And when did you last see a film on HBO or network TV? What about videocassettes? Have you rented any of them lately?

If you're like most people, you're hooked on movies, whether you see them in theaters or on TV. Somebody is making all those movies, and it isn't necessarily Paramount or Walt Disney. Many of the films you see are created by independent companies.

Starting an independent film production company requires relatively little capital, and the financial returns can be considerable. If you're careful, you can whip out a low-budget film for as little as $2 million. Even if you don't do well at the box office, you can still clear maybe $3 or $4 million from the TV rights and videocassette sales. Multiply that by, say, ten movies per year, and you have a $30 to $40 million business.

d. Who wouldn't jump at the chance to rub shoulders with Jennifer Jason Leigh, Spike Lee, Julia Roberts, Tom Cruise, Winona Ryder, Denzel Washington, Martin Lawrence, Michael Keaton, Marisa Tomei, and all the other box-office stars of the 1990s? Well, those are just some of the famous actors you'll meet when you visit the movie production company we're going to build together. Notice that I said "when" and not "if."

After you've heard my speech today, you'll agree that there's no better place to invest your cash than in our movie production company.

Although you'll be happy you made this investment, we all know that money isn't everything. You'll also have the prestige of working on Hollywood's most exciting movies with the biggest names in the business. Give me your attention for a few minutes as I talk about the movies we're considering right now.

5. In his role as chairman of the board of the Albany Civic Center Commission, Keys must give a speech outlining the center's financial position. The audience will include other board members, the mayor and members of the city council, and a group of 15 to 20 influential business and professional people. How should he handle the quantitative financial details?

a. He should prepare handouts that summarize the financial data in tabular and graphic form. As the audience arrives, he should give everyone a copy of the handout and refer to it during the speech.

b. Keys should write the information on a blackboard while he delivers the speech.

c. He should prepare simple overhead transparencies to use during the speech. As he concludes his remarks, he should tell the audience that detailed financial statements are available at the door for those who are interested.

d. Given the size and importance of the audience, he should show full-color 35 mm slides that summarize the financial information in tabular and graphic format. The slides should be professionally prepared to ensure their quality.[13]

Questions for Discussion

1. Would you rather (a) give a speech to an outside audience, (b) be interviewed for a news story, or (c) make a presentation to a departmental meeting? Why? How do the communication skills differ in each situation?

2. How might the audience's attitude about a topic affect the amount of audience interaction during or after a presentation?

3. Have you ever attended a presentation or a speech in which the speaker's style seemed inappropriate? What effect did that style have on the audience?

4. What similarities and differences would you expect to see in the introduction to a formal presentation and the introduction to a formal report?

5. What problems could result from using visual aids during your speech?

6. From the speaker's perspective, what are the advantages and disadvantages of responding to questions from the audience throughout a speech or presentation? From the listener's perspective, which approach would you prefer? Why?

Exercises

1. Attend a speech at your school or in your area, or watch a speech on television. Categorize the speech as one that motivates or entertains, one that informs or analyzes, or one that persuades or urges collaboration. Then compare the speaker's delivery and use of visual aids with the Checklist for Speeches and Oral Presentations. Write a two-page report analyzing the speaker's performance and suggesting improvements.

2. Analyze a speech given by someone introducing the main speaker at an awards ceremony, a graduation, or some other special occasion. Does the speech fit the occasion, relate to the audience's interests, and grab attention? How well does the speech motivate the audience to listen to the featured speaker? Does the speech provide the information necessary for the audience to understand, respect, and appreciate the speaker's background and viewpoint? Put yourself in the shoes of the person who made that introduction. Draft a brief (two-minute) speech that prepares the audience for the featured speaker.

3. You've been asked to give an informative ten-minute talk on vacation opportunities in your home state. Draft your introduction, which should last no more than two minutes. Then pair off with a classmate and analyze each other's introductions. How well do these two introductions arouse the audience's interest, build credibility, and preview the presentation? Suggest how these introductions might be improved.

4. Which media would you use for the visual aids that accompany each of the following speeches? Explain your answers.

a. An informal ten-minute speech to 300 assembly-line employees explaining the purpose of a new training program
   b. An informal ten-minute speech to 5 vice presidents explaining the purpose of a new training program
   c. A formal five-minute presentation to the company's 12-member board of directors explaining the purpose of a new training program
   d. A formal five-minute speech to 35 members of the press explaining the purpose of a new company training program

5. For the next meeting of the student government, you're preparing a presentation about the diversity of your college's student population. Prepare an introduction using humor, an introduction using a story, and an introduction using a question. Swap introductions with a classmate and critique how well each of your introductions gets attention. Which works best? Why?

6. With three classmates, practice audience analysis by analyzing the audience of a particular television program. Note the age, gender, race, marital status, relationships, and occupations of the characters. Also pay attention to the commercials that run during the program. On the basis of these clues, who do you think watches this program? Now choose a topic this audience is likely to feel strongly about. How would you prepare a speech on that topic if you believed the audience would probably be hostile? What would you do differently if you believed the audience would be sympathetic? Present your group's analysis to the class, and defend your answers.

FORMAT AND LAYOUT OF BUSINESS DOCUMENTS

An effective letter, memo, or report does more than store words on paper. It communicates with the right person, makes an impression, and tells the recipient who wrote it and when it was written. It may even carry responses back to the sender, if only to relate how and by whom it was received and processed.

Over the centuries certain conventions have developed for the format and layout of business documents. Of course, conventions vary from country to country, and even within the United States few hard-and-fast rules exist. Many organizations even develop variations of standard styles to suit their own needs, adopting the style that's best for the types of messages they send and for the kinds of audiences that receive them. The conventions described here are more common than others. Whether you handle all your own communication via computer or rely on your secretary to handle it for you, knowing the proper form for your documents and how to make them attractive to your readers is crucial.

FIRST IMPRESSIONS

A letter or other written document is often the first (sometimes the only) contact you have with an external audience. Memos and other documents used within an organization represent you to supervisors, colleagues, and employees. So it's important that your documents look neat and professional and that they're easy to read. Your audience's first impressions come from the paper you use, the way you customize it, and the general appearance of your document. These elements tell readers a lot about you and about your company's professionalism.

Paper

From your own experience, you know that a flimsy, see-through piece of paper gives a much less favorable impression than a richly textured piece. Paper quality is measured in two ways: The first measure of quality is weight, specifically the weight of four reams (each a 500-sheet package) of letter-size paper. The quality most commonly used by business organizations is 20-pound paper, but 16- and 24-pound versions are also used. The second measure of quality is the percentage of cotton in the paper. Cotton doesn't yellow over time the way wood pulp does, and it's both strong and soft. In general, paper with a 25 percent cotton content is an appropriate quality for letters and outside reports. For memos and other internal documents, lighter-weight paper and paper with a lower cotton content may be used.

In the United States the standard size of paper for business documents is 8 1/2 by 11 inches. Standard legal documents are 8 1/2 by 14 inches. Executives sometimes have heavier 7-by-10-inch paper on hand (with matching envelopes) for such personal messages as congratulations and recommendations.[1] They may also have a box of correspondence note cards imprinted with their initials and a box of plain folded notes for condolences or for acknowledging formal invitations.

Stationery may vary in color. Of course, white is standard for business purposes, although neutral colors such as gray and ivory are sometimes used. Memos are sometimes produced on pastel-colored paper so that internal correspondence can be more easily distinguished from external, and memos are sometimes typed on various colors of paper for routing to separate departments. Light-colored papers are distinctive and often appropriate, but bright or dark colors make reading difficult and may appear too frivolous.

Customization

For letters to outsiders, U.S. businesses commonly use letterhead stationery printed with the company's name and address, usually at the top of the page but sometimes along the left-hand side or even at the bottom. Other information may be included in the letterhead as well: the company's telephone number, fax number, cable address, product lines, date of establishment, officers and directors, slogan, and symbol (logo). The idea is to give the recipient of the letter pertinent reference data and a better idea of what the company does. Nevertheless, the letterhead should be as simple as possible. Too much information gives the page a cluttered look, cuts into the space needed for the letter, and may become outdated before the supply of letterhead has been used. If you correspond frequently with people in foreign countries, be sure your letterhead is intelligible to foreigners, and make sure it includes the name of your country as well as your cable, telex, or fax information.

In the United States, company letterhead is always used for the first page of a letter. Successive pages are typed on plain sheets of paper that match the letterhead in color and quality or on specially printed second-page letterhead bearing only the company's name. Other countries have other conventions. For example, Latin American companies use a cover page with their seal printed in the center.

Many companies also design and print standardized forms for memos and for reports that are written frequently and always require the same types of information (such as sales reports and expense reports). These forms may be printed in sets for use with carbon paper or in carbonless copy sets that produce multiple copies automatically with the original. More and more, organizations are using computers to generate their standardized forms.

Appearance

Most business documents are produced using either a typewriter or a letter-quality (not a dot matrix) printer. Some short informal memos are handwritten, and it's appropriate to handwrite a note of condolence to a close business associate. Of course, the envelope is handwritten or typed to match the document. However, even a letter on the best-quality paper with the best-designed letterhead may look unprofessional if it's poorly produced.

Companies in the United States make sure that documents (especially external ones) are centered on the page, with margins of at least an inch all around (unlike documents produced in Latin America, which use much wider margins and thus look much longer). Using word-processing or desktop publishing software, you can achieve this balanced appearance simply by defining the format parameters. If you're using a typewriter, such balance can be achieved either by establishing a standard line length or by establishing a "picture frame."

The most common line length is about 6 inches. Lines aren't usually right-hand justified because the resulting text can be hard to read without proportional spacing and the document generally looks too much like a form letter. Varying line length looks more personal and interesting. If the typewriter printer has larger, pica type, each line will have 60 characters; if smaller, elite type is used, each line will have 72 characters. Sometimes a guide sheet, with the margins and the center point marked in dark ink, is used as a backing when producing a page on a typewriter. The number of lines between elements of the document (such as between the date line and inside address in a letter) can be adjusted to ensure that a short document fills the page vertically or that a longer document extends to at least three lines of body on the last page.

Another important aspect of a professional-looking document is the proper spacing after punctuation. For example, U.S. conventions include (1) leaving one space after commas and semicolons and (2) leaving two spaces after periods at the ends of sentences and after colons (unless your typeface is proportional, requiring only one space). Each letter in a person's initials is followed by a period and a single space. Abbreviations for organizations, such as P.T.A., may or may not have periods, but they never have internal spaces. Dashes are typed as two hyphens with no space before, between, or after. Other details of this sort are provided in your company's style book and in most secretarial handbooks.

Finally, messy corrections are dreadfully obvious and unacceptable in business documents. Be sure that any letter, report, or memo requiring a lot of corrections is retyped or reprinted. Self-correcting typewriters and word-processing software can produce correction-free documents at the push of a button.

LETTERS

For a long time, letters have begun with some sort of phrase in greeting and have ended with some polite expression before the writer's signature. In fact, books printed in the sixteenth century prescribed letter formats for writers to follow.

Styles have changed some since then, but all business letters still have certain elements in common. Several of these elements appear in every letter; others appear only when desirable or appropriate. In addition, these letter parts are usually arranged in one of three basic formats.

Standard Letter Parts

All business letters typically include seven elements, in the following order: (1) heading, (2) date, (3) inside address, (4) salutation, (5) body, (6) complimentary close, and (7) sig-

nature block. The letter in Figure A.1 shows the placement of these standard letter parts. The writer of this business letter had no letterhead available.

Heading

Letterhead (the usual heading) shows the organization's name, full address, and (almost always) telephone number. Executive letterhead also bears the name of an individual within the organization. If letterhead stationery is not available, the heading consists of a return address (but not a name) starting 13 lines from the top of the page, which leaves 2

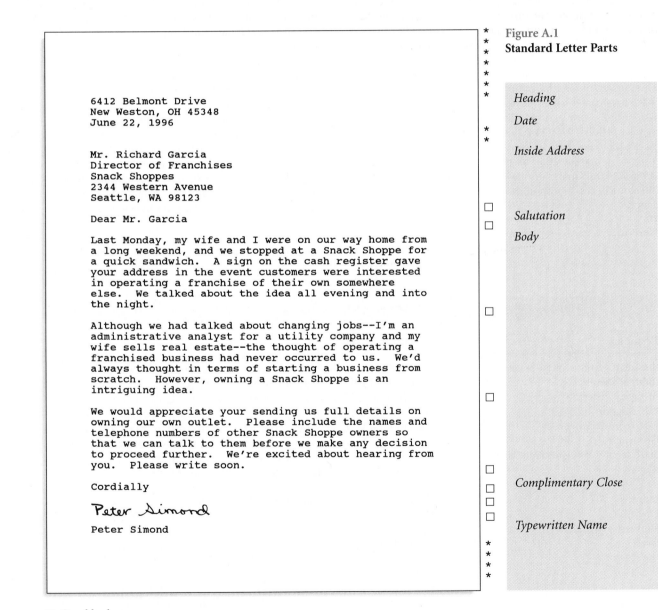

Figure A.1
Standard Letter Parts

```
6412 Belmont Drive
New Weston, OH 45348
June 22, 1996


Mr. Richard Garcia
Director of Franchises
Snack Shoppes
2344 Western Avenue
Seattle, WA 98123

Dear Mr. Garcia

Last Monday, my wife and I were on our way home from
a long weekend, and we stopped at a Snack Shoppe for
a quick sandwich.  A sign on the cash register gave
your address in the event customers were interested
in operating a franchise of their own somewhere
else.  We talked about the idea all evening and into
the night.

Although we had talked about changing jobs--I'm an
administrative analyst for a utility company and my
wife sells real estate--the thought of operating a
franchised business had never occurred to us.  We'd
always thought in terms of starting a business from
scratch.  However, owning a Snack Shoppe is an
intriguing idea.

We would appreciate your sending us full details on
owning our own outlet.  Please include the names and
telephone numbers of other Snack Shoppe owners so
that we can talk to them before we make any decision
to proceed further.  We're excited about hearing from
you.  Please write soon.

Cordially

Peter Simond

Peter Simond
```

Heading

Date

Inside Address

Salutation

Body

Complimentary Close

Typewritten Name

□ *One blank space*
Variable spacing, depending on length of the letter, except for the top margin, which should be 2 inches

inches between the return address and the top of the page. It is also acceptable to start the return address directly below the signature block.

Date

If you're using letterhead, place the date at least one blank line beneath the lowest part of the letterhead. Without letterhead, place the date 13 lines from the top, leaving a 2-inch margin. Spacing between the date and the inside address varies according to the length of the letter.

The standard method of writing the date in the United States uses the full name of the month (no abbreviations), followed by the day (in numerals, without *st, rd,* or *th*), a comma, and then the year: July 14, 1995 (7/14/95). The U.S. government and some U.S. industries place the day (in numerals) first, followed by the month (unabbreviated), followed by the year—with no comma: 14 July 1995 (14/7/95). This convention is similar to the one used in Europe, except that European convention replaces the U.S. solidus (the diagonal line) with periods when the date appears all in numerals: 14 July 1995 (14.7.1995). The international standard places the year first, followed by the month and the day, using commas in the all-numeral form: 1995 July 14 (1995,7,14). To maintain the utmost clarity, always spell out the name of the month in dates for international correspondence.[2]

When communicating internationally, you may also experience some confusion over time. Some companies in the United States refer to morning (A.M.) and afternoon (P.M.), dividing a 24-hour day into 12-hour blocks so that they refer to four o'clock in the morning (4:00 A.M.) or four o'clock in the afternoon (4:00 P.M.). The U.S. military and European companies refer to one 24-hour period, so that 0400 hours (4:00 A.M.) is always in the morning and 1600 hours (4:00 P.M.) is always in the afternoon.[3] Make sure your references to time are as clear as possible, and be sure you clearly understand your audience's time references.

Inside Address

The inside address identifies the recipient of the letter. For U.S. correspondence, type it one or more lines below the date, depending on how long the letter is. Precede the addressee's name with a courtesy title, such as *Dr., Mr.,* or *Ms.* (the accepted courtesy title for women in business—although a woman known to prefer the title *Miss* or *Mrs.* is always accommodated). When unable to find out whether the recipient is a man or a woman, don't use a courtesy title at all. Spell out any other titles, such as *Professor* or *General* (see Table A.1 for the proper forms of address for dignitaries). The person's organizational title, such as *Director,* may be included on this first line (if it is short) or on the line below; the name of a department may follow. If the name of a specific person

---

Table A.1 **FORMS OF ADDRESS FOR DIGNITARIES**

Personage	Name in Address	Salutation
President of the United States	The President	Dear Mr. or Madam President
Cabinet member	The Honorable [first and last name]	Dear Mr. or Madam Secretary
Attorney general	The Honorable [first and last name]	Dear Mr. or Madam Attorney General
U.S. senator	The Honorable [first and last name]	Dear Senator [last name]
U.S. representative	The Honorable [first and last name]	Dear Mr. or Ms. [last name]
Governor	The Honorable [first and last name]	Dear Governor [last name]
State senator or representative	The Honorable [first and last name]	Dear Mr. or Ms. [last name]
Mayor	The Honorable [first and last name]	Dear Mayor [last name] or Dear Mr. or Madam Mayor
Judge	The Honorable [first and last name]	Dear Judge [last name]
Lawyer	Mr. or Ms. [first and last name]	Dear Mr. or Ms. [last name]
University president	Dr. [first and last name], President	Dear Dr. [last name]
Dean	Dr. [first and last name], Dean of [school or college]	Dear Dr. [last name]
Professor	Professor [first and last name]	Dear Professor [last name]
Rabbi	Rabbi [first and last name]	Dear Rabbi [last name]
Protestant clergy	The Reverend [first and last name]	Dear Dr., Mr., or Ms. [last name]
Roman Catholic priest	The Reverend Father [first and last name]	Reverend Father or Dear Father [last name]
Roman Catholic nun	Sister [name]	Dear Sister

is unavailable, you may address the letter to the department or to a specific position within the department.

This example shows all the information that may be included in the inside address and its proper order for U.S. correspondence:

```
Ms. Linda Coolidge, Vice President
Corporate Planning Department
Midwest Airlines
Kowalski Building, Suite 21-A
7279 Bristol Avenue
Toledo, OH 43617
```

Canadian addresses are similar, except that the name of the province is usually spelled out:

```
Dr. H. C. Armstrong
Research and Development
Commonwealth Mining Consortium
The Chelton Building, Suite 301
585 Second Street SW
Calgary, Alberta T2P 2P5
```

When addressing correspondence for other countries, follow the format and information that appear in the company's letterhead:[4]

H. R. Veith, Director	Addressee
Eisfieren Glaswerk	Company name
Blaubach 13	Street address
Postfach 10 80 07	Post office box
D-5000 Köln 1	District, city
Germany	Country

Be sure to get organizational titles right when addressing foreign correspondence. Unfortunately, job designations vary around the world. In England, for example, a managing director is often what U.S. companies call their chief executive officer or president, and a British deputy is the equivalent of a vice president. In France responsibilities are assigned to individuals without regard to title or organizational structure, and in China the title *project manager* has meaning, but the title *sales manager* may not. To make matters worse, businesspeople in some countries sign correspondence without their names typed below. In Germany, for example, the belief is that employees represent the company, so it's inappropriate to emphasize personal names.[5]

Salutation

The salutation agrees with the first line of the inside address. If the first line is a person's name (*Mary Jones*), the salutation is *Dear Ms. Jones*. If at all possible, use the person's name in the salutation of your letter. Base the formality of the salutation on your relationship with the addressee. If in conversation you would say "Mary," your letter's salutation should be *Dear Mary* followed by a colon. Letters to people you don't know well enough to address personally include the courtesy title and last name, followed by a colon. Presuming to write

Dear Lewis instead of *Dear Professor Chang* demonstrates a disrespectful familiarity that a stranger will probably resent. If the first line of the inside address has no courtesy title, include none in the salutation (*Dear Pat Brown* or *Dear V. S. Smith*). If the first line is a position title (*Director of Human Resources*), then use *Dear Director*. Finally, if the first line is plural (*Production Department* or *The Worthington Company, Inc.*), then use *Ladies and Gentlemen*.

In the United States some letter writers use a salutopening on the salutation line. A salutopening omits *Dear* but includes the first few words of the opening paragraph along with the recipient's name. After this line the sentence continues a double space below as part of the body of the letter, as in these examples:

Thank you, Mr. Brown,	Salutopening
for your prompt payment of your bill.	Body
Congratulations, Ms. Lake!	Salutopening
Your promotion is well deserved.	Body

Don't overlook an especially important point with personalized salutations: Whether they're informal or formal, make sure names are spelled right. A misspelled name is glaring evidence of carelessness, and it belies the personal interest you're trying to express.

Body

The body of the letter is your message. Almost all letters are typed single-spaced, with double spacing (one blank line) before and after the salutation or salutopening, between paragraphs, and before the complimentary close. The body may include indented lists, entire paragraphs indented for emphasis, and even subheadings. If so, all similar elements should be treated in the same way. Your department or company may select a format to use for all letters.

Complimentary Close

The complimentary close is typed on the second line below the body of the letter. A number of alternatives for wording are available, but currently the trend seems to be toward using one-word closes, such as *Sincerely* and *Cordially*. In any case the complimentary close reflects the relationship between you and the person(s) you're writing to.

Avoid closes that are too cute, such as *Yours for bigger profits*. If your audience doesn't know you well, your sense of humor may be misunderstood.

Signature Block

After leaving three blank lines for a written signature below the complimentary close, the sender's name is typed (unless it appears in the letterhead). The person's title may appear on the same line as the name or on the line below:

Cordially,

Raymond Dunnigan
Director of Human Resources

Your letterhead indicates that you're representing your company. However, if your letter is typed on plain paper or runs to a second page, you may want to emphasize that you're speaking legally for the company. The accepted way of doing that is to type the company's name in capital letters a double space below the complimentary close and then type the sender's name and title four lines below that:

Sincerely,

WENTWORTH INDUSTRIES

(Mrs.) Helen B. Taylor
President

If the writer's name could be taken for either a man's or a woman's, a courtesy title indicating gender should be included in the typewritten name, with or without parentheses. Also, women who prefer a particular courtesy title should include it.

Additional Letter Parts

Letters vary greatly in subject matter and thus in the identifying information they need and the format they adopt. The following elements may be used in any combination, depending on the requirements of the particular letter, but generally in this order:

1. Addressee notation
2. Attention line
3. Subject line
4. Second-page heading
5. Company name
6. Reference initials
7. Enclosure notation
8. Copy notation
9. Mailing notation
10. Postscript

The letter in Figure A.2 shows how these additional parts should be arranged.

Figure A.2
Additional Letter Parts

Addressee Notation

Attention Line

Subject Line

Worldwide Talent Agency
2314 Hollywood Boulevard
Hollywood, California 90021-1654
(213) 695-2864

November 18, 1996

CONFIDENTIAL

Attention Scheduling Coordinator
Peachtree Lecture Bureau
2920 S. Bennett Parkway
Albany, GA 31702-1324

Ladies and Gentlemen:

Subject: Contract No. 27-83176

I have put together some additional information for
you to consider. Please note especially the dates

□ *One blank space*
Variable spacing, depending on length of the letter

Addressee Notation

Letters that have a restricted readership or that must be handled in a special way should include such addressee notations as *Personal, Confidential,* or *Please Forward.* This sort of notation appears two lines above the inside address in capital letters.

Attention Line

Although an attention line is not commonly used today, you may find it useful if you know only the last name of the person you're writing to. An attention line can also be used to direct a letter to a position title or department. An attention line may take any of the following forms or variants of them: *Attention Dr. McHenry, Attention Director of Marketing,* or *Attention Marketing Department.* When you use an attention line, make sure to place it on the first line of the inside address.[6]

Subject Line

The subject line lets the recipient know at a glance what the letter is about; it also indicates where to file the letter for future reference. It's usually typed below the salutation—against the left-hand margin, indented the same distance as the paragraphs in the body of the letter, or centered on the

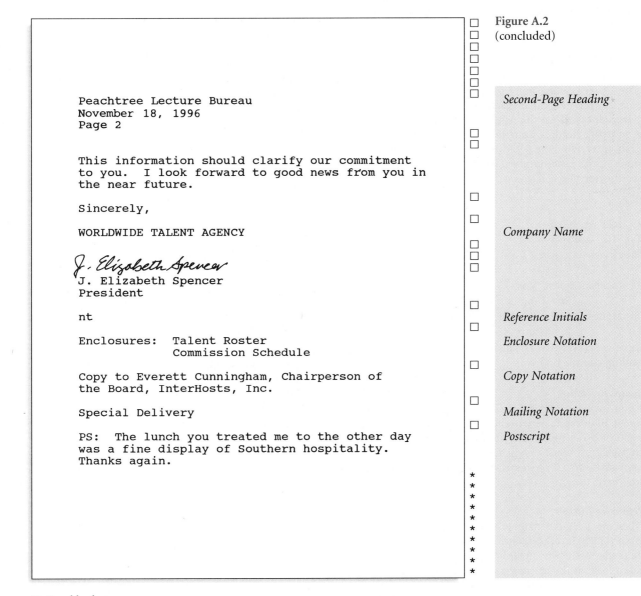

Figure A.2
(concluded)

Second-Page Heading

Peachtree Lecture Bureau
November 18, 1996
Page 2

This information should clarify our commitment to you. I look forward to good news from you in the near future.

Sincerely,

WORLDWIDE TALENT AGENCY

J. Elizabeth Spencer
J. Elizabeth Spencer
President

nt — *Reference Initials*

Enclosures: Talent Roster
             Commission Schedule — *Enclosure Notation*

Copy to Everett Cunningham, Chairperson of
the Board, InterHosts, Inc. — *Copy Notation*

Special Delivery — *Mailing Notation*

PS: The lunch you treated me to the other day
was a fine display of Southern hospitality.
Thanks again. — *Postscript*

Company Name

□ *One blank space*
**Variable spacing, depending on length of the letter*

line. Sometimes the subject line is typed above the salutation or at the very top of the page. The subject line may take a variety of forms, including the following:

Subject: RainMaster Sprinklers

About your February 2, 1995, order

FALL 1995 SALES MEETING

Reference Order No. 27920

Sometimes the subject line (or the last line of a long subject "line") is underscored. Some writers omit the word *Subject* and put the other information all in capitals to distinguish it from the other letter parts.

Second-Page Heading

If the letter is long and an additional page is required, use a second-page heading. Some companies have second-page letterhead, with the company name and address on one line and in smaller type than the regular letterhead. In any case, the second-page heading bears the name of the person or organization receiving the letter (as in the first line of the inside address), the page number, and the date of the letter; you can also include a reference number. All the following are acceptable:

Ms. Melissa Baker
May 10, 1995
Page 2

Ms. Melissa Baker, May 10, 1995, Page 2

Ms. Melissa Baker -2- May 10, 1995

Triple-space (leave two blank lines) between the second-page heading and the body.

Company Name

If you include the company's name in the signature block, type it all in capital letters a double space below the complimentary close. You usually include the company's name in the signature block only when the writer is serving as the company's official spokesperson or when letterhead has not been used.

Reference Initials

When one person dictates or writes a letter and another person produces it on computer or typewriter, reference initials are used to show who helped prepare the letter. Reference initials appear at the left margin and are typed a double space below the last line of the signature block. When the writer's name has been typed in the signature block, only the preparer's initials are necessary. If only the department name

appears in the signature block, both sets of initials should appear, usually in one of the following forms:

RSR/sm

RSR:sm

RSR:SM

The first set of initials is the writer's; the second set is the typist's.

Sometimes the writer and the signer of a letter are different people. In that case, at least the file copy of a letter should bear both their initials as well as those of the typist: JFS/RSR/sm (signer, writer, typist).

Enclosure Notation

Enclosure notations also appear at the bottom of a letter, one or two lines below the reference initials. Some common forms:

Enclosure

Enclosures (2)

Enclosures: Résumé
             Photograph

Attachment

Copy Notation

Copy notations may follow reference initials or enclosure notations. They indicate who's receiving carbon copies or photocopies (*cc* or *pc* or just *c*) of the letter, preferably in order of rank or in alphabetical order. Among the forms used:

c: David Wentworth

pc: Martha Littlefield

Copy to Hans Vogel

Addresses may be included, along with notations about any enclosures being sent with the copies.

On occasion, the sending of copies is not done to benefit the person who receives the original letter. In that case, place the notation *bc, bcc,* or *bpc* (for blind copy, blind carbon copy, or blind photocopy) with the name, where the copy notation would appear—but only on the copy, not on the original.

Mailing Notation

You may place a mailing notation (such as *Special Delivery* or *Registered Mail*) after reference initials, enclosure notations, and copy notations at the bottom of the letter; or you may place it at the top of the letter, either above the inside address on the left-hand side or just below the date on the right-hand side. For greater visibility, mailing notations may be typed in capital letters.

Postscript

Letters may also bear postscripts: afterthoughts to the letter, messages that require emphasis, or personal notes. The postscript is usually the last thing on any letter and may be preceded by *P.S., PS., PS:*, or nothing at all. A second afterthought would be designated *P.P.S.*, meaning "post postscript."

Postscripts usually indicate poor planning, so generally avoid them. However, they're commonly used in sales letters, not as an afterthought but as a punch line to remind the reader of a benefit for taking advantage of the offer.

Letter Formats

Although the basic letter parts have remained the same for centuries, ways of arranging them do change. Sometimes a company adopts a certain format as its policy; sometimes the individual letter writer or secretary is allowed to choose the format most appropriate for a given letter or to settle on a personal preference. In the United States, three major letter formats are commonly used:

- *Block format.* Each letter part begins at the left margin. The main advantage of this format is that letters can be typed quickly and efficiently (see Figure A.3).

Figure A.3
Block Letter Format

Mattel Toys

Mattel, Inc.
5150 Rosecrans Avenue
Hawthorne, CA 90250-6692
Telephone 213 978 5150
TELEX 188155 or 188170

September 5, 1996

Mr. Clifford Hanson
General Manager
The Toy Trunk
356 Emerald Drive
Lexington, KY 40500

Dear Mr. Hanson:

You should receive your shipment of Barbie dolls and accessories within two weeks, just in time for the holiday shopping season. The merchandise is being shipped by United Parcel Service. As the enclosed invoice indicates, the amount due is $352.32.

When preparing to ship your order, I noticed that this is your fifteenth year as a Mattel customer. During that period, you have sold over 3,750 Barbie dolls! We sincerely appreciate the part you have played in marketing our toys to the public.

Your customers should be particularly excited about the new Barbie vacation outfits that you have ordered. Our winter advertising campaign will portray Barbie trekking through the jungle in her safari suit, climbing mountains in her down parka, and snorkeling off a coral reef in her skin diving gear.

Next month, you'll be receiving our spring catalog. Notice the new series of action figures that will tie in with a TV cartoon featuring King Arthur and the Knights of the Round Table. As a special introductory incentive, you can receive a 15 percent discount on all items in this line until the end of January. Please send your order soon.

Sincerely,

Rhonda Rogers
Ms. Rhonda Rogers
Customer Service Representative

jhb

Enclosure

□ *One blank space*
Variable spacing, depending on length of the letter

Figure A.4
Modified Block Letter
Format

JCPenney

*
*

June 3, 1996

□

Ms. Clara Simpson, President
League of Women Voters of Miami
P.O. Box 112
Miami, FL 33152

□

Dear Ms. Simpson:

Thank you for inviting us to participate in the League
of Women Voters' Spring Fashion Show. We will be delighted to provide some clothing samples for the May 15
event.

□

You indicated that you would like us to supply about 12
outfits from our designer collection, all in a size 6. We
can certainly accommodate your request. To give your audience a representative overview of our merchandise, I suggest we provide the following: three tailored daytime
dresses or suits, two dressy dresses, one formal ball gown,
four casual weekend outfits, and two active sports outfits.

□

Please give me a call to schedule a "shopping" trip for you
and your committee members. Together, I'm sure we can find
exactly what you need to stage a well-rounded show. In the
meantime, you might enjoy looking through the enclosed
catalog. It will introduce you to some of the options.

Sincerely,

□
□
□
□

Vera O'Donnell
(Mrs.) Vera O'Donnell
Director, Public Relations

□
□

bcg

□

Enclosure

*
*
*
*
*

J. C. Penney Company, Inc., 6501 Legacy Drive, Plano, Texas 75024

□ *One blank space*
*Variable spacing, depending on length of the letter

- *Modified block format.* Same as block format, except the date, complimentary close, and signature block start near the center of the page (see Figure A.4). The modified block format does permit indentions as an option. This format mixes typing speed with traditional placement of some letter parts. It also looks more balanced on the page than the block format does.
- *Simplified format.* Instead of using a salutation, this format often works the audience's name into the first line or two of the body and often includes a subject line in capital letters (see Figure A.5). It also omits the complimentary close—so you sign your name between the body of the let-

ter and the typewritten name (customarily typed in all capital letters). The advantages include convenience when you don't know your audience's name. However, some people object to this format because it seems mechanical and impersonal (a drawback that may be overcome with a warm writing style). In this format, the elimination of certain letter parts changes some of the spacing between the lines.

These formats differ in the way paragraphs are indented, in the way letter parts are placed, and in some punctuation. However, the elements are always separated by at least one blank line, and the typewritten name is always separated from

Figure A.5
Simplified Letter Format

```
BLACK&DECKER®
701 East Joppa Road
Towson, Maryland 21286
410-716-3900
Telex 87-930
```

```
October 3, 1996


Mr. Arnold Bremer
Sunbelt Appliances
8970 Commerce Avenue
Hot Springs, AR 71901

NEW PRODUCT INFORMATION


Thank you, Mr. Bremer, for your recent inquiry about Black
& Decker's product line.  We appreciate your enthusiasm for
Black & Decker products, and we are confident that your
customers will enjoy the improved performance of the new
product line.

I have enclosed a package of information for your review,
including product specifications, dealer prices, and an
order form.  The package also contains reprints of Black &
Decker product reviews from leading technical magazines
and a comparison sheet showing how our products measure up
against competing brands.

Please call with any questions you may have about shipping
or payment arrangements.

        Wayne Sutherland
WAYNE SUTHERLAND
Western Region Sales Administrator

hm

Enclosures
```

□ *One blank space*
Variable spacing, depending on length of the letter

the line above by at least three blank lines to allow space for a signature. If paragraphs are indented, the indention is normally five spaces.

The most common formats for intercultural business letters are the block style and the modified block style. Use either the U.S. or the European format for dates. For the salutation, use *Dear (Title/Last name)*. Close the letter with *Sincerely* or *Cordially,* and sign it personally.

In addition to these three letter formats, letters may also be classified according to the style of punctuation they use. *Standard,* or *mixed, punctuation* uses a colon after the salutation (a comma if the letter is social or personal) and a comma after the complimentary close. *Open punctuation* uses no colon or comma after the salutation or the complimentary close. Either style of punctuation may be used with block or modified block letter formats. Because the simplified letter format has no salutation or complimentary close, the style of punctuation is irrelevant.

E NVELOPES

The quality of the envelope is just as important for first impressions as the quality of the stationery. In fact, letterhead

Figure A.6
Prescribed
Envelope Format

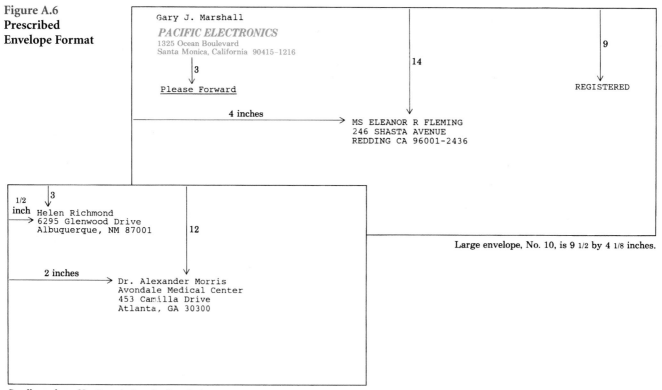

Large envelope, No. 10, is 9 1/2 by 4 1/8 inches.

Small envelope, No. 6 3/4, is 6 1/2 by 3 5/8 inches.

and envelopes should be of the same paper stock, have the same color ink, and be imprinted with the same address and logo. Most envelopes used by U.S. businesses are No. 10 envelopes (9 1/2 inches long), which are sized to contain an 8 1/2-by-11-inch piece of paper folded in thirds. Some occasions call for a smaller, No. 6 3/4, envelope or for envelopes proportioned to fit special stationery. Figure A.6 shows the two most common sizes.

Addressing the Envelope

No matter what size the envelope, the address is always single-spaced and typed in block form—that is, with all lines aligned on the left. The address on the envelope is in the same style as the inside address and presents the same information. The order to follow is from the smallest division to the largest:

1. Name and title of recipient
2. Name of department or subgroup
3. Name of organization
4. Name of building
5. Street address and suite number, or post office box number
6. City, state or province, and ZIP code or postal code
7. Name of country (if the letter is being sent abroad)

Because the U.S. Postal Service uses optical scanners to sort mail, envelopes for quantity mailings, in particular, should be addressed in the prescribed format. As in the mailing address on the No. 10 envelope in Figure A.6, everything is typed in capital letters, no punctuation is included, and all mailing instructions of interest to the post office are placed above the address area. Canada Post requires a similar format, except that only the city is typed all in capitals and the postal code is placed on the line below the name of the city. The post office scanners read addresses from the bottom up, so if a letter is to be sent to a post office box rather than a street address, the street address should appear on the line above the box number. Figure A.6 also shows the proper spacing for addresses and return addresses.

The U.S. Postal Service and the Canada Post Corporation have published lists of two-letter mailing abbreviations for states, provinces, and territories (see Table A.2), to be used without periods or commas. Nevertheless, some executives prefer that state and province names be typed out in full and that a comma be used to separate the city and state or province names. Thus the use of a comma between the name of the city and the state or province name is an unresolved issue. Most commonly, the comma is included; sometimes, however, the comma is eliminated to conform with post office standards.

Quantity mailings follow post office requirements. For letters that aren't mailed in quantity, a reasonable compromise is to use traditional punctuation and uppercase and lowercase letters for names and street addresses but two-letter state or province abbreviations, as shown here:

Mr. Kevin Kennedy
2107 E. Packer Drive
Amarillo, TX 79108

For all out-of-office correspondence use ZIP codes and postal codes, assigned to speed mail delivery. The U.S. Postal Service has divided the United States and its territories into ten zones, each represented by a digit from 0 to 9; this digit comes first in the ZIP code. The second and third digits represent smaller geographic areas within a state, and the last two digits identify a "local delivery area." Canadian postal codes are alphanumeric, with a three-character "area code" and a three-character "local code" separated by a single space (K2P 5A5). ZIP codes and postal codes should be separated from state and province names by one space. As an alternative, a Canadian Postal Code may be put on the bottom line of the address all by itself.

The U.S. Postal Service has introduced ZIP + 4 codes, which add a hyphen and four more numbers to the standard ZIP codes. The first two of the new numbers may identify an area as small as a single large building, and the last two digits may identify one floor in a large building or even a specific department of an organization. The ZIP + 4 codes are especially useful for business correspondence. The Canada Post Corporation achieves the same result with special postal codes assigned to buildings and organizations that receive a large volume of mail.

Table A.2 TWO-LETTER MAILING ABBREVIATIONS FOR THE UNITED STATES AND CANADA

State/Territory/Province	Abbreviation	State/Territory/Province	Abbreviation	State/Territory/Province	Abbreviation
UNITED STATES					
Alabama	AL	Michigan	MI	Utah	UT
Alaska	AK	Minnesota	MN	Vermont	VT
Arizona	AZ	Mississippi	MS	Virginia	VA
Arkansas	AR	Missouri	MO	Virgin Islands	VI
American Samoa	AS	Montana	MT	Washington	WA
California	CA	Nebraska	NE	West Virginia	WV
Canal Zone	CZ	Nevada	NV	Wisconsin	WI
Colorado	CO	New Hampshire	NH	Wyoming	WY
Connecticut	CT	New Jersey	NJ		
Delaware	DE	New Mexico	NM		
District of Columbia	DC	New York	NY		
Florida	FL	North Carolina	NC	**CANADA**	
Georgia	GA	North Dakota	ND	Alberta	AB
Guam	GU	Northern Mariana Islands	CM	British Columbia	BC
Hawaii	HI	Ohio	OH	Labrador	LB
Idaho	ID	Oklahoma	OK	Manitoba	MB
Illinois	IL	Oregon	OR	New Brunswick	NB
Indiana	IN	Pennsylvania	PA	Newfoundland	NF
Iowa	IA	Puerto Rico	PR	Northwest Territories	NT
Kansas	KS	Rhode Island	RI	Nova Scotia	NS
Kentucky	KY	South Carolina	SC	Ontario	ON
Louisiana	LA	South Dakota	SD	Prince Edward Island	PE
Maine	ME	Tennessee	TN	Quebec	PQ
Maryland	MD	Trust Territories	TT	Saskatchewan	SK
Massachusetts	MA	Texas	TX	Yukon Territory	YT

Figure A.7
Letter Folds for Standard-Size Letterhead

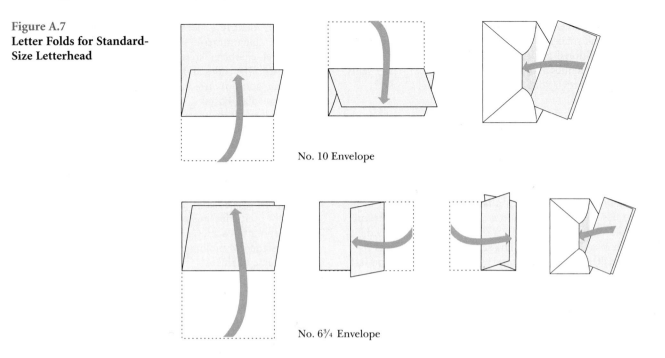

No. 10 Envelope

No. 6¾ Envelope

Folding to Fit

Trivial as it may seem, the way a letter is folded contributes to the recipient's overall impression of your organization's professionalism. When sending a standard-size piece of paper in a No. 10 envelope, fold it in thirds, with the bottom folded up first and the top folded down over it (see Figure A.7); the open end should be at the top of the envelope and facing out. Fit smaller stationery neatly into the appropriate envelope simply by folding it in half or in thirds. When sending a standard-size letterhead in a No. 6 3/4 envelope, fold it in half from top to bottom and then in thirds from side to side.

NTERNATIONAL MAIL

When sending mail internationally, remember that postal service differs from country to country. For example, street addresses are uncommon in India, and the mail there is unreliable.[7] It's usually a good idea to send international correspondence by airmail and to ask that responses be sent that way as well. Also, remember to check the postage; rates for sending mail to most other countries aren't the same as the rates for sending mail within your own country.

Three main categories of international mail are the following:

- *LC mail.* An abbreviation of the French *Lettres et Cartes* ("letters and cards"), this category consists of letters, letter packages, aerograms, and postcards.

- *AO mail.* An abbreviation of the French *Autres Objets* ("other articles"), this category includes regular printed matter, books and sheet music, matter for the blind, small packets, and publishers' periodicals (second class).

- *CP mail.* An abbreviation of the French *Colis Postaux* ("parcel post"), this category resembles fourth-class mail, including packages of merchandise or any other articles not required to be mailed at letter postage rates.

The U.S. Postal Service also offers Express Mail International Service (EMS), a high-speed mail service to many countries; International Priority Airmail (IPA), an international service that's as fast as or faster than regular airmail service; International Surface Air Lift (ISAL), a service providing quicker delivery and lower cost for all types of printed matter; Bulk Letter Service/Canada, an economical airmail service for bulk mailings of letters to Canada weighing 1 ounce or less; VALUEPOST/CANADA, a reduced postage rate for bulk mailings of certain types of printed matter; International Electronic Post (INTELPOST), a service offering same- or next-day delivery of fax documents; International Postal Money Orders, a service for transferring funds to other countries; and several optional services. To prepare your mail for international delivery, follow the instructions in U.S. Postal Service Publication 51, *International Postal Rates and Fees.*

M EMOS

Interoffice memos aren't distributed outside the organization, so they may not need the best-quality paper. However, they still convey important information, so clarity, careful arrangement, and neatness are important. As with the guidelines for letters, those for formatting memos help recipients understand at a glance what they've received and from whom.

Many organizations have memo forms printed, with labeled spaces for the recipient's name (or sometimes a checklist of all departments in an organization or all persons in a department), the sender's name, the date, and the subject (see Figure A.8). If such forms don't exist, you can use plain paper or sometimes letterhead.

When using plain paper or letterhead, include a title such as *MEMO* or *INTEROFFICE CORRESPONDENCE* (all in capitals) centered at the top of the page or aligned with the left margin. Also include the words *To, From, Date,* and *Subject*—followed by the appropriate information—at the top with a blank line after each one, as shown here:

MEMO

TO:

FROM:

DATE:

SUBJECT:

Sometimes the heading is organized like this:

MEMO

TO: DATE:

FROM: SUBJECT:

You can arrange these four pieces of information in almost any order. The date is sometimes typed without the heading *Date*. The subject may also be presented without a heading,

but type it in capital letters so that it stands out clearly. You may also include a file or reference number, introduced by the word *File*.

If you send a memo to a long list of people, include in the *To* position the notation *See distribution list* or *See below.* Then list the names at the end of the memo. Arranging such a list alphabetically is usually the most diplomatic course, although high-ranking officials may deserve more prominent placement. You can also address memos to groups of people—*All Sales Representatives, Production Group, Assistant Vice Presidents.*

You don't need to use courtesy titles anywhere in a memo; in fact, first initials and last names, first names, or even initials alone are often sufficient. As a general rule, however, use a courtesy title if you would use one in face-to-face encounters with the person.

The subject line of a memo helps busy colleagues find out quickly what your memo is about. Although the subject "line" may overflow onto a second line, it's most helpful when it's short (but still informative).

Start the body of the memo on the second or third line below the heading. Like the body of a letter, it's usually single-spaced. Separate paragraphs with blank lines. Indenting them is optional. Handle lists, important passages, and subheadings as you do in letters. If the memo is very short, you may double-space it.

If the memo carries over to a second page, head the second page just as you would head the second page of a letter.

Unlike a letter, a memo doesn't require a complimentary close or a signature, because your name is already prominent at the top. However, you may initial the memo—beside the name typed at the top or at the bottom of the memo—or even sign your name at the bottom, particularly if the memo deals with money or confidential matters. Treat all other elements—reference initials, enclosure notations, and copy notations—as you would in a letter.

Memos may be delivered by hand, by the post office (when the recipient doesn't work at the same location as the memo writer), or through interoffice mail. Interoffice mail may require the use of special reusable envelopes that have spaces for the recipient's name and department or room number; the name of the previous recipient is simply crossed out. If a regular envelope is used, the words *Interoffice Mail* are typed where the stamp normally goes so that it won't accidentally be stamped and mailed with the rest of the office correspondence.

Informal, routine, or brief reports for distribution within a company are often presented in memo form (see Chapter 12). Don't include such report parts as a table of contents and appendixes, but write the body of the memo report just as carefully as you'd write a formal report.

TIME-SAVING MESSAGES

If there's a way to speed up the communication process, the organization stands to gain. Telephones and electronic mail systems are quick, as are mailgrams, telegrams, faxes, and the like. In addition, organizations have developed special formats to reduce the amount of time spent writing and typing short messages:

▪ *Memo-letters.* Printed with a heading somewhat like a memo's, memo-letters provide a space for an inside address so that the message may be sent outside the company (see Figure A.9). Folded properly, the address shows through a

**Figure A.9
Memo-Letter**

MEMO

TO: Green Ridge Gifts
           1786 Century Road
           Nashua, NH 03060
           USA

FROM: Whiteside Import/Export, Ltd.
           1601 Ronson Drive
           Toronto, Ontario M9W 5Z3
           CANADA

DATE: October 11, 1996

SUBJECT: Order for Royal Dorchester china
           completer sets

MESSAGE:

The six Wellington pattern completer sets that you ordered by telephone October 9 are on their way and should reach your shop by October 18.

The three Mayfield pattern completer sets are coming from the factory, however, and will not arrive here until October 26 or 27. That means you will get them around November 2 or 3.

Do you still want the Mayfield sets? Would you like us to bill you for the Wellington sets only so that you can pay for the Mayfield order separately? Please add your reply below, retain the yellow copy for your records, and send us the white and pink copies.

SIGNED: *Barbara Hutchins*

REPLY: *PLEASE SEND THE MAYFIELD SETS AS SOON AS POSSIBLE. YOU MAY BILL FOR BOTH MAYFIELD AND WELLINGTON SETS*

DATE: *Oct. 15, 1995*

SIGNED: *William L. Smith*

window in the envelope, thereby eliminating the need to address the envelope separately. Memo-letters often include a space for a reply message so that the recipient doesn't have to type a whole new letter in response; carbonless copy sets allow sender and recipient to keep on file a copy of the entire correspondence.

- *Short-note reply technique.* Popular in many organizations, this technique can be used even without a special form. The recipient of a memo (or sometimes a letter) simply handwrites a response on the original document, makes a copy for the files, and sends the annotated original back to the person who wrote it.
- *Letterhead postcards.* Ideal for short, impersonal messages, letterhead postcards are preprinted with a list of responses so that the "writer" merely checks the appropriate response(s) and slips the postcard into the mail. Organizations such as mail-order companies and government agencies frequently use these time-saving devices to communicate with individuals by mail.

The important thing to realize about memo-letters, short-note replies, letterhead postcards, and all other message formats is that they've developed over time to meet the need for clear communication and to speed responses to the needs of customers, suppliers, and associates.

R EPORTS

You can enhance your report's effectiveness by paying attention to its appearance and layout. Follow company guidelines, but remember to be neat and consistent throughout. If it's up to you to decide formatting questions, the following conventions may help you decide how to handle margins, headings, spacing, indention, and page numbers.

Margins

All margins on a report page are at least 1 inch wide. Margins of 1 inch are customary for double-spaced pages, and margins of between $1\frac{1}{4}$ and $1\frac{1}{2}$ inches are customary for single-spaced pages. The top, left, and right margins are usually the same, but the bottom margin can be $1\frac{1}{2}$ times wider. Some special pages also have a wider top margin. Set the top margin as wide as 2 inches for pages that contain major titles: prefatory parts such as the table of contents or the executive summary, supplementary parts such as the reference notes or bibliography, and textual parts such as the first page of the text or the first page of each chapter.

If you're going to bind your report at the left or at the top, add half an inch to the margin on the bound edge (see Figure A.10). Because of the space taken by the binding on left-

Figure A.10
Margins for Formal Reports

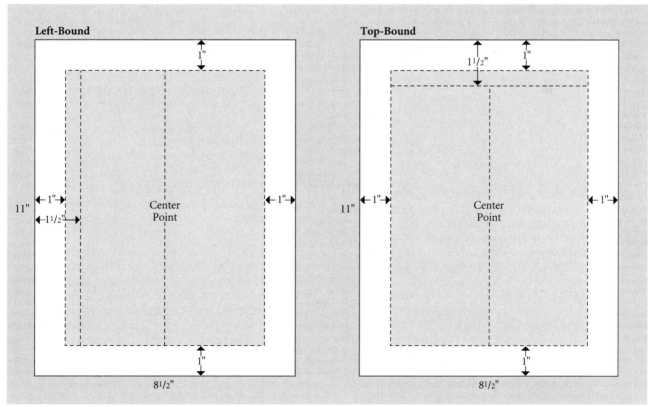

bound reports, make the center point of the typed page a quarter inch to the right of the center of the paper. Be sure that centered headings are centered over the typed portion, not centered on the paper. Other guidelines for formatting a report can be found in the sample in Chapter 14.

Headings

Headings of various levels provide visual clues to a report's organization. Figure 12.7, in Chapter 12, illustrates one good system for showing these levels, but many variations exist. No matter which system you use, be sure to be consistent.

Spacing and Indentions

The spacing and indention of most elements of a report are relatively easy. If your report is double-spaced (perhaps to ease comprehension of technical material), indent all paragraphs five character spaces (or about 1/2 inch). In single-spaced reports, you can block the paragraphs (no indentions), leaving one blank line after each paragraph.

Properly spacing the material on the title page is more complicated. For reports that will be bound on the left, start a quarter inch to the right of center. From that point, backspace once for each two letters in the line so that the line will appear centered once the report is bound.

To correctly place lines of type on the title page, first count the number of lines in each block of copy, including blank lines. Subtract the total from 66 (the total number of lines on an 11-inch page) to get the number of unused lines. To allocate these unused lines equally among the spaces between the blocks of copy, divide the number of unused lines by the number of blank areas (always one more than the number of blocks of copy). The result is the number of blank lines to devote to each section. The title page of the sample report in Chapter 14 shows how this procedure produces a balanced-looking page.

Page Numbers

Remember that every page in the report is counted but that not all pages have numbers shown on them. The first page of the report, normally the title page, is not numbered. All other pages in the prefatory section are numbered with a lowercase roman numeral, beginning with ii and continuing with iii, iv, v, and so on. The unadorned (no dashes, no period) page number is centered at the bottom margin.

Number the first page of the text of the report with the unadorned arabic numeral 1, centered at the bottom margin (double- or triple-spaced below the text). In left-bound reports, number the following pages (including the supplementary parts) consecutively with unadorned arabic numerals (2, 3, and so on), placed at the top right-hand margin (double- or triple-spaced above the text). For top-bound reports and for special pages having 2-inch top margins, center these page numbers at the bottom margin.

MEETING DOCUMENTS

The success of any meeting depends on the preparation of the participants and on the follow-up measures they take to implement decisions or to seek information after the meeting. Meeting documents—agendas and minutes—aid this process by putting the meeting plan and results into permanent, written form. Although small, informal meetings may not require a written agenda, any meeting involving a relatively large number of people or covering a lot of ground will run more smoothly if an agenda is distributed in advance. A written agenda helps participants prepare by telling them what will be discussed, and it helps keep them on track once the meeting begins. The typical agenda format (shown in Figure A.11) may seem stiff and formal, but it helps structure a meeting so that as little time as possible is wasted. It also provides opportunities for discussion, if that's what is called for.

The presentation, a special form of meeting that allows for relatively little group interaction, may also require an agenda or a detailed outline. Special visual aids such as flip charts help attendees grasp the message, and copies of the charts are often provided for future reference.

After a meeting the secretary who attended prepares a set of minutes for distribution to all attendees and to any other interested parties. The minutes are prepared in much the same format as a memo or letter, except for the heading, which takes this form:

MINUTES
PLANNING COMMITTEE MEETING
MONDAY, AUGUST 21, 1995

Present: [All invited attendees who were present are listed here, generally by rank, in alphabetical order, or in some combination.]

Absent: [All invited attendees who were not present are listed here, in similar order.]

The body of the minutes follows the heading and notes the times the meeting started and ended, all major decisions reached at the meeting, all assignments of tasks to meeting participants, and all subjects that were deferred to a later meeting. In addition, the minutes objectively summarize important discussions, noting the names of those who contributed major points. Outlines, subheadings, and lists help organize the minutes, and additional documentation (such as tables or charts submitted by meeting participants) are noted in the minutes and attached.

Figure A.11
Agenda Format

```
                       AGENDA

              PLANNING COMMITTEE MEETING
               TUESDAY, AUGUST 21, 1995
                      10:00 A.M.
               EXECUTIVE CONFERENCE ROOM


         I. Call to Order

        II. Roll Call

       III. Approval of Agenda

        IV. Approval of Minutes from Previous Meeting

         V. Chairperson's Report

        VI. Subcommittee Reports

              A. New Markets

              B. New Products

              C. Finance

       VII. Unfinished Business

      VIII. New Business

              A. Carson & Canfield Data

              B. Reassignments

        IX. Announcements

         X. Adjournment
```

At the end of the minutes, the words *Submitted by* should be added, followed by a couple of blank lines for a signature and then the preparer's typed name and title (if appropriate). If the minutes have been prepared by one person and typed by another, the typist's initials should be added, as in the reference initials on a letter or memo.

An informal meeting may not require minutes. Attendees simply pencil their own notes onto their copies of the agenda. Follow-up is then their responsibility, although the meeting leader may need to remind them through a memo, phone call, or face-to-face talk.

DOCUMENTATION OF REPORT SOURCES

Documenting a report through source notes and a bibliography is too important a task to undertake haphazardly. When you provide information about your sources, the facts and opinions you present gain credibility. By documenting your work, you also give readers the means of checking your findings and pursuing the subject further. Finally, documentation is the accepted way to give credit to the people whose works you have drawn on.

The specific style you use to document your report may vary from the style recommended here. Not only do experts disagree on the "correct" form, but you may also find that your company or organization has adopted a form somewhat different from any suggested by the experts. Don't let this discrepancy confuse you. If your employer specifies a form, use it; the standardized form is easier for colleagues to understand. If the choice of form is left to you, however, adopt a style like one of those described here. Just be consistent within any given report, using the same order, punctuation, and so on from one source note or bibliography entry to the next.

S ECONDARY SOURCES

Chapter 13 describes the difference between primary data and secondary data and tells how to gather both kinds. Most of this appendix describes how the results of secondary research are reported in source notes and bibliographies. (Studies and surveys that you conduct yourself as the basis for a report are usually documented through descriptions of your methods and findings within the text of the report.) Before review-ing documentation formats, consider how to get enough information. Most business research depends on secondary sources, which are traditionally stored in libraries.

A Library's Resources

Today the first hurdle in getting information is to figure out which library to visit or to phone with your query. The *American Library Directory* lists more than 30,000 public, college, university, and special libraries in the United States and 3,000 in Canada. In addition, many companies have their own libraries. However, most libraries harbor the same types of information sources.

Basic References
Once you've decided which library to use, head for the reference section. A librarian with specialized knowledge of general sources of information can direct you to the appropriate dictionaries, encyclopedias, almanacs, atlases, biographical reference books, handbooks, manuals, directories of companies and associations, and perhaps even a collection of corporations' annual reports. In the absence of a knowledgeable reference librarian, consult *Reference Books: A Brief Guide* or *Business Information Sources,* or refer to Figure B.1, which lists the major reference books used by business researchers.

Books and Articles
Both books and articles provide in-depth coverage of specific topics. Although articles are more timely than books, books have a broader focus. A combination of the two often provides the best background for your report.

- *Biography Index:* Indexes biographical data from more than 2,400 periodicals as well as from English-language books

- *Books in Print:* Lists more than 425,000 books in 62,000 subject categories currently available from over 6,000 U.S. publishers. Also indexes books by author and by title.

- *Business Periodicals Index:* Lists articles from about 280 business-related periodicals; companion is *Canadian Business Index.*

- *Current Biography:* Features biographical data about individuals who have achieved fame during the period covered.

- *Directory of Directories:* Indexes several thousand business, industrial, and professional directories.

- *Dun & Bradstreet, Inc., Million Dollar Directory:* Lists more than 120,000 U.S. companies by net worth. Includes names of officers and directors, goods and services, approximate sales, and number of employees.

- *Encyclopedia of Associations:* Indexes thousands of associations by broad subject category, by specific subject, by name of association, and by geographic location.

- *Moody's Manuals:* In a series of publications for specific industries—such as banks and financial institutions, public utilities, and international companies—lists financial data of the sort found in corporate annual reports.

- *Reader's Guide to Periodical Literature:* Indexes articles in some 190 popular periodicals by subject and author.

- *Standard & Poor's Register of Corporations:* Indexes more than 37,000 U.S., Canadian, and major international corporations. Lists officers, products, sales volume, and number of employees.

- *Standard Periodical Directory:* Describes more than 66,000 U.S. and Canadian periodicals.

- *Statistical Abstract of the United States:* Presents U.S. economic, social, political, and industrial statistics.

- *Survey of Current Business:* Features national business statistics on construction, real estate, employment and earnings, finance, foreign trade, transportation, communication, and other key topics.

- *Thomas Register of American Manufacturers:* Presents information on thousands of U.S. manufacturers, indexed by company name and product.

- *U.S. Government Publications: Monthly Catalog:* Lists titles of more than 1,000 new U.S. government publications in each issue.

- *Who's Who in America:* Summarizes the achievements of living U.S. citizens who have gained prominence in their fields; *Canadian Who's Who* and *Who's Who in Business and Finance* are similar.

- *World Almanac and Book of Facts:* Presents statistical information about many events, people, and places. Index contains both general subject headings and specific names. Similar information is available in the *Canadian Yearbook* and the *Corpus Almanac of Canada.*

- Other indexes of articles in newspapers, magazines, and journals:

  Accountants' Index
  Applied Science and Technology Index
  Art Index
  Biological and Agricultural Index
  Computer Literature Index
  Education Index
  Engineering Index
  General Science Index
  Humanities Index
  Index Medicus
  Index to Legal Periodicals
  The New York Times Index
  Predicasts (U.S. and international editions)
  Public Affairs Information Bulletin
  Social Sciences Index
  The Wall Street Journal Index

Figure B.1
Major Reference Works

So many books and articles are published every year that a library must be selective when choosing those to put on its shelves. So for specialized information, a public library isn't very useful. You'll have better luck finding books and articles on technical subjects at college libraries (assuming the college offers courses in those subjects) and in company libraries.

All libraries provide bibliographies of the books and back issues of publications they stock. The traditional card catalog contains vast numbers of index cards organized by subject, title, and author; a code on each card directs you to the shelf where the book or publication is located. However, some libraries have converted their card catalogs to microfilm or microfiche, which takes up far less space. Inserted into a special viewing device, microfilm and microfiche tell you where to find what you want. Other libraries have computerized information about their holdings.

Abstracts

One way to find out a lot relatively quickly is to consult abstracts. Instead of just supplying a categorized list of article titles, as indexes do, abstracts summarize each article's contents as well. Many fields are served by abstracts that regularly review articles in the most useful periodicals. Here are the names of a few abstracts that may prove useful:

ABS Guide to Recent Publications in the Social and Behavioral Sciences

Book Review Digest

Business Publications Index and Abstracts

Computer Abstracts

Dissertation Abstracts International

Educational Research Information Center (ERIC)

Personnel Management Abstracts

Psychological Abstracts

Sociological Abstracts

Government Documents

When you want to know the exact provisions of a law, the background of a court decision, or population and business patterns, you can consult the government documents section of a library. This sort of research can be rather complicated, but a librarian will direct you to the information you need. All you need to know is the government body you're interested in (U.S. Congress, Ninth Court of Appeals, or Department of Labor) and some sort of identification for the specific information you need (such as the Safe Drinking Water Act of 1974, *Price* v. *Shell Oil*, or 1990 Census). If you have a date and the name of a publication containing the document, so much the better.

Computerized Databanks

One resource available in some companies is a computerized database (referred to as a management information system) containing company-generated statistics on sales and expenses, product specifications, inventory status, market research data, and perhaps reports and correspondence as well. Employees can often tap into that information directly through the computers or terminals on their desks, or they may be able to ask the data-processing department to get them a printout of the information they need.

Your access to information expands greatly when you also subscribe to one of the commercial databases, such as Management Contents, National Newspaper Index, and Trade and Industry Index. (More and more libraries are also database subscribers.) Their extensive files are continuously updated, thoroughly indexed, and readily accessible over standard telephone lines.

Note Cards

Many people check out library books containing the information they need, or they make photocopies or printouts of articles and other documents so that they can study them more carefully in their own offices. (Good researchers carefully note all necessary bibliographic information so that they don't have to go back to the library or supply incomplete information in their documentation.) Photocopying is legal as long as you're not doing it to avoid buying the publication or to resell it.

Sometimes you won't need the whole document. When you want to note only a point or two, you'll find note cards useful. Make a separate note card for each fact, quotation, or general concept you want to record. Summarize in your own words unless you think specific data or quotations may be useful.

The reason for using note cards is to help you remember and retrieve useful information for your report. As a practical matter, then, write the author's name, the title of the book or article, and other necessary bibliographic information at the top of each card. (As an alternative when you're collecting several pieces of information from each source, you might prepare a bibliography card for each, number the cards, and then use these numbers to cross-reference your note cards.) It's also helpful to note at the top of the card the general subject of the material (either in a simple phrase or with identifying numbers from your preliminary outline) so that you can sort your notes more easily when it comes time to write your report. Figure B.2 shows a sample note card.

COPYRIGHT AND FAIR USE

You have an important reason for carefully documenting the sources you consult during secondary research: Although ideas belong to no one person, the way they're expressed provides a livelihood for many scholars, consultants, and writers. To protect the interests of these people, most countries have established copyright laws. If you transgress those laws, you or your company could be sued, not to mention embarrassed.

In addition to covering printed materials such as books and magazines, copyright law covers audiovisual materials, many forms of artistic expression, computer programs, maps, mailing lists, even answering machine messages. However, copyright law does not protect

- Titles, names, short phrases, and slogans
- Familiar symbols or designs
- Lists of ingredients or contents
- Ideas, procedures, methods, systems, processes, concepts, principles, discoveries, or devices (although it does cover their description, explanation, or illustration)

A work is considered copyrighted as soon as it's put into fixed form, even if it hasn't been registered.[1]

How do you avoid plagiarism (presenting someone else's work as your own)? Here are a couple of guidelines:

- Whenever you quote another person's work, whether published or unpublished, tell where you found the statement.

> II-B-2a
>
> William Hoffer, "Businesswomen: Equal but Different," Nation's Business August 1987, 46–47.
>
> Liz Claiborne, Inc., launched by Elisabeth Claiborne Ortenberg, Arthur Ortenberg, & Leonard Boxer w/ $250,000 initial funding (p. 47)

This rule applies to books, articles, tables, charts, diagrams, song lyrics, scripted dialogue, letters, speeches, anything that you take verbatim (word for word) from someone else. Even if you paraphrase (change the wording somewhat), give credit to the person who has found an effective way to express an idea.

- You do not, however, have to cite a source of general knowledge or specialized knowledge generally known among your readers. For example, everyone knows that Franklin Roosevelt was elected to the presidency of the United States four times. You can say so on your own authority, even if you have read an article in which the author said the same thing.

The way to provide credit through source notes is detailed in the rest of this component chapter.

Merely crediting the source is not always enough, however. The fair use doctrine says that you can use other people's work only as long as you don't unfairly prevent them from benefiting as a result. For example, if you reproduce someone else's copyrighted questionnaire in a report you're writing (even if you identify the source thoroughly), you're preventing the author from selling a copy of that questionnaire to your readers.

Generally, you do best to avoid relying to such a great extent on someone else's work. When you can't avoid it, however, write to the copyright holder (usually the author or publisher) for permission to reprint. You'll usually be asked to pay a fee.

Fair use is decided in the courts on a case-by-case basis. So you won't find any hard-and-fast rules about when to get permission. In general, however, you would probably get permission to use

- More than 250 words quoted from a book
- Any reproduction of a piece of artwork (including fully reproduced charts and tables) or excerpt from commercially produced audiovisual material
- Any dialogue from a play or line from a poem or song
- Any portion of consumable materials, such as workbooks
- Multiple copies of copyrighted works that you intend to distribute widely or repeatedly, especially for noneducational purposes

You do not need permission to use materials published before 1907, news articles more than three months old, or materials originally published by the government. Nor do you need permission to use copies as the basis for "criticism, comment, news reporting, teaching, scholarship, or research."[2]

When deciding whether you may use someone else's work without permission, remember that the courts (if they get involved) will consider the length of your quotation in relation to the total length of the work from which it is taken, the type of work you are taking it from, your purpose, and the effect your action has on the original author's efforts to distribute the work. If you think you may be infringing on the author's rights, write for permission and provide a credit line. In any case, be sure to acknowledge the original author's work with a source note.

SOURCE NOTES

Traditionally, source notes are presented as footnotes at the bottom of report pages. However, endnotes, typed at the end of each chapter or the end of the report (just before the bibliography), have also become quite common. Each practice has advantages and drawbacks. Footnotes are harder to type within the margins of the page, but they're handier for the reader. Endnotes, on the other hand, are much easier to type, but the reader may become annoyed at having to flip to the end of the report.

The solution to the dilemma may lie, in part, in distinguishing between two types of notes. **Source notes** are used to document quotations (word-for-word selections from another work), paraphrased passages (someone else's ideas stated in your own words), and visual aids. Any information taken from another source requires a source note. **Content notes** supplement your main text with asides about a particular issue or event, provide a cross-reference to another section of your report, or direct the reader to a related source, explaining the connection between one thing and the other. Any note that contains more than a simple reference to another work is a content note.

For the reader's convenience, content notes are easily located when presented at the bottom of the appropriate page, and source notes are less distracting when placed at the end. A report sometimes presents source notes as endnotes and content notes as footnotes. As a less-confusing alternative, consider which type of note is most common in your report; then choose whether to present them all as endnotes or all as footnotes. Regardless of the method you choose for referencing textual information, both content notes and source notes pertaining to visual aids are placed on the same page as the visual aid.

Mechanics

Notes of all varieties are single-spaced and separated from one another by a double space. In footnotes to textual information, the identifying number is indented five spaces, placed on the line, and followed by a period. Two spaces are left after the period, and then the entry begins (see the section containing examples). Endnotes, however, begin at the left margin (see the "Notes" section of the sample report in Chapter 14). Notes referring to visual aids are handled differently too: A source note, preceded by the underlined (italicized) word *Source* and a colon, is placed at the bottom of the visual aid; content notes, if any, are listed below the source note. Figure 14.2, in Chapter 14, shows the placement of these notes on visual aids.

When using footnotes, plan carefully to leave enough space for the footnote at the bottom of the page and still maintain the standard margin. A line about $1\frac{1}{2}$ inches long (15 spaces in pica type, 20 in elite), made with the underscore key on a typewriter, separates the footnote(s) from the text. Some word-processing software can handle the layout and numbering of footnotes for you.

Reference Marks

Content notes and source notes pertaining to text are signaled with superscripts, which are arabic numerals placed just above the line of type. Usually superscripts come at the end

of the sentence containing the referenced statement; but occasionally, to avoid confusion, a superscript is placed right after the referenced statement:

```
Rising interest rates put a damper on third-quarter
profits in all industries,[1] and profits did not pick up
again until the Federal Reserve loosened the money
supply.[2]
```

The first superscript in this example comes after the comma. Superscripts follow all punctuation marks except the dash, which is placed after the superscript.

Reference marks are numbered consecutively throughout the report. (In very long reports, they may be numbered consecutively throughout each chapter instead.) If a note is added or deleted, all the reference marks that follow must be changed to maintain an unbroken sequence. If you change the reference marks, be sure to renumber the notes as well (most word-processing software contains a footnote feature that will do this for you automatically). Content notes appearing in visual aids are marked with asterisks and other symbols (or italicized lowercase letters if the visual aids contain many numbers).

Quotations

Quotations from secondary sources must always be followed by a reference mark. However, quotations may appear in one of two forms, depending on their length. A brief quotation (three lines or less) can be typed right into the main body of the text. Quotation marks at the beginning and end of the quotation separate the other person's words from your own.

Longer quotations must be set off as extracts. An extract begins on a new line, and the left margin is indented five to seven spaces (indenting the right margin is optional). No quotation marks are needed. Although the main text may be single- or double-spaced, an extract is always single-spaced.

You'll often want to leave out some part of a quotation. Ellipsis points (or dots) are the three periodlike punctuation marks that show something is missing:

```
Brant has demonstrated . . . a wanton disregard for
the realities of the marketplace.  His days at the helm
are numbered. . . .  Already several lower-level execu-
tives are jockeying for position.[3]
```

In this example you can see how ellipsis points are handled between sentences: A period is followed by the three dots. Note also that ellipsis points are typed with spaces between them.

Form

Many schemes have been proposed for organizing the information in source notes. All break the information into two main parts: (1) information about the author and the work and (2) publication information. The first part includes the author's name, the title of the work, and such other identifying information as the edition and volume number. The second part includes the place of publication, the publisher, and the date of publication, followed by relevant page numbers. A few details about these elements are described in the sections that follow.

Author's Name

If the author of the work is only one person, spell out her or his name and follow it with a comma. For two authors, list the names similarly, with *and* separating them. For three authors, separate the names with commas and insert *and* before the last author's name. You can handle four or more authors more concisely: After the first author's name simply insert *et al.* or *and others* with no preceding comma.

Title of the Work

Titles are usually typed uppercase and lowercase, which means that the first and last words start with a capital letter, as do all nouns, pronouns, verbs, adverbs, and adjectives. However, prepositions, conjunctions, and articles start with a lowercase letter; exceptions are prepositions that are an inseparable part of an expression (as in "Looking Up New Words") and, often, prepositions and conjunctions with more than four letters.

Works often have a two-part title; a colon should be used to separate the two parts:

Managerial Communications: A Strategic Approach

Leave two spaces after the colon, and capitalize the letter that comes right after the colon.

Titles of books, periodicals (journals and magazines published at regular intervals), and other major works are usually italicized (or underlined on a typewriter). Sometimes they're typed all in capitals, with no underlining, to make the typing task easier and to make the title stand out more. Titles of articles, pamphlets, chapters in books, and the like are placed in quotation marks.

Publication Information

Source notes referring to periodicals don't usually include the publisher's name and place of business (see sample source notes 7, 12, and 13), but source notes for books, pamphlets, and other hard-to-find works do. Such publication information is set off in parentheses.

In a reference to a book, the first item following the opening parenthesis is the city where the publisher is located. If the city is large and well known and if there are no other well-known cities by the same name, its name can appear alone. However, if necessary for proper identification, the state, province, or country should also be indicated. Abbreviations (not the two-letter postal abbreviations) are used for states and provinces, but the names of countries are spelled out. A colon follows the name of the place.

The publisher's name comes after the colon, often in a shortened form. For example, McGraw-Hill, Inc., can easily be identified when shortened to McGraw-Hill. If you begin with shortened publishers' names, be sure to carry through with the same short forms throughout your source notes and bibliography. Use a publisher's full name if it's not well known or if it might be confused with some other organization.

The publication date is the most recent year on the copyright notice. Ignore the dates of printing. After the date, close the parentheses.

A source note often refers to a specific page number. If so, the closing parenthesis is followed by a comma, which in turn is followed by the page number(s).

Repeated Source Notes

When you cite the same reference more than once in the course of your report, you can save time and effort by using a full citation for the first source note and a shortened form for later references. If your report has a comprehensive alphabetical bibliography, you may opt to use the short form for all your source notes, not just first citations.

The information in repeated source notes can be handled in one of two ways: The formal style uses Latin abbreviations to indicate certain information; the informal style uses shortened versions of the source information instead.

Here are some repeated source notes using the formal style:

4. Lewis A. Presner, The International Business Dictionary and Reference (New York: Wiley, 1991), 62-63.

5. Ibid., 130. [refers to page 130 in the Presner book]

6. Roger C. Parker, Looking Good in Print: A Guide to Basic Design for Desktop Publishing (Chapel Hill, N.C.: Ventana Press, 1990), 110.

7. Les L. Landes, "Down with Quality Programitis," IABC Communication World, February 1992, 31.

8. Parker, op. cit., 28. [refers to a new page in the book cited in note 6]

9. Landes, loc. cit. [refers to page 31 of Landes]

Ibid. means "in the same place"—that is, the same reference mentioned in the immediately preceding entry but perhaps a different page (indicated by giving the page number). *Op. cit.* means "in the work cited"; because it's used when at least one other reference has come between it and the original citation, you must include the last name of the author. You must also use a new page number; otherwise, you would use *loc. cit.* ("in the place cited") and omit the page number.

The informal style, which is commonly used today, avoids Latin abbreviations by adopting a shortened form for the title of a reference that is repeated. In this style, the previous list of source notes would appear as follows:

4. Lewis A. Presner, The International Business Dictionary and Reference (New York: Wiley, 1991), 62-63.

5. Presner, <u>The International Business Dictionary and Reference</u>, 130.

6. Roger C. Parker, <u>Looking Good in Print: A Guide to Basic Design for Desktop Publishing</u> (Chapel Hill, N.C.: Ventana Press, 1990), 110.

7. Les L. Landes, "Down with Quality Program-itis," <u>IABC Communication World</u>, February 1992, 31.

8. Parker, <u>Looking Good in Print</u>, 28.

9. Landes, "Down with Quality Program-itis," 31.

Note that only the author's last name, a short form of the title, and the page number are used in this style of repeated source note.

Examples

With these few general guidelines in mind, take a closer look at how the form of a source note depends on the type of reference being cited. You'll find some additional examples in the sample report in Chapter 14.

Books

In their simplest form, references to books look like source notes 4 and 6 in the preceding set of examples. Sometimes, however, you'll want to note the edition of a book:

10. Charles Conrad, <u>Strategic Organizational Communication: An Integrated Perspective</u>, 2d ed. (Fort Worth, Tex.: Holt, Rinehart and Winston, 1990), 25.

When you need to cite a volume number, place *vol. 3* (or the correct number) after the title or edition number and before the publication data.

On other occasions you'll use the name of an editor instead of an author:

11. Warren K. Agee, Phillip H. Ault, and Edwin Emery, eds., <u>Perspectives on Mass Communications</u> (New York: Harper & Row, 1982).

Periodicals

The typical periodical reference looks like source note 7 in the previous examples. The article author's name (if there is one) is handled as a book author's is, but the title of the article appears in quotation marks. Like the title of a book, the title of the magazine or journal appears either in italics (underlined) or in all capital letters.

The rest of the periodical note can be tricky, however. For popular and business magazines, you need include only the date and page number(s) after the title. (Notice that the date is inverted, unlike dates used in text.)

12. "Time to Call In the Boss," <u>Brandweek</u>, 27 July 1992, 34.

For scientific or academic journals, however, include the volume number and treat the page number as shown here:

13. Kevin G. Lamude and Joseph Scudder, "Compliance-Gaining Techniques of Type-A Managers," <u>Journal of Business Communication</u> 30, no. 1 (1993): 64. [volume 30, number 1, page 64]

As a rule of thumb, use the more scholarly style of source note 13 if your report is weighted heavily toward serious research in professional journals; if popular and trade magazines dominate your references, you may stick with the simpler style that leaves out the volume number. Another option (used in this text) is to employ both styles, depending on the type of periodical being cited. Your guiding principle in choosing a style should be to provide the information that your readers need to find your source easily.

Newspapers

When a newspaper article doesn't have an author, the citation begins with the name of the article. The name of the newspaper is treated like the title of a book or periodical. Many of the best-known newspapers—such as *The New York Times, The Wall Street Journal,* and *The Christian Science Monitor*—are rarely mistaken for other newspapers, but many smaller newspapers are harder to identify. If the name of the city (plus the state or province for obscure or small cities) doesn't appear in the title of these newspapers, put the place name in brackets after the title. Finally, a newspaper reference specifies the date of publication in the same way a magazine does, and it ends with a section name or number (if appropriate) and a page number:

14. "Forecasters Predict Economy in 10 Years Won't Change Much," <u>Wall Street Journal</u>, 12 October 1993, A16.

Public Documents

Government documents and court cases are often useful in business reports, but source notes referring to them are hard to construct. As you struggle with a complex set of "authors" and publication data, remember that the goal is to provide just enough information to identify the work and to distinguish it from others. Here are some examples of source notes for government and legal documents:

15. U.S. Department of Commerce, Task Force on Corporate Social Performance, <u>Corporate Social Reporting in the United States and Western Europe</u> (Washington, D.C.: U.S. Government Printing Office, July 1979), 3. [identifies the group issuing the document as specifically as possible]

16. U.S. Congress, House Committee on Labor, <u>An Investigation Relating to Health Conditions of Workers Employed in the Construction and Maintenance of Public Utilities</u>, 74th Cong., 2d sess., 16-29 January 1936.

17. <u>Simpson</u> v. <u>Union Oil Co. of California</u>, 377 U.S. 13 (U.S. Sup. Ct. 1964). [provides the name of the

case, the volume and page numbers of the law report, the name of the court that decided the case (the U.S. Supreme Court here), and the date of the decision]

For more information on documenting specialized sources like these, consult the librarian in the documents section of the library or one of the style books cited at the end of this appendix.

Unpublished Material

Theses, dissertations, and company reports—which are usually prepared for a limited audience of insiders—are handled similarly. The title, like an article title, is in quotation marks, and "publication" data that will help the reader find the work is in parentheses:

18. John Peter Randolph, "Development and Implementation of Public Access Through Cable Television" (Master's thesis, San Diego State University, 1975), 73-74.
19. Frances Asakawa, "Recommendations for Replacing the Sales Fleet Based on a Comparison of Three Midsize Automobiles" (Report to Daniel Standish, Director of Sales, Midwest Marketing, Inc., 17 November 1988), 17.

This format can be used for any written source that doesn't fall into one of the other categories, such as a sales brochure or a presentation handout. Identify the author, title, and place and date of publication as completely as you can so that your readers have a way to refer to the source.

Letters, speeches, interviews, and other types of unprinted references are also identified as completely as possible to give readers some means of checking the source. Begin with the name, title, and affiliation of the "author"; then describe the nature of the communication, the date and possibly the place, and if appropriate, the location of the files containing the document:

20. Nancy Sjoberg, President, Del Mar Associates, welcoming address at CRM Reunion, San Diego, California, 15 August 1994.
21. Victor Schoenberg, letter to Barbara Parsons, 10 February 1988.
22. Dorothy Gabbei, interview with the writer, Emporia, Kansas, 14 July 1992.

You may want to weave references to these sorts of sources into the text of your report. If you have many of them, however, you may just as well put them into notes so that they won't be distracting to readers.

Electronic Media

Television and radio programs, films, computer programs, and the like are also documented. It may be more difficult for a reader to refer to these media (especially television and ra-

dio programs), but you still want to acknowledge ideas and facts borrowed from someone else.

You can often weave references to electronic media into the text of your report. When source notes are preferable, however, the citations look something like this:

23. Mike Wallace, "60 Minutes," CBS-TV, 22 August 1993.
24. Group Productivity (Del Mar, Calif.: CRM/McGraw-Hill Films, 1985), videotape, 22 min.
25. PROCOMM PLUS (Columbia, Mo.: Datastorm Technologies, 1991), software for IBM computer.

The exact information you provide depends on your subject and audience and on the context of the reference. For example, when citing a film, it may be appropriate to note the scriptwriter or director. When it comes to electronic media, use good judgment in constructing source notes.

BIBLIOGRAPHIES

The reason for including a bibliography in a report is to give your readers a complete list of the sources you consulted. In addition, a bibliography serves as a reading list for readers who want to pursue the subject of your report further. The bibliography therefore presents, in alphabetical order, every source that appears in the notes and perhaps additional references that you didn't specifically refer to in the body of your report.

If all your sources are listed in endnotes, you may find that a bibliography is unnecessary. However, the longer and more formal the report, the greater the need for a separate bibliography. Also, because a bibliography may serve as a reading list, you may want to annotate each entry—that is, comment on the subject matter and viewpoint of the source, as well as its usefulness to your readers:

Baldridge, Letitia. Complete Guide to Executive Manners. New York: Rawson Associates, 1985. Thorough review of etiquette as it relates to the business world. Two parts: Human Relations at Work and Business Protocol; 499 pages.

Annotations may be written in either complete or incomplete sentences.

Mechanics

Depending on the length of your report and the complexity and number of your sources, you may either put the entire bibliography at the end of the report (after the endnotes) or put relevant sections at the end of each chapter. Another way to make a long bibliography more manageable is to subdivide it into categories (a classified bibliography), either by type of reference (such as books, articles, and unpublished material) or by subject matter (such as government regulations, market forces, and so on).

When typing the bibliography, start each entry at the left margin, with the author's last name first. In general, the content of the entries and the order of the elements are the same as in source notes. Like source notes, bibliographic entries are single-spaced, with a double space between them. However, some of the punctuation is different, and bibliographic entries are indented (customarily five spaces or as few as two) after the first line (hanging indent). The sample report in Chapter 14 includes a complete bibliography.

Examples

To point out the differences between source notes and bibliographic entries, the following examples use the same works as sample source notes 10 through 19. The major content difference is that bibliographic entries do not include page numbers (unless they're articles or chapters in books) because the reader is being referred to the work as a whole.

To be sure you have all the information you need when it's time to construct a bibliography, use this same format during your research. Many writers use a separate index card for each work consulted, which makes alphabetizing the entries relatively painless.

Books

Note that only the first author's name is typed in reverse order and that parentheses are not used around the publication data:

Agee, Warren K., Phillip H. Ault, and Edwin Emery, eds. Perspectives on Mass Communications. New York: Harper & Row, 1982.

Conrad, Charles. Strategic Organizational Communication: An Integrated Perspective. 2d ed. Fort Worth, Tex.: Holt, Rinehart and Winston, 1990.

For more than one work by the same author, use six hyphens in place of the author's name, but repeat the name if one of the books is by a single author and another is by that author with others.

Periodicals

Use the same information that appears in the source note, but use inclusive page numbers (page numbers for the whole article):

"Time to Call In the Boss." Brandweek, 27 July 1992, 32-36, 60.

Lamude, Kevin G., and Joseph Scudder. "Compliance-Gaining Techniques of Type-A Managers." Journal of Business Communication 30, no. 1 (1993): 63-79.

Note the differences in punctuation between bibliographic style and source note style. Also, bibliographic entries that have no author are listed alphabetically by title.

Newspapers

Again, the major difference is in the punctuation:

"Forecasters Predict Economy in 10 Years Won't Change Much." Wall Street Journal, 12 October 1993, A16.

Because no author is listed, this entry would be alphabetized by the first word of the article title (*Forecasters*) instead of by the author's name.

Public Documents

Here, in alphabetical order, are bibliographic entries for sample source notes 15, 16, and 17:

Simpson v. Union Oil Co. of California. 377 U.S. 13 (U.S. Sup. Ct. 1964).

U.S. Congress. House Committee on Labor. An Investigation Relating to Health Conditions of Workers Employed in the Construction and Maintenance of Public Utilities. 74th Cong., 2d sess., 16-29 January 1936.

U.S. Department of Commerce. Task Force on Corporate Social Performance. Corporate Social Reporting in the United States and Western Europe. Washington, D.C.: U.S. Government Printing Office, July 1979.

Legal cases are often not listed in bibliographies, just mentioned in the text or cited in source notes.

Unpublished Material

Letters, casual interviews, and telephone conversations are rarely included in bibliographies. Theses, dissertations, company reports, and formal interviews may be included if the source is accessible to readers. Here are two examples, in alphabetical order:

Asakawa, Frances. "Recommendations for Replacing the Sales Fleet Based on a Comparison of Three Midsize Automobiles." Report to Daniel Standish, Director of Sales, Midwest Marketing, Inc., 17 November 1988.

Randolph, John Peter. "Development and Implementation of Public Access Through Cable Television." Master's thesis, San Diego State University, 1975.

Electronic Media

Here, in alphabetical order, are bibliographic entries for sample source notes 23 through 25:

Group Productivity. Del Mar, Calif.: CRM/McGraw-Hill
    Films, 1985. Videotape, 22 min.

PROCOMM PLUS. Columbia, Mo.: Datastorm
    Technologies, 1991. Software for IBM computer.

Wallace, Mike. "60 Minutes." CBS-TV, 22 August
    1993.

The information provided in these entries is sufficient to give readers a clear idea of the works you consulted, but more information may be needed if readers are to easily consult the works themselves.

REFERENCE CITATIONS

Another method of documenting report sources has become popular in recent years. In an attempt to eliminate the need for separate source notes and bibliography, references are listed at the ends of chapters or at the end of the report, in much the same format as a regular bibliography. However, superscripts and source notes are eliminated. Three popular ways of handling so-called reference citations are explained here. All three have been designed to streamline the report and to eliminate some of the tedium of preparing both source notes and bibliography.

Author-Date System

One simple system uses regular bibliographic style for the list of references. However, if the reference list has many instances of multiple works by one author or if the report writer wants to highlight the currency of the research, the date of publication may be moved to the spot just after the author's name.

In the text, reference to a given work is documented mainly with the author's last name and the date of publication (with a page number added when necessary):

. . . a basic understanding of the problem (Randolph
1975, 67).

An alternative is to weave the name of the author into the sentence:

According to Randolph (1975), no solution is likely to
come . . .

When no author is named, use a short form of the title of the work. If the "author" is an organization, shorten the name of the organization. In either case, make sure a reader can easily find the entry in the bibliography:

. . . with an emphasis on environmental matters (U.S.
Department of Commerce 1979).

If this entry were identified as "Department of Commerce," a reader would be searching the *D*'s instead of the *U*'s for the correct reference.

When listing more than one work by the same author, rely on the year of publication to distinguish between them. A lowercase letter (*a*, *b*, and so on) after the year differentiates two or more works by the same author published in the same year.

Key-Number System

The second approach numbers each bibliography entry in sequence, with an arabic numeral followed by a period. Sometimes the "bibliography" is arranged in order of the appearance of each source in the text instead of in alphabetical order.

In the text, references are documented with numbers. The first is the number assigned to the source, the second is the page number:

. . . a basic understanding of the problem (12:7).

This reference cites page 7 of item 12 in the reference list.

MLA Simplified Style

Like the author-date system, the documentation system recommended by the Modern Language Association lets you weave references into the text. However, instead of using the author's name with the date of publication, MLA simplified style uses the author's name and a page reference:

. . . giving retailers some additional options (Quelch
and Cannon-Bonventre 166).

Often, parenthetical references can be reduced to just the page number or eliminated entirely (when you refer to the work as a whole instead of specific pages):

In her chapter on international business manners,
Baldridge emphasizes Japanese customs (171-76).

Conrad offers specific guidelines for handling problems
with organizational communication.

The reference list at the end of the document (usually labeled "Works Cited" or, when uncited works are included, "Works Consulted") is arranged alphabetically in a format much like the bibliography format recommended in this appendix. The main difference is that the publication information—especially the names of months, the names of easily recognized periodicals, and portions of publishers' names—is often abbreviated:

United States Dept. of Commerce. Task Force on Corporate Social Performance. Corporate Social Reporting in the United States and Western Europe. Washington, D.C.: GPO, 1979.

In addition, punctuation is minimized in newspaper and periodical citations:

"Forecasters Predict Economy in 10 Years Won't Change Much." Wall Street Journal 12 October 1993, A16.

"Time to Call in the Boss." Brandweek 27 July 1992: 34.

The goal, as in other methods of using reference citations, is to simplify the traditional documentation style.

F URTHER INFORMATION ON DOCUMENTATION

As mentioned earlier, a wide variety of style books provide information on constructing source notes and bibliographies. These are a few of the guides most commonly used:

Achtert, Walter S., and Joseph Gibaldi. *The MLA Style Manual.* New York: Modern Language Association, 1985. Basis of the note and bibliography style used in much academic writing and recommended in many college textbooks on writing term papers; provides lots of examples in the humanities.

American Psychological Association. *Publication Manual of the American Psychological Association.* 3d ed. Washington, D.C.: American Psychological Association, 1983. Details the author-date system, which is preferred in the social sciences and often in the natural sciences as well.

Campbell, William Giles, Stephen Vaughan Ballou, and Carole Slade. *Form and Style: Theses, Reports, Term Papers.* 6th ed. Boston: Houghton Mifflin, 1982. Compares documentation styles recommended by the Modern Language Association and by *The Chicago Manual of Style.*

The Chicago Manual of Style. 14th ed. Chicago: University of Chicago Press, 1993. Known as the *Chicago Manual* and widely used in the publishing industry; detailed treatment of documentation appears in Chapters 15, 16, and 17.

Shields, Nancy E., and Mary E. Uhle. *Where Credit Is Due: A Guide to Proper Citing of Sources—Print and Nonprint.* Metuchen, N.J.: Scarecrow Press, 1985. Invaluable for its exhaustive treatment of troublesome sources, such as pamphlets, reports, oral messages, and electronic media.

Turabian, Kate L. *A Manual for Writers of Term Papers, Theses, and Dissertations.* 4th ed. Chicago: University of Chicago Press, 1973. Based on the *Chicago Manual,* but smaller and limited to matters of concern to report writers; many examples of documenting nonstandard references.

U.S. Government Printing Office Style Manual. Rev. ed. Washington, D.C.: U.S. Government Printing Office, 1973. Known as the *GPO Manual;* particularly useful for styling references to government documents.

FUNDAMENTALS OF GRAMMAR AND USAGE

Grammar is nothing more than the way words are combined into sentences, and usage is the way words are used by a network of people—in this case, the community of businesspeople who use English. You'll find it easier to get along in this community if you know the accepted standards of grammar and usage. What follows is a review of the basics of grammar and usage, things you've probably studied but may have forgotten. Without a firm grasp of these basics, you risk not only being misunderstood but also damaging your company's image, losing money for your company, and possibly even losing your job.

1.0 GRAMMAR

The sentences below look innocent, but consider the bombs they contain:

We sell tuxedos as well as rent.

(You might sell rent, but it's highly unlikely. Whatever you're selling, some people will ignore your message because of a blunder like this.)

Vice President Eldon Neale told his chief engineer that he would no longer be with Avix, Inc., as of June 30.

(Is Eldon or the engineer leaving? No matter which side the facts are on, the sentence can be read the other way. You may have a hard time convincing either person that your simple mistake was not a move in a game of office politics.)

Now look at this sentence:

The year before we budgeted more for advertising sales were up.

Confused? Perhaps this is what you meant:

The year before, we budgeted more for advertising. Sales were up.

Maybe you meant this:

The year before we budgeted more for advertising, sales were up.

The meaning of language falls into bundles called sentences. A listener or reader can take only so much meaning before filing a sentence away and getting ready for the next one. So writers have to know what a sentence is. They need to know where one ends and the next one begins.

Anyone who wants to know what a thing is has to find out what goes into it, what its ingredients are. Luckily, the basic ingredients of an English sentence are simple. They're called the parts of speech, and the content-bearing ones are nouns, pronouns, verbs, adjectives, and adverbs. They combine with a few functional parts of speech to convey meaning. Meaning is also transmitted by punctuation, mechanics, and vocabulary.

1.1 Nouns

A noun names a person, place, or thing. Anything you can see or detect with one of your other senses has a noun to name it. Some things you can't see or sense are also nouns—ions, for example, or space. So are things that exist as ideas, such as accuracy and height. (You can see that something is accurate or that a building is tall, but you can't see the idea of accuracy or the idea of height.) These names for ideas are known as abstract nouns. The simplest nouns are the names of things you can see or touch: car, building, cloud, brick.

1.1.1 Proper Nouns and Common Nouns

So far, all the examples of nouns have been common nouns, referring to general classes of things. The word *building* refers to a whole class of structures. Common nouns like *building* are not capitalized.

However, if you want to talk about one particular building, you might refer to the Glazier Building. Note that the name is capitalized, indicating that *Glazier Building* is a proper noun. Here are three sets of common and proper nouns for comparison:

Common	Proper
city	Kansas City
company	Blaisden Company
store	Books Galore

1.1.2 Plural Nouns

Nouns can be either singular or plural. The usual way to make a plural noun is to add s to the singular form of the word:

Singular	Plural
rock	rocks
picture	pictures
song	songs

Many nouns have other ways of forming the plural. Letters, numbers, and words used as words are sometimes made plural by adding an apostrophe and an s. As a rule, 's is used with abbreviations that have periods, lowercase letters that stand alone, and capital letters that might be confused with other words when made into plurals:

Spell out all *St.*'s and *Ave.*'s.

He divided the page with a row of *x*'s.

Sarah will register the *A*'s through the *I*'s at the convention.

In other cases, however, the apostrophe may be left out:

They'll review their *ABC*s.

The stock market climbed through most of the 1980s.

Circle all *the*s in the paragraph.

In these examples, *letters* and words used as words *are italicized* (discussed later in the chapter).

Other nouns, like those below, are so-called irregular nouns; they form the plural in some way other than simply adding *s*:

Singular	Plural
tax	taxes
specialty	specialties
cargo	cargoes
shelf	shelves
child	children
woman	women
tooth	teeth
mouse	mice
parenthesis	parentheses
son-in-law	sons-in-law
editor-in-chief	editors-in-chief

Rather than memorize a lot of rules about forming plurals, use a dictionary. If the dictionary says nothing about the plural of a word, it's formed the usual way—by adding *s*. If the plural is formed in some irregular way, the dictionary shows the plural or has a note something like this: pl. *-es*.

1.1.3 Possessive Nouns

A noun becomes possessive when it's used to show the ownership of something. Then you add *'s* to the word:

the man's car   the woman's apartment

However, ownership does not need to be legal:

the secretary's desk   the company's assets

Also, ownership may be nothing more than an automatic association:

a day's work   a job's prestige

An exception to the rule about adding *'s* to make a noun possessive occurs when the word is singular and already has two s sounds at the end. In cases like the following, an apostrophe is all that's needed:

crisis' dimensions   Mr. Moses' application

When the noun has only one s sound at the end, however, retain the *'s*:

Chris's book   Carolyn Nuss's office

With hyphenated nouns (compound nouns), add *'s* to the last word:

Hyphenated Noun	**Possessive Noun**
mother-in-law	mother-in-law's
mayor-elect	mayor-elect's

To form the possessive of plural nouns, just begin by following the same rule as with singular nouns: add *'s*. However, if the plural noun already ends in an *s* (as most do), drop the one you've added, leaving only the apostrophe:

the clients~~'s~~ complaints   employees~~'s~~ benefits

1.2 Pronouns

A pronoun is a word that stands for a noun; it saves repeating the noun:

> *Drivers* have some choice of weeks for vacation, but *they* must notify this office of *their* preference by March 1.

The pronouns *they* and *their* stand in for the noun *drivers*. The noun that a pronoun stands for is called the antecedent of the pronoun; *drivers* is the antecedent of *they* and *their*.

When the antecedent is plural, the pronoun that stands in for it has to be plural; *they* and *their* are plural pronouns because *drivers* is plural. Likewise, when the antecedent is singular, the pronoun has to be singular:

> We thought the *contract* had been signed, but we soon learned *it* had not been.

1.2.1 Multiple Antecedents

Sometimes a pronoun has a double (or even triple) antecedent:

> Kathryn Boettcher and Luis Gutierrez went beyond *their* sales quotas for January.

Kathryn Boettcher, if taken alone, is a singular antecedent. So is *Luis Gutierrez*. However, when both are the antecedent of a pronoun, they're plural and the pronoun has to be plural. Thus the pronoun is *their* instead of *her* or *his*.

1.2.2 Unclear Antecedents

In some sentences the pronoun's antecedent is unclear:

> Sandy Wright sent Jane Brougham *her* production figures for the previous year. *She* thought they were too low.

Which person does the pronoun *her* refer to? Someone who knew Sandy and Jane and knew their business relationship might be able to figure out the antecedent for *her*. Even with such an advantage, however, a reader still might receive the wrong meaning. Also it would be nearly impossible for any reader to know which name is the antecedent of *she*. The best way to clarify an ambiguous pronoun is usually to rewrite the sentence, repeating nouns when needed for clarity:

> Sandy Wright sent her production figures for the previous year to Jane Brougham. *Jane* thought they were too low.

Repeat the noun only when the antecedent is unclear.

1.2.3 Gender-Neutral Pronouns

The pronouns that stand for males are *he, his,* and *him.* The pronouns that stand for females are *she, hers,* and *her.* However, you'll often be faced with the problem of choosing a pronoun for a noun that refers to both females and males:

> Each manager must make up (his, her, his or her, its, their) own mind about stocking this item and about the quantity that (he, she, he or she, it, they) can sell.

This sentence calls for a pronoun that's neither masculine nor feminine. The issue of gender-neutral pronouns responds to efforts to treat females and males evenhandedly. Here are some possible ways to deal with this issue:

> Each manager must make up *his* . . .
> (Not all managers are men.)

> Each manager must make up *her* . . .
> (Not all managers are women.)

> Each manager must make up *his or her* . . .
> (This solution is acceptable but becomes awkward when repeated more than once or twice in a document.)

> Each manager must make up *her* . . . Every manager will receive *his* . . . A manager may send *her* . . .
> (A manager's gender does not alternate like a windshield wiper!)

> Each manager must make up *their* . . .
> (The pronoun can't be plural when the antecedent is singular.)

> Each manager must make up *its* . . .
> (*It* never refers to people.)

The best solution is to make the noun plural or to revise the passage altogether:

> Managers must make up *their* minds . . .

> Each manager must decide whether . . .

Be careful not to change the original meaning.

1.2.4 Case of Pronouns

The case of a pronoun tells whether it's acting or acted upon:

> *She* sells an average of five packages each week.

In this sentence *she* is doing the selling. Because *she* is acting, *she* is said to be in the nominative case. Now consider what happens when the pronoun is acted upon:

After six months Ms. Browning promoted *her*.

In this sentence the pronoun *her* is acted upon. The pronoun *her* is thus said to be in the objective case. Contrast the nominative and objective pronouns in this list:

Nominative	Objective
I	me
we	us
he	him
she	her
they	them
who	whom
whoever	whomever

Objective pronouns may be used as either the object of a verb (like *promoted*) or the object of a preposition (like *with*):

Rob worked with *them* until the order was filled.

In this example *them* is the object of the preposition *with* because Rob acted upon—worked with—them.

Here's a sample sentence with three pronouns, the first one nominative, the second the object of a verb, and the third the object of a preposition:

He paid *us* as soon as the check came from *them*.

He is nominative; *us* is objective because it's the object of the verb *paid*; *them* is objective because it's the object of the preposition *from*.

1.2.5 Possessive Pronouns

Possessive pronouns are like possessive nouns in the way they work: They show ownership or automatic association.

her job	their preferences
his account	its equipment

However, possessive pronouns are different from possessive nouns in the way they are written. That is, possessive pronouns never have an apostrophe.

Possessive Noun	Possessive Pronoun
the woman's estate	her estate
Roger Franklin's plans	his plans
the shareholders' feelings	their feelings
the vacuum cleaner's attachments	its attachments

Note that *its* is the possessive of *it*. Like all other possessive pronouns, *its* doesn't have an apostrophe. Some people confuse *its* with *it's*, the contraction of *it is*. Contractions are discussed later.

1.3 Verbs

A verb describes an action:

They all *quit* in disgust.

It may also describe a state of being:

Working conditions *were* substandard.

The English language is full of action verbs. Here are a few you'll often run across in the business world:

verify	perform	fulfill
hire	succeed	send
leave	improve	receive
accept	develop	pay

You could undoubtedly list many more.

The most common verb describing a state of being instead of an action is *to be* and all its forms:

I *am, was,* or *will be*   you *are, were,* or *will be*

Other verbs also describe a state of being:

It *seemed* like a good plan at the time.
She *sounds* impressive at a meeting.

These verbs link what comes before them in the sentence with what comes after; no action is involved. (See Section 1.7.5 for a fuller discussion of linking verbs.)

1.3.1 Verb Tenses

English has three simple verb tenses: present, past, and future.

Present:	Our branches in Hawaii *stock* other items.
Past:	When we *stocked* Purquil pens, we received a great many complaints.
Future:	Rotex Tire Stores *will stock* your line of tires when you begin a program of effective national advertising.

With most verbs (the regular ones), the past tense ends in *ed*; the future tense always has *will* or *shall* in front of it. However, the present tense is more complex:

Singular	Plural
I stock	we stock
you stock	you stock
he, she, it stocks	they stock

The basic form, *stock,* takes an additional *s* when *he, she,* or *it* precedes it.

In addition to the three simple tenses, there are three perfect tenses using forms of the helping verb *have.* The present perfect tense uses the past participle (regularly the past tense) of the main verb, *stocked,* and adds the present-tense *have* or *has* to the front of it:

(I, we, you, they) *have stocked.*

(He, she, it) *has stocked.*

The past perfect tense uses the past participle of the main verb, *stocked,* and adds the past-tense *had* to the front of it:

(I, you, he, she, it, we, they) *had stocked.*

The future perfect tense also uses the past participle of the main verb, *stocked,* but adds the future-tense *will have:*

(I, you, he, she, it, we, they) *will have stocked.*

Keep verbs in the same tense when the actions occur at the same time:

When the payroll checks *came* in, everyone *showed* up for work.

We *have found* that everyone *has pitched* in to help.

Of course, when the actions occur at different times, you may change tense accordingly:

A shipment *came* last Wednesday, so when another one *comes* in today, please return it.

The new employee *was* ill at ease, but now she *has become* a full-fledged member of the team.

1.3.2 Irregular Verbs
Many verbs don't follow in every detail the patterns already described. The most irregular of these verbs is *to be:*

	Singular	**Plural**
Present:	I *am*	we *are*
	you *are*	you *are*
	he, she, it *is*	they *are*
Past:	I *was*	we *were*
	you *were*	you *were*
	he, she, it *was*	they *were*

The future tense of *to be* is formed the same way the future tense of a regular verb is formed.

The perfect tenses of *to be* are also formed as they would be for a regular verb, except that the past participle is a special form, *been,* instead of just the past tense:

Present perfect:	you *have been*
Past perfect:	you *had been*
Future perfect:	you *will have been*

Here's a sampling of other irregular verbs:

Present	**Past**	**Past Participle**
begin	began	begun
shrink	shrank	shrunk
know	knew	known
rise	rose	risen
become	became	become
go	went	gone
do	did	done

Dictionaries list the various forms of other irregular verbs.

1.3.3 Transitive and Intransitive Verbs
Many people are confused by three particular sets of verbs:

lie/lay   sit/set   rise/raise

Using these verbs correctly is much easier when you learn the difference between transitive and intransitive verbs.

Transitive verbs convey their action to an object; they "transfer" their action to an object. Intransitive verbs do not. Here are some sample uses of transitive and intransitive verbs:

Transitive	**Intransitive**
The workers will be here on Monday to *lay* new carpeting.	We should include in our new offices a place to *lie* down for a nap.
That crate is full of stemware, so *set* it down carefully.	Even the way an interviewee *sits* is important.
They *raise* their level of production every year.	Salaries at Compu-Link, Inc., *rise* swiftly.

The workers *lay* carpeting, you *set* down the crate, they *raise* production—each action is transferred to something. In the intransitive sentences, one *lies* down, an interviewee *sits,* and salaries *rise* without (at least grammatically) affecting anything else. Intransitive sentences are complete with only a subject and a verb; transitive sentences are not complete unless they also include an object, or something to transfer the action to.

Tenses are a confusing element of the *lie/lay* problem:

Present	**Past**	**Past Participle**
I *lie*	I *lay*	I have *lain*
I lay (something down)	I *laid* (something down)	I have *laid* (something down)

The past tense of *lie* and the present tense of *lay* look and sound alike, even though they're different verbs.

1.3.4 Voice of Verbs

Verbs have two voices, active and passive:

Active: The buyer paid a large amount.
Passive: A large amount was paid by the buyer.

The passive voice uses a form of the verb *to be*.

Also, the passive-voice sentence uses eight words, whereas the active-voice sentence uses only six words to say the same thing. The words *was* and *by* are unnecessary to convey the meaning of the sentence. In fact, extra words usually clog meaning. So be sure to opt for the active voice when you have a choice.

At times, however, you have no choice:

Several items *have been taken,* but so far we don't know who took them.

The passive voice becomes necessary when the writer doesn't know (or doesn't want to say) who performed the action, but the active voice is bolder and more direct.

1.3.5 Mood of Verbs

You have three moods to choose from, depending on your intentions. Most of the time you use the indicative mood to make a statement or ask a question:

The secretary *mailed* a letter to each supplier.

Did the secretary *mail* a letter to each supplier?

When you wish to command or request, use the imperative mood:

Please *mail* a letter to each supplier.

Sometimes, especially in business, a courteous request is stated like a question; in that case, however, no question mark is required.

Would you *mail* a letter to each supplier.

The subjunctive mood, most often used in formal writing or in presenting bad news, expresses a possibility or a recommendation. The subjunctive is usually signaled by a word such as *if* or *that*. In these examples the subjunctive mood uses special verb forms:

If the secretary *were to mail* a letter to each supplier, we might save some money.

I suggested that the secretary *mail* a letter to each supplier.

Although the subjunctive mood is not often used anymore, it's still found in such expressions as *Come what may* and *If I were you.*

1.4 Adjectives

An adjective modifies (tells something about) a noun or pronoun:

an *efficient* staff	a *heavy* price
brisk trade	*poor* you

Each of these phrases says more about the noun or pronoun than the noun or pronoun would say alone. Adjectives always tell us something we wouldn't know without them. So you don't need to use adjectives when the noun alone, or a different noun, will give the meaning:

a *company* employee
(An employee ordinarily works for a company.)

a *crate-type* container
(*Crate* gives the entire meaning.)

At times, adjectives pile up in a series:

It was a *long, hot,* and *active* workday.

Such strings of adjectives are acceptable as long as they all convey a different part of the phrase's meaning.

Verbs in the *ing* form can be used as adjectives:

A *boring* job can sometimes turn into a *fascinating* career.

So can the past participle of verbs:

A freshly *painted* house is a *sold* house.

Adjectives modify nouns more often than they modify pronouns. When adjectives do modify pronouns, however, the sentence usually has a linking verb:

They were *attentive.*	It looked *appropriate.*
He seems *interested.*	You are *skillful.*

Most adjectives can take three forms: simple, comparative, and superlative. The simple form modifies a single noun or pronoun. Use the comparative form when comparing two items. When comparing three or more items, use the superlative form.

Simple	**Comparative**	**Superlative**
hard	harder	hardest
safe	safer	safest
dry	drier	driest

The comparative form adds *er* to the simple form, and the superlative form adds *est*. (A *y* at the end of a word changes to *i* before the *er* or *est* is added.)

A small number of adjectives are irregular, including these:

Simple	Comparative	Superlative
good	better	best
bad	worse	worst
little	less	least

When the simple form of an adjective is two or more syllables, you usually add *more* to form the comparative and *most* to form the superlative:

Simple	Comparative	Superlative
useful	more useful	most useful
exhausting	more exhausting	most exhausting
expensive	more expensive	most expensive

The only exception might be a two-syllable adjective that ends in *y*:

Simple	Comparative	Superlative
happy	happier	happiest
costly	costlier	costliest

If you choose this option, change the *y* to *i*, and tack *er* or *est* onto the end.

1.5 Adverbs

An adverb modifies a verb, an adjective, or another adverb:

Modifying a verb:	Our marketing department works *efficiently.*
Modifying an adjective:	She was not dependable, although she was *highly* intelligent.
Modifying another adverb:	His territory was *too* broadly diversified, so he moved *extremely* cautiously.

Most of the adverbs mentioned are adjectives turned into adverbs by adding *ly*, which is how many adverbs are formed:

Adjective	Adverb
efficient	efficiently
high	highly
extreme	extremely
special	specially
official	officially
separate	separately

Some adverbs are made by dropping or changing the final letter of the adjective and then adding *ly*:

Adjective	Adverb
due	duly
busy	busily

Other adverbs don't end in *ly* at all. Here are a few examples of this type:

often	fast	too
soon	very	so

1.6 Other Parts of Speech

Nouns, pronouns, verbs, adjectives, and adverbs carry most of the meaning in a sentence. Four other parts of speech link them together in sentences: prepositions, conjunctions, articles, and interjections.

1.6.1 Prepositions
Prepositions are words like these:

of	to	for	with
at	by	from	about

They most often begin prepositional phrases, which function like adjectives and adverbs by telling more about a pronoun, noun, or verb:

of a type	*by* Friday
to the point	*with* characteristic flair

1.6.2 Conjunctions, Articles, and Interjections
Conjunctions are words that usually join parts of a sentence. Here are a few:

and	but	because
yet	although	if

Using conjunctions is discussed in Sections 1.7.3 and 1.7.4.

Only three articles exist in English: *the, a,* and *an.* These words are used, like adjectives, to specify which item you are talking about.

Interjections are words that express no solid information, only emotion:

Wow!	Well, well!
Oh, no!	Good!

Such purely emotional language has its place in private life and advertising copy, but it only weakens the effect of most business writing.

1.7 Sentences

Sentences are constructed with the major building blocks, the parts of speech.

Money talks.

This two-word sentence consists of a noun (*money*) and a verb (*talks*). When used in this way, the noun works as the first requirement for a sentence, the subject, and the verb works as the second requirement, the predicate. Now look at this sentence:

They merged.

The subject in this case is a pronoun (*they*), and the predicate is a verb (*merged*). This is a sentence because it has a subject and a predicate. Here is yet another kind of sentence:

The plans are ready.

This sentence has a more complicated subject, the noun *plans* and the article *the;* the complete predicate is a state-of-being verb (*are*) and an adjective (*ready*). Without these two parts, the subject (who or what does something) and the predicate (the doing of it), no collection of words is a sentence.

1.7.1 Commands

In commands the subject (always *you*) is only understood, not stated:

(You) Move your desk to the better office.
(You) Please try to finish by six o'clock.

1.7.2 Longer Sentences

More complicated sentences have more complicated subjects and predicates, but they still have a simple subject and a predicate verb. In the following examples, the simple subject is underlined once, the predicate verb twice:

Marex and Contron enjoy higher earnings each quarter.
(Marex [and] Contron did something; enjoy is what they did.)

My interview, coming minutes after my freeway accident, did not impress or move anyone.
(Interview is what did something. What did it do? It did [not] impress [or] move.)

In terms of usable space, a steel warehouse, with its extremely long span of roof unsupported by pillars, makes more sense.
(Warehouse is what makes.)

These three sentences demonstrate several things. First, in all three sentences the simple subject and predicate verb are the "bare bones" of the sentence, the parts that carry the core idea of the sentence. When trying to find the simple subject and predicate verb, disregard all prepositional phrases, modifiers, conjunctions, and articles.

Second, in the third sentence the verb is singular (*makes*) because the subject is singular (*warehouse*). Even though the plural noun *pillars* is closer to the verb, *warehouse* is the real subject. So *warehouse* determines whether the verb is singular or plural. Subject and predicate must agree.

Third, the subject in the first sentence is compound (*Marex* [and] *Contron*). A compound subject, when con-

nected by *and,* requires a plural verb (*enjoy*). Also in the second sentence, compound predicates are possible (*did* [not] *impress* [or] *move*).

Fourth, the second sentence incorporates a group of words—*coming minutes after my freeway accident*—containing a form of a verb (*coming*) and a noun (*accident*). Yet this group of words is not a complete sentence for two reasons:

- *Accident* is not the subject of *coming*. Not all nouns are subjects.
- A verb that ends in *ing* can never be the predicate of a sentence (unless preceded by a form of *to be,* as in *was coming*). Not all verbs are predicates.

Because they don't contain a subject and a predicate, the words *coming minutes after my freeway accident* (called a phrase) can't be written as a sentence. That is, the phrase can't stand alone; it can't begin with a capital letter and end with a period. So a phrase must always be just one part of a sentence.

Sometimes a sentence incorporates two or more groups of words that do contain a subject and a predicate; these word groups are called clauses.

My interview, because it came minutes after my freeway accident, did not impress or move anyone.

The independent clause is the portion of the sentence that could stand alone without revision:

My interview did not impress or move anyone.

The other part of the sentence could stand alone only by removing *because:*

(because) It came minutes after my freeway accident.

This part of the sentence is known as a dependent clause; although it has a subject and a predicate (just like an independent clause), it's linked to the main part of the sentence by a word (*because*) showing its dependence.

To summarize, the two types of clauses—dependent and independent—both have a subject and a predicate. Dependent clauses, however, do not bear the main meaning of the sentence and are therefore linked to an independent clause. Neither can phrases stand alone, because they lack both a subject and a predicate. Only independent clauses can be written as sentences without revision.

1.7.3 Sentence Fragments

When an incomplete sentence (a phrase or dependent clause) is written as though it were a complete sentence, it's called a fragment. Consider the following sentence fragments:

Marilyn Sanders, having had pilferage problems in her store for the past year. Refuses to accept the results of our investigation.

This serious error can easily be corrected by putting the two fragments together:

> Marilyn Sanders, having had pilferage problems in her store for the past year, refuses to accept the results of our investigation.

Not all fragments can be corrected so easily:

> Employees a part of it. No authority or discipline.

Only the writer knows the intended meaning of these two phrases. Perhaps the employees are taking part in the pilferage. If so, the sentence should read:

> Some employees are part of the pilferage problem.

On the other hand, it's possible that some employees are helping with the investigation. Then the sentence would read:

> Some employees are taking part in our investigation.

It's just as likely, however, that the employees are not only taking part in the pilferage but are also being analyzed:

> Those employees who are part of the pilferage problem will accept no authority or discipline.

In fact, even more meanings could be read into these fragments. Because fragments like these can mean so many things, they mean nothing. No well-written memo, letter, or report ever demands the reader to be an imaginative genius.

One more type of fragment exists, the kind represented by a dependent clause. Note what *because* does to change what was once a unified sentence:

> Our stock of sprinklers is depleted.

> Because our stock of sprinklers is depleted.

Although it contains a subject and a predicate, adding *because* makes the second version a fragment. Words like *because* form a special group of words called subordinating conjunctions. Here's a partial list:

since	though	whenever
although	if	unless
while	even if	after

When a word of this type begins a clause, the clause is dependent and cannot stand alone as a sentence. However, if a dependent clause is combined with an independent clause, it can convey a complete meaning. The independent clause may come before or after the dependent clause:

> We are unable to fill your order because our stock of sprinklers is depleted.

> Because our stock of sprinklers is depleted, we are unable to fill your order.

Another remedy for a fragment that is a dependent clause is to remove the subordinating conjunction. That solution leaves a simple but complete sentence:

> Our stock of sprinklers is depleted.

The actual details of a transaction will determine the best way to remedy a fragment problem.

The ban on fragments has one exception. Some advertising copy contains sentence fragments, written knowingly to convey a certain rhythm. However, advertising is the only area of business in which fragments are acceptable.

1.7.4 Fused Sentences and Comma Splices

Just as there can be too little in a group of words to make it a sentence, there can also be too much:

> All our mail is run through a postage meter every afternoon someone picks it up.

This example contains two sentences, not one, but the two have been blended so that it's hard to tell where one ends and the next begins. Is the mail run through a meter every afternoon? If so, the sentences should read:

> All our mail is run through a postage meter every afternoon. Someone picks it up.

Perhaps the mail is run through a meter at some other time (morning, for example) and is picked up every afternoon:

> All our mail is run through a postage meter. Every afternoon someone picks it up.

The order of words is the same in all three cases; sentence division makes all the difference. Either of the last two cases is grammatically correct. The choice depends on the facts of the situation.

Sometimes these so-called fused sentences have a more obvious point of separation:

> Several large orders arrived within a few days of one another, too many came in for us to process by the end of the month.

Here the comma has been put between two independent clauses in an attempt to link them. When a lowly comma separates two complete sentences, the result is called a comma splice. A comma splice can be remedied in one of three ways:

- Replace the comma with a period and capitalize the next word: ". . . one another. Too many . . ."
- Replace the comma with a semicolon but do not capitalize the next word: ". . . one another; too many . . ." This rem-

edy works only when the two sentences have closely related meanings.

- Change one of the sentences so that it becomes a phrase or a dependent clause. This remedy often produces the best writing, but it takes more work.

The third alternative can be carried out in several ways. One is to begin the blended sentence with a subordinating conjunction:

> Whenever several large orders arrived within a few days of one another, too <u>many came</u> in for us to process by the end of the month.

Another way is to remove part of the subject or the predicate verb from one of the independent clauses, thereby creating a phrase:

> Several large <u>orders arrived</u> within a few days of one another, too <u>many</u> for us to process by the end of the month.

Finally, you can change one of the predicate verbs to its *ing* form:

> Several large <u>orders arrived</u> within a few days of one another, too <u>many</u> coming in for us to process by the end of the month.

At other times a simple coordinating conjunction (such as *or, and,* or *but*) can separate fused sentences:

> You can fire them, *or* you can make better use of their abilities.

> Margaret drew up the designs, *and* Matt carried them out.

> We will have three strong months, *but* after that sales will taper off.

Be careful using coordinating conjunctions: Use them only to join simple sentences that express similar ideas.

Because they say relatively little about the relationship between the two clauses they join, avoid using coordinating conjunctions too often: *and* is merely an addition sign; *but* is just a turn signal; *or* only points to an alternative. Subordinating conjunctions such as *because* and *whenever* tell the reader a lot more.

1.7.5 Sentences with Linking Verbs

Linking verbs were discussed briefly in the section on verbs (Section 1.3). Here you can see more fully how they function in a sentence. The following is a model of any sentence with a linking verb:

> A (verb) B.

Although words like *seems* and *feels* can also be linking verbs, let's assume that the verb is a form of *to be:*

> A *is* B.

In such a sentence, A and B are always nouns, pronouns, or adjectives. When one is a noun and the other's a pronoun, the sentence says that one is the same as the other:

> She is president.

When one is an adjective, it modifies or describes the other:

> She is forceful.

Remember that when one is an adjective, it modifies the other as any adjective modifies a noun or pronoun, except that a linking verb stands between the adjective and the word it modifies.

1.7.6 Misplaced Modifiers

The position of a modifier in a sentence is important. Note how the movement of *only* changes the meaning in the following sentences:

> *Only* we are obliged to supply those items specified in your contract.

> We are obliged *only* to supply those items specified in your contract.

> We are obliged to supply *only* those items specified in your contract.

> We are obliged to supply those items specified *only* in your contract.

In any particular set of circumstances, only one of these sentences would be accurate. The others would very likely cause problems. To prevent misunderstanding, modifiers such as *only* must be placed as close as possible to the noun or verb they modify.

For similar reasons, whole phrases that are modifiers must be placed near the right noun or verb. Mistakes in placement create ludicrous meanings:

> Antia Information Systems has bought new computer chairs for the programmers *with more comfortable seats.*

The anatomy of programmers is not normally a concern of business writing. Obviously, the comfort of the chairs was the issue:

> Antia Information Systems has bought new computer chairs *with more comfortable seats* for the programmers.

Here is another example:

> I asked him to file all the letters in the cabinet *that had been answered.*

In this ridiculous sentence the cabinet has been answered, even though no cabinet in history is known to have asked a question. *That had been answered* is too far from *letters* and too close to *cabinet*. Here's an improvement:

I asked him to file in the cabinet all the letters *that had been answered.*

In some cases, instead of moving the modifying phrase closer to the word it modifies, the best solution is to move the word closer to the modifying phrase.

2.0 PUNCTUATION

On the highway, signs tell you when to slow down or stop, where to turn, when to merge. In similar fashion, punctuation helps readers negotiate your prose. The proper use of punctuation keeps readers from losing track of your meaning.

2.1 Periods

Use a period (1) to end any sentence that is not a question, (2) with certain abbreviations, and (3) between dollars and cents in an amount of money.

2.2 Question Marks

Use a question mark after any direct question that requests an answer:

Are you planning to enclose a check, or shall we bill you?

Don't use a question mark with commands phrased as questions for the sake of politeness:

Will you send us a check today.

2.3 Exclamation Points

Use exclamation points after highly emotional language. Because business writing almost never calls for emotional language, you will seldom use exclamation points.

2.4 Semicolons

Semicolons have three main uses. One is to separate two closely related independent clauses:

The outline for the report is due within a week; the report itself is due at the end of the month.

A semicolon should also be used instead of a comma when the items in a series have commas within them:

Our previous meetings were on November 11, 1995; February 20, 1996; and April 28, 1996.

Finally, a semicolon should be used to separate independent clauses when the second one begins with a word such as *how-*

ever, therefore, or *nevertheless* or a phrase such as *for example* or *in that case:*

Our supplier has been out of part D712 for 10 weeks; however, we have found another source that can ship the part right away.

His test scores were quite low; on the other hand, he has a lot of relevant experience.

Section 4.4 has more information on using transitional words and phrases like these.

2.5 Colons

Use a colon (1) after the salutation in a business letter and (2) at the end of a sentence or phrase introducing a list, a quotation, or an idea:

Our study included the three most critical problems: insufficient capital, incompetent management, and inappropriate location.

In some introductory sentences, phrases such as *the following* or *that is* are implied by using a colon.

A colon should not be used when the list, quotation, or idea is a direct object or part of the introductory sentence:

We are able to supply

staples   wood screws
nails   toggle bolts

This shipment includes 9 videotapes, 12 CDs, and 14 cassette tapes.

2.6 Commas

Commas have many uses, the most common being to separate items in a series:

He took the job, learned it well, worked hard, and succeeded.

Put paper, pencils, and paper clips on the requisition list.

Company style often dictates omitting the final comma in a series. However, if you have a choice, use the final comma; it's often necessary to prevent misunderstanding.

The second place to use a comma is between clauses. A comma should separate independent clauses (unless one or both are very short):

She spoke to the sales staff, and he spoke to the production staff.

I was advised to proceed and I did.

A dependent clause at the beginning of a sentence is also separated from an independent clause by a comma:

Because of our lead in the market, we may be able to risk introducing a new product.

However, a dependent clause at the end of a sentence is separated from the independent clause by a comma only when the dependent clause is unnecessary to the main meaning of the sentence:

> We may be able to introduce a new product, although it may involve some risk.

A third use for the comma is after an introductory phrase or word:

> Starting with this amount of capital, we can survive in the red for one year.

> Through more careful planning, we may be able to serve more people.

> Yes, you may proceed as originally planned.

However, with short introductory prepositional phrases and some one-syllable words (such as *hence* and *thus*), the comma is often omitted:

> Before January 1 we must complete the inventory. Thus we may not need to hire anyone.

Fourth, commas are used to surround parenthetical phrases or words, which can be removed from the sentence without changing the meaning:

> The new owners, the Kowacks, are pleased with their purchase.

Fifth, commas are used between adjectives modifying the same noun:

> She left Monday for a long, difficult recruiting trip.

To test the appropriateness of such a comma, try reversing the order of the adjectives: *a difficult, long recruiting trip.* If the order cannot be reversed, leave out the comma (*a good old friend* isn't the same as *an old good friend*). A comma is also not used when one of the adjectives is part of the noun. Compare these two phrases:

> a distinguished, well-known figure

> a distinguished public figure

The adjective-noun combination of *public* and *figure* has been used together so often that it has come to be considered a single thing: *public figure.* So no comma is required.

Sixth, commas should precede *Jr., Sr., Inc.,* and the like:

Cloverdell, Inc.   Daniel Garcia, Jr.

In a sentence, a comma also follows such abbreviations:

Belle Brown, Ph.D., is the new tenant.

Seventh, commas are used both before and after the year when writing month, day, and year:

> It will be sent by December 15, 1995, from our Cincinnati plant.

Some companies write dates in another form: 15 December 1995. No commas should be used in this case. Nor is a comma needed when only the month and year are present (December 1995).

Eighth, a comma may be used after an informal salutation in a letter to a personal friend. (In business letters, however, salutations are followed by colons.)

Ninth, a comma is used to separate a quotation from the rest of the sentence:

> Your warranty reads, "These conditions remain in effect for one year from date of purchase."

However, the comma is left out when the quotation as a whole is built into the structure of the sentence:

> He hurried off with an angry "Look where you're going."

Finally, a comma should be used whenever it's needed to avoid confusion or an unintended meaning. Compare the following:

> Ever since they have planned new ventures more carefully.

> Ever since, they have planned new ventures more carefully.

2.7 Dashes

Use a dash to surround a parenthetical comment when the comment is a sudden turn in thought:

> Membership in the IBSA—it's expensive but worth it—may be obtained by applying to our New York office.

A dash can also be used to emphasize a parenthetical word or phrase:

> Third-quarter profits—in excess of $2 million—are up sharply.

Finally, use dashes to set off a phrase that contains commas:

> All our offices—Milwaukee, New Orleans, and Phoenix—have sent representatives.

Don't confuse a dash with a hyphen. A dash separates words, phrases, and clauses more strongly than a comma does; a hyphen ties two words together so tightly that they almost become one word.

When typing a dash, type two hyphens with no spacing before, between, or after.

2.8 Hyphens

Hyphens are mainly used in three ways. The first is to separate the parts of compound words beginning with such prefixes as *self, ex, quasi,* and *all:*

self-assured	quasi-official
ex-wife	all-important

However, hyphens are usually left out and the words closed up when using such prefixes as *pro, anti, non, un, inter,* and *extra:*

prolabor	nonunion
antifascist	interdepartmental

Exceptions occur when (1) the prefix occurs before a proper noun or (2) the vowel at the end of the prefix is the same as the first letter of the root word:

pro-Republican	anti-American
anti-inflammatory	extra-atmospheric

When in doubt, consult your dictionary.

Hyphens are also used in some compound adjectives, which are adjectives made up of two or more words. Specifically, you should use hyphens in compound adjectives that come before the noun:

an interest-bearing account	well-informed executives

However, do not hyphenate when the adjective follows a linking verb:

> This account is interest bearing.

> Their executives are well informed.

You can shorten sentences that list similar hyphenated words by dropping the common part from all but the last word:

> Check the costs of first-, second-, and third-class postage.

Finally, hyphens may be used to divide words at the end of a typed line. Such hyphenation is best avoided, but when you have to divide words at the end of a line, do so correctly (see Section 3.4). A dictionary will show how words are divided into syllables.

2.9 Apostrophes

Use an apostrophe in the possessive form of a noun (but not in a pronoun):

> On *his* desk was a reply to *Bette Ainsley's* application for the *manager's* position.

Apostrophes are also used in place of the missing letter(s) of a contraction:

Whole Words	Contraction
we will	we'll
do not	don't
they are	they're

2.10 Quotation Marks

Use quotation marks to surround words that are repeated exactly as they were said or written:

> The collection letter ended by saying, "This is your third and final notice."

Remember: (1) When the quoted material is a complete sentence, the first word is capitalized. (2) The final comma or period goes inside the closing quotation marks.

Quotation marks are also used to set off the title of a newspaper story, magazine article, or book chapter:

> You should read "Legal Aspects of the Collection Letter" in *Today's Credit.*

The book title is shown here in italics. When typewritten, the title is underlined. The same treatment is proper for newspaper and magazine titles. (Appendix B explains documentation style in more detail.)

Quotation marks may also be used to indicate special treatment for words or phrases, such as terms that you're using in an unusual or ironic way:

> Our management "team" spends more time squabbling than working to solve company problems.

When using quotation marks, take care to put in both sets, the closing marks as well as the opening ones.

Although periods and commas go inside any quotation marks, colons and semicolons go outside them. A question mark goes inside the quotation marks only if the quotation is a question:

> All that day we wondered, "Is he with us?"

If the quotation is not a question but the entire sentence is, the question mark goes outside:

> What did she mean by "You will hear from me"?

2.11 Parentheses

Use parentheses to surround comments that are entirely incidental:

> Our figures do not match yours, although (if my calculations are correct) they are closer than we thought.

Parentheses are also used in legal documents to surround figures in arabic numerals that follow the same amount in words:

Remittance will be One Thousand Two Hundred Dollars ($1,200).

Be careful to put punctuation (period, comma, and so on) outside the parentheses unless it is part of the statement in parentheses.

2.12 Ellipses

Use ellipsis points, or dots, to indicate that material has been left out of a direct quotation. Use them only in direct quotations and only at the point where material was left out. In the following example, the first sentence is quoted in the second:

The Dow Jones Industrial Average, which skidded 38.17 points in the previous five sessions, gained 4.61 to end at 3213.84.

According to the Honolulu *Star Bulletin,* "The Dow Jones Industrial Average . . . gained 4.61" on June 10.

The number of dots in ellipses is not optional; always use three. Occasionally, ellipsis points come at the end of a sentence, where they seem to grow a fourth dot. Don't be fooled: One of the dots is a period.

2.13 Underscores and Italics

Usually a line typed underneath a word or phrase either provides emphasis or indicates the title of a book, magazine, or newspaper. If possible, use italics instead of an underscore. Italics (or underlining) should also be used for defining terms and for discussing words as words:

In this report *net sales* refers to after-tax sales dollars.

The word *building* is a common noun and should not be capitalized.

3.0 MECHANICS

The most obvious and least tolerable mistakes a business writer makes are probably those related to grammar and punctuation. However, a number of small details, known as writing mechanics, demonstrate the writer's polish and reflect on the company's professionalism.

3.1 Capitals

You should, of course, capitalize words that begin sentences:

Before hanging up, he said, "*We'll* meet here on Wednesday at noon."

A quotation that is a complete sentence should also begin with a capitalized word.

Capitalize the names of particular persons, places, and things (proper nouns):

We sent *Ms. Larson* an application form, informing her that not all *applicants* are interviewed.

Let's consider opening a branch in the *West,* perhaps at the *west* end of *Tucson, Arizona.*

As *office buildings* go, the *Kinney Building* is a pleasant setting for *TDG Office Equipment.*

Note that Ms. Larson's name is capitalized because she is a particular applicant, whereas the general term *applicant* is left uncapitalized. Likewise, *West* is capitalized when it refers to a particular place but not when it means a direction. In the same way, *office* and *building* are not capitalized when they are general terms (common nouns) but are capitalized when they are part of the title of a particular office or building (proper nouns).

Titles within families, governments, or companies may also be capitalized:

My *Uncle David* offered me a job, but I wouldn't be comfortable working for one of my *uncles.*

We've never had a *president* quite like *President* Sweeney.

In addition, always capitalize the first word of the salutation and complimentary close of a letter:

Dear Mr. Andrews: *Yours* very truly,

Finally, capitalize the first word after a colon when it begins a complete sentence:

Follow this rule: When in doubt, leave it out.

Otherwise, the first word after a colon should not be capitalized.

3.2 Abbreviations

Abbreviations are used heavily in tables, charts, lists, and forms. They're used sparingly in prose paragraphs, however. Here are some abbreviations often used in business writing:

Abbreviation	Full Term
b/l	bill of lading
ca.	circa (about)
dol., dols.	dollar, dollars
etc.	et cetera (and so on)
FDIC	Federal Deposit Insurance Corporation
Inc.	Incorporated

L.f.	Ledger folio
Ltd.	Limited
mgr.	manager
NSF or N/S	not sufficient funds
P&L or P/L	profit and loss
reg.	regular
whsle.	wholesale

Note that *etc.* contains a word meaning *and;* therefore, never write *and etc.*

3.3 Numbers

Numbers may correctly be handled many ways in business writing, so follow company style. In the absence of a set style, however, generally spell out all numbers from one to ten and use arabic numerals for the rest.

There are some exceptions to this general rule. First, never begin a sentence with a numeral:

> *Twenty* of us produced *641* units per week in the first *12* weeks of the year.

Second, use numerals for numbers one through ten if they're in the same list as larger numbers:

> Our weekly quota rose from *9* to *15* to *27.*

Third, use numerals for percentages, time of day (except with *o'clock*), dates, and (in general) dollar amounts.

> Our division is responsible for *7* percent of total sales.

> The meeting is scheduled for *8:30* A.M. on August *2.*

> Add *$3* for postage and handling.

Use a comma in numbers with four digits (*1,257*) unless the company specifies another style.

When writing dollar amounts, use a decimal point only if cents are included. In lists of two or more dollar amounts, use the decimal point either for all or for none:

> He sent two checks, one for *$67.92* and one for *$90.00.*

3.4 Word Division

In general, avoid dividing words at the ends of lines. When you must, follow these rules:

- Don't divide a one-syllable word (such as *since, walked,* or *thought*); an abbreviation (*mgr.*); a contraction (*isn't*); or a number expressed in numerals (*117,500*).
- Divide words between syllables, as specified in a dictionary or word-division manual.
- Make sure that at least three letters of the divided word are moved to the second line: *sin-cerely* instead of *sincere-ly.*

- Do not end a page or more than two consecutive lines with a hyphen.
- Leave syllables consisting of a single vowel at the end of the first line (*impedi-ment* instead of *imped-iment*), except when the single vowel is part of a suffix like *able, ible, ical,* or *ity* (*respons-ible* instead of *responsi-ble*).
- Divide between double letters (*tomor-row*), except when the root word ends in double letters (*call-ing,* not *cal-ling*).
- Divide a hyphenated word after the hyphen only: *anti-independence* instead of *anti-inde-pendence.*

4.0 VOCABULARY

Using the right word in the right place is a crucial skill in business communication. However, many pitfalls await the unwary.

4.1 Frequently Confused Words

Because the following sets of words sound similar, be careful not to use one when you mean to use the other:

Word	Meaning
accede	to comply with
exceed	to go beyond
accept	to take
except	to exclude
access	admittance
excess	too much
advice	suggestion
advise	to suggest
affect	to influence
effect	the result
allot	to distribute
a lot	much or many
all ready	completely prepared
already	completed earlier
born	given birth to
borne	carried
capital	money; chief city
capitol	a government building
cite	to quote
sight	a view
site	a location
complement	complete amount; to go well with
compliment	to flatter
corespondent	party in a divorce suit
correspondent	letter writer

Word	Meaning	Word	Meaning
council	a panel of people	ordinance	law
counsel	advice; a lawyer	ordnance	weapons
defer	to put off until later	overdo	to do in excess
differ	to be different	overdue	past due
device	a mechanism	peace	lack of conflict
devise	to plan	piece	a fragment
die	to stop living; a tool	pedal	a foot lever
dye	to color	peddle	to sell
discreet	careful	persecute	to torment
discrete	separate	prosecute	to sue
envelop	to surround	personal	private
envelope	a covering for a letter	personnel	employees
forth	forward	precedence	priority
fourth	number four	precedents	previous events
holey	full of holes	principal	sum of money; chief; main
holy	sacred	principle	general rule
wholly	completely		
		rap	to knock
human	of people	wrap	to cover
humane	kindly		
		residence	home
incidence	frequency	residents	inhabitants
incidents	events		
		right	correct
instance	example	rite	ceremony
instants	moments	write	to form words on a surface
interstate	between states	role	a part to play
intrastate	within a state	roll	to tumble; a list
later	afterward	root	part of a plant
latter	the second of two	rout	to defeat
		route	a traveler's way
lead	a metal		
led	guided	shear	to cut
		sheer	thin, steep
lean	to rest at an angle		
lien	claim	stationary	immovable
		stationery	paper
levee	embankment		
levy	tax	than	as compared with
		then	at that time
loath	reluctant		
loathe	to hate	their	belonging to them
		there	in that place
loose	free; not tight	they're	they are
lose	to mislay		
		to	a preposition
material	substance	too	excessively; also
materiel	equipment	two	the number
miner	mineworker	waive	to set aside
minor	underage person	wave	a swell of water, a gesture
moral	virtuous; a lesson	weather	atmospheric conditions
morale	sense of well-being	whether	if

In the preceding list only enough of each word's meaning is given to help you distinguish between the words in each group. Several meanings are left out entirely. For more complete definitions, consult a dictionary.

4.2 Frequently Misused Words

The following words tend to be misused for reasons other than their sound. A number of reference books (including *The Random House College Dictionary,* revised edition; Follett's *Modern American Usage;* and Fowler's *Modern English Usage*) can help you with similar questions of usage.

a lot: When the writer means "many," *a lot* is always two separate words, never one.

correspond with: Use this phrase when you are talking about exchanging letters; use *correspond to* when you mean "similar to." Use either *correspond with* or *correspond to* when you mean "relate to."

disinterested: This word means "fair, unbiased, having no favorites, impartial." If you mean "bored" or "not interested," use *uninterested.*

etc.: This is the abbreviated form of a Latin phrase, *et cetera.* It means "and so on" or "and so forth." The current tendency among business writers is to use English rather than Latin.

imply/infer: Both refer to hints. Their great difference lies in who is acting. The writer *implies;* the reader *infers,* sees between the lines.

lay: This is a transitive verb. Never use it for the intransitive *lie.* (See Section 1.3.3.)

less: Use *less* for uncountable quantities (such as amounts of water, air, sugar, and oil). Use *fewer* for countable quantities (such as numbers of jars, saws, words, pages, and humans). The same distinction applies to *much* and *little* (uncountable) versus *many* and *few* (countable).

like: Use *like* only when the word that follows is just a noun or pronoun. Use *as* or *as if* when a phrase or clause follows:

> She looks *like* him.
>
> She did just *as* he had expected.
>
> It seems *as if* she had plenty of time.

many/much: See *less.*

regardless: The *less* ending is the negative part. No word needs two negative parts, so it is illiterate to add *ir* at the beginning.

to me/personally: Use these phrases only when personal reactions, apart from company policy, are being stated (not often the case in business writing).

try: Always follow with *to,* never *and.*

verbal: People in the business community who are careful with language frown on those who use *verbal* to mean "spoken" or "oral." Many others do say "verbal agreement." Strictly speaking, *verbal* means "of words" and therefore includes both spoken and written words. Be guided in this matter by company usage.

4.3 Frequently Misspelled Words

All of us, even the world's best spellers, sometimes have to check a dictionary for the spelling of some words. People who've never memorized the spelling of commonly used words must look up so many that they grow exasperated and give up on spelling words correctly.

Don't expect perfection, and don't surrender. If you can memorize the spelling of just the words listed below, you'll need the dictionary far less often and you'll write with more confidence.

absence	competitor	gesture
absorption	concede	grievous
accessible	congratulations	
accommodate	connoisseur	haphazard
accumulate	consensus	harassment
achieve	convenient	holiday
advantageous	convertible	
affiliated	corroborate	illegible
aggressive	criticism	immigrant
alignment		incidentally
aluminum	definitely	indelible
ambience	description	independent
analyze	desirable	indispensable
apparent	dilemma	insistent
appropriate	disappear	intermediary
argument	disappoint	irresistible
asphalt	disbursement	
assistant	discrepancy	jewelry
asterisk	dissatisfied	judgment
auditor	dissipate	judicial
bankruptcy	eligible	labeling
believable	embarrassing	legitimate
brilliant	endorsement	leisure
bulletin	exaggerate	license
	exceed	litigation
calendar	exhaust	
campaign	existence	maintenance
category	extraordinary	mathematics
ceiling		mediocre
changeable	fallacy	minimum
clientele	familiar	
collateral	flexible	necessary
committee	fluctuation	negligence
comparative	forty	negotiable

newsstand	procedure	sincerely
noticeable	proceed	succeed
	pronunciation	suddenness
occurrence	psychology	superintendent
omission	pursue	supersede
		surprise
parallel	questionnaire	
pastime		tangible
peaceable	receive	tariff
permanent	recommend	technique
perseverance	repetition	tenant
persistent	rescind	truly
personnel	rhythmical	
persuade	ridiculous	unanimous
possesses		until
precede	salable	
predictable	secretary	vacillate
preferred	seize	vacuum
privilege	separate	vicious

4.4 Transitional Words and Phrases

The following two sentences don't communicate as well as they might because they lack a transitional word or phrase:

> Production delays are inevitable. Our current lag time in filling orders is one month.

A semicolon between the two sentences would signal a close relationship between their meanings, but it wouldn't even hint at what that relationship is. Here are the sentences, now linked by means of a semicolon, with a space for a transitional word or phrase:

> Production delays are inevitable; _____, our current lag time in filling orders is one month.

Now read the sentence with *nevertheless* in the blank space. Now try *therefore, incidentally, in fact,* and *at any rate* in the blank. Each substitution changes the meaning of the sentence.

Here are some transitional words (called conjunctive adverbs) that will help you write more clearly:

accordingly	furthermore	moreover
anyway	however	otherwise
besides	incidentally	still
consequently	likewise	therefore
finally	meanwhile	

The following transitional phrases are used in the same way:

as a result	in other words
at any rate	in the second place
for example	on the other hand
in fact	to the contrary

When one of these words or phrases joins two independent clauses, it should be preceded by a semicolon and followed by a comma, as shown here:

> The consultant recommended a complete reorganization; moreover, she suggested that we drop several products.

CORRECTION SYMBOLS

Instructors often use these short, easy-to-remember correction symbols and abbreviations when evaluating students' writing. You can use them too, to understand your instruc tor's suggestions and to revise and proofread your own letters, memos, and reports. Refer to Appendix C for additional information on grammar and usage.

CONTENT AND STYLE

Acc	Accuracy. Check to be sure information is correct.
ACE	Avoid copying examples.
ACP	Avoid copying problems.
Adp	Adapt. Tailor message to reader.
Assign	Assignment. Review instructions for assignment.
AV	Active verb. Substitute active for passive.
Awk	Awkward phrasing. Rewrite.
BC	Be consistent.
BMS	Be more sincere.
Chop	Choppy sentences. Use longer sentences and more transitional phrases.
Con	Condense. Use fewer words.
CT	Conversational tone. Avoid using overly formal language.
Depers	Depersonalize. Avoid attributing credit or blame to any individual or group.
Dev	Develop. Provide greater detail.
Dir	Direct. Use direct approach; get to the point.

Emph	Emphasize. Develop this point more fully.
EW	Explanation weak. Check logic; provide more proof.
Fl	Flattery. Avoid flattery that is insincere.
FS	Figure of speech. Find a more accurate expression.
GNF	Good news first. Use direct order.
GRF	Give reasons first. Use indirect order.
GW	Goodwill. Put more emphasis on expressions of goodwill.
H/E	Honesty/ethics. Revise statement to reflect good business practices.
Imp	Imply. Avoid being direct.
Inc	Incomplete. Develop further.
Jar	Jargon. Use less specialized language.
Log	Logic. Check development of argument.
Neg	Negative. Use more positive approach or expression.
Obv	Obvious. Do not state point in such detail.
OC	Overconfident. Adopt more humble language.

OM	Omission.	Spec	Specific. Provide more specific statement.
Org	Organization. Strengthen outline.	SPM	Sales promotion material. Tell reader about related goods or services.
OS	Off the subject. Close with point on main subject.	Stet	Let stand in original form.
Par	Parallel. Use same structure.	Sub	Subordinate. Make this point less important.
Plan	Follow proper organizational plan. (Refer to Chapter 6.)	SX	Sexist. Avoid language that contributes to gender stereotypes.
Pom	Pompous. Rephrase in down-to-earth terms.	Tone	Tone needs improvement.
PV	Point of view. Make statement from reader's perspective rather than your own.	Trans	Transition. Show connection between points.
RB	Reader benefit. Explain what reader stands to gain.	UAE	Use action ending. Close by stating what reader should do next.
Red	Redundant. Reduce number of times this point is made.	UAS	Use appropriate salutation.
Ref	Reference. Cite source of information.	UAV	Use active voice.
Rep	Repetitive. Provide different expression.	Unc	Unclear. Rewrite to clarify meaning.
RS	Resale. Reassure reader that he or she has made a good choice.	UPV	Use passive voice.
SA	Service attitude. Put more emphasis on helping reader.	USS	Use shorter sentences.
Sin	Sincerity. Avoid sounding glib or uncaring.	V	Variety. Use different expression or sentence pattern.
SL	Stereotyped language. Focus on individual's characteristics instead of on false generalizations.	W	Wordy. Eliminate unnecessary words.
		WC	Word choice. Find a more appropriate word.
		YA	"You" attitude. Rewrite to emphasize reader's needs.

*G*RAMMAR, USAGE, AND MECHANICS

Ab	Abbreviation. Avoid abbreviations in most cases; use correct abbreviation.	Cap	Capitalize.
		Case	Use cases correctly.
Adj	Adjective. Use adjective instead.	CoAdj	Coordinate adjective. Insert comma between coordinate adjectives; delete comma between adjective and compound noun.
Adv	Adverb. Use adverb instead.		
Agr	Agreement. Make subject and verb or noun and pronoun agree.		
		CS	Comma splice. Use period or semicolon to separate clauses.
Ap	Appearance. Improve appearance.		
Apos	Apostrophe. Check use of apostrophe.	DM	Dangling modifier. Rewrite so that modifier clearly relates to subject of sentence.
Art	Article. Use correct article.		
BC	Be consistent.	Exp	Expletive. Avoid expletive beginnings, such as *it is*, *there are*, and *there is*.

F	Format. Improve layout of document.	Prep	Preposition. Use correct preposition.
Frag	Fragment. Rewrite as complete sentence.	RC	Restrictive clause. Remove commas that separate clause from rest of sentence.
Gram	Grammar. Correct grammatical error.		
HCA	Hyphenate compound adjective.	RO	Run-on sentence. Separate two sentences with comma or semicolon.
lc	Lowercase. Do not use capital letter.	SC	Series comma. Add comma before *and.*
M	Margins. Improve frame around document.	SI	Split infinitive. Do not separate *to* from rest of verb.
MM	Misplaced modifier. Place modifier close to word it modifies.	Sp	Spelling error. Consult dictionary.
NRC	Nonrestrictive clause. Separate from rest of sentence with commas.	Stet	Let stand in original form.
P	Punctuation. Use correct punctuation.	S-V	Subject-verb pair. Do not separate with comma.
Par	Parallel. Use same structure.	Syl	Syllabification. Divide word between syllables.
PH	Place higher. Move document up on page.	WD	Word division. Check dictionary for proper end-of-line hyphenation.
PL	Place lower. Move document down on page.	WW	Wrong word. Replace with another word.

PROOFREADING MARKS

Symbol	Meaning	Symbol Used in Context	Corrected Copy
═	Align horizontally	meaningful result	meaningful result
‖	Align vertically	1. Power cable 2. Keyboard	1. Power cable 2. Keyboard
(uc)	Capitalize	Do not immerse.	DO NOT IMMERSE.
≡	Capitalize	Pepsico, Inc.	PepsiCo, Inc.
◡	Close up	self- confidence	self-confidence
ℓ	Delete	harrassment and abuse	harassment
(STET)	Restore to original	none of the	none of the
∧	Insert	turquoise shirts	turquoise and white shirts
⋏	Insert comma	a, b and c	a, b, and c
⊙	Insert period	Harrigan et al	Harrigan et al.
/	Lowercase	TULSA, South of here	Tulsa, south of here
⊏	Move left	Attention: Security	Attention: Security
⊐	Move right	February 2, 1996	February 2, 1996
⊔	Move down	Sincerely,	Sincerely,
⊓	Move up	THIRD-QUARTER SALES	THIRD-QUARTER SALES
⊐ ⊏	Center	Awards Banquet	Awards Banquet
⌐	Start new line	Marla Fenton, Manager, Distri-bution	Marla Fenton Manager, Distribution
⌒	Run lines together	Manager, Distribution	Manager, Distribution
¶	Start paragraph	¶The solution is easy to determine but difficult to implement in a competitive environment like the one we now face.	The solution is easy to determine but difficult to implement in a competitive environment like the one we now face.
#	Leave space	real-estate testcase	real estate test case
◯	Spell out	(COD)	cash on delivery
(SP)	Spell out	Assn. of Biochem. Engrs.	Association of Biochemical Engineers
∿	Transpose	airy, light, casaul tone	light, airy, casual tone

Chapter 1

1. Adapted from James Bennet, "Saturn, G.M.'s Big Hope, Is Taking Its First Lumps," *New York Times*, 29 March 1994, A1, A12; David Woodruff, "Suddenly, Saturn's Orbit Is Getting Wobbly," *Business Week*, 28 February 1992, 34; David Woodruff, "May We Help You Kick the Tires?" *Business Week*, 3 August 1992, 49–50; Carol J. Loomis, "Dinosaurs?" *Fortune*, 3 May 1993, 36–42; Raymond Serafin, "The Saturn Story," *Advertising Age*, 16 November 1992, 1, 8, 13, 16; "General Motors' Saturn: Success at a Price," *The Economist*, 27 June 1992, 80–81; Fara Warner, "The Marketers of the Year: Donald Hudler," *Brandweek*, 16 November 1992, 21; "Saturn Gears Up Another Blockbuster Ad," *Adweek*, 4 January 1993, 8.

2. Joseph N. Scudder and Patricia J. Guinan, "Communication Competencies as Discriminators of Superiors' Ratings of Employee Performance," *Journal of Business Communication* 26, no. 3 (1989): 217–229; Joseph F. Coates, "Today's Events Produce Tomorrow's Communication Issues," *IABC Communication World*, June–July 1991, 20–25.

3. Vanessa Dean Arnold, "The Communication Competencies Listed in Job Descriptions," *Bulletin of the Association for Business Communication* 55, no. 2 (1992): 15–17.

4. J. Michael Sproule, *Communication Today*, (Glenview, Ill.: Scott Foresman, 1981), 329.

5. Jaesub Lee and Fredric Jablan, "A Cross-Cultural Investigation of Exit, Voice, Loyalty and Neglect as Responses to Dissatisfying Job Conditions," *Journal of Business Communication* 23, no. 3 (1992): 203–228; Barron Wells and Nelda Spinks, "What Do You Mean People Communicate with Audiences?" *Bulletin of the Association for Business Communication* 54, no. 3 (1991): 100–102.

6. J. David Pincus, Robert E. Rayfield, and J. Nicholas DeBonis, "Transforming CEOs into Chief Communications Officers," *Public Relations Journal*, November 1981, 24.

7. Jim Braham, "A Rewarding Place to Work," *Industry Week*, 18 September 1989, 18.

8. Donald O. Wilson, "Diagonal Communication Links with Organizations," *Journal of Business Communication* 29, no. 2 (1992): 129–143.

9. Brian Dumaine, "Who Needs a Boss?' *Fortune*, 7 May 1990, 52, 54.

10. Valorie A. McClelland and Richard E. Wilmot, "Communication: Improve Lateral Communication," *Personnel Journal*, August 1990, 32–38; Valorie A. McClelland and Dick Wilmot, "Lateral Communication: As Seen Through the Eyes of Employees," *IABC Communication World*, December 1990, 32–35.

11. Donald B. Simmons, "The Nature of the Organizational Grapevine," *Supervisory Management*, November 1985, 40; Carol Hymowitz, "Spread the Word: Gossip Is Good," *Wall Street Journal*, 4 November 1988, B1.

12. Maureen Weiss, "Manager's Tool Kit: Tapping the Grapevine," *Across the Board*, April 1992, 62–63.

13. Gilbert Fuchsberg, "Disaster Plans Gain New Urgency," *Wall Street Journal*, 20 October 1989, B1.

14. "2 Major PR Problems, 2 Approaches," *San Diego Union*, 21 January 1990, I1.

15. "Presumed Guilty: Managing When Your Company's Name Is Mud," *Working Woman*, November 1991, 31.

16. John Huey, "Wal-Mart: Will It Take Over the World?" *Fortune*, 30 January 1989, 56; Patricia Sellers, "Getting Customers to Love You," *Fortune*, 13 March 1989, 39; Stephen Phillips and Amy Dunkin, "King Customer," *Business Week*, 12 March 1990, 91; Charles Leerhsen, "How Disney Does It," *Newsweek*, 3 April 1989, 52.

17. Phillip G. Clampitt and Cal W. Downs, "Employee Perceptions of the Relationship Between Communication and Productivity: A Field Study," *Journal of Business Communication* 30, no. 1 (1993): 5–28.

18. Douglas McGregor, *The Human Side of Enterprise* (New York: McGraw-Hill, 1960), 33–34, 47–48.

19. William G. Ouchi, *Theory Z: How American Business Can Meet the Japanese Challenge* (Reading, Mass.: Addison-Wesley, 1981), 17.

20. Shlomo Maital, "Zen and the Art of Total Quality," *Across the Board*, March 1992, 50–51; James C. Shaffer, "Seven Emerging Trends in Organizational Communication," *IABC Communication World*, February 1986, 18.

21. A. Thomas Young, "Ethics in Business: Business of Ethics," *Vital Speeches*, 15 September 1992, 725–730.

22. Bruce W. Speck, "Writing Professional Codes of Ethics to Introduce Ethics in Business Writing," *Bulletin of the Association for Business Communication* 53, no. 3 (1990): 21–26; H. W. Love, "Communication, Accountability and Professional Discourse: The Interaction of Language Values and Ethical Values," *Journal of Business Ethics* 11 (1992): 883–892; Kathryn C. Rentz and Mary Beth Debs, "Language and Corporate Values: Teaching Ethics in Business Writing Courses," *Journal of Business Communication* 24, no. 3 (1987): 37–48.

23. Joseph L. Badaracco, Jr., "Business Ethics: Four Spheres of Executive Responsibility," *California Management Review*, Spring 1992, 64–79; Kenneth Blanchard and Norman Vincent Peale, *The Power of Ethical Management* (New York: Fawcett Crest, 1991), 7–11.

24. David Grier, "Confronting Ethical Dilemmas: The View From Inside—A Practioner's Perspective," *Vital Speeches*, December 1989, 100–104.

25. John D. Pettit, Bobby Vaught, and Kathy J. Pulley, "The Role of Communication in Organizations," *Journal of Business Communication* 27, no. 3 (1990): 233–249; Labich, "The New Crisis in Business Ethics," 167, 168, 172, 176; Kenneth R. Andrews, "Ethics in Practice," *Harvard Business Review*, September–October 1989, 99–104; Priscilla S. Rogers and John M. Swales, "We the People? An Analysis of the Dana Corporation Policies Document," *Journal of Business Communication* 27, no. 3 (1990): 293–313; Larry Reynolds, "The Ethics Audit," *Business Ethics*, July–August 1991, 120–122.

26. Jules Harcourt, "Developing Ethical Messages: A Unit of Instruction for the Basic Business Communication Course," *Bulletin of the Association for Business Communication* 53, no. 3 (1990): 17–20.

27. Gray Allen, "Valuing Cultural Diversity: Industry Woos a New Work Force," *IABC Communication World*, May 1991, 14–17.

28. Fred Klein, "International Technical Communication," *Technical Communication*, Second Quarter 1992, 264–268; Rose Knotts and Mary S. Thibodeaux, "Verbal Skills in Cross-Culture Managerial Communication," *European Business Review* 92, no. 2 (1992): 5–7.

29. Claire Gouttefarde, "Host National Culture Shock: What Management Can Do," *European Business Review* 92, no. 4 (1992): 1–3.

30. Mohan R. Limaye and David A. Victor, "Cross-Cultural Business Communication Research: State of the Art and Hypotheses for the 1990s," *Journal of Business Communication* 28, no. 3 (1991): 277–299; Joseph F. Coates, "Business Communication in Millennium III," *IABC Communication World*, May–June 1990, 129–134; Coates, "Today's Events Produce Tomorrow's Communication Issues," 24; Arnold, "The Communication Competencies Listed in Job Descriptions," 15–17.

31. Dianna Booher, "Don't Put It in Writing," *Training and Development Journal*, October 1986, 46; Lynn Asinof, "Copious Copies," *Wall Street Journal*, 28 August 1986, 1; Jaclyn Fierman, "Fidelity's Secret: Faithful Service," *Fortune*, 7 May 1990, 92.

32. Mintzberg, "The Manager's Job," 166.

33. "1992, Cost of a Business Letter," *Dartnell Target Study*, Dartnell Institute of Business Research, 1993.

34. Selwyn Feinstein, "Remedial Training," *Wall Street Journal*, 20 February 1990, A1.

35. See note 1.

Chapter 2

1. Maureen Martin, coordinator, employee communications, Ben & Jerry's Homemade, personal communication, 22 January 1990; Donna Lewis, "Making It Work Together," *Franchising World*, January–February 1994, 10–14; Ben & Jerry's Homemade 1993 Annual Report; Fleming Meeks, "We All Scream for Rice and Beans," *Forbes*, 30 March 1992, 20; Mark

Bittman, "Ben & Jerry's Caring Capitalism," *Restaurant Business,* 20 November 1990, 132; Jim Castelli, "Management Styles: Finding the Right Fit," *HR Magazine,* September 1990, 38; Steven S. Ross, "Green Groceries," *Mother Jones,* February–March 1989, 48; Bill Kelley, "The Cause Effect," *Food and Beverage Marketing,* March 1990, 20; Ellie Winninghoff, "Citizen Cohen," *Mother Jones,* January 1990, 12; Erik Larson, "Forever Young," *Inc.,* July 1988, 50; Jeanne Wegner, "This Season, Sharp-dressed Dairy Products Are Wearing Green," *Dairy Foods,* September 1990, 72; Daniel Seligman, "Ben & Jerry Save the World," *Fortune,* 3 June 1991, 247.

2. David Givens, "You Animal! How to Win Friends and Influence Homo Sapiens," *The Toastmaster,* August 1986, 9.

3. Mark L. Hickson III and Don W. Stacks, *Nonverbal Communication: Studies and Applications* (Dubuque, Iowa: Brown, 1985), 4.

4. Gerald H. Graham, Jeanne Unrue, and Paul Jennings, "The Impact of Nonverbal Communication in Organizations: A Survey of Perceptions," *Journal of Business Communication* 28, no. 1 (1991): 45–62.

5. David Lewis, *The Secret Language of Success* (New York: Carroll & Graf, 1989), 67, 170.

6. Dale G. Leathers, *Successful Nonverbal Communication: Principles and Applications* (New York: Macmillan, 1986), 19.

7. Margaret Ann Baker, "Reciprocal Accommodation: A Model for Reducing Gender Bias in Managerial Communication," *Journal of Business Communication* 28, no. 2 (1991): 113–127; Graham, Unrue, and Jennings, "The Impact of Nonverbal Communication in Organizations," 45–62.

8. Graham, Unrue, and Jennings, "The Impact of Nonverbal Communication in Organizations," 45–62.

9. Stuart Berg Flexner, "From 'Gadzooks' to 'Nice,' the Language Keeps Changing," *U.S. News & World Report,* 18 February 1985, 59.

10. Claudia H. Deutsch, "The Multimedia Benefits Kit," *New York Times,* 14 October 1990, sec. 3, 25.

11. Phillip Morgan and H. Kent Baker, "Building a Professional Image: Improving Listening Behavior," *Supervisory Management,* November 1985, 35, 36.

12. Augusta M. Simon, "Effective Listening: Barriers to Listening in a Diverse Business Environment," *Bulletin of the Association for Business Communication* 54, no. 3 (1991): 73–74.

13. Irwin Ross, "Corporations Take Aim at Illiteracy," *Fortune,* 29 September 1986, 49.

14. Some material adapted from Courtland L. Bovée, John V. Thill, Marian Burk Wood, and George P. Dovel, *Management* (New York: McGraw-Hill, 1993), 537–538.

15. Much of the material contained in the entire section on communication barriers has been adapted from Bovée, Thill, Wood, and Dovel, *Management,* 549–557.

16. Adapted from C. Glenn Pearce, Ross Figgins, and Steve F. Golen, *Principles of Business Communication: Theory, Application, and Technology* (New York: Wiley, 1984), 520–538.

17. Bovée, Thill, Wood, and Dovel, *Management,* 555.

18. See note 1.

Chapter 3

1. Adapted from Art Garcia, "Reversal of Fortune," *World Trade,* June 1992, 56–63; Neil Gross and Kathy Rebello, "Apple? Japan Can't Say No," *Business Week,* 29 June 1992, 32–33; Neil Gross, "Is It Finally Time for Apple to Blossom in Japan?" *Business Week,* 28 May 1990, 100–101.

2. Gus Tyler, "Tokyo Signs the Paychecks," *New York Times Book Review,* 12 August 1990, 7.

3. Tzöl Zae Chung, "Culture: A Key to Management Communication Between the Asian-Pacific Area and Europe," *European Management Journal* 9, no. 4 (1991): 419–424.

4. Larry A. Samovar and Richard E. Porter, "Basic Principles of Intercultural Communication," in *Intercultural Communication: A Reader,* 6th ed., edited by Larry A. Samovar and Richard E. Porter (Belmont, Calif.: Wadsworth, 1991), 12.

5. Kathleen K. Reardon, "It's the Thought That Counts," *Harvard Business Review,* September–October 1984, 141.

6. Otto Kreisher, "Annapolis Has a New Attitude Toward Sexual Harassment," *San Diego Union,* 30 July 1990, A6.

7. Robert O. Joy, "Cultural and Procedural Differences That Influence Business Strategies and Operations in the People's Republic of China," *SAM Advanced Management Journal,* Summer 1989, 29–33.

8. "Pakistan: A Congenial Business Climate," *Nation's Business,* July 1986, 50.

9. David A. Victor, *International Business Communication,* (New York: HarperCollins, 1992), 234–239; Mohan R. Limaye and David A. Victor, "Cross-Cultural Business Communication Research: State of the Art and Hypotheses for the 1990s," *Journal of Business Communication* 28, no. 3 (1991): 277–299.

10. Carley H. Dodd, *Dynamics of Intercultural Communication,* 3d ed. (Dubuque, Iowa: Brown, 1991), 215.

11. Edward T. Hall, "Context and Meaning," in *Intercultural Communication: A Reader,* 6th ed., edited by Larry A. Samovar and Richard E. Porter (Belmont, Calif.: Wadsworth, 1991), 46–55.

12. Dodd, *Dynamics of Intercultural Communication,* 69–70.

13. Samovar and Porter, "Basic Principles of Intercultural Communication," 5–22; David A. Victor, personal communication, 1993.

14. Laray M. Barna, "Stumbling Blocks in Intercultural Communication," in *Intercultural Communication: A Reader,* 6th ed., edited by Larry A. Samovar and Richard E. Porter (Belmont, Calif.: Wadsworth, 1991), 345–352.

15. Sharon Ruhly, *Intercultural Communication,* 2d ed., MODCOM (Modules in Speech Communication) (Chicago: Science Research Associates, 1982), 14.

16. Karen P. H. Lane, "Greasing the Bureaucratic Wheel," *North American International Business,* August 1990, 35–37; Arthur Aronoff, "Complying with the Foreign Corrupt Practices Act," *Business America,* 11 February 1991, 10–11; Bill Shaw, "Foreign Corrupt Practices Act: A Legal and Moral Analysis," *Journal of Business Ethics* 7 (1988): 789–795.

17. Harris and Moran, *Managing Cultural Differences,* 260.

18. Judy F. West and Judy C. Nixon, "International Business Communication Opportunities: A Key to Success," *1989 Proceedings of the Sixteenth International Convention of the Association for Business Communication,* 232; Marguerite P. Shane Joyce, "Intercultural Business Communication: Prescription for Success," speech before the Tenth Annual Conference on Languages and Communication for World Business and the Professions, Eastern Michigan University (Ypsilanti, Mich.), 3 April 1991, 9; Stephen Karel, "On Language," *American Demographics,* May 1989, 54.

19. David A. Ricks, "International Business Blunders: An Update," *B&E Review,* January–March 1988, 12.

20. Vern Terpstra, *The Cultural Environment of International Business* (Cincinnati: South-Western, 1979), 19.

21. Retha H. Kilpatrick, "International Business Communication Practices," *Journal of Business Communication* 21, no. 4 (1984): 36.

22. Victor, *International Business Communication,* 36.

23. Doreen Mangan, "What's New in Language Translation: A Tool for Examining Foreign Patents and Research," *New York Times,* 19 November 1989, sec. 3, 15.

24. Victor, *International Business Communication,* 39; Harris and Moran, *Managing Cultural Differences,* 64.

25. Geert Hofstede, *Cultures and Organizations* (London: McGraw-Hill, 1991), 211.

26. Richard W. Brislin, "Prejudice in Intercultural Communication," in *Intercultural Communication: A Reader,* 6th ed., edited by Larry A. Samovar and Richard E. Porter (Belmont, Calif.: Wadsworth, 1991), 366–370.

27. Dodd, *Dynamics of Intercultural Communication,* 142–143, 297–299.

28. Susan A. Hellweg, Larry A. Samovar, and Lisa Skow, "Cultural Variations in Negotiation Styles," in *Intercultural Communication: A Reader,* 6th ed., edited by Larry A. Samovar and Richard E. Porter (Belmont, Calif.: Wadsworth, 1991), 185–192.

29. See note 1.

Chapter 4

1. Adapted from Katherine Burger, "Demystifying the Glass House at MetLife," *Insurance & Technology,* July–August 1991, 18–25; Lura K. Romei, "Publishing Pays Off," *Modern Office Technology,* October 1988, 59–62; Patricia M. Fernberg, "Putting the 'E.T.' in Met Life," *Modern Office Technology,* November 1988, 72, 74; Darlane Hoffman, "Have You

Compressed Your Data Today?" *Best's Review,* May 1988, 48–54; Marilyn Gasaway and Anna Welke, "How Leading Insurers Use Technology to Compete," *ICP Insurance Software,* Autumn 1986, 14–23; "The Automated Office: Waging a Paper War," *ICP Insurance Software,* Spring 1984, 8.

2. Eric J. Adams, "A Real Global Office," *World Trade,* October 1992, 97–98.
3. *Dialog Database Catalog 1993,* 62–63, 130.
4. *The PC Zone Catalog,* Winter 1992, 36.
5. Rosalind Resnick, "Calling Up Trade," *International Business,* November 1992, 64–65.
6. John Markoff, "Computers Advancing Rapidly Back to the Pen," *New York Times,* 6 January 1993, C2.
7. Gene Bylinksy, "At Last! Computers You Can Talk To," *Fortune,* 3 May 1993, 88–91.
8. Frank Andera, "An Analysis of the Usage of Electronic Dictation by Business Executives," *The Bulletin of the Association for Business Communication* 54, no. 2 (1991): 46–50.
9. Jack Nimersheim, "Grammar Checker Face-Off," *Home-Office Computing,* July 1992, 49–53.
10. Eric J. Adams, "The Fax of Global Business," *World Trade,* August–September 1991, 34–39.
11. Lawrence Magid, "E-Mail Explained," Prodigy Interactive Personal Service, 14 May 1993.
12. Carla Lazzareschi, "Wired: Businesses Create Cyberspace Land Rush on the Internet," *Los Angeles Times,* 22 August 1993, D1.
13. Jolie Solomon, "As Electronic Mail Loosens Inhibitions, Impetuous Senders Feel Anything Goes," *Wall Street Journal,* 10 December 1990, B1–B2.
14. Solomon, "As Electronic Mail Loosens Inhibitions," B1–B2.
15. Mike Bransby, "Voice Mail Makes a Difference," *Journal of Business Strategy,* January–February 1990, 7–10.
16. Harris Collingswood, "Voice Mail Hangups," *Business Week,* 17 February 1992, 46.
17. Andrew Kupfer, "Prime Time for Videoconferences," Fortune, 28 December 1992, 90–95.
18. Michael Finley, "The New Meaning of Meetings," *IABC Communication World,* March 1991, 25–27.
19. Chris Campbell, "Outerstreaming: The Fourth Communication Paradigm," *IABC Communication World,* December 1990, 18–22.
20. Mark Mabrito, "Computer-Mediated Communication and High-Apprehensive Writers: Rethinking the Collaborative Process," *Bulletin of the Association for Business Communication* (December 1992): 26–29; Susan M. Gelfond, "It's a Fax, Fax, Fax, Fax World," *Business Week,* 21 March 1988, 138.
21. Jeffrey Young, "Knowing the Way to Santa Fe," *Forbes ASAP,* 29 March 1993, 112–116.
22. See note 1.

Chapter 5
1. Adapted from Mattel 1993 Annual Report, 2–6; Michelle Green and Denise Gellene, "As a Tiny Plastic Star Turns 30, the Real Barbie and Ken Reflect on Life in the Shadow of the Dolls," *People,* 6 March 1989, 186–189; Denise Gellene, "Forever Young," *Los Angeles Times,* 29 January 1989, D1, D4; Ann Hornaday, "Top Guns: The Most Powerful Women in Corporate America," *Savvy,* May 1989, 57, 60; Jennifer Roethe, "Dolls and Dollars Go Together like Ken and Barbie," *Cincinnati Business Courier,* 10 July 1989, 1.
2. Mary K. Kirtz and Diana C. Reep, "A Survey of the Frequency, Types, and Importance of Writing Tasks in Four Career Areas," *Bulletin of the Association for Business Communication* 53, no. 4 (1990): 3–4.
3. Ruth Yontz, "Providing a Rationale for the Process Approach," *Journal of Business Communication* 24, no. 1 (1987): 17–19; Annette Shelby, "Note on Process," *Journal of Business Communication* 24, no. 1 (1987): 21; Mary Cullinan and Ce Ce Iandoli, "What Activities Help to Improve Your Writing? Some Unsettling Student Responses," *Bulletin of the Association for Business Communication,* 54, no. 4 (1991): 8–10.
4. Peter Bracher, "Process, Pedagogy, and Business Writing," *Journal of Business Communication* 24, no. 1 (1987): 43–50.

5. Constance Pollard, "Streamlining the Writing Process in Business Communication," *Bulletin of the Association for Business Communication* 54, no. 2 (1991): 29–31.
6. Janis Forman, "Collaborative Business Writing: A Burkean Perspective for Future Research," *Journal of Business Communication* 29, no. 3 (1991): 233–257.
7. Terry R. Bacon, "Collaboration in a Pressure Cooker," *Bulletin of the Association for Business Communication* 53, no. 2 (1990): 4–8.
8. Sanford Kaye, "Writing Under Pressure," *Soundview Executive Book Summaries* 10, no. 12, p. 2 (1988): 1–8.
9. William P. Dommermuth, *Promotion: Analysis, Creativity, and Strategy* (Boston: Kent Publishing, 1982), 282.
10. Morgan W. McCall, Jr., and Robert L. Hannon, *Studies of Managerial Work: Results and Methods,* Technical Report no. 9 (Greensboro, N.C.: Center for Creative Leadership, 1978), 6–10.
11. Ernest Thompson, "Some Effects of Message Structure on Listener's Comprehension," *Speech Monographs* 34 (March 1967): 51–57.
12. Laurey Berk and Phillip G. Clampitt, "Finding the Right Path in the Communication Maze," *IABC Communication World,* October 1991, 28–32.
13. Al Schlachtmeyer and Max Caldwell, "Communicating Creatively," *IABC Communication World,* June–July 1991, 26–29.
14. Mohan R. Limaye and David A. Victor, "Cross-Cultural Business Communication Research: State of the Art and Hypotheses for the 1990s," *Journal of Business Communication* 28, no. 3 (1991): 277–299.
15. Berk and Clampitt, "Finding the Right Path in the Communication Maze," 28–32.
16. Berk and Clampitt, "Finding the Right Path in the Communication Maze," 28–32.
17. See note 1.

Chapter 6
1. Adapted from Erica Gordon Sorohan, "When the Ties That Bind Break," *Training & Development,* February 1994, 28–33; Blayne Cutler, "Corporate Victims," *American Demographics,* May 1989, 19; Diane Cole, "What's New in Outplacement," *New York Times,* 14 February 1988, sec. 4, 15; Dana Bottoff, "The Velvet Boot," *New England Business,* 19 October 1987, 24–28; Lisa Spooner, "Outplacement Eases Termination Woes," *Savings Institutions,* March 1986, 99, 101.
2. Carol S. Mull, "Orchestrate Your Ideas," *The Toastmaster,* February 1987, 19.
3. Based on the Pyramid Model developed by Barbara Minto of McKinsey & Company, management consultants.
4. Iris I. Varner, "Internationalizing Business Communication Courses," *Bulletin of the Association for Business Communication* 50, no. 4 (1987): 7–11.
5. Elizabeth Blackburn and Kelly Belanger, "You-Attitude and Positive Emphasis: Testing Received Wisdom in Business Communication," *Bulletin of the Association for Business Communication* 56, no. 2 (1993): 1–9.
6. John S. Fielden, Jean D. Fielden, and Ronald E. Dulek, *Business Writing Style Book* (Englewood Cliffs, N.J.: Prentice-Hall, 1984), 7.
7. See note 1.

Chapter 7
1. Adapted from Dyan Machan, "Great Hash Browns, but Watch Those Biscuits," *Forbes,* 19 September 1988, 192–196; Brian Bremner, "The Burger Wars Were Just a Warmup for McDonald's," *Business Week,* 8 May 1989, 67, 70; Richard Gibson and Robert Johnson, "Big Mac Plots Strategy to Regain Sizzle; Besides Pizza, It Ponders Music and Low Lights," *Wall Street Journal,* 29 September 1989, B1; Penny Moser, "The McDonald's Mystique," *Fortune,* 4 July 1988, 112–116; Thomas N. Cochran, "McDonald's Corporation," *Barron's,* 16 November 1987, 53–55; Lenore Skenazy, "McDonald's Colors Its World," *Advertising Age,* 9 February 1987, 37.
2. Iris I. Varner, "Internationalizing Business Communication Courses," *Bulletin of the Association for Business Communication* 50, no. 4 (1987): 7–11.
3. Kevin T. Stevens, Kathleen C. Stevens, and William P. Stevens, "Measuring the Readability of Business Writing: The Cloze Procedure Versus Readability Formulas," *Journal of Business Communication* 29, no. 4 (1992):

367–382; Alinda Drury, "Evaluating Readability," *IEEE Transactions on Professional Communication* PC-28 (December 1985): 11.

4. Portions of this section are adapted from Courtland L. Bovée, *Techniques of Writing Business Letters, Memos, and Reports* (Sherman Oaks, Calif.: Banner Books International, 1978), 13–90.

5. Randolph H. Hudson, Gertrude M. McGuire, and Bernard J. Selzler, *Business Writing: Concepts and Applications* (Los Angeles: Roxbury, 1983), 79–82.

6. Peter Crow, "Plain English: What Counts Besides Readability?" *Journal of Business Communication* 25, no. 1 (1988): 87–95.

7. Judy E. Pickens, "Terms of Equality: A Guide to Bias-Free Language," *Personnel Journal*, August 1985, 24.

8. Rose Knotts and Mary S. Thibodeaux, "Verbal Skills in Cross-Culture Managerial Communication," *European Business Review* 92, no. 2 (1992): 5–7.

9. Lisa Taylor, "Communicating About People with Disabilities: Does the Language We Use Make a Difference?" *Bulletin of the Association for Business Communication* 53, no. 3 (1990): 65–67.

10. Taylor, "Communicating About People with Disabilities," 65–67.

11. Varner, "Internationalizing Business Communication Courses," 7–11.

12. Drury, "Evaluating Readability," 12.

13. Portions of the following sections are adapted from Roger C. Parker, *Looking Good in Print*, 2d ed. (Chapel Hill, N.C.: Ventana Press, 1990).

14. Raymond W. Beswick, "Designing Documents for Legibility," *Bulletin of the Association for Business Communication* 50, no. 4 (1987): 34–35

15. Beswick, "Designing Documents for Legibility," 34–35.

16. "The Process Model of Document Design," *IEEE Transactions on Professional Communication* PC-24, no. 4 (December 1981): 176–178.

17. See note 1.

Chapter 8

1. Adapted from Jim Milliot, "Superstore Strength Results in 21% Sales Increase at B & N," *Publishers Weekly*, 20 February 1995, 107; Myron Magnet, "Let's Go for Growth," *Fortune*, 7 March 1994, 60, 62, 64, 68, 70, 72; Richard Phalon, "A Bold Gamble," *Forbes*, 28 February 1994, 90–91; Barnes & Noble 1993 annual report; Kate Fitzgerald, "Bookstores in Competitive Thriller," *Advertising Age*, 12 April 1993, 12; John Mutter, "The Fine Print: Walden Edges Toward Borders," *Publishers Weekly*, 23 May 1994, 38–39; John Mutter, "A Chat with Bookseller Len Riggio," *Publishers Weekly*, 3 May 1992, 33–34, 36, 38.

2. Lennie Copeland and Lewis Griggs, *Going International: How to Make Friends and Deal Effectively in the Global Marketplace*, 2d ed. (New York: Random House, 1985), 24–27.

3. Linda Beamer, "Learning Intercultural Communication Competence," *Journal of Business Communication* 29, no. 3 (1992): 285–303.

4. See note 1.

5. Adapted from *Music Design Wholesale Catalog and Price List*, Fall 1991.

6. Adapted from Florence Fabricant, "Forget That 'Java Jive.' America Is Humming 'Tea for Two,'" *New York Times*, 30 March 1994, B1, B4.

7. Adapted from Computer Discount Warehouse catalog, Spring 1994, 35; Linda Stern, "The Fee-Setting Debate," *Home-Office Computing*, October 1993, 40, 42.

8. Adapted from Shelley Cryan, "Multimedia Presentations," *Byte*, April 1994, 189–195.

9. Adapted from Bruce V. Bigelow, "Magnificent Magnetics," *San Diego Union-Tribune*, 24 November 1993, E1, E5.

10. Adapted from Kenneth L. Woodward (with Anne Underwood, Tim Pryor, Karen Springen, and Steven Levin), "Angels," *Newsweek*, 27 December 1993, 52–57.

11. Adapted from Zina Moukheiber, "A Lousy Day for Golf," *Forbes*, 9 May 1994, 60, 64.

12. Adapted from Associated Press, "Flood of Imports into Argentina Delights Shoppers, Riles Local Industry," *Los Angeles Times*, 6 January 1992, D4.

13. Adapted from Rose-Marie Turk, "Just a Touch," *Los Angeles Times*, 20 December 1991, E20; Business Notes, "Lipstick with a Conscience," *Time*, 7 October 1991, 45.

14. Adapted from Richard L. Hudson, "U S West to Become Partner in Firm Russia Is Forming for Phone Network," *Wall Street Journal*, 31 March

1994, B7; Don Bishop, corporate sales representative, Computerland, San Diego, California, personal communication, 16 June 1994.

15. Adapted from Market Watch, "Bookstore Landscape Changing in Burlington, VT," *Bookselling This Week*, 25 April 1994, 4–5; advertising flyers, Andrea Jeffery, Calgary, Alberta, Canada, Spring 1994.

Chapter 9

1. Adapted from 1993 Campbell Soup Annual Report; Joseph Weber, "Campbell: Now It's M-M-Global," *Business Week*, 15 March 1993, 52–54; Pete Engardio, "'Hmm. Could Use A Little More Snake,'" *Business Week*, 15 March 1993, 53; Joseph Weber, "Campbell Is Bubbling, But for How Long?" *Business Week*, 17 June 1991, 56–57; Joseph Weber, "From Soup to Nuts and Back to Soup," *Business Week*, 5 November 1990, 114, 116; "Here Are the Women to Watch in Corporate America," *Business Month*, April 1989, 40; Alix Freedman and Frank Allen, "John Dorrance's Death Leaves Campbell Soup with Cloudy Future," *Wall Street Journal*, 19 April 1989, A1, A14; Claudia H. Deutsch, "Stirring Up Profits at Campbell," *New York Times*, 20 November 1988, sec. 3, 1, 22; Bill Saporito, "The Fly in Campbell's Soup," *Fortune*, 9 May 1988, 67–70; biography of Zoe Coulson from *Marquis Who's Who*, accessed on-line, 24 May 1992.

2. Daniel P. Finkelman and Anthony R. Goland, "Customers Once Can Be Customers for Life," *Information Strategy: The Executive's Journal*, Summer 1990, 5–9.

3. Cathy Goodwin and Ivan Ross, "Consumer Evaluations of Responses to Complaints: What's Fair and Why," *Journal of Consumer Marketing* 7, no. 2 (Spring 1990): 39–46.

4. Susan Stobaugh, "Watch Your Language," *Inc.*, May 1985, 156.

5. Adapted from Donna Larcen, "Authors Share the Words of Condolence," *Los Angeles Times*, 20 December 1991, E11.

6. See note 1.

7. Adapted from Hilary Appelman, "Xerox Breaks into the Japanese Market," *Los Angeles Times*, 3 February 1992, D3.

8. Adapted from Timothy Aeppel, "Chlorine-Free Paper Is Clean but Unpopular," *Wall Street Journal*, 4 April 1994, B1, B6.

9. Adapted from Jeanne Wright, "Another Lifetime of Worry over DES," *Los Angeles Times*, 11 February 1992, E1.

10. Adapted from Matthew Kopka, "The Nuts and Bolts of Audio-Only," *Publishers Weekly*, 4 April 1994, 29–30.

11. Adapted from Andrew Pollack, "It's Asians' Turn in Silicon Valley," *New York Times*, 14 January 1992, sec. d, 1, 5.

12. See note 1.

13. Adapted from Anthony Ramirez, "Hot-Wiring Overseas Telephone Calls," *New York Times*, 9 January 1992, sec. d, 1, 6.

14. Adapted from Larry Reibstein (with Martha Brant and Nina Archer Biddle), "The Battle of the TV News Magazine Shows," *Newsweek*, 11 April 1994, 60–66.

15. Adapted from Julie Edelson Halpert, "Aluminum Is Put to the Test by Ford," *New York Times*, 3 April 1994, sec. 3, 7.

16. Adapted from Toni Mack, "Michael Dell's New Religion," *Forbes*, 6 June 1994, 45–46; Company News, "Expansion Planned for Dell's Irish Plant," *New York Times*, 7 April 1994, C3.

17. Adapted from Bernard Weinraub, "Young and Smart, but Not Too Smart to Lead a Studio," *New York Times*, 4 April 1994, B1, B2.

18. Adapted from Sylvia Nasar, with Alison Leigh Cowan, "A Wall St. Star's Agonizing Confession," *New York Times*, 3 April 1994, sec. 3, 1, 8; Michael Siconolfi, "Bear Stearns Forced Kudlow to Depart; Economist Says He Has Drug Problem," *Wall Street Journal*, 4 April 1994, B10.

Chapter 10

1. Adapted from Thomas R. King, "Ad Frenzy Is Planned to Mark 40th Birthday of Peanuts Gang," *Wall Street Journal*, 25 October 1989, B6; Craig Wilson, "He's a Good Man, Mr. Schulz," *USA Today*, 4 October 1989, 1D; Michael Barrier, "Working for 'Peanuts,'" *Nation's Business*, November 1988, 64–67; Carla Lazzareschi, "Fortune Grows from 'Peanuts' for Schulz, a Reluctant Tycoon. Good Grief!" *Los Angeles Times*, 29 November 1987, D1; William Scobie, "Happiness Is . . . Snoopy," *Reader's Digest*, May 1986, 99–104.

2. James Calvert Scott and Diana J. Green, "British Perspectives on Organizing Bad-News Letters: Organizational Patterns Used by Major U.K. Companies," *Bulletin of the Association for Business Communication* 55, no. 1 (1992): 17–19.

3. Iris I. Varner, "Internationalizing Business Communication Courses," *Bulletin of the Association for Business Communication* 50, no. 4 (1987): 7–11.

4. Ram Subramanian, Robert G. Insley, and Rodney D. Blackwell, "Performance and Readability: A Comparison of Annual Reports of Profitable and Unprofitable Corporations," *Journal of Business Communication* 30, no. 2 (1993): 49–61.

5. Jane R. Goodson, Gail W. McGee, and Anson Seers, "Giving Appropriate Performance Feedback to Managers: An Empirical Test of Content and Outcomes," *Journal of Business Communication* 29, no. 4 (1992): 329–342.

6. Howard M. Bloom, "Performance Evaluations," *New England Business,* December 1991, 14.

7. David I. Rosen, "Appraisals Can Make—or Break—Your Court Case," *Personnel Journal,* November 1992, 113.

8. Craig Cox, "On the Firing Line," *Business Ethics,* May–June 1992, 33–34.

9. Cox, "On the Firing Line," 33–34.

10. See note 1.

11. Adapted from Hannah Holmes, "Keepers: Better Bike Mirror," *Garbage,* June–July 1993, 53.

12. Adapted from International Tesla Society Museum Bookstore Catalog, Fall 1993.

13. Adapted from Michael A. Champ and Michael D. Willinsky, "Farming the Oceans," *The World & I,* April 1994, 200–207.

14. Adapted from John M. Glionna, "Owner of Julian Surfing Store Makes Waves with 14-Foot Sign," *Los Angeles Times,* 6 January 1992, B1, B3; Bob Rowland, "Surfing Sign Makes Big Waves in Julian," *San Diego Union,* 10 January 1992, B1, B4.

15. Adapted from Janet Guyon, "Fairness Issue: Inequality in Granting Child-Care Benefits Makes Workers Seethe," *Wall Street Journal,* 23 October 1991, A1, A7.

16. Adapted from Robert Johnson, "Your Little Monkey Is So Cuddly. Here, Let Me—OUCH!" *Wall Street Journal,* 2 December 1991, A1, A14.

17. Adapted from Barbara Foley, "Stepping into Something, Um, Ugly," *Los Angeles Times,* 18 December 1991, E1, E8.

18. Adapted from Fleming Meeks, "Shakespeare, Dickens & Hillegass," *Forbes,* 30 October 1989, 206, 208, 209.

19. Adapted from "A Color Printer to Be Shared," *Byte,* April 1994, 252.

20. Adapted from "I.R.S. Error of $40 Million," *New York Times,* 7 February 1992, sec. c, 4.

Chapter 11

1. Adapted from Margie Markarian, "Fundraising in Tough Times," *Black Enterprise,* December 1993, 77–78, 81–82; "Fundraising: The Bottom Line," *Black Enterprise,* December 1993, 82; Caroline V. Clarke, "Redefining Beautiful," *Black Enterprise,* June 1993, 243–244, 246, 248; Matthew S. Scott, "A Higher Calling," *Black Enterprise,* February 1992, 227–228, 230; United Negro College Fund 1994 Annual Report.

2. Jeanette W. Gilsdorf, "Write Me Your Best Case for . . .," *Bulletin of the Association for Business Communication* 54, no. 1 (1991): 7–12.

3. Gilsdorf, "Write Me Your Best Case for . . .," 7–12.

4. Mary Cross, "Aristotle and Business Writing: Why We Need to Teach Persuasion," *Bulletin of the Association for Business Communication* 54, no. 1 (1991): 3–6.

5. Gilsdorf, "Write Me Your Best Case for . . .," 7–12.

6. Jeanette W. Gilsdorf, "Executives' and Academics' Perceptions on the Need for Instruction in Written Persuasion," *Journal of Business Communication* 23 (Fall 1986): 67.

7. Teri Lammers, "The Elements of Perfect Pitch," *Inc.,* March 1992, 53–55.

8. William North Jayme, quoted in Albert Haas, Jr., "How to Sell Almost Anything by Direct Mail," *Across the Board,* November 1986, 50.

9. "The Ideal Collection Letter," *Inc.,* February 1991, 59–61.

10. See note 1.

11. Adapted from Claudia H. Deutsch, "Rewarding Employees for 'Wellness,'" *New York Times,* 15 September 1991, sec. c, 21; Hilary Stout, "Paying Workers for Good Health Habits Catches On as a Way to Cut Medical Costs," *Wall Street Journal,* 16 November 1991, B1, B5.

12. Adapted from Fara Warner, "Kellogg Launches a Cereal for Charity," *Adweek's Marketing Week,* 11 November 1991, 6.

13. Adapted from Suein L. Hwang, "Ding-Dong: Updating Avon Means Respecting History Without Repeating It," *Wall Street Journal,* 4 April 1994, A1, A4; Claudia H. Deutsch, "Relighting the Fires at Avon Products," *New York Times,* 3 April 1994, sec. 3, 6.

14. Adapted from David A. Avila, "Mentally Ill Find Health in Flowers," *Los Angeles Times,* 15 January 1992, B2.

15. Adapted from Matthew L. Wald, "Two Technologies Join to Assist Lost Drivers," *New York Times,* 30 March 1994, sec. a, 13.

16. Adapted from Joanne Lipman, "Consumers Rebel Against Becoming a Captive Audience," *Wall Street Journal,* 13 September 1991, B1.

17. Adapted from Tim Friend, "Health Care That's Also Fiscally Fit," *USA Today,* 5 December 1991, D1, D2.

18. Adapted from Roger Thuron, "Seeing the Light," *Wall Street Journal,* 20 September 1991, R1, R2; Erin Kelly, "Business School in Prague Trains Future Capitalists," *Los Angeles Times,* 12 January 1992, D3.

19. Adapted from Laurie M. Grossman, "PepsiCo Plans Big Overseas Expansion in Diet Cola Wars with Its Pepsi Max," *Wall Street Journal,* 4 April 1994, B4.

20. Marcia Joseph, Deodorant Stones of America, personal communication, 14 July 1994; DSA product literature.

21. Adapted from Karen E. Klein and Steve Scauzillo, "The Fuel Cell Future," *The World & I,* April 1994, 192–199.

22. Adapted from Marc Levinson, "Riding the Data Highway," *Newsweek,* 21 March 1994, 54–55.

23. Adapted from Rod Riggs, "Mother of Invention," *San Diego Union-Tribune,* 29 March 1994, C1, C2.

24. Rancho San Diego Vision Care Center Optometry, personal communication, 15 July 1994.

Chapter 12

1. Adapted from "All Strung Up," *The Economist,* 17 April 1993, 70; "Pass the Parcel," *The Economist,* 21 March 1992, 73–74; "Federal Express," *Personnel Journal,* January 1992, 52; Gary M. Stern, "Improving Verbal Communications," *Internal Auditor,* August 1993, 49–54; Gary Hoover, Alta Campbell, and Patrick J. Spain, *Hoover's Handbook of American Business 1994* (Austin, Tex.: Reference Press, 1993), 488–489.

2. Roger P. Wilcox, *Communication at Work: Writing and Speaking* (Boston: Houghton Mifflin, 1977), 49–51.

3. See note 1.

4. Adapted from J. Roberto Whitaker-Penteado, "Oil Cos. Pump Up Advertising in Brazil," *Adweek,* 6 September 1993, 14.

5. Adapted from Nancy Jeffrey, "Preparing for the Worst: Firms Set Up Plans to Help Deal with Corporate Crises," *Wall Street Journal,* 7 December 1987, 23.

Chapter 13

1. Adapted from Harley-Davidson 1993 Annual Report; Brian S. Moskal, "Born to Be Real," *Industry Week,* 2 August 1993, 14–18; Martha H. Peak, "Harley-Davidson: Going Whole Hog to Provide Stakeholder Satisfaction," *Management Review,* June 1993, 53–55; Gary Slutsker, "Hog Wild," *Forbes,* 24 May 1993, 45–46; Kevin Kelly and Karen Lowry Miller, "The Rumble Heard Round the World: Harleys," *Business Week,* 24 May 1993, 58, 60; James B. Shuman, "Easy Rider Rides Again," *Business Tokyo,* July 1991, 26–30; Holt Hackney, "Easy Rider," *Financial World,* 4 September 1990, 48–49; Roy L. Harmon and Leroy D. Peterson, "Reinventing the Factory," *Across the Board,* March 1990, 30–38; John Holusha, "How Harley Outfoxed Japan with Exports," *New York Times,* 12 August 1990, F5; Peter C. Reid, "How Harley Beat Back the Japanese," *Fortune,* 25 September 1989, 155–164.

2. Iris I. Varner, *Contemporary Business Report Writing,* 2d ed. (Chicago: Dryden Press, 1991), 135.

3. F. Stanford Wayne and Jolene D. Scriven, "Problem and Purpose Statements: Are They Synonymous Terms in Writing Reports for Business?" *Bulletin of the Association for Business Communication* 54, no. 1 (1991): 30–37.

4. All references to Lowry & Associates adapted from Jim Lowry, personal communication, December 1986.
5. Rudolf Flesch, "How to Say It with Statistics," *Marketing Communications,* 8 December 1950, 23–24.
6. Flesch, "How to Say It with Statistics," 23–24.
7. See note 1.

Chapter 14

1. Adapted from N. R. Kleinfield, "Penn State's $20 Million Touchdown," *New York Times,* 12 September 1987, sec. 3, 1, 8; Bruce Walker, "The Demand for Professional League Football and the Success of Football League Teams: Some City Size Effects," *Urban Studies,* June 1986, 209–219; "The Way We Were: The Tenuous Economics of the Gridiron," *Canadian Business,* September 1988, 118; Glen Waggoner, "Money Madness: The True Story about the Crazy Economics of Professional Sports," *Esquire,* June 1982, 49; John Merwin, "Dumb Like Foxes," *Forbes,* 24 October 1988, 703–724.
2. Material on plagiarism adapted from Courtland L. Bovée and John V. Thill, *Business Communication Today,* 4th ed. (New York: McGraw-Hill, 1995), 444–445.
3. See note 1.
4. Adapted from Suzanne Alexander, "College 'Parties' Get High Marks as Sales Events," *Wall Street Journal,* 23 October 1992, B1.
5. Adapted from David J. Jefferson and Thomas R. King, "'Informercials' Fill Up Prime Time on Cable, Aim for Prime Time," *Wall Street Journal,* 22 October 1992, A1.

Chapter 15

1. Adapted from Bob Smith, "The Evolution of Pinkerton," *Management Review,* September 1993, 54–58; Bob Smith, "Pinkerton Keeps Its Eye on Recruitment," *HR Focus,* 6 September 1993, 1, 6; "Oscar's News," *Security Management,* 14 June 1993, 14; Pinkerton 1993 Annual Report.
2. Pam Stanley-Weigand, "Organizing the Writing of Your Resume," *Bulletin of the Association for Business Communication* 54, no. 3 (1991): 11–12.
3. Robert G. Nesbit, "A Headhunter Rates Your Résumé," *Industry Week,* 6 February 1990, 19.
4. Janice Tovey, "Using Visual Theory in the Creation of Resumes: A Bibliography," *Bulletin of the Association for Business Communication* 54, no. 3 (1991): 97–99.
5. Myra Fournier, "Looking Good on Paper," *Managing Your Career,* Spring 1990, 34–35.
6. Adapted from Burdette E. Bostwick, *How to Find the Job You've Always Wanted* (New York: Wiley, 1982), 69–70.
7. Louis S. Richman, "How to Get Ahead in America," *Fortune,* May 1994, 46–51; Bruce Nussbaum, "I'm Worried About My Job," *Business Week,* 7 October, 1991, 94–97.
8. William J. Banis, "The Art of Writing Job-Search Letters," *CPC Annual, 36th Edition* 2 (1992): 42–50.
9. See note 1.

Chapter 16

1. Adapted from A. J. Vogl, "Risky Work," *Across the Board,* July–August 1993, 27–31; Kenneth Labich, "Hot Company, Warm Culture," *Fortune,* 27 February 1989, 74–78; George Melloan, "Herman Miller's Secrets of Corporate Creativity," *Wall Street Journal,* 3 May 1988, A31; Beverly Geber, "Herman Miller: Where Profits and Participation Meet," *Training,* November 1987, 62–66; Robert J. McClory, "The Creative Process at Herman Miller," *Across the Board,* May 1985, 8–22; Tom Peters and Nancy Austin, *A Passion for Excellence* (New York: Random House, 1985), 204–205.
2. Charlene Marmer Solomon, "How Does Disney Do It?" *Personnel Journal,* December 1989, 53.
3. Peter Rea, Julie Rea, and Charles Moonmaw, "Training: Use Assessment Centers in Skill Development," *Personnel Journal,* April 1990, 126–131.
4. Barron Wells and Nelda Spinks, "Interviewing: What Small Companies Say," *Bulletin of the Association for Business Communication* 50, no. 2 (1992): 18–22; Clive Fletcher, "Ethics and the Job Interview," *Personnel Management,* March 1992, 36–39.

5. Joel Russell, "Finding Solid Ground," *Hispanic Business,* February 1922, 42–44, 46.
6. Microsoft 1992 Annual Report, 5–6.
7. Robert Gifford, Cheuk Fan Ng, and Margaret Wilkinson, "Nonverbal Cues in the Employment Interview: Links Between Applicant Qualities and Interviewer Judgments," *Journal of Applied Psychology* 70, no. 4 (1985): 729.
8. Dale G. Leathers, *Successful Nonverbal Communication* (New York: Macmillan, 1986), 225.
9. Shirley J. Shepherd, "How to Get That Job in 60 Minutes or Less," *Working Woman,* March 1986, 119.
10. Shepherd, "How to Get That Job," 118.
11. Gerald L. Wilson, "Preparing Students for Responding to Illegal Selection Interview Questions," *Bulletin of the Association for Business Communication* 54, no. 2 (1991): 44–49.
12. Jeff Springston and Joann Keyton, "Interview Response Training," *Bulletin of the Association for Business Communication* 54, no. 3 (1991): 28–30; Gerald L. Wilson, "An Analysis of Instructional Strategies for Responding to Illegal Selection Interview Questions," *Bulletin of the Association for Business Communication* 54, no. 3 (1991): 31–35.
13. Stephen J. Pullum, "Illegal Questions in the Selection Process: Going Beyond Contemporary Business and Professional Communication Textbooks," *Bulletin of the Association for Business Communication* 54, no. 3 (1991): 36–43; Alicia Kitsuse, "'Have You Ever Been Arrested?'" *Across the Board,* November 1992, 46–49; Christina L. Greathouse, "10 Common Hiring Mistakes," *Industry Week,* 20 January 1992, 22–23, 26.
14. Marilyn Moats Kennedy, "Are You Getting Paid What You're Worth?" *New Woman,* November 1984, 110.
15. Harold H. Hellwig, "Job Interviewing: Process and Practice," *Bulletin of the Association for Business Communication* 55, no.2 (1992): 8–14.
16. See note 1; Some questions adapted from Gregory Stock, *The Book of Questions* (New York: Workman Publishing, 1987), 39.

Chapter 17

1. Adapted from Srikumar S. Rao, "Welcome to Open Space," *Training,* April 1994, 52–56; Claudia H. Deutsch, "Round-Table Meetings with No Agendas, No Tables," *New York Times,* 5 June 1994, sec. 3, 5; Charles D. Bader, "These Shoes Are Made for Walkin'," *Bobbin,* November 1991, 118–121.
2. Edward F. Walsh, "Telephone Tyranny," *Industry Week,* 1 April 1991, 24–26.
3. Madeline Bodin, "Making the Most of Your Telephone," *Nation's Business,* April 1992, 62.
4. Beverly Davenport Sypher, Robert N. Bastrom, and Joy Hart Seibert, "Listening, Communication Abilities, and Success at Work," *Journal of Business Communication* 26, no. 4 (1989): 293–301.
5. Augusta M. Simon, "Effective Listening: Barriers to Listening in a Diverse Business Environment," *Bulletin of the Association for Business Communication* 54, no. 3 (1991): 73–74.
6. Sypher, Bastrom, and Siebert, "Listening, Communication Abilities, and Success at Work," 293–301.
7. Thomas L. Means, "A Unit to Develop Listening Skill," *Bulletin of the Association for Business Communication* 54, no. 3 (1991): 70–72.
8. Phillip Morgan and H. Kent Baker, "Building a Professional Image: Improving Listening Behavior," *Supervisory Management,* November 1985, 35–36.
9. Lyman K. Steil, Larry L. Barker, and Kittie W. Watson, *Effective Listening: Key to Your Success* (Reading, Mass.: Addison-Wesley, 1983), 21–22.
10. J. Michael Sproule, *Communication Today* (Glenview, Ill.: Scott, Foresman, 1981), 69.
11. Sproule, *Communication Today,* 69.
12. Sproule, *Communication Today,* 69.
13. Thomas L. Brown, "The Art of the Interview," *Industry Week,* 1 March 1993, 19.
14. B. Aubrey Fisher, *Small Group Decision Making: Communication and the Group Process,* 2d ed. (New York: McGraw-Hill, 1980), 145–149.
15. William C. Waddell and Thomas A Rosko, "Conducting an Effective Off-Site Meeting," *Management Review,* February 1993, 40–44.
16. See note 1.

Chapter 18

1. Adapted from Trudy Gallant-Stokes, "Brady Keys Does Franchising Right," *Black Enterprise,* September 1988, 56–62; Cynthia Legette, "The New Entrepreneur: Nobody Does It Better," *Black Enterprise* 19 (December 1988): 56–60; Bill Carlino, "Keys Opens Doors for Minorities," *Nation's Restaurant News* 22 (10 October 1988): 1; Marsha Westbrook, "Burger King Honors a Pioneering Food Franchisee," *Black Enterprise* 18 (February 1988): 40.

2. Sherron B. Kenton, "Speaker Credibility in Persuasive Business Communication: A Model Which Explains Gender Differences," *Journal of Business Communication* 26, no. 2 (1989): 143–157.

3. Walter Kiechel III, "How to Give a Speech," *Fortune,* 8 June 1987, 180.

4. *Communication and Leadership Program* (Santa Ana, Calif.: Toastmasters International, 1980), 44, 45.

5. *How to Prepare and Use Effective Visual Aids,* Info-Line series, Elizabeth Lean, managing ed. (Washington, D.C.: American Society for Training and Development, October 1984), 2.

6. Kathleen K. Weigner, "Visual Persuasion," *Forbes,* 16 September 1991, 176; Kathleen K. Weigner, "Showtime!" *Forbes,* 13 May 1991, 118.

7. Eric Arndt, "Nobody Does It Better," *IABC Communication World,* May 1988, 28.

8. Daniel Goleman, "For Victims of Stage Fright, Rehearsal Is the Therapy," *New York Times,* 12 June 1991, sec. b, 1.

9. Judy Linscott, "Getting On and Off the Podium," *Savvy,* October 1985, 44.

10. Iris R. Johnson, "Before You Approach the Podium," *MW,* January–February 1989, 7.

11. Sandra Moyer, "Braving No Woman's Land," *The Toastmaster,* August 1986, 13.

12. Teresa Brady, "Fielding Abrasive Questions During Presentations," *Supervisory Management,* February 1993, 6.

13. See note 1.

Appendix A

1. Patricia A. Dreyfus, "Paper That's Letter Perfect," *Money,* May 1985, 184.

2. Linda Driskill, *Business & Managerial Communication: New Perspectives* (Orlando, Fla.: Harcourt Brace Jovanovich, 1992), 470.

3. Driskill, *Business & Managerial Communication,* 470.

4. Lennie Copeland and Lewis Griggs, *Going International: How to Make Friends and Deal Effectively in the Global Marketplace,* 2d ed. (New York: Random House, 1985), 24–27.

5. Copeland and Griggs, *Going International,* 24–27.

6. Jerry W. Robinson et al., *Century 21: Keyboarding, Formatting, and Document Processing,* 5th ed. (Cincinnati, Ohio: South-Western Publishing, 1994), 222.

7. Copeland and Griggs, *Going International,* 24–27.

Appendix B

1. Dorothy Geisler, "How to Avoid Copyright Lawsuits," *IABC Communication World,* June 1984, 34–37.

2. Robert W. Goddard, "The Crime of Copying," *Management World,* July–August 1986, 20–22.

ACKNOWLEDGMENTS

Text, Figures, and Tables

4 (Figure 1.1): From David J. Rachman and Michael H. Mescon, *Business Today*, 5th edition, p. 27. Copyright © 1987 McGraw-Hill, Inc. Reprinted by permission of the publisher. **7** (Figure 1.3): From David J. Rachman and Michael H. Mescon, *Business Today*, 5th edition, p. 127. Copyright © 1987 McGraw-Hill, Inc. Reprinted by permission of the publisher. **8–9** (Behind the Scenes at Amtrak): John Jacobsen and Sue Martin, personal interview, June 1989. Used with permission. **10** (Table 1.1): From Claudia Reinhardt, "How to Handle a Crisis," *Public Relations Journal*, November 1987. Reprinted by permission. **24** (Figure 2.1): From Philip I. Morgan et al., "Building a Professional Image: Improving Listening Behavior," *Supervisory Management*, November 1985. Copyright © 1985 American Management Association, New York. All rights reserved. Reprinted by permission of the publisher. **32–33** (Behind the Scenes at Federal Express): Jon Sutton, personal interview, June 1989. Used with permission. **50–51** (Behind the Scenes at Parker Pen): Roger Axtel, personal communication, June 1989. Used with permission. **59, 71–73:** From Lura K. Romei, "Publishing Pays Off." Adapted from the October 1988 issue of *Modern Office Technology*, and copyrighted 1988 by Penton Publishing, subsidiary of Pittway Corporation. **64–65** (Behind the Scenes at Mike's Video): Mike Negra, Alan Abruzzo, and Wanda White, personal communication, June 1989. Used with permission. **69** (Figure 4.2): Copyright © CompuServe Incorporated. **82–83** (Behind the Scenes at Allstate Insurance): Patrick Williams, personal interview, June 1989. Used with permission. **104–105** (Behind the Scenes at General Electric): David Warshaw, personal interview, June 1989. Used with permission. **116, 138–141:** From Dyan Machan, "Great Hash Browns, but Watch Those Biscuits," *Forbes*, September 19, 1988. Reprinted by permission of *Forbes* magazine. © Forbes Inc., 1988. **119** (Figure 7.2): Adapted from Robert Gunning, *The Technique of Clear Writing* (New York: McGraw-Hill, rev. ed., 1973). Used with permission of the copyright owners, Gunning-Mueller Clear Writing Institute, Inc. **132–133** (Behind the Scenes at the La Jolla Playhouse): Constance Harvey, personal interview, May 1992. Used with permission. **156–157** (Behind the Scenes at the Phoenix Symphony): Gail Warden, personal interview, April 1992. Used with permission. **174–175** (Behind the Scenes at Citibank): Jane Wolchonlok, personal interview, June 1989. Used with permission. **177** (Figure 9.1): Letterhead courtesy of Woolworth. **187** (Figure 9.3): Courtesy of Carnival Cruise Lines, Inc. **190** (Figure 9.4): Letterhead courtesy of TWA. **202, 223–225:** From Michael Barrier, "Working for 'Peanuts.'" Adapted with permission from *Nation's Business*, November 1988. Copyright 1988 U.S. Chamber of Commerce, **208–209** (Behind the Scenes at America West): Daphne Dicino, personal interview, March 1992. Used with permission. **242–243** (Behind the Scenes with John Keil): Adapted from John M. Keil, *The Creative Mystique* (New York: Wiley, 1985), pp. 46–48. Copyright © 1985. Reprinted by permission of John Wiley & Sons, Inc. **268–269** (Behind the Scenes at the San Diego Zoo): Rick Barongi, personal interview, May 1992. Used with permission. **309** (Figure 13.5): From David J. Rachman and Michael H. Mescon, *Business Today*, 5th edition. Copyright © 1987 McGraw-Hill, Inc. Used by permission of the publisher. **312–313** (Behind the Scenes at Gannett Company): Sheila J. Gibbons, personal interview, June 1989. Used with permission. **322–323** (Behind the Scenes at the Rocky Mountain Institute): Adapted from L. Hunter Lovins, personal interview, April 1992. Used with permission; James R. Udall, "Prophets of an Energy Revolution," *National Wildlife*, December-January 1992, pp. 10–13; *Water Efficiency: A Resource for Utility Managers, Community Planners, and Other Decisionmakers*, Rocky Mountain Institute, November 1991. **331** (Figure 14.1): From Gene Zelanzy, *Say It with Charts*, p. 112. Richard D. Irwin, Inc., © 1984. Reprinted with permission. **333** (Figure 14.6): Data from *Nation's Restaurant News*, August 3, 1987, p. 7. Copyright *Nation's Restaurant News*. **333** (Figure 14.7): From John M. Lannon, *Technical Writing*, 3d edition. Reprinted by permission of HarperCollins College Publishers. **334** (Figure 14.8): Adapted from Robert Lefferts, *How to Prepare Charts and Graphs for Effective Reports*. Copyright © 1981 by Robert Lefferts. Reprinted by permission of The Balkin Agency. **335**

(Figure 14.9): Adapted from Stephen Conley, "Spanning the Globe," *USA Today*, September 16, 1993. Copyright 1993 *USA Today*. Reprinted with permission. **336–337** (Report Writer's Notebook): From David M. Kroenke and Kathleen A. Dolan, *Business Computer Systems: An Introduction*, © 1987 McGraw-Hill, Inc. Reprinted with permission. **337** (photo): From Timothy N. Trainor and Diane Krasnewich, *Computers!*, 3d edition (Watsonville, CA: Mitchell McGraw-Hill, 1992), p. 198. **376–377** (Behind the Scenes at Mobil Corporation): Henry Halaiko, personal interview, June 1989. Used with permission. **379** (Table 15.1): Excerpts from Tom Jackson, *The Perfect Résumé*. Copyright © 1981 by Tom Jackson. Used by permission of Doubleday, a division of Bantam Doubleday Dell Publishing Group, Inc. **410–411** (Behind the Scenes at IBM): Jim Greenwood, personal interview, June 1989. Used with permission. **430** (Figure 17.1): Copyright Dr. Lyman K. Steil, President, Communication Development, Inc., St. Paul, Minnesota. Prepared for the Sperry Corporation. Reprinted with permission of Dr. Steil and Unisys Corporation. **435** (Figure 17.2): Adapted from J. Michael Sproule, *Communication Today*, 1981, by permission of J. Michael Sproule. **436–437** (Behind the Scenes at 3M): Virginia Johnson, personal interview, June 1989. Used with permission. **444, 461–462:** From Trudy Gallant-Stokes, "Brady Keys Does Franchising Right," *Black Enterprise*, September 1988, pp. 56–62. Copyright September 1988 The Earl G. Graves Publishing Co., Inc., 130 Fifth Avenue, New York, NY 10011. All rights reserved. Used with permission. **456–457** (Behind the Scenes with Charles Osgood): From Charles Osgood, *Osgood on Speaking*. Copyright © 1988 by Charles Osgood. Reprinted by permission of William Morrow & Company, Inc. **468** (Table A.1): From Amy Vanderbilt, *The Amy Vanderbilt Complete Book of Etiquette*. Revised by Letitia Baldridge. Copyright © 1978 by Curtis B. Kellar & Lincoln G. Clark as executors of the estate of Amy Vanderbilt and Doubleday. Used by permission of Doubleday, a division of Bantam Doubleday Dell Publishing Group, Inc. **473** (Figure A.3): Letterhead courtesy of Mattel Toys. **474** (Figure A.4): Letterhead courtesy of J. C. Penney. **475** (Figure A.5): Letterhead courtesy of Black & Decker.

Photos

3: Courtesy of Saturn Corporation. **6:** Courtesy of McDonald's Inc. **7:** Courtesy of General Electric. **11:** AP/Wide World. **14:** Courtesy of Time Life Custom Publishing/Peter Garfield Studios. **22:** AP/Wide World. **26:** UPI/Bettmann. **28:** NBC photo by Ken Regan. **29:** Courtesy of Avon Products, Inc. **30:** Courtesy of Ameritech. **40:** David Joel/Tony Stone. **41:** AP/Wide World. **43:** Safra Nimrod. **47:** Reuters/Bettmann. **51:** AP/Wide World. **60:** Karl Nembecek, M. L. I. Co. Photo Bureau. **61:** Copyright © George Bennett. **66:** Courtesy of Weyerhaeuser. **69:** Courtesy of Digital Equipment. **71:** Courtesy of Eastman Kodak Company. **77:** John Coletti/Stock, Boston. **78:** Cynthia Johnson/Gamma-Liaison. **79:** Courtesy of General Motors Corp. **80:** Courtesy of Reebok International Ltd. **81:** Courtesy of Nynex Service Co. **95:** Mark Sherman. **96:** Courtesy of Ford Plastic Products Division. **97:** AP/Wide World. **109:** David Levenson/Black Star. **110:** Courtesy of Microsoft. Photo by Kathleen King. **117:** AP/Wide World. **118:** Courtesy of Walt Disney Company. **121:** Courtesy of CBS News. **125:** James Schnepf. **128:** UPI/Bettmann. **147:** AP/Wide World. **148:** AP/Wide World. **153:** Courtesy of Bell Labs. **154:** Bill O'Leary/The Washington Post. **159:** Courtesy of Lorraine Scarpa. **171:** McGraw-Hill Photo. **172:** AP/Wide World. **180:** Courtesy of Colonial Mortgage Company. **186:** Courtesy of Avon Products, Inc. **189:** Mark Thomas. Courtesy of Hal Riney & Partners. **203:** Reprinted by permission of UFS, Inc. **204:** AP/Wide World. **206:** Newsweek/Shel Secunda. **208:** Courtesy of Metropolitan Life Insurance Company. **215:** Courtesy of American Express Company. **233:** Haviv/Saba. **234:** Courtesy of Mary Kay Cosmetics. **235:** Courtesy of The Black & Decker Corporation. **236:** Roger Ressmeyer/Starlight. **239:** Courtesy of the National Easter Seal Society. **265:** George Disario/Stock Market. **269:** Courtesy of the United States Supreme Court. **273:** Courtesy of Simpson/Bruckheimer Productions. **277:** Courtesy of Liz Claiborne, Inc. **284:** Tim Naprestek. **295:** Courtesy of Harley-Davidson, Inc. **296:** Courtesy of Capitol Cities/ABC, Inc. **302:** Exley/Gamma-Liaison. **305:** Shahn Kermani/Gamma-Liaison. **308:** Jim Graham/Gamma-Liaison. **319:** AP/Wide World. **324:** Bill Ray. **326:** Courtesy of Apple Computer. Photo by Carolyn Caddes. **327:** Copyright © Larry Ford. **359:** Courtesy of Computer Associates International, Inc. **371:** Peter Kelly/Impact Visuals. **374:** Courtesy of AT&T, Inc. **375:** Claudio Edinger/Gamma-Liaison. **383:** Courtesy of Godfather's Pizza. **387:** Najlah Feanny/Saba. **401:** Courtesy of Herman Miller Co. **407:** AP/Wide World. **408:** Courtesy of Gittings. **409:** Courtesy of FireKing International, Inc. **414:** Courtesy of Levi Strauss. **427:** Debra Hershkowitz. **428:** Courtesy of McGuffy's Restaurant. **431:** Courtesy of US West Communications. **438:** Courtesy of Aetna Life & Casualty. **439:** John Troha/Black Star. **445:** Courtesy of the Keys Group. **446:** C. Bankenhorn/Black Star. **450:** Courtesy of Success Strategy, Inc. **452:** Ann States/Saba. **458:** Courtesy of the Xerox Corporation.

ORGANIZATION/PRODUCT/NAME INDEX

Abruzzo, Alan, 64–65
Academy of Motion Picture Arts and Sciences, 370, 394
Aetna Life & Casualty, 438
Airborne Express, 264
All-Pro Fried Chicken, 461
Allstate Insurance Company, 82–83
Allstate Now, 82–83
America West, 208–209
American Airlines, 254
American Express, 215
American Society for Training and Development, 16
American Telecast, 367
Ameritech Information Systems, 30
Amtrak, 8–9
Andahazy, Joe, 198
Annenberg, Walter, 232
Apple Computer, 39, 48, 56, 305, 326
Apple Pacific, 39, 56
Ash, Mary Kay, 234
AT&T, 10, 59, 153, 374
Atlantic-Arco, 292
Audi, 199
Audio-Forum, 367
Avon Products, 5, 29, 186, 257–258

Bally's Health and Tennis Corporation, 259
Banc One, 230
Barad, Jill, 76–77, 91
Barbie, 76–77, 91
Barnes & Noble, 146–147, 162
Barongi, Rick, 268–269
B. Dalton Bookseller, 146, 162
Beals, Vaughn, 125
Bear Stearns, 200
Beauvais, Edward, 208
Beavers, Robert M., 6
Bell Laboratories, 153
Ben & Jerry's Homemade, 21–22, 35–36
Birnbach, Lisa, 371
Blecher, Mark, 260
Body Shop, 109
Bolton, Michael, 254
Bookstop, 146
Borders, 146, 162
Boschulte, Alfred F., 81
Bowers, Chris, 274
Bradford, Martina L., 374
Brokaw, Tom, 28
Bruckheimer, Jerry, 273
Burger King, 461
Burnham, Sophie, 167

Cain, Herman, 383
California Peach Growers Association, 168

Calloway, Wayne, 455
Cameron, Irma, 88, 89
Campbell Soup, 170–171, 193, 293
Campus Fest, 366
Carlisle, Van, 409
Cavallo, Domingo, 168
CBS, 121
Champ, Michael A., 227
Chase Manhattan Private Bank, 43
Chasman & Bem Booksellers, 169
Children's Hospital (Los Angeles), 91
Cholish, Daniel W., 196
Chudnow, Randy, 169
Chung, Lia, 277
Citibank, 174–175
CitiCorp, 25
Claiborne, Liz, 277
Cliffs Notes, 229
CNN, 61
Coca-Cola, 254, 260
Coca-Cola Company, 452
Cohen, Ben, 21
Coleman, Debi, 326
Coleman, Stacy L., 43
College Fest, 366
Colonial Mortgage Company, 180
Colson, Joseph S., Jr., 153
Columbia Pictures, 200
Communication Skills Institute, 277
Computer Associates International, 359
Computer Discount Warehouse, 166
Conway, Michael, 208
Cosby, Bill, 172
Coulson, Zoe, 170, 193
Creative Associates, 202–203, 223
Cross Pointe Paper, 197
Crown Books, 146, 162

Daily News (New York), 10
Daniels, Gregory L., 284
Dawson, Ken, 408
Dawson, Sheryl, 408
Dawson and Dawson Management Consultants, 408
Dell, Michael, 200
Dell Computer Corporation, 200
Deodorant Stones of America, 260
Department of Commerce, 297–298
DePree, D. J., 400
DePree, Max, 419–420
DHL International, 264
Dicino, Daphne, 208–209
Diery, Ian, 39, 56
Digital Equipment Corporation, 69, 230
Discovery Toys, 234
Disney, 6, 118

Disneyland, 9
Doc Martens, 229
Doubleday, 146
Dow Jones, 254
Drake Beam Morin, 94–95, 111–112
Dun & Bradstreet, 159
Dunn, Keith, 428

Eastman Kodak Company, 71
Edcadassa, 168
EDS, 254
E. I. Du Pont de Nemours & Company, 46
Eisner, Michael D., 118
Eli Lilly, 197
Environmental Protection Agency (EPA), 323
Erickson, Rodney A., 319, 362
Esso, 292
Estée Lauder, 26
Exxon, 254

Farmer, Lillian, 398
Federal Express, 6, 32–33, 264–265, 287, 324
Fidelity Investments, 16
Fields, Dawna, 10
Fields, Debbie, 14
FireKing International, 409
Fireman, Paul, 80
First Boston, 228
Fisher, Lucy, 200
Ford Motor, 51, 96, 199–200
Fresh Foot, 260
Frito-Lay, 254
Fuente, David, 167–168
Fuji Xerox Company, 196

Gadra, David, 259–260
Gannett, 312–313
Garcia, Nina, 258
Gates, William, 110
Gault, Stanley, 10
General Electric, 7, 59, 104–105, 259–260
General Mills, 88, 89
General Motors, 2, 18, 79, 323
Giarla, David, 116
Gibbons, Sheila L., 312–313
Giusti, Ruthann, 197
Godfather's Pizza, 383
Goizueta, Roberto, 452
Gold, Christina A., 258
Goldsberry, Ronald E., 96
Gordon, Sandra, 239
Goya, Donna L., 414
Graham, Katharine, 11
Gray, Sue, 228
Gray, William H., III, 232, 254
Greenfield, Jerry, 21
Greenwood, Jim, 410–411
Grove, William Robert, 260
Guess?, 366
Guggenheim Museum, 166

Hal Riney and Partners, 189
Halaiko, Henry, 376–377
Harley-Davidson, 125, 294–295, 313–314
Harris, Chuck, 226
Harvey, Constance, 132–133
Hastings, Arnold, 277
Health Club Television Network, 259
Hegranes, Marcia, 228
Henson, Lisa, 200
Herman Miller, 6, 400–401, 419–420
Hertz Rent A Car, 258
Hewitt, Don, 199
Hewlett-Packard, 7
Historic Fishing Village of Puget Sound, 293
Honda, 199
Hotz, James, 259
Hudson, Katherine M., 71
Hungary, 259–260
Hyatt Hotels, 11

IBM, 167, 410–411
In Touch, 7
In-a-Minute, 423
International Discount Telecommunications, 199
International Tesla Society, 227
Ipiranga, 292

J. C. Penney, 254
J. Walter Thompson, 292
Jeffrey, Andrea, 169
Jell-O, 172
Jemison, Mae C., 204
Jobs, Steve, 305
Jock's Rock, The, 260
Johansen, Gary, 277–278
Johnson, Jerry, 431
Johnson, Virginia, 436–437
Johnson & Johnson, 10, 257
Jonas, Howard, 199
Jones, Leonade D., 154
Julian Surf & Sport, 227–228

Keil, John M., 242–243
Kellogg Canada, 257
Kellogg's, 257
Kessler, David, 439
Keys, Brady, 444, 445, 461
Keys Group, The, 444, 461
KFC, 444, 461
Kmart, 146, 162
Knights Technology, 198
Kodak, 71, 172
Koppel, Ted, 296
Korn/Ferry International, 380
Kroch's, 146
Kudlow, Larry, 200–201

La Jolla Playhouse, 132–133
Lauder, Estée, 26

Laura Ashley, 264
Layer, Meredith, 215
LeFauve, Richard, 2, 7, 17–18
L'Eggs, 242
Leinberger, Chris, 71
Lesser & Weitzman, 71
Levi Strauss, 414
Life Savers, 242
Lindgren, W. Barry, 167
Lions Pride, 362
Listen 2 Books, 198
Liu, Shao Hung, 198
Livesey, William D., 59, 72
L. L. Bean, 196
Lovins, Amory, 322–323
Lovins, Hunter, 322–323
Lowry, Jim, 297–298

M.A.C., 168
Mandela, Nelson, 41
Mariage Frères, 166
MarketSource Corporation, 366
Martin, Sue, 8–9
Mary Kay Cosmetics, 234
Mathis, Keith, 440
Mattel, 76–77, 91
Mazda, 40
McDonald's, 6, 116, 138–139
McGregor, Douglas, 11
McGuffey's Restaurants, 428
Menem, Carlos, 168
Mercury Sable, 199
Merrill Lynch & Company, 375
Mersereau, Susan, 66
Metropolitan Life Insurance, 59–60, 72, 208
Metschke, C. J., 166
Microage, 169
Microsoft, 110, 403, 404
Mike's Video, 64–65
Mobil Corporation, 59, 376–377
Monterey Press, 166
Morin, William J., 111
Morris, Larry, 260
Mrs. Fields Cookies, 14
Music Design, 165

National Association of Railroad Passengers, 8
National Easter Seal Society, 239
National Semiconductor, 264
NationsBank, 254
Nature's Crystal, 260
NBC, 28
Negra, Mike, 64–65
Nemeth, Lane, 234
Nesbit, Robert, 380
Newman, Edwin, 148
NeXT, 305
Nike, 80
Nissan, 45
Nittany Lions, 319, 362
Noonan, Marilyn, 261

Noonan Design, 261
Notorious, Inc., 398
Novalle, Miriam, 166
Nutrific, 257
Nynex, 258
NYNEX Service Company, 81

O'Connor, Sandra Day, 269
O'Toole, Andy, 338
Office Depot, 167–168
ONSI Corporation, 260
Osgood, Charles, 456–457
Ouchi, William, 11
Owen, Harrison, 440

Pacific Gas & Electric, 323
Parker Pen Company, 50–51
Paterno, Joe, 319
Pauley, Jane, 97
Paulson, Lynda R., 450
Pavlenko, Victor, 169
Peace Pops, 36
Peanuts, 202–203, 223
Pennsylvania State University, 319, 362
Pentair, 197
Pepsi, 46
PepsiCo, 260, 455
Pepsi Max, 260
Perrier, 189
Petrino, Ralph, 362
Philips, 45
Phoebe-Putney Memorial Hospital, 259
Phoenix Symphony, 156–157
Pinkerton, 370, 394
Plummer, Roger, 30
Post-it Notes, 436
Powell, Colin, 47
Pure & Natural, 260

Quaker Oats, 13, 170
Quantum Magnetics, 167
Quinn, Jane Bryant, 206

Rainforest Crunch, 36
Rancho San Diego Vision Care Center, 262
Rand, Barry, 458
Rather, Dan, 121
Red Cross, 284
Reebok International, 80, 426
Rein, Catherine, 208
Reverby, Susan, 76
Revlon, 366
Riggio, Leonard, 146, 162
Riney, Hal, 189
Rivers, Jill, 273
R. J. Reynolds, 9
Roadmaster tires, 398
Roché, Joyce, 186
Rockport, 426, 440

Rockwell International, 59
Rocky Mountain Institute, 322–323
Roddick, Anita, 109
Rubbermaid, 10
Rucker Fuller, 166–167

Safire, William, 78
Sagan, Carl, 128
Salk, Jonas, 308
San Diego Zoo, 268–269
Saturn, 2, 7, 17–18, 189
Scarpa, Lorraine C., 159
Schneider, Don, 260
Schneider Trucking, 260
Schreyer, William A., 375
Schultz, Charles, 202–203, 223
Schwartzkopf, H. Norman, 446
Scotch tape, 436
Seabold Engineering, 273
Shell Oil, 292
Sidewalk Sergeant, 261
Silicon Valley Bank, 198
Simpson, Don, 273
Sims, John L., 69
Sinclair, Chris, 260
Smith, Frederick W., 264–265, 287, 324
Smith, Jennifer, 438
Southern California Gas Company, 260
Stigman, Dave, 36
Stuef, William, 200
Styer, Jim, 362
Success Strategies, 450
Sun Microsystems, 6
Sutton, John, 32–33
Swanson, 189
Sweeney, Peter, 197

Tab X-Tra, 260
TBS, 61
Teerlink, Richard F., 294–295, 313–314
Tenneco, 45
Tesla, Nikola, 227
Texaco, 292
Texas Instruments, 254
Thai Deodorant Stone, 260
Thanks-A-Bunch, 258
Thorbeck, John, 426, 437, 440
3M, 436–437
Tokyo Electric Power Company, 197
Tokyu Corporation, 197
Toskan, Frank, 168
Toy Manufacturers of America, 91
Toyota, 45, 196, 242, 366
Translations, 167
Trident Aquaculture, 227
TriTech Industries, 338

Trotman, Alex, 51
Tungsram, 259–260
Turner, Ted, 61
TWA, 190
Tylenol, 10

Ultra-Light Touring Shop, 226
United Auto Workers, 2, 18
United Negro College Fund (UNCF), 232,
   254
United Parcel Service (UPS), 264
Uptown cigarettes, 9
USA Today, 312
U S West, 169, 431
U.S. Food and Drug Administration, 439
U.S. Postal Service, 264

Verdugo, Raymond, 277
Vertical Club, 258–259

Wachner, Linda J., 327
Wal-Mart, 11, 254
Waldenbooks, 146, 162
Waldron, Hicks, 5
Walt Disney Company, 6, 118
Walthen, Thomas, 370, 394
Walton, Sam, 11
Wang, Charles B., 359
Warden, Gail, 156–157
Warnaco, 327
Warner Bros., 200
Warshaw, David, 104–105
Washington Post, 11
Washington Post Company, 154
Welch, Jack, 7
Weyerhauser Information Systems, 66
Wherehouse Records, 165
White, Wanda, 64–65
Whopper, 461
Williams, Patrick, 82–83
Willinsky, Michael D., 227
Wolchonok, Jane, 174–175
World Bank, 323
Worthing, Marcia, 29
Wynn, R. J., 180

Xerox Corporation, 11, 196–197, 458

Young, Shirley, 79

Zaman, Ellen, 91
Zerbe, Richard, 228

SUBJECT INDEX

Abbreviations:
  common business, 508–509
  for state names, 477
  punctuation of, 506
  spacing with, 466
Abstract nouns, 496
Abstraction, 120, 235
Abstracts, of articles, 485–486
Acceptance, letter of, 322, 417
Accuracy:
  of information, 81
  of messages, 28
  of reports, 265–268
Achievements, on résumé, 378
Acronyms, 14, 122
Action phase (of AIDA), 236, 245–246
Action terms, 244
Action verbs, 350, 498
Active listening, 429
Active voice, 126–127, 500
Address, forms of, 468
Addressee notation, 471
Addresses:
  international, 469
  in letters, 469
  on envelopes, 476–477
Adjectives, 121, 125, 244, 500–501, 504, 506, 507
Adjustments (*See* Claims and adjustments)
Adverbs, 121, 125, 501, 512
Advertisements:
  culture and, 46, 56
  responding to, 388, 391
Africa, 49
African Americans, 47, 232
Age bias, 124
Agenda, 438, 482, 483
  hidden, 435
AIDA plan, 235–236, 240
  for job application letters, 384–390
Alcohol testing, 402
Alphanumeric system, 301
Alternatives, comparing, 299
American Heritage Dictionary, electronic, 66
American Library Directory, 484
Americans with Disabilities Act, 124
Analysis:
  of audience, 34, 79–84, 233, 445–446
  of data, 308–311
Analytical assignments, 299
Analytical reports, 103, 268–269, 274–279, 280, 295–296, 311
  example of, 338–356
Annual reports, 36, 104–105, 305
Antecedents, 497
AO mail, 478
Apology, 204, 206, 207
Apostrophe, 496, 507

Appeals:
  emotional vs. logical, 233–234
  negative, 249–250
  positive, 248–249
Appearance:
  of business documents, 66–68, 136–138, 465
  for job interviews, 403, 407–408
  personal, 23, 403, 407–408
Appendix, for reports, 337, 357
Application forms, 390, 391–392
Applications, job, 384–393
Appreciation, messages of, 189–191
Arabs, 43, 49, 147
Articles (part of speech), 501
  unnecessary, 127
Artwork (*See* Visual aids)
Attention, 29, 30, 427
  holding audience's, 451–452
Attention-getting devices, 235, 236–237, 240–243, 386–387, 450
Attention line, 471
Attention phase (of AIDA), 235, 240–243
Audience:
  composition of, 80, 445
  defining, 240
  expectations of, 60
  gaining confidence of, 450
  interaction with, 453–454
  lack of familiarity with, 27
  likely reaction of, 80, 101, 102, 445–446
  motivating, 233–235
  needs of, 15, 80–84, 233, 267, 271, 452
  primary, 80
  questions from, 453, 459–460
  receptivity of, 269, 271–272, 276, 297, 311
  relationship with, 80, 105, 270, 283, 446
  size of, 80, 445
Audience analysis, 34, 79–84, 233
  for speeches, 445–446
Audience-centered approach, 15, 297
Audiotapes, 455
Audiovisual aids, 455
Author-date system, 493
Authoring tools, group, 61
Authority, references to, 100
Authorization, letter of, 322
Averages, 308–309
Awkward pointers, 130

Back translation, 122
Backgrounds, differing, 29
Bad news, in reports, 273
Bad-news messages, 202–222
  checklist for, 212–213
  collection letters as, 253
  declining job offer, 417–418

Bad-news messages (*cont.*):
    declining requests for favors, 215
    denying routine requests, 213–215
    about orders, 209–212
    organizational pattern for, 102, 203–209
    about people, 219–222
    about products, 212–213
    refusing adjustments, 216–218
    refusing credit, 218–219
    rejecting job applications, 221
    resigning job, 418
    terminating employment, 221–222
Balance, in design, 137
Bar charts, 332
Bargaining (*See* Negotiation)
Benefits:
    for audience, 235, 236, 239–240, 243–244
    job, 412–413
Berlitz language courses, 45
Bias-free language, 122–124
Biases, personal, 267
Bibliographies, 356, 357, 491–493
Binding, of reports, 481–482
Block format, 473
    modified, 474
Body, 102
    of bad-news messages, 205–207
    of direct requests, 147, 148–149
    of interviews, 433
    in job application letters, 387–389
    of letters, 469
    of persuasive messages, 235, 237, 243–245
    of positive messages, 171–172, 173
    of proposals, 359
    of reports, 327, 346
    of speeches, 451–452
Body language, 22–24, 429
    culture and, 14, 43–44, 55
    in job interviews, 403, 407, 409
    in speech delivery, 459
    (*See also* Nonverbal communication)
Boilerplates, 64
Boldface type, 137
Books:
    in bibliographies, 492
    reference, 484–485
    source notes for, 490
Bragging, 106
Brainstorming, 84
Brazil, 292
Brevity, 83–84
Bribes, 44
Buffer, 204–205, 210, 211, 212, 215, 216, 218
Bulgaria, 14, 43
Bulk Letter Service/Canada, 478
Business Information Sources, 484
Business technology (*See* Technology)

Call management systems, 70
Camouflaged verbs, 122

Campus recruiters, 376–377, 408, 410–411
Canadian addresses, 469
Canadian postal codes, 476, 477
Capitalization, 489, 508
Captions, design of, 136
Card catalog, 485
Career: The Annual Guide to Business Opportunities, 373
Career Information Center, 371
Career objective, on résumé, 375
Career planning, 371–373
Case, of pronouns, 497–498
Categorical organization, 298
Cause and effect, for paragraph development, 135
Cause-effect relationship, 309
CD-ROMs, 62
Central idea (*See* Main idea)
CEOs, 16
Chalkboards, 455
Channels, communication, 4, 25, 26, 34, 86–90
Charts, 331–334
China (Chinese), 41, 42, 53, 126
Chronological organization, 298
Chronological résumés, 379–380
Citation, of sources, 328–329, 355, 493–494
    (*See also* Documentation)
Claims and adjustments requests, 158–160
    checklist for, 160
    refusing, 216–218
    responding favorably to, 178–180, 181
Classification, for paragraph development, 135
Clauses, 125–126, 130, 502
Clichés, 121
Clip art, 65
Close, 102
    of bad-news messages, 207–208, 210
    complimentary, 469
    of direct requests, 148, 149
    editing of, 118
    of interviews, 433
    in job application letters, 389
    of persuasive messages, 236, 237, 245–246
    of positive messages, 172, 173
    of short reports, 286
    of speeches, 452–453
Closed-ended questions, 432
Closing, of interviews, 411–413
Clothing, 23, 51, 407
Coherence, 134
Collaborative writing, 78, 320
Collection messages, 247–253
    checklist for, 252–253
Collection series, 250–253
College Placement Annual, 373
College placement office, 373
Colons, 505
Color:
    cultural meanings of, 14
    in visual aids, 336
Comfort zones, 24
Comma splice, 503–504
Commands, 502

Commas, 125, 505–506, 512
Common nouns, 496
Communication:
  audience-centered approach to, 15, 297
  basic forms of, 22–25
  channels of, 4, 25, 26, 34, 86–90
  crisis, 9–10
  effective, 11–17
  ethical, 11–13, 31–32
  improving, 33–35
  inefficient, 32
  internal, 3–7
  legal considerations in, 12
  moral considerations in, 12–13
  (*See also* Intercultural communication; Nonverbal
    communication)
Communication barriers, 27–32
Communication climate, 4, 11, 33
Communication flow (*See* Information flow)
Communication process, 25–27
Communication skills:
  benefits of, 3
  intercultural, 50–52
  training in, 16–17, 27
Communication technology, 14–15, 60–72
  for electronic communication, 68–69
  for oral communication, 69–70
  for printed documents, 61–68
Company image, 110, 179
Company policy, 205
Comparative form, of adjectives, 500–501
Comparison and contrast, for paragraph development, 135
Compensation, job, 371–372
Compiled lists, 247
Complaints, customer, 158–160, 178–189, 216–218
Complex sentences, 125–126
Complimentary close, 469
Compliments, 109, 188
Composing, 77, 94–110
  on a computer, 63–64, 78
Composition process, 77–78, 117
Compound adjectives, 507
Compound nouns, 497
Compound sentence, 125
CompuServe, 68
Computer-aided design, 334–335
Computer conferencing, 90
Computerized databases, 486
Computers, 14–15
  for creating printed documents, 61–68
  for creating visual aids, 336–337
  for electronic communication, 68–69
  for form letters, 174
  for presentations, 455
  for producing reports, 320
  writing with, 61, 63–64, 65–66, 78, 320
Conclusions, 309, 311
  drawing, 309–310
  placement of, 311, 327, 328
  in reports, 267, 271, 272, 277, 327–328, 354
Concrete language, 34

Concreteness, 120
Condolence messages, 191, 466
Conferences, electronic, 70, 89
Confidence, in job interviews, 406
Conflict-resolution interviews, 431
Conformity, 436
Congeniality, 33
Congratulations, 189, 190
Conjunctions, 125–126, 501, 503, 504, 512
Conjunctive adverbs, 512
Connotative meaning, 28, 120
Consistency, in design, 137
Content:
  decisions about, 26–27
  editing of, 117, 118
  (*See also* Body; Main idea)
Content listening, 429
Content meaning, 29
Content notes, 488
Content words, 102
Contents, table of, 324, 341
Context, cultural, 43
Contractions, 507
Coordinating conjunctions, 504
Copy notation, 472
Copyright, 329, 486–487
CorelDraw, 65, 166
Corporate culture, 11, 372
Correction symbols, 513–516
Correlations, 309
Correspondence (*See* Letters; Memos)
Counseling interviews, 431
Courtesy, 109–110, 159, 216
Cover, of reports, 321
CP mail, 478
Credibility, 33, 82–83, 108–109, 234
  acknowledging sources, and, 329
  establishing, 450–451
  in oral communication, 429
Credit references, 182
Credit requests, 160–162
  approval of, 180–182
  denial of, 218–219
Crediting, of sources, 328–329
Crisis communication, 9–10
Criteria, 299
Critical listening, 429
Criticism, 107
Cultural bias, in language, 122
Cultural context, 43
Cultural diversity, 13–14, 40, 52
Culture, 14
  defined, 40
  differences in, 41–44
  job applications and, 384
  job interviews and, 407
  nonverbal communication and, 24, 43
  word meanings and, 28
  (*See also* Intercultural communication)
Customers:
  complaints by, 158–160, 178–189, 216–218

Customers (*cont.*):
    goodwill relations with, 188–192
    requests to, 154–157
Cut and paste, 65–66

Dangling modifiers, 131
Dashes, 506
    typing of, 466
Data:
    analyzing and interpreting, 308–311
    collecting, 304–308
Databases, 62, 486
Dates:
    format for, 468, 506
    on letters, 468
    on memos, 479
Deception, 12
Decimal system, 301
Decision making:
    cultural differences in, 42
    in groups, 436–437
Decision-making meetings, 438
Decoding, 26, 428
Deductive approach (*See* Direct approach)
Defamation, 217–218
Definitions, in reports, 326
Delivery, of speeches, 456–461
Demographics, 240
Denmark, 14
Denotative meaning, 28, 120
Departments, communication between, 6
Dependent clause, 125, 126, 502, 503, 505–506
Description, as type of detail, 100
Descriptive headings, 301, 302, 311, 349
Descriptive synopsis, 324–325
Design, of written documents, 136–137, 325
Desire phase (of AIDA), 235–236, 245
Desktop publishing (DTP), 61, 66–68, 336
Diagrams, 334–335
Dictation, 62–63
Dictionary of Occupational Titles, 373
Dignitaries, forms of address for, 468
Diplomacy, 110
Direct approach, 101–102, 103
    for bad-news messages, 208–209, 216
    for claims and adjustments requests, 158
    for direct requests, 147–149
    for good-news messages, 101–102, 171–172
    for goodwill messages, 101–102, 171–172
    for positive messages, 171–172, 174, 179, 183, 184
    for reports, 269, 270, 271–272, 273, 276, 277, 286, 328
    for routine requests, 152, 153–154
    for speeches, 446
Direct Mail List Rates & Data, 247
Direct-mail package, 246
Direct open-ended questions, 432
Direct requests, 101, 146–162
    checklist for, 158–159
    for claims and adjustments, 158–160
    for credit, 160, 162
    inquiries as, 156, 162

Direct requests (*cont.*):
    intercultural, 147
    organization of, 147–149
    placing orders, 149–151
    for routine information and action, 151–157
    for time extensions, 416–417
Directed interviews, 402
Directives, 185
Disability bias, 124
Disasters, 9
Disciplinary interviews, 431
Discretion, 267
Discrimination, in hiring, 409–411
Distortion, 4, 31
Distractions, 32–33, 34–35, 428
Diversity, cultural, 13–14, 40, 52
Division, rules of, 300
Documentation, of sources, 304, 484–494
Documents:
    appearance of, 66–68, 136–138, 465
    designing, 136–137, 325
    electronic, 68–69
    government, 486, 490, 492
    meeting, 482–483
    number and cost of, 15
    printing and distribution of, 68
    as research sources, 305
    revision of, 64–66, 116–138
    (*See also* Letters; Memos; Reports)
Downward information flow, 5
Draft, first, 103–104
Drawings, 334–335
Drug testing, 402

E-mail, 68–69, 71, 90
Econobase, 62
Editing, 117–124
Education, on résumé, 375
Egypt, 44
Electronic communication, 87, 89–90
Electronic documents, 68–69
Electronic media, source notes for, 491, 493
Ellipsis points, 488, 508
Emotions:
    appeals to, 82, 233–234
    interpretation of messages and, 29
    nonverbal communication and, 22
Empathic listening, 429
Empathy, 15, 29, 51, 107
Emphasis:
    audience needs and, 81
    positive, 107–108
    in sentences, 126, 132–133
Employees:
    communicating with, 82–83
    communication among, 3–7
    interviews with, 430–431
    letters of appreciation for, 189–190
    performance reviews of, 221
    termination of, 221–222, 431
    writing skills programs for, 16

Employment, information about, 372–373
Employment interviews (*See* Job interviews)
Employment search, 371–393
Enclosure notation, 472
Encoding, 25–26
End notes, 487–491
Ending (*See* Close)
English:
   as business language, 44, 45
   plain, 119
Enthusiasm, in business messages, 129, 234
Envelopes, 475–478
   preaddressed stamped, 156, 307
Environment, work, 372
Equal Employment Opportunity Commission, 402, 411
Ethical communication, 11–13, 31–32
Ethical dilemmas, 12
Ethical lapses, 12
Ethics, 11
   in intercultural communication, 44
   in sales letters, 239
Ethnic bias, 124
Ethnocentrism, 47
Etiquette, culture and, 44
Euphemisms, 108
Evaluation, of messages, 428, 429
Evaluation interviews, 431
Evidence, supporting, 100–101, 234, 267, 309
Exaggeration, 283
Examples, as type of detail, 100
Exclamation points, 505
Executive summary, 325, 343–344, 358
Exit interviews, 431
Expectations, audience's, 15
Experiments, 308
Expletives, 130
Express Mail International, 478
External communication network, 7–11
External reports, 268
Extracts, 488
Eye behavior, 23, 24
Eye contact, 43, 403, 429, 459

Face-to-face communication, 31, 86
Facial expressions, 22, 23, 459
Factoring, 297–300
Facts, 100, 266
Fair Debt Collection Practices Act, 247
Fair use, 487
Familiar words, 121
Familiarity, in business messages, 105
Fax machines, 68, 89–90
FCR worksheet, 85
Feedback, 25, 31, 35, 449, 453–454
   defined, 26
   in intercultural communication, 46
   in oral communication, 427, 429
Feelings (*See* Emotions)
Figures (*See* Visual aids)
File merge, 64
Filmstrips, 455

Filtering, 28
Flattery, 106
Flowcharts, 333–334
Fog Index, 118, 119
Folding, of envelopes, 478
Follow-up messages:
   to job applications, 392–393
   to job interviews, 413–418, 419–420
Footnotes, 329, 487–491
Form letters, 155, 174, 175
Formal communication network, 4–6, 31
Formal reports:
   checklist for, 360–361
   components of, 320–337, 357
   example of, 338–356
Formality:
   in intercultural communications, 53
   in reports, 281–283, 320, 344
   of speeches, 449
   style and, 105
Format:
   for bibliographies, 491–493
   desktop publishing and, 67
   for envelopes, 475–478
   for letters, 473–475
   for memos, 478–480
   for press releases, 187–188
   for proposals, 357–361
   for reports, 267–270, 320–357, 481–482
   for résumés, 373–374
   for sales letters, 240
   for source notes, 488–491
   of written documents, 138, 465
Forms:
   for reports, 270
   standardized, 466
Fragments, sentence, 502–503
France (French), 42, 49, 53
Fraud, 239
Freehand, 65
Functional résumés, 379, 381
Functional words, 120
Fused sentences, 503–504

Gatekeepers, 28
Gender, nonverbal communication and, 24
Gender bias, 122–123
Gender-neutral pronouns, 123, 497
General purpose, 78–79
Generalizations, 271
Geographic organization, 298
Germany (German), 44, 46, 53, 126
Gestures, 14, 22, 23, 43, 55
Gift giving, 44, 49
Glossary, in reports, 357
Going to Work (Birnbach), 371
Good-news messages, 184–185, 186–188, 417
   about employment, 184–185
   organizational pattern for, 101–102, 171–172
   about products and operations, 186–188
Goodwill messages, 188–192

Goodwill messages (*cont.*):
   checklist for, 192
   organizational pattern for, 101–102, 171–172
Government documents, 486, 490, 492
Grammar, 24, 118, 495–505
   correction symbols for, 515
Grammar checker, 66, 138
Grapevine, 6–7
Graphics, software for, 64–65
Graphs, 331–332
Greece, 42
Grooming, 23, 403, 407–408
Group authoring tools, 61
Group communication, technology for, 70
Group decision support systems, 70
Group dynamics, 435–437
Group-maintenance roles, 435
Groups, 434–439
   decision making in, 436–437
   interaction in, 435–437
   norms in, 436
   roles in, 435
Groupthink, 436
Groupware, 61

Handouts, 455
Handwritten documents, 466
Headings, 136
   in outlines, 301, 302, 311, 447
   in reports, 284, 285, 325, 349, 482
   in résumés, 374
   in table of contents, 325, 341
Hedging, 129–130
Hidden agenda, 435
Hierarchy, communication, 4, 5, 31
Hiring (*See* Job applications; Job interviews)
Honesty tests, 402
Hong Kong, 14
Horizontal information flow, 6, 31
Hospitality, 49, 50–51
House lists, 246
Humor, 106, 450–451
Hyphens, 506, 507, 509
Hypotheses, 297, 299

Idea (*See* Main idea)
Idiomatic expressions, 46
Illustration, for paragraph development, 135
Illustrations, list of, 324, 342
Image, company's, 110, 179
Imagesetter, 68
Imperative mood, 500
Impersonal style, 283
Impressions:
   appearance and, 23, 403, 407–408
   created by business documents, 465
Impromptu speaking, 456–457
Indefinite pronouns, 130
Independent clause, 125, 502, 503, 505, 512
Index, in reports, 357

India, 41, 44, 478
Indicative mood, 500
Indirect approach, 101, 102
   for bad-news messages, 203–208, 210–211, 215
   for reports, 269, 270, 272, 276, 286, 328
   for speeches, 446
Indirect questions, 405
Inductive approach (*See* Indirect approach)
Industrial Marketing, 372
Infinitive phrase, 296–297
Informal communication network, 6–7, 10–11
Informal reports, checklist for, 286–287
Information:
   accuracy of, 81
   analyzing and interpreting, 308–311
   gathering, 302, 304–308
   negative, 172
   relevant, 266
   unnecessary, 96
Information chain, 3
Information flow, 3
   downward, 5
   efficient, 15–17
   horizontal, 6
   technology and, 71
   upward, 5–6, 11
Information interviews, 431
Information overload, 29–30
Informational assignments, 298–299
Informational meetings, 438
Informational reports, 103, 268–269, 272–274, 275, 295, 296, 311
Informative headings, 301, 302, 311, 349
Informative presentations, 445
Informative synopsis, 324–325
Inquiries, about people, 162
Inquiry:
   in collection series, 250–251
   letters of, 156
   regarding a hiring decision, 415
Inside address, 468–469
Insincerity, 109
Instructions, written, 185–186
Intercultural communication, 39–56
   bad-news messages in, 203
   barriers to, 29, 44–47
   channels for, 86
   checklist for, 48–49
   defined, 41
   ethnocentric reactions to, 47
   legal considerations in, 44
   oral, 46–47, 54–56, 427, 458
   references to time in, 468
   tips for, 47–56
   written, 45–46, 53–54, 466, 468, 475
Interest phase (of AIDA), 235, 243–245
Interference, 34
Interim progress reports, 273, 274
Interjections, 501
Internal communication, 3–7, 82–83
   barriers to, 29–30
   (*See also* Memos)
Internal reports, 268, 276–277

International Electronic Post, 478
International mail, 478
International Postal Money Orders, 478
International Postal Rates and Fees, 478
International Priority Airmail, 478
International Surface Air Lift, 478
Internet, 68
Interoffice mail, 479–480
Interpretation:
    of information, 25
    of messages, 428
Interpreters, 458
Interruptions, 30, 83
Interviews, 430–434
    checklist for, 434
    for data collection, 305
    planning of, 432–434
    structure of, 433–434
    types of, 401, 402, 408, 430–431
    (*See also* Job interviews)
Intimacy, in business messages, 106
Intransitive verbs, 499
Introduction:
    in proposals, 358–359
    in reports, 326–327, 345
Invasion of privacy, 402
Irregular verbs, 499
Italics, 137, 508

Japan (Japanese), 39, 40, 42, 43, 53–54, 126, 196–197
Jargon, 14, 121
Job applications, 384–393
    rejection of, 221
Job descriptions, 3
Job-inquiry letters, 390–391
Job interviews, 401–413
    on campus, 376
    checklist for, 412–413
    common questions in, 405
    handling, 408–413
    legal considerations in, 409–411
    preparing for, 403–408
    process for, 401–402, 409
    résumé and, 373
    sequence of, 401
    stages of, 409–413
    types of, 402
Job offers, 184–185, 412, 416, 417
Job openings, 373
Job search, 371–393
Job titles, cultural variations in, 469
Journalistic approach, 85
Justification, of type, 136, 466
Justification report, 276–277

Kenya, 14
Key-number system, 493
Key points, 34, 99
    number of, 85–86
    in reports, 270–271, 326

Key points (*cont.*):
    restatement of, 452
    in speeches, 448, 452
Keyboarding, 63
Korea, 14

Language, 28
    bias-free, 122–124
    (*See also* Grammar; Words)
Language barriers, 40, 44–47
Language learning, 45, 48, 51
LANs, 68
Laser printers, 68
Latin Americans, 42–43, 466
Law (*See* Legal considerations)
Layout (*See* Format)
LC mail, 478
Leadership, 435, 438
Learning, of communication skills, 16–17, 27
Legal considerations:
    in approving credit, 180
    in business communications, 218
    in citing sources, 328–329, 486–487
    in collection messages, 247–248
    in credit references, 182
    in denying credit, 219
    ethics and, 12
    in intercultural communication, 44
    in job interviews, 409–411
    in performance reviews, 221
    of photocopying, 486
    in possible defamation, 217–218
    in using letterhead, 174
    in writing job offers, 185
    in writing recommendation letters, 183
    in writing reports, 267
    in writing sales letters, 239
Length:
    of interviews, 433–434
    of messages, 83–84, 85–86
    of paragraphs, 134
    of reports, 270, 272, 283, 320
    of résumés, 374, 383
    of sales letters, 246
    of sentences, 126
    of speeches and presentations, 448–449
    of words, 121
Letter of acceptance, 322
Letter of authorization, 322
Letter of transmittal, 323–324, 327, 358
Letterhead, 467–468
Letterhead postcards, 481
Letterhead stationery, 174, 466
    for press releases, 187
Letters:
    accepting job offer, 417
    acknowledging orders, 172–173
    advantages of, 87–88
    applying for job, 384–390, 391, 392–393
    of appreciation, 189–191
    approving credit, 180–182

Letters (*cont.*):
    with bad news about orders, 209–212
    claim, 158–160
    collection, 247–253
    condolence, 191–192
    of congratulation, 189, 190
    cost of producing, 16
    declining job offer, 417–418
    denying routine requests, 213–215
    elements of, 466–473
    following up on job applications, 392–393
    following up on job interview, 414–418, 419–420
    form, 155, 174, 175
    formats for, 473–475
    inquiring about a job, 390–391
    of inquiry, 156
    international, 45–46, 53–54, 55, 466, 468, 469, 475
    to job applicants, 184–185
    length of, 246
    making direct requests, 147–149
    making routine requests, 151, 153–157
    paper for, 466
    persuasive, 235–238
    placing orders, 149–151
    of recommendation, 183–184
    refusing adjustment of claims, 216–218
    refusing credit, 218–219
    refusing to write recommendation, 219–220
    replying to routine requests, 173–177
    for reports, 270, 273, 282
    requesting credit, 160–162
    of resignation, 418
    responding negatively to inquiries, 212–216
    sales, 238–247
    terminating employment, 221–222
    thank-you, 414–415
Libel, 183, 184, 217
Library research, 304, 484–486
Limitations, of reports, 327
Line charts, 331
Line length, 466
Linking verbs, 498, 504, 507
List of illustrations, 324, 342
Listening, 25, 29, 428–430, 436, 438
    in job interviews, 409
    process of, 428–429
    types of, 429
Lists, 284
Literacy, 25
Local area networks (LANs), 68
Location:
    for meetings, 438
    for speeches, 458
Logical appeals, 234

Mail:
    answering, 110
    international, 478
    interoffice, 479–480
    time for, 83

Mail (*cont.*):
    volume of, 16
    (*See also* Letters)
Mail merge, 68
Mail response lists, 247
Mailing abbreviations, 476, 577
Mailing lists, 246–247
Mailing notation, 472–473
Main idea, 34, 84–86, 99, 171, 446
Main question, in reports, 271
Management by Walking Around (MBWA), 7
Management styles, 11, 31
Managers:
    communication by, 3
    use of reports by, 265
    schedule of, 83
Manners, 44
Maps, 334
Margins, 136, 466, 481–482
Marketing, 8
Marketing communication, 8
MCI Mail, 68
Mean, 308–309
Meaning:
    content, 29
    conveyed by nonverbal communication, 22–24
    cultural context and, 43
    denotative vs. connotative, 120
    grammar and, 495
    interpretation of, 25, 26, 28
    relationship, 29
    semantics and, 234–235
    shared, 27, 28
Media richness, 31
Median, 309
Medium, communication, 26, 31, 34
    selection of, 86–90
Meetings, 426, 434–439
    arranging for, 437–438
    checklist for, 439
    conducting, 438–439
    documents for, 482–483
    electronic, 70, 89
    open-space, 440
    purpose of, 436, 437–438
Memo letters, 480–481
Memorization, of speeches, 456
Memory, listening and, 429
Memos, 89
    advantages of, 87–88
    bad news in, 209, 213
    directive, 185
    format for, 478–480
    making routine requests, 151, 152–153
    paper for, 466
    persuasive, 236–238
    for reports, 268, 270, 274, 275, 276, 280–282, 480
    responding to routine requests, 177
Mental map, 27
Messages:
    competition among, 30

Messages (*cont.*):
　complexity of, 30
　conflicting, 23
　decoding of, 26, 428
　encoding of, 25–26
　formulation of, 26–27, 34, 103–110
　length of, 83–84, 85–86
　number of, 16, 32
　persuasive, 232–253
　planning of, 77, 78–90
　positive, 171–191
　purpose of, 78–79
　scope of, 85–86
　timeliness of, 16
　(*See also specific types of messages*)
Mexico, 42, 44
Microfilm/microfiche, 485
Microsoft Bookshelf, 62
Minutes, for meetings, 438, 439, 482–483
Miscommunication, 13
Mission statement, 36
Misunderstanding, 41, 45
MLA simplified style, 493–494
Mock interviews, 406–407
Mode, 309
Modern Language Association (MLA) style, 493–494
Modified block format, 474
Modifiers, 500–501
　dangling, 131
　misplaced, 504–505
　placement of, 132
Mood, of verbs, 500
Morality (*See* Ethics)
Motivational needs, of audience, 81–82
Ms., 123, 468

Names, in intercultural communication, 50
Napoleonic Code, 44
Narration, as type of detail, 100
Native Americans, 43
Needs, of audience, 15, 80–84, 233, 267, 271, 452
Negative appeals, 249–250
Negative information, 172
Negative messages (*See* Bad-news messages)
Negative terms, 108
Negative words, 206
Negotiation:
　intercultural, 52–53
　of job benefits, 412–413
Networking, 10
News releases, 187–188
Noise, 27, 32, 33–34
Nominative case, 498
Nonverbal communication, 22–24, 427, 428, 429, 449
　cultural context and, 43
　in job interviews, 403, 407, 409
Norms, group, 436
Notations, in letters, 472–473
Note cards:
　for library research, 486, 487

Note cards (*cont.*):
　speaking from, 456
Notes, in reports, 328–329, 355
Notification, of overdue bill, 250
Nouns, 121, 125, 496–497
　long sequences of, 131
Numbering, of visual aids, 335
Numbers:
　cultural meanings of, 14
　style for, 509

Objective, career, 375
Objectivity, 283
Observation, 305
Obsolete language, 128–129
Occupational Outlook Handbook, 372
Offensive terminology, 108
Open-ended interviews, 402
Open-ended questions, 405, 432
Opening, 102
　for bad-news messages, 204–205
　of direct requests, 147, 148
　editing of, 118
　of interviews, 433
　of job application letters, 385–387
　of persuasive messages, 235, 236–237, 240–243
　of positive messages, 171, 173
　for proposals, 358–359
　for reports, 283–284, 326–327
　of sales letters, 240–243
　of speeches, 450–451
Optical character recognition (OCR), 64
Oral communication, 24–25, 427–429, 444–460
　advantages of, 86, 87, 427
　drawbacks of, 427
　intercultural, 46–47, 427, 458
　technology for, 69–70
Oral presentations (*See* Presentations, oral)
Order blanks, 149–150
Orders:
　acknowledging, 172–173
　bad news about, 209–212
　checklist for, 151
　placing, 149–151
Organization, of messages, 95–103
　editing of, 117, 118
　(*See also* Outline; Outlining)
Organization chart, 4, 5, 333
　for messages, 99
Organizational plans:
　for bad-news messages, 102, 203–209
　for direct requests, 147–149
　for longer messages, 103
　for persuasive messages, 102–103, 235–236
　for reports, 267–269, 270–280, 311
　for résumés, 379–383
　for sales letters, 240–243
　for short messages, 101–103
　for speeches, 446–447
　(*See also* Direct approach; Indirect approach)

Organizations:
    communication barriers in, 27–32
    communication technology and, 71
    ethical behavior in, 13, 31–32
    information flow in, 3–7, 29–31
Osgood Files, The, 456
Outline:
    final, 311–312
    for investigations, 297–302
    preliminary, 300–302
    for speeches, 446–447, 448
Outlining, 98–99
    rules of division for, 300
    software for, 62
Overhead transparencies, 70, 455
Overload, information, 29–30

Page numbers, in reports, 341, 342, 345, 346, 482
Pagers, 70
Pages, second, 466, 470, 472
Pakistan, 41, 42, 49
Panel interviews, 401
Paper:
    for business documents, 465–466
    for envelopes, 476
Paragraphs, 134–136
Parallelism, 130, 284, 301, 454
Parentheses, 507–508
Parts of speech, 496–505
Passive voice, 126–127, 131, 500
Pay (*See* Salary requirements)
PBX (private branch exchange) system, 70
Pen-based computers, 63
Perception:
    culture and, 14
    differences in, 27–28
Performance reviews, 221
Periodicals, 485–486
    in bibliographies, 492
    source notes for, 490
Periods (punctuation), 505
Permission, for using copyrighted materials, 487
Personal activity reports, 273–274, 275
Personal appearance, 35, 403, 407–408
Personal biases, 310
Personal data, on résumé, 378
Personal space, culture and, 42–43
Personalization:
    of collection letters, 251
    of form letters, 174
    of sales letters, 246
Persuasion, 108, 233
Persuasive interviews, 431
Persuasive messages, 232–253
    collection letters as, 247–253
    job application letters as, 384
    organizational pattern for, 102–103, 235–236
    proposals as, 358
    requests for action as, 236–238
    sales letters as, 238–247
Persuasive presentations, 445

Phone systems, 69–70
Photocopier, 68
Photocopies, 16
Photocopying, 486
Photographs, 335
Phrases:
    parallel, 130
    transitional, 135, 284–286, 512
Physical appearance, for job interviews, 403, 407–408
Physical attractiveness, 23
Physical distractions, 32–33, 34–35
Pie charts, 332–333
Plagiarism, 328–329
    avoiding, 486–487
Plain English, 119
Planning:
    of business messages, 77, 78–90
    career, 371–373
    checklist for, 90
    of interviews, 432–434
    of long reports, 295–312
    for meetings, 437–438
    of printed documents, 61–62
    of sales letters, 239–240
    of short reports, 269–272
Plural nouns, 496, 497
Plural pronouns, 497
Pointers, awkward, 130
Pompous language, 128–129
Positive appeals, 248–249
Positive messages, 171–191
    checklist for, 178
    direct plan for, 171–172
    good-news, 178–188
    goodwill, 188–192
    replying to requests, 172–177
Possessive nouns, 496–497, 498, 507
Possessive pronouns, 498
Postal requirements, 476–477
Postcards, letterhead, 481
Postscripts, 473
Posture:
    as nonverbal communication, 23
    in speech delivery, 459
Practical Home Energy Savings (Lovins), 322
Practicing:
    for job interviews, 406–407
    of speeches, 456, 458
Praise, 188, 191
Preaching, 106
Predicate, 125, 502
Prefatory parts:
    for proposals, 357–358
    for reports, 321–325, 327, 482
Prefixes, 507
Preparation:
    for job interviews, 403–408
    for oral presentations, 445–449
Prepositions, 498, 501
Presentation software, 65
Presentations, oral, 444–460
    organizational pattern for, 103

Presentations, oral (*cont.*):
    technology for, 70
    (*See also* Speeches)
Press releases, 132–133, 187–188
Prewriting techniques, 84–85
Price, in sales letters, 244–245
Primary research, 304–308
Print shop, 68
Printed documents, creating, 61–68
Printers, 68
Privacy, invasion of, 239
Problem and solution, for paragraph development, 136
Problem factoring, 297–300
Problem-solving approach, 277, 299
Problem statement, 295–297
Products:
    bad news about, 212–213
    good news about, 186–188
    selling points of, 239–240, 243–244
Progress reports, 273, 274
Promptness, 110, 408
Pronouns, 497–498
    gender and, 123, 497
    indefinite, 130
    relative, 127
Pronunciation, 46
Proofreading, 133, 137–138
Proofreading marks, 516
Proper nouns, 496
Proposals, 277, 278–279, 302
    advantages of, 88
    checklist for, 360–361
    components of, 357–361
Prospecting letter, 385
Psychographics, 240
Public relations, 8–10
Punctuality, 24, 408
Punctuation, 505–508, 512
    in letter formats, 475
    of quotations, 488, 507
    with reference marks, 488
    source notes, 489–491
    spacing after, 466
Purpose:
    of business messages, 78–79
    of longer messages, 103
    of meetings, 436, 437–438
    of reports, 266, 275, 296–297
    of short messages, 99
    of speeches, 445

Qualifications:
    in job application letters, 388
    on résumé, 375
Question-and-answer chain, 85, 271
Question-and-answer period, following speeches, 453–454
Question-and-answer stage, in job interviews, 409–411
Questionnaires, 305, 306–307
Questions:
    to ask interviewers, 406
    from audience, 453, 459–460

Questions (*cont.*):
    in job interviews, 403–406
    main, 271
    in making direct requests, 148–149
    for surveys, 306–307
    types of, 432–433
Quotation marks, 488, 505, 507
Quotations, format for, 488

Racial bias, 124
Random list, 85
Rational arguments, 82
Readability, 118, 119
Reading, 25
    of speeches, 456
Reason, appeals to, 82, 234
Receiver, of messages, 26
Reception, of messages, 428
Recommendation letters, 183–184
    refusing to write, 219–220
Recommendations, in reports, 272, 277, 278, 328, 354
    developing, 310–311
    placement of, 311, 328
Recruiting, campus, 376–377, 408, 410–411
"Red flag" system, 6
Redundancy, 127
Reference books, 484–485
Reference Books: A Brief Guide, 484
Reference citations, 493–494
Reference initials, 472
Reference marks, 488
References, for reports, 304, 356, 484–494
Relationship meaning, 29
Relative merits, 299
Relative pronouns, 127
Reliability, of research, 306
Remembering, of oral messages, 429
Reminder notice, 250
Repetition, needless, 128
Reports:
    advantages of, 88
    analytical, 103, 268–269, 274–279, 280, 295–296, 311
    annual, 36, 104–105, 305
    characteristics of good, 265–269
    checklist for, 286–287
    components of, 320–337, 357
    defined, 265
    documentation of, 484–494
    format for, 267–270, 320–357, 481–482
    informational, 268–269, 272–274, 275, 295, 296, 311
    length of, 270, 272, 283
    long, 319–361
    in memo format, 268, 270, 274, 275, 276, 280–282, 480
    organization of, 103, 267–269, 270–280, 311–312
    planning of, 269–272, 295–312
    production of, 319–320
    purpose of, 266, 275, 296–297
    readability of, 280–286
    "red flag" feature in, 6
    short, 264–286
    types of, 268–269

Reports (*cont.*):
    uses of, 265, 266
    work plan for, 302, 303, 304
Request for proposal (RFP), 273, 357–358
Requests for action, 236–238
    (*See also* Direct requests)
Resale information, 173, 179, 180, 211
Research:
    conducting, 302, 304–308
    for job interviews, 403, 404
    technology for, 61–62
Resignation, letter of, 418
Response, to reports, 320
Restatement, of main points, 452
Restatement questions, 433
Résumés, 373–383
    checklist for, 384–385
    common problems on, 383
    layout for, 373–374
    length of, 374, 383
    organizational plans for, 379–383
Revising, 77, 116–138
    checklist for, 138
    on computer, 65–66
Rewriting, 125–136
Role-playing, 435
Roles, culture and, 41–42
Routine messages, organization of, 101–102, 171–172
Routine reports, 268
Routine requests, 151–157
    checklist for, 158
    denying, 213–215
    replying to, 173–177, 178
Rules of division, 300
Russia (Russians), 46

Salary requirements, 371–372, 388–389, 412
Sales letters, 238–247
    AIDA plan for, 240–246
    checklist for, 248–249
    format for, 240
    packaging for, 246–247
    planning of, 239–240
Sales promotion, 173, 179, 180
Salutation, 469
Salutopening, 469
Sans-serif typefaces, 136–137
Scanners, 64, 65
Schedule, for producing reports, 320
Scheduling, 78
Screening interviews, 401, 408
Search and replace, 66
Secondary research, 304
Secondary sources, 484–486
Self-mailer, 246
Self-oriented roles, 435
Selling points, 239–240, 243, 244, 358–359
    in job application letters, 387–389
Semantics, 234–235
Semicolons, 125, 505, 512
Sender, 25

Sentence fragments, 502–503
Sentence structure, style and, 104
Sentence style, 126–133
Sentences, 125, 495, 501–505
    emphasis in, 132–133
    fused, 503–504
    hedging, 129–130
    length of, 126
    parallel, 130
    strung-out, 129
    topic, 134, 346
    types of, 125–126
Sequential organization, 298
Serif typefaces, 136–137
Sexual harassment, 23
Sicily, 43
Signature block, 469–470, 472
Simple sentence, 125
Simplified letter format, 474, 475
Sincerity, 188, 189, 234
Skills, on résumé, 378
Slander, 217
Slang, 14, 45, 122
Slides, 455
Smoking, 408
Social values, 41
Soft Energy Paths (Lovins), 322
Software, 62, 64–65, 66
    graphics, 336–337
    for multimedia presentations, 166–167
Solicited application letters, 385–386, 387, 391
Sound bites, 65
Source notes, 328–329, 355, 487–491
Sources:
    crediting of, 328–329, 487, 484–494
    for research, 304–308
South Africa, 41
Space, nonverbal communication and, 23–24, 42–43
Spacing:
    in letters, 469, 470–471
    in reports, 482
Spain, 49
Span of control, 4, 5
Spatial organization, 298
Speaking, 24–25, 427–428
    Charles Osgood on, 456–457
    rate of, 448
Special reports, 268
Specific purpose, 78–79
Speech, parts of, 496–505
Speech mannerisms, 407, 459
Speeches, 444–460
    audience analysis for, 445–446
    checklist for, 460
    delivery of, 456–461
    formal, 449–456
    location for, 458
    organization of, 446–447
    preparing for, 445–449, 458
    purpose of, 445
    visual aids for, 454–456
Spell checkers, 66, 138

Spelling, 511–512

Stage fright, 456, 458–459

Standard & Poor's Register of Corporations, Directors, and Executives, 372–373

Standard Rate and Data Service, 247

Standardization, of messages, 16

Standardized forms, 466

Statement of purpose, 296–297

Statement of qualifications, 359

States, abbreviations for, 477

Stationery, letterhead, 174, 466

Statistical analysis software, 62

Statistics, 100, 308–309

Status:
    as barrier to communication, 30
    culture and, 42
    nonverbal communication and, 22

Stereotyping, 47, 124

Storyteller's tour, 85

Stress interviews, 402

Structure, organizational, 4, 5, 31

Strung-out sentences, 129

Style, 104–110
    editing for, 117, 118, 119
    for job application letters, 384
    for public speaking, 449
    for reports, 267–269, 282–283
    sentence, 126–133
    speaking, 427–428
    (*See also* Tone)

Style books, 494

Style sheets, 67

Subcultures, 40–41

Subdivision, of topics, 298–300

Subheadings, 136

Subject line, 471–472, 479

Subjective case, 498

Subjunctive mood, 500

Subordinating conjunctions, 503

Substitutions, in filling orders, 211

Subtopics, arrangement of, 298–299

Suggestions, employee, 6

Summary:
    executive, 325, 343–344, 358
    in proposals, 360–361
    in reports, 327–328

Summary of qualifications, 375

Superlative form, of adjectives, 500–501

Superscripts, 488

Supplementary parts, 337, 357

Surface charts, 331–332

Surveys, 305–306

Symbols, correction, 513–516

Sympathy, 191–192

Synopsis, 324–325, 327, 358

Table of contents, 324, 341

Tables, 312, 329–330, 353

Tact, 109–110, 205, 207
    in job interviews, 410

Taiwan, 14, 43

Targeted résumés, 379, 382–383

Task-facilitating roles, 435

Tax Notes Today, 62

Team approach, 2, 434
    for doing research, 310
    for writing reports, 320

Technology, communication, 6, 14–15, 60–72

Telecommuting, 71

Teleconferencing, 70, 89

Telephone, 69–70

Telephone skills, 428

Tense, verb, 498–499

Termination interviews, 431

Termination letter, 221–222

Testing, preemployment, 402

Thank-you messages, 191, 414–415

Theory X, 11

Theory Y, 11

Theory Z, 11

Thesaurus, computer, 66

Thoroughness, 81

Time:
    concepts of, 23, 42
    references to, in international communication, 468

Time extension, request for, 416–417

Title, of reports, 321, 339

Title fly, 322

Title page, 322, 339, 482

Tone, 104–110
    in bad-news messages, 203, 204, 206
    in collection letters, 252
    of direct requests, 147
    editing for, 118
    of positive messages, 172
    in reports, 273, 281–283
    in requests for claims and adjustments, 158
    of speeches, 450
    vocal, 428

Topic, 84

Topic sentence, 134, 346

Touching behavior, 23

Training, in communication skills, 16–17, 27

Transitions, 134–135, 284–286, 352, 512
    in speeches, 451

Transitive verbs, 499

Translation, 45, 46
    back, 122

Transmittal letter (memo), 323–324, 327, 340, 358

Transparencies, 70, 455

Trend analysis, 309

Troubleshooting reports, 277–278, 280–282

Trust, 30–31, 82

Trustworthiness, 234

Turkey, 44

Type, for visual aids, 454

Typefaces, 136–137

Ulrich's International Periodicals Directory, 373

Ultimatum, in collection series, 251–252

Underlining, 137, 508

United Kingdom, 44

U.S. Department of Human Services, 9
U.S. Department of Labor, 411
U.S. Foreign Corrupt Practices Act, 44
U.S. State Department, 45
Unsolicited application letters, 385–386, 390
Upward information flow, 5–6, 11
Urgent notice, in collection series, 251
Usage, 495, 509–511

Validity, of research, 306
VALUEPOST/CANADA, 478
Values, social, 41
Variables, 308, 309
Verbal communication, defined, 24
Verbiage, excess, 127–128
Verbs, 121, 125, 244, 498–500, 504
    action, 374
    camouflaged, 122
    linking, 498, 504, 507
Videoconferencing, 70
Videotapes, 455
Videotaping, 89
Visual aids, 100
    color, 336
    computer creation of, 336–337
    designing, 454
    numbering of, 335, 347
    placement of, 336, 346, 348, 357
    for reports, 311–312, 325, 329–337
    software for, 64–65
    source notes for, 488
    for speeches and presentations, 454–456
    types of, 329–335, 454–455
Vocabulary, 28
    style and, 104
Vocal characteristics, 22, 23, 407, 459
Voice, active vs. passive, 126–127, 500
Voice mail, 70, 89
Voice recognition systems, 63
Voluntary reports, 268

Wall Street Journal, 62
Warm-up questions, 405
White space, 136, 374, 383
Whiteboards, 455
Witness, 8
Women, culture and, 41–42
Word choice, 118–124
    in intercultural communication, 53
Word division, 509
Word processors, 61, 63–64, 65–66, 78, 320, 466
Word usage, 495, 509–511
Words:
    abstract vs. concrete, 120
    connotative vs. denotative, 28
    in English language, 24
    functional vs. content, 120
    obsolete, 128–129
    parallel, 130
    short vs. long, 121
    spelling of, 511–512
    strong vs. weak, 121
    transitional, 135, 451, 512
    unnecessary, 127
Wordsmiths, 120–121
Work ethic, 41
Work experience, on résumé, 376–378, 379–380
Work plan, 302, 303, 304, 359
Workforce, diversity in, 13, 40, 52
"Works Cited," 493
Writing, 25
    collaborative, 320
Writing skills, training in, 16
Written communication, advantages of, 86–88

"You" attitude, 106–107, 148, 173, 188, 203, 244, 387, 414, 428, 446

ZIP codes, 477